Women in American History

Series Editors
Mari Jo Buhle
Nancy A. Hewitt
Anne Firor Scott

A list of books in the series appears at the end of this book.

A HARD FIGHT FOR WE

A
HARD
FIGHT
FOR
WE

LESLIE A. SCHWALM

Women's Transition
from Slavery to
Freedom in
South Carolina

UNIVERSITY OF ILLINOIS PRESS

URBANA AND CHICAGO

© 1997 by the Board of Trustees of the University
of Illinois
Manufactured in the United States of America
1 2 3 4 5 C P 5 4 3 2

This book is printed on acid-free paper.

Library of Congress Cataloging-in-Publication Data
Schwalm, Leslie A. (Leslie Ann), 1956–
    A hard fight for we : women's transition from
slavery to freedom in South Carolina / Leslie A.
Schwalm.
      p.   cm. – (Women in American history)
    Includes bibliographical references and index.
    ISBN 0-252-02259-9 (alk. paper). –
    ISBN 0-252-06630-8 (pbk. : alk. paper)
    1. Women slaves–South Carolina–History–19th
century. 2. Plantation life–South Carolina–History–
19th century. 3. Slaves–Emancipation–South
Carolina. 4. Afro-American women–South Carolina–
History–19th century. 5. South Carolina–History–
Civil War, 1861–1865. 6. Reconstruction–South
Carolina. I. Title. II. Series.
E445.S7S39   1997
975.7'00496–dc21   96-45866
                                              CIP
Digitally reprinted from the second paperback printing

TO MY FAMILY

CONTENTS

Illustrations follow pages 46 and 144

ACKNOWLEDGMENTS

I had the tremendous good fortune of studying women's history with a wonderful group of scholars at the University of Wisconsin at Madison, in the graduate women's history program founded only with the vision, determination, and courage of Gerda Lerner. The faculty and students I worked with there made becoming a historian more important and more rewarding than I ever imagined. My colleagues in the Women's History Dissertation Group, including Kathleen Brown, Eileen Findlay, Maureen Fitzgerald, Joyce Follet, Andrea Friedman, Nancy Isenberg, Marie Laberge, Nancy Maclean, Leisa Meyer, Mary Peckham, Leslie Reagan, and Susan Smith, were astute, provocative, and generous in reading proposals and drafts and responding to my speculations. Deeply engaged conversations with them and the other students who came to Madison to study women's history remain the most memorable hallmarks of my graduate-school experience. I am also deeply indebted to Linda Gordon, who supervised the dissertation on which this book is based, for her generous intellect and feminist insight, her clearheaded guidance, and her special ability to ask hard, good questions about women's history. I would also like to thank Jeanne Boydston, Vanessa Northington Gamble, Judith Walzer Leavitt, Stan Schultz, Richard Sewell, and Steve Stern for their various offers of support, their criticism, and their inspiration. Nellie Y. McKay and William Van Deburg, faculty in the Department of African American Studies at Wisconsin, also shared their expertise and friendly enthusiasm for my work. Although Tom Schick died before this book was well underway, I also would like to acknowledge my gratitude for his example of warm-hearted intellectual excellence. Three "fellow travelers" at Madison—Bobby Buchanan, Earl Mulderink, and Edward Pearson—also read proposals and offered helpful suggestions as this project first began, and many conversations since then with Ted have greatly advanced my understanding of South Carolina slavery, for which I owe him very special thanks. In addition to their help in the Women's History Dissertation Group, Kathleen Brown, Leslie Reagan, and Susan Smith have given generously of their time and their critical faculties to indulge endless consultations about history and the mystery of book writing. Beyond their constant support for this book, all three have deeply shaped my work and identity as a historian, and in their own book projects they have taught me much about the challenges and politics of women's lives.

xii

Several other scholars helped nurse this project along. Noralee Frankel, Laura Edwards, Malcolm Rohrbough, and Dan Goldstein read (some even reread) all or parts of this work and shared their expertise and excellent suggestions. Noralee has been especially helpful and enthusiastic in her support for this project for many years, and her own insight into the history of Mississippi freedwomen has been an inspiration. I also benefited from the critical observations offered by audience members and the comments of Kathleen Berkeley, Elsa Barkley Brown, Steven Hahn, Tera Hunter, Daniel Letwin, Randy Shifflett, and Brenda Stevenson as various aspects of this book were presented before the Berkshire Conference on the History of Women, the Southern History Association, the American Historical Association, and the North American Labor History Conference.

Readers for the University of Illinois Press, including Nancy Hewitt, Jacqueline Jones, and, in particular, an anonymous reviewer, were also thoughtful and generous in the substance of their advice and comments. My editor, Karen Hewitt, was tremendously helpful and made the book-production process far smoother than I ever expected. Carol Bolton Betts, my copyeditor, has an excellent and sensitive eye.

I would like to acknowledge the wonderful help I received from the staff at a number of archives, including the South Caroliniana Library at the University of South Carolina; the South Carolina Department of History and Archives; the South Carolina Historical Society at Charleston; the Southern Historical Collection at the University of North Carolina at Chapel Hill; the Manuscripts Department at Perkins Library of Duke University; and the National Archives.

In these times of waning financial support for the work of historians, I wish also to thank those institutions that supported this project in its various stages. Very important support for the dissertation came from a Ford Foundation Women's Studies Dissertation Grant, an American Association of University Women Dissertation Fellowship, and the University of Wisconsin Department of History. Further dissertation support came in the form of a one-year editing fellowship sponsored by the National Historical Publications and Records Commission at the Freedmen and Southern Society Project at the University of Maryland, where I spent a memorable twelve months working with and learning from Ira Berlin, Steven Miller, and Leslie Rowland. Leslie Rowland was also generous as I began my research, artfully steering me through the maze of record groups at the National Archives and offering important advice and suggestions as I began to think about this project.

More recently, the University of Iowa—especially the Provost, the Office of the Vice President for Research, and the Department of History—has been unstinting in supporting the research and writing required to finish this book. I have also been especially fortunate to enjoy the able research assistance of David Coleman, Shannon Fogg, Scott Grau, and Patti Reid, all graduate students at the University of Iowa.

Throughout my work, the loyal, good-natured, and loving support of my late mother, as well as my father and brother—Olive Schwalm, Ray Schwalm, and Bruce Schwalm—seemed inexhaustible. I would like them to know that their confidence in my ability to carry this project through has made all the difference.

Included in the family to whom this book is dedicated is my partner, Doris Stormoen. This is truly a small acknowledgment of my very deep gratitude to her for listening, reading, challenging, demanding greater clarity, and relentlessly editing. In these and innumerable other ways she has contributed to this project and supported the work that went into it. Not only have her insights helped make this a better book, but more important, her daily presence has made life inestimably richer.

Introduction

This book is about enslaved African-American women's transition from slavery to freedom. The story of how they experienced and shaped the end of slavery has three parts: their experience of slavery immediately before and during the Civil War; their participation in the wartime collapse and destruction of slavery; and their efforts as freedwomen to reconstruct life and labor in the postbellum South. As they encountered and accelerated the revolutionary changes affecting plantation society during and after the war, slave and freed women approached freedom with an eye on their own enslaved past, vigilant to ensure a different future. Slave women's transition to freedom, while deeply desired, prayed for, and actively pursued, was a treacherous and ambiguous process. Far from passive recipients of the liberating powers of the Northern army, slave women played a critical role in pushing the Union to accept emancipation as a war goal. Yet the final destruction of slavery, however devoted slave women were in their pursuit of it, came at the cost of war's violence and chaos. Furthermore, the meaning and consequences of slavery's end were deeply contested in the postbellum South by freedwomen in the rice fields, planter residences, and their own homes. For freedwomen, this postemancipation struggle was inextricably tied to their experience of slavery and of war.

In the last fifteen years, American historians have produced an impressive body of work reexamining the South's transition from slavery to freedom during and after the Civil War. Virtually all of this scholarship substantiates the premise that slaves were important participants in the wartime destruction of slavery. By virtue of their flight to Union lines, and through the contributions of their labor, their information, and their military service, slaves forced a reluctant nation to accept the imperative of black freedom. Recent scholarship on Reconstruction similarly reveals the involvement of former slaves in transforming the South into a free society. The contested disposition of Southern lands, the reorganization of the Southern economy, as well as the struggle to recast the relations of power in Southern societies have been subjected to vigorous reinvestigation. The result has been a wave of studies bringing to light new information and a clearer understanding of the process, and implications, of American emancipation.[1] Most of this scholarship, however, omits gender as an important category of analysis in the investigation of how slaves experienced their transition to freedom.

The groundwork in African-American women's history laid by Deborah Gray White and Jacqueline Jones, offering the first sustained analyses of women's experience of slavery and Reconstruction, has made it possible to ask new questions about women's transition from slavery to freedom.[2] Although many scholars have followed in their pioneering footsteps, White and Jones first posited the importance of both productive and reproductive labor in the lives of slave women, and both brought to light slave women's distinctive experience of exploitation under slavery as well as women's unique contributions to the efforts of their communities to resist the horrific conditions and consequences of slavery. As synthetic overviews, both works allowed their authors to raise some of the big questions that continue to drive scholarship today, but they also clarified the need for more focused studies that could test these larger questions in the great variety of economies, regions, and circumstances that belie the notion of a monolithic South.

The women studied in this book lived and labored on the large rice plantations found in lowcountry South Carolina. The antebellum lowcountry rice economy included many of the South's largest plantations, its wealthiest planters, and some of its largest and most culturally resilient slave communities. In 1860, an estimated 33,800 rice plantation slaves shared the Carolina coastline with a diverse lowcountry society, including about 109,000 additional slaves who labored on large Sea Island cotton plantations, in Charleston, or on smaller farms and plantations. That lowcountry society also included a varied population of whites, not only planters but also yeoman families employed on, or subsisting apart from, the plantation economy.[3] But the specific physical and demographic landscape, unique African-American culture, and distinctive system of slave labor that marked life and labor on lowcountry rice plantations helped create a distinctive plantation experience, which is the focus of this study. Knowing that African-American women's experiences elsewhere in the South were quite different, I offer here a detailed study attentive to the workings of a specific regional experience, both fleshing out and confronting the level of generalization that prevails in the existing literature on slave and freed women.

This book also offers a new periodization for the study of slave and freedwomen. It places enslaved African-American women at the center of the South's wartime and postbellum transition from a slave society to a free-labor society. The history of African-American women in slavery and freedom is inseparable from the history of their own communities. It is deeply entwined as well in women's complex relationships with slave-owners, with the mobilized wartime forces of South Carolina, the Confederacy, and the Union, and later with the Northern agents of Reconstruction.[4] Therefore, this is also a history of slave and freed women's encounters with the state, both during and after the war. Their confrontations with the institutionalized power of state authorities—whether Confederate officials, Union soldiers, or Freedmen's Bureau agents—reveal how gender and race informed the articulation of power, the development of postbellum social and economic policy in particular, and the material consequences of that policy.[5]

Women and Slavery

Women's experiences in slavery varied widely, deeply affected by features such as the process and organization of farm or plantation production, the size and regional stability of the slave population, and the impact of the internal and African slave trades on local slave populations. All of these factors created substantial differences in the material conditions of slavery, in the kinds and amount of work a woman was forced to perform, and in a mother's ability to maintain a family and a household, while also affecting her ties to community and her ability to resist exploitation. Labor—including field work and domestic production—was obviously central to women's experience of slavery.

For more than five generations, the coerced labor of African and African-American women had proven critical to the successful development of rice agriculture and the profitable plantation economy of lowcountry South Carolina. Women cleared trees and brush from new fields, constructed and maintained the elaborate tidal rice plantations that lined the coastal waterways, and cultivated the region's primary agricultural export. Slave women also performed the skilled domestic labor that was essential for the support of their own families, for the larger plantation slave labor force, and for the comfort of their owners' households. The labor extracted from enslaved women, whether in lowcountry mud or mansions, helped to make the region's plantation economy enormously profitable.

On the eve of the Civil War, rice agriculture rested squarely on the shoulders of slave women whose lives were spent in the fields and ditches that marked the distinctive lowcountry terrain. This exploitation was not an unusual or isolated development in the American South, nor in the Atlantic plantation complex. As in other advanced plantation regimes, a significant number of the "prime" field hands on lowcountry rice plantations were women.[6] Their daily labor in the rice fields was organized under the task system, so that the work of preparing fields and cultivating and processing the rice crop was assigned by the task—a portion of an acre for hoeing, a certain number of linear feet for ditch-digging, a certain number of rice sheaves cut and tied. This distinguished slave women's field labor on rice plantations from women's dawn-to-dusk labor on cotton or sugar plantations. The pace of task labor was set by slaves, who—with considerable effort—could often complete their tasks by midafternoon. For slave women, this translated into more time for the labor of raising and caring for families and for a variety of economic activities unrelated to the plantation's staple crop. Slave women's experience as rice workers and domestic servants also influenced the specific ways they resisted slavery, their wartime struggle to escape or destroy slavery, and the ways in which they defined freedom.

Women and War

Lowcountry slaveowners feared—and enslaved women and men on their plantations hoped—that slavery could not survive the Civil War. The blockade of Southern ports and the subsequent disruption of trade, the withdrawal of white men from agriculture to military service, and demands by the Confederate military and state authorities for slave labor, food, and material goods all disrupted the patterns of plantation life and production in the lowcountry.[7] Shortages in food and clothing, and the displacement of slave laborers through impressment and removal to the state's interior, further undermined the traditional cycle of rice culture that for many generations had anchored lowcountry plantation production and slavery. With the occupation of Port Royal by Union forces early in the war, the threat posed by the proximity of the enemy exacerbated the war's domestic interruptions.

These wartime conditions translated into incremental disruptions of the traditions, customary rights, social relations, and domestic networks that lowcountry slaves had forged over several generations of struggle against slavery. The standard of living in the slave quarters deteriorated significantly. Yet even as material conditions worsened on lowcountry rice plantations, slave women accelerated slavery's collapse by slowing plantation production, resisting the new forms of exploitation introduced during the war, and escaping lowcountry plantations and making their way to the fleet of federal ships blockading the coast. When slave women seized the opportunities presented by the war to weaken further the institution of slavery or to secure their own freedom, they also challenged the declining living conditions on rice plantations.

It bears stressing that war affected not only the material conditions of lowcountry slavery but also the relationships of power that were a part of slavery. The interests, needs, and demands of the state and the Confederacy weakened not only the actual power of lowcountry slaveowners, but also their appearance as powerful masters. Planters became increasingly unable to purchase or afford the most basic necessities; their plantation products and slaves were subject to impressment; they, their overseers, and their sons became vulnerable to conscription; and increasing numbers of plantation mistresses assumed unprecedented and unanticipated responsibility for plantation operations in the absence of husbands and sons. Slaves watched the art of domination that had pervaded lowcountry slavery weaken and change shape. Slave women not only observed but tested and acted upon the wartime crisis in slaveowner hegemony, exploiting newly exposed weaknesses in the bedrock of slavery. They were determined to make the war's trajectory toward emancipation irreversible.

Women and Freedom

The substance of former slave women's defining acts of freedom on South Carolina's rice plantations varied widely in the first months of freedom. Such acts included attacking former overseers, raiding planter residences and storehouses, confiscating or destroying planter property, and clothing themselves and their children in finery "in pride of their freedom."[8] Former slave women also turned their attention to the nature of postemancipation agriculture. They insisted upon their right to live and work—independent of white supervision or intrusion—on the land where their ancestors lay buried, the land they and generations of their ancestors had improved and worked as slaves. When forced by the terms of Reconstruction to work for planters under a military-imposed system of contract labor, freedwomen persisted in their efforts to define freedom on their own terms. They sought increased control over their labor in the fields and in domestic

service; they rejected what they regarded as overly arduous or demeaning labor; and they struggled to distinguish their work from slavery's relationships of dominance and subordination. Freedwomen vociferously—
sometimes violently—challenged the reappearance of planters, white
overseers, and former slave drivers on lowcountry rice plantations, defending their right to live and work without the intervention, exploitation, and
abuse they had known as slaves. Determined not to sacrifice any of the
prerogatives or autonomy they had gained under the task system, freedwomen vigorously defended their privileges against encroachment by
planters or by agents of the state who wished to install wage-labor relationships between planters and former slaves.

Women also made new claims. Now free, they insisted on their right
to select their own labor supervisors. They worked in groups of their own
choosing. They insisted on determining for themselves the number of
hours that they and their families would work for the planter. They rejected the Freedmen's Bureau counsel about the benefits of wage labor and a
ten-hour workday. Looking to the past and to the future, they insisted on
remaining free of white intervention in the workplace and on the inviola-
bility of their homes and family life in the quarters.

The portrayal of Reconstruction in lowcountry South Carolina offered
here, of freedwomen's active and public role in the contested social and
economic landscape of the postbellum South, departs significantly from
the prevailing discussions of freedwomen in some of the most recent histories of Reconstruction. Freedwomen are usually described as withdrawing from agricultural and, to a lesser extent, domestic employment in the
postwar period. These descriptions draw from the findings of economic
historians working with census data from cotton-producing areas, and from
a plethora of contemporary observations, sampled from across the South.[9]
Interpretations of the meaning of women's withdrawal from the workforce
have varied. Some historians assert that freedwomen gladly yielded to their
husbands' demands that they withdraw from agricultural employment, that
they voluntarily collaborated with their husbands' postemancipation claims
to the privileges and prerogatives of a patriarchal family and household.
Other historians suggest that freedwomen were imitating white behavior,
anxious to claim for themselves the privileges they perceived in elite white
women's domesticity—not the least of which was an escape from the
physical demands of field work and the demeaning labor of domestic service.[10] Still other historians of Reconstruction describe women's withdrawal
as their singular or most significant defining act of freedom, as an assertion of their liberation from the dominion of white slaveowners, an exer-

cise of freedwomen's claim over the right to allocate their labor exclusively within their own households and for the benefit of their own families.
The historians Jacqueline Jones and Gerald Jaynes, in particular, have
emphasized freedwomen's creative attempts to choose productive and
reproductive labor in their own and their families' best interests.[11]

The vital connection between freedwomen's pursuit of family autonomy and their influence over the evolution of free labor in plantation fields
and planter residences remains unexplored. This is probably because freedwomen are still by and large ignored as actors on the public postbellum
landscape, the landscape from which historians typically draw the "facts"
of Reconstruction. Freedwomen across the South are believed by many
historians to have preferred limiting their expectations about the consequences of freedom to the more private domain of their homes and family life, caring for spouses, children, and extended families in the role of
full-time wives and mothers—a privileged role denied to them under slavery. Yet their very important endeavor to reconstruct African-American
family life in the wake of emancipation was not divorced from other more
public struggles to define the consequences of black freedom in the South.
Unfortunately, the prevailing assumption of freedwomen's allegedly universal withdrawal has reinforced a notion that freedwomen were observers of, not participants in, the interrelated struggles to define freedom and
free labor in the postbellum South. Besides marginalizing freedwomen in
the historiography of Reconstruction, this has also discouraged scholars
from considering the pervasive significance of gender in the reconstruction of the South.[12]

On lowcountry rice plantations, freedwomen did not withdraw from the
contested terrain of plantation life and labor, nor did their actions suggest
that they regarded their social and reproductive labor as work that was isolated from or unaffected by other areas of postbellum and postemancipation conflict and dispute. Lowcountry freedwomen spoke to the importance
of their paid and unpaid labor with their words and their actions, when they
attempted to shape their agricultural and domestic employment as well as
their social and reproductive labor, according to their own expectations. In
seeking control over their field labor, women sought to distance themselves
from the power and control of former slaveowning whites *outside* of the rice
fields as much as *in* them. Freedwomen pursued that autonomy—readily
acknowledged as the goal when freedpeople resisted restoration of plantation lands—through every phase of negotiating plantation labor and also in
reconstructing household economies.

While I have found considerable agreement between freedwomen and freedmen about how they wanted to reconstruct the rice plantation economy, this does not mean that conflict did not arise among freedpeople. Testimony by newly freed women and men suggests that domestic conflict was not unusual, and that their ideas about the relationship between gender and authority in their communities was in flux. Their traditional beliefs were buffeted as much by the implications of men's military experience as by federal policies that promulgated specific gender roles as part of the larger agenda of spreading the gospel of free labor in the postbellum South. The conflicts that emerged between freedwomen and freedmen remind us that gender was inseparable from many of the key issues both confronted after the war: the meaning of free labor, of independence and dependence, of kinship relations and citizenship, as well as the changing formulation of racism in a postemancipation society.

The Setting: Slavery on Lowcountry Rice Plantations

In 1820, Mrs. Charlotte Petigru Allston observed of her slaveowning neighbors in Georgetown, South Carolina, that "the Majority of the People here . . . make Rice to buy Negroes and Buy Negroes to make Rice."[13] It was by rice and slaves that Allston's family and other white planters of the South Carolina lowcountry became the elite of Southern planters in the eighteenth century, with the highest per capita wealth among the colonies; by 1790, their wealth reflected unusually high holdings in land and slaves. Just before the Civil War, lowcountry rice planters dominated the slaveholding elite—the 1 percent of American planters who owned more than 100 slaves.[14] Years after the postwar decline of the lowcountry rice industry, white descendants of the rice barons and the few remaining rice planters grudgingly acknowledged that the elaborate rice plantations and the wealth they had created were the product of slave labor: "like the pyramids, slave labor only could have accomplished it." The former slaves, on the other hand, knew precisely what they and their forebears had been forced to accomplish in the lowcountry; in the words of one former slave, "all dem rice-field been nothing but swamp. Slavery people cut kennel (canal) and dig ditch and cut down woods—and dig ditch through the raw woods. All been clear up for plant rice by slavery people."[15]

South Carolina's earliest white settlers, in the 1670s, brought with them from Barbados a familiarity with the plantation as a mode of agricultural production and the use of African slaves, as well as a model of government that recognized and protected the complete domain of slaveowners over their human property. When Carolina's Anglo-Barbadian colonizers began to experiment with rice cultivation in the last decade of the seventeenth century, unfree black labor (as well as Native American slavery) was already an established feature of the region's mixed economy—which at that time included the export of naval stores and lumber products, livestock, and deerskins. In the next two decades, rice cultivation began to transform not only the landscape but also the demography and the economy of the low-country: white settlers imported increasing numbers of African slaves to carve rudimentary rice plantations out of inland swamps, and enslaved blacks became the majority of the lowcountry population.

African slaves were essential to the successful development of lowcoun-try agriculture, not only because of their labor, but also because of their superior knowledge about rice and indigo cultivation.[16] In fact, as the re-search of the historian Edward Pearson in a variety of Africa sources has confirmed, the contributions of African slaves to the technical refinements of American rice agriculture came most likely from the women, who, in West Africa, were the primary cultivators of rice. By 1720, when rice be-came South Carolina's most valuable export, the lowcountry had already begun its agricultural evolution into a plantation society.[17]

A new and more profitable method of rice cultivation introduced in the 1750s guaranteed that even with the demise of indigo production, the low-country's plantation regime would thrive for another century. The new tech-nique of tidal rice cultivation utilized the force of tides to flood and replen-ish rice fields located along freshwater rivers and completely dominated rice agriculture by the early nineteenth century.[18] The relocation of rice planta-tions from the decreasingly fertile inland swamps to the coastal river sys-tem accelerated when planters discovered that the regular flooding of rice fields would endlessly replenish the soil. The last half of the eighteenth cen-tury was the period of South Carolina's most intense involvement with the African slave trade. Charleston's slave market provided access to the large labor force required for the necessary large-scale land improvements. Plant-ers bought increasing numbers of slaves and set them to work on the dig-ging of ditches and canals and the clearing of woods. With the labor of their slaves, they created the lowcountry tidal rice plantations.

Along eleven river systems of the South Carolina lowcountry, where the freshwater flow was affected by tidal forces, African and African-Ameri-can slaves built the efficient and profitable tidal rice plantations. Several of the "rice rivers"—the Waccamaw, Black, Pee Dee, Sampit, and Santee—were in the area surrounding Georgetown; others lay to the south, between Charleston and Savannah.[19] Slaves transformed the landscape of these lowcountry river systems, clearing the land and enclosing it from the rivers with hundreds of miles of sturdy earthen banks. They divided and subdivided the fields into standardized squares by canals (fifteen feet wide, several feet deep), which opened into the river, and smaller irrigation ditches (eighteen inches wide, about two and a half feet deep). The flow of water in and out of the canals was controlled by wooden floodgates and culverts, crafted by slave carpenters, which were alternately opened and closed by slave trunkminders to take advantage of the tide to flood or drain the field. The canals were wide and deep enough for navigation by flat-bottomed boats, which carried the harvested rice to the barn for threshing and then to the schooners headed for the market.[20]

This tremendous gridwork of banks, canals, and ditches was constructed at great cost to the increasing numbers of African men and women forced into the Carolina lowcountry during the eighteenth century. Haphazard shelter, inadequate diets, and bad water intensified the impact of fever and respiratory disease, exposure and exhaustion, all of which took a heavy toll on African men and women already physically and psychically devastated by the experience of enslavement, dislocation, and transport. The accelerating demands of plantation agriculture introduced new hazards, as well. As one nineteenth-century observer noted, rice agriculture was "by far the most unhealthy work in which the slaves were employed . . . they sank under it in great numbers."[21]

The increased importation of Africans into the lowcountry raised the overall mortality rate among slaves and rendered the labor-hungry colony dependent on new imports to maintain, let alone increase, the slave population. High mortality rates among newly imported African slaves, and the very high ratio of adults to children and of males to females among the human imports, impeded the transition from an African-born to a self-reproducing, African-American population. African control over the supply side of the Atlantic slave trade helped keep the proportion of men to women in the Atlantic slave trade at about two to one (female slaves were highly valued among Africans for their productive and reproductive potential), and as a consequence most of the slaves imported to the colony were males.[22] Because many newly imported slave women were unable or unwilling to bring children into lowcountry slavery, and because slave infants faced a high mortality rate, eighteenth-century planters relied on "fresh imports" to maintain their slave workforce.[23]

Those women who were sold to South Carolinian buyers were among the early settlers and pioneers of the lowcountry, helping to clear the fields where later generations of enslaved women would cultivate crop after crop

NORTH CAROLINA

SOUTH CAROLINA

81°   80°   79°

34°

Black River

Pee Dee River

Waccamaw River

Murrell's Inlet

Santee

Britton's Neck

Plantersville

River

Sampit R.

Pineville

Moncks Corner

N. Santee R.

S. Santee R.

North Island

Winyah Bay

South Island

33°

Ashley R.

Cooper R.

Bull's Bay

Ashepoo River

Charleston

Mt. Pleasant
Ft. Sumter
Ft. Moultrie
Charleston Harbor
Ft. Johnson
Secessionville
Stono Inlet

Combahee R.

Wadmelaw

Folly Is.

Port Royal Is.

Edisto Is.

N. Edisto R.

Savannah R.

Broad R.

Beaufort

S. Edisto R.

St. Helena Sound

Colleton R.

St. Helena Island

Port Royal Entrance

Hilton Head Is.

Ogeechee River

GEORGIA

32°

ATLANTIC OCEAN

Catherine Island

Sapelo Island

Altamaha R.

St. Simon's Island

0 10 20 30 40 50
Miles

81°   80°   79°

Domier

of rice.[24] Several developments later in the eighteenth century allowed planters to capitalize more effectively on both the productive and the reproductive potential of slave women. The lowcountry plantation regime became more settled, agricultural labor more regularized, and the economic advantages of a self-reproducing slave labor force more urgent. But most important, as the numbers of first-generation African Americans in the lowcountry's slave population increased, so did slave women's fertility and the rate of reproduction.[25]

Eighteenth-century South Carolinians' investment in rice and slaves contributed to the development of distinct regional characteristics within lowcountry rice-plantation agriculture; rice planters accumulated considerable wealth and unusually large holdings of slaves, and the slave population developed several significant and distinctive demographic characteristics.[26] First, lowcountry black society was heavily infused with various African cultures, since Africans—particularly from the Gambia region, the Windward coast, and Angola—predominated in South Carolina's eighteenth-century slave population.[27] Second, the population of lowcountry South Carolina became predominantly black and enslaved. By 1810, all lowcountry parishes were more than 80 percent black. Immediately before the Civil War, slaves constituted about 85 percent of the population of Georgetown, the premier rice-producing district of lowcountry South Carolina, much higher than the South's average of about 32 percent.[28] Nearly 68 percent of the population of the lowcountry region was made up of black lowcountry residents, most of whom were enslaved.[29] Third, lowcountry slaves were also increasingly concentrated on very large plantations. In 1790, in two sample lowcountry parishes, more than half of the slave population resided on plantations of one hundred or more slaves. By 1820, more than 80 percent of the slaves in one Georgetown parish belonged to planters owning more than one hundred slaves; by 1860, although only one-third of the South's slaves lived in units of fifty or more, the median slaveholding unit in Georgetown was 135.[30]

The long-term trends within the lowcountry's slave population—toward creolization, a more balanced sex ratio, and regional stability—eased the process of establishing family and community by and among rice plantation slaves. With family and community came the creation of additional social and cultural institutions and traditions, infused with diverse African customs and worldviews, from which lowcountry slaves drew meaning and identity.[31] Gullah, the language created by slaves who combined English with several African dialects, endures today as evidence of this process of cultural syncretization.

The growing numbers and concentration of slaves in the lowcountry, and in particular their resistance to the agricultural revolution that forced most lowcountry slaves into the plantation regime, also evoked a repressive response from white South Carolinians. Planters, sensitive to the fact that they were outnumbered by their slaves, became anxious about their ability to control the slaves in their midst. The 1739 Stono Rebellion and the 1822 Denmark Vesey Conspiracy prompted tighter codification and regulation of slavery. The Stono Rebellion, occurring during the intensification of plantation slavery in the colony and at the high point of African slave importation, led to temporary restrictions on slave imports in the 1740s. It also resulted in the immediate passage of the extensive Negro Act, stringently limiting slaves' personal liberties and increasing the role of the state in regulating and controlling the slave population. Similarly, the planter-dominated state legislature reacted to the 1822 Vesey conspiracy by imposing new limitations on slave mobility, prohibiting white people from teaching slaves to read, and curtailing the religious organization and instruction of slaves.[32] The restrictive slave codes made life under the institution more difficult particularly for urban slaves, while the rural black majority of the lowcountry continued to live and labor under constraints defined largely by the demands of rice cultivation.

Although many whites across the South blamed absentee slaveowners for a range of evils associated with slavery, including slave rebellion, patterns of absenteeism among land owners took firm root on lowcountry plantations during the eighteenth century as planters sought to protect themselves against the environment of disease in the malarial lowcountry swampland. African slaves demonstrated a relative degree of resistance to the swamp fevers, convincing lowcountry whites that African labor was indeed the linchpin of successful rice production. Rice planters and their families typically fled from the threat of malaria and yellow fever during the summer months, moving to "pine-land retreats," villages such as Pineville or Pinopolis; to Charleston; or to coastal summer houses. The most attentive planters made day trips to their plantations in the months after the rice was sown in May and before the fall harvest was completed.[33]

Absentee planting only reinforced what other lowcountry conditions (a black majority, large slaveholdings, planters' desire for discipline and control over the plantation slaves) made evident to rice planters: that a sophisticated system of labor management was needed. As the mid-eighteenth-century observer William De Brahm noted, "the tasking of a Negroe and providing Employ . . . is one of a Planters principal Studies, since the preventing of Idleness is the Art, from which depends the whole Dis-

cipline of the Negroes and the Planters Success."[34] The labor system that
evolved relied upon white overseers as well as black drivers (selected from
among the slaves) to allocate and supervise slave labor.[35]

The nature of slavery and plantation agriculture in the lowcountry presented special problems in organizing slave labor. The large workforce
required for profitable rice cultivation, the superior expertise of Africans
in rice agriculture and their likely influence over the labor process itself,
and the periods of slack time inevitable in rice agriculture all contributed
to the evolution of the task system as the core of the rice plantation regime. Under the task system, each field hand was ranked according to age
and capability as either a full or a partial hand. Gender was not a determi-
nant of task rating, and task rating was in turn irrelevant to the plantation
sexual division of labor. Unlike the organization of slave labor on the sugar islands or on large cotton plantations into closely supervised gangs that
worked dawn to dusk, daily work assignments, or "tasks," on rice plantations were based on standard portions of an acre (one-half to one-quar-
ter)—measured off by irrigation ditches—which planters and slaves negotiated as a reasonable day's work. Under this system, field labor became
uniquely well defined and predictable. Furthermore, although assigned
individual tasks, slaves often performed their labor in gangs. Several rice
planters used sex-segregated gangs.[36] While each field hand was assigned
her or his own task, the completion of a day's task was often a cooperative effort among slaves in the field. Regardless of their task rating, the more
able slave laborers assisted the less able. Planters and overseers not only
recognized slaves' preference to work cooperatively but also occasionally
took advantage of it, assigning overly demanding tasks to some slaves,
expecting others to assist in their completion.[37]

A greater latitude for unsupervised activities was granted to slaves
under the task system than under the dawn-to-dusk gang labor typical on
cotton and sugar plantations in other parts of the South. Planters found
that the task system was, to a certain extent, self-regulating: slaves drew
on their familiarity with rice agriculture, and they worked at a self-deter-
mined pace. While slaves gained some control over the process of production, even a partially self-regulating slave labor force alleviated some of the
pressure on planter and overseer to plan, organize, supervise, and evaluate each day's labor on plantations where slave laborers might number
several hundred. By accepting and even encouraging slaves' self-subsistence (providing slaves with their own provision plots, for instance), lowcountry planters also successfully transferred to slaves some of the burdens of provisioning that other systems of labor placed on planters.

While accommodating an unusual degree of self-direction among slaves, the system of task assignments also reinforced the authority of overseers and drivers, giving their orders and directions the weight of "custom" and an entire system of labor. Slaves who challenged drivers or overseers took on the burden of challenging a regional institution, for both slaves and planters across the lowcountry were conversant with the division of rice agriculture into steps and stages measured as tasks. The standardized labor assignments of the task system stood as a buffer between slaves and their supervisors.

The historian Philip Morgan has provided evidence that, early in the development of the task system, slaves attempted to carve out a measure of independent market activity. Morgan has identified repeated legislative efforts in the late seventeenth and early eighteenth centuries to impose restrictions on the internal market system by which lowcountry slaves peddled the variety of goods they produced after the completion of their tasks, including groundnuts, benne (sesame seed), calabashes, peppers and an array of other vegetables, as well as hogs and poultry. This extent of slave production probably preceded the formal organization of the task system, when South Carolina's first slaves struggled to meet their own subsistence needs. By 1751, slaves' insistence on producing and marketing surplus goods resulted in both legislative recognition of slave marketing and increased legal obligations on planters to purchase rice and corn grown by their slaves. Slave men and women were able to transform opportunity into customary rights, while planters believed they had gained a new link in the chains of lowcountry slavery—that the accumulation of property among slaves would lessen their motivation to run away.[38] After all, reasoned the overseer on Pierce Butler's plantation, "no Negro, with a well stocked poultry house, a small crop advancing, a canoe partly finished, or a few tubs unsold, all of which he calculates soon to enjoy, will ever run away."[39]

By the beginning of the nineteenth century, rice agriculture and lowcountry slave society already shared a long history, out of which had emerged a unique plantation regime in the slaveholding South. Set apart in the American South by the wealth of its planters, by unusually large and relatively stable plantation communities, and by a regional population that was predominantly black and heavily infused with the African heritages of its enslaved immigrants, this plantation regime was also characterized by the essential labor performed by enslaved female agriculturalists, from the very beginnings of lowcountry rice culture to its antebellum maturity. Our focus turns, in the following chapter, to the specific contours of slave women's work—the process and organization of field and domestic labor.

Part 1

Slavery

1 "Women Always Did This Work": Slave Women and Plantation Labor

On antebellum rice plantations, field work was slave women's work. The preparation of fields, the planting, cultivation, harvesting, and processing of rice, and the maintenance of the elaborate plantation irrigation systems occupied the daily lives of most plantation slave women. It was a pattern of female labor that can be traced to the late colonial period.[1] While male slaves provided the essential labor in bringing in lumber and constructing and maintaining plantation buildings and fences, as well as in a range of artisanal production, slave women were more consistently, and in greater numbers, assigned to labor in the rice fields. Antebellum slave inventories suggest that on the large rice plantations of the lowcountry, slave women were often the majority of prime field hands.[2] Just as women's labor was central to rice agriculture, field labor was central to women's experience of slavery. As noted in the introduction to an anthology on slave labor in the Americas: "Slaves worked," and the particulars of that labor "determined, in large measure, the course of their lives."[3] A detailed examination of slave women's field work can tell us much about the day-to-day experience of slave women in the lowcountry rice plantation regime.

The Backbone of Field Labor

During December, January, February, and March, with morning temperatures dropping below freezing and the fields occasionally layered with ice, women and men were sent out to prepare for the new rice crop.[4] Before the soil could be broken by hoe or plow, the tall stubble and rubbish left on the field from the previous year was burned off. On many plantations "burning" was executed exclusively by women, always in gangs, sometimes by adults joined by young girls.[5] Sometimes, too, the task was assigned to a gang of "lusty women, as the phrase is here for women in the family way."[6] One planter recalled that

> burning stubble was usually done by women, who dragged the fire with their hoes. When the stubble was thoroughly dry and a stiff breeze blowing, they sometimes had to jump across the quarter ditches to avoid the advancing fire. There was considerable excitement in this work, and the women seemed to enjoy it. Their dresses were tied up to their knees and did not hinder them from jumping the ditches when they were caught in a close place by the fire. "Look out, Sister!" they would often call to each other. "Don't let dat fire ketch 'ona. Jump across de ditch."[7]

This relatively light task, which required watchfulness and quick response rather than strength or endurance, was undoubtedly preferable to the heavy work that followed, in which workers wielded clumsy hoes with eight-inch blades.

As women burned off last year's stubble, overseers sent out plowmen to begin turning up the soil in the burned-off fields. Prior to 1830, plows were not used in rice cultivation; as one observer noted, "the clumsy iron hoe is, almost everywhere, made to do the work of pick, spade, shovel, and plow."[8] Most planters would have agreed with Pierce Butler that "the whole land was too moist" for efficient plowing. But slaves believed that there were other reasons for the exclusion of the plow from the rice fields; Butler's own slaves were of the opinion that he refused to use plows "'cause horses [were] more costly to keep than colored folks." Not until slave prices began to climb in 1830 were plows brought into the rice fields, freeing slaves for other work; as one planter noted, "mules can draw harrows, but they can't clean ditches, raise, and make banks."[9] Among field slaves, there was "a regular jubilee among the negroes thereat," for the backbreaking work with hoes was significantly eased as plows were introduced.[10] Plowing would remain the only component of antebellum rice agriculture that used animal labor.

Although women were frequently assigned plow work in other areas of the slave South, on rice plantations such work was exclusively assigned to slave men. As plowmen, these individuals were often categorized as skilled slaves rather than simply field laborers.[11] Superficially, this designation reflected the high degree of specialization that the larger plantation workforce permitted. But the almost exclusive assignment of what planters and overseers considered specialized or skilled occupations to male slaves raises important points about how ideas about gender shaped the way both slaves and planters perceived agricultural production. For example, the slaves themselves may have viewed the elevation of male slaves to a higher status as consistent with traditional Old World (African) gender relations and strategies. Other factors might also have encouraged slaves to support this sexual division of labor. Because plowing took place concurrently with burning, slave women might have resisted being removed from the easier labor and camaraderie of the burning gang. In addition, early in the region's history, only men or boys tended cattle, horses, mules, and oxen; a horse- or mule-drawn implement may thus have come under the responsibility of those who tended the animals.[12]

The exclusive assignment of specialized, and therefore named, occupations to male slaves (plowman, watchman) was also evidence that ideas about gender shaped the way planters and overseers viewed and recognized the special skills and knowledge associated with agricultural slave labor. Only that work performed exclusively by men earned a slave the title and status of a skilled or specialized laborer. Although planters conceded that the agricultural work regularly performed by slave women required special skill, this work was very rarely designated "skilled labor." In the daily plantation records kept by planters and overseers, slave women did not accrue titles, status, or recognition for their specialized agricultural skills or knowledge. Instead, rice planters encouraged a social hierarchy on plantations in which overseers, (male) slave drivers, and (male) slave artisans, ranked in that order, enjoyed a privileged status.[13]

Female field hands on plantations throughout the slaveholding South and in the Caribbean spent most of their time with what could be considered the universal implement of slavery—the hoe. In this regard, the work performed by slave women on rice plantations was similar to that performed by slave women who cultivated other crops.[14] Throughout the yearly cycle of rice cultivation, slave women were more likely than slave men to be assigned hoeing tasks. Slave women's consequent association with the hoe drew comment by various observers; Frances Kemble once described lowcountry slave women as "human hoeing machine[s]," and Frederick Law Olmsted noted women who "struck their hoes as if they were strong, and well able to engage in muscular labor."[15]

In lowcountry rice agriculture, weeks of work with the hoe followed burning and plowing. "Chopping," "turning," "mashing," and "cutting down the land," slaves loosened and leveled the soil in the fields, first with the cumbersome eight-inch hoes, then with four-inch hoes. The driver made sure that the women took care to level the fields, bedding low spots and cutting away high ones, for when rice fields were flooded, high spots might not be covered with water, and low spots might fail to drain properly.[16]

Women also followed the plow into the plantation provision fields to level, and in some cases, to manure the land. Overseers sent slave women to collect barnyard manure; the women then carried it in baskets atop their heads, and hoed it into the upland fields with their "great, long-handled, heavy, clumsy hoes."[17] The monotonous and taxing work of land preparation continued until mid-March.

With the rice fields prepared and soon to be planted, the overseer set slaves to work repairing and maintaining the plantation's irrigation system.[18] Although this system required constant attention and maintenance, there were two periods when overseers devoted a significant proportion of the slave labor force to repairing and maintaining the ditches and banks that crisscrossed the rice fields: at the end of the growing season and, later, immediately before planting. This labor, usually referred to by slaves as well as slaveowners as "mudwork," involved repairing breaks in the banks, replacing or repairing floodgates, cleaning drains, and digging mud and raking trash out of the ditches. With good reason, slaves considered "mudwork" to be the most burdensome task associated with rice agriculture; it was hard, dirty work, performed in hip-deep water or mud. One traveler described slaves repairing the banks that protected rice fields from a flooding river as "working in a long string, exactly like a row of ants, with baskets of earth on their heads, under the superintendence of two under-drivers, likewise blacks. This labour appeared to be heavy, and as the day declined, some of the poor people, especially the women, looked tired enough."[19]

Contrary to the assertions of some scholars that planters did not assign women such difficult labor, a thorough reading of plantation records reveals that slave women regularly performed mudwork and that there was at best only minimal differentiation among the various aspects of mudwork that overseers assigned to men and women.[20] As one rice planter noted in 1835, "in ditching, particularly in canals, it is advisable to work in gangs of six or eight, in a given distance, consisting of men and women. A woman can do nearly as much work as a man, some of them being very expert at the axe and grubbing hoe. While the man is handling the axe or spade, she can be employed in hauling back the excavated earth."[21] Slave men were normally assigned the more occasional and strenuous excavation work, and they also assisted the plantation carpenters with the skilled work of repairing the wooden culverts and floodgates.[22] Many planters distributed spades only to slave men; one planter noted that on his plantation, "in the preparation of the Rice Lands, as ditching, embanking, etc., the *men* alone are engaged with the spade."[23] Another planter explained that both men and women used long-handled scoops to clear mud out of the ditches, but only men were assigned the yearly task of sinking the ditches a bit lower; "only men could do this, walking in the ditches and throwing out the mud with shovels."[24] There was no pattern of slave women's exclusion from mudwork.

In fact, labor routines on rice plantations were such that slave women were regularly assigned various tasks to work "in the mud": for example, while the men dug mud out of the ditches, the women carted it out to the fields. Women were also put to work raking out ditches in late winter, as one observer noted: "the women are rakeing out the vines &cs. which grew in the large ditches,—the rakeing of which is quite a job."[25] Other planters considered slave men and slave women equally competent at ditchwork, dividing them into men's and women's squads and sending them to the same tasks in different fields.[26] From Georgetown, South Carolina, to the Georgia plantations south of the Savannah, rice planters and their overseers assigned slave women task labor in the ditches and drains, repairing banks and dams, in all phases of mudwork.[27] Thus, it was not unusual for travelers in the South to happen upon the "very dreary scene" of "a company of . . . black women, armed with axes, shovels and hoes, and directed by a stalwart black man, armed with a whip, all slopping about in the black, unctuous mire at the bottom of the ditches."[28]

The rice fields were planted from mid-March to early June. In agricultural treatises and in personal memoirs, planters emphasized the skill with which slave women sowed the fields: "A group of women followed the trenches each with a large apron full of seed-rice before her. The rice was thrown with extraordinary precision with a forward movement of the hand."[29] One planter commented that "in fine April weather, it is pleasing to behold the steady, graceful progress of a good sower."[30] Planters were quick to point out that because open-broadcast sowing required "wonderful facility and precision," only "the best hands are chosen to sow rice." One rice grower noted, "Women always did this work, for the men used to say that this was 'woman's wuck,' and I do not recall seeing one of the men attempt it."[31] Even into the twentieth century, sowing continued to be done by women on those few plantations still operating and not using drills to sow the rice seed. "The women," observed a twentieth-century planter, "are very graceful as they sow the rice with a waving movement of the hands, at the same time bending low so that the wind may not scatter the grain; and a good sower gets it all straight in the furrow."[32] Lowcountry

planters rarely offered more glowing accounts of their slaves' skilled agricultural labor than the praise with which they described the female rice
sowers. Nonetheless, these female slaves were never given the status or
privileges enjoyed by male skilled slaves; nor were they ever designated
as specialists.

Like other slave artisans, the female rice sowers turned their skills to
their own advantage. One planter admitted that the sowers, with their skirts
"reefed up" around their hips, sometimes managed to hold "one or two
narrow sacks (under the skirt), which can hold a peck of rice, and some
of the sowers, if weighed on the homeward trip, would be found to have
gained many pounds."[33] But giving up a peck of seed rice—which the
women undoubtedly used to plant their own fields—was considered one
of the prices for a well-sown field. In fact, in 1854 one planter advised
readers of the *Southern Agriculturist* that "it is a good plan to make handsome presents to the best sowers after the planting," although most rice
planters seemed unconcerned about rewarding their female field hands.[34]

If a planter preferred the covered-trench planting method, the sowers
were followed by "coverers," who raked a thin layer of soil over the seed.
If open-trench planting was used, this step was bypassed and the field was
immediately flooded. In this method, the seed rice was specially prepared
to prevent it from floating to the surface once the sown field was flooded.
The rice was spread out on a barn floor and thoroughly mixed with wet
clay hauled in by young men. The mixing was done by young girls, who
"shuffled the rice about with their feet until the whole mass was thoroughly
clayed."[35] Even in this stage preparatory to planting, female slaves exclusively handled and prepared the seed.

The flooding of the rice fields was controlled by the trunkminder, a male
slave second-in-command to the black driver. His primary responsibility
was operating the floodgates, raising and lowering the level of water on
the fields, using the flooding process to sprout the grain, to control weeds
and grass, and to support the stalk as the ripening grain grew heavy.[36]
During the first flooding period, called the "sprout-flow," trunkminders kept
the fields covered with water until the rice sprout emerged, turned green,
and began to fork, at which point they drained the field. A variation of this
process was employed on plantations where the seed was covered with
earth; trunkminders flooded the fields only until the sprout began to
emerge, drained the fields to allow the sprout to mature, and flooded them
once again. Both procedures required that trunkminders carefully inspect
the fields and have an exacting familiarity with the cycle of the tides to
determine the moment when the fields were to be flooded or drained. Both

procedures also demanded very careful handling of the sprouts by field hands, who had to ease the young plants through each draining of the fields. According to the directions of one planter, Nathaniel Heyward, "the people are to raise the rice which has fallen, the leaves of which will be stuck to the ground by the scum left in the water, these they are to raise carefully, running their fingers under them in the manner of combing and breaking off dead leaves, they are to pick the rice very clean."[37]

As the rice required no further attention from the field hands for about two to three weeks after sprouting, overseers sent the slaves to tend the "upland" plantation crops, including corn, potatoes, and peas. Plowed, manured, hoed, and trenched by assigned tasks much as the rice fields had been, these fields were prepared, planted, and tended by both men and women, although women more frequently did this work. Also at this time— about the end of April—field hands were customarily given a day off in which to plant their own gardens and cash crops. On some plantations, this might be a rainy day or a day when the fields were too wet to be worked—when the overseer did not expect a good day's work out of the field hands. Whether allowed graciously or grudgingly, this time was one in which planters, over- seers, drivers, and slaves negotiated the demands of slavery.

When the rice sprout grew to about six inches, trunkminders lowered the water level in the fields, and field hands (men and women) were sent out to wade through the muddy, water-covered fields, to pull out the grass that always threatened to overtake the rice. The fields were cleaned off by being gradually drained, quickly reflooded, and drained again. Overseers sent men and women with long-handled rakes to pull weeds out of the ditches and cart them off the fields. After six or seven days the fields dried, and were hoed twice: first a deep hoeing with the smaller, four-inch hoes, then, ten or fifteen days later, when the roots of the crops were more de- veloped, a careful, light hoeing. Hoeing grass, a common task in rice pro- duction, was undoubtedly one of the most common aspects of women's agricultural slave labor, regardless of the crop.[38]

In early or mid-July, trunkminders flooded the fields with the harvest, or "layby," flow. For the next six to eight weeks the fields remained flood- ed. At least twice during this period slaves would be ordered to wade through the fields to pull off grass and weeds and to carry the trash out in baskets, but on the whole, the rice needed very little attention from any- one besides the trunkminder. Therefore, from mid-July to mid-August, most of the field hands were again occupied with the "upland" crops. Bank and trunk work also continued, as did the various chores associated with plan- tation upkeep.

During this slack period in rice culture, differences between men's and women's work again appeared: once more, women were far more likely to be assigned hoeing tasks, while men were given a greater variety of chores, such as cutting and transporting wood, and assisting carpenters and masons in making improvements to the plantation. Planters' obligation to contribute the labor of a gang of slaves to maintain the public roads was sometimes met during this period before the rice harvest. Slave women were apparently as likely to perform this labor as slave men, according to one mid-nineteenth-century observer, who watched slave women "driving the carts, loading them with dirt, and dumping them on the road; cutting down trees, and drawing wood by hand, to lay across the miry places; hoeing, and shovelling."[39] Just prior to the rice harvest, during early and mid-August, both men and women were set to work stripping fodder from cornstalks in the upland fields, a task described by one planter as "among the least inviting and healthful to the laborers."[40]

The rice harvest began in mid-August, as the rice ripened and the fields, one or two at a time, were drained by trunkminders overnight. Freshly sharpened short-handled scythes—rice hooks—were passed out to the field hands, and "as soon as the water left the surface of the field," the harvest began.[41] On most plantations, men and women shared in the harvest; on a very few, the rice was cut exclusively by the men, "while the women ma[d]e it up into bundles."[42] One planter described the sight, soon after dawn, of "the reapers . . . seen amid the thick hanging grain, shoulder high, mowing it down with the old-fashioned sickle, dealing brisk and dexterous, but noiseless strokes." The men and women "cut three rows at a time. Grasping the stalks with their left hands, they used the sickles with the right, laying the rice on the stubble behind them in order that the sun might dry it."[43]

A day's task, for a male or female field hand, was cutting down a half-acre section of field. Stacks of cut rice, left in the field to dry, were collected the next morning after the dew had burned off. They were tied into sheaves, the sheaves into bundles, and these were hefted onto the heads of men and women who carried their loads through muddy fields to the canals. "It was an amazing sight," recalled one planter, "to see a whole field of rice get up and walk to the barges."[44] Flats, the shallow-draft, flat-bottomed boats used in the rice plantation canals, carried the rice to the threshing yard, where the sheaves were stacked and protected from the night dew. This was perhaps the most vulnerable point in the cycle of rice culture, because it was precisely during August, September, and early October that storms would menace the coast. Either high tides, which threatened the banks and the crop with seawater, or freshets, sudden flooding from the streams and rivers, would ruin the year's work. If a bank was endangered by high water, the driver might send the men to make quick repairs while the women carried out the harvest.[45]

The laborers, too, were vulnerable to the severe weather; the harvest occurred at the hottest time of the year, and was acknowledged by the planters "to be exceedingly severe, and . . . very hazardous to the health, *even to the negroes.*"[46] In the lowcountry, no less than any other area of the slave South, harvest time was particularly hard for slaves; regardless of crop or location, there were more demands on slave labor, more stringent control of their lives both during and after completion of their tasks, more frequent punishment, and for the slaves, less recourse to "custom" as a means of alleviating the demands of the season. The harvest often lasted until mid-October, and most planters "rewarded" their slaves for the eight-week period of hard labor with an end-of-harvest dinner. Still, after the rice was in, there remained upland provision crops to be gathered. All harvesting on the plantation was usually completed before the processing of the rice began.

There were three stages in processing the harvested rice: threshing, winnowing, and milling. Until technological advances and capital accumulation allowed planters to build water- or steam-powered threshing and pounding mills, about 1830, most rice was processed by hand or sent to the largest plantations that had already invested in the machinery. Hand processing—which involved flailing the rice sheaves to loosen the grain from the stalks, winnowing or separating the grain from the chaff, and pounding the rice to release the grain from the hull—was sometimes performed by the entire slave force, but memoirs of lowcountry plantation life as well as drawings of the threshing process frequently portray this as women's work.[47]

During the last step of rice processing, the grain was placed in wooden mortars—constructed from hollowed-out logs—and pounded with wooden pestles. This work, while tedious, also required considerable skill, since broken grains could be marketed only at minimal prices and could not be used for planting. It was a job often (and perhaps typically) performed by women, judging from the extant drawings and photographs, which always portray women at work with the pestle and mortar. Within the first decades of the nineteenth century, the largest planters built hulling mills where the grain was speedily, if less carefully, processed. Seed-rice, however, was always threshed and pounded by hand, to protect the grain from any damage. Threshing coincided with the performance of wintertime plantation maintenance work and often lasted well into January. As in the late-summer slack time, slave women were more often assigned tasks directly relating to the rice crop, while slave men assisted artisans and performed a variety of chores relating to plantation maintenance.

Of all the factors involved in rice cultivation and processing, mill technology had the greatest effect on the labor process, sharply reducing the plantations' reliance upon skilled female threshers and replacing them with male artisans. Water- and, later, steam-driven rice mills began to replace the labor-intensive hand processing of rice, and technological improvements continued throughout the antebellum period. For example, the new thresher purchased by Charles Manigault and installed at his Argyle Island rice plantation in 1847 threshed his rice at such a rapid rate that it freed up most of the men previously engaged with threshing for ditching, draining, and banking during the early winter months—"which never happened to me before," Manigault commented.[48] In the mills, plantation engineers (slave men, never women) kept the machinery working smoothly, often replacing broken and worn-out parts with improvised repair work. Children, partially disabled adults, and elderly slaves all tended to various aspects of the process, assuring the smooth operation of mill machinery; however, it was very rare for prime female hands to work in the mill.[49] Once processed, the rice was packed into barrels or tierces and loaded onto the plantation schooner, which carried the grain to Charleston rice factors.

A diverse range of chores associated with plantation maintenance accompanied the work of threshing during the late fall and winter months. Overseers hurried to place the entire plantation in order for the next rice season; the irrigation system was repaired, the slave quarters cleaned or painted, the outbuildings repaired, fences, gates, and flats built or repaired, thread spun and cloth woven, the harvested crops transported to market; and, as winter stretched into the new year, slave women once again returned with their hoes to the rice fields.

Partial Hands and the Field Labor Force

Prime field hands were the strongest and most experienced anchor of the agricultural workforce, but partial hands—slaves judged by planters or overseers to be unable to perform a full task—were nonetheless a substantial proportion of the field labor force. Teenagers, pregnant or nursing mothers, ill or debilitated slaves, and the older, declining slaves were typically assigned three-quarter, half, or sometimes quarter tasks. Boys and girls under the age of twelve or thirteen were not sent to work regularly in the fields, but, as one planter noted, "all children were prospective field hands," and on many plantations they were expected to assist adults in the fields according to seasonal demands.[50] This same planter explained that "before [children] were old enough to work they knew the name of every [field] and the shortest way to it, for the first thing they were called upon to do was carry dinner to their parents working in the fields."[51] Young children were also expected to carry water to field hands and to run errands for the driver or overseer.[52] Other miscellaneous—yet not insignificant—chores assigned to young children included tending even younger children and infants, frightening away rice birds from the fields as the grain ripened, collecting manure for use in the fields, assisting in the mill and threshing house, and occasionally working with adults in gang labor, girls joining the adult women in raking and burning stubble, boys joining men driving the plows.[53]

Slightly older children (still preteens) might be assigned to a gang under an older woman, designated as a nurse or "foreman," who supervised their labor at certain tasks.[54] Daniel Heyward, planter at Rose Hill on the Combahee River, valued Abby Manigault, the foreman of Rose Hill slave children, as the best field hand he had ever known. She trained and supervised the children's labor at such tasks as loading the rice schooner with the processed grain: "They used to carry the rice in baskets from the rice house and dump it in the schooner's hatches, and Abby never let them linger either in the rice house or over the hatches. [O]ld Abby," Heyward recalled, "kept them moving. She always carried a bunch of switches in her hand, with which she constantly threatened them."[55] Whether the switches were intended for use or for the simple impression they made— on children or on planters—Abby Manigault and women like her were significant in the slave community for their role in guiding the transition from childhood into adult slavery.

Children usually entered the fields as quarter- or half-task hands, at the age of twelve to fourteen.[56] Given hoes with weight and handles proportioned to a child's size, these young field hands were often assigned work next to their parents (usually the mother), who then bore the responsibility not only of teaching them how to work the fields, but also of finishing whatever the child was unable to complete of his or her task.[57] One planter, Richard James Arnold, often assigned "little boys" to work alongside a gang of adult women, even as the women performed difficult mudwork (thus burdening the women not only with supervising the children's labor, but also with keeping the children safe from the danger of drowning and from the snakes, rats, and occasional alligators who lived in the canals and ditches).[58] This was another circumstance in which overseers and drivers recognized and took advantage of the emphasis on cooperation among field hands; they assigned overly strenuous tasks to young task hands, cognizant that adults would help the children rather than allow them to be punished.[59]

Between the ages of fifteen and nineteen, a young slave typically moved up to the next-highest rating—from quarter to half hand or half hand to three-quarter hand. In this way, older children moved up in their rating, until, by the age of twenty, they became full-rated hands. When a young slave first began regular field work, he was "assigned a task next to that of one of his parents, usually his mother, who was supposed to teach him how to do the work properly."[60]

These young workers also became initiated into the sexual division of labor, with girls and boys sometimes sent to learn an adult's responsibilities under the guidance of separate female and male gangs. Young girls joined with older women to learn how to rake and burn last year's stubble on the fields. They learned the art of even sowing from their mothers, while boys learned to guide the plow from their fathers. Thus children were not only productive members of the planter's workforce, but also received some of their instruction within the context of the separate social and productive roles of lowcountry men and women. This was perhaps best exemplified by the older girls who were sent by the overseer to join the "invalid" gang—usually made up of pregnant women—where the girls may have begun to learn how to endure the double burden of enslaved women's productive and reproductive labor on lowcountry plantations.

Slaves remained full hands for twenty-five to thirty-five years, until advancing age, illness, or debilitation from overwork so reduced their ability to work that the overseer was persuaded to reduce their rating. Older slaves might continue working a portion of a task until, reaching their sixties, they were assigned odd jobs on the plantation but no regular task work.

Slave Women's Work Outside the Rice Fields

On the large plantations that dominated the lowcountry landscape, slave women who worked neither in the rice fields nor in the planter or overseer residences might become dairy women, poultry minders, sheep herders, or gardeners. Still others might become nurses for the slave children and for the plantation hospital (these women might also serve as a "fore-

man" over the slave children first learning the meaning of fieldwork), plantation midwives (although this was not likely to be a full-time occupation),
or, on those plantations that provided one or two meals to all their hands
or those not in family units, cooks.[61] Although less numerous and perhaps
less prestigious than artisanal occupations held by slave men, these specialized jobs offered slave women distinct advantages, most important, a
degree of independence, an escape from direct, daily supervision, and a
means of avoiding the demanding, treacherous labor of the rice fields.
Some of these positions offered unique rewards. For example, poultry
women especially used their position as an opportunity to augment family meals, and also to market, surreptitiously (on the plantation or abroad,
when possible), any "surplus" eggs or poultry. Dairy women, of course,
were responsible for minding the plantation's cows while keeping the
owner's house (and, not so coincidentally, her own) supplied with milk,
cream, and butter. Despite the advantages slave women created in these
positions, however, there were also disadvantages: they were less able to
share the risks or the benefits of their positions with the larger slave community. They could neither contribute to nor derive benefit from the solidarity forged among field slaves as a way of preventing planters or overseers from exercising absolute control over their labor.[62] The labor of
women in these special occupations went largely unobserved and unre-
corded by overseers and planters; it was rarely mentioned in the antebellum plantation journals from which historians have been able to reconstruct
plantation life and labor among slaves.

One occupation in which slave women claimed a certain degree of
authority was that of plantation nurse. Charged with tending both children
and adult slaves in illness, nurses were highly valued by planters and overseers, who recognized that a good nurse provided vital services and helped
keep the plantation workforce healthy (without the expense of a doctor's
visit). In the opinion of one lowcountry planter who believed nurses had
considerable medicinal knowledge and expertise, a "raw field negro will
poorly answer the purpose of a nurse."[63] Some nurses, put in charge of
both the plantation hospital and the nursery, also supervised cooks and
assistant nurses.[64] It was perhaps a reflection of the nurse's status that
many rice planters listed the names of their nurses alongside the names
of their slave drivers in plantation inventories and journals. One planter
reported that he "found physicians of little service, except in surgical cases. An intelligent woman," he explained, "will in a short time learn the use
of medicine."[65] A modern authority on lowcountry plantation life respected the traditional herbal knowledge that slave women brought to their

special occupation as nurses; these women "knew the medicinal virtues of all the herbs in the surrounding woods and fields and could cure many childish and other ailments without calling upon the Doctor. This herb lore . . . was very efficacious, curing many a case."[66] According to descriptions by these and other planters, slave nurses regularly interceded between overseers or planters and sick or ailing slaves. The nurse was, perhaps, the only slave vested with the authority and the power to protect other slaves from misuse; certainly overseers and planters relied heavily on her "diagnosis" and her daily reports about the progress of slaves as they recuperated from various ailments.[67]

Most antebellum rice plantations included a considerable number of slave artisans among their slave men. Slave carpenters built the shallow-draft flats, as well as canoes, lighters (the barges used in unloading ships), rowboats, floodgates, outbuildings, and barns. Blacksmiths shod the horses and mended wheels and axles, while coopers crafted the barrels in which the harvested crop was shipped. Male slaves were not only more likely than females to be in "titled" occupations (as noted above in the discussion of plowmen), but also derived more benefits than did slave women from their specialized occupations. For example, slave men with valued skills or special training (like carpenters and blacksmiths) had far more opportunities for mobility than did their female counterparts. They were much more likely to be hired out to neighboring plantations than were women, thus gaining greater opportunities for mobility, earning wages, and sustaining relationships outside the immediate plantation community. The same skills that made male slave artisans valuable to their owners, however, also guaranteed the likelihood of frequent separations from kin and community when the artisan was hired out. Finally, many of these men labored under a system of piecework and had the opportunity to earn wages for work performed beyond the assigned quantity or task. Male artisans, more than any other plantation slaves, were probably the most removed from white supervision, and their highly valued skills lent them some authority—or at least a degree of leverage—in their relationships with whites on the plantation.[68]

Unlike female slaves with special skills or occupations, male slave artisans could also sometimes exercise some control over the pace of work on the plantation, which could be translated into a degree of power and authority in their relation to the overseer, the planter, and possibly the slave community, depending on how they exercised their power. In 1846, Stephen, the miller on Charles Manigault's Argyle Island rice plantation, controlled the rate of pounding and grinding by insisting that the plantation mill could not operate at full capacity. Manigault attributed Stephen's reluctance to a range of possible motives, but he never seemed to comprehend Stephen's effort to prevent a "speed-up" in the mill by regulating the rate of threshing and milling. Manigault purchased a "new Iron thresher" in order to process the grain more speedily, but the overseer soon found that even this new machine relied on the cooperation of the slave engineer and the millhands to run smoothly.[69]

The most powerful and prestigious occupation for any rice plantation slave, which planters reserved exclusively for slave men, was that of the driver. Planters frequently elevated their drivers from among the ranks of the plantation's field hands and tried to emphasize the driver's authority over other slaves by bestowing on him various privileges and benefits, which might include better housing, better housewares, improved rations, greater gardening privileges, and exclusive access to milk cows. But because the driver's authority was derived from the planter, and not from the slave community, the power that attended the position was tenuous.[70] Even more tentative than the driver's status in the plantation community was that of his family. While the driver's family members benefited from the material advantages provided by the planter, they were still expected to perform the same labor as other field hands. Some planters gave the driver's wife special privileges, but there was no general pattern of concessions.

Within the plantation slave community, the driver's reputation—and that of his family—hinged on the field hands' perception of whom the driver aligned with, revealed by his treatment of fellow slaves and whether he used his status and power for personal gain or to the advantage of the entire plantation community. Drivers who used their power to harass or rape slave women earned the deep enmity of fellow slaves. On plantations where the driver earned the enmity of the slave community, for whatever reason, the driver's family also suffered from it. For example, in 1837, the slaves on Waverly plantation murdered the driver and likewise threatened the driver's wife, who was forced to seek refuge in the planter's house. Other drivers were respected by fellow slaves as plantation community leaders. On one lowcountry plantation, two drivers were discovered to have been preaching to their fellow slaves, which according to the planter made the drivers "incapable of seeing or requiring work done by those who had been listening all night to their nonsense." The planter also discovered that the drivers and field hands had collaborated in concealing thousands of bushels of harvested rice, a scheme devised to discredit the plantation overseer. On yet a different plantation, thirteen slaves ran off to protest the overseer's mistreatment of the driver.[71]

Domestic Slavery

By the early nineteenth century, a significant proportion of the plantation slave force did not work under the task system, and in fact rarely, if ever, entered the rice fields. Anywhere from one-third to one-half of a rice plantation's workforce was comprised of domestic servants, artisans, and slaves with specialized occupations. Domestic servants, in particular, had an experience of slave labor very different from that of field hands or artisans. In contrast to the field hands, these slaves generally had received training in specialized skills or could claim special knowledge;[72] many had frequent, often intimate, contact with the planter family and enjoyed relatively advantageous material conditions. Without the differentiation between "master's time" and their own time that the task system established for field hands, however, house servants faced a more personal daily struggle to limit the demands made of them by the planter family or by the pace of plantation production.

The lives of rice-plantation servants and skilled slaves were similar to the lives of domestic or skilled slaves across the South, with the exception that domestic servants were likely to be more numerous and more specialized on the large rice plantations than on smaller plantations or farms. Included among the domestic corps that supported the planter family were personal servants or chambermaids, wetnurses and nurses (for the planter's children), waiting girls, cooks, seamstresses, and laundresses; among the slave men, butlers, manservants, coachmen, and occasionally assistants to the cook. On many plantations, one or two servants were also provided for the use of the overseer and his family. For house servants—mostly girls and women—there were material advantages of better clothing and a more plentiful and varied diet. Former slave women went so far as to assert that, given a servant's access to the planter's larder, it was her own fault if she and her family didn't eat better than the other slaves.[73] Unlike field hands, servants were rarely exposed to the elements, never stood for hours in the mud of the rice fields, never hauled earth to repair a broken bank, never wielded a rice hook or hoe.[74] But under the watchful eyes of the planter household, servants faced more obstacles and challenges in their efforts to shape their work lives and negotiate the terms and conditions of their labor.

Other historians have explored the work processes and social relations of domestic slavery common to the plantation South. The greater relative wealth of lowcountry rice planters, however, translated into more possessions needing repair, cleaning, and tending; elaborate, large residences also required added labor from household servants. Depending on their particular occupations, household slaves worked at innumerable tasks, all geared toward sustaining the high standard of living to which planter families were accustomed. In overheated and poorly ventilated kitchens and in smokehouses and pantries, slave women and girls cooked, baked, prepared, and preserved the daily foodstuffs as well as the elaborate meals required at parties and holidays. Those special entertainments also demanded the labor of preparing for overnight guests and other work required by the display of planter hospitality.

On a regular schedule, slave women had to clean windows and clean and press draperies; take up carpets and beat the dirt out of them; dust and polish the elaborate woodwork, including furniture, banisters, rails, bookshelves, mantles, window and picture frames; sweep the floors; change, launder, and repair bed linens; turn and repair mattresses; replenish washstands with newly laundered and pressed linens and fresh water; and empty slops. Clothing, of course, needed careful attention, from repair to laundering and ironing. Textile production occupied servants year round, from spinning to the manufacture of clothing for slaves and the planter family. Wood and kindling had to be carried in, fires lit and maintained. Besides the material production and maintenance of the planter residence and its furnishings, house slaves were expected to "serve" in a range of capacities relating to the personal needs of planter family members. Slave women had to nurse, feed, diaper, rock, walk, and dress infants; dress, feed, watch, and entertain children, and nurse them through repeated illnesses. Adults required close attendance from slave women for everything regarding personal care, such as assistance in dressing, nursing, running errands, and an enormous range of other demands.[75]

The yearly routine for the house servants of rice planters was dominated not by the cycle of rice cultivation but by the planter's annual exodus from the plantation to the city, to pine-woods retreats, or to summer homes on the coast, away from the summer "miasma" that brought deadly fevers to white and black alike. Every spring, house servants faced the complicated task of packing up and moving the planter household; every fall—usually by late October—there was also the return. On many plantations, it was not only the planter's family that slaves moved, but also the slaves' own families. The mistress at Hasty Point plantation, Mrs. Francis Weston, regularly relocated some fifty people during the annual exodus, as she believed that the spouses and families of the house servants could not spend half of each year separated.[76]

Planters' dependence on the "invisible" services that a house servant provided sometimes translated into a small degree of power for servants, as was the case for Mrs. Lavinia Ball, called "Maum Lavinia" by her mistress and owner. Lavinia was described by her owner as "a thoroughly trained, competent house-servant," whose "terrible temper" was tolerated only because of her highly valued services to the household.[77] But a servant's usefulness did not necessarily preclude punishment, as was the case with another house servant, Martha, whose "eternal and untireing tongue" inspired Martha's mistress to call "a Policeman, who conducted her to the work House, & had her well flogged." Even among treasured servants who were treated with tolerance, recalcitrance or resistance could yield severe retribution and punishment. Sarah, a servant on an Ashepoo River plantation called the Bluff, overstepped her authority when she challenged the driver's right to put her daughter out to field work; Sarah complained to the planter William Elliott that her daughter should follow in her footsteps, but Elliott reminded Sarah that "is not however for her to say."[78]

Relatively few slave men occupied positions as domestic servants. In 1845, on Charles Manigault's Savannah River rice plantation (Gowrie), five of twenty-six adult male slaves worked outside the rice fields, none of them as servants; whereas five of thirty-three adult female slaves worked as plantation cooks and nurses, and one as a maid for the overseer. In 1847, on one of the Sparkman plantations, only two of ten male slaves with special occupations worked within the planter residence, compared to half of the eight slave women with special occupations. In 1858, again on a Sparkman plantation, two of the ten slave men not working in the rice fields worked as servants for the planter or the overseer, compared to four of five slave women who were not field hands.[79] Both the advantages and the pitfalls of domestic service were largely the domain of female slaves.

House servants, assigned to quarters within close calling distance of the planter family, were slaves to the personal needs, whims, and constant demands of their owners and even their owners' children. One rice planter found it "odd" that although his house slaves were better clothed and fed than field hands, "every where the slaves preferred the field-work."[80] But despite the missed advantages of working under the task system, some house servants and slaves in occupations other than field work valued their special privileges, and some were removed to the field as a "demotion." In the spring of 1854, Jane, the nurse on Charles Manigault's East Hermitage plantation, was demoted to field labor when Manigault felt she had not properly attended to some of the sick slaves. Although Charles's son Louis declared it "one of the best Changes ever made" on the plantation, Jane apparently chose to run away rather than endure her demotion; she was captured, put in the Savannah jail for six months, and then sold at the New Orleans market.[81] Planters paid a "cost" for their constant demands on servants: theft by slaves, slaves' moodiness, and their acute awareness of, and willingness to manipulate, the white family's dependence on their skills, labor, and approval. Like task hands, house servants constantly negotiated the terms of their bondage and certain concessions. In instances where the plantation mistress was approachable and responsive to requests made by slaves, servants who had access to her undoubtedly viewed this as another valuable privilege. Although not all plantation mistresses acquiesced, many recorded the constant pleas for intervention and assistance that they received from their servants.[82]

The most significant contrast between field slaves and those with special occupations lay in the differences between men's and women's work in the arena outside of agricultural labor. No matter where their slavery held them—on plantations, in towns, on small farms—slave women who were house servants were vulnerable to sexual exploitation by the white men they served. According to Ben Horry, a former Georgetown slave, female house servants frequently bore children fathered by planters and overseers: "Not WANT 'em. HAB 'em," Horry emphasized.[83] Sexual abuse was inescapable for many female slaves in domestic service, and it often demarcated male and female experience in the "big house." Male and female house servants alike endured beatings, as well as assaults on their dignity, their sense of honor, and their ability to protect their loved ones; but for slave women, underlying their personal safety and their sexual expression and reproductive choices was the constant threat of violation, sexual abuse, and rape at the hands of white and black men empowered by the institution of slavery. Reinforcing the sexual objectification of female house servants was the planter families' tendency to seek what they considered "more decent looking" (oftentimes lighter-skinned) slaves as house servants, slaves whose "genteel and comfortable appearance" appropriately reflected the planter family's wealth, status, and gentility.[84]

Custom and Conflict on Lowcountry Rice Plantations

Planters, overseers, and some historians have argued that the system of lowcountry rice agriculture was entirely (and, according to some, humanely) standardized under the task system, that is, "settled by custom." As observed by Frederick Law Olmsted, "custom has settled the extent of the task, and it is difficult to increase it. . . . If it should be systematically increased very much, there is danger of a general stampede to the 'swamp.'"[85] Despite the appearance of a negotiated peace among slaves, slaveowners, and their overseers on lowcountry rice plantations, slave testimony and plantation records reveal that slaves struggled continuously against overseers and drivers to gain control over the process and pace of production, and they persistently tried to manipulate what appeared to be settled by custom to their own advantage. Slave women's challenges to custom were also often framed by pregnancy and childbearing. Women's encounters with the threat of rape and sexual abuse provided additional impetus for subtle, persistent resistance and occasional outbreaks of open rebellion. As the backbone of the plantation workforce, slave women were key figures in the collaborative traditions of lowcountry slave resistance.

As described above, field labor, even under the task system, was difficult and demanding work, and task assignments were intended to squeeze as much work as possible out of the workforce. Planters and overseers alike understood the central lesson of rice plantation slave management: "that because a negro knows how to do good work it does not follow that he will do it—*unwatched.*"[86] Threat of punishment for uncompleted work was as prevalent in the lowcountry as it was in other areas of the slave South. One former slave, Hagar Brown, recalled that in "Rebs time," when overseers "Gin you task [gave you a task], you rather drown than not done that task!" Slaves had to "clear task to keep from beat" [complete their task to avoid a beating]. Brown also recalled that her former owner beat her sister, Henritta, because she was too sick to complete her task, so that Hagar's mother "have to work he self to death to help Henritta."[87] Ben Horry recalled the cruelty of the black driver, as well, who "lay task on 'em she ain't able for to do."[88] Another former slave, Henry Brown, recalled that if slaves didn't complete their tasks, they faced a whipping.[89] When a slave on Pierce Butler's Georgia rice plantation failed to complete her assigned task and was consequently flogged, Butler explained to his outraged wife that "the whole thing was a regularly established law, with which all the slaves were perfectly well acquainted; and this case was no exception whatever."[90] His wife soon discovered that slave women were frequently punished—sometimes hung by their wrists or thumbs and flogged—for failing to complete their tasks, especially after childbirth.[91]

Overseers used the threat of punishment to control both the quantity and quality of labor performed by slaves. They flogged slaves for tasks performed sloppily, and drivers checked the tasks daily to ensure the proper completion of assigned work. Besides whippings and beatings, there always loomed the threat of being sold at the Charleston auction, away from family and community, if a slave repeatedly failed to perform his or her assigned tasks to the satisfaction of a driver or overseer. A planter from the Georgia lowcountry reported that an "old woman" who was "very troublesome & has a bad influence on all the rest" was threatened with a long visit to the Savannah jail, where confinement and whippings would bring her "to her bearings." With regularity, both men and women were sent there for this purpose. Slaves also became pawns in conflicts and jealousies between overseers, planters, and planter families; many a slave suffered blows intended to hurt someone else. Charlotte Allston, for example, admitted that the overseer on her family's plantation wanted to beat her slave "Mulatto Joe" only because the overseer knew it would "hurt and Displease me very much, as I think it will be only on my account as the People there say, it is because [the overseer] has an Ambition against me."[92]

The constant resorting to punishment by overseers contradicted the assertions by many lowcountry planters, including James R. Sparkman, that the task system was less exploitative of slaves than other systems of slave labor, because in the lowcountry "the ordinary plantation task is easily accomplished." Sparkman estimated that "during the winter months" a day's labor took "8 to 9 hours" to complete, "and in summer my people seldom exceed 10 hours labor *per day.*" Another rice planter concurred, portraying his slaves "working cheerfully and not too strenuously at tasks which would be completed by early afternoon (from one to four o'clock)." D. E. Huger Smith, in his memoir of rice planting, recalled that "it was seldom that any negro stayed in the field up to two o'clock, and most would have completed a day's work by one P.M." Frances Kemble, in her account of life in the Georgia lowcountry, noted that the workday often stretched from daybreak to six P.M., but she occasionally found women completing their tasks by midafternoon. Slaves and planters had very different impressions of how "reasonable" a day's work under slavery could be.[93]

There is abundant evidence that slaves covertly struggled to gain control over the process and the pace of production. One planter attributed to lowcountry slaves the saying, "De buckruh [white master] hab scheme, en de nigger hab trick, an ebery time de buckruh scheme once de nigger trick twice." This same planter conceded that "by all of [the slaves] combining their tricks, they came near to frustrating my well-laid scheme."[94] Slave women were key collaborators in the day-to-day resistance against slavery and slave labor that occurred across the rice fields of the lowcountry. In 1844, the rice planter Charles Manigault recognized and noted in his plantation journal the careful planning that went into resistance: "Negroes are cunning enough to remember that what they are harvesting they will have to thresh, & will tie as small sheaves as they can."[95] For Manigault's slaves, this meant their task of threshing—an assigned number of rice sheaves—would be effectively lessened. In 1856, Manigault also complained that even "the two primest, & best Negresses on the place (Betty & Cathrina)" were not attentive to the machinery of the mill, and he realized that "any accidental stopping pleases them all I fear, just as it used to be with us all at school I suppose."[96]

Rice planters marveled at slaves' pretensions at misunderstanding instructions "when it suited their purpose to do so." One nineteenth-century observer attributed rice planters' reluctance to try labor-saving devices and machinery to their slaves' reluctance to use new implements; the slaves had gained a reputation for purposefully misusing and breaking tools or machinery that interrupted the "customary" tasks and labor process. A Georgetown planter accused fellow planters of allowing their slaves' dislike for a particular variety of rice to stop them from cultivating it, even though it was a more profitable strain.[97] Finally, slaves' resistance extended beyond their efforts to control their daily labor. Frederick Law Olmsted attributed a great range of waste and carelessness in slave labor to slaves' outrage at being treated as "mere animal machines": "gates left open and bars left down, against standing orders; rails removed from fences by the negroes, as was conjectured, to kindle their fires with; mules lamed, and implements broken, by careless usage; a flat-boat, carelessly secured, going adrift on the river; men ordered to cart rails for a new fence, depositing them so that a double expense of labor would be required to lay them."[98] In even more covert resistance to their bondage, slaves used "superstitious" rituals and prayer to encourage rain, since on many rice plantations, slaves could not be made to work during heavy rains.[99]

Less frequently, but in cases notable for the reverberations they set off throughout the lowcountry, slaves sometimes joined together and openly resisted or rejected slavery. On one of the Manigault plantations on the Savannah River, "from a Real Cause of complaint almost every grown negro (male & female, principally the latter) pushed off in a body & went to Savannah" to lodge serious charges against the overseer with a business associate of the absentee owner. These slaves ran off fully aware that their owner's rule was to sell immediately any runaways at the New Orleans slave market.[100] In 1860, about thirty slaves ran off in a group from the Waccamaw River rice plantation, the Oaks; a local planter reported that "some trouble about work has been the cause."[101] Group resistance may have also taken more subtle forms. On R. F. W. Allston's Chicora Wood plantation there was a suggestion of collaboration among the slave women in resisting overstrenuous tasks, according to an overseer's report of having "flogged for howing corn bad Fanny 12 lashes, Sylvia 12, Monday 12, N Phoebe 12, Susanna 12, Salina 12, Celia 12, Iris 12."[102]

More often, slaves escaped slavery individually. As a form of individual resistance, running away included the rare permanent escapes and the more common practice of taking absence of the plantation for a few days. Slave women were far more likely to absent themselves for short periods of time, those with families having apparently arranged with friends or kin to take over their personal responsibilities until their return. Planters and overseers responded with minimal concern to these temporary departures, at least with individuals they felt sure would soon return—as in the case of Judy, at Gowrie plantation. The overseer explained to the planter, Charles Manigault, "Judy has walked off, but I hope she will feel rested and walk back in a few days."[103] Oftentimes, running away was more a matter of visiting with family and community of origin than an effort to secure permanent escape from slavery, a point understood by overseers and planters. Although rice plantation slaves most often ran away individually, their intent—especially slave women's—probably was to protect, maintain, or restore social and familial ties.[104] Maintaining the community and family ties that planters neither recognized nor respected was an important, and particularly female, manifestation of slave resistance.

Slaves occasionally fought back or ran away in response to work assignments or punishments that they judged unfair. This was the case with Margaret Bryant's mother. Bryant, once a slave in Georgetown, recalled that the overseer "couldn't manage my ma. Obersheer want to lick ma, Mary One say, 'Going drownded meself! I done my work! Fore I take a lick, rather drownded meself!'" One Cooper River rice slave recalled an instance where the overseer was whipping a slave woman, when she managed to take away his whip and turned it on the overseer himself. Similarly, Louis Manigault's slave Hector ran away after inflicting some minor damage on Manigault's flower garden while under the influence of alcohol. Preferring to live in the woods rather than endure punishment, he frequently visited the plantation community without the knowledge of the overseer. Two months later, he had armed himself with pistols and a sword and said "he will not be taken." Short of seeking freedom, other runaways sought some choice over whom their master might be, and where their slavery might hold them.[105]

Not only the slaves, but planters, overseers, and drivers also pushed at the boundaries of "custom." Women and men were often assigned a "full hand's" task by overseers or drivers even when age, disability, or illness prevented them from completing a full task; in this way, overseers exploited the cooperative nature of slave labor, relying on the relatives and friends of the overtaxed worker to complete the work assignment. Overseers and drivers whittled away at the time allocated to women to recuperate after childbirth, which resulted in increased back problems and prolapsed uteruses among women sent back to the field too early. Vagaries in the weather often provided ample justification for the planter to extract extra labor from his hands; a poor crop might warrant replanting, or high water might require working late at night to mend a break in the bank. Some planters persistently explored new ways to employ their otherwise "unproductive" elderly slaves, although by custom those no longer able to work were simply allowed to live out their few remaining years. In contradiction to this custom, H. W. Ravenel, writing in the pages of the *Southern Agriculturist,* repeatedly urged that elderly slaves—especially women—be put to work collecting trash, dung, and even human excrement to increase the manure piles that the lowcountry planter might use to replenish his fields.

Pregnancy and childbirth particularly inspired complaint, covert resistance, and open conflict in slave women of childbearing age.[106] Pregnant women often appealed directly to overseers for lighter tasks, but overseers were rarely inclined to lessen the work typically demanded from prime hands. More likely, the overseer would dismiss slave women's requests, as did the overseer on Frances Kemble's plantation, insisting that the women's assignment "was not a bit too much for them, and that constantly they were *shamming* themselves in the family way in order to obtain a diminution of their labor."[107] Sometimes, slave women appealed to a "higher authority": while a planter's wife was quite content to exploit the labor of her personal and household slaves, and however abusive her behavior toward them, a few plantation mistresses also gained a reputation among slaves for pressuring planters into reducing pregnant slaves' tasks.[108]

Some planters established a policy of having pregnant women assigned to separate gangs (who were presumably assigned lighter tasks) or lowered pregnant women's rating from full to three-quarter hands, and thus managed to continue profiting from the labor of pregnant women.[109] Other planters, and in turn their overseers and drivers, varied in their treatment of pregnant field hands; typically, those who assigned pregnant women lighter tasks did so out of interest in the potential addition to their slave holdings, rather than concern for the well-being of the mother. James R. Sparkman, a Georgetown planter, insisted in 1858 that "allowance is invariably made for the women so soon as they report themselves *pregnant* they being appointed to such light work as will insure a proper consideration for the offspring."[110] In June 1850, the overseer on one of R. F. W. Allston's plantations dutifully kept pregnant slave women out of the potentially dangerous damp rice fields, assigning women hoeing tasks in the upland crops instead.[111]

The treatment accorded female field hands during and after childbirth varied considerably. Nurses and granny midwives within the slave community attended to slave women during childbirth. On at least some plantations, slave women were expected to work their tasks right up to the onset of labor; "if a woman was taken in labor in the field," explained one lowcountry slave, "some of her sisters would help her home and then come back to the field."[112] Slaves on the large rice plantations were always given time off to recuperate from childbirth and to care for their infants—from three weeks to three months. But rather than lose the labor of their prime hands for any significant length of time, planters preferred to assign older, less productive slaves to infant and child care. Frances Kemble's *Journal of a Residence on a Georgia Plantation in 1838–1839* contains many references to the pleas of slave women for more time off before their return to the fields, hoping to avoid the debilitation that commonly resulted from a premature return to the field: "tree weeks in de ospital, and den right out upon the hoe again—*can we strong* dat way, missis? No!"[113] It is possible, too, that slave women, aware of the value planters placed on their labor as field hands as well as planters' disregard for slave parenting, veiled their desire to spend more time with their babies by emphasizing what they thought planters might respond more readily to—their physical capacity to perform field work.

While it is clear from the evidence that planters made concessions to the reproductive needs of slave women, the demands of the field usually prevailed when such accommodation conflicted with the labor needs of the plantation. Slave women were forced into the rice fields despite the pain of a prolapsed uterus; as a Yankee physician discovered during the Civil War, one woman's prolapse was "larger than my fist; it has been so ten years, the master made her work in the field, sometimes till she would drop down at work unable to stand."[114] From the perspective of planters and overseers—whose records of daily plantation labor usually referred to "hands" or "negroes," not men and women—the enslaved African-American women who worked their plantations were "women" only when motherhood interfered with their physical ability to labor. Because adult women typically comprised the majority of a plantation's prime hands, any "generous" accommodation to pregnant slaves or new mothers might have seriously impinged on the plantation workforce and threatened the

overseer's ability to cultivate a large and profitable crop.[115] Instead, planters and overseers offered material rewards to slave women with new babies; after all, extra cloth and rations were cheaper than prime hands.

According to the testimony of former slaves, much of women's most
overt resistance to slavery was a consequence of their efforts to avoid sexual
abuse and rape. Task assignments were often manipulated when planters,
overseers, or drivers were interested in sexually exploiting female field
hands. Slave narratives and other kinds of testimonial evidence from
former slaves describe sexual exploitation as a constant arena of struggle
between drivers and field hands. Ben Horry, once a slave on Brookgreen
plantation on the Waccamaw River, recalled:

> I see gash SO LONG . . . in my Mama—my own Mama! . . . If one them
> driver want you . . . they give you task you CAN'T DO. You getting this
> beating not for you task—for you flesh! . . . The worst thing I members was
> the colored oberseer. . . . He the boss over all the mens and womens and
> if omans don't do all he say, he lay task on 'em they ain't able to do. My
> mother won't do all he say. When he say, "you go to the barn and stay till
> I come," she ain't do 'em. So he have it in for my mother and lay task on
> 'em she ain't able for to do. Then for punishment my mother is take to
> the barn and strapped down on thing called the Pony. Hands spread like
> this and strapped to the floor and all two both she feet been tie like this.
> And she been given twenty five to fifty lashes till the blood flow. And my
> father and me stand right there and look and ain't been able to lift a hand!
> Blood on floor in that rice barn when barn tear down.[116]

Listening to the story, Horry's daughter attested that events like this
had been common.[117] A former slave from Beaufort explained that her
three children were not fathered by her husband but rather by the driver
when she was still a slave: "I had to give up to him or be licked, & I didn't
want to be whipped—." Other former slaves from the same plantation,
including the driver's immediate family, conceded the truth to her claim:
"he was the 'Driver' and he could take any of the young girls he wanted."[118]
Former slaves also recalled slave women's resistance to this exploitation:
Thomas Goodwater, once a slave of a Cooper River rice planter, recalled
that this particular planter "couldn' lick pa cus dey grow up togedder or at
least he didn' try. But he liked his woman slave. One day ma wus in de
field workin' alone an' he went there an' try to rape 'er. Ma pull he ears
almos' off so he let 'er off an' gone an' tell pa he better talk to ma. Pa wus
workin' in the salt pen an' w'en Mr. Winning tell him he jus' laugh cus e
know why ma did it."[119] Such persistent sexual exploitation of slave wom-

en was also devastating to slave men, like Ben Horry and his father, who were forced to watch, without interceding, when the driver beat his resistant mother. Such incidents also fueled further resistance. As a result of witnessing repeated acts of violence against slave women, reported one former slave, Solomon Bradley, "The sight of this thing made me wild almost that day. I could not work right and I prayed the Lord to help my people out of their bondage. I felt I could not stand it much longer."[120]

Some overseers also manipulated their responsibility for a healthy slave workforce to make what were always intrusive, and sometimes abusive, physical examinations of female slaves. Crude gynecological exams were apparently performed by overseers, as part of their obligation to keep absentee planters informed about the "soundness" of female slaves (who frequently suffered from such work-related disabilities as prolapsed uteruses and hemorrhoids). Louis Manigault's overseer kept him closely advised about the physical condition of the female slaves, and R. F. W. Allston was well-informed of the extent to which his own female slaves suffered from "female" disabilities.[121]

Gender mattered on rice plantations, not because it spared slave women from the hardest or most dangerous labor, but because it reserved for slave men the jobs that were labeled as skilled occupations and made slave women the all-season backbone of the field labor force. The few specialized occupations slave women did occupy brought none of the relative advantages enjoyed by slave men in skilled jobs—not the mobility, not the option of earning cash for extra work, not the prestige or power accrued by drivers.

Female field hands knew that planters and overseers thought that work and the reproduction of the slave workforce was the central purpose of their lives as slaves. Slave women resisted by limiting the degree and extent of the exploitation of their labor, but they also challenged this exploitative view of their womanhood over and over again when pregnancy, birth, and the demands (and pleasures) of new babies compelled them to rebel against standard work assignments in the rice fields.

Slave women predominated in the domestic workforce on the large rice plantations. Forced into daily intimate contact with planters and their families, some domestic servants found their womanhood an added vulnerability, a potential for exploitation and abuse by whites. Nearly all house slaves were forced to negotiate their household labor and service in a manner that avoided or lightened the burdens of coerced intimacy and exploitation.

The lowcountry rice plantation regime depended on the successful exploitation of slave women's labor, and slave drivers, overseers, and planters were willing to resort to violence to ensure the success of slave-cultivated rice crops and the "domestic tranquility" of their residences. Less obvious than slave women's labor in the rice fields and planter residences, however, was their social and reproductive labor—less obvious in the historical record, and less obvious in the ways historians have made use of that record. Slave women's reproductive work—their labor on behalf of slave households, families, and communities—was simultaneously shaped by the demands of rice agriculture and of lowcountry African-American culture. It is this more evasive, but no less important, realm of women's labor that is explored in the following chapter.

Mother and child (all sketches
by Alice R. Huger Smith, from
A Woman Rice Planter, by
Patience Pennington, 1913)

At work in the "quarters"

Girls "claying" rice seed to prepare it for planting

Women sowing rice seed

Child labor in the rice fields; carrying in the harvested rice

Women loading rice sheaves into flats

Women flailing the rice seed from the sheaves

Carrying rice from the
winnowing house

2 "Ties to Bind Them All Together": The Social and Reproductive Labor of Slave Women

The workday, for slave women, did not begin and end in the rice fields or planter residences. Slave women also worked in the quarters and in their own provision grounds, gardens, poultry yards, and hog pens. It was labor performed for the survival, comfort, and well-being of self, family, and community. Historians of slavery have sometimes isolated slaves' coerced field and domestic labor (especially that of women) from the "labor of love" that went into the support and care of the women's own families and communities. Separating the labor of slaves (especially women) into two distinct arenas, many of these historians argue, reflects more accurately the worldview and experience of the slaves themselves. Work performed for the master and mistress was performed under duress; work performed at home—in and around the slave quarters—was work through which enslaved men and women asserted their humanity, work that nurtured family and community survival and independence.

While this distinction has directed our attention to some of the ways in which African and African-American women actively shaped family and community culture under the regime of slavery, it also has somewhat romanticized family life under slavery and has allowed scholars to view family life uncritically and as the center of slave women's experience. This view, in turn, has obscured the significance of field labor to women's experience of (and resistance to) slavery, while also perpetuating the myth that women's housework and the care and nurture of family (what I refer to more comprehensively as social and reproductive labor) is not also work. To challenge these multiple and linked myths is not to dispute the idea that family was of central importance to African-American women and men in slavery. Instead, it is to argue that slave women's labor in the rice fields and their work in the quarters were both significant parts of their day-to-day experience of slavery.

In slave quarters and provision grounds, as well as in the rice fields and kitchens of their masters, slave women exercised a degree of authority over how labor was performed, influenced the social relations of that labor, and struggled to make their material and social surroundings reflect their own worldview. In both settings, slave women experienced the direct impact of slavery's regime, including conflict and contestation with planters, overseers, and their own men. They also experienced the burdens, exploitation, and many coercions associated with the material conditions and social relations of slavery. In several important ways, women's reproductive and productive labor on lowcountry rice plantations was significantly intertwined, rendering the seeming boundaries between these arenas of women's lives mutable in ways that must be explicitly addressed.

This chapter considers slave women's social and reproductive labor, but it also attempts to place slave women in the context of their extended families and communities. Twentieth-century debates about the form and function of African-American families, so often highly politicized and based on inaccurate or incomplete histories of American family life, have prompted many scholars to emphasize the importance slaves placed on long-lived conjugal relations and the significance of the nuclear family to African Americans both during and after the end of American slavery. As a result, slave women appear in much of the historical literature largely in the setting of nuclear families. Slave women's deep investment in consanguineous relations and in extended kin networks, and the relationship of these social ties to their experience of and resistance to slavery, are topics that fall outside a narrow focus on nuclear or conjugal families.[1]

In considering the mature lowcountry rice plantation regime, where the overlapping interests of slaves and planters created significant latitude for the formation of extensive kin and community ties among slaves, one may miss a larger picture by focusing exclusively on the nuclear family. By broadening that focus, we find that women played an important and instrumental role in antebellum slave communities, both in laboring in all-female gangs in the rice fields and in assuring the cross-generational continuity of lowcountry African-American culture in and around the slave quarters.[2] An exploration of women's role in the slave community is essential not only to our understanding of women's experience of slavery, but also to our understanding of slave resistance and the transition to freedom. The community was an important vehicle through which slave and freed women tried to establish the meaning and boundaries of African-American freedom.

Many of the details of slave life at its most private—the daily routines and relationships of the immediate family within the slave quarters—remain beyond the reach of historians. Too frequently plantation records, the written accounts left by slaveowners, and even testimony by former slaves provide inadequate evidence to allow a close analysis of intrafamily politics and behavior in the lowcountry. Historians often do not address these limitations on their understanding of slave life and their ability to cross the boundaries between the public and the private worlds of the slave. The extant sources overwhelmingly document only the more public aspects of slave life (such as field labor or publicly celebrated weddings). Still, a wide range of sources allows us to follow slave women from the setting of the smallest social group, the family residences referred to by slaveowners as "the quarters," to the largest, the slave community, whose setting was designated by planters and slaves alike as "the street," in reference to the physical grouping of slave quarters along a central avenue. Since the surviving sources for studying the social history of lowcountry slavery primarily shed light on the public aspects of family life among slaves at midcentury, the discussion that follows must also focus largely on the public, although noting the occasional intersections between public and private worlds of slavery.

Women and the Slave Family

The material subsistence and day-to-day substance of slave family life—no less than the labor performed in rice fields and planter residences—was one point at which enslaved African Americans and slaveowners negotiated their separate interests. When slave men in the late eighteenth century asked their owners for an increase in the number of slave women from which they could find wives, and planters then tried to import greater numbers of African slave women, planters hoped to "render the Negroes . . . happy and contented." More to the point, they sought to increase their own wealth through the reproduction of the slave workforce.[3] Yet, regardless of slaveowners' interest or intent in encouraging family formation among slaves, African and African-American slaves asserted not only their right to family life, but also their intent to shape, as much as possible, family life in ways that were consistent with their own traditions. When the distinct and usually opposing interests of slaves and planters coincided, as they did in this instance, it helped slave family life to develop in the lowcountry.

Even the physical environment of slave dwellings on rice plantations was a point of negotiation related to family formation. Although planters decreed the layout and form of barns, outbuildings, and slave dwellings, the structures were actually built (and sometimes designed as well) by slave carpenters. The slave quarters—typically located one hundred or two hundred yards from the planter residence, or "big house"—were usually uniform in construction. The numerous one-story, two-room cabins (or sometimes attached "duplexes," housing two families), often woodframe but occasionally brick or "tabby" (a mixture of lime, shells, and stones), faced a central avenue and were surrounded by small kitchen gardens, fruit trees, poultry yards, and hog pens. Running behind the cabins was an open ditch, functioning as an open sewer. On Robert F. W. Allston's plantation Chicora Wood, three separate slave "settlements" were needed to accommodate all 236 slaves. Each settlement on Chicora Wood contained about twelve houses, grouped along "the street"; one settlement included the plantation sickhouse, and the overseer's house was nearby. The meager quarters of Allston's and other Waccamaw Neck rice plantations housed slave families of from three to ten people (according to the research of the historian Charles Joyner), but accounts of other plantations place the number of family members residing together at five or six.[4] Allston's daughter noted that the slave families "lived more or less to themselves" in these "separate villages," in contrast to slave settlements in the upcountry, where "it was more like one large family."[5] Lowcountry slave settlements were larger and further removed from the planter residence, and the slave cabins better constructed, than their upcountry equivalents. Since planters and overseers rarely mention the furnishing of slave quarters, we can assume that the interior furnishings and arrangements were the product of slave handiwork, improvisation, and preferences.

The actual formation of slave families was a negotiated process between slave agency and the inevitable threat of separation. Despite the constant possibility of family disruption, the composition of slave families reflected the unusual stability of slave residence on lowcountry rice plantations. Extrapolating from the records of two rice planters, we can gain "snapshots" of slave families at midcentury. These are pictures of slaves living in family units headed by two parents, with two to four children. The records of James R. Sparkman's Dirleton plantation for the 1850s reveal that slave families commonly ranged in size from two to six members, in two-parent households (despite the fact that this plantation had probably changed hands at least four times in the preceding century). In 1854, of twenty-one slave families on Dirleton, three of the five female-headed families were the result of "abroad," or off-plantation, unions (the husband and his owner's names being included in the register); there were only two female-headed families with no notation of the identity of the children's father. The plantation register also revealed occasional instances where slave families adopted orphans. In no case did adult slave men live with young children without the presence of an adult female. Similar patterns of family size and formation appear in Robert F. W. Allston's register for True Blue plantation; in 1855, True Blue housed sixty-nine families, forty-two of which included two to four members. Only three of these families included more than six members. Allston also recorded slave births; from 1856 to 1865, 84 out of 104 recorded births were listed with both parents' names.[6]

Plantation inventories unfortunately reveal much more about how slaveowners defined slave families than they do about family life and the actual configuration of familial relationships among enslaved African Americans. Plantation records, for instance, do not typically document the paternity of slave children fathered by masters or overseers. The substance of those family relationships are difficult to uncover. Wartime observers, including former slaves, repeatedly describe familial relations and obligations reaching well beyond immediate (or coresident) family members to include extended kin. For example, "family" was not always synonymous with "household" among rice plantation slaves. Planters recorded nuclear family units as a means of keeping track of increases among their slaves and to allocate rations, clothes, blankets, and quarters to new families. In general such recordkeeping was an expression of their material interest in the reproduction of the slave workforce. But among slaves themselves, family extended far beyond the confines of the immediate household or the nuclear family. The importance of extended kin to slave family life was noted by Harry McMillan, a former Beaufort slave, who insisted that although children were closest to their parents, "they stand up for all their relations."[7] Robert Smalls, a former lowcountry slave and Civil War naval hero, reported that among extended family members, "their love is strong." Plantation slaves "regard their relations more than city people; they often walk fifteen miles on Saturday night to see a cousin."[8]

The testimony of former slaves in the pension applications of black Civil War veterans provides a few glimpses into slave family life. For example, when taken as a body, pension testimony indicates that for various reasons, lowcountry African Americans clearly distinguished between sexually intimate relationships and marriage. Not all sexual encounters were welcome; owners, overseers, and slave drivers claimed sexual access to slave women as part of the prerogatives of power on lowcountry rice plantations. Lydia Brown bore three children before she married, but everyone on her plantation knew that these births were the consequence of rape committed by the driver.[9] Lucy Brown had two children by her owner, George Fripp, possibly when she was living with her husband, Sandy Brown; she gave the two children her slave husband's name and considered her husband their real father.[10] Slave women were also vulnerable to assault by fellow slaves. Phoebe Brown "was very young" when another slave, Prince Robinson, "took advantage of her"; although he was a married man, he "got her in the family way." Phoebe kept the name of the child's father a secret; the other slaves on the plantation "did not know for some time who the father was."[11]

Neither were all consensual relationships intended as serious, lifelong commitments. Some children born before marriage were the result of youthful sexual liaisons or intentionally brief or casual relationships. Mary Higgins, who lived on the Colleton District plantation of William C. Heyward, bore a child but had not been married prior to her marriage to Brutus Nesbit; "I don't know who was the father of the child—I was then running about and picked up the child accidentally."[12] Participation in more casual relationships was not limited to unmarried slaves. Jane Washington had an "outside child" before her marriage to Hardy Mayrant, but the father, also a slave, was already married and had his own family.[13]

During the war, Ellen Corsee became acquainted with Moses Graham, another slave on a neighboring plantation, and for a brief period they lived together, despite the fact that Graham was already married and had three children. According to a fellow slave, Affy Lawton, although Graham "took up with" Ella Corsee, "he never left his wife." Graham and Corsee "merely cohabited together at times that was all." Lawton observed that "it made a heap of trouble" between Graham and his wife, although they remained married for several more years, until Graham's death.[14]

It is important to recognize that more permanent slave unions, while not invulnerable to human foible, were often the culmination of carefully developed relationships, and marriage ceremonies—although unrecognized by law—were important, memorable events in the community life of rice plantation slaves. Slave men and women sometimes courted each other for many years before electing to marry; some "knew each other all their lives," although they were not necessarily owned by the same planter or coresident on the same plantation.[15] Besides the apparently common consultations with parents of prospective spouses, off-plantation or "abroad" marriages demanded from slave men and women additional, and complicated, negotiations. According to the former slave Andy Marion,

"S'pouse you gits your marster's consent to [take a wife]? Look here, de gal's marster got to consent, de gal got to consent, de gal's daddy got to consent, de gal's mammy got to consent. It was a hell of a way!"[16] Luck Green had to present the owner of his prospective wife with a paper from his own owner, "which was the consent for our marriage," according to his wife, Mary.[17] Slave women also pursued marriage negotiations, approaching overseers, stating their cases as persuasively as possible, and seeking the permission of the planter.[18]

Slave weddings typically were performed at the plantation chapel, at "the white folks' house," or in the slave quarters. Tony Izard, a slave and blacksmith on Weymouth plantation and "a colored preacher licensed to marry and bury the dead among the colored people," presided over several marriages of Weymouth slaves. He performed a "home wedding, in the colored peoples quarters" for Hector Green and Rina Mitchell, and "there were a good many eye witnesses to the ceremony."[19] When he married Nathaniel Allston and Rebecca Nesbit at the quarters on a Monday night, all the plantation people, white and black, attended.[20] The Reverend Thomas Bonneau, a slave who was head carpenter for Robert F. W. Allston, performed slave marriages at Chicora Wood—in the plantation chapel he himself had built.[21] White preachers also performed slave weddings, as did planters themselves.[22] Jane Myers could remember when two fellow slaves, Mary and Luck Green, were married; "they went to the white folks house to be married—I stood on the piazza and could see thro' the window." It is not clear if any other slaves present were allowed to join the couple and the "white folks" inside the "big house."[23]

Planters tried to promote slave weddings and regulate slave marriages for several reasons. Most commonly slaveowners hoped slave marriages would yield children and thereby increase their wealth in chattel property; planters also hoped that stable, monogamous slave unions would produce more contented adults.[24] Other lowcountry planters, ignorant of the slaves' own systems of morality and values, viewed slave marriage ceremonies as a part of the planter's obligation to impart Christian values to their slaves. A Methodist missionary to the Santee River planters during the 1840s was impressed by the extent to which planters regulated slave life and noted that slave marriage was one of the "most particular," or exacting, areas of planter intervention into slave life.[25] For example, one former slave, Annie Frazier, reported that planters in the Georgetown, South Carolina, area did not permit their slaves "to live double lives or have two wives or husbands on the plantations or to leave one wife or a husband for another."[26] Nonetheless, it is apparent from the testimony of former slaves that some marriages were not monogamous (as in the case of Ellen Corsee and Moses Graham, noted above). Planters may have successfully regulated the performance of wedding ceremonies but evidently found it much more difficult to regulate or prohibit the relationships slaves formed with each other, including those between slaves of different owners.

For all the initial interest claimed by rice planters in promoting slave weddings and the monogamous morality of family life, once the ceremonies were performed and slave offspring were produced, planters were far less likely to acknowledge the slave family as a unit in the day-to-day operations of their plantations. The lines of communication and recognition between slaveowners and slave families flowed nearly exclusively from the planter or overseer through slave mothers; husbands or fathers were rarely acknowledged in the distribution of rations or clothing.[27] If Cheryll Ann Cody's intensive study of one particular lowcountry plantation community reveals behaviors typical of planters in the region, planters were also likely to retain daughters with mothers, and to separate both husbands and sons from slave family groups, when slaves were sold or moved in the course of estate dispersal.[28]

The lowcountry rice plantation regime was probably similar to that of other plantations in the United States in that slave mothers were more directly burdened than were slave fathers by slaveowners' interest in slave families. On one hand, most planters encouraged and rewarded safe and successful reproduction. They ordered slave women to report their pregnancies to overseers, usually instructed overseers to assign women in advanced stages of pregnancy to easier or dryer tasks, and rewarded women after childbirth with a short break from their work and increased allotments of food and clothing. But the assignment of field labor immediately before and only three or four weeks after delivery revealed planters' primary interest in plantation production and their disregard for slave women's social labor in reproduction. Slave mothers were made to assume dual and often conflicting work roles as prime field hands (or domestic servants) and as mothers. They asserted that they saw their maternal responsibilities as primary and sought to protect their own health and that of the fetus or infant, which brought them into conflict with planters and overseers over the assignment of overstrenuous task work.

Lowcountry Africans and African Americans defined their families through their ties not only to an extended network of living family members but also to their ancestors, buried on the plantation. The historian Margaret Washington Creel, a scholar of lowcountry African and African-American religiosity, has argued that lowcountry slaves considered their ancestors as integrated members of their families and their communities. Surviving family members played an important role in a deceased relative's successful passage to the spirit world. Creel's argument helps us understand how the unbroken tie between the living and the dead enhanced the meaning of the physical surroundings of the plantation community for slave families and communities. Slaves' ties to locale were not based only on a preference for the familiar or for well-cultivated gardens or cash crops; these links were infused with the same emotional and cosmological content that bound together the slave family and community. The involuntary separation of slave families split the living from the living, but also the living from the dead.[29]

Although planters often did not understand ties to ancestry or many other dimensions of slaves' beliefs, slave men and women won some concessions from them regarding the ways that slaves allowed kin and community ties to shape their lives. The planter Louis Manigault was surprised by the intense expression of grief by two of his teenaged slaves, Nancy and Able Hunt, when they lost their parents to a cholera epidemic. Manigault observed Able "rolling on the ground almost like a Crazy person & Calling his Father & Mother"; "he seems to be deranged at times . . . he imagines he sees his Father & Mother & that they are talking to him, & then he will strike up the funeral hymn." Nancy, too, suffered under "the great loss that has Come upon her."[30] Manigault acknowledged that he could not force Nancy and Able to ignore their grief; he could do little besides keep the two together, reduce their workload, and wait for their grief to pass.

Not only in death, but in many important life events—including marriage, the naming of infants, and involuntary separation through sale or estate dispersal—slaves demonstrated the great importance they placed on family ties. Some of the early historians of the slave family and community far underestimated the strength and resiliency of slave family formation and conflated planters' disregard for slave husbands or fathers with slaves' attitudes about family life.[31] As noted earlier, slaves seeking to marry off their own plantation were forced to seek the permission of both planters, but, conscious of their community's own standards, they might also seek the permission of parents.[32] By choosing a father's or grandfather's name for a newborn, slaves etched patrilineal descent onto the family tree, perhaps explicitly in opposition to planters' disregard (especially in estate dispersal) for ties between slave fathers and their children. When former slave men changed their last names to reflect their free status, their sons adopted their fathers' new names and again asserted and protected the importance of patrilineal descent.[33]

In the lowcountry, even one of the most horrible features of slavery—the buying and selling of slaves—reflected the influence of slave agency. As Keating Ball described it, the pending sale and separation of members of a slave community created a "general gloom" that settled on the plantation slaves "at the idea of parting with each other." Their "gloom" and "state of doubt" had, according to Ball, a decidedly negative effect on plantation labor.[34] Slaves' response to involuntary separation from their families so disrupted the peace and efficiency of the slave workforce that it became common wisdom among nineteenth-century rice planters that slaves should be purchased and sold in intact family groups. Otherwise, one planter acknowledged, "when you buy several small parcels & throw them all together among strangers They dont assimilate, & they ponder over former ties, of family, &c., & all goes wrong with them."[35] Charles Manigault followed this advice closely when he purchased nineteen slaves in 1857, a group that included valuable prime hands like the slave woman Miley, but also unproductive slaves such as "old" Daniel and "old, quite old" Eve. Planters like Manigault purchased unproductive slaves because they were part of a prime hand's family group: in this particular case, "old" Daniel was Miley's husband of six years, and "old, quite old" Eve, her "Anty."[36] Another rice planter (in lowcountry Georgia), on recapturing a runaway slave woman, decided to sell her as well as her sons and her parents. He preferred not to separate slave families, he admitted, but more important, the runaway tended to be troublesome, her family as a whole was unreliable, and if he kept the rest of her family he suspected that "the effect upon them in all probability will not be for the better."[37] Of course, only the wealthier planters, which included most of the rice planters in the lowcountry, could afford to sacrifice profits for the integrity of slave families. And even when planters could afford such purchases, there were always what the planter William Elliott tried to justify as "unavoidable hard cases—separation of husbands and wives—and parents and children."[38]

Rice plantation slaves defended their "right" to mold family formations and maintain family bonds just as they defended their "right" to influence the pace and process of rice cultivation. Ultimately, the ties with kin were so important among slaves that planters found greater benefits in accommodating those ties when they found it possible (and profitable) to do so. Lowcountry slave culture was nonetheless subject to the hard reality of planter power. Patrilineal naming, an emphasis on maternal kinship ties, and a dependence on extended rather than immediate family for emotional and material support were among the mechanisms that helped slaves cope with the possibility of involuntary separation.

Slave Women's Work in the Quarters

The slave family's day-to-day survival, like the efficient operation of the plantation, depended on labor that was performed largely, if not exclusively, by slave women. This labor included obtaining and processing food and preparing meals, nursing the sick and other kinds of health care, and making, washing, and repairing clothing. Unions between slaves were, according to some observers, based consciously on the exchange of these kinds of services and mutual material support. One former slave, Robert Smalls, explained, "My idea was to have a wife . . . to have somebody to do for me and to keep me. The colored men in taking wives always do so with reference to the service the women will render." Laura Towne, a Northerner and an instructor to former slaves on St. Helena, also described the significance of material support to slave marriage: "the wife is looked upon as a help" and was expected to labor on behalf of the family. The notable degree of respect and honor conferred upon lowcountry slave mothers may have been in part a recognition of the importance of their labor to the survival and comfort of slave families. Henry Judd, a general superintendent of Sea Island contrabands, noted that the families "depend almost altogether upon the mother." Yet women also relied on the labor and support of their husbands; a slave widow, Smalls noted, would seek a new husband only when "she is driven to it by want, and must have somebody to help her."[39]

Some historians have argued that slaves created a sexual division of household duties as a conscious act of resistance against the tendency of planters to ignore, if not purposefully violate, the gender conventions preferred by slaves.[40] But the limitations of source materials do not allow confident isolation of one cause for the sexual division of labor that evolved among slaves, especially since there is a range of possible explanations. For example, we know that many rice planters distributed rations and clothing to families through slave mothers, suggesting that these planters presumed and expected slave women would perform, or at least allocate, the work associated with feeding and clothing the family. But it is also possible that slaves chose to delegate the bulk of household labor to women as a conscious or unconscious safeguard against the constant threat of involuntary separation, in which children nearly always remained with the mother, not the father.[41] Plantation registers provide no examples of slave families where adult men took sole responsibility for children. Of course, with the initial formation of slave families, this division of labor may have replicated the sexual division of labor in the African slaves' natal cultures.

Many West African women today continue to carry the responsibility of growing the food to feed their families or earning the money to buy it.[42] Perhaps that tradition persisted over distance, as well as time.

Although rice planters as well as slave families relied upon and benefited from slave women's labor in the quarters, that labor was often invisible to the planters. Planters recorded and described the quantity and diversity of rations they provided for their slaves, but they rarely noted the amount of time slave women had to spend processing the items provided. Food production was a second "task" required of slave women after their field tasks were completed. It was also performed under varying degrees of adversity. "Many masters," complained one overseer, "think they give provision and clothing in abundance, but unless they use means to have these properly prepared, half the benefit is lost." He explained, "Any one that has spent a night on a plantation where the Negroes grind their own Corn, must recollect the horrible sound of a *hand-mill, all night*. It is this that wears them down." If they lacked the necessary time to process their corn or rice, slave women had to trade away the rations and find quicker or easier means to feed their families.[43]

One of the most frequently remarked-upon examples of women's survival struggles in slavery came from their responsibility for feeding their families. Slave women's skill at surreptitiously supplementing their families' meals was well known throughout the slave community and became a part of the oral history of slavery handed down in lowcountry African-American families. In her memoir of life in lowcountry South Carolina, Mamie Garvin Fields explained the source of one lowcountry superstition, passed down by slave women, that "you must never sweep at night":

> The women had to go down to the low, wet places to get the rice. To do that, they would hitch up their skirts and tie them. When they got ready to "fan" the rice that was dry enough, they used a wide fanner basket, and they kept their skirts knotted. I guess you can see what's coming. After pounding the rice to open the husks, they poured it onto a flat basket made like a tray. Then they threw the rice up in the air to let the husks fly away. Each time it came back down, they "fanned" it first one way and then the other, "some for you and some for we." What was "for we" fell into the knots and folds. The rest fell back onto the basket. When they got home, the women untied those big skirts and let their families' rice fall out. Now, if you would sweep your cabin out at night and you couldn't see in the dark what was going out the front door, then you might miss a few grains. When the owner passed by and saw them, she knew that you had been eating rice.[44]

On one of the few rice plantations continuing its operations early in the twentieth century, African-American women continued to appropriate rice for their families. As they sowed the rice, some of the women managed to conceal "many pounds" of rice in their skirts, which were "tied up around their hips" in a manner traditional to African-American women working in lowcountry fields.[45] Women's theft of rice to feed their families was part of a widespread slave tradition of appropriating the planter's property for their own use. It was also one way by which slave women tried to insist that their families took precedence over the production of profit for their owners.

Neither planters nor overseers appear to have expected unpaid after-task labor from slave husbands or fathers. On the other hand, slaveowners expected slave mothers and wives to perform a range of domestic production for the support of the slave workforce, from preparation of meals to the spinning and weaving that offset the cost of the clothing and bedding required by their families. Most planters held slave women responsible for cutting and sewing the clothing allotted each year (generally, two suits of clothing per person) for the entire plantation, allowing two weeks during the winter months to accomplish this major sewing task. Others assigned slave women responsibility for their own household's clothing requirements.[46]

The task system, which so fundamentally shaped women's field labor on lowcountry rice plantations, was no less important in the way it shaped slave women's work in the quarters. The task system alone allowed slave women to set aside daylight hours for domestic production; under the gang system, women's domestic work had to be accomplished between dusk and dawn or on Sundays.[47] On lowcountry rice plantations, task assignments clearly defined each day's labor, and energetic or ambitious slaves who were able to complete their tasks by midafternoon could carve out blocks of daylight hours for their own uses. This made the task system unusually accommodating to slave women who needed to appropriate time and other resources to meet the demands of domestic production, and care for infants, children, or elderly family members.

Slave women and men also used their "after-task time" to craft household utensils and furnishings necessary for their family's comfort. In the quarters, slave men made buckets, bowls, benches, and baskets, while women made mattresses, quilts, and rugs. Men and women contributed to the food supply. Slave men hunted, and both men and women caught fish and crabs to supplement the family larder; slave women tended kitchen gardens and watched over their poultry yards that lay just outside the

cabins, another supplement to the planter's provisioning.[48] Slave households may have also reallocated among themselves the extra labor that
planters required from slave women. One former slave recalled that the
entire family helped to make thread and cloth; children would gather wood
to feed the fire during late evening work and would help clean, card, or
spin cotton along with their parents. The parents' recitation of "Buh Rab-
bit" stories educated and entertained the children and kept them awake
to work.[49]

Under various plantation regimes across the South, slave women and
men carved out a niche in the monolith of slavery when they grew their
own crops, raised their own stock or poultry, or hired themselves out during "off-times" for wages. Described by historians as "independent production," this labor performed by slaves for their own benefit must be
understood in the context of slavery and the ongoing struggle between
masters and slaves.[50] Like slave women's tradition of labor in the quarters
for their families, the patterns of slaves' independent production were
shaped by the daily and seasonal labor requirements of a plantation's staple crop, as well as by the master's need to subsist their slaves. Some planters even saw independent production as a vehicle for social control; one
planter wrote to the *Southern Agriculturist* that "all my slaves are . . . supplied with sufficient land, on which [I] encourage, and even compel them
to plant and *cultivate* a crop. . . . This crop can be tended during their idle
hours, after task work is done, which otherwise would be spent in the
perpetration of some act that would subject them to severe punishment."[51]
Slaves themselves viewed independent production, like household labor,
as a way to raise their standard of living, as another method by which they
could exercise control over, and shape, their daily lives, and as a means of
appropriating their labor for their own benefit. The proceeds might go
toward immediate needs or toward long-term goals such as self-purchase,
the purchase of family members, or the securing of freedom or a better
standard of living for successive generations. Although independent production could be found in every imaginable setting of North American slavery, it took a particularly vibrant form in the lowcountry. On a daily basis,
according to one Northern observer, rice plantation slaves could "cultivate
land for themselves, raise poultry, pigs & on some places cattle, catch fish,
dig oysters or whatever they please," which they sometimes traded for
"finery" or "some luxury to eat."[52]

Slave women's access to time for independent production set lowcountry slavery apart from the patterns of independent production carved out
by slaves working on cotton or sugar plantations or in the piedmont's more

diversified crop economy.[53] Yet both time and land were the crucial build-ing blocks of independent production. By the nineteenth century, rice plan-tation rules and customs governing independent production by slaves varied, but full hands were typically allocated a "task," or quarter-acre lot of marginal land, for their own uses.[54] Slave women—even those who were married—had their own plots of land. Some planters allocated half-tasks of land to older children "capable of working"; the child's land would most likely be incorporated into what was described by planters as the family "holdings," the land already assigned to parents or other adult family members.[55] Slaves with more complicated family arrangements worked out their own land-use customs. Harriet Smith, who recalled that "my mistress always allowed me some land to work in my spare time," had her own plot of land to farm. Her husband lived on another plantation five miles away; according to Smith, "He had his things home to his house and I had mine to my house," and through her industry Smith had accumulat-ed, by the eve of the war, hogs, lard, fodder, poultry, corn, potatoes, and sugar.[56] Planters often provided not only land but also an occasional day off from plantation labor to allow slaves to plant or tend their own crops.[57] On many plantations slaves were also permitted to raise (and graze) their own hogs or cattle, and in some instances horses or mules.

Independent production evolved from a compromise made in the early years of the rice plantation regime to a customary right for slaves, as can be seen in slaveowners' adoption of rules and procedures to ensure that slaves' opportunities translated into benefits for planters. Louis Manigault, for example, reserved to slaves the exclusive right to raise and sell poultry to his own and the overseer's family because there was no land available on his plantation for independent cultivation by slaves.[58]

Skilled slaves, especially those not laboring under a variation of the task system, were occasionally granted substitute privileges by planters. Male artisans such as blacksmiths and coopers were permitted to earn "over-time" pay by working late afternoons, evenings, or weekends for their owners or neighboring planters. Rose Goethe, the slave of lowcountry farm-ers in Coosawatchie Swamp, attested she was a "midwife by profession, and made money before and during the war, besides what I made by crop-ping in my own time." She owned hogs, corn, beef, bacon, "a good lot of poultry," peas, syrup, rice and lard, in the period leading up to the Civil War.[59] This midwife was one of the few lowcountry slave women who entered the wage economy through a skilled occupation. Drivers were allocated additional land and were sometimes allowed to hire other slaves to work the land, or their wives were given extra time off to do so. Neighbors described Pompey Smith, the driver on W. Y. Smith's plantation, as "much indulged" and noted that Smith accumulated considerable property, "so much that he had money to lend at interest." Pompey described himself not as indulged but as hardworking; he insisted that "I got the property by hard work, made money and bought it."[60] The wife of the driver on William Heyward's plantation recalled that she and her husband were able to make "plenty of provisions and meat for our selves," and just before the war they owned hogs, grew several acres of rice on their own, and also raised sugar cane, which they independently processed into syrup. She also owned a yard full of poultry.[61] Robert Bryant, the driver on another plantation, purchased a mule with $167 he earned by "laborment." "The colored population," he explained, "had the privilege of working over time, and raising stock, hogs, and sich as that." Bryant also gained through his "laborment" a watch and "silver money."[62]

Through their independent production slaves also participated in what historians refer to as the internal, or slave, economy. Slaves raised provisions, cash crops, and fodder not only for home consumption; produce was also traded or sold to other slaves, to the overseer or planter, to neighboring plantations, or to the local crossroads store.[63] With independent production as one of the "rights" they claimed, lowcountry slaves were "at liberty to sell whatever they choose from the products of their own garden, and to make what they can by keeping swine and fowls."[64] Interwoven in this trade of slave-produced surplus goods was a trade in stolen crops, oftentimes corn or rice taken from the planter's harvest. This was a black market that lowcountry planters continually attempted (without apparent success) to eradicate. A group of eleven rice planters on the Ashepoo River tried to suppress the active river trade with slaves during the harvest season of 1836.[65] Despite the efforts by lowcountry whites to monitor the off-plantation slave economy, lowcountry slaves "always managed in one way or another to have something to sell, and to do some trading."[66]

Slaves' claims to the goods and commodities they produced were apparently recognized by planters, which is implied by planters' careful record keeping of cash owed slaves for various goods purchased from them. In 1857 alone, the planter James R. Sparkman purchased 190 chickens and ducks from fifteen of his slaves at his Birdfield plantation. Slaves not only traded or sold their produce for cash or exchange, but also made "gifts" of their produce to the planter or his wife, in exchange for certain "considerations": a lighter task for an ailing relative, medicine for a sickly child, permission to go off the plantation to visit family or friends. Such gifts were made regularly and were fully recognized by both parties.[67]

Through the process of accumulation, trade, and independent production, slave men and slave women alike acquired, and bequeathed to their children, some—and occasionally, considerable—personal property.[68] The slaves on Williams Middleton's Combahee River plantation kept their own poultry and penned their own hogs among the slave quarters; inside their houses were not only chairs and other furniture, but also wooden boxes (described by Middleton as "negro boxes") where slaves stored cloth, blankets, skillets, pots and pans, and sometimes the rarer "large silver watch."[69] One slave of Williams Middleton left his son, William Drayton, two hundred dollars' worth of gold and silver, which enabled Drayton to purchase a mule before the Civil War.[70] Abraham and Ann Goethe, while slaves of Eliza Goethe in Beaufort County, owned horses, hogs, and poultry, some of which they purchased with money that Abraham earned from blacksmithing in his spare time.[71] Plenty Green, a slave of Santee River planter James Maxwell, owned "20 fat hogs," four sows, twenty bushels of corn, twenty bushels of rice, ten fowls and thirty ducks.[72] Just prior the Civil War, Harriet Smith, slave of Julia R. Speaks, owned the bacon from five large hogs, and an additional two live hogs, forty fowls, "2 gourds full of lard," fodder, and twenty bushels of corn harvested from two acres that she cultivated on her own—as well as a few prized kitchen utensils.[73] Speaks once testified that one of her slave women killed and butchered five of her own hogs in one year alone.[74] Others accumulated enough money to lend it to fellow slaves—at interest.[75] In each of these instances, the former slaves acknowledged that it was by the permission of their former owners that they had the opportunity to accumulate both property and money; all stressed, however, that it was by their own initiative and hard work that they made whatever they could, creating the best situation possible for themselves and their kin within the bonds of slavery.[76]

On the rare occasions when a slave's rights of ownership over the produce of her independent labor were challenged by a planter or overseer, at least some women were quick to defend those "rights." One slave, Susannah, repeatedly told her owner that he could not shoot the hogs she had raised for the support of her family: "No, massa, you cawnt do it. What can I do for our children's winter shoes and our salt if our pigs are shot? You cawnt do it—you cawnt do it." When her owner ordered her to cease her impudence, she said that she did not mean impudence, but, she insisted, "you cawnt shoot my hogs."[77] Slave women may have been particularly insistent on defending this customary right, since the after-task household work required of them already ate into the time they would otherwise be free to spend in food or craft production for profitable sale or trade.[78]

Women and the Slave Community

By the mid-nineteenth century, South Carolina's rice economy had evolved into a mature plantation regime where slaves were concentrated into large plantation communities. According to the research of Charles Joyner, the fifteen rice planters in one Georgetown parish owned an average of 292 slaves each in the days just preceding the Civil War.[79] Wherever large slave holdings like these occurred, they translated into a double advantage for slaves. There was less risk of personal contact with the slaveowners, and more opportunity for independent social and culture development among the slaves; there were also, among slaves, greater human resources and generational depth for building families, communities, and cultures. The lowcountry rice plantation system incorporated an unusual degree of independence and autonomy among slaves, unique even among the one-third of the slaves in the Deep South living on large plantations of fifty or more slaves.[80] This was because numbers were only one important factor: demography was joined by the task system (which incorporated a degree of independent agency among slaves), the level of wealth among lowcountry rice planters, and the unusually high price of rice slaves, all of which created an environment in which slaves could and did mold relatively stable and autonomous plantation communities linked through several generations of residence in the area.[81] Suggestive of the stability of the lowcountry rice economy, it was reported of one Georgetown planter's 350 slaves that all but one had been born on the plantation.[82] On another Georgetown plantation in the mid-1840s, "Old Lincoln" and "Old Jenney," slaves born in 1777 and 1787, respectively, resided on the same plantation with their seven children and three grandchildren.[83]

Most of the slaves owned by Robert Allston had lived and worked in the Waccamaw area for generations. Consider, for example, the slaves belonging to Benjamin Allston, who headed the second generation of Allston family planters in the Carolina lowcountry. At the time of Allston's death in 1809, he owned 144 slaves, who subsequently were distributed among his six children and his widow. The majority of these slaves continued to live and labor at the Allston family's largest plantation operations, either at Waverly plantation (the family residence) or at Chicora Wood, a plantation that the family had purchased in 1806. The slaves on Waverly remained largely unseparated until 1837, when financial necessity led the Allstons to sell 51 members—nearly half—of the slave community there. Meanwhile, at least 25 slaves had been added to the Chicora Wood slave community, all owned by Benjamin Allston's son, Robert F. W. Allston, following the death of one of Robert's brothers in 1823 and of his mother in 1824. Many of these slaves undoubtedly originated at the Waverly slave community. In 1827, the slaves at Chicora Wood were separated when Robert Allston's sister, recently married, moved her share of the Allston slaves from their mother's legacy from Chicora Wood to her new husband's plantation. In 1828, outsiders were added again to Chicora Wood when Allston, seeking to expand his operations as a planter, purchased 64 additional slaves from a neighboring planter. Some he used to clear swamp land at Chicora Wood, and others he resold at a profit. Twelve years later, Allston inherited another large group of slaves, 58, from his aunt. In the 1850s, he purchased additional land and slaves (including Rose Bank and Pipe Down plantations) to enlarge his holdings to seven plantations and 630 slaves, and to establish his son as a planter.

During the course of fifty years, the Allston plantations had changed hands between siblings and heirs who sought to consolidate their holdings into adjacent lots; some plantations were tools of speculation, another, lost on a bad debt. As the land changed hands, so too did the slaves who worked those lands. But after the plantation regime of tidal rice agriculture had matured, most rice slaves were purchased or sold within the lowcountry. Rice planters demonstrated a clear preference for purchasing slaves from local, if not neighboring, plantations.[84] During his forty-six years as a planter, Robert Allston apparently only infrequently sold slaves, until the Civil War imposed financial hardship on the family.[85] Although the Chicora Wood slave community was occasionally broken by the sale of small numbers of slaves, the plantation was far more frequently disrupted through the addition of land and slaves.

Despite the protections that wealth and the habits of rice agriculture offered against the dispersal of slave communities through forced sales, Georgetown-area slaves were still at risk of separation, as all slaves were. Robert Allston's widowed sister-in-law, forced to sell her slaves, promised to find them a good master and pressured Allston to purchase them as a lot. He finally did so in 1859, after he was visited by deputations of the slaves, who sought to have some voice in the selection of their new owner. But despite Allston's gesture and the best efforts of the slaves to control their destiny, within six years only ten of the original thirty-four slaves remained together. Death, sickness, the war, the opportunity for escape, and perhaps financial strains on the planter had all conspired to separate the group whose members had worked so hard to maintain the fabric of their community.[86]

Although planters controlled the size and stability of the slave community, the social fabric of that community was significantly a product of slave agency. Some planters encouraged the formation of nuclear families among slaves, but slaves themselves placed great importance on the collection of close and extended kinship ties, as well as the extrafamilial relationships, that bound their communities into an integrated whole. Slave quarters could not contain slave life and culture, which overflowed onto porches and into the central "street." After-task work in kitchen gardens and animal pens brought slaves out-of-doors during daylight hours. Slave women gathered to share the grinding mills, or to piece quilts. Older slave men gathered to smoke and talk on the cabin porches. Socializing and religious activities regularly transformed the one-household cabins, intended by planters to promote nuclear families, into interdependent centers of community activity.

Both individual and community identities were linked to locale, in part through the extended kin and community relationships that typically stretched over several plantations and back through several generations of slavery.[87] The stability of the lowcountry rice slave force was unusual. It was a contrast to the three-quarters of all U.S. slaves who were involved in cotton culture, which rapidly exhausted the soil and forced the disruption of many plantation communities through emigration to the Southwest in the early decades of the nineteenth century.[88] Lowcountry slave "community-culture" was misunderstood by rice planters, who presumed that slaves' strong connection to locale was focused on the planter, his white family, the rice fields, and the "big house." Whites often misconstrued in what terms and why lowcountry slaves considered the lowcountry their home. For example, one planter recalled "that there were negroes in Mexico [plantation] working the same half-acre tasks that had come down in their families from the ancestor who came out of the slave ship."[89] He believed that slaves traced their connection to the lowcountry through the rice fields they had cleared and worked for generations. In fact, the link to locale expressed by most rice plantation slaves was focused in part on their own gardens and provision plots, but mainly on the social ties of kin and community that typically extended back through generations of life on a particular plantation or in a particular lowcountry neighborhood. In addition, the sacred grounds where ancestors were buried proved to be an especially crucial link to a specific plantation for families and communities of slaves.[90]

Former slaves themselves tell us a great deal about how they had created and defined their communities. In the pension files of black Civil War veterans and their families there is extensive testimony describing close and extended kin, fictive kin, and community ties, all reaching back through generations of slavery. In 1894, speaking from her home on a Georgetown rice plantation, the former slave Nellie Thompson stated, "I was born and raised here on this place and so were all my ancestors for many years."[91] Thompson, like many former slaves, described the social bonds of her individual and community identity as extending back through relations long deceased, which insured the generational continuity of African-American culture.

One former slave woman described several elements of her community's social ties, explaining that she and another freedwoman had known each other "from a child: we grew up together. We have lived near each other all our lives. We have belonged to the same church and same society. I am her own cousin."[92] According to the former slave Carolina Ellis, the slaves belonging to Robert Allston were scattered onto several different plantations but they were often brought together to work on various projects, so that they frequently visited each other and grew to be close friends.[93] Relationships were also forged between extended kin of different generations, as described by another former slave: "I was a woman when she was a child. My mother was her grand aunt. . . . I have visited her, and she has visited us; we have been backwards and forwards, ever since freedom."[94] The ties that drew individuals into a community were sometimes modeled on familial bonds: one former slave claimed of a friend, "I know him as well as I know my own brother"; and another stated, "I am not related to them but I know as much about them as I know about myself."[95] Bristo Habersham was not kin to Sina Grant but knew her "all my life"; "I sucked her breast the same I did that of my mother."[96] Grace Brown, a former slave, explained further how "fictive" kin ties were formed: "we were children together and grew up on the same plantation and belonged to the same man, and I have lived near them in the same neighborhood ever since."[97] Slave children purchased and brought to the plantation without their families were raised by adoptive families and thereby claimed as part of the plantation community. This was the case with the former slave and Civil War hero Prince Coit: "All of his raisen was right here."[98]

The basis of slave communities in familial relationships has been observed by nearly every historian writing on slave communities in the U.S. South. But in the historiography of the lowcountry, scholars have failed to recognize that the relationship between families and communities was especially important for slave women. Given slave women's responsibility for maintaining their families and the tendency of planters to retain children with their mothers even in the face of slave sales or estate dispersals, the conditions of slavery under the rice regime and the preferences of lowcountry slaves overlapped enough to reinforce a deep respect for slave mothers. One consequence, according to comments made by former slaves, was that "country people" (meaning plantation, as opposed to city, slaves) respected and obeyed their mothers more than their fathers. Henry Judd, a general superintendent of contrabands on several Sea Islands during the war, also reported that "there is a large distinction between the respect paid to the father and the mother; they depend almost altogether upon the mother."[99]

Even though slave women were accorded respect within their families and communities as mothers, they did not escape harassment or exploitation by fellow slaves, in particular, slave men. Some slave drivers were notorious for their persecution of female slaves.[100] While there is considerable evidence of the abuse of slave women by slave drivers, there is little documentation of other kinds of conflict between men and women in the slave community. Yet it would be wrong to assume that there was not also ill treatment of slave women by slave men who were not agents of the planters. Rather, the lack of evidence might be a thread in what Darlene Clark Hine has described as a "culture of dissemblance," an unwillingness of African-American women to divulge, particularly to Southern whites, incidents in which ordinary slave men attacked or brutalized slave women.[101] The narrative testimony made by former slave women, extant today as sources for historical research, was either taken when former slaves tried to obtain benefits or reimbursements, or was collected as part of the Work Projects Administration interviews with ex-slaves. In neither context were former slave women likely, let alone motivated, to divulge to white interviewers or examiners their intimate conflicts with husbands. But the likelihood that conflict did occur is suggested by the extent of post–Civil War testimony to conflict between freedmen and freedwomen.[102] Before the war, slave women may have chosen to air their grievances only within the slave community.

Planters, in using slave women (both biologically and socially) to reproduce the slave workforce, inadvertently reinforced a role through which slave women exercised considerable power in imparting slave culture and survival skills to young slaves. Seizing upon the opportunity created by their dual exploitation as workers and mothers, slave women maintained and strengthened community ties across the generations. They were the primary figures in raising the children of the slave community; in supervising and training children in the work that they would be forced to perform as adults; and in imparting to children the skills with which they, their kin, and their community might survive (and resist) lifelong enslavement.[103] From birth to young adulthood, most young slaves were nurtured and trained by slave women, kin and non-kin, field hands as well as skilled slaves, such as those removed from field labor to care for infants and children. In addition to acts of nurturing, slave women also ensured that the ties that bound them all together in opposition to slavery reached into each new generation. Slave men were not absent from training young people, but their roles as laborers and as fathers did not overlap to the extent that women's did. Slave men dominated in different arenas of work, training young apprentices in the exclusively male-occupied crafts (as coopers, carpenters, and blacksmiths, for example).

A particularly important and powerful role accrued to older slave women in their communities through their supervision of young adults as they entered into the community. Neither slave men nor slave women could claim exclusive dominion over the most important requirement for leadership and authority in their communities; age, rather than gender, was the primary characteristic of authority and leadership among lowcountry slaves. Elders—both men and women—enjoyed an elite status in the community and claimed for themselves the privileges and responsibilities of protecting and leading their communities along both traditional and improvised paths of survival, interdependency, and mutual responsibility. But slave women were especially important in "seeking," the coming-of-age experience through which young women and men joined the autonomous spiritual life of the adult plantation community.

Women's highly regarded status in slave families extended to their role in the community as "spiritual mothers," one of the most obvious and yet unexamined examples of fictive kin transmuting family ties into the relationships that maintained the slave community.[104] With family at the center of their social universe, slaves vested in their spiritual mothers the responsibility and authority to guide and control the entry of young women and young men into the realm of adulthood, with its spiritual duties and its mutual obligations to the community as a whole. Just as the slave midwives relied on years of experience and special skills to deliver newborns safely into the world, so spiritual mothers led young men and women through the travail of "seeking" and safely delivered them to the adult community. The older slave women who were revered as spiritual mothers taught young people how to pray and how to behave. They interpreted their dreams and visions and decided when the seekers were ready for presentation to the praise house—the community's autonomous place of worship. This was an extremely important role in a culture where, according to the research of Margaret Washington Creel, spirituality safeguarded "communal harmony, solidarity, and accountability." In essence, the religious experience of seeking was also a coming-of-age ritual, which marked a young person's transition into adulthood, when allegiances extended beyond immediate and extended family to the community as a whole. Coming of age and recognition from the community as an adult granted a new, more powerful status on young people. Nearly exclusively, older slave women retained control over the process.[105]

The status of spiritual mothers in their lowcountry communities must be considered as part of the larger oppositional nature of the religion that originated in the slave community. Southern planters attempted to Christianize their slaves and manipulate their membership in the church as a form of social control. In the lowcountry, this "mission" to the slaves gained momentum in the 1830s, as Methodists, Baptists, and Episcopalians built plantation chapels and brought preachers onto their plantations.[106] Planters also exercised a heavy hand in appointing "class leaders," elders, or deacons from the slave population to preside over the plantation congregation. Consistent with the planters' experience of organized religion, these chosen leaders were predominantly male.[107] Although lowcountry slaves generally participated in these plantation congregations, they maintained their own religious services and practices away from the eye, and intervention, of whites. The ownership of slaves clearly seemed to conflict with the message of Christianity promoted by whites. The persistent role of spiritual mothers, despite the "informal" nature of their authority, was yet another aspect of slaves' resistance to planters' efforts to "meddle" in the religious affairs of the slave community.[108]

As elder slave women, spiritual mothers often wielded additional powers in their community, accumulated through the primary benefit that age brought any community member. They were described as prophets, fortunetellers, women who wielded "tremendous influence" over their spiritual children, individuals whose wisdom, dignity, and special skills also made them powerful and respected community leaders.[109] Planters as well as white Northerners observed that these female elders held considerable power and authority in their communities, which included, but was not limited to, their affiliation with lowcountry religion. Frances Kemble described the tremendous power and authority of one slave woman, Scinda, who "passed at one time for a prophetess among her fellow slaves on the plantation."[110] During the Civil War, Harriet Ware, Laura Towne, Edward Pierce, and William Allen—all Northern observers—described older slave women who held positions of community leadership and authority, organizing praise-house meetings called "shouts," leading gangs of women workers in various protests and demonstrations, and speaking to whites on behalf of their communities. Older women also helped maintain the important distinction between the shuffle that accompanied the shout and the foot movements seen in secular dancing. An observer noted that when a young woman "showed the slightest tendency to move her feet too far apart, or to cross them, one of the older sisters would reprimand her sharply, often quoting the words of the spiritual—'Watch out, sister, how you walk on de cross! Yer foot might slip an' yer soul got los'."[111]

The spiritual mothers and leaders of lowcountry slave communities may have had antecedents in the female secret societies described by scholars researching the formulation of community in several West African societies. In these cultures, where elders accrued considerable power, the sex-segregated secret societies protected that power by controlling the admittance of young adults into the societies and the community as full adults. Once admitted, individuals exchanged allegiance to parents and kin for loyalty to community and the secret society. Among black South Carolinians we can expect to find a similar approach to community, rather than any direct reformulation of African societies or organizations. The sexual division of labor as well as the social organization of field and domestic work on rice plantations promoted group identity among women. In this fertile setting Africans and African Americans could recall and reformulate the sex-segregated secret societies that regulated most of community life. Margaret Washington Creel has looked to West African antecedents to place the "seeking" experience and the importance of the spiritual parents in a larger historical and cultural context. Many of the diverse ethnic groups of the upper Guinea region of Africa shared significant cultural features, including the role of the secret societies in regulating most of community life.[112] Certainly the importance of community to slave life in the lowcountry suggests that such factors as the ethnic origins of lowcountry slaves, their cultural autonomy and independence from white intervention, as well as the geographic—and hence cultural—isolation of the region provided an arena in which African Americans could forge social relations based on shared cultural memories and values.

In the years before the Civil War, the ties that bound rice plantation slaves into families and communities were viewed very differently by planters and by slaves. Rice planters exaggerated when they boasted that "we don't care what [slaves] do when their tasks are over—we lose sight of them until the next day."[113] In fact, planters expected slave mothers and wives to perform a range of after-task domestic duties that alleviated the planters' own responsibilities for subsisting his slaves. Planters hoped that slaves who participated extensively in independent production would in essence reinforce their ties to the plantation and to their enslavement. Certainly, independent production, no less than the growth of extended, stable families and communities, made life under slavery somewhat less brutal and exploitative to lowcountry African Americans. On the other hand, slaves themselves knew that in subsisting their own families in ways they saw fit, they appropriated their own labor for their own uses, nurtured their families and communities as they bound them together in mutual support, and reinforced a slave ethic of giving new meaning to slave labor. When the Civil War undermined the material basis of slave life and also threatened the bond of family and community, slaves and slaveowners were forced into new alliances and new conflicts. The shifting form of wartime lowcountry slavery affected slave men and slave women very differently, but had the same result: the wartime collapse of slavery on South Carolina's lowcountry rice plantations.

Part 2

Slavery's Wartime Crisis

3 "A Hard Fight for We": Slave Women and the Civil War

For slave women, the wartime battle between slavery and freedom was fought at home, in the slave quarters, the rice fields, their own provision grounds, the planter residences, and even the plantation nurseries and hospitals. It was on the home front that lowcountry slave women experienced the consequences of Confederate demands on Southern slaveowners. They negotiated planter responses to the exigencies of war, accelerated plantation slavery's wartime demise, and struggled to survive the war with their families intact. It was, according to one slave mother, a "hard fight," but it was a conflict that culminated in victory—the final collapse of slavery in South Carolina's rice regime.[1] The wartime battles slave women fought over the changing conditions and social relations of slavery shaped how both black and white Southerners viewed the progress of war. These conflicts also affected the potential consequences of emancipation.

Slave women were provoked to fight because their many contributions to the Confederate war effort were extracted by force. They now labored in new settings, suffered ever-worsening conditions of daily life, shouldered the burden of increasing demands for their work in the rice fields and planter households, and faced increasingly unpredictable separations of their families. Rice plantation slaves, both women and men, suffered these effects of the war at home, but not without exacting a price. They sabotaged the Confederacy's efforts to hire and impress slave laborers, applied long-standing traditions of resistance to the new settings in which they were forced to work, and created or seized new opportunities to resist and escape slavery itself. White South Carolinians could not prevent the decline in stability of plantation slavery, even with increasingly violent measures. Worsening conditions on lowcountry plantations and harsh repression drove many slaves to flight. But even if they made their way behind Union lines to Sea Island contraband camps, slave women found survival—not to mention the pursuit of their freedom—a daily struggle.

The traditions, customary rights, family ties, and community networks that rice plantation slaves had forged over several generations of opposition to slavery were disrupted even before war was declared. Late in 1860, white South Carolinians turned from the issue of secession (approved 20 December) to begin preparations for the anticipated battle over the reinforcement of the federal garrison at Fort Sumter. Before the new year, planters had taken hundreds of slave men from lowcountry rice plantations and put them to work constructing batteries and other coastal defenses on Morris and Sullivan's Island at the mouth of Charleston Harbor. By mid-April, when the battle over Fort Sumter had drawn the state and the Confederacy into war, the conflict had already produced "great annoyance and disorganization on the Plantation," so that, according to one planter, the "routine of work" was "entirely deranged."[2] Planters wondered if slavery could survive the disruptions and pressures of secession and war.[3]

The military conflict that had started in Charleston Harbor returned to South Carolina on 7 November 1861, when Union forces occupied Forts Beauregard and Walker at the mouth of Port Royal Sound, and then Hilton Head, St. Helena, Ladies, and Port Royal Islands, and eventually Edisto Island. Federal occupation of these islands south of Charleston placed the city and surrounding coastline under a threat of attack that lasted throughout the war. The close proximity of U.S. forces to rice plantations was key to the wartime collapse of lowcountry slavery; in trying to defend the vulnerable city and coastline, the state and the Confederate military command placed unprecedented demands on the institution of slavery, on lowcountry slaves, and on slaveowners. At the same time, slaves did not hesitate to take advantage of the war to pursue freedom.[4]

As much as the enemy's presence and other conditions of war threatened the institution of slavery, the actions of slave women and men helped transmute those threats into a wartime crisis. Enslaved women, far from neutral or passive observers of the military conflict, reacted and improvised new responses to the changing circumstances of lowcountry life and labor. Slaveowners discerned the change in their slaves, and some feared the worst. Charles Manigault suspected that his slaves were "polluted with evil thoughts" about the implications of war, and he declared "the perfect impossibility of placing the least confidence in any Negro." The wartime diarist Mary Chesnut found slave men and women "inscrutably silent" on the war, "in their black masks, not a ripple or an emotion showing"—even through the bombardment of Charleston, and as slave men were discovered arming themselves. From a Santee River rice plantation mistress came complaints early in the war of the "license" increasingly taken by slaves; her family's slaves "all think this a crisis in their lives that must be taken advantage of. . . . Times and slaves, have changed" since the onset of war.[5] The comments by the planter elite remind us that slaves not only observed but also tested and acted upon the weakening of planter authority. Slave women fueled each stage of the developing crisis, through traditions of quiet noncooperation, by their complaints, and even by overt opposition to wartime slavery.

Slaves and Wartime Shortages

Wartime shortages and inflation demanded changes in plantation life that were small at the start but blossomed into a large-scale interruption of daily routine. Slave women bore the consequences of that interruption. It was spring 1862 before the federal navy attempted to curtail maritime traffic from Savannah to Georgetown's Winyah Bay. But the "paper blockade" initiated by Lincoln reduced trade and inflated prices. The naval blockade off the South Carolina coast quickly exacerbated shortages—just as available stocks of mill-made cloth were being depleted for Confederate uniforms.[6] Although the lowcountry rice planter counted himself among the wealthiest of Southern men, the Union blockade of Southern ports, when combined with tremendous wartime demands on Southern agriculture and manufacturing, depleted the planter's pocketbook and the plantation larder. The shortages and rising prices prompted changes in the routine of plantation life that had a particularly profound impact on slave women.

The declining availability of cloth and clothing was felt by lowcountry slaves nearly as soon as the blockade was in place. Scarcity and inflation limited the quantity of slave clothing some planters were willing to purchase. Some rice planters tried to ignore the rising price of cloth in the autumn of 1861, apparently unaware or unconcerned that this shortage might worsen in the years to come or that Charleston merchants would find themselves unable to replace their depleted stock. One planter, Thomas Porcher Ravenel, economized by providing his slave men with pants but not coats; however "the [slave] women," he decided, "can do without." As for shoes, "all have to do without," he noted, "as none can be had."[7]

The factory-made shoes planters usually purchased for their slaves were needed instead to outfit Confederate soldiers. The footwear that planters could find was expensive. Even with the ingenious use of substitutes (including canvas, felt, and even wooden shoes), by the fall of 1862 many lowcountry slaves were working in the rice fields without shoes, clothed in rags.[8] Before the first year of war had passed, Elias VanderHorst, an Ashepoo River planter, could "neither . . . afford or buy the Blankets" he usually provided for his slaves, and instead had to "cut up the carpets for the negroes." His daughter's awareness that she must sacrifice the carpets or "lose the Negroes" suggests the extent to which these shortages were already disrupting lowcountry slavery.[9]

In the slave quarters, deprivation was worsened by its cumulative effects, as customary distributions of plantation goods to slaves dwindled and then ended entirely. Planters also assumed greater control over the allotting of what few goods could be purchased, suiting their own priorities but not, one suspects, those of the slave women and children left without shoes or clothing.[10] Want contributed to the apparent rise in sickness and deaths on rice plantations, and even the most mundane shortages had their impact. From overseers' complaints that "the vermin in their heads" were contributing to the sickly condition of slave children on the plantation, we realize that without combs, lice infestations among slave children could not easily be checked.[11] Slaves had to wonder why wealthy planters could not prevent this deterioration of conditions.

Slave women and men directed a steady stream of complaints about wartime shortages to overseers and planters. In November 1864, slaves on Chicora Wood plantation made "a great Complaint" about the lack of shoes and clothing. The overseer on a neighboring plantation complained he could "hardley Get aney thing out of the hands for thay have no shoes and [are] quite Bare for cloths." Overseers' reports that "the negroes are all Beging very hard for clothing" became commonplace.[12] Finding conditions increasingly intolerable, slaves protested, balked at demands on their labor, and generally refused to act as if worsening wartime conditions had not decisively altered their lives under slavery.

Slave women were forced to shoulder the larger burden of planter strategies to cope with wartime shortages. As the scarcity of cloth and clothing worsened, rice planters and plantation mistresses demanded an increase in slave women's domestic production (spinning, weaving, reworking old clothes into new), regardless of their primary assignment in the field or planter residence. Slave women thus found their workdays absorbed by new labor demands and stretching longer into the night. As one woman recalled, "my old Missus made me weave to make clothes for the soldiers till 12 o'clock at night & I was so tired & my own clothes I had to spin over night. She never gave me so much as a bonnet."[13] Planters brought out old hand looms that had fallen into disuse and had them put back into production by those older slave women "who understood [their] construction and working."[14] As the war continued, other items that planters had once purchased from merchants were replaced by substitutes that slave women manufactured on the plantation. Many planter families followed the example of Marjorie Spaulding Kell in entering, with slave women, "into the mysteries of Soap boiling, salt-making, & *shoemaking*."[15] Slave women's work in the slave quarters, while more hidden, also increased, as the women struggled to care for their families with fewer resources of time and materials.

Although we tend to emphasize the impact of wartime food shortages on the white communities from which bread riots arose, those shortages obviously affected slave communities as well. Planters cut the amount and diversity of slave rations, and experimented with substitutes.[16] One rice planter conceded that some of his Georgetown neighbors "put their negroes on half allowance" early in 1864, when it became difficult for planters to buy their provisions. By that year, many lowcountry slaves were apparently receiving meat rations only once a week, some not at all.[17] But the shortsighted economy of some planters had dangerous and even lethal consequences for malnourished slaves. Several Savannah River rice planters decided in the summer of 1862 that with corn, bacon, and molasses "almost impossible to procure" and prohibitively expensive, their slaves would have to subsist solely on rations of rice. The result, according to a local overseer, was that the "constant use of rice for so long a time" killed "many negroes," both children and adults. Their deaths began "with swelling of the feet and gradually rising until the entire person is swollen to an immense size the person dying in 3 or 4 days after being taken." Thirteen slaves on one plantation alone died in this manner. "Thus," declared the planter Charles Manigault, "does the Negro to some extent, experience his share of privation, during the continuance of this War."[18]

Rice plantation slaves had rarely relied exclusively on the rations provided by planters, but the deaths noted above reveal another dimension of wartime shortages. The scarcity of items related to food production in the slave quarters—such as shot and powder, fish hooks, and the materials used to make and repair fish nets—prevented slave men and women from supplementing their families' diet, intensified the impact of food shortages, and highlighted for slaves the growing constraints on their ability to cope with wartime conditions.[19]

The declining availability of salt was one of the earliest-felt, most persistent, and far-reaching wartime shortages, since salt accompanied meals as a seasoning, was fed to cattle and horses, and was used to preserve meat and fish. Although the blockade interrupted the lowcountry's importation of salt, the coastal waterways of South Carolina provided an ideal location for manufacturing it. By early 1862, South Carolinians became almost completely dependent on slave-produced, locally made salt. Its manufacture was also a profitable endeavor, since the price of a sack of salt in South Carolina skyrocketed to twenty-five dollars in 1862, from a low of fifty cents just two years earlier. When the blockade made the transport of rice to market increasingly difficult and expensive, the sale of salt became a ready source of cash for lowcountry rice planters.[20] The severity of the salt shortage, the rising cost of salt, the availability of state-sponsored loans for manufacturing setup costs, and the opportunity to offset sagging plantation incomes all served to encourage lowcountry planters to establish their own "saltworks" along the coast. These operations relied almost exclusively on slave labor, and "vast numbers" of slaves were soon encamped on the Carolina coast, making salt.[21] The size of the operations varied, from the numerous small ones near Charleston to the larger and more permanent saltworks closer to Georgetown, which commonly employed as many as twenty to thirty slaves.[22]

The labor involved in such an enterprise—maintaining a steady supply of cut wood, tending the boilers, bagging, selling, and transporting the salt—was often "carried on entirely by Negroes, without any white man in charge."[23] It also appears to have been carried on largely by slave men, which extended some of the features of the sexual division of labor in normal plantation routines, wherein slave men held most of the artisanal occupations. Slave women (in some instances, the men's wives) may have been brought in to prepare meals or to help bag the salt, but few seem to have been involved in the actual saltmaking process.[24] Nonetheless, the salt shortage affected slave women who remained on the plantation. Slave women's share of the work in the rice and provision fields of lowcountry plantations increased when slave men were reassigned to making salt. Planters' strategies to cope with the salt shortage separated families and communities and forced slave women to cope with the added burdens of work in the quarters.[25] Small wonder that conflict, complaints, rumors of conspiracies, and threats of escape came from the slave men assigned to the saltmaking operations as well as from the slave women who remained behind.[26]

Work in the rice fields continued during most of the war, unaffected

by the restrictions first urged by the Confederate Congress and later legis-
lated by Confederate states on cotton and tobacco production.[27] Confederate officials did, however, confiscate a proportion of the lowcountry rice
crop following the tax-in-kind legislation of 1863, and in October 1864 they
required rice planters to sell half their harvest to the Confederate army at
a set rate. In fact, many rice planters found in the Confederate quartermaster an important market for rice they could no longer export.[28] Even
so, rice production decreased over the course of the war. The reallocation
of plantation labor away from the rice fields to other kinds of production,
the difficulties in safely storing rice and transporting the crop to market,
and, ultimately, the relocation of the lowcountry slave population away
from the coast put an end to many rice plantation operations. Poor weather
and the deterioration of plantation irrigation systems also decreased the
wartime yield of rice crops.

Slaves and War Work

Slave labor, both on and off the plantation, was a critical resource in the
Confederacy's ability to wage war and sustain its armies. The Confederacy had limited means for an extended conflict with the Union (less man-
power, far fewer manufacturing establishments, and fewer facilities for
the transportation of soldiers, ordinance and supplies), making it necessary to employ slave labor in a variety of settings. But that strategic decision had unintended consequences for lowcountry slaves. Lowcountry
plantation slavery was deeply disrupted when slave men and women encountered new settings for the exploitation of their labor, new masters,
as well as new, unpredictable forces with the power to rend their families and communities.[29] The hiring out and impressment of slaves not
only severed family and community ties, but also interfered with slaves'
efforts to endure wartime hardships. As a consequence of impressment,
the work of family survival and support fell increasingly on the shoulders of slave women.

   Only slave *men* were volunteered and impressed to work on South Carolina's coastal defenses. In fact, the legislation enacting impressment in the
state specified the sole eligibility of slave men.[30] Whatever factors influenced
the decision not to impress women for military labor, it was a determination made without open dialogue between Confederate and state officials
and slaveowners. It seems therefore to have been a decision that was unre-
markable to those who made it. But before the war, slave women had reg-

ularly performed backbreaking labor in rice-plantation irrigation canals and ditches. Since both white and black South Carolinians described the work on coastal defenses as very similar to plantation "mudwork," it would seem that mudwork performed for military purposes was viewed as gendered in a way that field labor was not. Of course, the exemption of slave women might have been an effort to placate slaveowners by safeguarding the reproductive potential of their slave holdings.[31] Or, the economic pressures posed by the war may have led rice planters to appreciate the logic of offering the labor of slave men to the Confederate cause, while keeping their slave women laboring at essential plantation and domestic production.[32] Whether their slaves also appreciated this logic lies beyond what our sources tell us. We do know that despite their exemption, slave women suffered the consequences of impressment. The separation of their families and communities, as well as the reduction of the plantation workforce, meant greater burdens for slave women in the slave quarters and the rice fields.[33] Slave women's protests against the splintering of their families—and family strategies for survival—had added meaning at a time when the material conditions of plantation life were so steadily deteriorating.

Lowcountry planters were initially enthusiastic about volunteering supplies, tools, and slave men to erect embankments and fortifications, demonstrating their support for the Confederate cause while defending their own valuable plantations in the process.[34] Between December 1860 and the early spring of 1861, slaves who were volunteered, transported, and supervised by lowcountry planters had erected defense works at strategic points along the entire coast.[35] But neither planter patriotism nor the labor of hundreds of slave men kept pace with escalating military needs.[36] The subsequent turn to slave impressment strained the limits of Confederate nationalism among planters, who were reluctant to test the elasticity of the institution of slavery by relinquishing their slaves to a bureaucratic military authority, however great the need. Only the appointment of state impressment agents would force slaveowners beyond the Charleston area to contribute to the defense of the coast, but the legislature moved slowly and sporadically in responding to the military's repeated calls for slaves.[37] Slaveowners—from the lowcountry and the upcountry alike—were also reluctant to elevate state, let alone Confederate, priorities over the needs of local defense; state officials, for their part, were unwilling to subordinate state defense to the greater good of the Confederacy.[38] State inaction and the vulnerability of impressment legislation to political infighting meant that the plantations nearest the defense works continued to bear the brunt of impressment until February 1863.[39]

The Confederate impressment law passed in March 1863 only generated new controversies, given the army's intent to use South Carolina's
slaves on out-of-state projects.[40] In an effort to overcome slaveowners'
resistance, fines for evading impressment were raised twice, and when
these failed to yield compliance, the state legislature directed sheriffs to
arrest and deliver eligible slaves, costs to be borne by their owner.[41] In the
meantime, the Confederate military command seized as many lowcountry slave men within reach as it could.[42] Although thousands were impressed, neither state nor Confederate mechanisms managed to supply
the military with a sufficient labor force.[43]

Lowcountry rice planters were among the least compliant with impressment.[44] Many were appalled at what they came to understand as the misuse and mistreatment of their slaves at the hands of the Confederate military. To these planters, a war conducted in part to defend slavery should
not, in its prosecution, place slavery at risk.[45] And in fact, the conditions
of impressment justified their concerns.

The destinations to which impressed slave men were sent offered some
of the worst living and working conditions rice plantation slaves had ever
experienced. The hastily constructed encampments gained a reputation,
even among Confederate officials, as a "scene of disgraceful suffering and
want." Supplies of fresh water ran out, food rations were inadequate, and
by the time the men were released they were "almost in a state of nudi-
ty," according to their supervising engineers. Military authorities received
a steady stream of complaints about inadequate shelter, firewood, and
bedding for impressed slaves. Sickness swept through the labor camps.[46]
According to one camp supervisor, impressed slaves suffered from the
discomforts of "light cases of diarrhea or bad colds," as well as pneumo-
nia, dysentery, and tetanus. Lack of medical attention and inadequate
hospital facilities contributed to a high mortality rate among impressed
slaves, rates that worsened as the war dragged on and slaves arrived at
the camps already in rags, malnourished, and vulnerable to illness.[47] On
their return to plantations, slave men often required careful nursing to
restore their health.[48]

Besides the unhealthy conditions of the labor camps, the work itself
proved treacherous. During twelve-hour shifts, slave men were forced into
difficult and dangerous excavation and construction work, much of it performed in waist-high water and mud. Accidental deaths and drownings
were common. Enemy shells took their toll, as did Confederate soldiers
who occasionally found sport in attacking impressed slave men.[49]

Slave men left little in the way of direct testimony about their experience of wartime impressment, but we can piece together some of their responses from the observations of those who supervised them. Labor superintendents repeatedly complained that "our work is going on . . . disgustingly slow."[50] But they soon realized that the poorly performed work came "from a class . . . cunning in what may be deemed by them disagreeable service."[51] When ordered to fill and carry sandbags, slaves were found making and carrying "very small" bags; when ordered to carry other burdens, they ignored the handbarrows and carried smaller loads atop their heads; they straggled, and were "apt to skulk off at night," absenting themselves without permission.[52]

The inadequate supervision of their impressed slaves worried many rice planters.[53] The commander of local forces admitted that "the gangs of negroes" who should have been working on the fortifications were often "idle" in the streets of Charleston.[54] Thrown together with other slaves from across the state, intermingling with free men of color and recaptured runaways, slave men could easily move from seditious talk to plans for escapes or insurrections. Slave men came back from defense work changed; according to one plantation mistress, "Working on the public defenses has demoralized and made the men hard to manage."[55] Rice planters became increasingly convinced that the institution of slavery and their power over specific slaves could be permanently undermined by the influence of impressment. Certainly the abuse of their slaves by state and military authorities made it difficult for planters to maintain their claims to omnipotent authority over their households and the destinies of their dependents.

Many slave men did not return from their work on the coast. Instead they found the means and created the opportunity to flee the encampments and work sites. Many sought temporary or permanent refuge in Charleston, purchasing forged passes from semiliterate Confederate soldiers to gain entry to the city.[56] Others planned mass escapes, paying local slave men to ferry them back to the mainland.[57] They fled the backbreaking work, the unhealthy conditions, and the unpredictable duration of camp life to reunite with their families or to fight for freedom with the Union army.[58]

Even as the Confederacy tried to improve its mastery over impressed slave workers, slaves improvised new ways to manipulate their owners. Sensitive to their pivotal role in the conflict over impressment, slave men confirmed the suspicions of their owners that they were poorly treated, inadequately supervised, and exposed to seditious fellow slaves in the labor camps.[59] The dangers they described induced planters to search for the means to circumvent impressment.[60] Some slaveowners chose to pay fines rather than relinquish their slaves to impressment agents.[61] Others sent overseers to retrieve their slaves, provided slaves with illegal passes, or personally escorted their slaves back to the plantation (according to one engineering officer, "every owner who sees his negro in the city takes him off").[62] By the last year of the war, legislators were being elected on the basis of their opposition to impressment, and the failure of impressment was generally conceded: "The slaves themselves are very averse to this labor, and their owners sympathize with them, feel for them, and are disposed to screen them. . . . The owner has but to wink at evasions by the slaves and the best concerted efforts for arrest are foiled."[63] Slave men and rice planters together confounded the process of impressment, each in their own separate endeavor to influence the destiny of slavery during the war.

When the impressment of slave labor became more difficult and costly, state authorities turned to another vulnerable population to meet its labor needs. It was during the harvest season of 1862, when rice planters were particularly resentful of having their labor force reduced by impressment, that Governor Pickens first urged the state assembly to begin impressing free men of color in and around Charleston itself; "there are many necessarily idle all the time in such a place," he reasoned.[64]

Pickens's impression of the idleness of Charleston's free people of color was echoed by other whites, including elite women who also resented what they felt was the insulation free black men and women seemed to enjoy from the hardships of war. Ann VanderHorst complained that "Black Dandies & mulattoes . . . were dressed in expensive Broad cloth, whilst our poor ladies are obliged to turn & patch & fix off rusty old ribbons on their worn bonnets, I suppose the Dandies said poor Devils they are rather badly off—." Women like VanderHorst also resented the possibility that white women who accepted their share of wartime hardships were subject to the derision of free women of color: "these finely dressed mulattoe women observed in the market look at those poor white women loaded down with work, I would not carry[,] said Miss Mulatto[,] such weights—." VanderHorst recommended punitive action: the Confederacy should "work the Black and mulatto dandies on the Batteries." Her sentiments were echoed by Provost Marshal Francis S. Parker, who was disgusted that free people of color in Georgetown not only carried on business as usual, but had actually increased their profits due to the absence of competition from whites now in the military service.[65] The legislation to impress free blacks, enacted in September 1863, served the interests of lowcountry elites on a number of scores, alleviating some of the pressure on local planters for their slave laborers, suppressing the wartime autonomy free blacks seemed to enjoy, and forcing free women of color to shoulder their share of wartime sacrifice.

With free men of color subject to impressment, free black women were left, as slave women had been, to protect and subsist their families. Mary Orr, a resident of the small free black settlement known as Calf Pen, asserted that during the war "we free-born colored people were very much oppressed. . . . during the war we had no protection, while the slaves had their masters to protect them." She continued: "Not only were our able bodied men forced to work for the Rebel armies and when any one refused he was most unmercifully whipped, but they even took small boys off from the neighborhood and some have never come back." Orr herself was frequently threatened by white South Carolinians during the war, one man firing his gun at her. Other free blacks recalled the consequences of their vulnerability to impressment; like Orr, Rebecca Smith insisted that "free born colored people were indeed worse off during the war than slaves." In the spring of 1864, their men were "dragged away from . . . home to work for [the Confederates] and had to work with guards placed over [them] all the time." Sometimes, a neighborhood's entire population of able-bodied men was carried off. In slave communities as well as free black ones, women alone were left to maintain their families while deprived of the help of black men.[66]

Not all of the Confederacy's labor needs were met through impressment of black men's labor. The quartermaster and the Confederate Medical Department also employed scores of slave women and men over the course of the war. Rice planters eagerly sought employment for slaves they could no longer clothe or feed, or for slaves whom they suspected of spreading discontent or intending to escape—lending credence to the belief of Confederate military authorities that planters were in the habit of "dumping" recalcitrant slaves into war work.[67] Planters also relied on slave employment to generate income.[68]

Like impressment, wartime slave hiring led to unwelcome and unpredictable separations of slave families and communities. A number of slaves belonging to Robert Allston, for example, were hired out from 1861 through 1864. Allston's slaves were, as a consequence, scattered across the region during the war, employed by both private concerns and the military. They were hired to work on railroads, to work at the naval station on the Pee

Dee River north of Georgetown in Marion District, and to assist in the construction of gunboats; carpenters, blacksmiths, and coopers were constantly hired out to practice their skills in the service of the Confederacy.[69]

Although the Confederacy hired far fewer slaves than it impressed in South Carolina, hiring was nonetheless a common experience for slave men in the lowcountry rice regime (who were the largest proportion of slaves employed in the state), and even for lowcountry slave women, though they were hired out in fewer numbers.[70] At Charleston, the quartermaster employed hundreds of slave men over the course of the war to work in Confederate blacksmith and wheelwright shops, in government warehouses and granaries, as personal servants to officers, and—the largest numbers—as ostlers and teamsters. A very few slave women were also hired by the quartermaster's office, apparently as servants or cooks. If James Brewer's findings regarding Virginia slaves laboring in service to the Confederacy can be taken as a model for other Confederate states, slave women might also have been employed in ordnance production, as cooks and laundresses for workers at foundries and factories, and especially in hospitals—described by Brewer as "forgotten" black workers who numbered in the thousands.[71]

The majority of South Carolinian slave women to be found on the extant payrolls of the Confederacy were employed by the Confederate Medical Department, working primarily in the general hospitals established at Columbia, Summerville, and Charleston; some also worked in the many smaller field hospitals that served and followed specific regiments, often along the coast.[72] The patterns of slave women's employment in the hospitals varied widely; sometimes they were hired from several individual owners, and sometimes pairs (including mothers and daughters) or a group of slaves were hired from the same owner. Their terms of employment were unpredictable, varying from weeks to months or, for some, spanning years. The conditions of their labor were also shaped by the hierarchy of hospital work. For example, no slaves, men or women, were employed in supervisory positions such as matrons, ward masters, or hospital stewards. No slave women worked as nurses, an occupation in which we do find white men and women, as well as slave men. Fewer slave women than slave men, or whites of either sex, were employed as cooks. But nearly all hospital laundresses were slave women, with a few exceptional white women similarly employed. While we have little information on the actual work performed by slave men or women, we can gather a sense of the social dimensions of that labor by the fact that the larger hospitals included a majority of slaves among their employees. Hospital muster rolls also indicate that slave women worked in the same hospitals and occasionally in the same occupations with illiterate (and presumably non-elite) white women. And although slave women appeared at the bottom of the hospital hierarchy, their labor earned the same pay—sometimes more—as that earned by slave men employed as nurses or cooks.

Hired slaves did not necessarily enjoy better working conditions than impressed slaves. A foreman employed by one lowcountry rice planter to oversee his hired slaves reported back on the hardships they faced at work on the railroad: "your negroes ar verry much Disatisfide tha cant satisfy those men on the Road with all tha can doo." He warned the planter, as well, that any money the planter was making from the arrangement would have to go toward clothes and shoes for the slaves, if they were to endure working through the cold winter. Already, the foreman reported, one slave was dying, two had run away, and others he feared were conspiring to flee. "You will loose more than you will Make in this cold climit," he warned.[73]

Like many impressed slaves, hired slave laborers frequently had no set term of service. In order to see their families and assure themselves that their loved ones were surviving the privations of war, slave men constantly petitioned their employers and their owners for news from home and the opportunity to return home for visits.[74] A foreman hired by the planter Elias VanderHorst to oversee his slaves who were hired out on the North Carolina railroad reported back that the men had a "great desire to hear from their families," and he himself hoped that VanderHorst would write him "so as to enable me to tell the fellows how their families are[;] it would have a good effect," he assured the planter.[75] But it would take more than reassuring words to prevent slaves from intensifying their protests against family separations.

Wartime Flight

In July 1864, Lizzie, joined by her husband, Stephen, their children, and a fellow Allston slave, Toney (who left behind his wife and children), made their escape from the Allston farm and saltworks at Britton's Neck. As they made their way to Georgetown, the group was joined by eight slaves from four other plantations, and together they set out for either the federal fleet blockading Winyah Bay or the contraband camp Union forces had established on nearby North Island. For Lizzie and her family, the risks of discovery or recapture were apparently preferable to enduring the worsening conditions of wartime slavery, in particular the threat of family separation. Adele Allston—their owner and plantation mistress since the death of her husband that April—had ordered Stephen to leave his family and travel up to the Allstons' North Carolina refuge (an inland farm safe from the threatened coastline), where many other Allston slaves had been relocated. Before he could be carried off, and the family face an indeterminate separation, Stephen and Lizzie made their decision to escape with the family intact.

It was not Stephen's success but the fact that the entire family had escaped that surprised Allston; "How so many children got off safely I can't imagine, but Stephen is so completely acquainted with the face of the country the by paths & swamps that what would be difficult to others is easy for him comparatively." Stephen's antebellum mobility and knowledge of the surrounding countryside gave him the advantage that some other male slaves had used to escape both before and during the war. But Allston also suspected that the family had additional help; she believed that Lizzie's mother, Mary Grice, had helped engineer the escape. Lizzie was not the first member of her extended family to escape slavery. Two of her siblings had preceded her; one of her brothers had also escaped with his family, and Allston suspected that Mary Grice had played a role in all three incidents. "It is too many instances in her family for me to suppose she is ignorant of their plans and designs," Allston charged; she felt that Mary's position as "a highly favoured servant" had contributed to the success of the escapes. She surmised that Mary had hidden Lizzie's family, perhaps in the vacant Allston residence, in the course of their escape. Allston ordered the overseer to isolate Mary from her remaining children and grandchildren to prevent any further escapes, and threatened that any further misbehavior on the part of Mary Grice's family would be held as Mary's responsibility. But Allston could not contain the reverberations of yet another slave escape in the Allston slave community, and the overseer warned that he could "see since Stephen left a goodeal of obstenatry in Some of the Peopl. Mostly mongst the Women," he noted, "a goodeal of Quarling and disputeing & telling lies."[76]

Lizzie's escape, particularly in light of the immediate threat to separate her family, reminds us that the slave women who ran away from lowcountry rice plantations during the war were fleeing not only slavery but also the threat of separation posed by removal, assignment to salt works, impressment or hiring, as well as the declining material conditions on lowcountry plantations. The relative safety of staying in slavery lessened as wartime hardships and risks accumulated and undermined slaves' strategies for family survival. Furthermore, Lizzie's was not an unusual decision; in contrast to antebellum patterns of mostly male escapes, an unprecedented high proportion of slave women and children were among those who escaped slavery during the Civil War.[77] For slave women, the proximity of federal forces made escape—with or without family members—a more viable option; the risks of staying put increasingly outweighed the risks of flight. The decision by slaves to escape in family groups also signaled the depth of their commitment to the wartime destruction of slavery. For these families and communities, their flight reflected a wholesale commitment to securing freedom behind Union lines; they were transplanting their lives and their future to what they understood to be free soil. For slaveowners, the flight of their slave women and children meant far more than the immediate loss of property; it threatened the reproductive potential of their slaveholdings as well as the future of slavery in the region. The escape of women and children would also significantly shape the nature of life behind Union lines.

For Union authorities, the arrival of large numbers of women and children exposed the shortcomings of a military policy intended to undermine the Confederate employment of slave men's labor. Women, children, and the elderly did not fit well or easily into the pragmatic equation that a slave lost by the Confederacy became a military laborer or a soldier gained by the Union. Military authorities, increasingly hungry for the labor of fugitive slave men as "weapons of war," felt that the larger numbers of women, children, and elderly slaves who also fled to Union lines "could contribute nothing substantial to the war effort." Instead, those authorities viewed slave women and their families with "bewilderment and panic, forseeing the demoralization and infection of the Union soldier and the downfall of the Union cause." It was the Union's effort to cope with these noncombatants (particularly in the Mississippi Valley and the border states) that led to the brutal and unsuccessful policy of excluding fugitive slaves from army camps, as well as the subsequent policy of establishing contraband camps and regimental villages. And when slave men were tapped for military service beginning in the summer of 1863, the labor of slave women and older children became particularly important to the wartime organization of free-labor experiments behind Union lines throughout the occupied South. As central as the story of black soldiering has been to our view of slaves and war, it was the flight of noncombatant slaves to Union lines that forced Union policy in new and unpredictable directions during the course of the war.[78]

With great consequence for slave women like Lizzie and for South Carolina slavery as a whole, Union ships entered South Carolina's Port Royal

Sound in November 1861. As federal forces extended their presence over the course of the next three months to include at least fifteen Sea Islands, thousands of slaves evaded the efforts of Sea Island planters to evacuate them to "safety." These were the first lowcountry slaves to act on the opportunities that war presented to escape from slavery.[79] Despite the deteriorating conditions on lowcountry rice plantations and the disruptive impact of impressment and slave hiring, it was this third element of war—the presence of Union forces along the Carolina coast—that finally inspired both slaves and slaveowners to flight, attracting slaves with a possibility of freedom, while repelling slaveowners from the threat of attack, confiscation, the loss of their property, and slavery's ultimate demise.

Over the course of the next three and a half years, slaves from the surrounding islands and from the nearby mainland together transformed the federal blockade into what the historian Willie Lee Rose termed a "rehearsal for Reconstruction," as they rejected slavery to claim whatever kind of freedom they could forge on the Union-occupied islands. By virtue of their actions, these mainland and Sea Island slaves forced the Union to confront the meaning of slavery and freedom. The issue of their welfare and their labor drew the interest and attention of not only the War Department but also the Treasury Department and a multitude of missionary and aid societies, all sending teachers and agents to assist, manage, and exploit the contrabands in their claim for freedom and safety behind Union lines.[80]

Official Union policy toward the status of the fugitive slave women who made their way to the Sea Islands changed over the course of the war. The Union forces making their appearance at Port Royal Sound initially had no intention (nor the authority) to attack slavery in South Carolina, and they were even reluctant to employ fugitive slave laborers despite the permission of the War Department. But the unexpected presence of thousands of Sea Island slaves who had resisted planters' efforts to evacuate them, and an uninterrupted flow of fugitives from the mainland, left little room for Union equivocation; they were accepted into Union lines (although until March 1862, Union officers were within their rights to return fugitive slaves to owners claiming loyalty to the Union).

The contrabands' belief that they had gained their freedom in fact had no legal foundation until Lincoln's Emancipation Proclamation. Neither the First nor Second Confiscation Acts—intended to allow the Union army to claim the labor of slaves found working on behalf of the Confederate war effort and owned by disloyal Southerners—provided a basis for the freedom of the Sea Island fugitives, men or women, who had already escaped

the reaches of their owners. Furthermore, both the First and Second Confiscation Acts were implicitly gendered in their limited offers of protection
and freedom, since the great majority of slaves employed directly in military labor by the Confederacy were men. To the extent that the Militia Act
of July 1862 did hold out an offer of freedom to women and children, it
was limited to the families of slave men who offered their military labor
and service to the Union and whose owners were disloyal. Slave women
who escaped to Union lines alone or as heads of families, or those with
husbands who found some means of subsistence outside of work for Union
forces, were not eligible for the protection or the offer of freedom provided by the Militia Act. Despite the lack of legal grounding, mainland and
Sea Island slaves acted on their own conclusion that the war must bring
an end to slavery, forcing the Union military forces and strategists to deal
with their presence and their expectations for freedom. The presence of
Union military forces off the coast of South Carolina helped create an
opportunity for escape from slavery, but the determined actions of slaves
transformed opportunity into reality.[81]

Even in the microcosm of wartime South Carolina, the timing of slave
escapes varied considerably between the Sea Islands and Georgetown's
Winyah Bay. Slaves began running away from the plantations of the Savannah River as well as those north of Charleston as early as January 1861,
eleven months before the appearance of the federal fleet in Port Royal
Sound. With the arrival of the federal ships of the South Atlantic Blockading Squadron off the coast of South Carolina, slave women and men from
the mainland rice plantations (and from as far away as Savannah) began
slipping away to Union ships, using the coastal river systems as avenues
for escape.[82] The presence of the federal fleet sent shock waves throughout the lowcountry; "at once was a change discerned among the Negroes,"
noted the planter Charles Manigault. "They have very generally got the idea
of being emancipated when 'Lincon' comes in," he noted.[83] Because the
federal fleet arrived first at Port Royal Sound, slaves to the south of Charleston were among the very first to claim safety and freedom behind federal
lines. Rather than flee toward federal ships, these slaves simply had to resist
their owners' efforts to carry them off just prior to the arrival of the fleet.
Several thousand—many of them women and children—succeeded (one
of the Northern missionaries to the Sea Islands speculated that ten thousand slaves remained behind when the planters evacuated the islands).[84]
By the spring of 1862, thousands of slaves from the mainland between
Beaufort and Charleston joined those already on the islands.

At first, some planters doubted that the "Yankees desire to take the negroes away. It is preposterous," stated James Petigru, and impossible "without a vast number of ships."[85] But by spring and summer of 1862, the steady stream of slaves from lowcountry plantations to the blockade convinced planters that regardless of the federal navy's intent or capabilities, slaves were making their own way to the federal fleet in impressive numbers. Some Sea Island planters, reluctant to abandon such a significant portion of their wealth, pleaded with Confederate commanders to attempt the recapture of their slaves. Union control over some of the islands was tentative, and Confederate raiders were often successful, as was the case in August 1863, when a raid on Union-occupied Barnwell Island resulted in the recapture of thirty-seven women and children and four men.[86] Other planters made surreptitious visits to their own plantations in an effort to persuade or force their slaves to rejoin them. One Beaufort planter intent on so doing stumbled upon his former slave women, celebrating their new freedom: "Chloe, Stephen's Wife, [was] seated at Phoebes Piano playing away like the very Devil & two damsels up stairs dancing away famously."[87] Recaptured slaves faced the threat of permanent separation from their families, imprisonment, or execution. Eighty or ninety fugitive slaves belonging to James Legare were recaptured in 1862, "the women placed in jail, the men chained & put to work on the fortifications." Other recaptured slaves were sentenced to be hanged.[88]

For slaves on the rice plantations closer to Georgetown, it was the fortuitous and combined effects of the withdrawal of Confederate forces from Winyah Bay, the growing presence of the federal blockade, and also the presumption by slaves that the U.S. Navy would protect their freedom (rather than restore them to slavery) that created conditions ripe for a stream of runaways in 1862. The federal fleet explored the main river systems between Port Royal and Georgetown until March 1862, when the Union's South Atlantic Blockading Squadron intensified its efforts to make an effective blockade of Georgetown, hoping to shut down an important Confederate supply and shipping station.[89] Just as federal ships were increasing their presence along the South Carolina coast north of Charleston, the Confederacy suffered important losses in Tennessee, forcing a significant withdrawal of Confederate forces from lowcountry defensive positions to allow reinforcements to be sent to the interior of the South. Georgetown was left poorly defended from April 1862 until the end of the war, leaving exposed, as Governor Pickens complained to President Davis, "the richest country in the South, on Waccamaw and Santee, and . . . some sixty thousand negroes," as well as a valuable rice crop. Lowcountry planters had argued since the beginning of the war for

the vigorous defense of the lowcountry rice region; "these negroes," argued planter William Elliott,

> are the main source of our wealth, and the product of their labor is the only
> fund from which the Confederate States can hope to support the war, and
> pay the interest of our public debt, immense and still accumulating. More
> than this—every able bodied negro man—who is allowed to go over to the
> Enemy—is not only a valuable producer abstracted from us—but from the
> unprincipled conduct of our malignant and unscrupulous foe—becomes
> a recruit in his ranks—and is armed to cut the throat of his former master.
> It seems to me therefore a matter of life and death—and worth some risk
> and some actual loss—to prevent so great a calamity.[90]

According to one observer, the decision to withdraw Confederate defenses was also a sacrifice of "$200,000 worth of work building fortifications,"
as well as a substantial amount of harvested rice.[91]

Rice plantation slaves in the vicinity of Georgetown responded to this
convergence of wartime circumstances immediately and en masse; hundreds of slaves, especially slave families, made their escape in the spring
and summer months of 1862 to the ships patrolling the local bay and rivers.[92] Slaves came in such great numbers between April and June that by
July 1862, the federal fleet established a temporary colony for escaped
slaves on North Island, which separated the northern shore of Winyah Bay
from the Atlantic Ocean. That colony grew from eighty inhabitants in May
to over twelve hundred in July.[93] By the close of the war, thousands of
mainland lowcountry slaves from the Georgetown area—many of them
women, children, and the elderly—had decided that the presence of the
federal fleet offered a viable means of escaping slavery.

The proximity of federal forces had made the possibility of escape more
likely for the most vulnerable members of lowcountry slave communities.
As federal ships became more aggressive in exploring the lowcountry
waterways and more willing to escort slaves to safety, the greater mobility and knowledge of the terrain enjoyed by slave men became less critical to a successful escape. The proximity of federal forces on the Sea Islands also meant that slaves did not have to plan for lengthy journeys; they
were no longer forced to view their families—including small children and
the elderly—as insuperable obstacles to a successful escape. Sea Island
missionaries noted that "few men run away to us alone; as a rule they come
off bringing with them wives and little ones—often from great distances,
and at frightful risks."[94] Thomas Wentworth Higginson described in his

wartime memoirs several successful escapes that would have been impossible before the war. A family Higginson knew only by the name of Wilson had made the decision to separate, the youngest sibling staying behind to watch over the old mother on the plantation, but the rest of the siblings, including a sister and her children, braved the water and the Confederate pickets to make their escape by boat. Members of another family, known to Higginson as the Millers, were detected in an attempt to escape their Savannah River rice plantation. Even as the grandfather was given five hundred lashes, the grandmother gathered their children and grandchildren for the second and successful attempt that same night. She navigated her family aboard an old abandoned flat to a federal gunboat, and, according to Higginson, "when the 'flat' touched the side of the vessel, the grandmother rose to her full height, with her youngest grandchild in her arms, and said only, 'My God! are we free?'"[95]

Federal raids up lowcountry waterways also became an important avenue for the escape of slave families. One of the most successful of those raids occurred on the Combahee River in June 1863. Led by the former slave and famed spy and scout Harriet Tubman, federal forces brought 756 slaves from Combahee rice plantations to freedom on the islands. One of the Combahee slave men (one of 250 slaves who fled Charles Lowndes's plantation that day)[96] recalled the circumstances of this massive escape, later written down by a white officer: "De people . . . was a hoein' in de rice-field, when de gunboats come. Den ebry man drap dem hoe, and leff de rice. De mas'r he stand and call, 'Run to de wood for hide! Yankee come, sell you to Cuba! run for hide!' Ebry man he run, and, my God! run all toder way! Mas'r . . . say, 'Run to de wood!' and ebry man run by him, straight to de boat. . . . Lor, mas'r, did d't care notin' at all, *I was gwine to de boat.*" This same officer, Thomas Wentworth Higginson, participated in other similar lowcountry raids, including one in July 1863. The "moist meadows" of the rice plantations lining the river

> had become alive with human heads, and along each narrow path came a straggling file of men and women, all on a run for the river-side. I went ashore with a boat-load of troops at once. The landing was difficult and marshy. The astonished negroes tugged us up the bank, and gazed on us as if we had been Cortez and Columbus. They kept arriving by land much faster than we could come by water; every moment increased the crowd, the jostling, the mutual clinging, on that miry foothold. What a scene it was! With the wild faces, eager figures, strange garments, it seemed, as one of the poor things reverently suggested, "like notin' but de judgement day."

Presently they began to come from the houses also, with their little bundles on their heads; then with larger bundles. Old women, trotting down
the narrow paths, would kneel to pray a little prayer, still balancing the
bundle; and then would suddenly spring up, urged by the accumulating
procession behind. . . . Women brought children on their shoulders; small
black boys carried on their backs little brothers.[97]

Lowcountry rice planters found it nearly impossible to prevent the escape of large families—even entire plantation communities—to the Union
ships patrolling lowcountry waterways.[98] Charles Heyward reported that
in March 1862, fifteen of the slaves on his Combahee River rice plantation—including three women and one child—"left the plantation and went
over to the enemy on the islands." John Berkeley Grimball lost nearly eighty
slaves that month, "men women & children" who boarded a federal steamer and thus made their escape. Nearly all the slaves from three Georgetown rice plantations reportedly made their escape in March as well.[99] In
May 1862, Captain George A. Prentice, of the USS *Albatross,* was patrolling the Waccamaw River near Georgetown and picked up "a whole plantation of Negroes wishing our protection."[100] In May and June, a total of
thirty-eight slaves escaped from the plantation of Elias VanderHorst.[101]
Twenty-eight contrabands escaped in a group from William G. Magill, a
Georgetown planter, in July 1862; three of the slave men returned in November to carry their wives off the plantation but were caught and executed.[102] In July 1862, a pair of Union steamboats shelling saltworks that
lined the Georgetown waterways "took off the negroes who were willing
to go with them."[103] Among them may have been the 105 slaves who fled
from the Georgetown planter William Mayrant, some of Andrew Johnstone's Santee River slaves, and twenty-one slave men who slipped away
from another Georgetown planter, just as he prepared to remove them to
the interior of the state.[104] That August, a Union gunboat ascended Georgetown's Black River and escorted twenty-two willing slave men to freedom from William Ervine Sparkman's Springwood plantation.[105] Between
May 1862 and March 1863, at least five hundred refugees from the rice
planting district of the Santee River had made their way to Port Royal.[106]
Many of these escapees included slave women, who were among those
least likely to escape before the war.

Although the presence of Union forces presented new possibilities for
escape for women and their families, flight from slavery still demanded
difficult decisions and required tremendous risks. The unanticipated arrival of federal gunboats sometimes forced parents, spouses, and children

to make hard choices between escaping and remaining with their families.[107] John Emory Bryant, one of the white Union officers who participated in the June 1863 Combahee River raid, observed that on that and other occasions, the escaping slaves "were obliged to leave friends behind. Husbands left wives children brothers sisters. They came when they could get the chance and trusted in God to unite them." A lowcountry plantation mistress, describing a similar raid, also noted that the wives of several slave men had left them to make their escape; the slaves were so "wild with the idea of being free" that "the wives leave their husbands, the men their wives but," she noticed, "they all seem to cling to their children." Yet another planter who lost slaves to this particular raid observed that one of the escaping slaves left behind his wife, and that a neighboring planter "lost eleven some quite young leaving their parents."[108]

Northern observers frequently commented on slaves who, having escaped without their families, returned to plantations to bring their families to freedom as well.[109] But this was not always the case, and some family separations were clearly disturbing to rice plantation slaves, in particular those left behind who couldn't imagine that their spouses or families would go off without them. Adam preferred to believe that his wife, Diana, had been forced off by the Yankee soldiers, despite the evidence from other observers that "Diana deserted him of her own free will, she was down at the landing with her clothes in a bundle, waiting for the Gunboat . . . about an hour before any landing was made."[110] Diana, it would appear, pursued her freedom above all else.

The wartime flight of lowcountry slaves—especially of women, children, and the elderly—illustrates one of the many dramatic changes war brought to antebellum patterns of slavery and slave resistance. Not only had the war made the escape of families possible; the worsening wartime conditions on lowcountry rice plantations, and the unpredictable threat of family separations, made the relative risks of staying in slavery greater than the many risks of attempting escape.

The War behind Union Lines

Once fugitive slaves made their way to the temporary or permanent camps maintained by Union forces in Port Royal Sound or Georgetown's North Island, they became "contraband of war" and fell subject to Union jurisdiction and policy.[111] The War Department, the Treasury Department, and Northern missionaries contended for authority over the disposition of the Sea

Island plantations and the former slaves and, as a consequence, the policies that governed slave women's life and labor were erratically developed,
enforced, abandoned, or replaced. Sea Island contrabands found provisions
promised for their own subsistence and the support of their families sometimes lacking, their wages paid irregularly, and their new employers disinclined to consult the contrabands themselves about their future as free people. Perhaps worst of all was the sale of Sea Island plantation lands to
Northern speculators, despite the perceived proprietary rights of the contrabands and their efforts to file legal claim to the land. The confused and
chaotic process of preempting land, along with the expense, prevented most
Sea Islanders from gaining the land and, consequently, the independence
on which they felt their real freedom depended.[112]

"The refugees were vastly worse off than the plantation people," asserted one white observer, Elizabeth Botume, a contraband teacher. "They
literally had nothing to wear," having pieced together what little covering
they could from cast-off bagging, twine, and carpet.[113] While native Sea
Islanders often continued living in the quarters they had occupied before
the war, tending their own provision plots and working on the same plantations now under the supervision of Northern missionaries, the mainland
refugees (who constituted about 60 percent of the contrabands at Hilton
Head by February 1862, even before the larger stream of escapes that
spring and summer) were settled into makeshift camps.[114] Others were
distributed among the plantations, where they were sometimes regarded
as unwelcome strangers. The camps themselves varied; some refugees
were sheltered in little more than tents or barracks, while others were
housed in churches, storehouses, even jails and arsenals.[115] Some camps
were like the one established under the direction of General Rufus Saxton,
supervisor of contraband affairs, for the hundreds of slaves brought from
the rice plantations of the Ashepoo and Combahee Rivers in May and June
of 1863. As described by Elizabeth Botume, the best of these quarters
consisted of "a row of a dozen or more buildings, which resembled huge
wooden boxes. Each house was divided into four rooms or compartments,
and in each room was located one family of from five to fifteen persons.
In each room was a large fireplace, an opening for a window with a broad
board shutter, and a double row of berths built against the wall for beds.
One or more low benches, and a pine table with 'piggins,' home-made
cedar tubs, on it, completed the furniture."[116] Even in the worst of refugee
camps, women and children devoted themselves to raising sweet potatoes
and corn, along with other provisions, in small garden patches around or
near their dwellings.[117]

The contrabands, their numbers growing to between fifteen thousand and sixteen thousand from 1862 to 1864, had to support themselves, by either raising their own food crops or earning the wages to buy them.[118] Contraband men typically found employment in the Quartermaster's or Engineering Departments. In 1863, they were credited with having "done almost all the work in the Quartermaster's Department."[119] Men were employed in higher proportions than were women and appear to have found a far greater range of employment than did women.[120] The range of men's employment from 1862 through 1864 included repairing and building wharfs, tending the military's gardens, making coffins, digging graves, splitting wood for the wash and cook houses, and as boatmen, hospital attendants, engineers, carpenters, dock hands, teamsters, and stable hands. Women found work as "cooks and washers for single men," as nurses, attendants or laundresses in regimental hospitals, as prostitutes, or as cooks and general servants to individual officers and soldiers.[121] Large numbers of women found employment in army wash houses, laundering the uniforms and other clothing of military personnel. "The women are needed as laundresses and find an abundance of employment," according to one white observer, who noted that the "demand for labor really exceeds the supply."[122] As wage workers employed by the quartermaster's and other departments in these necessary but undervalued "female" occupations, however, contraband women were paid far less than men for a day's work. Even a highly skilled woman like Susie King Taylor, who worked as a teacher and a nurse in a black regiment, was officially employed (and underpaid) as a regimental laundress.

The exception to the disparities in pay was in agricultural labor, where men and women's equal abilities and earning capacity was widely commented upon by white observers.[123] The Sea Island "free-labor experiment" encompassed the various efforts of Northern abolitionists and businessmen to transform plantation agriculture into a model of free-labor production.[124] Sea Island plantation operations varied significantly between the abolitionists, who hoped to accelerate the contrabands' transition to freedom, and the entrepreneurs, who hoped to exploit the Sea Island plantations to benefit themselves, the Treasury Department, and, far more rarely, the slaves. For the contraband women and men, the question of whether they would be forced to cultivate cotton as opposed to provisions, the regularity and equity of their wages, their vulnerability to involuntary military conscription, and their concern about their ability to secure legal title to the land they cultivated were frequently the transcending issues of their wartime experience with free labor on the islands.

Not all contraband women turned to wage labor, the civilizing effects of which were so heavily touted by the Northern whites who came to the Sea Islands. Many former slave women, both refugees and native Sea Islanders, supported themselves and their families by marketing goods in the streets of Beaufort and other villages and by selling prepared foods to Union soldiers and officers in their camps. Sweet potatoes, melons, peanuts, corn, radishes, peas, eggs, milk, and butter were all regularly purchased by one Union soldier, who also admitted that "we have to pay pretty well" for the things sold by these enterprising marketers.[125] Corporal James Henry Gooding wrote from Hilton Head that he and other black soldiers were often visited by marketers from the "native population, who bring all sorts of little delicacies to sell, such as cakes, poultry, eggs, fruit and so on; but as the 54th is minus the circulating medium, they won't be enriched a great deal trading with us."[126]

Although civilians and soldiers alike on the islands depended heavily on the food sold by traders, some of the superintendents of the contrabands disapproved when women chose marketing over what the Northern whites considered "honest steady labor." One superintendent complained in August 1864, "This getting a precarious livelihood by doing a little at this thing, & a little at that is the very curse of the people. So far as possible they should be compelled to *steady labor.* Hence I would allow no peddling around camps whatsoever." "All persons," he continued, "whether in town or on plantations, white or black, who lived without occupation should either go to the poor house or be put in a place where they *must work*—a work house or chain gang, & if women where they could wash iron & scrub for the benefit of the public." He hoped a military order might secure better regulation and control of what he disdainfully described as "the floating Negro Population."[127] His suggestion was approved and issued in September 1864, by Major General Foster, commander of Union forces in South Carolina, who ordered that

> the practice of allowing negro women to wander about from one Plantation to another, and from one Post or District to another, on Government transports, for no other purpose than to while away their time, or visit their husbands serving in the ranks of the Army, is not only objectionable in every point of view, both to the soldiers and to themselves, but is generally subversive of moral restraint, and must be discontinued at once. All negro women, in future found wandering in this manner, will be immediately arrested, and compelled to work at some steady employment on the Plantations.[128]

Foster apparently agreed with the superintendent. African-American women who avoided wage labor and tried to support themselves and their families by marketing were, by Foster's orders, subject to the presumption that they were engaged in prostitution or promiscuous behavior with the troops.[129]

The voluntary and involuntary entry of contraband men into military service was another critical component of the wartime experience of escaped slaves, both men and women, on the Sea Islands. Between April and August of 1862, Sea Island and refugee men from the mainland alike were involuntarily pressed into the unauthorized black regiment formed by General David Hunter in Union-occupied South Carolina. Many slave men had escaped to the Sea Islands with the intent of joining the war as Union soldiers. But the involuntary nature of Hunter's conscription, and its disregard for the families of conscripted men, seemed to the contrabands more like their treatment at the hands of Confederate impressment agents than the treatment they expected from liberators. Hunter's regiment, although "kept hard at work on the entrenchments for four months," was disbanded in August when the War Department refused to supply uniforms, guns, or soldiers' pay.

General Rufus Saxton once again took up black enlistment in October 1862, this time with the permission of Secretary of War Edwin Stanton to employ five thousand military laborers and five thousand soldiers. Now guaranteed official sanction—and more important from the perspective of the contrabands, a soldier's pay—the 1st South Carolina Volunteers was organized and placed under the command of Thomas Wentworth Higginson.[130] Early in 1863, two additional regiments (the 2d and 3d South Carolina Volunteers, African Descent) were organized as well. But when enlistment began to lag, conscription was resumed and Sea Island contraband men again faced the use of force to secure their service to the state.[131] Then, as in the preceding year's sweeping military impressment, the contraband men evaded impressment and women and children tried to delay or obstruct the recruiters. Despite the evasions and protests of the former slaves and their employers on the islands, the military "press gangs" swept the plantations and the refugee camps for potential soldiers, undermining the contrabands' newfound safety, security, and strategies for family survival—especially since soldiers received monthly pay of seven dollars, rather than the ten to twenty-five dollars earned by employees of the Quartermaster's Department.[132] Treasury Department officials concerned about the successful cultivation of the Union-supervised Sea Island cotton plantations, employers of contraband men in the quartermaster's and engineer's departments, and military recruiters all competed for the services of military-aged men with relatively little regard for the preferences of the contrabands themselves.[133]

While life on the Union-occupied Sea Islands provided some safety from slavery, female contrabands discovered other dangers. For many former slave women, rape and the threat of rape were part of life on the Union-occupied Sea Islands, a brutal manifestation of the contempt with which black women were viewed by many Northern whites. All contrabands, men and women alike, encountered the "prejudice of color and race" on the part of the Union's army of occupation, which was "manifested in various forms of personal insult and abuse, in depredations on their plantations, stealing and destroying their crops and domestic animals, and robbing them of their money," as well as in official policy. But that "prejudice" was also brutally expressed when white soldiers attacked the former slave women "as the legitimate prey of lust."[134] Former slave women were victims of outrage and assault at the hands of the army press gangs, as well as by white soldiers, sailors, and officers, oftentimes despite the presence and protests of mothers, fathers, husbands, and other witnesses. A black minister in one of the camps called on the military command to intervene—"We have been trubled very often by these officers & Sailers & i think a stop aught to [be] Put to it"—when a woman was assaulted by three white officers who came into her house on the pretense of recruiting soldiers and raped her, apparently in the presence of her husband.[135] Esther Hawks, a white physician who worked as a missionary and teacher for the Freedmen's Aid Society during the wartime occupation of the Sea Islands, complained in 1862 that "no colored woman or girl was safe from the brutal lusts of the [white] soldiers—and by soldiers I mean both officers and men. . . . Mothers were brutally treated for trying to protect their daughters, and there are now several women in our little hospital who have been shot by soldiers for resisting their vile demands." Hawks complained that perpetrators were not punished, especially when the officers were as guilty as the men of such attacks. While General Saxton had "made it somewhat disgraceful to be caught abusing women and little children," Hawks believed that the only change brought by Saxton's policy was that such attacks, while no less frequent, were less openly committed.

Saxton became even less ambivalent in his attitude toward African-American women in the year to come, when he openly blamed slave women for encouraging the brutality of white soldiers. In his 1863 testimony before the American Freedmen's Inquiry Commission, Saxton described sexual restraint as though it were a female secondary sex characteristic, but one that the system of slavery and slave masters in particular had destroyed in slave women. The consequence, he believed, was that "the colored women are proud to have illicit intercourse with white men," causing "great difficulty in keeping the soldiers away from the women." Hawks, in treating some of the victims of the violence committed by Union soldiers, saw brutality manifested in a myriad ways against the former slaves. "Every indignity which human ingenuity could devise was heaped upon the poor negroes," complained Hawks, indignities perpetrated by the same soldiers whose arrival had been so welcomed by the slaves.[136]

Deprived of the income of their conscripted men, and subjected to the violent manifestations of hostility directed at former slave women by white soldiers, officers, and civilians, women in the Sea Island contraband camps endeavored to hold together family and community as best they could. They shouldered the support of children and extended family, despite heavy economic disadvantages (dependents in need of support represented a significant proportion of the Sea Island population—in the summer of 1862, Charles Nordhoff estimated that 48 percent of the Port Royal contraband population consisted of the elderly, the ill, and children too young to work even as quarter hands).[137] Contraband women found ways to care for themselves and each other. Women joined and led churches, and those with more secular claims to authority continued to watch over their communities as they probably had in slavery. Wartime observers identified "Maum Katie" as a "spiritual mother," a "fortune-teller," "prophetess," and "a woman of tremendous influence over her spiritual children," and similarly portrayed "Old Peggy" and Bina as spiritual mothers in their Sea Island contraband communities.[138] Christiana, widow of the driver on a Little Island plantation, "has for years exerted a wonderful influence over the slaves and now her word is law. All go to her for advice and do as she wishes."[139] Other former slave women, like Amarinta, "naturally stood forward as spokeswoman to get 'satisfaction'" about the conscription of the men, while "Old Grace' led a body of women to complain about the pay rate on cotton plantations operated under the auspices of the Treasury Department. Women also protested, and resisted, the sale of Sea Island land that they had preempted for their own uses.[140]

However difficult their experiences at the hands of military recruiters and employers, the contrabands deeply appreciated, and took full advantage of, the opportunities for education in the Union-occupied Sea Islands. By the hundreds, perhaps thousands, men, women, and children enrolled in regimental or camp schools, where they eagerly pursued a rudimentary education in reading, writing, and other studies. Regimental chaplains as well as the missionaries and teachers—African-American and white men and women sent South by Northern freedmen's aid societies to organize and operate the schools—marveled at the intense desire for learning expressed by contrabands of all ages.[141]

As 1864 drew to a close, General Saxton admitted to Secretary of War Stanton that "several occurrences had led [the contrabands] to doubt our good faith, who professed to come as their deliverers. They were fully aware of the contempt, oftentimes amounting to hatred, of their ostensible liberators."[142] Nonetheless, women and men who successfully escaped slavery on mainland rice plantations and ultimately made their way to Sea Island contraband camps gained a measure of freedom that was still out of reach on the mainland. Lowcountry mainland slaves who remained under the domain of their owners and the Confederacy found that the Union presence and the growing cracks in the foundations of slavery made black South Carolinians the target of increased repression by lowcountry whites.

The Wartime Crisis of Slavery

Running away was only the most overt of many forms of resistance employed by slave women during the course of the war. Plantation whites saw evidence of unrest in the uncontrolled "dancing and fighting" in slave quarters at night; in women's "obstenatry," "quarling and disputeing and telling lies"; in the surreptitious support slave women gave to runaways; in their "conceited," false obsequiousness and their ingratitude; and even in slaves' masking of their emotions, their thoughts, and their responses to wartime events.[143] Unwilling and sulky labor also suggested resistance. Although more than one rice planter or plantation mistress continued to believe that *their* slaves were loyal and contented, overseers more readily acknowledged the threatening signs of increased discontent.[144] With slave women and men abandoning in small but detectable increments the appearances of subordination, slaveowners and their agents sought to exert a more vigilant, forceful (and violent) dominion over them.[145]

Military and national interests joined with those of slaveowners and the state in seeking to prevent the wartime erosion of control over the slave population. Lowcountry planters emphasized the necessity of slave control as a wartime security measure but also warned of the potential financial ruin that the collapse of slavery would bring to the region and the Confederacy. When slaveowners, police, and soldiers therefore governed lowcountry slaves in an increasingly interventionist manner, their actions were influenced not only by the growing numbers of escapes but also by their perception of the costs attending the breakdown of white authority, power, and control over slaves.[146] The anxious, angry response of lowcountry whites to the resistance and flight of lowcountry slaves became increasingly virulent and violent.

Rice planters sought help to shore up their weakening mastery. They organized civilian patrols of the local waterways used as escape routes by slaves and also relied on Confederate pickets to block the flow of slaves to the enemy.[147] So significant was the "government of the negroes" to wartime concerns that South Carolina's executive council included a member whose responsibilities were largely defined as overseeing the policing of the state's slave population.[148] South Carolina's wartime Provost Guard aided in this endeavor.[149] In Georgetown, Dr. Francis Parker, a rice planter and provost marshal, included in his responsibilities "a wide and extended jurisdiction over the slaves and free persons of color within this district." For example, Parker persuaded local Confederate officials to increase the number of cavalry assigned to patrol the lowcountry slave population in the slack period following the harvest of 1862.[150]

Lowcountry rice planters also relied on traditional forms of slave punishment, control, and discipline to discourage overt challenges to the bonds of slavery.[151] Plantation mistresses who found their domestic servants impertinent, "excessively negligent & indifferent" relied on their male kin to deliver punishment.[152] Prisons and commercial workhouses in Charleston and Savannah saw a steady flow of wartime business.[153] The threat of sale was also used in the wartime effort to secure obedience from slaves.[154] In response to the growing number of slave escapes, some planters assigned additional watchmen and chained their slaves at night.[155] Others turned to increasingly harsh punishments for recaptured runaways or those suspected of plotting their escapes, including the use of what were called "dark-holes": "they dug a hole like a well with a door on top. This they called a dungeon keeping you in it two or three weeks or a month, and sometimes till you died in there. This hole was just big enough to receive the body; the hands down by the sides."[156]

Rice planters, their overseers, and local authorities also turned whippings, beatings, and the execution of restive and recaptured fugitive slaves—women and men—into public rituals intended to intimidate the slaves and free blacks who were forced to witness such events. When Big George tried to run off East Hermitage plantation before the eyes of the entire slave force, William Capers, the overseer, not only caught him but "gave him 60 straps in presents of those he ran off in presents of" as a deterrent to the entire community.[157] Slave women who dared to resist the escalating violence on wartime plantations found overseers like Capers less restrained than ever, apparently with the approval of his employer. After stripping and whipping one apparently "troublesome" slave woman, Capers assured his employer that "before she is turned loose" the slave would "know she is a negroe."[158]

Testimony by former slaves also revealed the extent of their wartime harassment and abuse by local authorities. One slave congregation was locked inside the house where they held their meetings and were not allowed out for several hours; their preacher believed they had been locked up because "we made a great deal of noise sometimes praying for the success of the Union cause," prayers that continued until the provost guard finally forbade them from holding meetings.[159]

The provost guard's surveillance also apparently extended to the low-country communities of free people of color. Men and women were beaten "for speaking for the Union." Thomas Jackson was "cut up by Rebel Soldiers for attempting to defend his family from outrage."[160] Whether they used the war as an excuse to act out their hatred and contempt for free and enslaved African Americans or were simply overzealous in their endeavor to monitor the threat posed by the "enemy within," the provost guard was violent enough to be portrayed by slave and free alike as nothing short of a lynch mob.

Efforts to restrain lowcountry slaves and free people of color went well beyond patrolling the coastal waterways and perpetrating sporadic acts of brutality. In November 1862, the provost martial court in Georgetown tried and executed three slave men who had escaped but were caught when they returned to help their wives escape. The execution was an elaborate public display meant to discourage local blacks, slave and free, from seeking refuge with the federal forces. According to one local planter, "the effect will not soon be forgotten."[161] Indeed, more than a decade after the execution it was quite clear in the memory of Job Mayzeck, a former slave who had purchased his freedom before the war, and whose Union sympathies were known by several local whites. A sergeant and four soldiers arrived at Mayzeck's house the morning of the execution and forced Mayzeck and other black workmen to construct the gallows for the hanging. Mayzeck tried to refuse, on the grounds that he had no carpentry skills, but "they said I had to do it or go to jail," recalled Mayzeck; "I told my wife I better put up the gallows." He was also forced to take the executed men down from the gallows and bury them. Mayzeck was almost joined by

Alonzo Jackson, a slave who had been ordered by the provost marshal, Dr. Francis Parker, "to assist in hanging 3 colored men at the jail in Georgetown." Jackson believed "that I had been ordered to assist in the hanging because I was suspected of being on the side of the Yankees." Like Mayzeck, Jackson initially refused to cooperate, but offered a more convincing excuse, insisting that he had to tend to some business for one of Georgetown's larger rice planters. Jackson was released from the work detail with the warning "if you don't look pretty sharp, you will be hung next."[162]

Despite tighter surveillance and harsher punishments, slaves became increasingly fractious, signaling the internal collapse of the discipline and routine on which the lowcountry rice regime was built. By the closing months of 1864, the combined effects of war were not only prompting slaves to escape but also inspired increased resistance to the demands made on them by planters and overseers. It was, reported the planter Charles Allston, "my first experience of unwilling labor; the hands were sulky."[163] Jesse Belflowers's letters to Adele Allston in October 1864 summed up the worsening state of slavery. The overseer warned, "Theare will not be much work done this winter." The plantation was "in such bad order," he reported, "it will be almost useless to Plant Rice." Within two weeks of this dim report of progress on the Allston plantation, Belflowers added that he could "see in the last two weeks some change in the Pople[.] [T]hey doant seem to care to obay orders & Jack the Drive[r] is not behaveing write he doant talk write before the People." Even worse, rumors in the area suggested that "an attac will be made on Georgetown and if that should be so, the Negros will all Go to them, or Pretty much all, for we have no force hear to prevent them."[164]

Reports of similarly unmanageable slaves came from other Allston overseers: "I see something working among some of the negroes . . . that I Doe not like," warned the overseer William Sweet, in November 1864. Indeed, the slaves on all the Allston plantations bitterly complained about wartime shortages; Sweet conceded that the slaves were so impoverished that "I can not Drive them as I wish to Doe." That winter, the deaths of children and adults among the Allston slaves reflected even more starkly the consequence of wartime conditions. One overseer warned of "several negroes that I think you had Best move" from the lowcountry to an inland refuge, a move that Belflowers also recommended for particular slave families on the plantation he suspected of planning their escape. Adele Allston anticipated the probable result of slave unrest; "If this war lasts two years longer," she ventured, "African Slavery will have ceased in these states."[165]

The Retreat to the Interior

The most dramatic step taken by lowcountry rice planters to protect their investment in slavery also became an unintended element in the wartime collapse of lowcountry plantation life: the removal of their slaves from the coast to "safer" inland locations. By the time most planters contemplated removal as a strategy to avoid further losses among their slaves, the war had already thrown the organization of plantation labor into disarray; impressment was regularly interfering with rice agriculture and subjected slave men to many new and dangerous conditions; shortages were wearing on the health and patience of slaves, and the introduction of new kinds of plantation production—from food crops to salt making—had further disrupted plantation routine. Lowcountry slaves were already demonstrating their desire and intention to make the war a vehicle for black freedom, and planters could not overlook the fact slave women and children—the reproductive future for slaveholdings—had joined in the flight from slavery. Removal was sometimes a preemptive move, but most planters viewed it as a last resort.

For good reason, planters were reluctant to make such a move, even when it was ordered by Confederate or state officials as a matter of military necessity. Without regular maintenance, the delicate and elaborate rice plantation irrigation systems would deteriorate beyond repair.[166] There would be no plantation income, and "refugeed" slaves were a heavy expense to maintain. Mary Elliott Johnstone ventured that "such a move could only be temporary I imagine—for in the pine region they were going to, there would be no provision or work to occupy them"; their prospects were "very bad."[167] Another lowcountry planter concurred that removal offered only dismal prospects: "There is no probability of making anything by the move. . . . All I can hope for is to preserve property which is now out of all danger from the Yankees—the expense of the move & the daily expense of feeding the negroes who will bring in nothing for at least a year is so great than I can not think of feeding ten animals to plough with."[168] James Sparkman complained that his "negroes removed to Clarendon, so far from being self-supporting, in the simple item of *bread* have cost me Thousands per year."[169]

Removing slaves meant forcing them to abandon their own crops, animals, gardens, and much of their personal belongings. In some cases it would require them to accept an indeterminate separation from family members, sacrifice their rapidly improving chances to flee slavery for federal lines, and head for the unfamiliar interior of the country where they

would be poorly cared for and the target of local suspicion. Planters anticipated their slaves' reluctance to leave; "they are not inclined to come, &
I think we will have to make a terrible example of many of them."[170] Some
slaves slated for removal were deemed so unwilling or so likely to make
an attempt to flee that overseers seized them at night and handcuffed
them.[171] When slaves got wind of their master's plans to move them, some
made their decision to escape to the coast while they could; others even
escaped in the very process of moving. A Georgetown planter "had 21 of
his men leave the *moving gang* to join the Yankees."[172] Lowcountry slaveowners cautioned each other to keep their plans for removal secret from
slaves, who might take to the woods. Other rice planters purposely separated families during removal, in effect holding the removed slaves hos-
tage to discourage family members who remained on the plantation from
escaping to federal lines.[173] Adele Allston threatened to remove the parents of some particularly troublesome slaves, "letting them understand they
would have to remain there until the end of the war, and desertion or rebellion in any of their children would be laid at their door."[174]

A few rice planters also had no choice about removal. Some had no
time to consider and weigh the options; faced with the escapes of their
own slaves or those of their neighbors, some planters simply made a last-
minute effort to hold onto the slaves they still had. John Grimball, who lost
nearly eighty slaves to a Union steamer, quickly located a temporary refuge for some of those slaves who remained and hired out the rest to a
planter who sheltered, fed, and clothed the Grimball slaves in exchange
for entitlement to any product of their labor.[175] The July 1863 raid on Combahee River rice plantations by U.S. forces prompted one of the few un-
touched planters to remove his slaves as quickly as possible; "Our negroes
must and should be removed immediately, as the demoralization is something awful." A flood of slave escapes from Santee River rice plantations
similarly prompted several planters in that area to remove their slaves.[176]

Although the Confederate Congress was reluctant to assume the financial liabilities that might result from a formal order to lowcountry civilians
to retreat to the interior, state officials in South Carolina viewed removal
as a potential military necessity early in the war. In January 1862, state
authorities established a commission to oversee, and if necessary, to compel the removal of slaves from the coast, and they loaned slaveowners the
funds they needed to transport their slaves and relocate to the interior of
the state.[177] Despite state and military interest in the removal of lowcountry slaves, and even the provision of state loans to cover the costs of removal, state officials acknowledged that "no general exodus could be ef-

fected," both for practical reasons and because of planter reluctance. Removal would by necessity occur primarily on a voluntary basis.[178]

For the Allstons, like many Georgetown rice planters, the decision to
move was a cumulative result of the Confederacy's relatively weak defense
of Georgetown, ongoing attacks and raids on Georgetown plantations by
the Union navy, and the increasing propensity of neighborhood slaves to
run off to Union gunboats.[179] Sympathetic friends offered places of refuge
to the Allstons during the summer of 1861, but the financial implications
of removal—loss of income, potential loss of property, lack of subsistence—
prompted the Allstons to delay any serious consideration of removal until
the fall of 1862.[180] That summer, even as the Allston slaves were at work
in the rice fields, Allston conceded that with the enemy "commanding our
waters . . . I may be broken up in the midst of the harvest." That summer,
some 1,700 slaves from the Georgetown area fled to the Union fleet—leading the Allstons (whose immediate neighbors alone lost some 150 slaves)
to realize that slaves throughout the neighborhood, including those they
claimed as their own, were pursuing the possibility of freedom with great
determination. Finally, that October, the Allstons found a likely refuge, a
1,900–acre farm on the Pee Dee River in Anson County, North Carolina,
which they purchased for $10,000.[181]

Fragmentary evidence shows slave women to represent about 59 percent of the adult slave population removed from the lowcountry in 1862.[182]
Patterns of removal varied widely and were shaped by several factors. On
one hand, many slave men were already absent from the rice plantations,
forced to labor at fortifications, at saltmaking operations, or hired out, so
that the population subject to removal was often the slave women and
children remaining on the plantations. On the other hand, the decision to
flee often came from a sense that the lowcountry had become a dangerous war zone. Some planters and overseers removed women and children
first in an emergency endeavor to protect the reproductive potential at the
core of the slave population. Others viewed women and children as potential hindrances to the speedy removal that an unanticipated Union invasion might necessitate. On Hobonny plantation, the overseer reported
that he was "moving all the children up to the place I have rented, & will
(with your consent) also send up all the Pregnant Women, who are but little
use to the place at present, & who would be much in the way in case of a
sudden move." The "prime" hands left behind could be depended upon
to make a hasty exit from the coast if threatened by the enemy.[183] Finally,
female domestic slaves were not only subject to removal as part of the slave
population but were also forced to accompany planter families who evac-

uated the coast and sought refuge in the interior of the state. Slave women were, as a result, frequently at the vortex of the disruptions caused by removal as it affected slave families and slave communities.[184]

The conditions of travel to the interior varied, with some slaves traversing the inland waterways on rice flats, others shipped by railroad freight cars, and still others forced to walk or, if unable to walk, carried by wagon. Even planters admitted it could be a "very fatiguing journey" for their slaves.[185] For some slaves—such as the Combahee River slaves of Charles Heyward—their removal to the interior was the first time many of them had been more than a few miles from the plantation (this would have been true particularly for female field hands). Heyward's overseer relied on each "settlement's" headman (or driver) to organize the slaves and assemble them near the local railroad depot. Although the slaves hastily bundled up their personal belongings and carried or drove their stock with them, Heyward permitted them to bring only poultry on the trip. Their hogs and other livestock were presumably left to forage on their own, a total loss to the slaves who had labored long and hard to accumulate the most minimal personal property. Gathered together, Heyward's slaves traveled partly by rail, but they traveled the last eleven miles on foot, with a wagon along to carry their belongings.[186]

Slave women and men begged their owners not to move them to the interior, while others threatened flight rather than see their families sundered.[187] Jenny threatened to run away "before she will leave her child," a threat taken seriously by the overseer, who kept Jenny and her child together.[188] Mothers separated from their children kept tabs on them through the slave grapevine and were quick to protest when their children went hungry. They persistently pleaded for their return. Hester, removed by the Allstons to their refuge, complained "that her uncle Will sent her word that her children were suffering for something to Eat that they do not get Enough to Eat. . . . she Begs you to let her Bring her children home." One mother, her entreaties ignored, apparently instigated rumors about probable rebellion at the refuge to hasten the return of her child and the other slaves.[189] Three of Charles Manigault's slave men attempted to run away when they learned of their master's intention to isolate them miles away from their families and community, and they had to be handcuffed for their journey.[190]

The splintering of plantation communities by selective removal might also have contributed to an escalation of the abusive treatment of slave women by overseers and drivers. Freedwomen's testimony in pension records speaks to the mistreatment and abuse they suffered after being separated from male kin. Slave men might not have been able to bodily prevent such attacks, but their presence—and at least the potential of their retaliation—might have constrained overseers and drivers from the kinds of brutalities described in pension testimony.[191]

The conditions slaves encountered at the inland farms were dismal. Abandoned outbuildings, storage cellars, and hastily erected cabins made poor slave quarters.[192] The change in diet and water contributed to the deteriorating health of refugeed slaves, as did the declining availability of provisions.[193] The shortage of provisions brought refugeed slaves into competition with local yeomen and working-poor whites for scarce resources, exacerbating the growing hostility and antagonism of upcountry residents toward the elite lowcountry whites and their slaves invading upcountry neighborhoods.[194] Some observers believed that the drain on local resources played a role in instigating upcountry bread riots, and that the perceived threat posed by large numbers of strange slaves increased the opposition to military service among local whites.[195] Given the apparently pervasive antagonism between the invading force of lowcountry elites and their slaves and upcountry residents, refugeed slaves found themselves the focus of considerable hostility. Even refugeed whites recognized that "the negroes have been quite nervous."[196] Removal may have protected slaves from an external enemy, but it increased the dangers posed to slavery from within the South.

For slave women, removal was disruptive not only because it entailed leaving home, provision plots, gardens, livestock, and other personal property, but also because they often faced new overseers, new kinds of farm or domestic work, new processes and organizations of production, new divisions of labor.[197] Domestic servants found it nearly impossible to perform the work their mistresses expected when they fled lowcountry plantations for hotels and boardinghouses in the interior.[198] Women's field work also became harder. One planter forced his refugeed slave women to undertake the plowing of fields, a task they had not traditionally performed on the rice plantation.[199] The slaves refugeed by A. H. Elliott were forced to cultivate crops without the help of animals to plow with because Elliott could not bear the expense of supporting his refugeed slaves as well as feeding the animals.[200] Charles Heyward's refugeed Combahee River slaves faced three and a half years of intensive labor to transform an inland cotton and corn plantation into a functioning rice plantation; they "spent the latter part of 1862 in clearing and ditching more land in the swamp, and also in increasing the length and height of the river bank."[201]

Slave women's response to planters' harsh or uncustomary labor demands drew on longstanding traditions of resistance, including slow and inattentive labor.[202] Lowcountry slave women—and even children—also responded to the duress of removal by attempting to escape and, in some cases, to reunite with family members from whom they had been separated. Dolly, a domestic slave owned by Louis Manigault, had been forced to accompany Manigault's family in its flight from the coast to a hotel in Augusta. There Dolly cultivated the friendship of a local black omnibus driver, who apparently aided in her successful escape. Neither the fifty-dollar reward offered by Manigault nor his harassment and intimidation of her fellow slaves secured her capture or return.[203] The story of the escape of two young girls was told by a former slave to the contraband relief worker Charlotte Forten Grimké:

> two girls, one about ten and the other fifteen, who having been taken by their master up into the country about the time of the "Gun Shoot," determined to try to get back to their parents who had been left on this island. They stole away at night, and traveled through woods and swamps, for two days without eating. Sometimes their strength w'ld fail and they w'ld sink down in the swamps, and think they c'ld go no further, but they had brave little hearts, and struggled on, til at last they reached Port Royal Ferry. There they were seen by a boat-load of people who had also made their escape. The boat was too full to take them but the people, as soon as they reached these islands, told the father of the children, who immediately hastened to the Ferry for them. The poor little creatures were almost wild with joy, despite their exhausted state, when they saw their father coming to them. When they were brought to their mother she fell down "jus' as if she was dead" as Tina expressed it.[204]

Planters appear to have been well aware of the increasing fragility of the ties of slavery, some instructing their overseers to take special care in their treatment of refugeed slaves. "You must be easy & not harsh to the people," instructed one planter, "As I can not afford to have them put into the woods. Tell the men & women who have left wives, husbands & children here that they are all well & I will arrange for their meeting as soon as it can be done," he advised.[205] But slaves' resistance and unrest, when added to the financial consequences of removal, prompted several of the refugeed rice planters between the Savannah River and Georgetown to return many of their slaves to the lowcountry and to resume a minor level of plantation production.

Thus, while removal may have protected their slaves from federal confiscation, many planters felt it had proved too burdensome for their finances. James Sparkman "risked the removal of a portion of them back to the Rice fields" when he could no longer afford to buy basic provisions for his refugeed slaves.[206] By 1864, four-fifths of the Allston slaves were back on the plantations, trying to repair the rice fields and irrigation systems now neglected for several years. Many Savannah River rice planters "were working their entire gangs" in 1864.[207] Others moved their entire slave labor force back and forth between the interior and the coast, as the threat from enemy forces changed.[208] Jane Pringle, another planter, had also returned the bulk of her slaves to the coast, keeping some slaves in the interior where they could at least grow their own provisions. But she too had grown weary of flight; her preference was "to stop quietly here and try by our presence to save something, instead of going on the rampage refugeeing *where*? that's the question, shew me a safe point and I'll go tomorrow, but no such happy Valley exists in the Confederacy."[209]

Despite the most diligent monitoring of their slaves, lowcountry rice planters could not stop what the war helped put into motion. By the spring of 1864, war had brought chaos and ruin to many plantations. One Confederate soldier stationed in the lowcountry described the war's impact on the region:

> The cotton fields are grown up in weeds and broom sedge, the trunks and dams of the rice fields are broken and the[y] themselves are overflowed and covered with a green and poisonous slime. The once proud families that had inherited these lands from their Revolutionary ancestors are now scattered over the up-country bearing the name of "Refugees" (which I am afraid has got to be a term of contempt), living Heaven knows how, in a famished land. Their thousands of contented negroes are among the Yankees (their worst enemies) dying like sheep of ill-treatment and disease. Such is the sad condition of a Country ravaged by war.[210]

Of course, it was not only the landscape of lowcountry South Carolina, but also its institution of slavery that had been ravaged by war. The war had altered the material conditions of slave life as well as the relationships of power that were integral to the lowcountry rice regime. Slaves had watched the appearance and substance of planter power weaken, as planters became increasingly unable to purchase or afford even the most basic necessities; as they became subject to impressment of their crops and their slaves; and as voluntary and involuntary removal uprooted the local and familial ties that had held plantation communities in place for generations. As a conclusion to more than a century and a half of plantation slavery, these four years of war were devastating and destabilizing to a system of slavery bound by custom, habit, and tradition in the exercise of power and in resistance to it. It was in part these profound disturbances of war that fueled the determination and vengeance with which black and white South Carolinians, women and men, approached the apocalypse of Confederate defeat, the final destruction of slavery, and their future together in the postwar South.

4 "Without Mercy": The End of War and the Final Destruction of Lowcountry Slavery

"Boys, this is old South Carolina, lets give her hell," shouted one of Sherman's soldiers as they invaded the state during the last months of war.[1] Former slave women would later give fulsome testimony to the fact that the "hell" Sherman's troops delivered was not reserved for Confederate sympathizers and slaveholders. The military historian Joseph Glatthaar has pointed out that the bitterness, anger, and resentment fomented among Sherman's troops by separation from families, deprivation, hard fighting, and marching "came to a head and were focused on" Southern blacks during the Georgia and Carolinas campaign.[2] Slave women, in particular, were enveloped by this chaotic maelstrom of violence that marked the end of war and slavery in the lowcountry between February and May 1865. The violence they experienced came not only from Sherman's armies but also from the Confederate forces retreating before Sherman's advance, and from the civilians, scouts, and guerrillas who attempted to reassert white authority and control over former slaves in the aftermath of Sherman's advance northward out of the region. During these last weeks of war, slave women were in a precarious position, attacked by soldiers on both sides, their freedom announced by Union soldiers one day and withdrawn by Confederate scouts the next. Their meager food, clothing, and possessions were taken by hungry, ragged, resentful, and greedy soldiers in both blue and gray uniforms. They and their families were forced away from their homes to Union lines by Sherman's troops, or back onto the plantations by bands of lowcountry whites. The turmoil of the closing weeks of war probably seemed very much like hell.

Yet even during these tumultuous final weeks of war, lowcountry slave women not only improvised a range of survival strategies but also fought to secure the final collapse of slavery. Their endeavors went far beyond pursuing the promise of freedom as put forward in Lincoln's Emancipation Proclamation. Self-emancipation relied on women's ability to transform their relationship to former owners, to diminish, irrevocably, the slaveowner's power and authority over them. Slave women pursued self-emancipation when they left the rice plantations for the safety (and freedom) of Union-controlled islands and towns, when they confronted planters and overseers, when they ransacked and destroyed lowcountry plantations. Far from passive recipients of the benefits of presidential proclamations or of military victory, slave women helped direct the war's path toward emancipation and shaped the South's final transition out of slavery. Their actions also helped define how Northern and Southern whites viewed the aftermath of war and emancipation in the postbellum South.

The simultaneity of total warfare and the destruction of slavery brought a violent conclusion to four years of civil war and many generations of slavery in lowcountry South Carolina. In February 1865, the hard years of wartime deprivation and the slow collapse of slavery suddenly seemed to draw to a close. To slave men and women, the evacuation of Charleston and the retreat of Confederate soldiers were welcome indications that the rice plantations and their residents were being abandoned to Union forces. Slaves carrying information and rumors between plantations brought word to planters and to their own communities that, by 18 February 1865, General William T. Sherman's forces had taken Columbia, Charleston had surrendered to General Quincy A. Gillmore, and Union control was being extended along the coast from Savannah to Charleston and also at the port at Georgetown.[3] Planters relied on slaves for news detailing the immediate approach of Union troops ("The negroes were well posted as to the movements of the Union Army," recalled one planter). The meaning of that news, and the fear and anxiety it evoked among slaveowners, was carefully interpreted and reported to the slave community, often by the slave women whose invisibility as house servants made them privy to fearful planter-family discussions about occupation and emancipation.[4]

Lowcountry slave women watched planter families become panicked by the "awful news" and "terrifying rumors" of surrender, incipient Union occupation, and emancipation.[5] Confederate authorities warned planters to remove their slave property behind Confederate lines, to prevent their employment by the approaching enemy. But, to the relief of many slaves, removal was no longer possible. The interior refuges lay in the path of Sherman's army, and transportation was nearly impossible, given the destruction of rail lines and the confiscation of mules and horses by both armies.[6] A few planters made final-hour efforts to remove and thereby preserve at least a small portion of their property in slaves, but in several instances slaves rejected this last bid to delay their freedom, managed to become "lost" en route, and purposefully made their way back to their lowcountry homes or to Union gunboats.[7] Other slaves were simply abandoned when planters, particularly in the Georgetown area, fled with their families, perhaps hoping that the scattering of their slaves at farms and upcountry refuges would prevent a complete loss.[8]

Slaves reacted with some apprehension when they heard the news of Confederate withdrawal from the lowcountry. They correctly suspected that the retreating Confederate army would make a final sweep of the plantations, impressing slave labor to help erect obstacles to Sherman's advance; slave men took to hiding in the swamps at night.[9] As Confederate forces evacuated Charleston and their posts along the coast, they confiscated corn and provisions from planters and slaves alike to feed themselves. They took horses and mules to prevent their falling into Union hands and burned anything that might prove useful to the enemy. Deserters simply stole what they needed or wanted from planters and slaves.[10] But as the Confederates disappeared and slaves reported the arrival of Yankee soldiers at neighboring plantations, the burden of fear shifted, at least temporarily, from slaves to the planter families. In the slave quarters, the news of the Union's advance raised hopes; it induced both house servants and field hands to abandon the veil of obedience and inspired a refusal to work, sullenness, and "aside speeches," reactions perceived by slaveowners as "incendiary."[11]

Lowcountry slaveowners feared not only Union soldiers but also the changes evident in their slaves. For many elite whites, emancipation was an even more frightening prospect than the occupation of their state by enemy forces. "What I most fear," complained one planter's daughter, "is not the Yankees, but the negroes, cut off from all help from across the river, and at their mercy, what will become of us?" Indeed, as she and others observed, the discipline of slavery was already disintegrating. "Disorder has already started," she noted; slaves ordered to work resisted, even departed, and forced overseers to leave the plantations.[12] As Yankee troops drew closer, the planter elite became terrified of slave insurrection and the revenge of armed black troops; "my head" cried one frightened white woman, is "full of negroes." False alarms—that Union troops were just down the road, were already on the plantation—left some panicked planter women begging slave women to join them in the "big house," as though to serve as protectors.[13]

Despite the fears many slaveowners held about the consequences of lowcountry emancipation, rice planters' Civil War memoirs frequently recount heroic acts by slaves to protect their owners, which they described as evidence of slave loyalty to the domestic order of the Old South and the system of slavery. Some slaves did protect individual whites from harm. Rose Washington, a house slave, took the safety of a Santee River planter family on her own shoulders when she smuggled contraband liquor ("medicinal" brandy) out of the house under the noses of Union soldiers who threatened to search for it; Nelson, the slave driver at Mount Arena plantation, carried the plantation mistress on his back into the woods to hide her from Union troops.[14] But these acts, even if indicative of affection for individual whites, could hardly be regarded as evidence of slaves' loyalty to the system of slavery. Planters rarely considered whether such feats might have come from slaves' uncertainty about the outcome of the war. Clearly, some slaves could not yet believe that the Confederacy's defeat was at hand, and this may have been reflected in the decision by some of them to maintain the illusion of loyalty to their owners, buying time until the violence that shook the region subsided and the consequences became clearer.

Some slave women, influenced by the planters' portrayal of Union troops as a brutal enemy, or perhaps having heard from other slaves about white Union soldiers' ill-treatment of slaves, fled from approaching Northern troops. Ellen Godfrey, a Georgetown slave, hid in the overseer's house at the sight of the approaching Yankee soldiers. When slaves on Keithfield plantation "saw the Yankees coming they ran away for fear they would be shot." Another former slave explained "we all got scared when we heard the guns shooting, & we ran."[15] Lowcountry slaves, women and men, feared the armed and uniformed white strangers, the exchange of gunfire, the war brought to their homes.

Both plantation mistresses and slave women had good reason to be particularly apprehensive about the treatment they might receive at the hands of Union soldiers. After all, rape had long been one of the prerogatives claimed by men waging war against an enemy's civilian population. Rape has also played a prominent role in wartime ideologies about the masculine defense of hearth and home—the threat against "their" women used to rally soldiers—and enemy soldiers have often been objectified through their portrayal as rapists.[16] Confederate ideology and the South's critique of Northern free-labor culture combined to produce a portrayal of white Union soldiers as just the sort of coarse, dishonorable men likely to assault defenseless women and children. General Benjamin F. Butler's infa-

mous General Order No. 28 (issued 15 May 1862), threatening rude treatment for Confederate women who insulted Union men on the streets of
Union-occupied New Orleans, drew a tide of invective from elite white wom-
en in the South. Butler's name became synonymous with acts of brutality
against Southern white women.[17] White Southerners' fears about Union
soldiers escalated with the enlistment of black soldiers into the Union army,
and the racist sexualization of black men immediately became a part of white
Southern discourse about Union soldiers. Besides its ideological or symbolic weight, rape was also a reality of the Civil War.[18] In lowcountry South
Carolina, white women of the planter class, as it turned out, encountered a
far different demeanor from the Union's black soldiers than what they were
accustomed to, but most found that their personal safety was not at risk
among the Yankees, white or black. During the closing months of war in
the lowcountry, Union naval officers helped escort white women and children to safety, away from the tumultuous rice plantations.[19]

In fact, it was slave women who had the most to fear at the hands of
the advancing Union army. In contrast to the protection extended (however grudgingly) by Union soldiers and sailors to elite white women, slave
women on the rice plantations and female contrabands behind Union lines
discovered they could expect neither safety nor protection at the hands
of white Union soldiers. Many of the Union soldiers moving through the
plantations of lowcountry South Carolina and Georgia "were so outrageous," according to white observers, "that the Negro men were obliged
to stay at their houses for the protection of their wives; and in some instances they rescued them from the hands of these infamous creatures."[20]
When Union soldiers made their appearance on one Santee River rice
plantation in March 1865, the soldiers "treated some of the negro girls
dreadfully," giving rise to a "dreadful howling" from the slave quarters.
Rose, an older house servant, immediately took charge of the younger slave
women, spiriting several away to a variety of hiding places on the plantation—in the planter residence, in the garden, under the slave cabins, in
the woods, and onto neighboring plantations. The white women of the
planter family—who only days before had begged Rose to come and comfort them as they fearfully awaited the arrival of Yankees—now laughed
"very heartily" at the Union soldiers' treatment of the slave women.[21]

Slave-owning women broke their customary silence on the sexual abuse
and exploitation of slave women by white men when the perpetrators were
enemy troops rather than their own husbands or male kin. They described
in diaries and correspondence the physical and sexual abuse of slave
women (and the wives of overseers as well) by Yankee troops, with tangi-

ble relief that the confirmation of their fears about Union soldiers came at the expense of slave women.[22]

How did slave women respond when the soldiers they hoped would help to end slavery raped them even as they announced their freedom? The nature of the evidence we have about slave women's experiences during the close of the war does not allow us to answer this question directly.[23] But certainly we cannot avoid considering the ramifications of some slave women's initial encounters with white Union soldiers as we try to assess women's experience during the transition from slavery to freedom, and as we begin to consider how former slave women defined freedom. We can assume that the experience or threat of assault would have injected a great deal of caution and mistrust into African-American women's dealings with white Union soldiers, during and after the war. Their male kinfolk, too, must have drawn upon their knowledge about the violence aimed at black women when making their own decisions, perhaps affecting patterns of black enlistment, residence, and labor. Finally, it would seem that the experience of violence at the hands of so-called allies in the lowcountry war against slavery would have reinforced freedpeople's desire to live in communities insulated from both Southern and Northern white interference.

There were, of course, many disciplined white soldiers in Sherman's army who did not mistreat slaves, who supported the abolition of slavery and enthusiastically played a role in the final destruction of slavery plantation by plantation. Even though some Union troops cruelly abused lowcountry slaves, the presence of the blue-uniformed soldiers was nonetheless a powerful signal to lowcountry rice planters of the Confederacy's imminent defeat.[24] Sympathetic soldiers assembled the slaves and announced the news of the Emancipation Proclamation. Black troops took a particular joy and pride in their role as liberators and also took a special interest in the vengeful ransacking and destruction of lowcountry plantations. Three soldiers of one black regiment "incited the slaves to commit depredations on the overseer's property and they had abused somewhat the overseer's wife."[25] Alonzo Reed, of the 102d United States Colored Troops, admitted that he and fellow black soldiers eagerly "ransacked every plantation on our way and burnt up everything we could not carry."[26]

White Union soldiers disapproved of the black soldiers' assumed role as liberators and agents of vengeance, but they were far from unified in their own understanding of what might be permitted by the end of slavery. Union soldiers' pronouncements about the close of slavery were often contradictory. On one plantation slaves might be told they were free but had to continue working; on a neighboring plantation soldiers might threaten to shoot slaves who continued working.[27] Furthermore, in the initial traverse of the lowcountry by Union forces, the destruction of slavery was not even the most immediate task at hand. Union forces were in the South Carolina countryside to intimidate and destroy the civilian base of an enemy army and to render interior rail lines unusable. They searched for Confederates and arms. Having marched through lowcountry swamps and in heavy late-winter rains, their own clothing, shoes, and blankets were soaked and ragged; so they sought dry replacements. Deep in the Confederacy without supply lines, Sherman's armies relied on whatever provision could be garnered from the countryside. Those who were greedy also pocketed or carried away valuable trinkets or tools or items that caught their eye. They were tired of the hardships of war and expressed it in their treatment of the people, their homes, and their belongings.[28]

Too often, in their appearances at lowcountry rice plantations, Union troops acted toward slaves very much as the retreating Confederates had. Some confiscated personal property and provisions from the plantations (including slave property); others forcefully "persuaded" slave men to labor on behalf of the (Union) army, too similar to the way retreating Confederates had impressed slave men as laborers; and, as noted above, some attacked and raped slave women.[29] According to one white observer, even the slaves in the path of the Northern army "prayed about as hard for Sherman to go as they had prayed for him to come."[30]

Former slave women unharmed by retreating Confederates, advancing Union forces, or the white guerrilla bands following in their wake still faced the challenge of trying to survive and subsist their families in a countryside swept free of provisions, animals, seed, and the most basic household furnishings. Sherman's "bummers," veteran troops well-practiced in the art of foraging and determined to employ destruction and pillaging as weapons of war, took a particularly severe toll on lowcountry South Carolina.[31] Union soldiers refused to believe that some of the property, provisions, stock, and poultry that they confiscated belonged to the former slaves and not the planters. When Robert Bates, a former slave, tried to explain that the animals they were taking belonged to the former slaves, the Union soldiers "said it was a damned lie."[32] Union soldiers—white and black—also commonly failed to credit lowcountry slave women and men with either the opportunity or the capacity to accumulate personal property. They correctly suspected that some planters, hoping to avoid confiscation, had distributed goods to slaves and intended to try to reclaim them. Many soldiers mistakenly believed that when they confiscated the slaves' "honey, poultry, pigs, cattle, etc." they were stealing from secessionist rebels; that when they "ransacked every plantation on our way and burnt up everything we could not carry away," it was the Confederate planter who would suffer, not the slaves themselves.[33]

Some Union troops deliberately stole from slaves, taking clothes, food, and furnishings out of their cabins. Former slaves were "robbed by the Yankees of their provisions and even the shoes they had on"; Ceasar Deas bitterly recalled "they even took the coat off my back."[34] Cupid Hamilton, formerly a slave of William Heyward, complained that "Sherman's Army came up the Broad River in boats and . . . took all the rice and provisions from the colored people on the place."[35] Another former slave from the same plantation elaborated: "They took every thing the people had. All their horses, all the Meat Rice and provisions . . . [and] there was nothing left for the people to eat. . . . The soldiers also took the people's blankets, beddings Clothes and pots—left them nothing. This was the first place they came to after leaving the river and they swept it clean."[36] Eliza Washington particularly recalled the soldiers' theft of her few household furnishings. The soldiers "took all our bed clothes such as Blankets, sheets and pillow cases. They shook the feathers and moss out of the beds and made bags of them to fill with Rice. They also took all our Clothes but what we had on."[37]

The invading Union armies, with their policy of provisioning troops off the land and destroying whatever could not be eaten, dealt a blow to all the residents of the lowcountry.[38] Several months after the war ended, when an overseer asked one older freedwomen how she had fared when the Yankees came through, she "threw up her hands" and said "My God, the Yankees cleaned us out, & never left us one pint of the corn you gave us." Georgia Ann Butler, another former slave, summed up the consequences of Sherman's march for lowcountry African-American women: "Couldn't find no corn seed! Couldn't find no cotton seed! Couldn't find no salt! . . . Sufferin' been in de neighborhood atter de war passes!"[39]

For freedwomen, the work of subsistence and survival had been made even more difficult by the actions of Union troops as they swept through the lowcountry, a region where slaves were already hard hit by wartime shortages, impressment, and confiscation. Stripped of whatever personal property they may have accumulated and clung to during the war, left without the seed or tools needed to prepare a new crop, many freedwomen—especially those with dependent children or elderly kin to care for— were pressured by Union soldiers to take their families to temporary contraband camps and then on to the Sea Islands, where the fortunate few found a place to live and work.[40] Many found themselves delivered into dependency on the army quartermaster's office for rations and clothing.[41] As one freedwoman explained, "When they had cleaned us out, they brought four wagons and put all the old people in the wagons, and the rest had to walk, and made us go to the River to a Steamboat which carried us to the Island where we received Rations from the Government officers."[42] One family of freedpeople had loaded up their wagon with their house-hold goods and headed away from the plantation, but then encountered so many Union soldiers "we just got out of the wagon and let them have" the wagon and its contents: "they wanted us to go along with them, but we took the first chance to get away and went home. The next day the Army came up to the plantation and broke up the place. They took every-thing the people had. All their horses, all the Meat Rice and provisions[,] wagon after wagon came and loaded up with our provisions and then ordered us to the Islands for there was nothing left for the people to eat and we had to be furnished with rations by the Government officers."[43]

Rebecca Smith, a free black farmer of Beaufort County, watched Union soldiers confiscate not only her livestock and provisions, but also all her household goods, including pots and pans, and blankets and quilts. Left without the means to clothe, feed, or support her five children, she ap-pealed to the commanding officer of the Union troops, General Hatch, for the return of some of her property. Hatch told Smith to bring her children behind Union lines; when she did so and reported back to Hatch, he sent Smith and her family on to Beaufort, and from there, to Port Royal, to draw government rations.[44] Agnes Jackson, also free, was forced to migrate when Union soldiers "took possession of my house and lot and every thing that was in it and ordered us to go [to] Pocotaligo. We went on foot with what little clothes we could carry and at Pocotaligo we were put into a Govern-ment wagon and sent to Port Royal Island. Here we were furnished with rations for about a month, when we had to shift for ourselves, and were often in a starving condition. I had three little girls with me and had a hard time of it."[45]

At the same time that Union troops forced the relocation of former slaves to the coast, other freed slaves took to the road on their own initia-tive. Thousands of former slaves had followed in the wake of Union forces as they moved through Georgia, and from Savannah through South Caro-lina.[46] When General Edward H. Potter returned to Georgetown from his early April raid against interior rail lines, he estimated that at least five thousand lowcountry slaves attached themselves to his army; a captain of a Massachusetts regiment reported the number higher, at six thousand.[47]

Former slaves followed Potter's army to the vicinity of Georgetown, joining troops and former slaves on plantations, until "hordes of blacks who
like vultures hung round the plantations here and by their numbers over-
awed the [local] negroes and got the lion's share of the booty."[48] Union
troops were impressed by the slaves' determination to gain their freedom,
but thousands of refugees interfered with the army's progress: "It was
extremely tedious to keep the contrabands in their places [at the rear of
the division]. There must have been as many as 3,000 of the latter of all
ages sexes and conditions. Old crippled men and women, little boys and
girls just able to toddle[,] women in the very agonies of child birth all
moving along each with 'we 'tings' on their heads. Some of the women
gave birth to children last night and more will do the same to night."[49]
Slowed by the logistical burden of thousands of black refugees, some Union
soldiers did their best to persuade them "to remain at home free" rather
than follow in the seemingly safe wake of Union army movement.[50]

In light of the problems posed by the black refugees, and following a
consultation with the Secretary of War and twenty local black leaders, in
January 1865 Sherman was authorized by Secretary of War Stanton to issue Special Field Order 15, which established the Sea Islands and a thir-
ty-mile strip of the coastal mainland, between Charleston and St. John's
River (Florida), as a settlement for the exclusive use of black refugees.[51]
As had been the case in the wartime preemption and sale of Sea Island
land to contrabands, soldiers' families and heads of households were entitled to claim up to forty acres of land in the settlement, and to receive
"possessory title," whose meaning was left for Congress to resolve.[52] Thus
only a small proportion of the refugees who made their way to the coast
or who were forced there by Union depredations were eligible for land
claims. Slave women who had risked all to escort their families to freedom,
or who had lost all to marauding soldiers, were not entitled to land claims.
Nonetheless, thousands of lowcountry freedpeople headed for the Islands
and the promise of independent homesteads, joining those who were being
virtually forced off mainland plantations and sent to the coast. By early
April, General Rufus Saxton estimated the population of black refugees on
the islands at 35,000; in Charleston, 30,000; in and around Georgetown,
15,000; in Savannah, 15,000. Of the 95,000 black refugees estimated to
be in the Department of the South at war's end, only 30,000 were thought
to be self-supporting.[53]

The contraband camps—such as Montgomery Hill and Mitchelville on
Hilton Head Island—were overwhelmed with what one historian has described as a "kind of refugee black population, of women, children, the

infirm, and the aged."[54] Some were the families of enlisted men, but many more were individuals and families left destitute by four years of war and Union liberation. Infectious disease—like measles and smallpox—swept through the black refugee population.[55] But regardless of their health, those who were brought to the camps—like thousands of wartime refugees who had fled slavery—found it was necessary to obtain some sort of employment, either under the quartermaster, or on the plantations operated by the Treasury Department agents and Northern entrepreneurs. Those without land, who remained in the army "annexes," were dependent on the army for rations, clothing, and some means of livelihood.

Slavery Destroyed

On the mainland, the wartime dissolution of slavery had accelerated with the arrival of Union troops; slaves eventually took matters into their own hands to secure slavery's final destruction.[56] Still, even their self-emancipation relied, in part, on the perceptions of former slaves and planters as to the strength and duration of Union presence. On a few lowcountry plantations, the long-anticipated arrival of Union troops seemed to bring an abrupt change in the relation between former slaveowner and former slave. In other instances, news traveled faster than Union troops, and soldiers found their announcement of emancipation "made no difference," because the former slaves "knew it before."[57] In some of the more remote regions, word—and Union soldiers—traveled slowly, so that some "freedpeople," making their way south from "liberated" upcountry refuges to their lowcountry homes, were arrested and jailed as runaway slaves in the countryside, where neither soldiers nor emancipation had made a convincing appearance.[58] On a very few plantations, where planters had taken it upon themselves to gather up their slaves and announce the end of slavery, Union soldiers skipped any formal pronouncements, leaving former slaves and planters to work out between themselves the meaning of black freedom.[59] A few lowcountry slaveowners refused to concede emancipation even as enemy soldiers drove home the meaning of Southern defeat. These included planters like Henry Ravenel, who believed (and hoped) that the occupying Yankee troops as well as emancipation were only temporary, until the winds of war shifted to the advantage of the South once more.[60]

On plantations where both slaves and slaveowners still resided, the appearance of Union forces was often necessary to finally force planters to acknowledge Southern defeat and slavery's end.[61] One rice planter complained that the arrival of Union troops seemed to have "snapped the ties suddenly" between him and his former slaves; another conceded that "only the Yankee bayonets put a stop to our work."[62] When friendly or sympathetic Union troops visited refuges and lowcountry plantations, the former rice slaves "hurrahed for liberty" and "went wild with joy."[63] Soldiers from an Ohio regiment "advanced through the rice plantations along the Cooper River, and told the negroes they were all free[.] They seemed so rejoiced they nearly went wild over the matter. Our band played while passing several of the plantations and the negroes came running out to the road as if crazy[.] They would dance in front of the musician and shout and clap their hands in a very ecstasy. Poor creatures they seem scarcely able to contain themselves."[64] Far from the organized, orderly emancipation celebrations that would eventually take place in towns and counties across the South, spontaneous and ecstatic outbursts erupted at the appearance of Union soldiers, as women and men joyfully greeted what appeared to be an irreversible step toward the final destruction of lowcountry slavery.[65]

During the late winter and early spring of 1865, neither Confederate nor Union forces could claim control over the Carolina countryside. It was a moment that reflected the wartime deterioration of slavery as well as the impact of Sherman's march through the state, but it preceded the wholesale entry of lowcountry residents into the contested terrain of black freedom. In this pause between slavery and freedom, lowcountry residents apparently sensed that slavery was on the brink of final collapse. Slave women responded by accelerating their efforts to make a permanent change in the relations of lowcountry plantation life, through dramatic, destructive, and wholesale attacks on planter residences, through the redistribution of plantation property, and by driving planters and overseers off the plantations.

An episode at one of the Allston plantations suggests both the intent and the drama attending this moment of transition. In a two-week period marked by the arrival of Union troops to the neighborhood, and the departure of "all the yonge men & boys [who had] gone down to them to go in the army," the former slave women and few remaining men compelled the overseer on Pipe Down plantation "to give up the Barn Key—or to suffer from their hands." Apparently encouraged by passing Yankee soldiers who had "turned the People loose to disturb the house," the freedpeople then began

> taking out every thing & then to the smoke hous and Store Room doing
> the same as in the house & took the Plough oxen & Kild some of them[.]

[T]he Pipe down People done this[.] [T]he hogs in the Pen is Kild & all the Stock is taken a way the horses is all taken a way. Some of the People owns some of them. the Pore mules has been Road to death all most[.] [A]fter this the People have Puld down the mantle Pieces Broke them to Pieces, taken of[f] all the doors & Windows, Cut the Banisters & sawd out all such as wanted and have taken a way the fenceing a Round the yeard, brok down the old Stabel & the Carpenter Shop.[66]

Everything from fine interior woodwork to fences and outbuildings became targets as former slaves turned the world of plantation relations upside down by vandalizing every symbol within reach of the planter's authority, status, and power. The overseer who witnessed the ritual of destruction at Pipe Down, spared from harm when he complied with the freedpeople's demand for the plantation keys, warned the plantation mistress that it was not safe for her to return: "if you had been on the plantation . . . you would have been hurt by the People." Neither the intensity nor the outcome of this episode was exceptional. In the Santee River rice plantation district, "everything is burnt & destroyed. Dwelling, outhouses, stable, barn & negro huts," and the destruction, a neighbor informed the planter Williams Middleton, was "principally instigated by your own negroes."[67] Passing Union soldiers sometimes attempted to interrupt the slaves' destruction ("Passed Mr. Gillyard's where I found the negroes running riot about the place. Drove them out and restored order as well as I could").[68]

The incident on the Allston plantation was part of a larger pattern of destruction on lowcountry rice plantations. In the earliest weeks of freedom, former slave women and men pillaged and burned dozens of planter residences. Barns and outbuildings, although often stripped or even burned, were less frequently the target of the kind or extent of damage done so purposefully to the planters' homes.[69] Former slaves seemed especially intent on taking apart crafted interiors, destroying paneling, banisters, furniture, rugs, even ornate window and door frames, all of which had also been the bane of domestic servants' housekeeping chores.[70] The plantations that had been abandoned by the planter families seemed most vulnerable, but many occupied plantations suffered some depredation as well.

The frequency, specificity, and intensity of former slave women's attacks on planter property signals to us the symbolic importance of these acts in the drama surrounding the transition from slavery to freedom. The fine, elaborately appointed homes were constant reminders (to black and white plantation residents) of the disparity between the lives led by white rice planters and the conditions of poverty in which slaves lived (worsened by the war).[71] Freedwomen expressed an acute understanding that planter wealth had been derived from the very flesh and blood of slaves. Phillis, former slave of St. Helena, responded to a Northern interviewer's inquiry about the cost of her former owner's beautiful mansion: "'Whar he git he money? Is dat what you ask—whar he got he money? *I* show you, massa.' Pushing up her sleeve, she showed a gaunt, skinny, black arm, and tapping it energetically with her fore-finger, exclaimed: 'You see dat, massa? Dat's whar he got he money—out o' dat black skin he got he money.'"[72] Similarly, another lowcountry freedwomen, pointing to a field of cotton, explained, "there you see our blood."[73] Here, former slave women were speaking to the predominance of women among field hands and the exploitation of their labor in the fields, as well as to profound cruelty and brutality. Here, lowcountry freedwomen seem also to be speaking to the literal sacrifice of flesh and blood—especially from the slave mothers whose children superadded to the wealth of lowcountry planters—that made the staple crop valuable and the beautiful planter homes possible.

Now stepping outside slave traditions of obsequiousness, dissemblance, and covert resistance, women like Phillis openly declared war on slavery and the ill-gotten gains derived from the exploitation of their flesh and blood. Their attacks on lowcountry rice plantations were, perhaps, acts of public redemption against the public humiliations and loss of dignity and status that slaves had endured under the domination of planter, overseer, and driver.[74]

By publicly redistributing the contents of planter homes and storehouses, the freedwomen and men gave new meaning to the slave tradition of secretly appropriating planters' property for their own uses. Former slave women no longer surreptitiously smuggled the planter's rice and meat into their cabins; as one overseer reported, "the People say they mean to have it."[75] Former slaves on one North Santee plantation took fifteen hundred bushels of rice, prepared for market, and were "feeding & distributing it to the Whole River."[76] Freedpeople on several Cooper River rice plantations opened several barns and storehouses ("forced the overseer Mr. Wm. C. Sloan by aiming fire arms at him several times to open the barn"), distributing salt, rice, grist, and corn "among the crowds of freedmen & freedwomen" there gathered.[77] At the Allston's Nightingale Hall plantation, former slave women brought in all the sheep from the fields, then slaughtered and consumed them.[78]

Freedwomen and men were thorough in their ransacking of the plantations: "not an article was left in the house, neither bed nor sheet, table or chair. . . . Every lock [was] taken off, and the doors taken off their hinges." On the same plantation, the meat house and storeroom had been plundered of their contents.[79] The slave quarters were soon furnished with bedsteads and other fine furniture, clocks, crockery, and various fineries confiscated from the "big house," but also, for the first time, bed linen, a variety of kitchen utensils, and other more elaborate household goods. At least some rice planters recognized that these were not random acts of vandalism; "the conduct of the negroes in robbing our house, store room meat house etc. and refusing to restore anything shows . . . they *think it right* to steal from us . . . as the Israelites did the Egyptians."[80] In a similar vein, Charles Manigault realized that when his former slaves "broke into our Well-furnished residences on each Plantation & Stole or Destroyed everything *therein,*" they did so because, "though [the property was] *useless to them* . . . they knew *its value to* us."[81]

The redistribution of plantation property by former slaves was not always a political statement or for the commonweal, but included the endeavors of individuals to gain possession of some particularly desired or valued item. A former slave at Morefield plantation who had long evaded work by shamming illness suddenly gained the strength to move books and even a piano from the planter house to his own cabin.[82] Another former slave, with ambitions to be a preacher and teacher, took the secretary out of the Weston plantation residence and carried it to his quarters.[83]

Freedwomen's appropriation of the treasured belongings of former owners was derided by plantation elites as an especially preposterous attempt at role reversal. According to one rice planter, the "leading Characterisks of *The NEGRO,* and . . . *The Times,* through *which we have recently passed,*" were exemplified in the actions of his former slave Peggy. He noted that as his former slaves plundered his plantation, Peggy "seized as Her part of the *spoils* my wife's Large & handsome Mahogany Bedstead & Mattrass & arranged it in her own Negro House *on which she slept* for some time" and in which, her former owner bitterly imagined, she enjoyed "*her Sweet Dreams of freedom.*" No less bitterly, her former owner derisively noted that "in the pride of *their freedom*" Peggy also took "some *Pink Ribands,* & tied in a dozen bows the woolly head of her Daughter, to the admiration of the other Negroes." Peggy's particularly maternal expression of her freedom, from her former owner's perspective, was as absurd as the theft and tumult that had turned the world of slavery and lowcountry race relations upside down. The rice planter Adele Allston may have had a similar response on being informed by an outraged neighbor that "yr. [former slave] woman

Lavinia claimed and took all the furniture" in Allston's fine summer residence at Plantersville. Another "negress" had claimed as her own another Allston residence and reportedly had even had the audacity to appeal to the federal fleet to gain "protection for her property."[84]

Just as freedwomen like Peggy insisted that freedom included their right to assert a new public maternal identity, freedmen also improvised new expressions of their manhood that were consistent with how they perceived their status as freedmen. In a few instances former slave men, apparently deeply affected by the commanding appearance of black men in uniform and their talk of emancipation, seized upon a paramilitary model of masculine camaraderie, leadership, and authority in their pursuit of both vengeance and freedom. At least six former slave men banded together, under the captaincy of a fellow slave, William Arnell, and initiated a particularly violent confrontation with the white men who had once claimed the power of life and death over them. They seized Joseph Ford's Georgetown plantation, forced his overseer into the woods where they shot and killed him, and threatened Ford and his nephew with a similar fate.[85] On John Irving's plantation, a band of seven freedmen seized the plantation keys from the overseer and made off with the contents of Irving's house as well as two hundred bushels of rice. During the course of the attack, the freedmen informed Irving that one of them had been made a lieutenant and acted with the authority of the U.S. Army; if Irving tried to interfere with the group, the "lieutenant" would "fetch him down." The same "lieutenant" also threatened the overseer and his wife, telling them that U.S. troops had gone to a nearby village to "make buzzard's meat of the white people."[86] While verbal confrontations with lowcountry whites, plantation plundering, and the redistribution of plantation goods were activities in which both freedwomen and freedmen participated, the claim to military authority and a military style of organization were attributed solely to freedmen. Although rarer than the widespread incidents of property destruction, these examples of paramilitary activities reflected one of the avenues through which freedmen assumed a new public style of masculine agency. Like freedwomen's assertion of new public identities in the aftermath of emancipation and Confederate defeat, freedmen's paramilitary activities seemed to be a response to former slaves' gendered experience of the relations of domination and subordination on lowcountry plantations.[87]

Freedwomen were not always content to wreak vengeance on the symbols of wealth and exploitation on rice plantations, and not all of the life-threatening attacks on lowcountry whites were by freedmen in paramilitary groups. Anxious to burn the bridges by which they might be returned to slavery, some lowcountry freedpeople chased planters and overseers off the rice plantations, threatening or attacking them, and burning down their homes. Former slaves at one plantation "begged the Yankees to burn the house" so that the owner could never return.[88] Three former slaves, Billy, George, and Smart, threatened to burn the residence on Bossis plantation around the heads of their former owners, the Irving family.[89] On Hammock plantation, near the Savannah River, Harriet, a former slave and mother of two children, saw to the burning of the planter residence herself.[90] Mazyck Porcher's former slaves retaliated against his support of the local Confederate forces by burning his plantation to the ground.[91]

At some of the Santee River plantations, freedmen and women discovered new allies when neighboring poor whites joined them in sacking the plantation houses and seizing plantation property, especially provisions. One white woman was overheard to comment to a former slave, as they trashed and scavenged from one planter house, that she was glad the planter families would have to go to work; "now they are equal to us."[92] Lowcountry planters like Thomas Porcher Ravenel were astounded to discover neighboring poor whites taking a part in the "shameful robbery on those who had been their friends and in some instances their supporters."[93] The defiant acts of lowcountry African Americans seemed to inspire the white yeomanry, as well.[94]

Later, when lowcountry planter families took measure of the condition of their rice plantations, the list of stolen property and damage was a long one. For some planter families, it offered an intense revelation of their former slaves' anger and hatred.[95] "Aunt Nenna's people, with few exceptions, behaved shamefully," wrote one shocked member of a planter family; "the Morefield negroes are crazy," she added. "The People have behaved Verry badly," reported one overseer to a planter; "I do think if you have been on the plantation you would have been hurt by the People."[96] The former slave men and women on various Allston plantations "behaved like devils," though particularly the women at Nightingale Hall were reported to have "acted in a frenzied way."[97] In every neighborhood, former slaveowners declared and believed that "the negroes here have behaved worse than any I have heard of yet."[98] Rice planters and overseers were deeply affected by the realization that former slaves, through their "crazy," "bad," and "perfectly insubordinate" behavior, had not only destroyed the plantations but also rejected the entire facade of subordination and reciprocity.

Concerned that Union forces had failed to restore or maintain order over the former slaves, and insistent that such order was essential both for the freedpeople's "own good" and so that a "large number [of whites] may escape the horrors of insubordination violence & ultimate starvation," a number of lowcountry whites organized to take matters into their hands.[99] Discharged Confederate soldiers, Confederate officers and soldiers separated from their companies during the evacuation of Charleston, along with overseers and members of planter families who had escaped the draft, joined into guerrilla bands that lowcountry whites called "scouts." Following in the wake of the Union troops who passed through the lowcountry, the loosely organized bands of civilian and former Confederate men initiated a new wave of reactionary violence, attempting to reassert white authority and restore order to the countryside through the subordination of the former slaves.

The motives for the organization and activities of the "scouts" seem apparent, given the "horrors of insubordination" that accompanied the final destruction of lowcountry slavery, but the scouts and their supporters rationalized their guerrilla activities in a number of ways. In the Georgetown area, planters claimed a respectable status for their civilian "militia," which they argued was organized solely to put an end to the plantation plundering that followed in the wake of the arrival of Union forces between February and April 1865.[100] In mid-May 1865, according to one planter, "some of our colored friends in Georgetown began to think stealing from what they considered a 'reb' was a safe and profitable business. . . . so I got some of my neighbors together; we armed ourselves, and pursued. There were about twenty of them, and only six of us. . . . They showed fight . . . but 'twas no use. We scattered them easily. Seven of them fell, five of the seven killed on the spot." The fact that this same planter kept a souvenir of his victory— the bullet-pierced skull of one of the fallen freedmen—suggests that the lethal defeat of their foes had more complex meanings for lowcountry rice planters than simply bringing an end to plantation plundering.[101]

In other lowcountry localities, the organization of white guerrilla activities was publicly acknowledged as a counterreaction to freedmen's paramilitary organizing—as though white men felt called to respond in kind to freedmen's public and occasionally violent assertion of a new, aggressive masculinity. In one particularly bloody incident, white scouts battled with a paramilitary company of neighborhood freedmen and free black men at Pineville, a Santee River village. According to local whites, at the close of the war the "negroes . . . seemed to get cross and did more mischief than the Yankees even—they stripped the houses and no doubt helped to burn." Former slaves and free blacks from the neighborhood also "formed a regular company with officers & armed with U.S. Rifles which were sent up to them." Besides visiting local plantations and confiscating and redistributing plantation goods, a local planter reported they were also "preparing & were about to commense an insurrection & a dreadful murder of the whites" when the scouts seized the initiative and attacked the freedmen on 26 March.[102]

It was not only the simple fact of freedmen's paramilitary activity and the general threat of violence that motivated the white response. The scouts' attack at Pineville was prompted—and later rationalized—in part by rumors circulated among local planters that Pineville's black paramilitary organization "had force[d] some of the females in PineVille to walk before the regt[.] stripped of their clothes."[103] Here, the implied defense of white womanhood against rapacious black men—a symbol that would fuel the lynching of thousands of black men in decades to come—was used by local whites to rationalize their violent suppression of freedmen in lowcountry South Carolina.[104] In this instance, the conflict between freedmen and lowcountry scouts came to a head in a battle; the scouts "had a regular fight with them, killed Pringle [one of the acknowledged leaders] & a good many of the other ringleaders, in all killed 28." According to one planter's account, which sounded very much like a dispatch from a wartime battlefield, "the negroes held their ground & fought well" until they were "finally routed." Pringle's heroism was described even by the planter families of the neighborhood; he was reportedly "wounded several times & fought desperately to the last, he dragged himself off for half a mile" before the scouts finally discovered and killed him.[105] By using military language and imagery, and by portraying freedmen as an able but defeated enemy force, local whites seemed to cast the scouts' activities as legitimate contestation between voluntary participants.

However, the violence perpetrated by lowcountry scouts was not limited to open battle between willing male participants. Slave and freedwomen were also targets. An armed band of whites lynched several former slaves, including the former slave driver on Hanover plantation who had threatened to reveal to Union soldiers the hiding place of the white scouts, as well as the driver's mother, Rose Washington. Only days after Rose had tried to protect other slave women from attacks by Union soldiers as they marched through the countryside, and just after the lynching of her son, the scouts "visited" Rose at her quarters, apparently in response to the rumor that she had stockpiled arms and ammunition belonging to a band of local slave men organized to fend off attacks by the whites. Sometime after their visitation, Rose's body was discovered, "left unburied just on the field where she had been tied & dragged & killed."[106]

The reign of terror conducted by lowcountry whites against freedpeople was far reaching. The scouts continued their visitations to the former slave quarters of the neighborhood plantations, punishing or murdering former slaves who acted as though they were free. For passing on information to the Union troops, or for threatening the livelihood of lowcountry planters by fleeing the old plantation, former slaves—men, women, and children—were "disappeared," a tactic that planters encouraged and thought far more effective in subduing the freedpeople than public corporal punishment. Henry W. Ravenel, for example, approved when Jonas, along with his wife and some of their children, were disappeared, apparently in response to insolence and the family's determination to leave their former owner and reach the relative safety of Charleston.

Planters encouraged the scouts in "disposing of" the "ringleaders" and "the really violent and insubordinate who are influencing others," and were not hesitant to include freedwomen among the ranks of the deserving offenders.[107] On some plantations, scouts gathered up the freedpeople and "told them they were not free, but slaves, and would be until they died; that the Yankees had no right to free them, and that they would go to work as they had always done with a driver." Scouts confiscated firearms from the former slaves and threatened to kill any of the individuals found off the plantation without a pass from the planter. The scouts temporarily revoked the freedom that some former slaves had enjoyed for only a short period, prompting one planter's granddaughter to observe, "the negroes freedom was brought to a close to-day."[108] Before the beginning of summer the scouts reinstituted slavery on a number of Santee River rice plantations and forced a number of freedpeople to return to slave labor. And despite scouts' occasional claims to be acting as protectors of white womanhood, getting former slaves back to work was their most important accomplishment. Whether they organized as militia or scouts, lowcountry whites offered proof that African-American freedom—given its multifaceted challenge to Southern white manhood—would require vigorous defense.[109]

The scouts' violent campaign failed to prevent either former slaves' continued assertions of freedom or their acts of revenge against the planters. Even those Pineville planters, who for a time had enjoyed the benefits of the presence of the scouts, still had to appeal to Union troops for protection from their former slaves. Rene Ravenel begged to be taken into protective custody, and Mazyck Porcher, whose refuge had served as headquarters for Confederate troops, found his place burned to the ground by his former slaves. These acts of retribution seem particularly bold in a neighborhood where armed whites were likely to extract murderous revenge.[110]

The successive waves of violence that accompanied the final destruction of slavery may have inspired some of the enlistment of lowcountry slaves and freedmen in the Union army and navy during the late winter and spring of 1865. Enlistment, like paramilitary activities, offered them another strategy for contending with the scouts, a way of assuring the defeat of the Confederacy, and also another means of burning the bridges leading back to slavery—all in the context of an exclusively male endeavor. Slave men who left lowcountry plantations only to reappear armed and in uniform offered an explicitly masculine affront to the authority of planters and former slaveowners. The sight certainly enraged the planter Henry W. Ravenel, who described black troops as "savages, the outlaws & runaways, & rogues of our plantations." "Their object," he believed, was "to endeavor by their position in the army, to be haughty & overbearing to the whites, as an example to the negroes at home[.] They wish to incite hostile feelings towards us, & do every thing in their power to destroy the respect & attachment which the domestics have for the whites. They . . . say they have the whites under their thumb, & mean to degrade them."[111]

The fact that some former slave men were able to confront their former owners, clothed in the dignity and authority of the U.S. uniform, has drawn the attention of many scholars interested in the social history of the Civil War. One historian has argued that nothing "more graphically demonstrated" the impact of the Civil War than the sight of "armed and uniformed black men, many of them recently slaves, operating as a liberation and occupation army."[112] Unfortunately, the dramatic image of black soldiers confronting former owners has typically substituted for a closer examination of the fuller context of the black military experience. The Union army was no less important in the lives of women and other civilians, as revealed by men's military experience beyond the battlefield and especially by the impact of army regulations and military policy on soldiers' families and their communities, and on the entire region's transition from war to peace.

Men, Women, and Their Military Experience

Although eager to further the war for black freedom, black soldiers and their families found soldiering a mixed experience. For the former slave men who enlisted or were recruited, as well as for their families and communities, military service once again divided war-torn families and rice plantation communities. Women left behind by the new recruits had to assume the burden of struggling with planters over the final collapse of lowcountry slavery and the meaning of black freedom. Black enlistment

also permitted the Union military establishment to assume an even greater role in the closing weeks of the war and in postwar lowcountry South
Carolina, subjecting not only the soldiers but also women and their families to the policies and prejudices of the white command structure and
military culture. Although by the time most mainland lowcountry ex-slaves
enlisted (February to April 1865) several major battles over discrimination
in the service had been fought and won, racism still shaped the actions
and attitudes of white soldiers and officers toward black soldiers and civilians. Racism also shaped the way white military authorities perceived,
and responded to, the unique culture and distinct gender conventions of
lowcountry African Americans.

Black Americans, north and south, had fought for their right to serve in
the military. They rightfully viewed the enlistment of black men as a victory
against discrimination and an assertion of African-American manhood. But
the Union's wartime enlistment of Southern African-American men had been
influenced by pragmatic issues as well, and pragmatism governed recruit-
ment in lowcountry South Carolina at the close of the war. By early March
1865, the Union military command in South Carolina had turned to a more
aggressive enlistment of slave men and the employment of their wives and
families within Sherman's reserve as a means of controlling and contain-
ing the refugee black population, and as a way of interrupting the pillaging
and destruction carried on by blacks against the planters in areas evacuated by Confederate soldiers.[113] New enlistments also allowed the quicker discharge of white war-weary veterans during the general postwar demobili-
zation that followed Lee's surrender.[114] These pragmatic issues were not far
from mind when the commander of Union forces in South Carolina instructed General Potter, on his raid into the state's interior, to have his troops "bring
in all the negroes they can" to Georgetown, where "an entire regiment" could
then be raised.[115] Mainland lowcountry slave men, enlisted by Potter's troops,
formed most of the companies of one South Carolina regiment, the 128th
U.S. Colored Infantry.[116] Hundreds of slave men on the lowcountry rice plantations answered the call to arms, and the consequences of their enlistment
in turn became one of the factors shaping the transition from slavery to freedom in the lowcountry.

Although the majority of slave men who enlisted in March and April
of 1865 came into the army too late to participate in any major battles,
they saw themselves as armed combatants in a war that would bring an
end to slavery. Certainly one of the motivations for the formation of the
scouts had been the threat they believed that black soldiers—and black
men who acted like soldiers—posed; perhaps white Southerners' visceral
response to armed black men in uniform likewise contributed to the deci-

sion of hundreds of lowcountry slave and freedmen to enlist in February, March, and April 1865.[117]

While former slave men's military service became an important setting for the expression of a new, postemancipation masculinity, some lowcountry slave men were not initially enthusiastic about enlistment. A number of lowcountry soldiers appear to have been pressed into service, as their families and friends watched, by the Union troops who appeared at their plantations. Harriet Lemmon, a freedwoman, recalled that U.S. soldiers physically took her brother, Cain Nesbit, and carried him away. According to Nesbit, "I was just about grown when the Yankees took me out of the big ditch at our place at Georgetown S.C. and carried me off."[118] Gabriel Brown reported that he and Pompey Gray, a fellow slave, "were taken by the soldiers when they came . . . & sent down the river to Charleston & put in the guardhouse until the next Sunday—when we were sent on a steamer to Beaufort & put in the 128th."[119] Rina Green, one soldier's widow, explained that "a crowd of Yankee soldiers came through Waymount Plantation and took soldier and some other colored men into Georgetown." But her husband, she emphasized, "was willing to go," suggesting that probably not all were. Jacob Vandross was proud to be among those who made his own way to town to enlist: "I was not recruited. There was an office in Georgetown where men could enlist and I went there voluntarily and recruited."[120] Clearly, enlistment was not a wholly voluntary process in lowcountry South Carolina.

The majority of black soldiers from the lowcountry mainland enlisted and served with men from their own and neighboring plantations. This may have been largely a consequence of recruiting practices, but it also reflected and reinvigorated the social and kinship bonds among slave men on lowcountry rice plantations. Frederick Allston's account of enlisting with several friends and relations was typical; his friend Cain Mayhams "& I & Nat & Tony & others all went at the same time" to enlist. Fellow enlistees had known each other since boyhood; they enlisted together, were shipped aboard the same steamers to their encampments, were often mustered into the same company together, were tentmates, and were mustered out of the service together. Those who were not mustered into the same regiment were frequently camped in the same area and saw each other often.[121] These shared experiences created close ties among men and cemented existing bonds, in a specific, male context. The meaning of that gender-specific experience would be influenced, however, not only by the nature of their shared histories and lowcountry community ties, but also by their encounter with the army's efforts to mold the former slave men into the military model of masculinity.[122]

White officers commanding black troops imagined themselves responsible for transforming dependent, docile, and cowardly slave "boys" into
self-reliant, disciplined, courageous soldiers. Many Americans believed that
men, white or black, were made more "manly" by the experience and
discipline of soldiering. Although freedmen may have felt their military
service offered *prima facie* evidence of their intrinsic masculinity, some
whites imagined that slave men were given their first real taste of manhood when they donned the U.S. uniform and came under the tutelage of
(white) military command and discipline.[123] Northern perceptions of slavery's impact on African-American men and women critically influenced
the training and discipline black soldiers were subjected to, as well as the
policies of the War Department and individual white officers toward the
families of soldiers. According to white commanders and civilians, men's
presumably emasculating experience of slavery was an enormous obstacle for military training to overcome. The commander of a black South
Carolina regiment, Colonel Thomas Wentworth Higginson, described slave
men not as adults but as childlike: he saw them as "soft," "sensitive," "sus-
ceptible," lacking the "moral strength" of free men. Higginson believed that
his soldiers had learned in slavery a habit of servility that was incompat-
ible with both military service and masculinity; "when they can unlearn
this servility and develop manhood, they become admirable soldiers," he
noted.[124] B. K. Lee, a superintendent of contrabands on the South Carolina Sea Islands, agreed that army training "has brought out the manliness
of these people and they realize that they have the rights of men." The
commander of Union forces in South Carolina concurred, believing that
military training would encourage among former slave men self-reliance
and self-support, also helping them to "develop their manhood."[125] Many
white commanders of black troops expected military service to transform
former slaves not only into better men but, more precisely, into men who
shared their own definitions of masculinity and their definition of men's
appropriate social, economic, and familial roles. Higginson was probably
unusual among his peers, in that he eventually understood that what appeared to be meek and passive behavior of one soldier and former slave
was in fact a cunning strategy common to a "crushed race."[126]

Neither Higginson nor other white Union commanders conceded that
their assumptions about slave men's masculinity were based on their own
culture's narrow and specific definitions of gender conventions, layered
with Northern racism and misperceptions about the institution of slavery.
The antislavery movements in the North, exercising considerable influence
on public discourse about slavery, unwittingly provided many whites and
some Northern blacks in the Union army with a vision of slavery as an

institution that had wiped away the humanity of enslaved men and women. In addition, the rhetoric and symbols of Northern free-labor ideology portrayed masculinity as a counterpoint to slavery; free men embodied independent power and authority, while many Northerners viewed slaves only in the context of their seemingly powerless relationship to planters. The vast majority of Northerners were complete strangers to slave communities and slave cultures, slaves' daily resistance to slavery and their construction of gender identities.

Most of the men of the 128th U.S. Colored Infantry enlisted too late in the war to prove their valor on the battlefield. Instead they spent their military service as an occupation army, drilling and performing fatigue duty—heavy physical labor.[127] While monotonous and menial duty was the lot of many soldiers, black and white, the constant tedium of drilling and fatigue duty could and did become hazardous for black soldiers. White officers often either believed that former slaves required heavier physical training and discipline than white troops, or believed the then-popular theories of racial difference that posited blacks as physiologically suited to harder labor than white men, able to endure more heat and exposure to sun than whites.[128] Black soldiers from the lowcountry were described by planters and white Northerners alike as "African savages," "the most ignorant & degraded of the negro race on the continent," apparently by virtue of their dark skins as well as their unique culture. White perceptions of their "strangeness" meant that black lowcountry soldiers were subjected to overtraining and suffered its consequences.[129]

Some white officers apparently believed that slavery had not only debilitated slave men's masculinity but had also destroyed the opportunities for, and inclination toward, family life among slaves. Officers stationed in the lowcountry were often surprised to discover black soldiers' strong ties to family and locale, and they were disappointed when these ties seemed an impediment to the black men's performance as soldiers. In August 1862, the commander of the South Atlantic Blockading Squadron was dismayed to encounter great difficulty in enlisting navy recruits among lowcountry contrabands who were willing to ship to the West Indies. The contrabands' "full sense of relief at the change in their physical and moral condition" was not sufficient to induce them to break "local attachments," to be "separated from their families and relations," according to Commander DuPont.[130]

In fact, in the lowcountry as in other areas of the South, the Union military command was unprepared not only for black soldier's feelings of attachment to their families, but also for the large numbers of women and children who were determined to flee slavery and to share both the advantages and the difficulties of army life with their enlisted male kin.[131] The growing population of noncombatants in and around the lowcountry army camps put tremendous strains on the Quartermaster's Department to feed and clothe the refugees. It also led the Union military command to begin the wartime process of establishing military policy relative to the presence, support, and employment of civilian contrabands.

During the war, late in 1863, an officer in a black South Carolina regiment pointed out that the men in his company were deeply disturbed by their lower pay (at that time, still not on par with white soldiers); the officer explained that "some of the men have large families unable to procure sufficient food and are in a deplorable condition" at the nearby contraband camps. His request for extra rations for his men's families, approved by his immediate superior, was ultimately denied by General Saxton, who viewed the starving condition of soldiers' families as an acceptable price for the independence that he believed the former slaves needed to learn. Saxton insisted that "a habit of dependence upon the Government for food and clothing ought to be discouraged . . . even at the risk of some suffering."[132]

The view of the army establishment toward slave families was both inconsistent and less than charitable. This was in part a consequence of the same racism and popular misperceptions about the experience of slavery that also informed the attitudes of white officers toward their black enlisted men; the views of Northern officers and soldiers alike toward slave and freed women in particular were strongly informed both by racist perceptions of black women in general and by popular notions about slavery's specific consequences for women. Included in those misguided notions was an assumption that slave women's sense of morality and sexual restraint had been destroyed. Saxton was among those white officers who believed that slavery had totally eradicated in slave women any self-restraint in their sexual expression. From his misinformed and distorted perspective on power relations in the slave South, Saxton believed that slave women had learned to respond enthusiastically to the planters' rewards for "breeding," and that slave women universally found it an honor to have sexual relations with white men.[133] Enough white soldiers shared Saxton's view that the abuse of black women by Union soldiers at Beaufort was endemic. It caused such an outcry that General Oliver O. Howard, commanding some of the forces involved in Sherman's invasion of South Carolina, urged a fellow officer to investigate and prosecute the guilty soldiers and force them to make amends to the injured parties.[134] A black soldier from Ohio, stationed at Beaufort, saw several examples of what he described as "the negro-hating element" among white soldiers who openly abused and stole from black women.[135]

Yet some Northern black soldiers expressed their share of disdain toward former slave women. Corporal James Henry Gooding, of the 54th Massachusetts Volunteers, reported from Hilton Head in February 1864 that among the daily visitors to the camps was "a young 'she regiment' from Beaufort to see their long absent Pompeys, Abe Linkuns, Joe Unions, Fridays, Mondays, Washingtons, belonging to the 2nd South Carolina Volunteers, who had just arrived from the scene of active operations. There were all sorts of greetings," he noted derisively, "which were a little on the principle of New Zealand etiquette."[136] Although less vicious in his observations than white officers, Gooding viewed female contrabands as sharing what he described as the universal superficialities of womanhood, along with the barbaric customs of an uncivilized culture.

Some female contrabands came to the encampments of Union soldiers simply to take advantage of the opportunity to visit and socialize. Some apparently spent a portion of their newly earned wages on finery available at Beaufort dry-goods dealers; "some of them too good looking, and they know it too," according to at least one Northern black soldier. Those who couldn't buy new would take a dress donated by Northern missionary groups but immediately "make it over to suit their wants." Dressed in their finery, the women would come into the camps to "see and be seen."[137] "Young women particularly flock back & forth by scores to Hilton Head, to Beaufort, to the country simply to while away their time, or constantly to seek some new excitement, or what is worse to live by lasciviousness," complained the general superintendent of Sea Island contrabands. Northern missionaries, contraband superintendents, officers, and the military command of the Department of the South concurred that the young women were "as great a curse to the soldier as to themselves," "subversive to good order" and a "fruitful source of vice and disease."[138] Young African-American women who enjoyed the freedom to travel, to look good and attract the attention of young men, were presumed, by Northern observers, to be idle and immoral. They were, in a word, dangerous.

When the low opinion Northern whites shared about female contrabands was put into policy, the wives and family members of black soldiers suffered. Typically harsh regulations against consorting with "camp followers," regulations that were officially imposed upon all Union soldiers, were exaggerated in their enforcement and prosecution against former slaves. In September 1864, Major General Foster, commander of Union forces in

South Carolina, ordered the arrest and forced labor of women with no visible means of support, women who visited their male kin in camp, and women who visited other plantations, camps, or villages. Such women, he believed, subverted the "moral strength" of his troops.[139]

Later in the war, regulations were relaxed to permit the legally married wives of black soldiers to visit encampments. This may have motivated at least some of the legal marriages (oftentimes between former slaves who already considered themselves married) performed by army chaplains, as when Eliza Middleton came to Beaufort from a Georgetown rice plantation to be married by a chaplain to a soldier, Washington Rutledge.[140] But similar visiting privileges were not provided for female kin. Cain Nesbit, who was "just about grown" when he began his military service, wrote to his younger sister, Harriet, to come join him on the coast. Harriet made her way to Beaufort to be near her brother, and helped him by doing his laundry. But she could not visit Cain in the camp, from which she was prohibited.[141]

Still, soldiers, their wives, and their kin often ran afoul of military policy that closely regulated the proximity and contact between soldiers and civilians. Hunger, the search for protection from abusive planters, the need to support infants and small children, even the inadequate provision of health care to black soldiers alternately (and sometimes cumulatively) led black soldiers and their wives to challenge military regulations. Soldiers often had to plead special circumstances to obtain the permission of their commanding officers for their wives and families to join them for extended periods. Although during the war Julia Tucker had been forced to the upcountry by her owners, as soon as the war ended she brought her newborn with her to the coast to be near her husband, Michael Tucker, a soldier in the 128th U.S. Colored Infantry. She went twice to Castle Pinckney to visit her husband. When he was encamped on Sullivan's Island, Michael "got permission from the Adjutant for me to stay on the island. . . . They put all the women off the island who did not have husbands," but since Julia and Michael had been married two years before, "they gave me permission to stay." She and her child, Josephine, lived in a house at a settlement on the island.[142] Brutus Nesbit asked his company sergeant for permission to bring his wife onto Morris Island where the company was encamped, so that she could draw rations.[143] Ann Frazier, whose husband, Daniel, left their plantation home on the Pee Dee River to enlist, went to stay with him at Beaufort. The soldier had been able to obtain permission for his wife to join him only when he had become so sick from mistreatment and inadequate shelter that "he could not do duty and . . . received permission for his wife to come and attend to him." Ann stayed there five or six months, nursing Daniel and making friends with several soldiers and officers—"I knew a good many of his comrades," she later recalled.[144]

Despite the employment of former slave women in crucial occupations, supporting the army as laundresses, nurses, cooks, teachers, and spies, some historians have suggested that military service assigned an active role to African-American men—and a passive one to African-American women—in winning the war and bringing the end to slavery. This may, in fact, have been the view of the military establishment, of white and black Northern observers, and even of some black soldiers. Later chapters will consider the long-term implications of that view, its influence over military and Reconstruction policy and on gender relations in the lowcountry African-American community. But in the immediate aftermath of enlistment, the freedwomen who remained on the lowcountry rice plantations played a very important yet unrecognized role in the struggle for freedom, at the "frontlines" in the face-to-face conflict over what free labor and a free life meant in the postwar rural South. Historians have long described the dramatic sense of empowerment and change of status that military service undoubtedly provided to former slave men. But while the new recruits became soldiers, the former slave women who remained on the plantations became deeply involved in their own crucial, immediate struggle—to define black freedom.[145]

Contrabands on the South Carolina Sea Islands (New Hampshire Historical Society #3909)

Sea Island contrabands (New Hampshire Historical Society #4024)

Former slave woman with a hoe (New Hampshire Historical Society #3808)

Wartime photograph of woman and child (New Hampshire Historical Society #3804)

Wartime workers on a Sea Island cotton plantation (New Hampshire Historical Society #3809)

Women, men, and children in a wartime Sea Island setting (New Hampshire Historical Society #3860)

Plantation workers assembled to hear terms of a labor contract (Penn School Collection at the Southern Historical Collection, University of North Carolina, Chapel Hill; reproduced with permission of Penn Center, Inc., St. Helena Island, South Carolina)

Mothers and infants; original photograph inscribed, "Excused from work—" (Penn School Collection at the Southern Historical Collection, University of North Carolina, Chapel Hill; reproduced with permission of Penn Center, Inc., St. Helena Island, South Carolina)

Part 3

Defining and
Defending Freedom

5 "The Simple Act of Emancipation": The First Year of Freedom

In his memoir of the events marking the end of the Civil War, the rice planter Charles Manigault described his former slave, Peggy, as though her actions exemplified the ways in which emancipation and Confederate defeat had turned his world upside down. Peggy's defining acts of freedom were not limited to taking a "Mahogany Bedstead" and other property of her former owners and using it as she saw fit. As revealed by Manigault's memoir, Peggy also assumed a very public and confrontational role in negotiating the consequences of emancipation and Confederate defeat. Shortly after the end of the war, Manigault came onto the plantation and (with the help of his son and a former overseer) immediately began to "pitch the Negro Effects" into two wagons, evicting the freedpeople who had resisted his authority and his right to control the plantation. In his description of the incident, Manigault pointed out that only Peggy ("the lady of the *Big Mahogany Bed*") tried to intervene: "placing her arms *akimbo,* said '*She* would go off to the Provost Marshal in town & *stop our unlawful proceedings with their property in their own homes.*'"[1] Peggy's confrontation with Manigault and his assistants seemed driven at least in part by her belief that they acted unlawfully, and that the occupying forces of the Union army would naturally protect freedpeople in their pursuit of freedom as they understood it. According to Manigault, Peggy was quite visibly dismayed when she realized that the very wagons Manigault was using were, in fact, government wagons, borrowed with the permission of the local military authorities.

Peggy's appropriation of her former mistresses' furniture, her use of contraband ribbons to style her daughter's hair, and her public challenge to Manigault's authority all signaled to Manigault that Peggy pursued her freedom with a literal vengeance, or what Manigault described as "recklessness and Ingratitude." In the actions of freedwomen like Peggy, and also in the responses that she and freedwomen like her provoked from former owners and from the civilian and military agents of Reconstruction, lies one of the most underexplored dynamics of the South's transition from slavery to freedom: the influence of former slave women's defining acts of freedom on the South's transition to freedom, and the impact of freedwomen's actions on how Northern and Southern whites viewed the aftermath of war and emancipation in the postbellum South.

Peggy's actions were typical for freedwomen on lowcountry rice plantations. In the public deeds of Peggy and women like her we find clues to some of the many ways in which former slave women distinguished their freedom from their slavery—ranging from the vengeful ransacking of their former owner's homes, to the assertion, through dress and hairstyle, of a new personal dignity, to "reckless" confrontations with the plantation whites who had defined the day-to-day nature of exploitation under slavery. When freedwomen assumed a defiant stance and challenged the right of former owners and planters to act with impunity, they were defining and defending black freedom as they understood it.

Peggy's confrontation with her former owner also foreshadowed other conflicts slave women would face in their transition to freedom. Although the Freedmen's Bureau had been created in March 1865 in part to assist former slaves in their transition to freedom, employing hundreds of Union army veterans and others to staff local bureau offices across the South, freedwomen who expected the Union army or Freedmen's Bureau agents to share their definition of freedom and to provide unilateral support in their conflicts with planters soon discovered otherwise. The military and the bureau pursued their own, sometimes conflicting, mandates in the aftermath of war. Although federal authorities would play a critical role in protecting lowcountry freedwomen from violence and exploitation at the hands of former slaveowners, freedwomen would discover in the course of 1865 that their expectations about the consequences of freedom and Confederate defeat were not shared by the army and bureau personnel, who were often the last resort for redress.

In 1865, determined to pursue freedom on their own terms, freedwomen—like freedmen—sought the means and the opportunity to live and subsist as free from white intervention as possible. In so doing, they encountered considerable opposition from several sources. It came from white vigilantes, from planters, mistresses, and overseers, all anxious for the return of a reliable and subordinate labor force. But, as Peggy discovered, opposition also came from military and bureau personnel who became frustrated by former slaves' unwillingness to embrace the tenets of the free-labor society many Northerners envisioned for the postwar South. The letters, reports, complaints, and official responses generated by freedwomen's observers and antagonists during this first year of freedom comprise a rich record of freedwomen's efforts to reconstruct life and labor on lowcountry rice plantations. They also reveal that an important part of the work of defining freedom lay in freedwomen's determined efforts to unveil and disrupt the relations of power and domination that had marked their lives as enslaved laborers in the rice fields and planter residences of lowcountry plantations. Those efforts—even when concealed by habits of language in which women were subsumed under references to "freedmen"—were critical to how observers and participants alike viewed the lowcountry's transition from slavery and war to peace and freedom.

Surviving the Peace

Setting 1865 apart from subsequent years of Reconstruction, the material consequences of war continued to have as great an impact on freedwomen's first year of freedom as it had on the last four years of their enslavement. Peggy, Charles Manigault's former slave, again offers an example: two months after her eviction, dumped with her few belongings outside the Manigault plantation, Peggy "died in misery," her three children "scattered about, with no one to care for them."[2] War had brought an end to slavery, but peace brought no sudden, dramatic improvement in the material conditions of lowcountry life for the formerly enslaved. The Union invasion of mainland South Carolina and the final destruction of lowcountry slavery had capped four years of deterioration and decline in the living conditions of lowcountry slaves. By March 1865, when the end of war and the collapse of chattel slavery were in sight, the countryside was largely "burnt & destroyed."[3]

Freedwomen discovered during the first postwar months that peace literally had to be survived if freedom was to be defended or enjoyed. Displaced from their homes and separated from their families by removal, impressment, escape, or military enlistment, and robbed by both Union and Confederate forces of provisions, animals, household utensils, and tools, many freedwomen found themselves stripped of the most basic means for subsistence. Despite Lee's surrender and the Confederacy's concession to defeat that soon followed, the devastating consequences of the military conflict continued to be felt by the lowcountry's former slaves.

One hardship freedwomen encountered in their first months of freedom were the epidemics that swept through their communities.[4] The two to three hundred freedpeople who had returned to Jehossee Island sometime in June "suffered dreadfully from the smallpox." A visiting Union officer noted that "a good many have died, and many are down with it."[5] That summer, a bureau agent surveying plantations along the Combahee found that "the small pox rages fearfully" among the freedpeople; crops so critical to their future subsistence were "wasting from want of care."[6] Along the Combahee River, one planter noted in August 1865 that "the negroes are *almost all dead* as far as we can learn—and indeed this is the case at Ashley River as far as the *young men & women* are concerned— The mortality under the beneficent care & rule of the Yankees has been almost incredible." The commander of military forces at Charleston predicted "that before the end of the year one half of those in his district would be dead at the rate they were dying."[7] Mainland refugees on the Sea Islands were dying from fever and exposure, while refugees from the interior placed onto government-held rice plantations on the mainland were also described as "suffering much from sickness, from an unhealthy situation to which they have not been accustomed and from the want of proper medicine or attendance." From the army commander at Georgetown came repeated calls for medical attention for the freedpeople, who were "dying for the want of it."[8] In Charleston, where "the negro hearses are going from morning till night," came dire predictions that at current mortality rates, at least a third of the state's black population would die by the end of the year, from smallpox, measles, and other diseases.[9]

From the perspective of many white Southerners, the high mortality rate among freedpeople was to be blamed on emancipation, African-American inferiority, and Yankee misjudgments about the ability of former slaves to live as free people. One held that "the abolitionists outwitted themselves, instead of having been the benefactors they have become the murderers of the slave."[10] There was an element of truth to the charge of Yankee blame; one consequence of Sherman's march for the thousands of South Carolinian slaves who followed his army was a high mortality rate from "exposure and insufficient clothing & food." Another result was the large number of orphaned children found among the Sea Island refugees.[11] Rice planters and lowcountry physicians were willing to blame Northerners (and indeed emancipation itself) for the high mortality rate among freedpeople, yet they were at that very moment colluding to drive home to former slaves the "cost" of freedom. In mid-March, a group of physicians had "decided not to attend any calls which are not authorized by proprietors of plantations, unless the fee is paid in advance." According to one approving planter, "They adopt this course to bring to the notice of the negroes, their dependent condition & to check the feeling of irresponsibility now prevalent."[12] With or without recourse to physicians, freedpeople here and throughout the lowcountry continued to rely on "their own female doctors" for care and relief, even as they had when slaves.[13]

Whether former slavewomen viewed the difficulties they encountered in 1865 as the result of war or of slavery, the survival struggles they faced included long, difficult trips back home from interior farms, cities and towns, army posts, and contraband camps. Women began the process of reuniting families, extended kin, and communities separated during or before the war by escape, removal, impressment, hiring out, or sale. Sometimes they rescued children still held in bondage. En route and back at home, they found that survival often meant foraging off the countryside because Union soldiers had taken not only the food but also the pans to cook it in.

Throughout the remaining months of 1865, freedwomen continued to return to their lowcountry homes from the interior and the Sea Islands. Various reports place the numbers of migrating freedpeople well into the thousands. A military expedition up the Santee River in April alone brought hundreds of former slaves from the interior of the state to the coast, including many who had been refugeed away from lowcountry rice plantations.[14] They were joined by former slaves originally from the upcountry who sought either the refuge of military protection or the promise of land along the seaboard. Over a thousand freedpeople passed through Columbia each month that spring as they made their way from upcountry refuges back to "the country in which they were born—'their old range,' as they express it."[15] A Freedmen's Bureau agent estimated at the end of July that about two thousand former slaves, "mainly the former Slaves in the same locality," had returned to the area bound by the Combahee and Ashepoo Rivers.[16] General Saxton received reports that between February and early August over seventeen thousand freedpeople had arrived at Beaufort alone.[17]

The movement of thousands of women and men into and out of Charleston also partially accounted for the general impression of mass mobility noted by white observers in 1865. Among those entering the city were former slaves from Charleston, removed by city slaveowners during or at the very close of the war; others were former plantation slaves from interior refuges or nearby plantations.[18] Some freedwomen came to the city to track down, or be near, husbands or kinfolk among the soldiers or other black immigrants. Others, familiar with the city from years of seasonal travel between plantation and town house, now seized the opportunity to occupy their former owners' abandoned city residences. Still other freedwomen were attracted to the city precisely because they had never been allowed to visit before. During the spring and summer of 1865, the city offered many attractions, including the presence of several black regiments in and around the city, which seemed to encourage freedpeople in breaking with the slave past. When white women shared with each other stories of the affronts they encountered on city streets, they revealed a city filled with former slaves who challenged the public rituals of a slaveowning society: "they are very insolent in the streets[,] never pretend to give place to you[.] [S]everal times I have had them to squeeze themselves in the inside & say 'look at dat rebel'[.]"[19] In April and May, local and visiting Northern black leaders and white abolitionists organized memorials to the Union dead as well as celebrations of General Lee's surrender and the Confederate defeat, attended by thousands of black Charlestonians. The city's free blacks and former slaves also held and attended public meetings addressing the future of Reconstruction, and openly challenged white city leaders attempting to regain political control over Charleston.[20]

The desire to educate children also drew many families to the city; "Little Grace [freedwoman Suckey's] daughter says her mother means to put her to school if it costs $500 a year."[21] Julia, her husband, Ben, and their children also headed to Charleston; according to his former owner, "Ben said he could not stay" for the wages he had been offered "as it was the duty of a Parent to educate his children & that he could not educate them for 2 dollars each per month" offered in wages by his former owner. Their wish to move to Charleston may also have been inspired by news that several schools had already been established for freedpeople in Charleston.[22] Hopeful, assertive, and aligned with the victorious Union cause, Charleston's free and freedpeople were described even by grudging former slaveowners as "so bright, so happy, so triumphant."[23]

Freedwomen found that the attractions of the city were not only of a social or political nature; from March until mid-May, Union forces distributed rice and corn confiscated from Confederate stores to destitute refugees both in and around the city. Despite the city's many advantages, the refugees who had streamed into the city since February encountered devastating circumstances. Freedpeople encamped around the city's outskirts—sometimes in the very camps where impressed slaves had resided—were suffering, malnourished, and barely clothed. In May, Esther Hawks, a Northern physician and teacher, inspected a contraband camp at Secessionville and concluded that its three hundred "dirty, ragged, *starving*" residents presented more "misery and utter destitution" than she had seen yet. On questioning a number of the camp residents, Hawks discovered that some had waited two to four weeks before receiving paltry government rations—a few quarts of rough rice. The distribution point for what few rations were available was five miles away. Women at the camp reported that they were living off blackberries. Along with the children and the elderly, they clearly bore the effects of disease and starvation, and they were "as nearly naked as possible and still be clothed."[24]

The attractions Charleston did offer would soon "prove illusory," at least according to one former slaveowner, when the military authorities began forcing freedpeople out of the city.[25] Both voluntary and involuntary migration of freedpeople out of Charleston back to the countryside and the Sea Islands began by early June, adding to the mass of freedpeople arriving from the interior. In mid-May, the commanding officer at Charleston—General Hatch—attempted to alleviate the strain on army and federal resources with orders that "colored people coming from the country are given ten days to leave the city and settle themselves upon the plantations set apart for their use by Gen. Sherman," at risk of being denied government rations in Charleston.[26] One white observer noted that within two weeks "the throngs of colored people that were visible in our midst some time ago have scattered and settled down on the plantations," a phenomenon he attributed to the dwindling of government-distributed provisions.[27] (Military authorities encouraged freedpeople to leave smaller lowcountry towns and military posts in similar fashion.)[28] The restoration of Confederate property (accelerated by President Andrew Johnson's Amnesty Proclamation of 29 May) similarly forced many freedpeople to leave, as white property owners returned to Charleston. With the assistance of federal soldiers, they compelled black squatters to vacate their town residences. White Charlestonians welcomed the crackdown on black refugees, having repeatedly complained to each other and to the Union command that Charleston had become unfit for white women or children, given the "wandering tribes of uncouth and unclean negroes that fill the streets day after day."[29] Despite Charleston's many draws (including the opportunity to transgress pre-emancipation racial etiquette), the city served largely as a temporary stopping-off place, as rural freedpeople made their way back to their homes on lowcountry rice plantations.

∾

These first months of peace, if a time of "chaos and disorder," were none-theless critical to the course of postwar Reconstruction in lowcountry South Carolina. It was a time when attempts to determine the path of the post-war, postemancipation South came from several competing sources. As evidenced by the destruction and pillaging on lowcountry plantations even before the close of war, former slave women lost no time in declaring the irrevocable break from slavery and claiming the prerogatives of their free-dom. They became deeply involved in the collisions and negotiations that cumulatively would give form and meaning to their freedom. At the same time, the occupation forces of the U.S. Army attempted to regulate the initial stages of Reconstruction, creating new policies and elaborating on wartime strategies designed to restore peace and social order and promote the free-labor plantation economy. Lowcountry rice planters, for their part, may have accepted the inevitability of defeat and emancipation, but with the plantation economy hanging in the balance, they also joined the con-test to direct the course of Reconstruction. Their efforts were charged with a vehement racism and an overriding concern with the material conse-quences of emancipation for the elite class of lowcountry "landed propri-etors" and their families.

Although former slave women had passed through the most dramatic change in status any American had ever experienced, in the spring of 1865 little about the meaning or consequences of that change had yet been settled in lowcountry South Carolina. The wartime destruction of slavery had not defined freedom. While a planter and former slaveowner might concede that "the breath of Emancipation has passed over the country," in his eyes emancipation simply meant that South Carolina stood "in that transition state between the new & the old systems—a state of chaos & disorder."[30] It was their effort to survive while directing the outcome of this chaos that made freedwomen's first year of freedom distinctive. For many freedwomen, their needs and preferences in the aftermath of war and slavery's destruction were best addressed by returning with friends and family to the lowcountry rice plantation lands they regarded as their homes.

Land and the Meaning of Freedom

From the perspective of many lowcountry freedpeople, their safety and survival, no less than freedom as they envisioned it, depended on their ability to secure autonomous control over the land as subsistence farm-ers. One of the unique characteristics of life under lowcountry slavery had been the relative stability of the slave population, which had allowed the creation of extensive familial and social networks within and between plantation communities. This stability had further provided an opportuni-ty to sink deep roots into the land itself: gardens were nurtured, favored fishing spots identified, river systems and swamps well traveled. The dis-tinctive lowcountry ecology also influenced the culture and folklife of the slave community. Most important, generations of ancestors linked lowcoun-try freedpeople to plantation burial grounds. Tied to the living as well as the dead, former slaves staked out their interest in the land their ances-tors had carved out of the swamps, the land that promised the possibility of sustenance and subsistence to present and future generations of free African Americans.

Former slave women, who had cautiously awaited the spring 1865 arrival of Union forces and confirmation of emancipation, were quick to desert upcountry refuges and join the exodus back to lowcountry rice plan-tations once it seemed safe to do so. Newly freed slaves at the upcountry refuges "pretended to be quite satisfied" where they were, but according to former owners were soon "dropping off by driblets till I suppose they will all soon return" to their homes and families in the lowcountry.[31] Plan-tation mistresses described the steady stream of groups of ex-slaves to the lowcountry as desertion.[32] Indeed, the stream of lowcountry freedpeople returning from interior refuges remained steady during the summer of 1865 and increased dramatically that fall.

Neither shortsighted nor impulsive assertions of freedom, the long and often painful journeys home were very frequently fueled by the desire to return and reunite with kin and community. Freedwomen at one of the Allston upcountry refuges undertook their hundred-mile return trip to the lowcountry with pots balanced on heads, bundles of clothes on their backs, and babies in their arms, sharing the road with the leavings of the Union army: dead horses, cows, hogs, and sometimes the bodies of men and women.[33] Many making the trip were former slave children, who had been among the first slaves to be removed to upcountry refuges by planters. As one former slave recalled, "when one young girl come back from refugin' wid de white folks, her feet were jes' ready to buss open."[34]

Reuniting families whose members had been separated in slavery and during the war was made more difficult by slaveowners who had not yet acknowledged emancipation. Rebecca Jane Grant, fifteen years old at the end of the war, was rescued from her former owner by an uncle, who cared for Jane until her grandfather came for her, and the two walked the sixty-four miles to her mother's home. At the same time, Grant's mother retrieved and guided five of her other young children back home.[35] Families faced other obstacles to reconciliation as well. Bella, the mother of a twelve-year-old daughter and formerly a slave on a lowcountry plantation, made the forty-mile trip back to the plantation from the Sea Islands alone, but she was evicted from her former home by the planter on the alleged suspicion that she had contracted smallpox (lowcountry planters did not always welcome the return of former slaves from the Sea Islands, given their new "Beaufort manners"). Undaunted, Bella returned to the islands, retrieved her daughter, again made the trip on foot to the plantation, and insisted on her intention to live with her daughter at her former home. The planter regarded the family as vagrants and appealed to military authorities for the power to evict them.[36]

After their difficult trips back home, freedwomen often found the plantations in a shambles, rice fields flooded from breached dams and weed-filled canals, barns and storehouses ransacked or destroyed, tools and personal belongings stolen, former communities scattered. Those who arrived in the lowcountry in July and August, too late to plant corn crops, turned to the federal government for subsistence rations and, when available, clothing.[37] Even in these circumstances, freedwomen claimed the land—and its potential—as their own. "I want to lay my bones in dat air bush . . . and don't want to go nowhare else," explained one freedwoman.[38]

Freedwomen shared with freedmen a critical expectation: that the land was now to be theirs. The legitimacy of their claim, according to former slave women, was based on many factors: generations of usage and residence ("I was born on this plantation," "I have never lived any place else in my whole life");[39] the value imparted to the land by virtue of their own skills and labor; the reparations owed them for the theft of their labor and the sundering of their families by slaveowning whites ("out o' dat black skin he got he money").[40] Women and men relentlessly petitioned Union officers with their claims; lowcountry freedpeople "had again and again" asked one Union officer "what good it did them to make them free, unless they were to own the land on which they had been working, and which they had made productive and valuable."[41] The desire for land was universal: in this postwar struggle, as in many others, freedwomen made their voices heard.

While former slaves' claims to the land were formulated from their own experiences and expectations about the meaning of freedom, those claims had also been encouraged by military authorities and Sea Island missionaries during the war. The First and Second Confiscation Acts (August 1861 and July 1862) had provided the legal basis for the wartime confiscation of Confederate property, and the Direct Tax Act (June 1862) gave Treasury Department agents the authority to seize Confederate land for nonpayment of federal taxes and to dispose of it by sale. Northern missionaries, sympathetic officers, and Treasury Department agents had reserved some of the lands for the use of the Sea Island contrabands. Sherman's Special Field Order 15 had drawn thousands of former slaves from the state's interior to the lowcountry. Yet freedwomen's desire for land was not limited to the area officially set aside for colonization by wartime precedent or Sherman's order. Well outside those borders, on the mainland and north of Charleston, freedwomen similarly pursued their right to live and work, independent of white intervention, preferably on the land that they had worked as slaves and where their ancestors lay buried.[42]

While freedpeople's ties to lowcountry plantation homes, burial grounds, and provision plots were generations deep and complex, their desire for autonomy from former owners and white overseers was sometimes even more compelling. Freedmen and women who were "unanimously impressed with the idea that they are never again to work for 'the Old Master' on any terms" chose wholesale eviction by the army or voluntarily moved elsewhere, rather than resume life and labor under their former owners.[43] Many preferred settling on nearby abandoned plantations; four or five hundred freedpeople, including many from Henry W. Ravenel's Pooshee plantation, moved onto Dean Hall, an abandoned Cooper River plantation, rather than work under their former owners.[44] Several freedpeople were similarly unwilling to remain on the plantation with the Georgetown planter Jane Pringle and, despite her offer of rice rations, left for nearby plantations where planters remained absent.[45]

Since many lowcountry planters chose to stay away for the 1865 growing season, thousands of freedwomen and men continued unchallenged in their occupation of rice plantations in 1865. Of fifty-nine Combahee River plantations surveyed by a Freedmen's Bureau agent in August 1865, "nearly all" were abandoned by whites but "to some extent occupied by freedmen [and women] 'bred and born' on the spot."[46] Another bureau agent estimated that between one-sixth and one-eighth of Georgetown's former population of slaves lived and worked on abandoned rice plantations for the 1865 planting season, in addition to those gathered on twenty-one other plantations abandoned by planters and held by the army as colonies for refugee freedpeople.[47]

President Johnson's Amnesty Proclamation restored confiscated prop-

erty to former Confederates who took the loyalty oath, but many rice planters who owned property worth more than $20,000 were not eligible to take
the oath and instead had to file a special appeal. Even eligible planters were
unsure about the future, about their new relationship to their former slaves,
and perhaps felt safer at their upcountry refuges.[48] The conflict between
Johnson's intent to restore land to Southern whites and the effort of Oliver O. Howard, commissioner of the Freedmen's Bureau, to secure his agency's jurisdiction over abandoned and confiscated lands would not be settled until mid-September, effectively delaying restoration of nominally
abandoned rice plantations until the next planting season. Insulated in this
manner from the full impact of the move toward restoration, large numbers of lowcountry freedpeople planted their own crops, "in anticipation
of being left to enjoy the fruits of their labors."[49] Before the summer of 1865
had passed, however, military and civilian agents of Reconstruction began
to take a key role in the reconstruction of rice plantation agriculture. Freedwomen seeking a full measure of freedom found that they had to negotiate their claim to the land with them, as well as with former owners and
planters.

Military Intervention

As Peggy, Charles Manigault's former slave, and thousands of other freedpeople learned, during the spring and summer of 1865 their sovereignty
on lowcountry rice plantations could be interrupted, directly or indirectly,
by Union military policy. After the initial appearance of Union troops on
mainland South Carolina in February and March, it would be nearly summer before federal control over South Carolina was anything more than
loosely established. Nevertheless, that spring Union forces began to respond to the pleas of rice planters for help in ending the pillaging and
destruction of plantation property by former slaves. Although some planters accused the Union army of having "abandoned us after revolutioniz-
ing our social system & left us in ruins," many sought and received military assistance in evacuating their families from the chaotic countryside
or in restoring their authority on various plantations. With Union forces
willing to interpose themselves between vengeful former slaves and their
former owners, and willing to protect plantation property from further
destruction, lowcountry planters were forced to view the army not only
as the conquering, hated enemy but also as a potentially powerful and
important ally.[50] Jane Pringle pointed this out to her fellow planter Adele

Allston, emphasizing the critical role of Union military forces in regaining and maintaining control over her plantation and its residents:

> You say you "acquiesce in the freeing of the blacks," but you evidently use a form of words which carries with it no relative idea of what is covered and comprised by the freeing of the blacks. If you come here all your servants who have not families so large as to burthen them and compel a veneering of fidelity, will immediately leave you. The others will be more or less impertinent as the humor takes them and in short will do as they choose. *Here* I have over them the abiding fear of the Yankee Capts. who go out and speak sharply to them and sustain my authority, but you are too far up to depend on the frequent visits which they make here and without which I believe a residence among negroes would be humiliating and impossible.[51]

According to Pringle, lowcountry planters could not expect to return to their plantations without the close backing of a local military force.

The promise of protection by military authorities, no less than Andrew Johnson's liberal amnesty program, prompted many rice planters to take the oath of allegiance or to appeal directly to Johnson. They paid back taxes on their property, ventured a visit to their plantations, and sometimes secured labor contracts with their former slaves, in order to "collect what they can" and avoid having their plantations deemed "abandoned."[52] Most of these planters made contracts and then left, returning only at the close of the season. Although this was the normal pattern of proprietorship on absentee rice plantations, misinformation about both amnesty and restoration circulated, encouraged at least in part by the somewhat incoherent federal policy of determining which plantations were abandoned. Cooper River planters understood that if they did not take the oath, they ran the risk of "being turned out of their homes & all property destroyed."[53] Georgetown planters speculated between themselves about their property rights; "your absence from this part of the country," one overly cautious planter warned another, "bars your claim for the present to any of your property."[54]

But planters had more than ill-defined federal policy to cope with in regaining control over their plantations, for freedwomen like Peggy, as well as freedmen, were prepared to defend their right to stay on the plantations and their claim to the land, and vigorously resisted some planters who reappeared in the late spring and summer of 1865. Although warned by fellow planter Jane Pringle that "the blacks are masters of the situation, this is a conquered country and for the moment law and order are in abeyance," Adele Allston attempted to reclaim her plantations in the spring of that year.[55] Much as Pringle had forewarned, the predominantly female community of former slaves on Chicora Wood plantation turned out to block Allston's path. When Allston ordered the former slave driver to relinquish his barn keys to her, freedwomen were among those who aggressively threatened that "blood'll flow" if the keys were surrendered. According to a memoir of the incident written by Allston's daughter, she and her mother were quickly surrounded by "a yelling mob of men, women, and children"; the freedwomen "revolved around us, holding out their skirts and dancing—now with slow, swinging movements, now with rapid jig-motions, but always with weird chant and wild gestures." A few freedmen set out to bring a Union officer to settle the issue but warned the women and men who remained, "'Don't let no white man een dat gate,' which was answered by many voices, 'No, no, we won't let no white pusson een, we'll chop um down wid hoe—we'll chop um to pieces sho'—and they brandished their large, sharp, gleaming rice-field hoes, which look most formidable weapons truly. Those who had not hoes were armed with pitchforks and hickory sticks, and some had guns."[56]

Similar confrontations occurred on other rice plantations. Francis Le-Jau Frost, a Georgetown planter, also encountered opposition when he returned to reclaim his Camp Main rice plantation on the North Santee. Frost was informed by local military authorities that, along with all the other land on the river, Camp Main had been confiscated as abandoned land, and that freedpeople's tenure there was protected until their crops were harvested. But Frost persisted until the "authorities" finally decided that the plantation was neither officially confiscated nor abandoned. They then even agreed to send an officer and armed guard along with Frost to the plantation, "to superintend the making of a contract."

Having won his case with Union officials in Georgetown, Frost still had to contend with the freedpeople residing at Camp Main. "I am a little afraid that the negroes may make some objection & that we may have trouble & not be sustained by the military," he admitted. "I have not yet been to the plantation, not having had time & thinking it best to feel the Yankees first & learn their propensities. I am afraid that the negroes are more or less unruly and insubordinate, & that they will object particularly" to the return of Frost's white overseer. "They cannot understand why that now that they are free they sh'd have any white man over them any longer & are altogether opposed to it." Frost's overseer heard the freedpeople pronounce "that they wish & mean to have nothing more to do" with Frost, and in fact that "the negroes object entirely to any white person being on the place at all." Not only were Frost and his overseer afraid of the North Santee freedpeople; three neighboring planters also remained absent from their plantations, "afraid of the negroes."[57]

Local military authorities did provide the assistance Frost needed to overcome his own apprehensions and the objections of the freedwomen and men at Camp Main; he secured a labor contract with the thirty-eight freedpeople on the plantation for a third of their rice and provision crops. A week later, the Camp Main freedpeople were further instructed by an army officer that "although their freedom has been secured as a result of the war, the lands, buildings, furniture, and animals, including the swine, still belong to the Planter and that they have no right or title" to them. If they failed to return the property, "they are liable to be punished."[58]

Forced to relinquish not only the goods they had confiscated from the planter residence but also, for the time being, their hopes for control over the land, the Camp Main freedpeople appear to have regained their hope when Frost left the plantation for several months. His return in December 1865 to take his share of the crops angered the women and men once again, suggesting that neither labor contracts nor military orders had lowered the Camp Main freedpeople's expectations for the future. "The very great majority of them are . . . evidently very much disturbed at my presence on the place," he noted. "They look upon me as one who has come to interrupt the entire freedom from any restraint whatever, which they have enjoyed for past 9 mos.—They had hoped too to possess this land. The dispelling of this delusion distresses them no little," Frost realized. Furthermore, he found that "their discomfature is much more increased when I tell them that they are to work just as they used to do, or leave the plantation. They cannot understand how it is that the Yankees sh'd set them free & give them no lands; how it is that they can have been born & raised on the soil & yet not inherit it upon becoming free."[59] Lowcountry freedwomen, like freedmen, defined freedom as their right not simply to survive, but also to work and thrive without white intervention on the land they had worked as slaves and where generations of their ancestors had lived, worked, and died.

Work and the Meaning of Freedom

On plantations where rice planters opted to ride out the chaos and disorder marking the closing weeks of war and the first months of freedom, freedwomen and men quickly made plantation labor a focus of the revo-

lutionary changes unleashed by emancipation. The most widespread development following emancipation on planter-resident lands was an immediate cessation of work by former slaves, which included their rejection of work orders and supervision by planter families and overseers alike.
"The field negroes are in a dreadful state," wrote one plantation mistress
that March; "they will not work, but either roam the country, or sit in their
houses." They refused to listen to their former owner's proposition for their
continued labor and seemed unsure about whether to remain on the plantation or not.[60] Former field hands throughout the parish of St. John's refused to work that spring, and the commanding officer of a Union steamboat found former slaves on Santee River rice plantations generally refusing
to work.[61] Daniel Heyward's former slaves were reported to be "kind
enough, but spoke to him sitting, and with their hats on." They "were
willing to help him along," but when Heyward suggested "working as formerly," the freedpeople insisted "oh, no, neva work as they did, and no
overseer and no drivers." In addition, the freedpeople were reportedly
"very much confounded and incredulous as to *his* ownership of the land."[62]
In Georgetown, Adele Allston's overseer on Chicora Wood wrote to her that
he was "not allowd to say any[thing] a bout Work."[63]

By refusing to work, freedpeople may have been responding to the
efforts of former owners to minimize the significance of emancipation.
Lowcountry rice planters often tried to dismiss the enormity of emancipation as an issue subordinate to the more important question of the future of the plantation economy: the formal announcement of emancipation was only "preliminary to another matter of much more immediate
importance, namely the cultivation . . . of rice." Planters who tried to limit the impact of emancipation or who acted too quickly to arrange the terms
of continued plantation labor met resistance by former slaves who demonstrated a determination to savor this transition and carefully consider
the future.[64]

Freedpeople's refusal to work was first challenged by military force; eventually, U.S. soldiers stationed throughout the lowcountry interceded frequently enough to assume a central role in formulating the terms of peace in 1865.
During the summer of that year, the military began to define their role in
the lowcountry more clearly: to establish peace and order by policing the
countryside, to ensure the end of slavery but at the same time to encourage
the resumption of plantation labor, with freedpeople—men and women—
receiving wages for the same labor they had performed as slaves. In fact,
the army's solution for most of the immediate problems plaguing postwar
South Carolina—including overcrowding and the shortage of provisions in

the vicinity of Charleston—was to reinstate plantation production as quick-ly as possible. In Summerville, Colonel James C. Beecher ordered the arrest and removal of any *"able bodied* man or woman at this post" who applied for government rations but refused to work.[65] This strategy became, for occupying military forces in South Carolina, the solution for restoring peace to the countryside and making self-sufficient the black and white residents of the lowcountry who they feared would otherwise become dependent on federal or civilian charity in the years to come.[66] It was a strategy that also relied on the implicitly race-based presumption that both women and men of African descent could and should work.

The commander of the Department of the South, as well as his subor-dinate in lowcountry South Carolina, advocated the resumption of planta-tion production as a "military necessity." By mid-April, the commander of Union forces at Charleston, General Hatch, proposed to the command-er of the Department of the South that any planter who offered to make fair contracts with the freedpeople should receive military protection of their property rights in their rice plantations.[67]

The contract labor system Hatch now proposed had first been used in the wartime occupation of southern Louisiana, where in 1862 General Benjamin F. Butler had instituted labor contracts as a way to alleviate the contrabands' drain on army supplies, benefit the Union by restoring the profitable sugar plantation economy, and support the Unionist inclinations of local planters. Like its wartime predecessor, the postbellum labor con-tract system was implemented in lowcountry South Carolina primarily to meet military and political goals, and not with the expectations of freed-people in mind. Hatch did believe that his proposal for a speedy return of plantation production would "secure a practical enforcement of the rights of labor to be justly remunerated."[68]

At the end of April, with the approval of the commander of the Depart-ment of the South, Hatch instructed planters north of Charleston and out-side the Sherman Reserve to take the oath of allegiance, inform their former slaves of their emancipation, and make equitable contracts with them for the new season. Hatch addressed his instructions not only to Charleston-area planters but to all the planters between Charleston and Georgetown, including those on the Santee, Black, Pee Dee, and Waccamaw Rivers. He thereby established the basis of the military's key role in resuming plan-tation operations throughout the mainland plantation economy in the af-termath of the war. Hatch warned planters of the loss of military protec-tion and property rights should they fail to implement or abide by the contract labor system.

Planters who followed his instructions were guaranteed military "encouragement and protection" to ensure the success of their efforts. While uncooperative planters (even those outside the boundaries of the Sherman Reserve) were threatened that their plantations might be confiscated as colonies for freedpeople, Hatch also promised planters the use of military force against freedpeople who were uncooperative laborers.[69] It may well have been Hatch's instructions that prompted Manigault to evict Peggy and other of his former slaves. Lowcountry freedpeople, like those on Manigault's plantation, quickly learned that the U.S. army was not unequivocally committed to defending black freedom as former slaves defined it.

Hatch discovered that lowcountry freedpeople expected more from their freedom than the military was offering. In the weeks following his effort to jump-start plantation agriculture, Hatch received letters, reports, and delegations from lowcountry rice planters as well as his own officers complaining of the various impediments to the resumption of plantation agriculture. From Cooper River came complaints of "roving bands of idle and dissolute people," wreaking havoc and destroying planter property, and of freedpeople on the east branch of the river who rejected outright Hatch's contract labor system, instead claiming the right to work the land on their own. Ashley River planters joined those from the Cooper River in informing Hatch that freedpeople "decline emphatically" to enter contracts. From his tour of the Santee River countryside, a Union officer reported the "intelligent and systematic operations of the blacks," including "a regularly organized corps and system of telegraphing," which they used to preempt unpopular military actions. Santee River freedpeople, he reported, "cannot as yet be made to understand" why they should be required to work ten hours a day when as slaves they had finished their tasks early in the day.[70]

When lowcountry rice planters tried to make the contract labor system into one more closely resembling their antebellum control over plantation workers, freedpeople found more reasons to resist the resumption of plantation work. Santee River planters were busy informing freedpeople that "their condition is now worse than when they were slaves; that they must pay for their own medicine, their doctors bills, clothing, etc." As a result, according to a military report, "the negro is amazed and generally refuses work altogether."[71] That June, Hatch intervened, voiding a form of contract used by some planters that introduced a system of perpetual peonage.[72] According to their delegate sent to speak with Hatch, planters on the Cooper River so feared the likelihood that their former slaves were about to do "something awful" in retaliation against lowcountry whites that Hatch, in response, sent a steamer to carry U.S. forces up the river, and a cavalry company to "disarm all the insubordinate and compel them to go to work."[73]

The contract labor system was vulnerable not only to freedpeople's resistance and planter misinterpretation, but also to interpretation and enforcement by the commanding officers at each local military outpost, as suggested by the admission of the headquarters of the Department of the South that there were "no prescribed terms regulating contracts with freedmen."[74] Troops assigned to duty in the military subdistricts throughout the lowcountry, making up a substantial part of the seven to eight thousand troops assigned to the department as a whole, were critical to the enforcement of the labor contracts.[75]

The military's efforts to nurture a speedy transition to free labor snagged on the outrage and fear of rice planters in encountering, among those forces on which the enforcement of the new system relied, black troops. Lowcountry planters protested that black soldiers should not be stationed in their districts; "Unless the colored troops are kept back the crops cannot be gathered as the freedmen induced by the troops will leave the plough and hoe to turn soldier," they warned. "These colored troops," planters further complained, "are averse to seeing their own color doing any labor at all, and by their conversations make the laborers dissatisfied."[76] From Georgetown rice planters came a number of complaints: that freedpeople anticipated that black troops—including several companies formed out of their own communities—would both "enlarge their privileges" and confirm their claims to plantation lands; that black troops were "not as pointedly a means of Military power against the Freedpeople as the white inhabitants think the condition of things demands"; and that black troops could not be relied upon to protect the property and person of lowcountry whites.[77] In private, the commander of the department, General Quincy A. Gillmore, was sympathetic to planter complaints about black troops; in August, he noted that "in many instances nearly all the laborers on large plantations under extensive cultivation have violated their contracts and suspended their work in consequence of the pernicious influence of a few bad colored soldiers, who were formerly slaves in the neighborhood." Yet Gillmore was also reluctant to remove the black troops, fearing a hostile reaction from freedpeople in the affected communities.[78]

Civilian complaints about the influence of black troops on the lowcountry were made forcefully and frequently enough that both the commander of the military division, Major General George G. Meade, as well as Secretary of War Edwin Stanton, were drawn into the controversy. Stanton asked Meade to investigate the complaints against black troops, particularly whether "they present a threatening aspect to the people of the Department in which they are employed." Meade reported back that while black troops did pose certain disruptions to "the laboring population," the complaints against them were not sufficient to justify their removal—although Meade did see fit to remove black troops from the interior of the state to the lowcountry, where he felt they would be more usefully employed.[79]

Some white military authorities believed it was the freedpeople themselves who posed the greatest obstacle to the lowcountry's transition to a free-market, free-labor economy. In June 1865, Captain Charles Soule, a white officer of a black regiment, the 55th Massachusetts, described his efforts to implement the contract labor system. Soule wrote from his post in Orangeburg, a district adjoining the northern border of Charleston district and one to which a large number of lowcountry slaves had been refugeed during the war and from which most had not yet left. According to Soule, the free-labor experiment there had met with cooperative and solicitous planters, but also former slaves with "false and exaggerated ideas of freedom." Soule believed that the former slaveholders offered "little danger to the welfare of society." Instead, it was the "ignorance, the prejudice, the brutality, and the educated idleness" of the freedpeople that threatened the free-labor future of the South. The former slaves, Soule argued, needed "to be watched and placed under restraint, to supply the place of the rigid plantation discipline now suddenly done away with." "Only actual suffering, starvation, and punishment" would drive them to work, Soule predicted. Indeed, it appeared that hunger—and planters' promises to distribute rations to contracted workers—drove many lowcountry freedpeople into accepting the contract system in 1865.[80]

Like their families and communities closer to the coast, freedpeople in Orangeburg expected the plantations to be divided among the former slaves. Freedwomen and men insisted on setting the terms of their labor: "besides receiving their food, cloth[e]s, the free rent of houses and gardens, and the privilege of keeping their hogs and poultry, they are to take for themselves all day saturday and sunday, and to receive half the crops." But Soule argued that "so low, uneducated and inefficient a class of laborers as these now suddenly freed, should not receive more pay than northern farm laborers," who, he pointed out, usually have "to pay all [their] wages for food clothing and house-rent." "Were the freedmen to receive more," warned Soule, "the relation between capital and labor would be disturbed and an undue value placed upon the latter." In fact, Soule and the other officers agreed with local planters that the compensation suggested by General Hatch—half the harvested crop—was "too much to give, if the laborers were also to be fed and clothed," so contract terms were left up to the planter's discretion. Unsurprisingly, Soule found former slaves "distrustful of all whites," that they "persist still in giving credit only to rumors set afloat by people of their own color, and believe that the officers who have addressed them are rebels in disguise."[81]

Soule's feelings about freedpeople and their expectations for freedom's benefits were shared not only by his superior officer and his commander, but also by other military personnel in South Carolina, among them Lieutenant Colonel A. J. Willard, commanding U.S. troops in Georgetown.[82] Since freedpeople had "subdivided the lands among themselves" and presented returning planters with "great difficulties . . . from their unwillingness to do anything except cultivate and harvest their own little plots," Willard expected that force would inevitably be brought to bear against such exaggerated notions of freedom.[83] It was his opinion that freedpeople's vision of subsistence farming "cannot be maintained for any length of time as it is contrary to the laws of nature and civilization, as I understand them." Willard, like Soule, came to realize in 1865 that "the laborers . . . have their own opinions and inclinations and are not disposed to place any large amount of confidence in the judgement of those whose duty it is to look after their interests."[84] As a consequence of the views held by Willard, Soule, and other army officials, freedwomen and men found themselves increasingly at odds with the military's definition of freedom.

In the early months of 1865, the occupation forces of the U.S. Army initiated a policy of restoring plantation production as quickly as possible. They assumed a policing role to assure former slaves of their right to be paid for their contracted labor, and to assure planters of their right to claim and operate their plantations under the new system of free labor. Like Peggy, freedwomen envisioned a different kind of freedom and a different role for the U.S. Army as midwife to that freedom, and so when military force was used to ease the birth of the resuscitated plantation economy, their dismay and disappointment were evident even to lowcountry planters. Small wonder that both the military and lowcountry planters viewed the Freedmen's Bureau, with its enlarged agenda for the postbellum South, as a meddler in the fragile postbellum peace.

The Freedmen's Bureau

The Bureau of Refugees, Freedmen and Abandoned Lands (the Freedmen's Bureau) was created by Congress before the close of the war as a federal agency with unprecedented responsibility for the general welfare of the Union-occupied South's former slave and white refugee population. Despite the radical implications of the agency's project, including its role in the disposition of abandoned lands, the bureau was created as a moderate compromise, a fact reflected both in its limited tenure—requiring yearly renewal by Congress—as well as by the fact that it was created without a budget. Forced to draw whatever resources it required from the War Department, the bureau had to rely on military personnel to fill key posts— local "subassistant commissioners" charged with distributing food (which had to be drawn from the Commissary General of the army), clothing (from the Quartermaster General) and medical supplies (from the Surgeon General) to the most needy. Bureau agents also provided invaluable institutional support for the educational and religious pursuits of local freedmen and women, and of course encouraged the resumption of agriculture within the plantation economy.[85]

In 1866 and 1867, the bureau would play an important role in defending freedwomen's most basic rights to live free of violence and to work free of the kind of exploitation they experienced as slaves. In the spring and summer of 1865, however, the bureau was slow to establish its presence in South Carolina. It was mid-June before Bureau Commissioner Oliver O. Howard appointed General Rufus Saxton the assistant commissioner over South Carolina, Georgia, and Florida. Saxton was delayed in assuming his responsibilities by illness, a delay compounded in Georgetown District where subordinate bureau agents were ill or absent from their posts for most of the summer.[86] These delays meant that bureau operations in South Carolina were initiated well after the planting season; freedpeople and planters had, in essence, begun the process of negotiating the transition to free labor. The bureau was essentially left to enforce the contract system already put into place by military authorities.[87]

Other obstacles also limited the bureau's influence over lowcountry labor relations in 1865; critical among these was a lack of personnel. Two months after Saxton became South Carolina's chief bureau officer, he still had only seventeen subassistant commissioners to cover the state's thirty-one counties. By the year's end, Saxton relied on only twenty-four subassistant commissioners and twenty doctors to meet the needs of more than four hundred thousand freedpeople in the state. These local agents assumed their posts in a vacuum of funding and support, relying heavily on local military posts and the army quartermaster for personnel and goods.[88]

Subassistant commissioners included civilians, officers from the Veteran Reserve Corps, and active-duty officers borrowed from local military posts. All of them varied widely in their understanding of their responsibilities, in their experiences, and in their attitudes toward the former slaves and the former slaveowners. Furthermore, bureau agents and military authorities often believed that their respective duties and mandates placed them at cross-purposes. Bureau agents complained, for example, that planters had quickly learned which military authorities could be relied upon to press even the most unfair contract terms onto the freedpeople.[89]

Before Saxton and his subordinate local agents had assumed their official roles in lowcountry affairs, the occupation forces of the army had overseen the transition from war to peace, simply extending many of the wartime policies that had guided military occupation in the lowcountry and the treatment of former slaves. Besides implementing the contract labor system, the army had also expanded its role in mediating and adjudicating conflict among lowcountry residents by establishing circuit and superior provost courts in the Department of the South in July 1865.[90] Although neither the army nor the bureau had members either entirely dedicated to the uplift of freedpeople, or entirely opposed to it, consistent conflict between them reflected the different goals and strategies of the two organizations. The army's primary duty of coping with the immediate effects of the military conflict, restoring and protecting the peace and social order by careful policing of civilians and former Confederates (especially in the absence of civil government), placed the military in a different relationship to freedpeople than the bureau.

These and other differences led to open conflict between the personnel of the two agencies, erupting in 1865 when the bureau tried to become more involved in reconstructing labor and race relations on lowcountry plantations. Rice planters preferred dealing with the military over the bureau, arguing that the bureau agents "demoralized" freedpeople, and that freedpeople believed the bureau to be an agency "organized for the sole purpose of protecting them in the enjoyment of the most extravagant pretensions and the largest license."[91] For lowcountry freedpeople, the conflict that emerged between the two organizations meant they were subject to contradictory policies, delaying either organization from effectively assisting them, and undoubtedly alienating freedpeople from the men and the agencies ostensibly charged with the job of helping them in their transition to freedom.

The conflict that developed between military authorities and bureau agents, and its implications for lowcountry freedpeople, became particularly evident in the case of Colonel James C. Beecher (brother of Henry

Ward Beecher and Harriet Beecher Stowe), a white commander of a black regiment who was assigned at the close of the war to a military subdistrict in lowcountry South Carolina, along the Combahee River south of Charleston. Beecher considered himself a longtime advocate for freedpeople and black soldiers, a career officer who had sacrificed his advancement within the military by advocating so strongly on behalf of African Americans. Northern whites visiting in Charleston believed him "too active a man among the colared people and hates rebs too much to be allowed to remain here longer," and rumors flew that General Hatch reassigned Beecher from Charleston to the remote countryside, in June 1865, in order to remove "so formidable an advocate of the people."[92]

But in his haste to prevent the threat of famine and civil disruption that he believed would result from freedpeople's refusal to work and their continued claims to abandoned plantations, and to encourage a more rapid transition to "free labor" in the lowcountry, Beecher soon resorted to draconian measures (including pistol-whipping) when his orders failed to win obedience. Freedwomen and freedmen began to complain to local Freedmen's Bureau agents about Beecher's use of physical force, and the agents complained in turn to Assistant Commissioner Saxton.[93] Beecher's reputation among Freedmen's Bureau agents was not improved when he denied government rations to "ablebodied" freedpeople and threatened arrest, confinement, and even involuntary servitude for any who dared apply.[94]

As a result of Beecher's increasingly harsh interpretation of military necessity in postwar South Carolina, freedwomen and men under his jurisdiction were forced into labor contracts, late in the growing season, that gave half of what they had independently grown and harvested to absentee planters; underage orphans were removed from school with Beecher's approval to be apprenticed to former owners for ten-year terms and more; and freedpeople were physically assaulted by Beecher and men under his command for openly resisting his directives. Beecher rejected criticisms of his strategies and techniques, and ignored accusations that planters were motivated by greed and a reluctance to acknowledge emancipation.[95] Bureau agents who knew of Beecher's earlier reputation as an advocate for slaves and black soldiers were astounded at his new sympathy for Southern planters.[96]

Beecher argued that his harsh actions were based on a realistic assessment of lowcountry residents and their capacities. He believed that bureau agents acted under misguided, naive stereotypes in their approach to freedpeople and former slaveowners alike. He was not alone in this belief; General Gillmore similarly denounced civilian bureau agents as "more mischievous and troublesome than beneficial—mere doctrinaires and agitators."[97] Unlike many of the recently arriving bureau agents, Beecher had seen, during and at the close of the war, former slaves' capacity for revenge as well as their violent defense of freedom and independence. Indeed, the men and women Beecher observed and policed had demonstrated a willing recourse to violence in defense of what they perceived as the rights of free people, a capacity that Beecher felt was overlooked by bureau agents who saw former slaves only as "poor, ignorant oppressed creatures."[98]

Beecher believed that the naivete of civilian bureau agents threatened to undermine the peace he had labored to bring to the lowcountry.[99] When bureau agents tried to circumvent Beecher's policies, he threatened to arrest "any man not my superior officer who either ignorantly or viciously interferes & incites the Freed people to violence or laziness—within the limits of my command."[100] Beecher maintained that the strictest policing of the lowcountry and a hasty resumption of plantation production were the only solutions to the deplorable material and social conditions and the threat of violent confrontations that existed at the end of the war.[101] He forwarded copies of orders from the commander of his department to local bureau agents, who responded by forwarding to him and other military authorities copies of their own orders and circulars from Howard, the bureau commissioner. Only an uneasy division of labor between the bureau and the military allayed the kind of conflict that arose from Beecher's command in the lowcountry.

Critical to the division of labor between the bureau and the military forces of occupation was the army's initial and larger role in instituting and enforcing the contract labor system in 1865. In Georgetown, bureau agents investigated and supervised the operation of abandoned plantations, but army personnel continued, whether under the policies established by Hatch and Gillmore or at the request of understaffed bureau offices, to oversee labor arrangements on restored and other planter-resident plantations. In Georgetown District, the local military force drew up over two-thirds of the 112 labor contracts entered into by planters and freedpeople in 1865.[102] The contracts themselves tell us more about the military's intent to bring order to the disheveled state of plantation production in the lowcountry than they do about the actual contours of free labor in the first year of freedom.[103]

What did contract labor entail for lowcountry freedpeople? Typical was a contract entered into by Adele Allston and the forty-six freedpeople on Chicora Wood plantation. Any freedperson who placed an "X" by his or her full name agreed to labor "industriously and faithfully" at whatever labor the planter or her chosen agent directed the worker to do, "in the mode and manner usual to rice-lands." All plantation tools, boats, and wagons were to be used with care and returned to the planter at the end of the contracted year. The planter agreed to subsist the laborers until provisions were harvested, and to give them half of what they harvested after seed for the next year's crop was deducted from the total. The lieutenant, who wrote out, witnessed, and approved this and many other contracts, added a clause that guaranteed any laborers evicted from the plantation before the close of the year full payment for their labor.[104]

The terms of the contracts varied, but nearly all revealed facile attempts by planters to retain elements of their antebellum domination over the labor force. Most contracts specified restrictions on the behavior, and especially the mobility, of the former slaves. Some stated that freedpeople were to be "obedient" and "respectful," and to solicit the permission of the planter for any deviation from antebellum norms on the plantation.[105] Other contracts stipulated the continuation of specific antebellum customs; the former slaves were to "occupy the Houses they have heretofore lived in," or to work "as hitherto usual in this part of the State," or simply "to labor as formerly."[106] The nature of some of the limitations and prohibitions contained in the contracts suggests a multitude of ways by which planters hoped to circumscribe the impact of emancipation: the contracts banned weapons of all sort, from firearms to dirks; freedpeople were prohibited from feeding or sheltering anyone whose name did not appear on the contract, in an effort to regulate residence on or visitors to the plantation; freedpeople were required to seek permission from the planter to leave the plantation ("not to ramble about the country during work hours"). Several contracts restricted the number of dogs, mules, hogs, or horses that freedpeople could keep on the plantation, apparently seeking to limit self-subsistence that might undermine their investment in the staple crop. Contracts also attempted to regulate freedpeople's behavior and social and leisure activities; the workers were instructed to avoid "gross immorality" as well as "Idleness bad language & drunkenness" and to display obedience and respectfulness toward the planters. Nearly every contract stated that the freedpeople were to labor under the task system and to maintain the irrigation system as they always had; furthermore, the planter or the planter's assigned agent would direct and evaluate their labor. Finally, there were very few examples of gender-specific labor assignments or restrictions. This first year of contract labor bore no evidence of efforts by either planters or the freedpeople themselves to insist that men's and women's labor be treated differently.

Only 2,521 freedpeople—of Georgetown's estimated 18,000 freedpeople—signed onto these contracts.[107] And despite the army's assumption that the contracts would secure a new labor system to replace slavery, in practice the greatest accomplishment of the contract labor system was that it secured rations for contracted freedpeople (provided by planters) as well as the basic assurance to planters and to freedpeople of a share of a crop. The many clauses planters inserted into the contracts to regain their former power and authority over the workforce ultimately proved unenforceable as well as cumbersome, prompting a great many appeals by planters and freedpeople alike to the military provost courts.

Other factors undermined the utility of the contracts: the lateness of their imposition (most in June, July, and after), and the fact that as written documents they were inaccessible to the vast majority of freedpeople (and even if freedpeople could read the contracts, they were not provided with copies). Most of the 1865 contracts in Georgetown (unlike those in years to follow) excluded the last names of the former slaves, suggesting that when the contracts were drawn up freedpeople were not closely consulted. In other parts of lowcountry South Carolina—south of Charleston, for example—contract terms were closely contested by freedpeople.[108] Whether freedpeople accepted the contract system or not, their responses to the resumption of rice plantation production in the immediate wake of emancipation were less concerned with the formal terms of the contract system than with their day-to-day interactions with both Northern and Southern whites.

Freedwomen Define and Defend Black Freedom

By the late summer and early fall of 1865, their claim to lowcountry plantation lands undermined by military authorities, and the potentially revolutionary consequences of freedom constrained by federal authorities' concerns for law and order in the chaotic lowcountry countryside, freedwomen and men turned their efforts to expanding the consequences of freedom in the local settings where land and labor were still in flux. That fall and winter, Georgetown planters complained with greater frequency of freedpeople's insolence, of their leaving the plantations without the permission of the planter, of refusing work orders, and of making threats against planters. South of Charleston, planters accused former slaves of keeping irregular hours and of being saucy, insolent, intractable, disobedient, and dangerous. Planters complained that freedpeople "not only will not work now, but tell you so openly & plainly."[109] Even in this general climate of insolence and labor's unmanageability, men and women of the lowcountry planter class, white overseers, soldiers, and agents of the Freedmen's Bureau all complained pointedly about the insubordinate behavior of former slave women.

The record of freedwomen's actions in the late summer and autumn of 1865 emphasizes not only the content of their demands, but also the manner in which those demands were made. Freedwomen were refusing to comply with the ritualized codes of conduct that had required from slave women subordinate verbal and physical posturing in their interactions with whites. Freedwomen not only challenged the right of planters and overseers to define their freedom; they added to their antebellum repertoire of evasive tactics and deceptive appearances a new public strategy of insubordination and direct confrontation.[110] One planter, Richard Cumming, and his wife agreed that the freedwoman Jane, who rejected work orders and slapped Mrs. Cummings, was "an audacious creature."[111] William Robert complained to local military authorities that his former slave MaryAnn "boldly or unblushingly" confronted him in the field, refused his assignment of work unrelated to the present crop, and "frequently contradicted me and spoke to me as roughly and as defiantly as if I had been the meanest old negro in the country." Robert was as alarmed by MaryAnn's defiant bearing toward him as by her insistence on determining for herself which work she would and would not perform. W. M. Robertson characterized freedwomen on the plantation he was attempting to operate as idle and insolent, vagrant, playing sick, and doing no work. The driver's wife thought she was "too fine a lady to think of doing any work," and even Eve, while admittedly "an old woman," he described as "very impertinent." It was the behavior of women like these that prompted the agent on one lowcountry rice plantation to complain that "the more kindness offered to them the more ingratitude & abuse we receive," an unwitting admission that freedwomen were challenging the facade of reciprocal relations that underlay antebellum paternalism.[112]

The growing number of complaints from rice planters after the 1865 harvest were concerned with the declining productivity of plantation labor. Military authorities concurred that while planters had typically met their part of the labor contracts, freedpeople were "in no manner performing the part of hired laborers." More precisely, from the perspective of freedpeople, it was the part of a slave that they refused to play.[113] Endless complaints that freedpeople were not working did not indicate a general work stoppage, as had been the case earlier that year, but instead indicated a refusal to perform specific, postharvest tasks. In the fall of 1865, lowcountry freedpeople, regardless of the stipulations of their labor contracts, began to insist that their obligation as free workers ended with the harvest of the current rice and provision crop. They refused to perform any of the postharvest work they had performed as slaves. Their refusal quickly escalated into one of the most crucial labor battles fought in the first season of emancipated labor. It was no less apparent to former slaves than to planters that the rice plantations, their elaborate canal, trunk, and dam systems neglected or destroyed during the war and now in need of extensive repairs and maintenance, could never reach their former level of production without considerable construction, repair, and maintenance. But as "croppers," freedpeople were making an important distinction between their former "enslavement to the plantation" and their current status as independent workers oriented toward crop production.

This was an especially important point in the fall of 1865, when land was rapidly being restored to planters, when freedpeople's claim to the plantation lands was significantly eroded, and when "military necessity," the contract system, and the course of Johnsonian Reconstruction seemed to accelerate the threat against freedom as former slaves understood it. Freedwomen reminded planters of their crucial role in the postwar economy when they refused to perform a range of tasks important to plantation maintenance that had typically been performed after the rice harvest. "Mudwork," the repair of flats, fences, and outbuildings, and the chopping of firewood for the planter's woodpile, according to bureau agents, was "wholly neglected."[114] Freedpeople also refused any labor that was not directly related to the present crop—on Stephen Doar's plantations, this included refusing to thresh rice that had been grown in 1864.[115]

As croppers, lowcountry freedwomen and men were particularly insistent that they would not perform the most hated aspect of plantation labor, the maintenance of the plantation irrigation system. Cleaning the irrigation ditches meant days of hard labor standing in water and mud, heavy digging, and hauling, and bureau agents reported that the freedpeople "as a general thing refuse to perform this work, claiming that with a division of the crops their labors are at an end." The rejection of this labor greatly alarmed the planters, for on most plantations the ditches and canals had not been properly maintained during the war, and future crops depended on the repairs that were needed. Planters in the Georgetown area even tried to persuade the Freedmen's Bureau to force former slaves to perform the hated mudwork by claiming that the unrepaired ditches presented a serious threat to "public health"—a manipulation that failed.[116]

There were other important issues also at stake when freedpeople insisted they would work only as croppers. Former slave men and women on Hammock plantation, in St. Peter's Parish, refused to cut and gather fodder after the harvest, "saying that 'they could not eat fodder,'" a critical point on this plantation where corn rations had not been provided for the laborers for at least three weeks leading up to this protest. The withholding of rations was a tactic regularly used by lowcountry rice planters to force freedpeople to work when and at whatever tasks the planter so ordered.[117] The shortage of provision crops—a consequence of late planting, a shortage of seed and implements, ill health among the laborers, and poor growing weather—put tremendous pressure on freedpeople's few resources. What small crops they managed to produce might have subsisted those who had raised them, but the fall of 1865 saw a steady stream of freedpeople returning to the lowcountry who needed to be fed. The bureau agent at Columbia estimated that his office provided transportation to the lowcountry for at least 250 men, women, and children each week between September and January. "People who formerly lived upon the plantations—but were carried away by their old masters[,] are now returning to their old homes, & seldom if ever bring either provisions or money with them. . . . Unless help comes from some source, great suffering must ensue."[118]

Freedwomen's rejection of postharvest labor also reflected a newly developing family economy among former slaves. Freedpeople were still in a state of extreme deprivation as a consequence of the war as well as the short crops of 1865. Families of ex-slaves sought a balance between their ties to specific communities and their claim to the land, with their need for cash or food and basic goods. After the harvest, freedmen (husbands and fathers) left the plantations in pursuit of day labor, marketing fruit, firewood, or farm produce in nearby towns or to steamers, or found other temporary avenues into the wage or cash economy.[119] The result, according to one planter, was that "all male hands but two have left the place. . . . So I have my houses, filled with women and children, 12 (twelve) women who are full hands, but will not work, 6 (six) half hands, 4 (four) old and crippled[,] 21 (twenty one) children fit for no work of any kind, 43 (forty three) in all."[120] Freedwomen—often wives and mothers—remained on the rice plantations and assumed a frontline role in the battle over postharvest labor while caring for family and independent crops. This strategy not only deepened planters' concern about securing essential postharvest labor from freedpeople, it also placed freedwomen in direct conflict with planters. Freedwomen like MaryAnn, who "shewed the virago from the start," insisted they would perform no postharvest labor for their white employers. Her former owner complained that "since gathering the corn & potatoes she has refused to rake[,] fence[,] or do any work," leading him to fear that her behavior "will poison all the rest of the people of the place."[121]

Freedmen, joined by single freedwomen, female kin of soldiers, and other freedpeople, contributed to a brisk "local retail trade" at Hilton Head, Charleston, and other gathering places. Rice planters feared that much of the trade was in goods and crops stolen from their plantations. They urged military authorities to curb the nearly universal ownership of boats among freedpeople and to regulate the sale of agricultural products during and after the harvest season. Planters complained of what they felt was a direct relationship between this active trade and freedpeople's refusal to enter labor contracts and to perform postharvest labor. Planters like William Roberts resented freedpeople's efforts to make an independent living, as well as their attention to their own gardens and crops, which he felt came at a cost to the plantation crop and his own pocketbook. Others, like J. S. Bostick, found the women and children remaining on the plantations unrelenting in their battle against planters; he complained to military authorities that a freedwoman and a boy armed with a sword "tried to give a beating" to him.[122]

Freedwomen fueled the escalating labor conflict on rice plantations with their refusal to perform postharvest domestic chores for planters. Prior to the war, planters typically held female field hands responsible for a range of postharvest labor unrelated to field work, including spinning and weaving, the manufacture of clothing, butchering and the preservation of meat, as well as other kinds of domestic production that were critical to the maintenance and support of plantation operations. That labor had eaten into the hours slavewomen might otherwise have spent with, and working for, their own families. In the fall of 1865, freedwomen may have rejected that labor because their own survival and that of their families depended on doing so. Freedwomen who had contracted to work as field hands were no longer willing to perform "double duty" in domestic production for their employers. One planter's wife reported that in order to get former slaves to work even half tasks in the field, chores related to domestic production, such as spinning, had to be totally abandoned. Another plantation mistress found herself reported to a local bureau agent for trying to compel freedwomen to do her spinning and weaving. Even a young woman like sixteen-year-old Margaret Brown rejected "weaving after night" for her employer, who took her refusal as provocation enough for a beating with his bare hands and with a stick.[123]

According to bureau and military records, freedwomen were sometimes forced to pay a dear price for insisting on their right to define freedom on their own terms. Their experience of violence at the hands of an outraged employer was not unusual. In October, Hagar Barnwell was ordered by her former owner to go into the kitchen and work, but "she refused . . . as she had contracted to work in the field." When he persisted, Barnwell vowed she would leave the plantation rather than work in his kitchen, at which point he threatened her with his pistol, insisted he would have killed her if he didn't have to get his crop in, and then took her to a shed where he tied her up by her thumbs so that her feet barely touched the ground. Barnwell went to three different army officers as well as a local magistrate before she found someone who would investigate her mistreatment.[124]

One bureau agent described how "a Woman named Sarah . . . was tied up by the thumbs" by a planter and two accomplices; "Sarah was pregnant and . . . she was kept suspended for nearly two hours," reported the agent, and "in consequence of this brutality the birth of the child was forced." The infant "was dead when delivered" and Sarah "has not been expected to live." Besides Sarah, two other freedwomen, as well as two boys, were flogged by a party of eight to ten white men "until the blood ran from their bodies." "The pretext for whipping these persons," reported the agent, "was that they were visiting on this place and that . . . was against orders."[125] In another incident, a husband and wife and two other freedmen refused a planter's proposal that they sign a contract for life; the men were shot, while the freedwoman was stripped bare, given fifty lashes on her back, and forced to walk fifty miles to return to the planter's place. For a week, she was forced to plow by day and was confined at night without being fed, until a U.S. officer discovered the situation and intervened.[126]

During the fall of 1865, freedwomen struggling to redefine plantation life and labor in the lowcountry did so as political Reconstruction gathered steam. Antebellum experience and wartime developments had combined to make land claims extremely important to lowcountry freedpeople; the rejection of those claims became, in turn, a significant motivation prompting freedpeoples' vigorous opposition to the efforts of planters, bureau agents, and military authorities to control plantation life and labor. The sense of betrayal felt by freedwomen when the Union army failed to support their expectations for what freedom might mean fueled lowcountry freedpeople's drive for independence from whites in general and their distrust of the agents of Reconstruction in particular. Those freedpeople who were on abandoned land became increasingly determined to defend that land against restoration, resorting to arms and barricading plantations in a few notable instances. With the option of obtaining land in the Sherman Reserve no longer available and the tenure of those with possessory title in doubt, freedpeople in the mainland lowcountry turned with greater determination than ever to the immediate task of defining and defending their own freedom.[127] The conflicts over plantation life and labor provided political fodder for whites' fears for the future.

The Politics of Presidential Reconstruction and Local Responses

President Johnson's lenient policy toward former Confederates, particularly his willingness to restore to planters their property, was irreconcilable with any plan to resettle freedpeople on so-called "abandoned" lands. As a result, early in September, the military commander in South Carolina ordered a cessation to the confiscation of abandoned land for the use of freedpeople. Johnson was also unwilling to challenge the sanctity of property rights, even in the defeated South, and so instructed the head of the Freedmen's Bureau, General Oliver O. Howard, to revoke the full impact of the Sherman Reserve and restore to pardoned planters their land. In so doing, Johnson gained cooperation and political support from some white Southerners, but at the same time he conveyed to former slaves further proof that the federal government was an unreliable ally. Freedpeople already settled on bureau-held lands faced eviction at the conclusion of the fall harvest. As Johnson moved Reconstruction policy more consistently toward restoration and away from the redistribution of abandoned and confiscated lands, the level of conflict between freedpeople and planters would escalate, gaining momentum and greater urgency during the fall of 1865.[128]

Late that summer, Benjamin Perry, named the state's provisional governor by President Johnson, called for the election of constitutional convention delegates and directed the convention's reluctant steps toward Presidential Reconstruction during its September meeting. The all-white convention met the barest requirements to satisfy Johnson's overt demands by recognizing the abolition of slavery and repudiating secession.[129] The convention also assigned a committee to create an elaborate legal framework, South Carolina's black code, for restoring white domination in postemancipation race and labor relations. The constitutional convention's delegates, alarmed by the persistent labor unrest that kept their

households as well as their rice fields in disarray, hoped that the imposition of new controls on the former slaves would restore the economic stability of the state as well as the social and racial relations that had prevailed
prior to emancipation.[130]

For the freedmen and women of the lowcountry who continued to live
and work on lowcountry rice plantations, the black code represented a
threat by former slaveowners and other white South Carolinians to deny—
or at best, severely circumscribe—black freedom. For example, the code
would force freedpeople to labor under stringent terms; would exclude free
and slave-born black South Carolinians from all but the most menial occupations; would permit the arrest of unemployed freedpeople for vagrancy
and force them into involuntary labor as punishment; and would establish severe reprisals in instances where freedpeople violated their contracts.
It also proposed capital punishment for African Americans convicted of
various crimes, including raising an insurrection and assaulting a white
woman or "impersonating her husband for carnal purposes."[131] The code
attempted to force postwar social and labor relations into a mold more like
black slavery than black freedom.

Lowcountry rice planters were among the proposed code's critics,
charging its upcountry authors with failing to provide adequately stringent
regulation of former slaves. The lowcountry elite believed that the success
of the plantation economy depended not simply on compulsory labor ("to
enable them to hold the same despotic sway as they engaged under the
unrestrained use of the lash," according to one critic)[132] but also the systematic subordination of all African Americans (few lowcountry whites
distinguished between slave- and freeborn in their reference to black South
Carolinians). Rice planters unanimously believed their plantations could
not be worked by white labor, and that black labor required compulsion:

> The rice planters all say, with one accord, that not only must they have black
> labor to succeed, but compulsory black labor, and nothing else. For the
> white man to attempt to inhabit, much less to work upon a rice plantation
> in the hot season, is certain death. This being the case, and compulsory
> labor being (as the negroes have learned to say) "played out," it is clear
> that the rice planters are in a very bad way, and that unless something
> should turn up to prevent, the cultivation of rice in South Carolina will, ere
> long, be a thing of the past.[133]

Lowcountry planters and other whites could not even fathom lowcountry
life without the system of racial subordination and domination that most

whites believed had made life possible for them in the black-majority low-country.[134] Former slaveowning women concurred: "I do not see how we are to live in this country without any rule or regulation."[135]

Freedpeople had good reason to expect former slaveowners and planters to pursue every possible return to black slavery. "As far as making the negroes work," commented one lowcountry planter, E. P. Miliken, ". . . No Sheriff & Posse or Patrol, under civil rule, will suit our wants. We must have *mounted Infantry.*" Indeed, Miliken's call for a forceful restoration of slavery was answered in some parts of the region; between Sherman's mid-February march through South Carolina and the effective occupation of the lowcountry in April, slaves who had been "freed" by Union forces were essentially re-enslaved, told by Confederate scouts and guerrillas "they were not free, but slaves, and would be until they died; that the Yankees had no right to free them, and that they were to go to work as they had always done . . . and the first one caught out without a ticket would be killed."[136] During the summer of 1865, planters were not only "tyrannical" but also made "violent threats of what they will do when the Yankees leave." Even as late as October of that year, former slaveowners exchanged rumors that black freedom was to be severely circumscribed. Mary Pringle reported as reliable the news she had heard from white Charlestonians that "all the negroes were to be placed under a seven years apprenticeship on their former owners' plantations, and made to cultivate them."[137] For the duration of 1865, freedom was threatened not only by organized violence like that perpetrated by guerrillas and scouts in the closing weeks of war, but also by the efforts of white South Carolinians to deploy the state as a tool of white supremacy.

The constitutional convention's efforts to shore up white-dominated Southern society did not go unanswered by black South Carolinians. Building on their disappointment over Johnson's leniency toward former Confederates, they responded with a series of local meetings leading up to a statewide freedmen's convention, held in Charleston on 20–25 November, where the black code was a key topic of discussion. The official delegates to the convention were all men (newspaper accounts of the convention proceedings fail to indicate whether women were part of the audience), and many of them were from a class that the historian Thomas Holt has described as "the freeborn petite bourgeoisie" of Charleston. These participants in the state's first convened assembly of elected black delegates created a new arena for black political and public life. To the existing examples of military service, they added mass meetings on abandoned plantations, organized committees through which Sea Islanders governed their communities and called for land redistribution, and paramilitary organizations on the mainland.[138] All of these new venues for public life were apparently the domain of men, but the impenetrably scant evidence of their internal workings makes it difficult to draw out the implications for gender relations among freedpeople.

While we know little of the local meetings leading up to it, the proceedings of the statewide convention suggest the emergence of important differences among the perceived self-interests of black Carolinians.[139] While they came together to oppose the black code, the delegates left no record of any discussion that may have addressed the specific interests and concerns of freedwomen or men who labored in the lowcountry rice fields. Even the three Georgetown delegates represented that town's freeborn black elite—not former slaves from the rice plantations—at the convention. Apparently exceptional among the delegates were Ishmael Moultrie and Henry Bram, elected from Colleton District, both of whom had been and would continue to be active in the organized movement among Sea Island freedpeople for land redistribution. Moultrie and Bram left the convention early, apparently in order to make their way to Jehossee Island, where as many as three hundred freedpeople were resisting the government's efforts to impose contract labor on the people who had lived on and cultivated the plantation independently for some time. Two weeks after leaving the convention, Moultrie was accused of organizing and drilling a paramilitary company among Jehossee Island freedmen.[140] Moultrie and Bram represented a minority interest at the freedmen's convention; the delegates who dominated the gathering were more concerned with the black code's threat against the privileges they had enjoyed as freeborn men, than with the land and labor conflicts unfolding on lowcountry rice plantations.[141]

Even with its failure to address the concerns of rice plantation workers, and the apparent exclusion of freed or freeborn women from its roster of delegates and speakers, the convention was an important public platform from which freeborn men and freedmen responded to the reports of the black code then being drawn up by a committee of the state constitutional convention.[142] The black code threatened not only a return to slavery but also a severe limitation on the rights to which the state's elite black men now aspired. "The simple act of emancipation, if it stops there, is not worth much," stated one of the Charleston delegates, expressing a universally shared sentiment among former slaves, women and men, that freedom meant more than the simple destruction of slavery.[143]

If they were denied a role or a voice in the discussion at South Carolina's freedmen's convention, rural freedwomen were neither absent nor silent during the transition from slave to free labor on lowcountry rice plantations. Their struggle to define freedom on their own terms continued, unaddressed by convention delegates but increasingly the subject of military and bureau reports and planter complaints. Their involvement in the escalating labor conflict of fall 1865 was noted by the overseers, former owners, and lowcountry elites who were as outraged at freedwomen's studied violation of antebellum rituals of deference and subordination as by the content of their demands. Although conflict and resistance had been part of the fabric of day-to-day life under slavery, by the late summer of 1865 freedwomen were clashing with former slaveowners and other whites in a new, more public, and openly declared arena. Freedwomen challenged former slaveowners' and overseers' expectations of ritualized, deferential behavior as they set out in fairly clear terms and with definitive action how they believed life and labor should differ in freedom from their experience under slavery.

Stalemate

With white South Carolinians seeking to reinstate a kind of slavery, and with freedwomen challenging planters and plantation mistresses over the terms and nature of their labor, by late 1865 the escalating conflict led the military commander in Georgetown District, Lieutenant Colonel A. J. Willard, to concede that the system of free labor was "not working well." Despite Willard's best efforts to explain to the former slaves how free labor worked in the North, they freely violated their labor contracts, preferred working under the task system, "positively refuse[d]" to perform postharvest labor, and advocated a work ethic that was "contrary to the laws of nature and civilization," generally manifested in their "indisposition to continuous and regular labor" and their continued preference for dividing up the plantations among themselves in order to cultivate and harvest their own plots. Local planters shared Willard's frustration with the freedpeople's work habits, their expectations for the meaning of freedom, and even his lack of influence over the freedpeople.[144]

The fragile negotiations over land and labor arrangements in the closing months of 1865 were further threatened by two waves of new arrivals to lowcountry rice plantations. One of these was a significant postharvest migration of freedpeople from upcountry refuges returning for the first time since the war to their lowcountry homes.[145] Many of these new arrivals had suffered several months of scarcity in the interior, and they brought few resources with them. One recently returned freedwoman described the conditions in the interior that had killed many of her fellow former slaves: "No shoe, no cloes, an' den de fros' git up into deir body, tell when de sun come down so hot, dey dies too fas'. Tight livin' what do 'em so; not'in to eat. . . . Dear Christ . . . I most' starve to death."[146]

Some of these newly arrived refugees still expected to claim abandoned plantation lands for their own use, and their hopes seemed to revive the aspirations for land even among those freedpeople who had already negotiated their first year of contract labor.[147] Freedpeople maintained their expectations for lowcountry lands even in light of the visit of Commissioner O. O. Howard to Edisto, in October, to convey the disappointing news of Johnson's policy of restoration. Howard's message of the federal government's betrayal of their hopes for land seemed to have been blunted by his appointment of a commission to overview the process of restoration; Saxton, South Carolina's assistant commissioner, played his role in delaying restoration as well. In short, the bureau offered an ambivalent message about restoration in the same breath in which it betrayed the legacy of wartime and postbellum land redistribution.

A second wave of new arrivals also appeared late in 1865: planters who returned for the first time to reclaim control over their plantations, with an eye toward the 1866 planting season. Freedwomen and men made it clear that planters were still unwelcome. From Camp Main, where freedpeople looked upon the returning planter as "one who has come to interrupt the entire freedom from any restraint whatever, which they have enjoyed the last 9 mos.," to the Sea Island plantation of Thomas R. S. Elliott, where freedpeople reacted to Elliott's return by "getting on their high horse & say they intend to fight for the land," lowcountry freedpeople held onto their claim to the land regardless of presidential, bureau, or military policy. In the Georgetown area, where a number of freedpeople had contracted with rice planters to guard the estates from further destruction, they too regarded their uninterrupted residence on the land as encouragement, and they harbored hopes that their presence would translate into a legitimate claim to the land. Other freedpeople simply rejected planters' bids to enter contracts for the upcoming year's labor, stating that they intended on having forty acres and planting it for themselves.[148]

The conflict and contention that had marked the transition from slavery to freedom since February 1865 had still not subsided. Freedwomen's many efforts to shape the transition to freedom and to invest their freedom with particular meaning spoke to their determination, but the reactions they evoked from former owners and other lowcountry whites often generated more wretchedness, more violence, more conflict. The provision crops they harvested were well short of their immediate needs, yet by refusing postharvest labor, freedpeople risked evictions or having their rations cut off. They repeatedly appealed to military authorities for protection and some semblance of justice, even when some white soldiers seemed inclined to whip, beat, or torture complainants into abandoning their grievances.[149] Freedpeople expected bureau agents and the military's provost courts to enforce planters' obligations under the labor contracts, and yet freely violated the terms of those contracts themselves. Above all else, freedpeople held onto their claim to the land, yet every fight with planters over postharvest labor or to prevent returning planters from assuming control over the plantation placed them at risk of being evicted from the very land they yearned for. The months that had passed since the close of the war had not resolved the many conflicts surrounding lowcountry life and labor; in fact, by the end of 1865, conflict was steadily escalating, as evidenced by the renewed claims among freedpeople for land.

Encountering labor unrest and insubordination from their domestic servants, their field hands, and even the children of their former slaves, and convinced that the bureau was helpless to force order and discipline onto the former slave population, lowcountry planters feared the worst in November and December 1865. In Georgetown, white citizens' fear of a rebellion among former slaves spurred them to complain to Provisional Governor Perry that "an entire gang from one of the plantations came into town yesterday and[,] on being ordered by the Col. to disperse [and] go back to their homes and work or they would be put in jail[,] declared with one voice that they would go to jail and it resulted in their returning to the plantation declaring that they would not work."[150] Other incidents added to the sense of impending danger for lowcountry whites. One agent for a Georgetown planter "was run off and threatened with death by a mob of 30 or 40 negroes armed with rails sticks &c."; on another plantation, the freedpeople threatened to tie up the overseer or "burn him out at night if he did not leave the place." These and other events, the Georgetown whites complained, had all happened within the last ten days "and are rapidly thickening. . . . We are rapidly drifting to a condition of lawlessness and violence which must end in open insurrection and the extermination of our race in this section unless instant aid be afforded."[151]

In the winter of 1865–66, lowcountry planters petitioned the bureau, the military command, and their newly elected governor, James Orr, to

suppress what many whites claimed was inevitable—a Christmas uprising by local blacks to kill all lowcountry whites. As Orr explained in his
appeal for help to General Daniel E. Sickles: "during Christmas week which
has always been a holiday for the negroes they will congregate in large
numbers at the villages & towns where they will get liquor & while under
its influence I fear that collisions will occur between them & the whites.
When once commenced no one can tell where the contest will end."[152]
Late in December, Jane Pringle appealed directly to the commander of
military forces in South Carolina, "in behalf of the women of this doomed
district," with the "positive information that an insurrection of the negroes
is to take place next Sunday night—It will be a general rising in the district." She insisted, "The negroes must now be taught that their former
masters will be protected by the U.S. authorities against all attempts to take
land and life."[153]

Rice planters' near-hysterical fear of an insurrection revealed an almost
automatic tendency to view freedpeople's self-assertion in matters of land,
labor, and independence as evidence of a racial uprising, rather than as a
conflict over the disposition of land and the terms of free labor in the
postslavery, postwar South.[154] The military commander in South Carolina
felt that these end-of-year conflicts were, instead, labor-related: "those who
have been so recently slaves," he pointed out, "look with ignorant yet in-
stinctive distrust upon the obligations and restraints and uncertainties of
contract service." Sickles predicted that a soothing flow of investment
capital would enter the state once planters succeeded in restoring "kindly
relations" with the former slaves.[155] The case for free labor, Sickles believed,
would be made and would win over both black and white South Carolinians. But many white planters feared that as long as freedwomen and men
remained independent of the planters, "stuffed with the idea of proprietorship" over the abandoned lands, their willingness to perform wage labor
for the planters was doubtful. Planters insisted that the freedpeople's "feeling of security and independence has to be eradicated," that it must be
"effectually extirpated before we wish to put seed in the ground."[156] And
so, at the close of 1865, the meaning of black freedom was still under
contention.

6 "In Their Own Way": Women and Work in the Postbellum South

Following the end of the Civil War, freedwomen attempted to expand the consequences of emancipation beyond the destruction of slavery. They escalated the lowcountry battle to define black freedom when they fought to retain their autonomous control over plantation lands, when they negotiated and reconstructed plantation and domestic labor, and when they defended the new autonomy of their families and household economies from exploitation by rice planters and unwelcome intervention by Northern agents of reconstruction. Linking freedwomen's participation in these specific and publicly negotiated issues was their concern that the nature, process, and organization of their paid work, that work's impact on their unpaid household labor, as well as their relationship to former slaveowners, overseers, and slave drivers all reflect the dramatic change in status that they had undergone. Work, which had been so central to women's experience of slavery, became critical to women's definition and experience of freedom.

There were also other important arenas in which former slave women tried to give meaning and substance to their freedom. In fact, freedwomen's (and men's) efforts to increase their autonomy and their resources were intertwined with their desire to build, staff, and sustain schools, churches, mutual and benevolent societies, and a host of other independent institutions.[1] When Radical Reconstruction opened the political arena to freedmen, freedwomen also brought forward their own claims to citizenship, to political meetings and rallies, to voter registration, to the polls.[2] Labor was not, therefore, the only arena where freedwomen or freedmen negotiated their freedom. But an important part of the work of defining freedom lay in revealing and transforming the social relations of power, authority, and domination that had constituted slavery on lowcountry rice plantations.

187

In the context of the reprisals, coercion, and threat of violence with which their efforts were met, freedwomen's determination to shape their work became all the more crucial to their definition and exercise of freedom. Their refusal to withdraw from disputes over the meaning of black freedom meant that freedwomen became targets for physical attack, resulting in a record of brutality that historians of the postbellum South are only beginning to plumb.[3]

In 1866 and the years to follow, freedwomen's pursuit of freedom was seen in their defense of former slaves' control over land; in their negotiation and reconstruction of plantation labor; and in their resistance to white intervention into their households and family life. When freedwomen insisted on working "in their own way and as such times as they think fit," they were articulating a politics of Reconstruction in which women's experience of gender, race, and a history of enslavement were inseparable. They made the issue of reconstructing work their own.

Despite the anxieties of lowcountry rice planters like Jane Pringle of Georgetown, who feared that "thousands of *armed negroes*" would overrun the white inhabitants of "this doomed district" during the closing days of 1865, no insurrection by former slaves brought in the New Year. (Freedpeople did, however, indulge in several days of celebration in Georgetown, "dancing, with little intermission, day & night, on the different plantations in turn," while anxious, armed whites waited them out, listening to the sounds of drums and shooting that accompanied the plantation gatherings.)[4] Similar fears recurred among planter elites at Christmas in 1866 and 1867, but they were dismissed by one lowcountry bureau agent as a seasonal rumor "from time immemorial," the residue of white anxiety about the brief respite from plantation routine that Christmas celebrations had offered to slaves.[5] At the close of 1865, however, some of the fear of insurrection arose as lowcountry whites anticipated the disappointment of freedpeople's expectations for the New Year, that the Freedmen's Bureau would transfer the plantations to the control of the former slaves. As for the freedpeople themselves, the bureau agent at Georgetown reported, "The 1st of January 1866 was a date vividly impressed on their minds that something, greatly to their future welfare and ease was to happen."[6] Many rice planters anticipated freedpeople's disappointment with a mixture of relish and fear: relish, that the federal government had implied through the policies of Presidential Reconstruction that the property rights of even defeated

Confederates were sacred; fear, that former slaves would respond violently and vengefully when the Christmas holidays passed without the redistribution of land to former slaves. Planters and bureau agents alike were to learn that freedpeople's disappointment and anger were channeled not into unfocused racial insurrection but toward shaping the terms under which the former slaves would continue to participate in the lowcountry rice plantation economy.

Local conflict and contests over the meaning and consequences of black freedom coincided with the intensely debated, federal-level contest over the political reconstruction of the former Confederate states. Between 1865 and 1867 there were significant changes in the players, the path, and the goals of Reconstruction, alternately giving hope to, then discouraging, freedpeople's expectation for autonomous control over the land. At the federal level, the victors of the war fought among themselves for control over the Republican party and over Reconstruction. Congress, increasingly alarmed by the actions of the state governments restored under President Andrew Johnson's guidelines (including the election of secessionists to office and the creation of the black codes in South Carolina and Mississippi), refused to admit the recently elected Southern congressmen and also established the investigatory Joint Committee on Reconstruction, signaling to Johnson and to former Confederates that Reconstruction would not be accomplished so effortlessly. Conflict over Reconstruction policy at the federal level escalated as Congress debated the Freedmen's Bureau Bill and the Civil Rights Bill—the latter intended, as Eric Foner points out, to "define in legislative terms the essence of freedom."[7] Freedom, it soon became clear, would not include the redistribution of Southern lands to the formerly enslaved. The moderates in Congress easily rejected Thaddeus Stevens's effort to attach a Radical proposal to the bureau bill turning confiscated Confederate land over to former slaves; in its place, the ineffectual and nonpunitive Southern Homestead Act easily won congressional support.

Yet even the moderates then prevailing in Congress were stunned when Johnson chose to veto both the bureau bill and the civil rights bill in February. Both bills, Johnson argued, would promote an unwarranted expansion of federal authority, would permit federal agencies to overtake state and local responsibilities, would encourage dependence rather than self-help among freedpeople, and would expand the rights of African Americans by eroding those of white citizens. Suspicious of Johnson's claims to have made speedy progress toward the Reconstruction of the South and unwilling to ignore testimony to the contrary before the Joint

Committee on Reconstruction, Congress passed both bills over presidential vetoes in July, extending the life of the bureau for two more years and providing the necessary funds for its support.[8] Congress thus began to seize control over Reconstruction. This was largely accomplished by March 1867, when the Reconstruction Act began the process of establishing the citizenship and civil rights of African Americans in the South and placed the region under military control until such rights were established in law and in practice.

The military and civilian officials directing Reconstruction at the state and local level in South Carolina did not escape the effects of the federal-level struggle to seize control over the Reconstruction plan and process. Both the assistant commissioner of the Freedmen's Bureau in South Carolina and the commander of military forces in the state were replaced in 1866: Saxton because of his continued advocacy for the redistribution of land in opposition to Johnson's program of restoration, Gillmore for his unwillingness to lend support to the bureau and its work in the state. Now headed in South Carolina by Robert K. Scott, the bureau came closer in agreement with the goals of the military command in the state (now under General Daniel E. Sickles) insofar as they agreed that the promulgation of free labor would best answer the concerns of former slaves that their rights would be protected, and those of former slaveowners, that planters have reliable access to a cooperative workforce. Both the military and the bureau hoped that white and black South Carolinians would come to recognize and appreciate what Northerners regarded as their mutual interests under a free-labor system.[9]

To Hold the Land

The end of 1865 and the beginning of 1866 also saw former slaves—women and men—continue their fight to live on and cultivate lowcountry plantation lands without the interference of whites. On the Sea Islands, including John's, Wadmalaw, Edisto, and James Islands, freedpeople held public meetings, organized commissions, appointed delegations, and formed paramilitary guards to protest the accelerating process of restoration, and to prevent returning white landowners from setting foot on the islands and usurping their own claims to the land.[10] On the mainland, from Georgetown to the Savannah River, freedpeople moved to block the restoration of planter control over the rice plantations where they had lived and worked since the close of the war. Late in the spring of 1866, freedpeople's persisting claim of entitlement to lowcountry plantation lands was described by a Cooper River rice planter:

> notwithstanding all the efforts that have been made by their former own-
> ers, as well as the constituted military authorities of the United States and
> agents of the Freedmen's Bureau, to impress upon the under standing of
> the negroes that they own not an inch of land on which they had lived as
> slaves, it is very manifest they are nevertheless slow to relinquish the pleas-
> ing hope that they have a sort of undefined right, title and interest in the
> land, and that it followed as a matter of course with the acquisition of their
> freedom. . . . In all probability they will continue to encourage the idea, and
> to flatter themselves that they are "*tenants at will*," so long as they are al-
> lowed to occupy the very houses perhaps in which they were born, the old
> cradle it may be in which they were rocked still standing in it, and the warm
> fires still there.[11]

Freedpeople's resistance to restoration meant forcing planters and over-seers off the plantation, confronting bureau agents and armed guards of U.S. soldiers, and refusing to cooperate with restored landowners. Even in the defense of individual land claims, freedpeople's resistance to resto-ration occurred as community struggles rather than individual battles.[12] Some plantations, like Jehossee (on the South Edisto river) and Delta (near Savannah), became battlegrounds as hundreds of freedpeople (including those on Delta who "had been born on the plantation and thought they had a life estate in it") "crowded together in a solid phalanx" against the dispatched military force and "swore more furiously than before they would die where they stood" before surrendering their claims to the land.[13]

Freedwomen's opposition to restoration and their involvement in even the most violent confrontations with planters and agents of Recon-struction have sometimes been obscured by the tendency of observers to describe participants as undifferentiated crowds of freed*men* or "ne-groes." But the records of freedwomen who were arrested and jailed for their resistance to restoration reveal their active role. The vehemence with which freedwomen attempted to obstruct restoration seemed to mirror the depth of their exploitation and oppression under slavery—as victims of sexual abuse and unwanted intimacy, as survivors of labor demands that consumed their daily lives and threatened the health and safety of childbearing women as well as their infants, and as witnesses to the abuse and sale of their parents, their children, their husbands, their kin and community.

Charlotte and Sarah, two among more than 260 former slaves who had occupied and cultivated the Georgetown plantation Weehaw for over a year on their own, opposed the owner when he returned in 1866. When he reappeared in person to try and take control of the plantation, Charlotte and Sarah—joined by Fallertree—attacked him. Charlotte's role in the attack was deemed especially egregious by the local military command, who saw fit to sentence her to thirty days in the Georgetown jail, while the other two received lesser sentences.[14]

Eight or ten freedwomen also played a critical role in the physical defense of Keithfield plantation against restoration. The white overseer of Keithfield had been driven off by the freedpeople in March 1865, and for the rest of the year about 150 freedwomen and freedmen worked the plantation on their own, and cultivated at least a partial crop of rice.[15] But early in 1866 Keithfield's absentee owner, a widow, asked a neighboring planter to help her retake control of Keithfield. She could not have chosen a figure more hated by former slaves in the area, for this neighbor, Francis Parker Sr., as the local Confederate provost marshal, had helped carry out the public execution of recaptured fugitive slaves during the war.[16] Adding to the potential for conflict, Parker attempted (with the approval of the Georgetown Freedmen's Bureau agent) to install as overseer Dennis Hazel, the former slave driver.[17]

In March 1866, according to Parker and Hazel's account, Parker sent his son and Hazel to deliver work orders to the people at Keithfield, but the men's authority to direct plantation labor was repudiated by Abram, whom the freedpeople had appointed their foreman. Parker's son threatened to bring Abram before the local provost marshal and "break him," but he then left the plantation. Abram called the women and men in from the field. The work gang turned their tools—"Axes hatchets hoes and poles"—into weapons, and attacked Hazel, threatening to kill him. Hazel escaped and, that afternoon, returned to the plantation with Parker's son and two soldiers. On their appearance, the people assaulted them with their tools and pelted them with bricks and stones.

Sukey and Becky entered the fray armed with heavy clubs. Joined by Jim, they exhorted their fellow laborers to join the fight, "declaring that the time was come and they must yield their lives if necessary—that a life was lost but once, and they must try and kill" the intruders. The crowd was then joined by eight or ten "infuriated women," including Charlotte Simons, Susan Lands, Clarrisa Simons, Sallie Mayzck, Quashuba and Magdalen Moultrie, who were armed with heavy clubs and hoes, and backed by four or five men. The women made a point of their particular hatred for the former slave driver, Hazel, by focusing their attack on him; the soldiers' efforts to defend Hazel from their blows were "entirely ineffectual." Parker pleaded with the women to let up their attack on Hazel, promising to leave and let Freedmen's Bureau authorities settle the matter, but, as he recalled, "the mob was not to be reasoned with." The freedmen called to the women, "kill him, now is your time, don't let him get away." Three times, Parker called on the freedmen to "exert themselves," to stop and force back what he described as "the maddened women." The freedmen replied to Parker that he "had no business over there anyhow—that no white man could control them now they were free."

Sukey and Becky then turned their attack from Hazel onto Parker. Sukey took a hickory stick out of Parker's hands and beat him with it over his back; both she and Becky delivered a series of heavy blows to his head. One of the soldiers, "his face covered with blood" and apparently disarmed by the freedpeople, "beseeched his comrade to shoot" at the mob, but Parker insisted no shooting take place, "fearing such a measure might further madden the desperate mob." Parker and Hazel turned to make a hasty retreat, begging the men to keep the women back, but before Parker could escape he was "struck very heavily over my right eye with a club in the hands of a woman Becky—the blow bringing blood instantly, and making me stagger with blindness—[.]" He noted that "vigorous efforts to strike me again were continued by women among whom I recognized Sukey, Becky, Quashuba, Charlotte Susan." Now fearing for his life, Parker (followed by Hazel) made the only escape he could, by jumping into the river and swimming out to their boat, "under a shower of missiles." Parker and Hazel left the soldiers to make their own escape by foot, bloodied and disarmed by the freedpeople.

Later, an armed guard of U.S. soldiers settled the incident by arresting several of the ringleaders. Three of the freedmen were charged with inciting the freedwomen to violence; five of the women served sentences in the local jail. Labor unrest at Keithfield would recur in the year to follow, when freedpeople continued to reject Parker's efforts to direct their labor.[18] Although the Freedmen's Bureau agent called the violence attending the Keithfield incident "unusual," reports from across the lowcountry noted the vigor of women's participation in resisting rice planters who attempted to reclaim their plantations and to reinstate overseers and former slave drivers. The reports confirmed the fears of bureau agents who knew that freedpeople were cultivating so-called abandoned lands "in anticipation of being left to enjoy the fruits of their labors." Agents anticipated that the return of planters would invariably lead to "serious difficulties," but they seemed surprised at the role played by women.[19]

Negotiating a Return to Labor

Planters and overseers were so intent on regaining control of the rice plantations (and bureau and military personnel so determined that this was in
the best interests of all lowcountry residents) that they failed to realize what
freedwomen and men soon demonstrated: Restoration was only an incremental concession.[20] It was just the beginning of a long process of negotiation on lowcountry plantations. It was not unusual for rice planters, their
land restored, to discover that freedpeople still "were not willing to make
any contracts, inasmuch as the contract system would tend to bring them
back into a state of slavery again."[21]

Along the Santee River, a region the Georgetown bureau agent described
as "in a very unsettled state," planters quickly discovered how freedpeople
could render restoration a hollow victory for planters. Many rice planters
simply found that they could not negotiate with freedpeople; "the word of
the planters to the freedpeople has no weight." The apparent accidental
burning of a Santee river planter residence, following restoration, dissuad-
ed other planters from returning.[22] In 1866, and continuing at least through
1868, many freedpeople left restored plantations for nearby pinelands, squat-
ting where they could clear small patches of land and cultivate provision
crops, rather than accept the terms offered by planters or the Freedmen's
Bureau. In 1866, one bureau agent estimated that perhaps three hundred
freedpeople in the parishes of St. Thomas, Santee, and St. James were living and planting small subsistence crops in the pinelands.[23]

Combahee River planters reported that even on their restored plantations, freedpeople rejected all efforts, by planters and the bureau, to contract for the upcoming season.[24] Backed by federal military force in their
repossession of plantation lands, planters could threaten resident freedpeople who refused to contract with eviction, but as one Santee River planter noted, freedpeople remained "entirely indisposed for any thing like
regular, systematic work, What they want is to be left alone."[25] Oliver Middleton reported that when he returned to his restored plantation with an
escort of U.S. soldiers, his former slaves turned their backs on him and
"they simply asked the guard 'what had they brought *that man there for*'"
and "refused most positively" to enter into a labor contract with him.[26]

The owner of two Waccamaw River rice plantations returned in early
1866 to discover that nearly sixty women and men, formerly his slaves,
had resided on and cultivated the plantations in his absence, and now, "in
a state of utter insubordination, refused to contract, claiming the right to
remain on the places." They insisted "they will only work in their own way

& at such times as they think fit, without the supervision of an agent or any white man & insist upon renting the lands, they to fix the amount to be paid us according to their notions of justice."[27] The former slaves' determination to cultivate plantation crops without the planter's intervention led him to call in Union soldiers to help him gain control over the workforce, but the freedpeople repelled the soldiers, pelting them with stones and beating them. A "strong detachment" of soldiers was necessary to force off those freedpeople who refused to work under the planter, but a few of the "most turbulent" left the plantation voluntarily, apparently unwilling to work for their former owner under any terms.[28]

Williams Middleton also discovered that restoration of his several plantations late in November 1865 was only a partial victory. Repeated visits by his overseer had proven fruitless in gaining any agreement from freedpeople to contract for the new planting season. This proved to be the case on many Combahee and Ashepoo River rice plantations, that freedpeople "even with the prospect of starvation staring them in the face refuse to contract for work of any kind."[29] According to Middleton's overseer, "they say further, that if they consent to work for or under their former owners, it is like returning again to slavery." By mid-February, they refused to contract and refused to leave the plantation; Middleton's overseer wrote that the freedpeople "speak in very defiant terms & say you had better not come on the plantation—nothing can be done there until you go or send and get a military force and put off all the leaders, they tell me they will not contract with you and will not leave the place." (Later that spring, Middleton was able to persuade a very small force of freedpeople to cut and sell lumber from his land, but even that small operation was dependent on Middleton's ability to furnish the workers with rations.)[30] Middleton eventually leased most of his plantation lands to local men and a "Yankee Captain" who had some degree of success in raising crops.

Another planter, Arnoldus VanderHorst, also encountered the delaying tactics of freedpeople; four months after the restoration of his Chickasee plantation, VanderHorst returned but discovered that "the Negroes refused to make any contract with him the first day saying that they would not work for any man, on the second day they cooled off & showed indications of a better feeling"—he expected to make terms with them as soon as he could get an officer to visit from Walterborough. The freedpeople "looked like fiends upon him," but forty-six eventually signed the labor contract.[31]

Even with the threat of bureau intervention and evictions, freedpeople appear to have gained considerable leverage by not accepting the contract labor system, even temporarily; "the continuance of this state of determination for a very few weeks longer will effectually render vain any attempts at planting in the coming year."[32] Thus, at some point, freedpeople's absolute refusal to sign labor contacts evolved into a tactical delay. According to observers, some lowcountry freedpeople withheld their consent to labor contracts (and thus their labor power) deliberately, manipulating the planter's concern for the crop, thereby gaining better contract terms.[33] Although complaints and reports about the delay in contracting did not single out the role of freedwomen, their participation is suggested by the antebellum division of labor; in rice agriculture, sowing rice seed was designated as "women's work," and any delay in planting would have relied heavily on freedwomen's cooperation and support.

The impact of the delay in agreeing to contract terms was nearly universally intensified by the refusal of freedpeople in the previous fall and winter to prepare the rice fields and irrigation systems for the 1866 crop.[34] Delays in planting also threatened to place the maturing rice crop at risk of the depredations of rice birds, or bobolinks.[35] At a time when landowners were especially dependent on a good year's crop to ward off further debt and impoverishment, such delays threatened not only the immediate crop but also the planters' ability to survive the financial crisis of the postwar period.[36] As one South Carolinian explained from the pages of the *Charleston Daily Courier:* "A strike among factory operatives may stop the engines and looms for a few days or weeks, but the work can then be resumed without serious damage to anyone. But the suspension of labor in an agricultural region for a month or two, is quite a different affair, and plantations left without laborers for such a period must suffer, and if this continues much longer, the damage will be irreparable at least for twelve months to come."[37]

When Lieutenant Colonel B. F. Smith assumed command of the military post at Georgetown at the close of 1865, he found that every labor contract made that year had been broken; that the crops raised were barely sufficient to keep people from starving; that no contracts had been made for the upcoming season; and that the small military force under his command was quite inadequate to lend the authority of the state to the planters in the region, particularly in the area of the Santee River, which was "very unsettled."[38] One month later, Smith described the strategies deployed by freedpeople in resisting contracts for the year. Freedwomen and men, he reported, "now positively refuse to make any Contracts unless they have the control of the crops themselves, the planters to have little or nothing to say in the matter, but to receive a portion of the crop raised. It is really wonderful, how unanimous they are[,] communicating like magic, and now holding out, knowing the importance of every day in regards to the welfare of the next crop, thinking that the planters will be obliged to come to their terms." Smith also recognized the collaborative nature of freedpeople's resistance and believed that when some freedpeople finally agreed to sign labor contracts with planters, other freedpeople would eventually follow suit. But for the time being, the freedpeople in Georgetown District were not agreeing to the terms deemed reasonable by rice planters, the military, or the bureau. Large numbers of freedpeople were, at the behest of planters, being forcibly evicted from plantations by the army—filling nearby roads and woods with vagrants. This last job, complained Smith, required a larger military force than he had at his disposal, but he tried to honor the requests by planters that freedpeople refusing to contract for the next year be evicted.[39]

In 1865, military and civilian agents of Reconstruction viewed freedpeople's resistance to restoration and contract labor as a threat to the immediate peace and good order of the lowcountry, an obstacle to the military's efforts to prevent further starvation and its efforts to bring peace to the Southern countryside. By 1866, freedpeople's continued resistance to the restoration of the lowcountry rice plantation economy was construed by some military and civilian agents of Reconstruction as a conscious and ill-informed rejection of the tenets of free labor during the crucial, first full year of freedom.[40] Freedpeople' resistance, the refusal of so many planter families to acknowledge defeat and accept the consequences of emancipation, and the efforts of South Carolina's newly restored state legislature to reinscribe slavery through the black code all predicted the continued intervention of the War Department (through the military and the bureau) in the reconstruction of the state and the plantation economy. The escalation of federal debates over the politics of Reconstruction, which had resumed in the December session of the Thirty-ninth Congress, did not bode well for a quick and easy replacement of military occupation with civil government.

The local military command, still a crucial player in the reconstruction process, turned in 1866 to redressing the missteps taken by South Carolina's restored state government. Complying with instructions from General-in-Chief Ulysses S. Grant, the commander of the Department of South Carolina, General Sickles, ordered that "all laws shall be applicable alike to all the inhabitants" of the state. Yet Sickles's order went much further than simply abrogating the black code; in essence, his order replaced the black code's attempt to regulate lowcountry labor relations. The order attempted to assure that "the rights and duties of the employer, and the free laborer respectively, may be defined; that the soil may be cultivated and the system of free labor fairly undertaken," asserting the property rights of the planter and the right to employment among former slaves. To accomplish this unimpeded transition to free labor, Sickles not only demanded the abrogation of any law applied to one race and not another, but also sought to remove any other constraints on the free market, including "combinations or agreements" to set compensation for labor or to prevent the sale or hire of land. Sickles threatened to evict freedpeople who refused reasonable employment; established the responsibility of freedmen for the support of "their relatives"; and threatened "vagrants" (freedpeople who refused reasonable employment) with involuntary labor at the discretion of district commanders, on roads, fortifications, or other public works. The army was ordered to regulate the distribution of rations to freedpeople in such a way as to assure that relief did not encourage idleness or vagrancy. Finally, Sickles expanded the responsibilities of commanding officers of districts, subdistricts, and posts by authorizing them to perform the duties of Freedmen's Bureau agents in the absence of such agents.[41]

Military authorities and bureau agents, from the Savannah River north to Georgetown, faced a daunting task in enforcing Sickles's orders. A Cooper River agent described "large numbers of freedmen . . . collected on vacant plantations, refusing to engage to work"; bureau agents and army officers alike anticipated "some trouble" from these "idlers" in forcing them to enter labor contracts for the year.[42] When Sickles's orders were read to freedpeople on one Georgetown plantation, they "said that they were free and would follow there own orders."[43] By late February, in the vicinity of Georgetown, bureau agents had convinced only a portion of the people on plantations to enter into contracts; freedpeople continued to "squat" on unrestored plantations, further frustrating the bureau's efforts to organize plantation labor.[44]

Along the Combahee River, freedpeople continued to "refuse to work for wages at any price." They were in such agreement on this matter that the local commander, General James C. Beecher, thought them to be acting in concert; he believed "there is a settled combination to refuse contracts of any kind on Combahee River plantations," for which he blamed "Freedmen's Bureau waiverings and Civilian stupidity."[45] Beecher was also aware of how quickly resistance spread among lowcountry freedpeople; it was common in his district for one plantation community's resistance to fuel unrest on neighboring plantations, and freedpeople readily fled restored plantations for nearby "abandoned" lands. Lowcountry rice planters quickly realized that labor unrest often had an impact beyond the immediately affected plantation. They knew no one would rent in an area of labor unrest until, as one prospective lessee noted, "the negroes are put down."[46]

The gathering of freedpeople on abandoned plantations had an unsettling impact on neighboring restored plantations, and because of this Beecher insisted that "it is absolutely necessary to organize labor on *all* the plantations. Otherwise," he explained, "those refusing to contract will simply go on these unorganized plantations and squat there, to be uprooted again when the owners come."[47] Beecher believed that the "stalemate" between landowners and laborers in the rice plantation district of the Combahee and Ashepoo Rivers would result in a year's loss both for the planter and the freedpeople—who would then either starve or rely, for another year, on government support. Dependence would, in turn, jeopardize the success of free labor in the lowcountry. Believing that the contract system's offer of fair work for fair wages was preferable to starvation or pauperism ("two years of honest free labor for fair wages will better fit the majority of freedpeople for Citizenship than the gift of 40 or 400 acres will do"), Beecher began systematic evictions of freedwomen and freedmen from plantations where they continued to reject contract labor outright. By late January 1866, Beecher had "cleared out" eight plantations. On plantations not yet restored to planters, Beecher was far less successful at persuading freedpeople to agree to contract labor.[48]

The Contract Labor System

Eventually, a sizable number of lowcountry freedwomen and men entered the labor contract system. Yet given the extent of their initial and ongoing resistance, it is unlikely that they saw in the system what bureau agents hoped they did: an opportunity to "develop the habits of a free labor economy, and come to understand their fundamental harmony of interests" with former owners and planters. While providing the basis for bureau enforcement of their rights as specified under the contracts and offering some level of protection against unscrupulous employers, the contracts also exacted a heavy price from freedpeople. Contracts bound laborers to terms they may not have understood and certainly could not reread for clarification; circumscribed their mobility and right to leave an abusive or exploitative employer; and rendered them dependent upon the understaffed and too frequently unsympathetic bureau and military posts for enforcement and redress.[49] Contracts based on wages rather than shares also significantly undervalued freedwomen's labor.

Why, then, did freedpeople ultimately "consent" to the contract labor system? Perhaps enough planters made use of the "Yankees'" threat "to turn them, everyone, off the plantation" if they failed to sign,[50] and perhaps freedpeople's ties to specific locations were ultimately too important to sacrifice. Starvation most likely left thousands of freedpeople without other choices; first the military department and then the bureau decided to withhold rations from freedpeople they deemed capable of earning a living ("all able-bodied negroes") but refusing to sign labor contracts. Planters viewed this as a successful strategy—for those planters who could afford to offer laborers rations as part of their labor arrangements. One planter described the ability to provide rations to workers as "the sine qua non of success" in resuming some semblance of plantation production. Planters who could not found themselves still without workers.[51]

The imposition of the contract labor system insinuated the army and the bureau more fully into the reconstruction of rice plantation labor, since it fell upon these organizations to approve, adjudicate, and settle the final disposition of contracts.[52] (Garret Nagle, a bureau agent posted in Colleton District, reported adjudicating two hundred cases in a five-month period in 1866.)[53] While planters, in turn, hoped the closely supervised labor system might help secure a reliable and malleable workforce,[54] freedpeople saw otherwise. Affixing their mark to labor contracts did not end freedpeople's involvement in labor conflict or negotiations over plantation labor, any more than restoration had completed the reconstruction of the plantation economy. Instead of becoming acquiescent, freedwomen and men turned to a new series of battles with former slaveowners: making the terms and conditions of their work as emancipated laborers and their lives as plantation residents distinct from what they had been forced to endure as slaves.

Freedpeople who yielded to the contract labor system may have become less inclined to attack returning planters, but their resentment and considerable resistance continued unabated. In some cases, the hostility of contracting freedpeople toward former owners and planters was palpable. In January 1867 E. B. Heyward returned to Amsterdam plantation for the first time since the war. He reported of his former slaves, "It is very evident that they are disappointed at my coming here; they were in hopes of getting off again this year and having the place to themselves. They received me very coldly; in fact it was some time before they came out of their houses to speak to me. . . . They are as familiar as possible and surprise me in their newly acquired 'Beaufort manner.'"[55] Five months later, Heyward was hoping their attachment to the plantation would prevail over their disappointment with his return. Heyward ridiculed their sense of the plantation as home; "they love it, *most exceedingly*—'dey hang pon um.'" But in the context of the postwar labor shortage, Heyward also recognized the usefulness of, and so manipulated, their attachment; "now I avail myself of this, to attach them still more to it." Heyward's former slaves did remain on his plantation but, in their newly acquired bold and assertive manner, informed Heyward "that the land ought to belong to the man who (alone) *could work it*—That I couldn't do more than sit in the house and lay my foot on the table and write on the paper." Heyward, like many lowcountry planters, soon realized that keeping the freedpeople on his plantation was one thing, controlling their labor, another. Conflict loomed, never far distant.[56]

Like the men and women on Heyward's plantation, many freedpeople entered into labor contracts for the 1866 season (more than four thousand freedpeople entered contracts in Georgetown District alone) but worked according to their own preferences, frequently disregarding the terms set forth in the written contracts.[57] The exacting language of the contracts, and the activities planters tried to prohibit or closely regulate through them, offer one window onto specific areas of debate within the contract labor system. Other evidence of specific areas of conflict between planters and plantation laborers is found in the many complaints filed with bureau agents and officers at local military posts, sometimes describing in great detail the kinds of disputes likely to erupt during the lowcountry's contested transition to a free-labor future.

Because of their preemptive language, labor contracts are particularly useful as models of what planters hoped postemancipation labor would *not* look like. They also indicate areas the planters believed could become points of contention. Bureau agents also tried to anticipate problems via the contracts, for example, inserting clauses that assured even those workers discharged for violations of the contract some payment for their labor. While freedpeople often contested the terms and language of contracts and sought changes before agreeing to them, they also attempted to renegotiate their work in practice, as specific issues developed. Contracts are therefore not especially useful as evidence of what happened after they were approved. Neither can they be taken to represent the larger universe of plantation arrangements; more plantations apparently operated without contracts than with them, and the contracts now extant may not even represent the small universe of contracts that once were entered into. Also, rarely did either planters or freedpeople adhere closely to the terms and regulations established by the contracts. Still, there is such significant agreement among the extant lowcountry contracts in the ways they attempted to circumscribe behavior and regulate labor that they merit our consideration.[58]

Unlike 1865 labor contracts, between 1866 and 1868 nearly all lowcountry contracts specified the labor to be performed (oftentimes an exhaustive list of chores followed by the sweeping phrase, "all such labor . . . as may be connected with & necessary for the raising, harvesting & protecting of the crop").[59] They spelled out the obligations of the employer (typically to provide rations, clothing, garden space, and acreage where freedpeople could cultivate independent rice crops) and the terms of remuneration (among lowcountry contracts, typically a half or third share of the crop), specifying fines for absence or contract violations.

Lowcountry planters and bureau agents also used labor contracts to introduce regulations or prohibitions addressing particular aspects of plantation life and labor, areas that had been significant points of disagreement in 1865. A great many contracts specifically required laborers to perform mudwork—work that freedpeople had refused to perform in the previous year. Their refusal had prompted many complaints to the bureau from planters. Nonetheless, bureau agents and many local military commanders had declined to force freedpeople to perform this or any other postharvest work that had not been specified in the 1865 labor contracts. To assure themselves that the yearly maintenance of the irrigation system— indeed, the repairs that five years of neglect now required—would be performed, planters inserted in many labor contracts a requirement that freedpeople perform the hated work or pay, out of their share of the final crop, the labor costs of having the work performed by outside laborers.[60] In so doing, planters were essentially trying to shift, to freedpeople, some of the costs of plantation operations in the new economy (one contract even specified the withholding of one-tenth of the crop as a way of sharing operation costs between freedpeople and planters).[61]

Planters also tried to use contracts to regulate specific areas of plantation life well beyond the rice fields. They prohibited the sale of agricultural products by freedpeople, a stipulation sometimes reinforced with regulations against freedpeople's ownership of boats. In freedom no less than in slavery, planters sought to repress the active trade among lowcountry African Americans in rice, cotton, and other goods that were sometimes stolen out of the fields and barns and sold in an active trading network along lowcountry waterways. In their efforts to prevent theft, however, planters attempted to prohibit all independent trade, even when contracts set aside land and time for freedpeople to cultivate independent crops for market.[62]

Many contracts also instituted fence laws; freedpeople were required to fence their own animals and, sometimes in addition, to fence their own crops against planters' free-ranging stock.[63] Not all freedwomen accepted such a fundamental alteration in traditions of land use. One freedwoman on Windsor plantation directly and positively refused orders from the planter's son to pen up her poultry or to replant his damaged corn crop. "This woman of whom I complain," he wrote to the bureau, "skreeches out that no one can make her leave her house to set out [replant] the corn destroyed."[64]

Two additional points of anticipated conflict were reflected in prohibitions against visitors, gatherings, and meetings ("They will neither have, nor allow any meetings or gatherings of people on said plantation")[65] and against impertinence and insubordinate language (including "any improper or disorderly conduct" and "using improper or insulting language to our employers or their agents").[66] Planters and bureau agents hoped labor contracts would either preempt disputes about the terms and conditions of rice plantation labor, or deny freedpeople the opportunity to meet and organize around their grievances. Conflicts nonetheless arose very frequently and were recorded in the records of complaints filed with the Freedmen's Bureau and the local military command.

One of the most common complaints made by planters was that freedwomen and men, in sundry ways, disregarded the contracts they had entered into and insisted that they alone determine the important distinction between slave and free labor on lowcountry rice plantations. For example, freedpeople on William R. Maxwell's plantation insisted that "they control both their time & their Labour," and worked far shorter days than Maxwell believed they should. In addition, he complained, "they are striving with all that lack of days labour to obtain Saturday entire as a day of rest, & I object, as the Contract specially provides against it." The freedpeople on his plantation may have pushed for Saturdays off when they discovered that the printed contract forms supplied by the Freedmen's Bureau that year—used by some of their neighbors—gave freedwomen who were also heads of families half of each Saturday off.[67] Also according to Maxwell's complaint, the freedpeople on his plantation gained some confidence in challenging the terms of their contracts from the fact that three neighboring plantations were still abandoned, "overtaken" with freedpeople who refused contract labor altogether, and who used the abandoned plantations as a "place of refuge."[68]

Regardless of the terms of their contracts, lowcountry freedpeople—men and women—made use of the rating assigned to individual laborers under the task system (as prime or full hands, half-hands, quarter-hands, etc.) to reject the burden of work they had performed as "prime" slaves. Freedpeople who as slaves had been rated "prime" hands by owners or overseers insisted on contracting, or working, as partial hands instead. Many simply contracted for a share of the final crop, deciding to make a smaller crop by working less than full time.[69] This was not only a defense of the task system, as the historian John Scott Strickland has suggested;[70] it was an effort by freedpeople to deploy and even extend the leverage they had recourse to under that system. John Irving, a Cooper River rice planter, was frustrated that nothing could persuade the freed people to contract as full hands—not even stern lectures to freedwomen and men by the assistant commissioner of the Freedmen's Bureau in South Carolina on the necessity of contract labor. "Even the firmest men," Irving complained, "when they came to sign, would only pledge themselves to do *half* task, and in many instances *quarter* task, thereby curtailing the daily labor so much as to put it entirely out of the power of my neighbors to plant more than half a crop." Irving reported that "when some of the freedmen came up to sign their contracts," freedpeople insisted that the contract be altered to indicate they would not perform mudwork, labor under white supervision, or accept anyone's decision but their own as to how much task work they would perform.[71] From his post at Georgetown, Lieutenant Colonel B. F. Smith similarly complained that freedwomen and men worked only partial tasks, and only until noon; "no reasoning can induce them to do more," he reported. By the end of June, freedpeople were still working less than rice planters and Northern agents of reconstruction wanted them to; "it has been impossible," noted Smith, "to persuade them to perform more than their allotted tasks."[72] One planter, Olney Harleston, similarly complained that the thirty-three freedpeople who signed his contract would agree to perform half tasks only, disregarding both his advice and direction.[73]

Women and Field Labor

Although both freedmen and freedwomen insisted on setting the terms of their labor according to their own ideas about what freedom meant, it was freedwomen's refusal to work as they had under slavery that planters and Northern agents of reconstruction commented on most bitterly and most frequently. More than one planter complained to the Freedmen's Bureau that he was "forced to discharge my freedwomen for neglect and refusal to do less than reasonable tasks."[74] The planter E. B. Heyward's complaints in 1867 were typical:

> The women have got rather lazy and try your patience severely. The work progresses very slowly and they seem perfectly indifferent. . . . The women appear most lazy, merely because they are allowed the opportunity. They wish to stay in the house, or in the garden all the time—If you chide them, they say "Eh ch! Massa, aint I mus' mind de fowl, and look a' me young corn aint I mus watch um." And to do this, the best hand on the place will stay at home all day and every day.

Heyward also noted that the "men are scarcely much better"; men and women both seemed to "feel bound as a slave and work under constraint, are impudent, careless and altogether very provoking." As a consequence, Heyward was cautious in his interactions with them, saying, "If the women get mad I am gone, for they run in their holes like Fiddlers and won't come out. I therefore never quarrel. . . . I avoid all difficulties, and make a kind of retreating fight." The freedwomen working on his cousin's plantation also "come out on a kind of frolic and sow and cover his rice doing it of course abominably. All the work is badly done."[75]

John DeForest, a bureau agent in upcountry South Carolina, was among the first to label freedwomen's rejection of a "prime" hand's labor and their seeming withdrawal from field labor as the "evil of female loaferism." DeForest—whose memoir is frequently cited by historians as contemporary evidence of women's universal rejection of field labor—noted that "myriads of women who once earned their own living now have aspirations to be like white ladies and, instead of using the hoe, pass the days in dawdling over their trivial housework, or gossiping among their neighbors." DeForest's characterization of women's social and reproductive labor as "trivial" was undoubtedly as firmly rooted in the devaluation of (white) women's house work in the North, as in the judgment he was also making about freedwomen's unpaid labor in and connected to the support of their own households. Yet his comment serves to point out that the characterization of "female loaferism" was as concerned with the kind of work freedwomen were choosing to perform as with their rejection of field work for the planter. Both issues were important to the way Northern and Southern whites viewed the decisions freedwomen were making.

What was the extent of women's withdrawal? Even DeForest was careful to add that he "did not mean that all women were thus idle; the larger proportion were still laboring afield, as of old; rigid necessity held them up to it." The withdrawal of some women from the waged workforce, he concluded, was gaining popularity among freedpeople just as it had "among us white men and brethren."[76] Most observers commenting on freedwomen's seeming rejection of field labor failed to qualify its extent, as DeForest had; planters from across the state reported that freedwomen would simply stay in their cabins if starvation didn't drive them to work. Freedwomen "generally decline to work altogether and depend on their lords [husbands] for their support," reported one planter in May 1866, although another nearby planter relied on a plantation labor force composed of two freedwomen to every freedman.[77]

Freedwomen's efforts to shape their labor on lowcountry rice plantations from within the contract labor system are partially documented in the surviving labor contracts filed by lowcountry planters with the Freedmen's Bureau between 1865 and 1868. Although labor contracts offer at best an incomplete record of labor arrangements in the postwar era, they do suggest some important trends in the labor force participation of men and women, trends that appear consistent with the descriptive examples from other sources provided so far.[78]

Freedwomen's enrollment on the labor contracts (see table 1) suggests that they were continuing to work in the lowcountry rice fields, but they increasingly rejected *full-time* field labor between 1866 and 1868. During those years, in Georgetown District (the lowcountry's penultimate rice-growing region), freedwomen's names were consistently about half of those signed to the contracts—which was very close to the proportion of slave women who were working in the rice fields before the war.[79] Nonetheless, their intent to decrease the amount of agricultural labor they performed for planters was demonstrated by their signing the contracts not as prime or full hands but as three-quarter or half hands. While a large number of contracting freedwomen continued to work as full hands, there were many women who insisted on working less than a full hand would. Drawing on a subset of labor contracts (where the assigned men and women were rated as full or partial hands), we learn that the percentage of freedwomen contracting as full hands on Georgetown plantations had declined from nearly 69 percent of the women in 1866 to 34 percent in 1868. During the same years, in this same subset of all contracted hands, the percentage of freedmen contracting as full hands also declined, but at a much slower rate—from 81 percent to 70 percent.[80]

Table 1. Georgetown Labor Contracts, 1866–68

	1866		1867		1868	
	Women	Men	Women	Men	Women	Men
Number of rated hands	800	749	812	669	191	161
(total rated and unrated)	(2088)	(2267)	(1461)	(1409)	(586)	(601)
Percentage contracting as						
full hands	68.75	81	54.4	81.3	34	70
¾ hands	11	6	16.2	6.27	31.9	18
½ hands	17.75	7.87	27	9.27	29.3	11
¼ hands	2.5	2.8	1.9	3.1	4.7	—
Number of contracts with rating	57		45		14	
(total number of contracts)	(171)		(88)		(38)	

Sources: Labor Contracts, Ser. 3210 and 3211, Georgetown, South Carolina, Subassistant Commander, and Reports of Contracts Approved in the Subdistricts, Ser. 2930, South Carolina Assistant Commander, both in RG 105.

For freedwomen, freedom differed from slavery in part because they could control the extent and the rate of their entry into the plantation labor force.[81] This undoubtedly became more critical as the bureau, the army, and lowcountry planters deployed a range of strategies to convince or coerce freedpeople to enter contractual labor arrangements. Freedwomen were not withdrawing from field labor; the proportion of women in the contracting workforce was not declining; instead, they were battling, with planters, the military, and local bureau agents, over their right to shape the conditions and terms of their plantation labor, thereby seeking greater control over the allocation of their paid and unpaid work.

Women and Domestic Employment

The strategies employed by freedwomen during the transition from slave to free labor in the rice and provision fields of lowcountry plantations were mirrored by those whose employment brought them into planter residences. Just before the war, from one-third to one-half of the slave workforce on lowcountry rice plantations had consisted of domestic servants, artisans, and other slaves with specialized work assignments.[82] These slaves, who maintained plantation operations outside the rice fields or waited on the planter families, had an experience of slavery very different from that of field hands. Without the apparent separation between "master's time" and their own time that the task system permitted, house servants faced a more personal and daily struggle to limit the demands made on them, either by the planter family or by the pace of plantation production. Female house servants were subject to the disadvantages of a forced intimacy with slaveowning families, which included a degree of vulnerability to sexual exploitation. This had been a pervasive feature of African-American women's experience of domestic service in slavery, and it especially demarcated male and female experience in the "big house." With the arrival of Union troops, and their plantation-by-plantation appearance throughout the lowcountry, former slave women began to challenge the subservience that had permeated their labor and their relations with whites as domestic servants.

In the immediate aftermath of war, female domestic servants, like field hands, had first resorted to a work stoppage. Following the appearance of Union troops during March 1865, planters' families frequently complained to each other of having to perform their own domestic labor such as washing, cooking, and cleaning, "their servants having all left them."[83] Servants who violated the work stoppage risked reprimand from kin or other former slaves. One plantation mistress reported, in March 1865, that her former slave Ruis "gave his wife (Ellen) a fearful beating" because she ignored the general work stoppage on the plantation and waited on her former owner.[84] On another plantation, a former slave woman named Gabriella "ordered" two servant women to leave the planter household and join the other freedpeople in the fields instead.[85]

In the first year of freedom, some servants preferred to leave their former owners and find new employers, rather than fight with former owners over what they would and would not continue to do as free laborers. And still others, such as fifteen-year-old Rebecca Jane Grant, sought only to reunite with their families. "We had been done freed," she noted; her uncle "stole me by night from my Missus," so that she could return to her own family, from whom she had been sold away.[86] Planters, however, viewed the training of new servants as burdensome, and some forcibly prevented their former servants from seeking employment elsewhere. While ex-Confederate guerrillas were harassing former slaves in the Santee River neighborhoods of Charleston District, local planters asked them also to track down and return house servants who fled their former owners.[87]

Some freedwomen who tried to exercise their new mobility suffered the painful consequences of a domestic slave's constant proximity to slaveowners. Mistresses who had treated their domestic slaves' children as pets resisted separation from those children when freedwomen decided it was time to leave. Even worse, the children themselves may have resisted separation, having formed strong attachments to the white women who undoubtedly had more time to spend with them than did their enslaved mothers. The wartime diarist Mary Chesnut recorded the drama of a three-year-old child, "a great pet," who "did not wish to go even with his mother." The child was "torn" from the arms of the mistress by "ruthless Yanks" and turned over to his mother. The mother—whose torment and fury over slavery's interference with her child's loyalties and attachments can only be imagined—was described by the mistress as running away with her child, "whipping this screaming little rebel darky every foot of the way." Like other former slaves who found their freedom so quickly revoked, this mother and her child were soon forcibly returned by rebel pickets. The three-year-old was denied the opportunity to renew his attachments; both mother and child were banished from the house by the angry and jealous mistress.[88]

When house servants began to reappear voluntarily at the planter residences during the summer and fall of 1865 in search of employment, they tried to implement significant changes in their work and in their relations with the white women who now employed, rather than owned, them. Freedwomen continued in 1866 and 1867 to press forward those changes. In attempting to distinguish their work as wage laborers from their experience of slavery, freedwomen focused many of their efforts on undermining the fundamental characteristic of domestic service in slavery: slaveowners' demand for the undivided attention and loyalty of servants. Freedwomen did this in two fundamental ways: by trying to focus their employment on the tasks to be performed rather than the people to be served; and by explicitly preferring labor arrangements designed to accommodate their own familial interests and responsibilities.

To the provocation of many women of the planter families, freedwomen insisted that domestic service be broken down into several tasks or occupations: washing, cooking, cleaning, and nursing became separate jobs, so that freedwomen could limit the kinds of work they performed. Rather than assume responsibility for all the personal and household needs of the planter family, freedwomen now pushed to define their work as domestic servants in terms of specific tasks and skills. In turn, plantation mistresses had to hire the services of several freedwomen rather than rely on one "Jill-of-all-trades" to serve at the beck and call of the planter family. For example, Hagar, a former slave and house servant, insisted she "was not strong enough" to do the laundry, and she refused to wash "even a towel fit to look at." She could carry water and clean the rooms, but she would not do the laundry, nor would she turn and beat the mattresses. Months later, her employer still had not found a house servant who would agree to do washing as well as cooking.[89]

Incrementally, freedwomen employed in domestic service had begun to distinguish slave from free labor. Freedwomen also began to insist on their right to reject particularly arduous or demeaning labor, prompting complaints by women of one planter family when a domestic servant refused to wash her employer's "necessaries"—her menstrual rags.[90] Freedwomen may have gained considerable satisfaction not only from freeing themselves of what they felt was demeaning labor, but also from knowing that former slaveowning women were now forced to perform such labor on their own.

Making their family responsibilities an explicit consideration in their labor arrangements, some freedwomen insisted, for example, on bringing their children along to their employer's house, in order to balance the demands of wage work and child care; others limited the hours or days of their labor.[91] Freedwomen pursued various employment strategies to accommodate their own families' needs.[92] As a consequence, most white women began to view the families of domestic servants as encumbrances and distractions; they tried their best to employ servants without families, a "quality" some prospective employers valued above cleanliness, industry, and even deference.[93] Employers resented the demands of younger children on their domestic servants ("her infant monopolizes her attentions," one plantation mistress complained)[94] but welcomed the employment of mothers who were willing to put their older children to work as well.[95]

Freedwomen in domestic service also challenged the very nature of their relationship to planter families, seeking a new level of dignity even as servants. "Have you noticed with the negroes at home," inquired one planter's wife to another, "that when you call they will never answer, every body up here finds it the case, they seem to think it is a sign of their freedom, heard one of them say, 'My Miss don't like it because I won't answer, but I ain't got no call to answer now.'"[96] Former mistresses complained (largely to each other) that former slave women studiously transgressed the rituals of subservience; they "just drop down into a chair if they come to talk to you about anything & are as free as possible."[97] White employers sometimes faced the difficult choice of firing servants or finding a way to put up with the changes freedom was bringing into their households; others began what seemed like an endless search for the perfectly deferential and obedient servant, as promising servants proved themselves too assertive for the job ("she was too impudent for anything").[98]

When female domestic servants attempted to define their own terms of labor, their efforts were made all the more difficult by the fact that plantation mistresses—no less than planters—were unwilling to concede the end of slavery and their loss of ownership and control over former slaves. White women treasured those servants they could hire who still acted "humble & civil."[99] When freedwomen struck at the core of the antebellum mythology of domestic servitude—that slave women had no lives, priorities, or identity outside their service to white families—slaveowners-turned-employers planned and schemed to prevent the return of formerly enslaved servants to their family and friends. Freedwomen became the targets of considerable hostility and bitter resentment when they chose to abandon their former owners in search of their own families.[100]

Setting new boundaries and new terms on their household labor, freedwomen also challenged their employers' presumptions of intimacy and mutual dependency with their former slaves, while at the same time undermining the plantation mistress's veneer of authority in her ability to command and manage a household of servants.[101] Freedwomen's efforts to distinguish free labor from slavery in their domestic work aroused deep feelings of betrayal in white women.[102] Thus, the "servant problem" described by so many elite white South Carolinians in the postbellum period referred not only to the shrinking supply of labor, but also to the assertiveness of freedwomen in shaping the terms and conditions of their employment.

Behind the Veil of Withdrawal

Freedwomen's insistence on working less and differently than they had as slaves was part of their strategy to take absolute control over their time and their labor, but it also may have reflected their efforts to cope with the conditions of lowcountry life after the war. Freedwomen faced the first years of freedom without the most basic necessities of domestic production and household support, forced to seek out food wherever and however it could be obtained: from the crops still in planters' fields, from the Freedmen's Bureau, from the forests and streams of the countryside. Freedwomen also improvised their employment patterns to maximize their access to food. For many, the material condition of their households was worse than it had been in slavery, and military and bureau officials had conveniently forgotten their own role in making this so.

Besides rebuilding their households, finding food, and making do with inadequate tools, freedwomen had additional responsibilities. The health of the lowcountry's former slave population had been devastated by the combined effects of wartime deprivation and hardship, by the poor crops of the immediate postwar period, and by the spread of infectious disease among lowcountry freedpeople—including smallpox and measles.[103] The provision of health care—such as it had been under slavery—had been withdrawn by rice planters as one of the punitive costs of freedom. While the Freedmen's Bureau operated hospitals and employed physicians, its overall provision of health care to freedpeople was woefully inadequate.[104] The burden of nursing the sick and dying, and burying and mourning the dead, fell heavily on families struggling to survive and to cope with the continued absence of enlisted men. The support of elderly freedpeople, also rejected as a punitive measure by planters, increased the burden of household responsibilities. The physical devastation of the countryside, the shortage of food, clothing, and the most basic necessities, and the poor crops of the 1860s all heavily increased the freedwomen's labor in their own homes. When freedwomen sought greater control over their paid and unpaid labor, they were driven not only by their determination to shape the meaning of freedom in lowcountry rice fields and planter residences, but also by the necessity of family and household survival. The survival of their families lay in the balance; laziness or an escape from hard work were luxuries they could not easily afford.

Yet white observers seemed convinced that it was a desire not to work that motivated freedwomen. Former slaveowners and other Southern whites ridiculed freedwomen's efforts to negotiate the terms of their contracted work, or to devote more of their time and resources to the direct care and support of their families, households, and independent crops. This suggests that proslavery ideology continued to affect how Southern whites viewed the actions of former slave women and the events unfolding since the war. One such assessment came from the Reverend C. W. Howard, a white Georgian familiar with these postwar events on lowcountry rice plantations, who authored a report published by the U.S. Commissioner of Agriculture in 1867.[105] Howard described the efforts by lowcountry freedpeople to shape the terms and conditions of their work, arguing that their actions revealed "the inherent defects of the race, indolence and want of thought for the morrow." These racially determined "defects," according to Howard, were evidenced in freedpeople's preference for labor arrangements that remunerated workers with ready cash rather than a share of the crop at the close of the season; in their resistance to contract labor; and in their rejection of full-time employment. According to Howard, these preferences revealed an innate desire not to work, rather than an effort to determine the conditions and terms of work.

Howard offered more than a racist analysis of lowcountry labor relations; he also made explicit the misogynistic implications of that racism. Howard's assessment of laziness as one of the "inherent defects of the race" also prompted him to assert that freedpeople were similarly averse to the work of raising and supporting a family. According to Howard, freedpeople's aversion to work not only threatened the postemancipation plantation economy but also the very survival of their race; freedpeople's supposedly characteristic laziness meant that "comparatively few negro infants will be hereafter raised."

Howard had moved easily into a discussion of infanticide (referring to African-American infants much as if discussing any other of the South's staple crops). "Infanticide," according to Howard, "was often prevented on large plantations with extreme difficulty by the most vigilant care of the mistress," reiterating the proslavery argument that slave infant mortality could be blamed on the inadequate mothering instincts of the women of an inferior race rather than on malnutrition, the overwork of pregnant and postpartum women, and the conditions of slave life in the plantation South.[106] In the aftermath of war and emancipation, Howard warned, infanticide had become more frequent; freedwomen were not only "relieved from the control [of slaveowners]" but were also "unwilling to be burdened with the expense and care of children." Although never referring explicitly to freedwomen, Howard was in fact arguing that their choices and instincts in motherhood were as degraded as their attitude toward and performance of field labor. His pronouncements echoed the arguments of proslavery idealogues like George Fitzhugh, that slavery was the only institution that could elevate the "conjugal, parental, and filial feelings" of African Americans and also compel them to work.[107] Howard's assertion that lowcountry freedwomen were racially unequipped for childraising implicitly excluded them from civilized society, even denying their basic humanity.[108]

Although Howard's statements were unusually explicit in this regard, lowcountry rice planters offered similarly degrading and dehumanizing portrayals of freedwomen. The postbellum attack on "female loaferism" by bureau agents and Southern whites was no less vicious an attack on freedwomen, given its refusal to acknowledge the conditions and obstacles freedwomen encountered in the aftermath of war and emancipation; the label also suggests how easily some Northern and Southern whites found common ground in the demonization of freedwomen.

Who's in Charge?

Another of the critical battles freedwomen waged in their effort to distinguish slavery from freedom was their refusal to labor under former slave drivers and overseers, insisting on selecting their own foremen—regardless of the fact that most of the bureau-approved labor contracts specified that foremen were to be appointed by planters. Planters anticipated former slaves' refusal to work under former overseers; one planter wrote to another, "whatever may have been the ability & fidelity of your overseer at Combahee to yourselves—I suppose there is no doubt of the ill will of the slaves to him—and in any case I do not think you could expect to renew your relations there or elsewhere *through any overseer formerly employed*— . . . the petty despot who came between you & them will never be submitted to."[109] But the refusal of Southern whites to admit the specific grounds for freedpeople's hatred of former overseers—their exploitation of the productive and reproductive labor of slaves, their sexual violence against slave women—was also a denial of the extent to which freedpeople now rejected the relations of domination so critical to their experience of slavery.[110] While Southern white men defended the sensitivities of white women to the horrors so recently perpetrated by Northern whites (they "would be averse, for the present at least, to intimate social relations with those who have been . . . connected with the suffering which they have endured"),[111] African-American women were afforded no such recognition. When these former slaves claimed the right to live and work free from their former tormentors, elite whites responded with derision. When freedwomen on El Dorado plantation secured the right to work under a foreman of their own choosing, the plantation mistress ridiculed the fact that "the 'foreman' escorts the women with an air of gallantry" to the fields, directing their labor "in the most courteous manner," addressing them as "ladies" even as they wielded their hoes in the field.[112]

The fight against the reinstatement of white overseers and former slave drivers was a struggle in which freedwomen gained particular notoriety. Freedwomen explicitly challenged the power and authority of their former overseers, purposefully and publicly violating the ritualized behavior of subservience, obedience, and submission demanded from them while slaves, at the same time escalating the protracted battle over the terms and conditions of their labor. Some overseers found freedwomen's verbal attacks on their authority so sharp as to threaten "manhood and common sense." Even agents of the Freedmen's Bureau concurred, reporting that while freedmen were "tolerably civil" toward former masters, "the women, especially those advanced in age, are abusive, with remarkable aptitude at 'billingsgate,'" the vituperative verbal weaponry exercised by women in London's famous open-air fish market.[113] Edwin Tilton, twelve years the overseer on Waverly plantation, complained in January 1866 that he was "subject of the most gross abuse" by the freedwomen, formerly slaves on the plantation, who candidly expressed their feelings about his employment on the plantation. On another plantation, freedwomen rebuked the white overseer when he attempted to revoke privileges won in slavery, such as the right to the open range of their poultry and farm animals on the plantations; in addition, they had become fierce defenders of their right to perform their labor without his supervision. One freedwoman, he reported, "has used verry abusive and somewhat threatening language to me for shooting hogs in the field," and a second freedwoman "has ordered me out of her task, saying if I come in her task again she would put me in the ditch." When the same overseer tried to take a seat in a boat being used to transport seed rice, one of the freedwomen demanded to know, as he reported, "who told me to sit down in the boat." Daunted by freedwomen's direct challenge to his authority on the plantation, this particular overseer appealed for the support of an armed guard from local military authorities.[114]

Freedwomen's repudiation of the legitimacy of overseers' authority may have been prompted by reasons beyond their outrage at their own recent and accumulated experiences of exploitation; freedwomen may also have been acting strategically on behalf of their communities, aware that sometimes the risks were different for freedmen and freedwomen who challenged whites. One overseer explained that while freedwomen challenged him, "I did not mind it so much, but when the men took to backing up the women by some of the same talk I asserted my rights as an American Citizen under abuse by at once knocking down and trouncing one of the abusers" (the same overseer suggested that the provost marshal would "be surprised" at the "actions and language" of the freedwomen and freedmen).[115] Still, overseers could and did take their revenge with freedwomen who spoke their minds.[116]

Freedpeople's resistance to the reinstatement of white overseers evoked complaints to bureau and military officials from planters throughout the lowcountry.[117] According to Olney Harleston, a Cooper River rice planter, the freedpeople he employed refused to obey his foreman; Harleston was even informed "that the hands consider my presence in the field to examine the work as offensive."[118] A planter in Georgetown District, J. Rees Ford, complained that "the negroes have refused to allow the Foreman to measure off their tasks today, they wish to appoint their Foreman and I won't consent to his acting." Ford asked the local military command to send a soldier to the plantation, to explain to the people "that I have the right and intend to appoint my Foreman."[119] Francis Bryant, a freedman on Rice Hope plantation, was arrested and charged with using disrespectful language for loudly declaiming to a white overseer that he was "damned if he would work for any White Son of a Bitch upon Rice Hope Plantation."[120] The entire workforce on Jane Pringle's plantation refused to work, even after signing a labor contract, when they discovered that their labor was to be supervised by a white man; a large number of them went into town "to get the Contract altered as they would not work under a white man!" Pringle insisted that the military take charge and force the people to work; throwing them in jail, she pointed out, would do her no good; "they can't till the land there."[121]

Freedpeople's refusal to labor under white supervision grew out of their antebellum experiences under abusive overseers and drivers, as well as the white planters' and overseers' disregard for black freedom since the war. It was prompted also by the inadequate protections offered by the agents of the state against brutal or exploitative overseers. Typical was the incident in 1865 that inspired two freedmen, Cupid Coaxan and Plenty Small, to travel more than one hundred miles to make a report to a Charleston bureau agent. At their Horry District plantation, an overseer joined by five other local whites and their bloodhounds had hunted down six former slaves who had fled the plantation on fear of being whipped by the overseer for their tardiness in getting to work that day. The white men shot one of the freedmen in the chase and delivered the others to the local jail, where they were held for a month. The overseer then escorted the freedmen back to the plantation, where he and about twenty other white men hanged the five freedmen. Coaxan and Small reported this to the local army officer, whose response was to instruct the overseer that "shooting and whipping were done with," and order the freedpeople to obey the overseer. The freedpeople, about one hundred in number, were quite unwilling to resume work under this overseer for the remainder of 1865, and they undoubtedly put little trust thereafter in the army's willingness to bring murderous or abusive white overseers to justice.

Aware of this and incidents like it, General R. K. Scott, assistant commissioner of the Freedmen's Bureau in South Carolina, acknowledged that, especially in 1866, "many of the officers in command of troops manifest an aversion to the bureau, and do not seem disposed to carry out its provisions, and I regret to say that the freed people in many localities fear the troops as much as they do their former masters. From remote districts . . . they have come on foot from 100 to 150 miles to ask justice at may hands, having no confidence in the officers commanding troops stationed near them."[122] It was not only the actions and attitudes of officers from "remote districts" that alienated the trust of freedpeople; General Beecher, overseeing the Combahee River region, grew notoriously hostile toward freedpeople and their complaints by early 1866. As one lowcountry planter understood him, "Genl. Beecher who has entirely changed his views since coming to the South, has written a long & strong report upon the condition and prospects here which he showed to one of my friends before sending on to the President. He states his opinion decidedly that the only mode of avoiding the necessity of providing food & clothing for the negroes by the government, until they die out, is to restore the plantations to their owners & refrain entirely from interference."[123] With men like Beecher posing as their friends and advocates, freedpeople may have been demonstrating remarkable foresight by avoiding labor arrangements they feared would force them to rely on bureau or military protection.

Freedwomen's opposition to the reinstatement of former overseers, like their opposition to the return of planters, indicated their concerns about what might happen outside the rice fields as well as in them. Freedwomen and men had worked under many overseers and owners who had freely violated the bodies and homes of slaves. Since the close of the war, many of those same men had made it clear that they still considered their recourse to violence as a tool of domination and labor control an "inalienable" right. That effort to reclaim power epitomized the extent to which "family" and "labor" issues were deeply entangled in the postbellum plantation economy.

The symbolic violation of freedpeople's homes became one avenue by which planters and their agents attempted to circumscribe the consequences of emancipation, avenge freedpeople's depredations on planter residences at the close of the war, and reassert the threat of violence that underlay their antebellum control over slaves. Former owners and overseers entered and searched freedpeople's homes ostensibly to reclaim property that was alleged by the planter to have been stolen from his family or the plantation. In the process of these searches, planters and their agents performed a ritualistic return to antebellum relations of power on lowcountry plantations, reclaiming their prerogative to violate, and denying freedpeople's claims to the privilege of an inviolable family sphere. Given the enthusiasm with which freedpeople had ransacked the planter residences at the close of the war, it was possible—even probable—that many planters actually were trying to recover stolen property. But no less important than the reclamation of that property was the right claimed by planters and overseers to search freedpeople's homes and persons. Even the threat of searches became a ritual contest of power, suggested when one freedwoman sent word to her former mistress that "she has nothing of mine, & she hopes we will carry her into court as then she might get back the things she lost of her own."[124]

Searches were sometimes accomplished with the assistance of an armed guard from a local military post, evoking disappointment—and outrage—among lowcountry freedpeople. They felt betrayed by Northerners' complicity in what they clearly regarded as an invasion and a return to the past, let alone a fulfillment of the threat of violence that often accompanied such searches.[125] When a search of this type occurred on Hagley plantation early in 1866, there was trouble "when the freedpeople resisted the soldiers while the latter were making a search of the former's houses for furniture belonging to the estate. One of the men Corporal Freck was severely beaten by them, and later in the darkness of the evening missiles were thrown" at an officer and the planter.[126] On another plantation, a planter and a bureau agent made a search of the freedpeople's homes, removing property that the planter identified as stolen. They ordered the freedpeople to carry the items back to the planter residence, but the people refused, saying that their work was done for the day. According to the bureau agent, the freedpeople were "most unruly and impertinent"; they "acknowledged that they had no right in the furniture but wanted to be obstinate." Having accomplished the search on this plantation, the bureau agent then went to a neighboring plantation and performed the same service there.[127]

It was not unusual for the bureau to approve searches by planters and overseers of freedpeople's homes for the purpose of recovering stolen crops. For example, Warren Thompson, a white planter on the Santee River, was charged with trespass by two different freedwomen for his unauthorized entry into their homes. But when brought before the Moncks Corner bureau agent, Thompson insisted he had found rice stolen from him; the bureau responded by recommending that Thompson bring suit against the women in the civil court system. Bureau-approved labor contracts sometimes included clauses permitting planters to enter and search the homes of contracting freedpeople.[128]

Late in 1867, a search resulted in the death of a newborn infant. The ensuing provost court trial offers closer insight into the conduct of these searches and the responses of freedwomen and men during and after. When George Singleton, a freedman, filed his complaint before the provost judge, he characterized the search of his house as "not only unlawful and cruel but also indecent."[129] According to trial records, moments after Singleton's wife had given birth to their child, two white boys and one adult white man appeared at their home with a search warrant that the overseer (the planter's son-in-law) had secured from the local magistrate (the planter's father) to search the house for stolen cotton.

Singleton tried to stop them at the door; "I asked why they searched my house instead of others? They said they had a search warrant: that I had stolen something—I asked what had I stolen? and Sam Ravinel did not answer—J. H. Porcher said they would not tell me till they had searched my house." Singleton described how the search was conducted; that after searching other rooms, Sam Ravenel

> went in my wife's room—I told him my wife was just brought to bed—he said, he did not care, he went in & knocked the window open, & went up to my wife's bed, & searched under neath it—after that he pulled the blanket off my wife, & felt all around under neath it—They were just dressing the child by the fire—when he took the blanket off, my wife had a thin dress on—he stayed in the room about one half hour, with the windows open[,] talking to me—

Singleton charged that "the searching of the bed & room of my wife by Sam Ravinel did her harm—gave her a bad cold." In a cautiously understated reference to his wife's feelings about the violation, Singleton simply asserted, "My wife did not like her be[d] being searched."[130] Perhaps suspecting that neither his wife's feelings nor his effort to protect her counted for much to the white men gathered to hear his case, Singleton chose to emphasize the death that he felt had resulted: "I think the child died from the window being open." The three white men, he concluded, left the cabin without finding the stolen cotton they later claimed to be seeking.

Although Singleton's wife did not testify at the trial, other freedwomen did. Annette Manigault, one of the attendants at the birth, had not allowed the violation of Mrs. Singleton's privacy and person to go unchallenged; she had confronted the men. "I told them that it was not right for young unmarried men to search the room where a woman was just confined." Rachel Taylor, George Singleton's aunt, was also present, and similarly challenged them: "I asked Sam. Ravenel, if he was going into the room, of a woman just put to bed, & he said he did not care, that was nothing." Taylor and Manigault were evidently claiming a prerogative for their gender that the white men felt was reserved for the women of their own race.

The men testified in court that they had been invited into the bedroom by the women attending the infant and claimed not to have touched the bed or Mrs. Singleton. They pointed out that they were threatened (without cause) by George Singleton, who "said if we went in that room, we would not come out again." Young Ravenel's open disregard for Singleton's wife and Singleton's right to defend her, even when challenged by the other women present, suggests that insult and violation were an intended part of the search. Rachel Taylor also confirmed what the freedpeople present believed was a consequence of the search: "I think the child was made sick & died from the window being opened."

In his closing statement for the defense, magistrate Rene Ravenel (the planter who initially issued the warrant) ignored the insulting and inappropriate nature of the search, blamed the midwife for the baby's death, and urged the judge to ensure that "the innocent," meaning the white men, "be protected, against the selfish and unprincipled attempts of those who desire to revenge themselves for imaginary *wrongs trespasses* and *enormities.*" Ravenel could not have made his point more clearly; freedpeople's claim that the search had violated their right to privacy, dignity, and self-defense was "imaginary." According to Ravenel and the men who conducted the search, the property rights of white planters superseded any rights claimed by freedpeople. Ravenel did not mention that the overseer had been involved in earlier disputes with freedpeople living and working at Pooshee plantation about the extent of his and the planter's authority.[131] Ravenel's rationale ultimately held sway, for although the provost judge found the young white men guilty of "Wrongs and Enormities" in their invasion of the Singleton household and fined them fifty dollars and court costs, the case was ultimately dismissed "for irregularity," four months after the trial, by the military commander.

Violence, or the threat of it, continued to be one of the means by which planters tried to control the plantation workforce. The extent and frequency of white violence against freedpeople, and the obstacles to prosecuting white perpetrators, seemed to encourage planters and their agents to see violence as one of many strategies still at their disposal. Some white South Carolinians scoffed at the idea of being legally prosecuted for their abusive treatment of the former slaves in any circumstance. Local magistrates often refused to respond to freedpeople's complaints, as was the case in Colleton District when "three or four young men gave an unmerciful beating to a couple of freedwomen." The women reported the incident to the local bureau agent, who directed them to the civil authorities; "the women returned and informed me that the magistrate told them that if they would prosecute the young men, they (the women) would have to go to jail, or give security in the sum of ($300.00) three hundred dollars that they would appear against them." In another incident, a plantation mistress noted the arrest of five local white "gentleman" by an officer of the local military post. She supposed "it must make him feel badly to arrest gentlemen" for beating former slaves, and that they would little more than "make Henry pay something for beating that negro."[132]

Planters frequently resorted to violence when freedpeople resisted their efforts to control or direct their labor. Hitting, kicking, slapping, and beating the freedmen as he had when they were slaves, William Maxwell was further enraged when they complained about his violence to the local military authorities. The Georgetown planter Benjamin Allston, apparently unable to pay market prices for seed rice for the 1866 season, had insisted that his former slaves sell their seed rice to him; when they refused, Allston struck one of them on the head with a stick. In his complaint to the local military command, the freedman insisted "I had given him no impertinent language when he struck me," as though such language would have been seen as justifying Allston's attack.

Some whites resorted to violence whenever they perceived an insult, such as when freedpeople challenged their orders. The overseer on Waverly plantation, anxious to recover tools lost during the war, insisted that the freedman Washington return an ax. Washington denied having it, and insisted that the driver knew this to be true. When a soldier finally intervened, he did so not to stop the fight that developed between the overseer and the freedman but rather to prevent any freedpeople from interfering while the overseer beat Washington. When planters and overseers used violence and violation as tools to restore their former domination, and military or bureau officials failed or were unable to prevent it, freedmen and freedwomen more aggressively pursued the independence and autonomy that they believed was not only a part of their freedom, but possibly its only protection.[133]

In the struggle between planters and freedpeople to shape free life and labor, each to their own advantage, many of the points of conflict that first arose in 1865 and 1866 continued in years after to generate discord on lowcountry rice plantations. In fact, several of these points of conflict had roots in slavery and slave resistance. The myth of task labor being "settled according to custom" was no more true in the postbellum lowcountry than it had been during slavery; the definition of tasks and task labor remained a volatile source of dispute. Fifty freedpeople on Richmond plantation decided in September 1866 not only to work as half hands but also to define for themselves what amount of work a half hand would perform. In 1867, a Colleton River plantation overseer sounded a familiar complaint: "the negroes lay up much and give much trouble about task."[134] The division of crops at the end of each year, attended by so many disturbances and disappointments, continued to inspire the fears of lowcountry whites about the possibility of insurrection by freedpeople. As a result, when freedpeople met to discuss and organize around specific contract demands for the new year, their meetings were frequently misread as paramilitary actions.[135] End-of-the-year disputes were further aggravated when military authorities evicted freedpeople who refused to enter contracts for the new year.[136]

Freedmen and women's refusal to perform mudwork on the rice plantations also remained an ongoing source of conflict, especially when they rejected such work not only after the harvest at the end of the contract year but also during the winter at the beginning of the next season's contract year.[137] This work was critical to the repair, upkeep, and continued productivity of rice plantations; a break in a bank could destroy an entire crop overnight. Planters feared that "the cultivation of Rice must languish— That custom of cleaning ditches by working them, waist deep in mud and water, cannot be continued—Compulsory labor alone continued it during slavery."[138] Along the Santee River freedpeople used planters' apprehensions to negotiate higher pay for mudwork; after the harvest of 1867, they "still refuse[d] to go into the ditches . . . they have come to this determination all along the River," noted one planter, "unless they are paid higher wages first." Without these repairs and maintenance to irrigation systems, planters' hope for future crops would be greatly diminished.

Ultimately, several rice planters considered recruiting Chinese and Irish immigrants to perform plantation mudwork, with gangs of Irish day-laborers (often hired out of Savannah) proving most available and most effective.[139] They were hired to work in the North Santee area, where freedmen refused the work unless they were paid higher wages. By the 1870s, "Irishmen in great numbers were in the habit of seeking work upon our Savannah River rice plantations during the Winter season," explained one Georgia planter; "they come out in squads of 5 or 6, and are under the head of a foreman with whom your contract is made. These men occupy any ordinary negro house, and are quiet, and orderly, in demeanor," and performed the work to many planters' satisfaction.[140] There is no evidence that freedpeople protested the employment of Irish ditch-diggers; it appears, instead, that they were glad to be free of that labor most strongly associated with slavery on lowcountry rice plantations.

Some planters believed that only a return to the particular power relations through which they had dominated and controlled their enslaved workforce before emancipation could restore the profitability of the rice plantation economy. Yet others were surprisingly adaptive as they endeavored to wield free labor into a system that planters could control and profit from. The most savvy planters took every advantage and opportunity—legal and extralegal—to increase the return on their investment in rice crops, attempting to restore their plantations to the profitable level they had known so recently.[141]

According to military officials as well as bureau agents, planters became "tenacious of the 'terms of the contract' which they themselves have disregarded throughout the season, and now wish to hold the freedman subject to all the penalties that can be imposed by it."[142] E. B. Heyward, a lowcountry planter, believed that "decent work" could not be gotten from people who were forced to remain on a plantation against their will, but his neighboring planters had learned that they could rely on the bureau to forcibly return laborers who had broken their contracts and left.[143] Other planters knew they would find a sympathetic ear in the bureau when they made complaints about freedpeople's violations of labor contracts; as one planter put it, "I do not think it is humanity to indulge such people any longer & it is high time they should be taught the sacredness of Contracts." He facetiously suggested that if freedpeople were not punished for breaking contracts, then they were denied "a fair chance of becoming good citizens."[144]

Planters were quick to learn to turn labor contracts to their own advantage; by 1866, many contracts enumerated various penalties to which freedpeople fell subject for every imaginable infraction of their contracts. Fines were assessed for each perceived act of insolence, as well as for days missed due to illness, childbirth, and unexcused absences, all carefully recorded by overseers and planters. At the division of the crop, the accounts were produced and the accumulated fines drawn against freedpeople's share of the harvest, contributing to the tension and conflict attending crop divisions and to freedpeople's distrust of planters and overseers. For example, at Fairfield plantation, a bureau agent attempted to divide and distribute the crop but freedpeople refused to accept their shares, believing they had been cheated; they "used the most insulting language & gestures toward myself & Mr. Doar," complained the agent.[145] Less scrupulous planters took to dismissing workers immediately before the harvest in an attempt to defraud workers of their share of the harvest.[146]

Some of the more forward-looking planter families found a new and profitable business in the operation of plantation stores. The catastrophe of war had left many lowcountry freedpeople too impoverished, with too few resources, to engage in much household manufacture; for both their basic necessities and those few small luxuries they sought, many turned to the plantation stores. Williams Middleton, for example, when pondering the labor arrangements he might make with freedpeople for 1866, considered setting up "a small shop to sell suitable goods and provisions to the 'freedmen' chiefly in return for their labor, if they will condescend to enter into this arrangement."[147] John Berkeley Grimball's overseer operated a store on Grimball's plantation, and in 1869 described in detail its place in the local plantation economy:

> On each plantation there is a store with a general assortment of every thing, corn, groceries Dry goods, Shoes, Hats, hardware & fancy articles from a Mosquito net down to a Waterfall & walking cane. Each day when I am through in the field I open the store for a couple of hours & answer any demands that may be made on it. The hands are paid off every week. . . . On those days the run on the stores is tremendous . . . the pay off [is] in printed Due Bills redeemable Jany. 1st in Greenbacks but *current now* in the *store*. Of course the object is to get as many in as possible as the store profits are large & we would shame a King's Street clerk by the energy with which we extol the beauties of a fancy bonnet or some tinsil jewelry. At this place last year Frost issued $5500 in Due Bills & in Jany last had to redeem only about $150 in Greenbacks.[148]

In one day alone, when he opened the store on payday to "answer the demands of this influx of capital," the overseer reportedly "took back some sixty dollars in sums varying from 5 cts to a dollar, generally in small sums, for groceries of all kinds, dry goods, knick knacks etc."[149]

The bureau agent at Colleton District complained that planters "add at least (50) fifty per cent to the price of everything they purchase for the plantation and in the end the Freedmen are the victims."[150] Again, overseers and planters kept account books where the charges and interest accumulated until, by the end of year, freedpeople found their share of the harvest drastically reduced—on occasion, they found themselves indebted to the planter.[151]

. Plantation stores absorbed a considerable portion of freedpeople's earnings, and several bureau agents saw these emporiums as vehicles used by planters to perpetuate freedpeople's indebtedness and their obligation to continue as part of the plantation workforce.[152] The stores also prompted planters to begin using scrip to pay freedpeople's wages, in the fashion described above by Grimball's overseer.[153] Whether the scrip was used to delay paying cash wages (as was the case on Grimball's plantation) or, as elsewhere, served to limit freedpeople's spending power to the local plantation store, freedpeople's perception that the scrip system was used to their disadvantage ultimately contributed to an 1876 strike by rice workers.[154]

By targeting freedwomen's developing consumer tastes as well as their new consumer power as wage earners, women in the planter families helped make the stores even more profitable by sewing new dresses or offering their old ones for sale and developing strategies to best attract buyers: "I don't think any of the negroes have ready money to buy the dresses, *perhaps* if you were to send some of them up you might sell them, you know seeing a thing yourself might tempt you to buy," recommended one white woman to another.[155] Another advised, "Do tell Sall that she cannot get $10 for her dress . . . the trimming & skirt are both old fashioned. You know how fastidious our ladies of color are now."[156]

The operation of plantation stores quickly became an integral part of the plantation economy, and planters attacked their competitors—the traders who traveled the waterways, "inducing" freedpeople to rob from the fields, or trading freedpeople's share of the rice crop and their provisions for "wretched finery," whiskey, and "counterfeit jewelry." Fifteen lowcountry planters petitioned the bureau to keep traders off the river until the 1866 crop was harvested and divided (which was also a period of great demand at plantation stores).[157] Neither planters nor bureau officials stopped at simply preventing the river traders from gaining access to freedpeople employed on lowcountry plantations. Although lowcountry freedpeople had enjoyed the right to market and trade their own surplus crops or hand-manufactured goods even when slaves, they encountered increasingly restrictive regulations designed to prevent their participation in the extensive marketing and trade that took place both in city and town, and on the lowcountry waterways.[158] By 1867, for example, the bureau was using printed labor contracts specifying that any rice or cotton found on the person or premises of freedpeople could be presumed stolen. Some bureau-approved contracts also specified that freedpeople could not sell any agricultural product without planter consent.[159]

Planters and Northern agents of reconstruction alike justified their interference in this extensive system of trade by arguing that freedpeople, vulnerable to "underhand dealing by traders" and "dishonest bargains," would "waste the entire proportion of the Rice Crop" to which they were entitled, leaving them no alternative to starvation but to rely on government support.[160] Other planters made no bones about the fact that freedpeople's participation in local trading networks competed with their own trading schemes, reason enough for some planters to seek restrictions on freedpeople's trading activities. Williams Middleton described his joint venture with the overseer in selling lumber and the unwelcome competition he encountered from freedpeople: "One of the difficulties we have had to contend with was that thousands of negroes have been at work devastating the neighboring island plantations, cutting the woods, *houses, bridges* etc. & selling them from their rowboats along the wharves & thus spoiling our market."[161]

The Two-Day Compromise

By the close of 1866, every indication was that the contract labor system had met with another year of failure. Both the military and bureau agents had, throughout the year, been overwhelmed by calls to adjudicate grievances and intervene in outbreaks of violence. Hunger—indeed, starvation—had driven many freedpeople off the plantations even before crops were harvested, seeking food or the wage work that allowed them to purchase provisions. Once crops were harvested, freedpeople refused once again to perform the hated mudwork or any other plantation labor and insisted they work as croppers. For their part, planters attempted to defraud plantation laborers by dismissing them before the harvest was divided or having them arrested on frivolous charges, in an effort to deny them their share for their year's labor. With the weather playing havoc on growing conditions, the final crop was small, and freedpeople saw little proceeds from their first full year of work under the contract labor system. Many freedpeople refused to contract for the year to come.[162]

Building on their desire to avoid white supervision of their labor, to resist entering into wage-labor relationships with former owners, and to exercise as much control over their own land and labor as possible, freedwomen and men began to prefer a two- or three-day work-rent system of labor on rice plantations. The system was based on freedpeople's exchange of two or three day's task labor in the planter's rice fields for a share of the crop and the use of plantation land (which freedpeople could cultivate without planter supervision).[163] The work-rent system minimized the extent to which the freedpeople had to work under an overseer's or planter's supervision, and maximized freedpeople's ability to manage and apply their labor in their own best interest. Freedwomen preferred it because it better accommodated their "double burden" of social and reproductive labor as well as their contracted field labor.

The work-rent system also built upon lowcountry freedpeople's insistence that they contracted to work as croppers, a claim they made with the harvests of 1865 and 1866. Insisting that their obligation to an employer (and a plantation) ended with the harvest of the crop, freedpeople performed none of the postharvest, fall and winter maintenance work (in particular, mudwork) that had been required of them as slaves. As croppers, freedpeople were determined to bring an end to their "enslavement to the plantation," but also tried to increase their ability to respond to seasonal demands.

The two-day system was also an improvised response to hunger, bureau policy, and freedpeople's preference for employment strategies that met their most pressing needs. The most devastating seasonal stress occurred during the weeks preceding the harvest of provision crops, when many freedpeople were literally starving, and the rice crop required little attention. In 1866 freedpeople who had contracted as full hands began to leave the plantations two or three days each week in order to find a way to feed their families. As one bureau agent explained, "the several rivers, the bay and ocean furnish them plenty of fish, which in catching necessarily takes the people from their proper work."[164] In the rural areas surrounding Charleston, starving freedpeople resorted to eating green corn, pond lily beans, and alligator meat.[165] Planters like L. W. Winningham complained to the bureau that "although I gave them double rations last week they say it is not enough & only work until Wednesday." When the bureau stopped issuing rations to freedpeople who worked under labor contracts, they had to pursue "a scanty & uncertain subsistence by working occasionally for people in the neighborhood." Their labor, although already contracted, went to the planters "capable of feeding them."[166]

Freedwomen and freedmen insisted on the two- or three-day work-rent system out of preference as well as necessity. Again, in some instances, it was evident that both freedwomen and men drew on their identity as croppers in making the transition to work-for-rent arrangements. This was the case on Henry W. Ravenel's Pooshee plantation, where despite the terms under which they had originally contracted, after the rice harvest the freedpeople "made the extraordinary claim to the right to go off three days in each week, to work for themselves." Ravenel would allow them to leave the plantation occasionally to find day work, but he resisted their claim to the right of independent movement. The freedpeople were so assured of the legitimacy of their claim that they appealed directly to the local bureau agent. The overseer, in turn, appealed to the assistant commissioner, R. K. Scott, who backed the overseer's interpretation of the labor contract. Freedpeople on plantations in Moncks Corner were similarly "doing what they please & going where they please."[167] Cooper River planters also appealed to the bureau to enforce the terms of the labor contracts against freedpeople's determination to come and go at will.[168] Closer to Georgetown, bureau agents reported similarly that freedpeople were seeking day employment, in some cases to buy provisions, thereby forcing a change in the terms of their labor to a version of the work-rent system.[169] By 1867, Scott acknowledged "a great disposition on the part of some freedmen, not to contract upon such terms, as would give the entire control of their time to the landlord." That September, Scott also affirmed freedpeople's right to reject labor not specified in their contracts and not related to the current season's crop.[170]

The work-rent system, which had first emerged in 1865, grew in popularity and apparently dominated lowcountry agriculture through the 1880s, although planters still complained that "this system is not working satisfactorily," because "the labor is not so easily controlled as when cash wages are paid."[171] Yet many planters saw some advantage to the two-day system in the first years after the war. Planter finances had been so devastated by the war that it was not possible to make weekly or monthly payrolls for workers contracting under a wage system. "Even under the share system a certain amount of capital is needed," complained one planter to another; "and I can't command a dollar for the purpose." Plantations required expensive repairs; any contract with workers meant "the purchase of mules—food—tools, and an infinite number of things, required for the business—and there is no money to do all this," conceded one lowcountry rice planter. The two-day system greatly reduced the capital planters needed to cultivate a crop.[172]

Like most postbellum labor arrangements, the work-rent system evolved over time, reflecting the changing needs of planters and freedpeople as well as changing markets for labor and for rice.[173] While the exchange of task labor for the use of plantation land remained constant, the details of how much task work was performed, who performed the task labor, and under whose supervision were negotiated on individual plantations. Also negotiated were such issues as whether freedpeople had to pay planters for the use of plows, mules, or other tools.[174] Among the variations in the work-rent system that evolved over time were those in the sexual division of labor and the family economy. On rice plantations along or near the Savannah River, for example, the gendered division of labor that emerged in 1865 persisted: freedmen tended to leave the plantations in search of waged day work at neighboring plantations or in the city, while freedwomen stayed on the plantation, caring for children and tending provision and cash crops. A similar division of labor appears to have developed in Georgetown District; freedmen sought day work in the vicinity while freedwomen and children remained on the plantations.[175] In more isolated areas of the lowcountry, freedmen's day work was restricted to other plantations or farms.[176] On one Moncks Corner plantation, "a Day's work," explained the planter, "is simply the old task—a man and his wife do a task apiece the first day, & one between them the next—."[177] But on another plantation, "they would not contract with Papa the other day, they all wanted the contract changed, they did not wish their wives to work at-all & the men only wanted to work the day & a half, which of course Papa would not listen to, he threatened to turn them off, but I believe they are going to work on Monday under last year's contract."[178] Given planters' refusal to relinquish control over their plantations, or to rent or lease their plantations to freedpeople, and alternately, freedpeople's insistence on gaining as much autonomy from the planters as possible, the work-rent system seemed to offer the best possible reconciliation of interests the former slaves could attain.

Whether they approved of the two-day system or not, lowcountry planters grew frustrated by the repeated failures of the contract labor system to restore the rice plantation economy. Some planters insisted on contract terms that explicitly prohibited freedpeople from seeking employment of any sort off the plantation.[179] Others blamed the share-wage system for repeated crop failures; in 1868, repeating the pattern established three years before, freedpeople ran out of provisions, "& it becomes necessary for them to work elsewhere to secure their supplies. Indeed this form of contract has *entirely* failed through this neighborhood," declared one overseer.[180] By 1869, as the labor shortage became more acute, rice planters were forced to lure workers with the most competitive contract terms they could offer, and freedpeople made it clear that the two-day system was their preference.[181] As one planter observed early in 1867, "without laborers land is worth very little now & everyone is straining every nerve to retain all that he can in hope of better times hereafter."[182]

The bureau and the local military authorities were not of one mind on the two-day system. In Moncks Corner, the local agent accepted contracts under the work-rent system only if they met certain conditions; bureau approval was important to planters, since it determined whether workers were eligible to receive government rations or would be forced to leave the plantation in search of food. Thus one planter yielded to terms that satisfied the bureau's requirements:

> Mr. Porcher was obliged to apply to the Bureau for aid in supplying Provisions for the plantation, & so he had to conform to the requisitions made by the Agent, which are very disadvantageous to us. The negroes are not to work but one day and a half for their rent of land &tc. & are to be hired if necessary for two more days & a half if Mr. P.[orcher] requires for which they are to be paid in Government Rations. . . . Major Donaldson says he will come up sometimes to see how the negroes are working, as he will not engage to furnish rations to people who may not be able to return them after harvest.[183]

But by 1867, when the two-day system had become increasingly popular among lowcountry freedpeople, the bureau more strongly opposed the system. Agents described the work-rent system as "productive of much evil," "a perfect swindle," a "miserable form of contract," in part because they believed that freedpeople were not fairly remunerated under the system. But they also opposed it because it was not predicated on wage labor, because it allowed freedpeople to enter the market economy on their own terms.[184] One Edisto Island bureau agent described the two-day system as a major obstacle to black workers attaining "parity" with white laborers in the North.[185] Most bureau agents also believed that the work-rent system encouraged subsistence agriculture, thereby slowing the freedpeople's integration into a profit- and consumption-oriented wage-labor economy. These agents believed that without the incentive of personal gain and material appetites, the former slaves would never learn to labor for self-interest nor would they ultimately submit to the market.[186] Convinced of the advantages of its own vision of the postwar South, the bureau actively discouraged the increasingly popular labor arrangement—although enough agents supported freedpeople's insistence on working as croppers to convince Governor Orr that the bureau actually supported the emerging compromise.[187]

Freedmen's Bureau agents mounted their fight against the spread of the two-day system in a number of ways. The bureau manipulated South Carolina's new lien law, established in September 1866, to the disadvantage of freedpeople working under the two-day system; bureau policy tried to insist that renters could not make a primary claim on a mortgaged crop, although wage or share laborers could.[188] In February 1867, General R. K. Scott, the Freedmen's Bureau assistant commissioner in South Carolina, ordered his subordinates to "prevent any freedpeople from entering into unjust [work-rent] Contracts." Instead of approving work-rent contracts, he directed that agents advise freedpeople to procure wage-paying employment.[189] As a consequence, when bureau agents were presented with labor contracts based on the work-rent system, the agents refused to approve them and informed both planters and workers that the bureau would consider the contract an arrangement for a third of the crop to the worker.[190] By mid-June, the bureau agent in the rural district surrounding Charleston ordered that rations, which the bureau frequently advanced to freedpeople in need, be cut off if the applicant labored under the two-day system; "there is plenty of work for them to do, at good wages," the subassistant commissioner insisted. Regardless of the bureau's disapproval and its active measures to prevent it, in late 1866 when freedpeople met to discuss labor arrangements for the year to come, they agreed on their preference for the two-day system. In 1867, "this system was discouraged in every way . . . but without effect, on account of the extreme desire of the people to have land to work for themselves." By 1868, when a great many lowcountry freedmen and freedwomen insisted on the two-day system as the only arrangement under which they would labor for planters, freedpeople and planters in portions of Beaufort District simply agreed not to submit their contracts to the bureau, knowing the bureau would refuse to approve them.[191]

By opposing restoration, delaying the implementation of labor contracts, resisting wage labor, and even abandoning plantations restored to white planters, freedwomen sought to gain some control over the lowcountry's transition to a free-labor society, a process that civilian and military officials hoped both to direct and to accomplish quickly. Even once the contract system was in place, freedwomen insisted on working when and how they chose: as fractional hands, working only at tasks associated with the immediate crop. They rejected the restoration of overseers, challenged their authority, and fought to keep overseers (among other whites) out of the rice fields and out of their homes. In nearly every arena of labor conflict, freedwomen sought to replace the antebellum configuration of plantation power relations with a new autonomy, one that protected their freedom both in the rice fields and outside them. Denied their most important measure of freedom—autonomous control over the plantation lands—freedwomen helped move the rice economy toward a new organization of labor under the work-rent two-day system. Far more than the sharecropping or wage systems, the work-rent system permitted freedwomen greater freedom of movement between their household and family economies and the plantation economy, greater insularity from the supervision of overseers and other hated figures from their recent past, and the option of making their own decisions about how best to allocate their time and their labor.

In March 1867, South Carolina entered a new and important stage in the process of Reconstruction: Congress had returned the South to military control, and later that spring, the enfranchisement of freedmen opened up to lowcountry African Americans the formal process of political organizing, registration, campaigning, and electing their chosen representatives and office holders. Although the reservation of the right to vote and to hold office to men eventually interjected new distinctions in the communities of freedpeople, initially both men and women viewed the franchise as a means of community empowerment. Freedwomen as well as children left the rice fields when it was time to register, attended political meetings and rallies where their influence over the lowcountry vote was recognized and manipulated, and were found at the polls on election days.[192] The right to vote was not merely symbolic; it offered freedpeople the possibility—and for a time, the reality—of bringing local and some state offices into the control of African-American men. And, while South Carolina's officeholders may have ultimately disappointed former slaves, for a time black South Carolinians reinforced their efforts in the rice fields to define black freedom with political power. While the behavior and expectations of freedpeople relating to the franchise and political office offer important indicators of their desire for citizenship rights, there were con-current struggles occurring in the homes and families of freedwomen that were no less important to the immediate and long-term struggle to define and defend black freedom.

7 "And So to Establish Family Relations": Race, Gender, and Family in the Postbellum Crisis of Free Labor

In July 1866, a freedwoman appeared at the office of the local Freedmen's Bureau agent at St. James Santee to file an official complaint against her husband, Bungie. According to the bureau agent, C. V. Wilson, Clarender's complaints against Bungie were several. He had been unfaithful; even worse, when Clarender "caught him in a corn field with a woman and reproached him for his conduct," he had whipped her so severely that she had suffered from it for several days. Clarender appeared before the local bureau agent not only to complain about the violence she had suffered at the hands of her husband, but also, it seems, to obtain a measure of revenge. Rather than continuing to support herself by working on a local plantation, Clarender now wanted to take the bureau's pronouncements about the sanctity of marriage and the obligations of husbands and use them to force her husband to provide for her; according to Wilson, she "says she will not work any more but make him support her." But in order for Clarender to rely solely on the support that the bureau had so often noted was the responsibility of husbands to provide, she would have to withdraw from her labor contract.

In deciding how to act on Clarender's complaint, Wilson was forced to choose between his agency's manifold efforts to regularize both the form and function of freedpeople's familial relationships, on the one hand, and the bureau's ongoing efforts to persuade both freedmen and women to submit to the obligations and discipline of the contract labor system, on the other. In this instance, Wilson decided to hold Clarender's labor contract inviolable. He reprimanded Clarender's errant husband, assessed a fine out of Bungie's share of the current crop to be paid to his wife, and urged Clarender to "try and make home pleasant for her husband."[1]

Wilson's record of this incident provides little insight into Clarender's feelings about how he handled her complaint. But Clarender's complaint does reveal that the transition to freedom introduced new sources of conflict into the family lives of freedpeople, and offered new alternatives for settling intrafamily disputes. Clarender's actions also reveal that she had intended to work until her husband's abuse prompted her to pursue a very material revenge against him, and only then did she invite the bureau to intervene and enforce their pronouncements about marital and familial relations in her own marriage.

Part of freedom's promise lay in the possibility of reconstituting families and remaking households, family economies, and familial relationships in ways that made sense to lowcountry African Americans, finally free of white intervention and the burden of slavery. But in the contested aftermath of war and Reconstruction, freedwomen and their families were still embattled, deeply entangled in the contested supply, organization, and control of labor. In fact, freedwomen's persistent efforts to define free life and labor on their own terms—their repudiation of the authority of overseers, planters, and plantation mistresses, their insistence on contracting as partial rather than full hands, their preference for the two-day system, and their determination to see the benefits of freedom extend beyond the rice fields—contributed to what many scholars have described as the "crisis of free labor" in the postbellum, postemancipation South.[2]

The perception of a crisis of free labor, if shared by many Southern whites, arose primarily from the disappointment of Northern expectations for the unimpeded development of a free-market, liberal democratic society in the postwar South. The war had revived the appeal of the free-labor ideal to many Northerners, who overlooked the growing presence of a permanent class of wage workers (a presence that belied free labor's promise of social mobility and opportunity), and anticipated the southward spread of free labor in the wake of emancipation and the military defeat of the Confederacy.[3] However, developments in the postwar South (including freedwomen's efforts to expand the consequences of emancipation) raised significant and unexpected challenges to the implementation of the free-labor market economy by Northern agents of Reconstruction. Because of those challenges, the problem faced by bureau agents and military authorities, as explained by the historian Thomas Holt, "was not merely to make ex-slaves work, but to make them into a working class, that is, a class that would submit to the market because it adhered to the *values* of a

bourgeois society: regularity, punctuality, sobriety, frugality, and economic rationality." As Holt suggests, one of the goals of Reconstruction policy
was to overcome freedpeople's demonstrated reluctance to embrace the
social and economic relations, institutions, and values dictated by a free-
labor social order.[4]

Bureau agents and military authorities were determined to impart to
former slaves the benefits of full and unimpeded participation in the marketplace, but they were also enthusiastic about conveying the privileges
and prerogatives of those bourgeois family and gender relations they believed integral to a free-labor society. It was not necessary for bureau or
military policy makers to address gender relations apart from their endeav-
or to assure the smooth transition to the free market economy in the South;
ideas about gender and gender's "power to mean" were already fully integrated into Northern visions of such a system, determining notions of,
for example, who supported families, who was a dependent, and whose
labor lacked economic value.[5] To ignore the ways gender structured the
North's free-labor social order is to ignore the assignment of specific rights,
obligations, and privileges by gender, to disregard the construction of
unequal relationships between men and women in their families and
household economies, to dismiss the subordination of women and the
undervaluing of women's paid and unpaid labor.[6] It also means overlooking one of the sources of conflict between the policy makers and the targets of reconstruction policy, as freedwomen and men did not necessarily accept Northern visions of normative family relations ("the men in the
fields,—the women in their own homes,—the children at school").[7] As a
consequence, neither the postbellum crisis of free labor, the federal response to it, nor the continuously embattled position of freedwomen and
their families can be fully explained without unveiling the gendered imperatives of free-labor ideology and the social order envisioned by it.

The extent to which ideas about gender informed Northern advocacy
of a free-labor social order in the postwar South may not have been explicitly articulated at the time, but middle-class and elite Northern whites
invested the family—and their view of women's role and work within it—
with a vast reservoir of meaning about free-labor society. More important,
Northern agents of Reconstruction certainly acted as if they shared those
beliefs; as the crisis of free labor worsened, Reconstruction policy focused
more intently on freedpeople's families.[8] In the form of general orders,
circulars, and regulations issued by the military department and the bureau, several policies bore directly on the regulation of families among
former slaves—attempting to govern marriage and divorce, child custody,

and the support and residence of families whose members became involved in plantation labor disputes. As subjects of this policy, freedwom-
en and freedmen were urged to adhere to specifically gendered models
of obligations and privileges in their families and households. Along with
the more informal practices by which Freedmen's Bureau agents and
military officials mediated in instances of marital conflict, domestic abuse,
and family violence, the cumulative effect of both practice and formal
policy was to target African-American gender roles and family form and
function as part of the lowcountry's transition to a free-labor future.

Another of the consequences of the postbellum "crisis of free labor" was
that army officers and bureau agents across the lowcountry became less
inclined to blame the devastating impact of slavery for precipitating the crisis, beginning instead to blame freedpeople, as well as intransigent former
slaveowners. It became increasingly evident to Northern observers that the
destruction of slavery had not in itself created free labor's ascendancy in the
South, nor had it necessarily promoted the kind of family life and domesticity denied African Americans in servitude. Remaining unshaken in what
Thomas Holt has described as "their faith in their liberal democratic ideology" and their valorization of a particular view of free-labor society, Northern agents of Reconstruction turned to "racial explanations of freedmen's
behavior."[9] Bureau officials and military authorities became persuaded that,
in contrast to the image of docile, submissive, deprived slaves once portrayed
in the abolitionist press, freedpeople in fact "had their own opinions and
inclinations" that created obstacles to the ascendancy of a free-labor society in lowcountry South Carolina. In contrast to the wartime prevalence of
a more humanitarian if also paternalistic racism among Port Royal missionaries and federal agents, the postbellum agents of Reconstruction were increasingly persuaded of racial differences that emancipation could not erase
and that were contributing to free labor's failure in the postwar South.[10]
Lowcountry freedpeople were described by one "sympathetic" bureau agent
as "the most powerfully degraded class of colored people which ever slavery has the credit of forming."[11]

Northern agents of Reconstruction viewed the family and the behavior
and activities of men and women within it as critical indicators of the smooth
functioning of the social order, and it was often in the scrutiny of freedpeople's family arrangements and gender conventions that bureau agents and
military officials began to elaborate their ideas about racial difference and
African-American inferiority.[12] How ideas about gender and race affected
the way bureau agents, civilian missionaries, and military authorities understood and responded to the crisis of free labor would have a profound im-

pact on African-American women in the South, both in their immediate efforts to define freedom and long into the future. Neither Northern nor Southern whites attributed to lowcountry freedwomen the ability, inclination, cultural support, or traditions that would encourage them to make appropriate and proper choices for the support and nurture of their families. For freedwomen, the corpus of laws, orders, and policies that resulted added another heavy layer of burden to women's efforts to fashion their lives in freedom as they saw fit. When freedwomen pursued their own definition of freedom, what they encountered from military and civilian agents of Reconstruction was not only a racialized "explanation" for their resistance, but an explanation that was also heavily informed by bureau perceptions of the extent to which freedwomen failed—even refused—to conform to the gender roles idealized in Northern free-labor society. The end result was a near-demonization of freedwomen, especially those who improvised the support of their families outside the system of waged and contracted labor.

The greater the inclination among federal officials to blame the South's postbellum crisis on lowcountry African Americans—not as former slaves or victims of poverty but as people of African descent—the more easily bureau and military officials turned to coercive and punitive measures.[13] The tension between Northern ideals of free labor and the social reality of the postbellum, postemancipation South encouraged these officials to resort to coercive transitional institutions and expedient compromises. They freely rationalized their recourse to compulsion by emphasizing the active role played by lowcountry freedpeople in delaying the transition to the free market economy. Military and civilian agents of Reconstruction "claimed that devices such as vagrancy laws and compulsory contracts were merely temporary expedients needed to mediate the transition from slavery to freedom." Coercive policies targeted labor relations in the field, but they aimed also at family life and at labor and gender relations in the home. They were intended to accomplish freedpeople's submission not only "to the impersonal forces of the marketplace and to the rational and uniform constraints of law" but also to specifically gendered models of family relations and household economies. One could not be obtained without the other.[14] By denying the feasibility of free African-American family life under any other terms, proslavery idealogues and Northern officials alike offered tacit approval and, by extension, a tolerant environment for the continuing postbellum assault on the families of freedpeople.[15] When the implicit assumptions about gender and the tendency to resort to racist explanations converged in Reconstruction-era policies, it was often freedwomen who paid the price.

Marriage

To bureau agents in lowcountry South Carolina, one of the critical measures of the difference between slavery and freedom was the former slave's
right to claim the benefits of marriage. The abolitionist outcry against the
denial of civil marriage to slaves and the consequences of that denial—
supposed immorality and lack of sexual restraint among slaves—served
to emphasize marriage as a means of raising freedpeople to a new level
of civilization. Marriage, after all, served several important functions in a
stable and prosperous society; by establishing legitimate heirs, it helped
order and regulate the transfer of property between generations; it institutionalized men's privileges and obligations as heads of households, and
assured their entitlement to the unpaid labor of women on behalf of the
household; it also established the legally normative subordinate status of
married women in Northern society by subsuming their legal identities
under those of their husbands. Civil marriage regulated female sexuality
and ordered the family in ways that many Northern middle-class and elite
whites considered to be essential to social stability and civilization itself.

Anticipating the importance of civil marriage in the postwar program
for Reconstruction, the wartime Port Royal community of missionaries,
teachers, relief workers, and military and other federal personnel were
preoccupied with the disarray of contraband families. Observers had commented extensively on what they viewed as the degrading influence of
slavery on lowcountry African Americans, elaborating on their view of the
deficiencies of black family life. They particularly emphasized a perceived
lack of sexual restraint among slave women, even those with husbands.
Servitude, the Port Royal observers believed, "has had the effect of rendering bigamy, adultery, fornication . . . the norm." Elizabeth Botume admitted "all our preconceived ideas of propriety and the fitness of things
were set at naught."[16] When asked by the members of the American Freedmen's Inquiry Commission (established in 1863 to help the War Department determine how to deal with emancipated slaves) to comment on
women's sexual behavior, white observers were more than willing to ex-
pound. They declared contraband women—married or not, young and
old—to be "universally unchaste" with a propensity toward pre- and extramarital sexual activity. Rufus Saxton, when asked about the chastity of
contraband women, stated he did not think that anything of the kind existed. He blamed slavery for having "destroyed that feeling," and he also
noted that it was contraband women's desire for and pride in sexual relations with white men that made it difficult to keep the white Union sol-

diers away from them (an observation challenged by contrabands and female missionaries and relief workers, who documented the sexual assaults on contraband women by Union troops and officers). Saxton's opinions were not entirely representative of the officers on his staff; one aide believed that contraband women appreciated the value of chastity thoroughly, and he blamed incidents of prostitution on the influence of soldiers. Still, Saxton's attitudes were consistent with those affecting military policy. "Wandering" women were disruptive to the community, as the commander of Union forces in South Carolina asserted, not only because of their failure to work under labor contracts, but because their very presence was "subversive of moral restraint" among the soldiers—even when they were, in fact, married and traveling to visit their enlisted husbands.[17]

No wonder, explained another Northern observer, that the contrabands' home life and family relations seemed in such disarray, with mothers given to wandering and immoral excess. "Marriages" were abandoned for the slightest reasons, by both husbands and wives. The natural ties between parent and child seemed absent (one observer asserted that children had no real love or reverence for their parents). There was little evidence of the practices that most Northern middle-class whites associated with civilized home life. Families were not in the habit of eating together (fathers and sons eating first), and lacking tables, family members sat instead on their "haunches" around the campfire. A plantation superintendent on Ladies Island believed there was "no real domestic life" among the contrabands; "you cannot get civilization into their houses" because they "live . . . on a fearfully low plane." He hoped to "introduce the family table and a meal hour" by law. "I would like," he added, "authority to furnish every family with table and table cloths, knives and forks and dinner set, and so to establish family relations." Laura Towne concurred, believing that without these and other kinds of interventions, freedpeople would "relapse into barbarism."[18] Even those observers willing to defend the morality of contraband women still pointed out evidence of marital and familial disarray. Yet when these Northerners criticized the families of lowcountry contrabands, they stressed that it was the deprivation of the protections of civil law that had produced such disorder. Although their views of race and of slavery were complicated and predated their mission to the South, many of them believed that the behavior and attitudes of the contrabands could be blamed largely on the devastating consequences of slavery and could therefore be unlearned under their tutelage and, for slave men, in military service.[19]

The Freedmen's Bureau hoped to accelerate the transition to free labor in the South by promulgating its own view of appropriate family ties and responsibilities among freedpeople, stressing the importance of "legitimate" nuclear families and even mandating legal unions between former slaves. Toward that end the Reverend Mansfield French (chaplain to black troops and minister among the Port Royal contrabands beginning early in 1862) was appointed the bureau's Supervisor of Missions and Marriage Relations for South Carolina through 1868. One historian describes French as "the foremost advocate of marriage."[20] In August 1865, French issued his first postbellum instructions urging former slaves to pursue the legitimization of their slave marriages and offering guidelines for settling the varied and, from French's perspective, confusing array of family arrangements found in the communities of former slaves.[21] That circular attempted to apply the bureau's definition of legitimacy and illegitimacy to the relationships and families of freedpeople, declaring legitimate those marriages between slaves performed by churches (although state law had prohibited legal marriage between slaves since 1740), and illegitimate any marriages between slaves that had been declared with no more solemnity than their own or the planter's consent. Illegitimate unions, stated the bureau, required a new ceremony, performed by a church or a civil magistrate. Overreaching, perhaps, his influence over the community of former slaves, French warned that unless a proper ceremony was performed, the man and woman would not be allowed to live together.[22] French's regulations, however, were soon replaced by the state's black code, which provided legal recognition to all slave marriages consented to by both parties. According to the code, freedpeople with multiple partners were required to choose one by April 1866.[23]

Following instructions from General-in-Chief Ulysses S. Grant that military commanders in the South were to protect freedpeople from the enforcement of black codes, Freedmen's Bureau Commissioner O. O. Howard directed state assistant commissioners to provide freedpeople with clarification on "what the law demands of them in regard to marriage." French wrote another set of "Marriage Rules" in 1866, which were issued under General Orders No. 19 by Assistant Commissioner R. K. Scott.[24] French's new and very detailed set of regulations determined which freedpeople were "eligible to marriage," regulated who was authorized to grant marriage permits, established the authority of commissions composed of ministers and freedmen whose responsibility it was to dissolve marriage agreements (in the instance of separation prior to emancipation), and outlined the "duties of husbands to former wives." French's marriage rules also offered detailed instructions on reconciling the marital status of former slaves separated involuntarily by owners, and also for sorting out the status of former slaves who found themselves restored not just to one former mate, but to two or more. A freedman was required, in these instances, to chose as his wife the woman who was mother of his children; freedwomen's choices were not addressed. The rules also specified that in instances where a wife or husband willfully remained absent from a spouse and refused to resume "marriage relations," the injured party could petition for a release from responsibility, especially, in the case of the husband, his financial responsibility to support his wife and her children by him.[25] French's regulations provided for the dissolution of marriages for adultery and desertion and also asserted that freedpeople guilty of adultery or fornication would not be permitted to remarry. The responsibility for deciding which spouse received custody rights over children was turned over to the special marriage commission provided for in French's rules. Nonetheless, these aspects of the marriage rules remained in conflict with state law, which made no provision for divorce, apparently leading to some confusion among freedpeople as to whether first marriages could be annulled for any reason.

Not every Northern white observer in the lowcountry believed the bureau's marriage policy was effectively enforced. In April 1867 a Northern planter (in Beaufort since 1863) reported in the pages of the *New York Times:*

> Husbands and wives are constantly returning to their former companions to find them in new relations of long standing, and with new sets of children. Many church leaders, who are not ministers, are in the habit of marrying or of giving permission to live without marrying until a minister shall come around. . . . Divorces are granted by permission of church authorities composed entirely of blacks, so that it is impossible for them to be settled on any such permanent foundation as cases of such momentous occasion call for. Under the Freedmen's Bureau there is no practical system of divorces adopted—not here, at least.[26]

The participation of black church leaders in granting marriages and divorces, according to this particular planter, doomed French's regulations to failure.

It is difficult to measure the impact of the bureau's efforts to regulate and encourage legal marriage among freedpeople. Freedmen's Bureau officials clearly believed that marriage—legal and sanctified—was essential to the successful transition from slavery to freedom, in part because civil marriage would help ensure the institutions and self-discipline of bourgeois society. But to freedpeople, the attraction of legalizing their unions was mitigated by their own experiences of slavery, war, and the transition to freedom. For example, even with the relative advantages of living in large plantation communities, lowcountry slaves had been vulnerable to slaveowners' persistent disregard for their family ties and obligations. They had lived under the constant threat that their families might be separated by sale, as punishment, or in the process of dispersing the estate of a deceased planter. They knew the consequences of living in a family-centered slaveowning society as slaves whose own family ties were denied and violated at will. During the course of the war, lowcountry slaves had also encountered new threats to the integrity and survival of their families: the impressment of slave men, the hiring out of slave men and women alike, the separation of spouses and of parents from children, by removal, escape, or enlistment.

Freedpeople's appreciation for the benefits of legitimate marriage has been argued most strongly by Herbert Gutman in his landmark book on the black family in slavery and freedom. Gutman held that former slaves had "a strong desire to legalize slave marriages." He challenged the claims of earlier historians and sociologists that slavery had destroyed black family life; he asserted that freedpeople's rush to register and legitimate their marriages provided incontestable evidence of an imperative among the former slaves to gain legal recognition and protection for their marriages.[27] Gutman also argued that neither native whites nor Northern white missionaries—the latter being of such small numbers—could have motivated such a high interest among former slaves in marriage registration. The widespread desire to obtain legal recognition for their families, he concluded, reflected the former slaves' claim for entitlement under the law as well as the strength of their family ties. Indeed, some Northern observers in the South Carolina lowcountry also described what they believed was a profound respect among freedpeople for the ceremony, and the certificate, of legal marriage.[28]

Both during and after the war, there is evidence that lowcountry contrabands and freedpeople readily seized the opportunities offered to them to consecrate their marriages in legal ceremonies.[29] To the extent that black soldiers and their families reflected in part the experience of lowcountry freedpeople, there were many freedwomen and men who married or remarried after the war. Although the freedman Randol Ward testified, "[I] had my present wife before the war," he noted, "[I] married her after I came from the war. We were married by the Trial Justice, Mr. Flagg, [his former owner] at Brook Green." Sina Grant had been "married according to slave custom" but then was separated from her husband before the war; after the war, she and another man, Frank Grant, "commenced living together as man and wife and lived that way for about two years, then the law came out that colored folks living together must get married so we were married . . . by the Rev. 'Dick' Bryan at the African Methodist Church." Bashie Ladson, who visited her husband during the war while he was posted at Beaufort, and lived with him after the war, finally remarried him because "the law came out that we had to marry by certificate, and the Rev. Reed married us and gave us a certificate of marriage."[30]

While some lowcountry freedpeople related their marriages to the law and bureau policies, many freedpeople seem to have been motivated primarily by the dictates and requirements of their own churches (some of which undoubtedly conveyed the bureau's emphasis on marriage). Lucy Brown reported that before the war, she and Sandy Brown "took up together and lived together according to slave custom, and with consent of our owners, as man and wife, though we were not married by any ceremony." She and her "husband" were "regularly married by Robert Lesenton, a colored minister. . . . The reason we were married was in order that my husband might be a Deacon in the Church." Mary Nesbit noted that she had "lived with Brutus Nesbit a good long while before Preacher Jones married us by ceremony. I belonged to the church," she explained, "and wanted to 'insure my honor' so we got married in the right way." Tony Allston concurred; "the people were told by the preachers that they must come up and get married." Susan Grant also explained that she and Aaron Grant "were living together as were many others and in the churches the preachers told them that the[y] must get married and that they, as did many others, got up in church and were married." Judith Swinton, a freedwoman and a friend of Susan and Aaron Grant, explained that after the war the churches "compelled the members, who were living together as man and wife but not married to have these ceremonies performed." Swinton added, "They were all advised they must do so by the preacher."[31]

Yet it would seem that in defining their families and intimate relationships, no less than in defining their new role as free workers, freedwomen and freedmen felt "that they were free and would follow there own orders." When they yielded to any authority in such matters, it was frequently to the authority of their churches and not the bureau.[32] For example, not all freedpeople involved in long-term intimate relationships or with families chose to answer the demand by the bureau or their church for "legitimate" ceremonies. Some had been married in slavery and may have

considered the postwar emphasis on new ceremonies superfluous or perhaps insulting. Slave marriages had been important events in the lives of
slave families and entire plantation communities, and they were sometimes
attended by considerable ceremony and celebration that freedpeople recalled vividly decades later. Rebecca Nesbit and Nathaniel Allston offer one
such example; they had grown up together on Weymouth plantation and,
with the permission of their owner, were married by a fellow slave and
preacher at a large celebration in the slave quarters. As Rebecca later recalled, all the plantation people—white and black—attended the ceremony and celebration. Although separated by the war, Nathaniel and Rebecca resumed their life together afterward, and never felt it necessary to go
through a second, civil marriage ceremony.[33]

On the other hand, not all intimate relationships between freedmen
and freedwomen were destined, or even intended, to approximate marriage. In his pension testimony, Washington Rutledge stated, "I had a slave
wife, but I never lived with her after the war. I have had but one wife since
freedom, and I have her now." The slaves Pendar and Israel Carr "just took
up and lived with each other awhile and then separated" before the war.
Charlotte Washington met Frank Grant shortly after the war, and the two
lived together on the Rutledge rice plantation for a year. But, complained
Washington, "he drank so much whisky and was so no account I picked
up and left him and never had anything to do with him after that. We never
got married. We just lived together. I would have married him," she explained, "if I could have made a man of him but he drank so hard I couldn't
do it so I let him go." They had "no marriage ceremony," "were not considered man and wife," "had no children." Although this man had been a
soldier, she had never submitted a pension claim as his widow because "I
never had enough of a hold on him to do that, I was not his wife but just
his woman." Their neighbors "understood that." One bureau agent was
very disturbed by the fact that freedpeople in his upcountry district "still
adhere to the old custom of *taking up* with each other and living as man
and wife and consider it their right to part on the slightest provocation."
Tellingly, he complained that "it seems almost impossible to eradicate this
evil as it is the desire of both sexes that the custom should continue." A
lowcountry observer similarly complained that "persons by the score live
together 'just so,' without any form of marriage."[34]

Many contraband and freedwomen continued to measure their family relations and intimate relationships along their own standards—whether
secular or sacred—rather than the bureau's comparatively narrow, legally
constructed ideal. During the war, Jane Ferguson learned that Martin Barn-

well, her first husband, who had been sold away from her, was not only living but would soon be reunited with her. Although she had since taken another husband, Jane insisted that "Martin is my husband . . . an' the father of my child; and Ferguson [her second husband] *is a man,*" explaining that she and her second husband "had an understanding" about her prior attachments and that he would now "act like a man" and accept what was to Jane a welcome reunion. Jane's experience was multiplied hundreds of times over after the war.[35]

Bureau agents across the state complained of the difficulty created by "the freedom of traveling" that now restored long-absent spouses; from a Charleston agent came the report that "frequently I have before me two women claiming a man, and two men claiming a woman as their former wife or husband." An agent in Aiken District reported that "many cases are made by wives in regard to their husbands and by husbands in regard to their wives for leaving them and going to live with other parties. Many of these parties have never been married and it is somewhat of a puzzle to settle such complaints."[36]

Many freedwomen, of course, had long, committed, and loving marriages to freedmen.[37] But marriage was not the only, or even most important, familial relationship; many freedwomen spent the years immediately following the war caring not only for their children, but also their grandchildren, nieces and nephews, cousins, sisters, parents, aunts, and grandparents. Still others adapted their intimate relationships to the range of responsibilities and duties that lowcountry African Americans recognized not only as legitimate but also obligatory in their tightly woven families and communities. Although the freedwoman Ellen Cooper's husband, Mingo, had secured employment in a distant town and had to move, Ellen insisted that she had to remain in Georgetown in order to nurse her ill sister. Mingo left and subsequently became involved with Laura, an "outside woman," but also maintained his relationship with Ellen through occasional visits. When he died, Laura conceded to Ellen and her children the right to bury Mingo and to make an exclusive claim on his property. Ellen was also recognized in her community as the "chief mourner" at his burial.[38] Such arrangements evoked considerable complaint from bureau officers, but freedpeople had been forced as slaves to rely on the strength of adaptive relationships. Still, freedpeople were not universally accepting of "outside" relationships; Regina Toney left James Bracey, her husband, and married another man "because James didn't shew me proper respect—I heard that he had a woman."[39]

Although the Freedmen's Bureau urged freedmen and freedwomen to conform to a narrow model of family and married life, freedpeople had their own ideas about the form and function of their intimate relationships. Coresidence was not always the highest priority between married couples, despite the bureau's insistence that it should be. Amy Deas, who apparently had a legitimate land claim on Edisto Island, preferred to cultivate her land there rather than accompany her husband, Robert, back to the plantation where they had lived and worked as slaves. Only when the planter, John Berkeley Grimball, agreed to provide the family with land they could cultivate on their own did Amy apparently join her husband. Rose, a freedwoman formerly a slave at the same plantation, also refused to return; according to the former owner, she was "violently opposed" to returning and working for their former owner; she "was a furious woman when angry, which she very often was— a perfect tigress." Grimball believed that only with her unexpected death was her husband "at liberty to do as he wished," suggesting that freedpeople were not always in agreement among themselves about their obligations and duties as husband and wife.[40]

The devastating consequences of slavery and the war for slave family life were well understood by lowcountry freedpeople, who seemed disinclined to worsen the consequences of rape and sexual coercion by slaveowners, overseers, slave drivers, and even white Union soldiers by further shaming their victims. One Northern planter reported from Beaufort in 1867:

> Among the two plantations of people adjoining me on one side there is scarcely one young woman who has arrived at the age of 15 or 16 years who has not become a mother out of wedlock. Of these children thus born the large majority are half white and were born during the war. . . . and I know on these same places of eight married women who have the same evidence of their infidelity about them. In some of these cases the husband takes umbrage at the conduct of the wife and leaves her, in others not. The worst feature of the matter is that this conduct does not outcast the actors in it, nor is it so frowned upon as to render them obnoxious. . . . This fearful condition was brought about by Union officers and soldiers.[41]

When Lydia Brown and Murphy Allston married in 1866, she brought to their life together three children, all fathered by the slave driver, who had offered Lydia the "choice" of yielding to him or being whipped. The involuntary circumstances of Lydia's pregnancies were known to many of the slaves on her plantation, including the driver's own family; testimony to the fact reflected no tendency to blame Lydia.[42] At the time Lucy

Brown filed a pension claim as the widow of a deceased Civil War veteran, she testified having ten children by her husband. But she conceded on close examination by the pension examiner that only eight of those were actually the children of Sandy Brown; included in their family were two children who had been fathered by Lucy Brown's owner, George Fripp.[43] The consequences of sexual coercion were widely known in slave communities, and while no blame seemed to be attached to its victims, freedwomen also seem to have regarded such events as private matters, implying a degree of shame that women may have felt as victims of such abuse.

Even freedwomen's voluntary participation in pre- or extramarital sexual relationships was not necessarily a shameworthy act in lowcountry communities. During the war, refugee slavewomen from the mainland who made their way to the Sea Islands impressed the missionary teacher Elizabeth Botume with their "touching appeal" for "their down-fallen sisters." According to Botume, several of the refugee women "wished to bear united testimony" in the case of one "fallen" woman, "for they knew very well we would have nothing to do with one like her." Botume conceded that "their tenderness overcame our scruples. Their readiness to help the poor erring girl made me ashamed."[44] After the war, Jane Mayrant, a freedwoman, had a child outside of marriage, after the death of her husband. A friend insisted that despite the "pick up" child, Jane had not lived with any man since her husband's death—"the church would not allow that," he explained. And apparently Jane—although the mother of an illegitimate child—was regarded as having lived by the rules of her church.[45]

Although marriage regulations like those established by Mansfield French provide the most obvious evidence of bureau interest in and intervention into the families and familial relationships of freedwomen and freedmen, there were several other ways in which both the bureau and the military department intervened in or otherwise tried to influence family form and function among freedpeople. In fact, the significance of the marriage regulations—and freedwomen's responses to them—becomes clearer when they are considered in the context of related bureau and military policy. Marriage regulations were, for example, one of many tools available to the bureau to regulate and discipline the rice plantation workforce. Considerable bureau and military policy also followed up on a related issue addressed by French's marriage regulations: regulating the dependents of, and dependency among, freedpeople—issues deeply charged by Northern racial and gender ideologies.

Dependents and Dependence

Early after the war, some lowcountry rice planters began to appreciate that "the results of free and compensated labor, though perhaps less profitable in appearance, will be far more satisfactory in the end than those of the unpaid toil of slaves." The source of that improvement would be that "with free labor, it is within their power to choose and retain only the likeliest field hands and to rid themselves at once of the care of all superfluous negroes, including the young children, those too old to work and the sick; while, on the other hand, the use of slave labor necessarily saddles them with the support of an army of black dependents." Thus, argued this and other white South Carolinians, "the dreaded abolition has a bright side too for the planters."[46] Anxious to benefit from that "bright side" of emancipation during the summer of 1865, planters began refusing to provide rations to the uncontracted members of freedpeople's families. Given the conditions of the countryside that summer—the prevalence of impoverishment, starvation, and disease among former slaves—the planters' actions forced freedpeople either to work under terms and conditions determined by planters, or to starve. The military intervened, however, when it realized that planters were exerting pressure not only on freedpeople but on the fragile beginnings of free labor, as freedpeople were beginning to abandon plantations—and labor contracts—in search of food. Although military authorities ordered planters to feed the immediate families of contracted workers, they also required adult freedwomen to work as contracted hands if they wanted to receive rations. Freedwomen who were cultivating independent provision crops were therefore forced to abandon them and work for planters instead.[47]

Both the black codes and the earliest bureau policies, as they pertained to the legal standing of freedpeople's families, focused on establishing a husband's responsibility for the support of his wife and children. In the late fall of 1865, the black code extended liberal legal recognition to slave marriages, but it also threatened men who abandoned their wives and children with being bound out to involuntary labor for a term to be determined by the district judge, the profits of his labor to be applied to their support. It would seem that in the eyes of South Carolina's white legislators, legitimating freedpeople's marriages served primarily to transfer the responsibilities and liabilities of support of so-called dependent populations from former owners to freedmen. In the bureau's earliest marriage regulations husbands who refused to renew marital relations with their long-lost but recently returned wives were held responsible for the financial support of their wives and all their minor children. Furthermore, the requirement that a freedman with two wives take the mother of his children as his wife, regardless of his or her preferences, suggested that concern for the support of dependents, and not for the happiness of freedpeople or their right to make unimpeded choices, drove bureau policy. At least some Northern planters on the Sea Islands seem to have concurred; they believed that only by strict enforcement of the legal liabilities of husbands and fathers could sexual restraint be promulgated among freedpeople who, when left to their own devices, tended to "live together . . . like the hogs" and leave illegitimate children without adequate support.[48]

The transfer of the economic burden and legal responsibility for supporting "an army of black dependents" to male household heads was one of the long-term goals of bureau policies. Other objectives were to encourage specific kinds of family formations and to establish equality before the law for black South Carolinians in the matter of legal marriage. The consequences of these goals were far reaching. They freed planters from their earlier obligation (however minimally met) of providing for freed slaves who could not or would not work; altered the way labor conflicts were resolved; and possibly relieved the Freedmen's Bureau and the military from the degree of charity and relief work it did for former slaves, while reinforcing among freedpeople the duties and obligations that their release from slavery carried— including, bureau and military officials hoped, disciplined labor. Yet, curiously enough, the effort by Northern agents of Reconstruction to bring freedwomen and children into legally sanctioned families as dependents of black men offered only illusory promises of increasing freedmen's range of power or authority. The prerogatives of black masculinity envisioned by white bureau officials were apparently constrained to freedmen's domination over their wives and children. Reconstruction-era family policy attempted to transfer women and children from either autonomy or dependence on the state into legal and economic dependence on and subordination to men who were significantly disempowered themselves.

As freed families endured the strains and stresses of separations, or losses through death or desertion, apprenticeships became one of the easiest avenues by which intervening bureau or military officials could secure support for "dependent" children.[49] The apprenticing or fostering of orphans and children was a common nineteenth-century response to incidental and long-term impoverishment.[50] In postwar South Carolina, the assistant commissioner of the bureau first established a policy of apprenticing freed children in October 1865, authorizing the indenturing of freed orphans to "proper persons" in accordance with state law as it then governed the indenturing of white children. Bureau policy thus predated the implementation of apprenticeships under the state's black code, and it survived well past the annulment of the code in January 1866.[51] The bureau's frequent recourse to child apprenticeships suggests the agency's ignorance of extended families and the cultural significance of a community's sense of mutual duty and obligation among extended and fictive kin. It also reflects an active rejection of the notion of children's contributions to the household economy, a necessary part of family survival in the postwar lowcountry. This is shown in part by bureau efforts to have children bound out under apprenticeship contracts when immediate family members were dead or missing. Extended family members, such as uncles, aunts, or grandparents, were suspected by bureau agents of seeking to exploit the children rather than care for them.

Neither Northern nor Southern whites were reluctant to express their suspicions that freedwomen failed to act in the best interests even of their own children. Supporting the characterization of freedwomen as incompetent, if not abusive, parents was a range of opinions, including the argument of proslavery ideologues that freedwomen would just as soon murder their infants as have to work hard to support them.[52] Other Southern whites were more subtle in their condemnation of black mothers; one rice planter, for example, blamed freed mothers for purposefully teaching their children to drop all of the rituals of deference and respect they had been expected to exhibit as slaves; he complained that "the little Negroes who used to watch for me coming, to open the gates, & climb on the Sulky to take a little ride, were *now* taught *to shun me* & never to call me 'Master' again—'Heddy Massa' was Dead & gone."[53] Northern white observers who disapproved of freedpeople's family economies, where the labor of children was essential, suspected freedpeople of uncaring parenting:

> In the matter of rearing their children is where the true issue and true danger lies. They make them work with them in all kinds of labor to which they are adapted, but it is mainly enforced, as labor was enforced from themselves, without encouraging words of hope and cheerfulness and of course without the inculcation of those foundation principles of life on which all labor is founded and made honorable. They have not themselves sufficient weight of character to enforce that *steady* moral discipline so necessary to the growth of good habits and principles of life. Still, if these children get habits of *labor* simply, it is a great point gained, and the rest will come by slow degrees.[54]

The issue of dependency pervaded nearly all considerations of child custody; the ability to support a child without becoming dependent on government-issued rations was foremost in the minds of bureau agents who mediated custody and apprenticeship disputes. When the grandparents of five orphaned freedchildren appealed to the superintendent of a lowcountry orphanage for custody, the most important factor weighed by the superintendent was whether the grandparents would turn to charity for help in supporting the children. Forced to choose between the help offered by the bureau and the custody of their grandchildren, the grandparents were insistent; "They say they *can,* and *will* take care of them, without aid from Govt. They were drawing rations because it *assisted* them, but they would exert themselves to the utmost to keep them comfortable."[55]

The bureau's overriding concern with eliminating freedpeople's dependence on government support often led them to apprentice children to former slaveowners and other whites who, the bureau decided, had the resources to offer better or more secure material support to a child than did former slaves.[56] The historian Rebecca Scott, in her essay on child apprenticeships, has made the point that bureau agents were also disposed to hear the claims and arguments of white planters more sympathetically in these matters, oftentimes overriding the protests of an apprenticed child's parent. While local bureau and military officials were particularly vulnerable to the appeals of wealthier whites, cases appealed directly to the bureau's assistant commissioner were less likely to be subject to local pressures and to subvert parental wishes (although extended families were rarely accorded the same preference).[57]

Freedwomen—mothers, aunts, sisters, and grandmothers—opposed apprenticeships for a number of reasons, primary among them their belief that whites sought custody of black children in order to secure their forced labor and that an apprenticed child essentially faced a continued state of bondage. Certainly many of the disputed apprenticeships freedpeople brought to the bureau's attention involved the apprenticeship of children to former owners who claimed a special attachment to the child or the ability to provide superior support.[58]

Sometimes freedpeople opposed apprenticeships in order to regain custody of their own children; in other instances, as members of extended families, they asserted their obligation and entitlement to the care, custody, and labor of their kin's children. One particular case helps to illustrate how an extended family as well as an entire plantation community responded to such intrusive child apprenticeship. The authorities had apprenticed the freedwoman Sue's nephew, George, to William Cade, their former owner, much to the dismay and anger of George's family and the entire plantation community. When Cade came to George's grandparent's cabin to insist that they give him the clothes his grandmother had made for George, the grandparents refused. Freedpeople across the plantation, having seen Cade approach the cabin and anticipating trouble, left the fields and made their way to the cabin. Sue intervened when Cade began to treat George's grandmother rudely, and according to Sue's brother, Cade then threatened to shoot Sue, "struck her twice with his fist," and "struck her with a stick three times." As Sue took hold of Cade's shirt to return his attack, the gathered freedpeople became enraged at the white man's audacity. Sue's brother interceded and demanded that Cade stop, he "would not see his sister beaten." But Cade, aware and perhaps fearful of the fact that "dissatisfaction existed among the said Freedmen and women, for a month past, in consequence of [his] having the said Freed-boy George in his charge," pulled out his pistol, shot and killed Sue, and threatened to kill any other of the freedpeople who did not obey him. Although the military authorities ultimately overruled the inquest jury that had failed to find against Cade, no change in the custody of the freed boy is mentioned in the records.[59] Bureau officials usually insisted that unless "improper treatment" could be proven by freedpeople, apprenticeships would stand. When family members' claims on a child were even considered, the family or family member was subjected to close investigation—in search of moral impropriety—and was made to guarantee that he or she could provide for the material support of the child without seeking the assistance of the bureau (for rations, for example).[60]

Freedwomen's efforts to defend or reclaim their custody of children is extensively documented in bureau and military records from the postwar period. Susan Johnson, mother of fifteen-year-old Levinia as well as an eleven-year-old son and a three-year-old daughter, contracted for herself and her two oldest children to work for Elisha Durr and his wife for the year in exchange for twenty-five dollars. When Johnson scouted out her options at neighboring plantations and found better terms at one nearby, she returned to the Durrs to get her children, but her former employer now refused to yield custody of Levinia, threatening to set the dogs on Susan and kill her, at the same time warning Levinia she could not go with her mother. As directed by the local bureau agent to whom she first complained, Johnson took her case to a local magistrate, Rene Ravenel, who had his own record of abusively dealing with freedpeople. Ravenel scolded Johnson for bothering the bureau with her complaint and sent her back to the family who continued to hold Levinia. Instead, Johnson returned to the bureau and only with the help of an armed guard was able to get back her daughter; she lost her wages and the cost of traveling over two hundred miles between Ravenel, the bureau, and the Durrs.[61]

Freedpeople's challenges to bureau-approved apprenticeships led to considerable confusion among bureau agents themselves about settling apprenticeship and custody disputes. One agent queried his superiors about the frequent occurrence where a parent wished to retract or challenge a bureau-approved apprenticeship of his or her child. One official informed him that no indenture would be annulled unless improper treatment was alleged; a subsequent communication clarified that whenever a parent could support an apprenticed child, the contract could be voided. This left the agent confused about instances where the parent challenged the contract but the apprenticed child was well treated. His inquiry was answered, finally, that all apprenticeships were to stand unless he received other instructions in regard to specific cases.[62] Bureau administrators apparently felt their efforts to regulate and circumscribe black dependence were more important than the reconstitution and defense of black family life in ways that made sense to lowcountry freedpeople.

Charity and Dependence

In the summer of 1865, Assistant Commissioner Saxton had moved immediately to organize the distribution of food to impoverished white refugees and freedpeople throughout the state, drawing surplus rations from the army and distributing shipments of foodstuffs from Northern relief and missionary associations. Among the nine thousand people who received this kind of aid were freedpeople in camps, hospitals, and across the countryside. The need for relief was profound, yet by the fall of that year, the amount of rations distributed by the bureau dropped by two-thirds. One historian of bureau activities in South Carolina noted that "the Bureau, in fact, had rendered a humanitarian service of impressive proportion, but still one that fell considerably short of the actual need."[63]

Despite the importance of the rations and the real difference such relief made to the survival of lowcountry freedpeople, both the bureau and the military regarded it as a form of charity and were concerned about differentiating between the worthy and the unworthy poor. Even as early as August 1865, military authorities had begun to deny the distribution of rations to freedpeople—men and women—who refused to enter into labor contracts. The bureau manipulated the distribution of rations in other ways as well, insisting that freedpeople seeking custody of freedchildren first demonstrate their ability and intention to get by without relying on government relief.[64]

A Beaufort correspondent to the *New York Times* argued early in 1866 against the provision of charity or any form of government relief to freedpeople:

> To give these freedmen clothes, and food, and farms, will neither develop nor save them. All will be just so much harm done, unless strictest, steadiest discipline is enforced; and under no special code either, but under general laws. Indeed, the most dangerous process through which the negro goes when he becomes a freedman is that of receiving the gratuities of benevolence in the shape of food and clothing. If you wish to make them impudent, fault-finding and lazy, give them clothing and food freely. If you wish to make them self-reliant and manly, set their work before them and tell them they will get food when they have earned it, and not before.[65]

In Commissioner Howard's report to Congress on bureau operations at the end of 1865, he noted that when he took charge of the bureau, the distribution of rations had been very large, "and the idea seemed to prevail throughout large companies of freedmen and poor white refugees that they were to be the permanent recipients of food," leading him to order "great discrimination" in distributing relief, "so as to include none that are not absolutely necessitous and destitute." Otherwise, Howard warned, the coming winter would see "a large number of dependents, old men, women and children . . . become a tax to the general government." Howard did not address the role that the provision of rations to contracted workers played in supporting a planter's operations, that only the ability to provide provisions—if necessary, arrange for them through the bureau—encouraged freedpeople to sign contracts with lowcountry rice planters in 1866 and 1867. In essence, the provision of relief was as much charity to planters—who lacked the resources to pay regular cash wages—as it was to starving freedpeople. In his conclusion, Howard postulated a relationship between emancipation, the end of planters' responsibility for "the aged, the infirm, and the helpless negroes," freedpeople's imperfect family relations, and the growing number of freedpeople becoming "wards of the government." Howard warned that until the families of freedpeople could be regularized by law and shaped to more closely resemble Northern ideals of family life, large numbers of dependents would continue to rely on government support.[66]

The military command also linked eligibility to receive rations to the contract labor system when the commander of the Department of the South issued orders, at the beginning of 1866, that prohibited the issuance of rations to persons not contracting to work but capable of earning a living.[67] The order increased military intervention into lowcountry labor relations, providing a rationale for men like James Beecher to force freedpeople into contracted labor—as a means to prevent their dependence on government support.[68] By the beginning of the 1866 harvest season, the Secretary of War had ordered the Freedmen's Bureau to cease all issues of rations (or clothing, etc.) to freedpeople with very few exceptions, turning to the states to assume this as their own responsibility.[69]

In fact, the bureau did continue to provide rations to freedpeople, but largely as part of the ongoing effort to reorganize the lowcountry rice plantation economy. By mid-February 1866, planters understood that the bureau would issue rations to planters for their contracted workers, on the basis of a lien against the freedpeople's crop, with the planters liable in the case of crop failures. The offer was critical to the restoration of planting on several rice plantations.[70]

The bureau's provision of rations had kept many freedpeople alive when the bad weather of the two previous growing seasons produced poor harvests. Although in 1867 the bureau became increasingly insistent that only contracted laborers were eligible to receive rations, the devastation of the state's corn crop by drought in 1866 and the extensive damage to the rice crops by heavy June rains in 1867 prompted private organizations and the federal government to send provisions to South Carolina for distribution among the freedpeople.[71] In the long run, the bureau's insistence on linking eligibility for relief to the contract labor system, along with the poor postbellum harvests, may have contributed to freedpeople's increasing dependence on plantation stores.

Further evidence of the state's growing interest in freedpeople's families was revealed in the provision of free transportation to freedpeople by the bureau and the army. This was a charitable practice that had been widespread in 1865, to assist former slaves removed from their families by planters during the war, freedpeople assured of employment in other locations, and freedpeople who had a legitimate claim on Sea Island land. But in January 1866, the military commander of the Department of South Carolina decreed that transportation would be denied to freedmen who were not also joined by their families, as a means of preventing a male head of household from escaping his family obligations. Only in instances where freedwomen and children sought to rejoin their husbands could they obtain transportation, to enable freedmen to assume support of their families and so the women could join their "male protectors." Commissioner Howard of the Freedmen's Bureau issued a circular in April similarly limiting the provision of transportation to those who might otherwise become dependent on the government for support.[72] Thus when a freedman petitioned the Mount Pleasant bureau agent to provide free transportation to his two daughters, stranded in the upcountry with their former owner "in bad conditions," Assistant Commissioner Scott overruled the sympathetic bureau agent and insisted that the freedman should "work and pay the fare himself."[73] Despite such reactions, throughout 1866 the bureau continued to provide free transportation to freedwomen and their children who wished to return to their lowcountry homes from the interior of the state where their former owners had brought them during the war, apparently without comment or concern about the potential for becoming dependent on government relief.[74] Neither did bureau officials seem perturbed when lowcountry planters helped their former slaves apply for free transportation from interior wartime refuges back to the lowcountry, presumably to work on their plantations.[75]

Families and Labor Discipline

One aspect of bureau policy shaped implicitly by ideas about gender's role in family form and function was the effort to resolve and ultimately prevent labor disputes. In 1865, bureau rulings in several lowcountry labor conflicts indicated that the bureau tended to regard spouses and family members as individuals, each obligated to fulfill his or her own contract terms and individually entitled to fair treatment; the dismissal and eviction of a spouse or parent did not affect the rights of a spouse or other family members to remain on the plantation.[76] The bureau's treatment of families in the context of plantation production and labor conflict began to change by early 1866, however, possibly in response to the continued unsettled labor conditions in the lowcountry. The change in bureau policy might also have been an effort to address lowcountry planters' objections that freedmen dismissed from plantations pursued work off the plantation but continued to reside with their families on the plantation. The dismissal of individual workers was not enforcing the labor discipline so desired both by planters and bureau agents.

In January 1866, the bureau decreed that the wives and children of men who were deemed troublemakers and evicted from plantations would be forced to join the men off the plantation; "able-bodied freedmen, when they leave the premises in which they may be domiciled, shall take with them and provide for such of their relatives as, by the laws of South Carolina, all citizens are obliged to maintain."[77] Although the general order that established this new policy also provided that planters were still obligated to provide shelter for orphans, the elderly, and others too incapacitated by age or illness to work, the provision excluded even these protected groups if they were found guilty of disorderly behavior or misdemeanor, or if their family head had committed some similar offense. Thereafter, freedpeople—in particular, freedmen—who became embroiled in labor conflicts with planters risked not only their own dismissal, but the eviction of their entire families. This required different family strategies when freedpeople wanted to challenge the organization, terms, or conditions of their work—or in any way question the authority of planter or overseer. The order's focus on freedmen might have led freedpeople to believe that freedwomen's protests in the rice fields may not put families at the same risk as that of freedmen might; perhaps this encouraged some of freedwomen's very active participation in labor protests. Yet the order also undermined freedwomen's autonomy, making them subject to the consequences of their husband's actions. This was demonstrated in one particular incident following a conflict between a freedman and a planter, E. B. Heyward. Heyward said that "his poor wife came crying afterwards to me, fearing she and the children (and the poultry) would have to leave the place, but I told her to remain and that her husband was not discharged but only sent home for his impudence." The freedwoman attempted to placate the planter and appealed to him for mercy. Heyward responded that she "shows wonderful good sense" in appealing to him in this way.[78]

By the end of June, when the demands of rice culture eased, freedmen in particular began to pursue day work outside the plantation. The military saw this as a violation of their contracts and an unnecessary threat to the free-labor system; in trying to prevent it, the military commander in South Carolina went so far as to order that the children of any freedman charged with deserting legal employment would, along with the charged freedman, be bound out into involuntary apprenticeships. The order evoked almost an immediate response from planters intent on restricting the mobility of their contracted workers. Within days, one planter complained to bureau officials about the freedwoman Scilla, who, although a contracted worker, was traveling place to place in search of food for herself and children—to the neglect of the crop, and to the disadvantage of those people in the neighborhood who suspected Scilla was desperate enough to be stealing from them. The planter recommended, as dictated by Scott's order, that Scilla be taken up as a vagrant and her children bound out to proper and discreet persons. Again, the threats were mounting: the resistance that marked freedpeople's participation in the lowcountry plantation economy met with increasing threats to the independence and integrity of their entire families.[79]

Labor contracts in 1866 did not all adhere to the new policy; for example, many contracts approved by bureau agents specified that if a male or female head of household faced dismissal from the plantation for some infraction, the wages owed the worker would be distributed to family members remaining on the plantation. It seemed that bureau policy about labor unrest and its consequences was left largely up to the discretion of local agents. In fact, bureau agents, in mediating labor conflict, occasionally instructed planters not to dismiss the family members of evicted troublemakers. In one such instance, the planter appealed to the precedent established by Scott's order, pointing out that the freedman at issue would simply obtain day work nearby and continue to make the plantation—where his family still resided—his domicile. This was an outcome that the planter suspected was the freedman's intent from the start—to nullify the contract and obtain better employment nearby.[80]

In a circular addressed to the landlords and laborers of the state during the closing days of 1866, Assistant Commissioner Scott elaborated on how the bureau regarded families in the context of enforcing labor contracts. Scott announced that when a family head was dismissed from a plantation for *his* failure to meet the terms of the labor contract, his family would be dismissed along with him, since "its retention would in a measure relieve the laborer of the support of his family, which is his first duty."[81] Scott's circular included his extensive analysis of why wage labor had not yet succeeded in the lowcountry, and also offered his solutions to this failure—including increasing the pressure on freedmen to support their families, and pressuring planters to pay freedmen a "family wage." Scott believed that these two solutions would remove several of the causes for complaint and dissatisfaction that had disrupted free labor in the preceding years. Scott even indicated his willingness to allow wives of freedmen to withdraw from contract labor, "as long as they don't become dependent on the government."[82]

Following up on his orders, Scott directed the Georgetown bureau agent to evict the freedmen and their families who refused to work as agreed on John Read's Sampit River rice plantation. The freedmen had sought day work at neighboring plantations, in order to buy rations, while their wives and children took care of the seven-acre rice crop, as well as their own gardens. Scott insisted that since they failed to contract for proper terms, the men and their families should be evicted.[83] Although many labor contracts for 1867—both manuscript contracts and those printed by the bureau—failed to specify Scott's policy about the eviction of families, contracts rarely detailed any provision for how labor conflicts were to be settled.[84]

Family Politics

Freedwomen's responses to the family politics of reconstruction—the legal status of their unions, the vulnerability of freed families to involuntary child apprenticeships, the attendant risks when freedwomen and children were designated subordinates to male head of households—were informed and shaped by freedwomen's historical experience of slavery as well as the conflicts that had been unfolding in the South since the beginning of the Civil War. Freedwomen's understanding of this "war at home" overlapped their concerns about the terms and conditions of wage labor, the organization of family economies, and the struggle to keep planter and overseer authority at a distance. But this was also a war that encompassed disputes between family members over "real resources and benefits," conflicts that arose not simply from "personal aspirations but also from changing social norms and conditions," and that sometimes led to family violence.[85]

As this chapter's opening example of Clarender's complaint to her local bureau agent revealed, freedpeople apparently recognized and manipulated the bureau's interest in regulating and monitoring marriages and families, appealing to the bureau to intervene when their personal circumstances were unsatisfactory or when conflict arose between family members.[86] Unfortunately, few lowcountry bureau records of this type seem to have survived. But extant records kept by middle- and upcountry bureau agents in Greenville, Darlington, and Union District deserve our attention, in part because they reflect the bureau's systematic willingness to intervene in domestic relations when freedpeople requested their assistance, although particular circumstances varied widely.[87] In Orangeburg, Fanny, a married freedwoman, asked a bureau agent to prevent a married man from trying to coerce her to "go with him." One freedman, Thomas Scriven, complained of being robbed of his clothing by his wife, Lizzie; Lizzie, however, reported to the bureau that her husband had failed to repay a debt to her, and she had taken his clothes in lieu of payment.[88] Children sometimes appealed to the bureau to intervene, including in incidents involving family violence. A young girl, Amaretta, complained to the bureau agent that the freedman Jake, her father, was beating Lucy, her mother—which Jake denounced as a lie. In Barnwell District, in 1867, a son reported his father to the bureau for beating his mother, himself, and the other children.[89]

Freedwomen called on the bureau as well as the provost courts to intervene when they were being beaten by their husbands, negotiating the competing jurisdiction of military, bureau, and civilian authorities as they pursued claims against abusive husbands. South Carolina's provost courts—the most extensive system of military courts established in the South—assumed jurisdiction over all but the most severe cases involving freedpeople in 1865, hearing cases before a tribunal composed of an army officer and two civilians. At this time, the Freedmen's Bureau recorded and investigated charges of "outrages" perpetrated by whites against blacks and the reverse. The bureau and the military seemed eventually to reach an agreement that proximity dictated jurisdiction. Freedpeople could appeal to either authority, although the bureau was officially charged with the protection of freedpeople's legal rights, and the army and bureau occasionally clashed over when and how justice was administered to freedpeople. In June 1866, the assistant commissioner of the bureau in South Carolina, R. K. Scott, assumed control of military forces in the state, ostensibly combining military and bureau authority into one office, giving him jurisdiction over the provost courts—although Scott felt his actual authority over the military was "nominal." The following month the Freedmen's Bureau Bill expanded the bureau's authority over freedmen's affairs to include the civil rights of freedpeople until the state legislature opened the state courts and civil proceedings to freedpeople on an equal basis with whites, in the fall of 1866. Only the Sea Islands were exempt from the restoration of state authority; there, provost courts continued.

Complicating the picture even further, in 1865 Assistant Commissioner Saxton had tried to bring civil magistrates into the administration of civil justice, obtaining very mixed results. At that time one bureau agent described civil law as an "expensive luxury," because magistrates frequently demanded large bonds from freedpeople prior to acting on their behalf. Rene Ravenel, one of these civil magistrates, not only failed to take freedpeople's complaints seriously but also believed "negroes misrepresent things to such a degree that there is very little truth to be found from their story until after investigation." Freedpeople preferred to bring their complaints to the bureau or the provost courts.[90]

We have no way of estimating the extent or frequency of domestic violence among freedpeople, especially given the paucity of lowcountry records. Nonetheless, we know that bureau or military officials became aware of violence committed by freedmen against freedwomen when the women appealed to the bureau and the provost courts to intervene. Incidents of domestic violence were one of the relatively few instances when freedwomen invited the state to mediate in their personal and family lives. The freedwoman Laney complained to the Orangeburg bureau agent of being "beat about 30 lashes, with a leather strap, over her back and shoulders, by her husband Cesar." When called to explain his actions, Cesar both minimized and rationalized his attack on Laney. Only two of the cuts drew blood, and his attack was clearly justified, since he had whipped her "for laziness & being indifferent to his comfort or welfare, and not working, washing or mending his clothes, and for roaming about the country instead of remaining at home." Another freedwoman, Elsie, also complained to the bureau about being beaten; her assailant, the freedman Toney, retorted that Elsie "called him a son of a bitch several times, hit him with an ear of corn," at which he slapped her twice. John Gardner, a freedman, was reported to the Orangeburg bureau agent by the freedwoman Silvy, for brutally beating her; John insisted that Silvy "was acting very unchastely and sleeping with a man without being married." John apparently slapped her "several times" when she ignored his order to leave his house. Leah Perry brought her husband before the provost court in Beaufort because he had choked and beaten her in their home on Port Royal and again in the streets of Beaufort. In passing sentence, the judge of the provost court noted that "the matter of beating their wives is so common among the freedmen that pretty stern action is necessary to put a stop to it."[91]

Since their arrival on the Sea Islands during the war, Northern whites had commented on the prevalence of domestic violence among contrabands and freedpeople, including those from mainland rice plantations. Laura Towne, who complained of the mistreatment women received from their husbands in a variety of matters, also complained that freedmen felt that freedom brought to them the right to beat their wives. Another Northern observer simply found "that the colored men whip their wives."[92] An upcountry bureau agent also noted that "freedmen seem to think they have a perfect right to whip their wives on the slightest provocation and several have reported that they have been brutally beaten by their husbands."[93] Freedwomen's frequent and detailed complaints about physical abuse at the hands of freedmen indicate that abuse was occurring, but determining whether patterns of abuse preceded the war or developed only in the aftermath of war and freedom lies beyond the extant evidence. Certainly, testimony of freedmen brought before authorities on charges of attacking freedwomen suggests that these men felt fully justified in resorting to physical violence when their wives failed to behave or work as these men believed gender norms dictated. It is also true that in contrast to Southern whites' refusal to recognize the role of slave men as husbands and fathers, bureau and military policy focused considerable attention on freedmen. Fathers became the subject of policies that established their authority and obligations as heads of households; relief was distributed through freedmen as well as freedwomen (in contrast to the distribution of slave rations and clothing exclusively through mothers); freedmen's field labor, for the first time, was valued more highly than that of freedwomen, as reflected in bureau wage rates.

The free-labor endeavor in lowcountry South Carolina was infused with the effort to render freedmen "self-reliant and manly," an endeavor complemented by slave and freedmen's wartime and postbellum military experience as well.[94] Military authorities and civilian observers alike described the culmination of the transition from slavery to freedom for all former slaves in terms of the enhanced masculine authority and prerogatives of freedmen; there was no corollary—no universal description of freedom's benefits cast in terms of freedwomen's greater independence, or their accrual of greater respect or personal power. Yet the tendency of Northern civilians and military officials to emphasize and reinforce the power and privilege of masculinity, in the long run, tells us far more about the intent of Reconstruction policy than its actual impact on freedmen (and freedwomen).

For many of the freedwomen (upcountry and lowcountry) who sought out the bureau's intervention in domestic disputes, the primary concern they expressed was their husbands' failure to help support them or their children. This, too, had its wartime precedents; according to one military official, married contrabands "change about at pleasure—a man will not live with his wife because she does not treat him well, and a woman will not live with her husband because another man will provide for her better."[95] Although lowcountry slave culture had emphasized the exchange of material support and services between spouses, freedwomen seemed to have seized upon the bureau's rhetoric about men's responsibilities to support their families. Mrs. Rebecca Ann, of Beaufort, petitioned her local bureau agent to arrest her husband and force him to post a bond for her support; he had deserted her to live with another woman in Barnwell District. Flora Chisolm, also of Beaufort, brought similar charges against her husband, Landon, and also sought bonds for her support. In Orangeburg District, Lucy Jenkins, repeatedly beaten by her husband, who had finally thrown her out of their house, had no source of support besides her husband and so asked the bureau to authorize her return to the household. The freedwoman Charlotte Sally complained that she and her four children had been abandoned by her husband, who left behind no provision for their support.[96] In Barnwell District, Charity complained to the bureau agent that her husband had deserted her and left to her the sole support of her three children. The agent ordered her husband to return, to live with her, and to support her children.[97] James Anderson, a resident of Beaufort, was brought before the provost court, convicted of beating his common-law wife, Jane, with a club, and was fined and threatened with hard labor should he break the peace again. The beating had occurred after James had left Jane and their children to live with another woman; Jane, in turn, had stolen some of James's rice to feed their nine-month-old child, for which James had attacked her.[98] When James Bracey, father of a child borne by Regina Toney, attempted to bring her to court to sue her for custody rights, Toney "said the child was mine & that there was no way for me to get it without we'd cut it in half & divide it—I said before I'd do that it could stay—I then told her I would try it in law—she said I had never given the child anything. . . . I have had the care of that child since it was born[.] It has been well provided for all the time." Toney defended her custody rights by virtue of her sole support of the child.[99]

Other women appealed to the bureau not to gain their husbands' support, but rather to force their husbands to return property the men had stolen from them. When Nancy Bacon charged her husband, Titus, with deserting her and their many children, she sought to regain use of the four acres of land they had purchased with their joint earnings. The provost court transferred ownership of the land to Nancy, and, describing Titus as "domineering, unfaithful & living upon the labor of his wife," decreed that Nancy be freed "from his influence or authority as a husband," although the court admitted it lacked authority to grant a legal divorce.[100] In Darlington, the freedwoman Rose complained that after she had harvested an extra corn and fodder crop, her husband had taken it for himself; she asked the bureau to intervene and force him to return the crop to her. Margaret, another freedwoman, complained that her husband, who had recently deserted her, had sold a cow and calf that she had purchased with her own money; she asked the bureau to make him keep away from her and to leave her property alone.[101]

Other freedwomen seemed to have used the bureau to take revenge, to make a point, and even to enter paternity into the public record. Clarender's complaint to the bureau agent at St. James Santee offers one such example. M. A. Holland, a freedwoman of Horry District, also seizing on the bureau's interest in shaping the domestic affairs of freedpeople, appealed to the bureau not only to gain material support for herself and her children, but also to punish and teach her husband a lesson: "my Husband has treated me most cruel and shameful and sent me away with two little c[h]ildren and he has kept everything and says he will not give me any thing to live on[;] he kept some of our clothing too and says he will not do any thing for me. . . . I want you to take him and put him in Penetensuary or in some of your Forts and make him work and support me and his children that he has give me to live upon other people. . . . You are strange to me but I do earnestly trust that you will favor me."[102] The freedwoman Flora Murphy appealed to a local bureau agent that the father of her two young children be made to provide for their support; her appeal forced the agent to acknowledge that the bureau's ideas about family obligations were racially determined. The agent admitted that the bureau could probably do very little for her, as the father of Murphy's children was her former owner, a white man.[103]

Freedwomen and men alike used the provost courts when violence capped longstanding or complicated family feuds. This was the case in an attack by Hester Scott on Sarah Waite with an ax, for which the court fined Scott twenty-five dollars and court costs or sixty days confinement at hard labor. Court testimony revealed that the attack was the outcome of a confrontation between the two women over the support of Sarah and her four children. At the time of the confrontation that led to the violence, Hester had, for four months, been living with Paul, Sarah's estranged husband, to whom Sarah had been married "since I was young," about five years before the war. According to Paul's testimony, Sarah and Paul had separated when Sarah "disowned me . . . and went home to her father." Paul had since taken Hester "for my wife." Sarah, however, had charged Paul and Hester with an obligation to help support the four children Sarah had borne during her marriage to Paul. Sarah's ability to tend her crops had been limited by having four children to care for on her own, and she had unsuccessfully challenged her estranged husband to help in the support of the children. Sarah then approached Hester, who at the time was chopping firewood, and demanded from Hester her pea crop, as Sarah had "lost my peas on account of her." Hester rebuked the claim—"she would like to see the one who would make her share her crop"—and the two women began to fight, ending when Hester delivered a wounding blow to Sarah's head with the ax.[104]

At the same time that freedwomen seized upon the bureau's rhetoric about families and used it to their own advantage, there were constraints that made freedwomen reluctant to appeal to the bureau or the military about domestic disputes. Not all bureau agents took the women's complaints seriously. The agent at Orangeburg who heard and recorded many domestic complaints described the conflicts and made recommendations in a sarcastic, condescending tone: in a typical case, involving quarreling and infidelity, the agent advised the husband and wife "to forget their little troubles, forgive and forget, work hard; lay up something for a rainy day, and they won't have much time or inclination to quarrel, and above all be honest, industrious, and virtuous."[105] Other bureau agents felt they had little authority or leeway to act on freedwomen's complaints; one agent complained that in the upcountry districts, the civil courts refused to intervene in such cases, and he himself could not accomplish much, believing he lacked the necessary authority to arrest and punish the offenders.[106]

As freedwomen attempted to allocate their productive and reproductive labor according to their own ideas, they encountered the opposition of not only planters and overseers but also military and bureau authorities. These officials viewed the families of former slaves as the raw material out of which the bureau would form the free-labor society they hoped would replace the vestiges of Southern slavery. Convinced that slavery had prevented African-American men and women from developing the virtues on which a free-labor society was founded—including the self-discipline that regulated labor as well as sexuality—Northern agents of Reconstruction set out to rebuild lowcountry culture and society in their own image of a free-labor society.[107] Former slave families on lowcountry rice plantations became the targets of missionary efforts, policy, and informal intervention that neither recognized nor understood the traditional values that had guided and informed enslaved African American families for generations—including the important ties to and obligations among extended kin; the contributions of children to household production and survival; and the basis of marriage not only in affection but also in the exchange of services and labor. Instead, the bureau sought to remake slave marriages and slave families into legal marriages and households established in idealized domesticity.[108]

The social order envisioned and idealized by Northern agents of Reconstruction was distinctly gendered. Freedmen would become industrious, disciplined laborers, earning a family wage and supporting their wives and children, while freedwomen would create and maintain a "civilized" and pleasant domestic sphere. While freedwomen were expected to work in the fields at least temporarily to help their families "gain a little surplus"—after all, they have "been accustomed to field labor"—the bureau avoided any suggestion that freedwomen might become a permanent class of laborers as had most free African-American women in the North.[109] Freedwomen's crucial role in the immediate postbellum plantation workforce was rationalized by bureau agents as a temporary necessity. They believed freedwomen's contribution to the evolution of free labor in the South would ultimately come from a separate domestic sphere, dependent on the family wage earned by freedmen.[110]

The implications of the bureau's gendered policy were especially important after 1865, when the bureau became preoccupied with freedpeople's dependence on charity, be it food, clothing, or medical care. Overlooking the wartime devastation of the rice plantation infrastructure and the poor crops of the postbellum years, the Freedmen's Bureau "diagnosed" freedpeople's reliance on charity in distinctly racialized and, to a lesser extent, gendered terms: their dependence reflected the failure of a race of men to overcome their servility rather than the bleak material conditions created by slavery and war. The bureau was especially alarmed that freedmen had failed to support their families ("which is [their] first duty"), an indication that the bureau expected women and children to depend on freedmen's wages for their own livelihood rather than contribute to household subsistence.[111] As bureau policy makers and field agents sought to transfer freedpeople's dependency to male heads of households, their interest in controlling the labor force extended to defining legal marriages, parental rights and authority, the best interests of the children, and the distribution of labor within the family.[112] The bureau became a formidable, if bungling, vehicle of intervention into the social relations of the lowcountry African-American community.[113]

For at least two reasons, freedwomen could not and did not simply disregard bureau policies. The first of these concerns the bureau's power over lowcountry labor relations: the bureau dissolved contracts, evicted freedmen and their families, and denied rations to freedpeople who rejected bureau policies. The second reason relates to evidence that freedmen and freedwomen's own ideas about the relationship between gender and authority in their communities was in flux, buffeted in part by the impact of men's military experience, by freedmen's prominence in conventions and other political gatherings, as well as by the policies of the federal government that promulgated an unprecedented emphasis on fathers and husbands as part of their larger agenda in spreading the gospel of free labor in the postwar South. Freedwomen appealed to local bureau agents to intervene in intrafamily disputes over the support of households, questions of child custody, and cases of domestic violence, as they attempted to defend their own position in households profoundly altered by war and the destruction of slavery.

∞

In describing the actions of freedpeople in determining how, when, and for whom they would work, one lowcountry planter commented "the women are the controlling spirits."[114] However bitter, antagonistic, or exaggerated the response of rice planters and plantation mistresses toward lowcountry freedwomen who acted on their own authority, freedwomen did indeed give meaning to the immediate transition from slave to free labor.

The misperception that freedwomen universally withdrew from the plantation workforce or domestic service has had a very important impact on our view of African-American women during their transition to freedom and the South's transition to a free-labor society. We have for too long labored under the mistaken idea that freedwomen universally withdrew from some of the most important "battlefields" of freedom. In fact, it was on rice plantations, in planter residences, and in their own households that former slave women fought a protracted battle over the meaning of freedom. They had endured the brutalities of slavery, and survived the unprecedented violence and chaos of war and its aftermath, only through a careful negotiation of the exacting regime of rice plantation slavery—not by surrendering their own and their children's fate to the workings of the world of plantation slavery. Freedwomen insisted on working "in their own time, as they see fit"; on reconstituting their families in ways that made sense according to their own standards and expectations; on meeting their obligations and responsibilities not only as wives and mothers but also as sisters, aunts, grandmothers, and as women who knew too well the costs of slavery.[115] In so doing freedwomen helped assert their own and their community's autonomy from uninvited intervention and shaped the long-term consequences of that region's transition to black freedom and free labor.[116]

NOTES

Abbreviations

LC   Library of Congress

M   Microfilm Publication

Navy OR U.S. Navy Department. *Official Records of the Union and Confederate Navies in the War of the Rebellion,* 30 vols. Washington, D.C., 1894–1922.

OR   U.S. War Department. *The War of the Rebellion: A Compilation of Official Records of the Union and Confederate Armies,* 128 vols. Washington, D.C., 1880–1901.

PL   Manuscripts Department, William R. Perkins Library, Duke University

Pt.   Part

R   Reel

RABSP Kenneth M. Stampp, ed. *Records of Ante-Bellum Southern Plantations from the Revolution through the Civil War.* Frederick, Md.: University Publications of America, c. 1985–c. 1996.

RG   Record Group, National Archives

SC   South Carolina

SCDAH South Carolina Department of Archives and History

SCHS   South Carolina Historical Society

SCL   South Caroliniana Library, University of South Carolina

Ser.   Series

SHC   Southern Historical Collection, University of North Carolina, Chapel Hill

USCT United States Colored Troops

Bracketed letters and numbers (e.g., [A-7192]) refer to file numbers of documents copied from the National Archives by the editors of the Freedmen and Southern Society Project at the University of Maryland, source of the multivolume documentary history of emancipation, *Freedom: A Documentary History of Emancipation, 1861–1867.*

Introduction

1. See, for example, Ira Berlin, Joseph P. Reidy, and Leslie S. Rowland, eds., *Freedom: A Documentary History of Emancipation, 1861–1867,* Series II, *The Black Military Experience* (Cambridge: Cambridge University Press, 1982); Ira Berlin, Barbara J. Fields, Thavolia Glymph, Joseph P. Reidy, and Leslie S. Rowland, eds., *Freedom: A Documentary History of Emancipation, 1861–1867,* Series I, Vol. 1, *The Destruction of Slavery* (Cambridge: Cambridge University Press, 1985); Ira Berlin, Thavolia Glymph, Steven F. Miller, Joseph P. Reidy, Leslie S. Rowland, and Julie

Saville, eds., *Freedom: A Documentary History of Emancipation, 1861–1867,* Series I, Vol. 3, *The Wartime Genesis of Free Labor: The Lower South* (Cambridge: Cambridge University Press, 1990); Barbara Jeanne Fields, *Slavery and Freedom on the Middle Ground: Maryland During the Nineteenth Century* (New Haven: Yale University Press, 1985); Eric Foner, *Nothing But Freedom: Emancipation and Its Legacy* (Baton Rouge: Louisiana State University Press, 1983) and *Reconstruction: America's Unfinished Revolution, 1863–1877* (New York: Harper and Row, 1988); Thavolia Glymph and John J. Kushma, eds., *Essays on the Postbellum Southern Economy* (College Station: Texas A & M University Press, 1985); Thomas Holt, "'An Empire Over the Mind': Emancipation, Race, and Ideology in the British West Indies and the American South," in *Region, Race, and Reconstruction: Essays in Honor of C. Vann Woodward,* ed. J. Morgan Kousser and James M. McPherson (New York: Oxford University Press, 1982), 283–313; Gerald David Jaynes, *Branches without Roots: Genesis of the Black Working Class in the American South, 1862–1882* (New York: Oxford University Press, 1986); and Lynda J. Morgan, *Emancipation in Virginia's Tobacco Belt, 1850–1870* (Athens: University of Georgia Press, 1992).

   2. Deborah Gray White, *Ar'n't I a Woman? Female Slaves in the Plantation South* (New York: Norton, 1985); Jacqueline Jones, *Labor of Love, Labor of Sorrow: Black Women, Work, and the Family from Slavery to the Present* (New York: Basic Books, 1985). The literature on slave and freedwomen is quickly growing; see Kathleen M. Brown, *Good Wives, Nasty Wenches, and Anxious Patriarchs: Gender, Race, and Power in Colonial Virginia* (Chapel Hill: University of North Carolina Press, 1996); Elizabeth Fox-Genovese, *Within the Plantation Household: Black and White Women in the Old South* (Chapel Hill: University of North Carolina Press, 1988); Brenda Stevenson, "Distress and Discord in Virginia Slave Families, 1830–1860," in *In Joy and In Sorrow: Women, Family and Marriage in the Victorian South,* ed. Carol Blesser (New York: Oxford University Press, 1991), 103–24; Dorothy Sterling, ed., *We Are Your Sisters: Black Women in the Nineteenth-Century South* (New York: Norton, 1984); Susan A. Mann, "Slavery, Sharecropping, and Sexual Inequality," *Signs* 14, no. 4 (1989): 788–97; Noralee Frankel, "The Southern Side of 'Glory': Mississippi African-American Women during the Civil War," in *"We Specialize in the Wholly Impossible": A Reader in Black Women's History,* ed. Darlene Clark Hine, Wilma King, and Linda Reed (Brooklyn: Carlson, 1995), 335–42; Laura F. Edwards, "Sexual Violence, Gender, Reconstruction, and the Extension of Patriarchy in Granville County, North Carolina," *North Carolina Historical Review* 68, no. 3 (1991): 237–60; Catherine Clinton, "Reconstructing Freedwomen," in *Divided Houses: Gender and the Civil War,* ed. Catherine Clinton and Nina Silber (New York: Oxford University Press, 1992), 306–19; Victoria E. Bynum, *Unruly Women: The Politics of Social and Sexual Control in the Old South, 1840–1865* (Chapel Hill: University of North Carolina Press, 1992); and Orville Vernon Burton, *In My Father's House Are Many Mansions: Family and Community in Edgefield, South Carolina* (Chapel Hill: University of North Carolina Press, 1985). Two excellent collections of additional literature include Darlene Clark Hine, Elsa Barkley Brown, Tiffany R. L. Patterson, and Lillian S. Williams, eds., *Black Women in U.S. History: From Colonial Times to the Present* (New York: Carlson, 1990), and Patricia Morton, ed., *Discovering the Women in Slavery: Emancipating Perspectives on the American Past* (Athens: University of Georgia Press, 1995).

3. Figures cited from William Dusinberre, *Them Dark Days: Slavery in the American Rice Swamps* (New York: Oxford University Press, 1996), 457–58, and Peter A. Coclanis, *The Shadow of a Dream: Economic Life and Death in the South Carolina Low Country, 1670–1920* (New York: Oxford University Press, 1989), 112. On the diversity of the lowcountry plantation society, see Stephanie McCurry, *Masters of Small Worlds: Yeoman Households, Gender Relations, and the Political Culture of the Antebellum South Carolina Low Country* (New York: Oxford University Press, 1995), esp. chaps. 1 and 2. The rice-planting region of South Carolina—responsible for 98 percent of the state's rice production in 1859—embraced the lower districts of Charleston, Beaufort, Colleton, Georgetown, and, more marginally, Horry and Williamsburg. According to the Seventh U.S. Census, 446 rice plantations were to be found in the state; William Dusinberre estimates that 137 of these were large plantations (those with more than 100 slaves). Lowcountry agriculture was not limited to the large rice plantations; it also included cotton farms and plantations, producing 12 percent of the state's cotton crop, 15 percent of the state's corn crop, and 42 percent of the sweet potato crop (figures from 1859). The lowcountry region included about 16 percent of the state's improved farm acreage in 1859. See Alfred Glaze Smith Jr., *The Economic Adjustment of an Old Cotton State: South Carolina, 1820–1860* (Columbia: University of South Carolina Press, 1958), 62–63; Dusinberre, *Them Dark Days,* 460; and Lewis Cecil Gray, *History of Agriculture in the Southern United States to 1860,* 2 vols. (Washington, D.C.: Carnegie Institution, 1933), 2:722–23.

4. On emancipation and Reconstruction in lowcountry South Carolina, see Willie Lee Rose, *Rehearsal for Reconstruction: The Port Royal Experiment* (1964; rpt. New York: Vintage Books, 1967); Joel Williamson, *After Slavery: The Negro in South Carolina during Reconstruction, 1861–1877* (Chapel Hill: University of North Carolina Press, 1965); Thomas C. Holt, *Black Over White: Negro Political Leadership in South Carolina During Reconstruction* (Urbana: University of Illinois Press, 1977); Charles Joyner, *Down by the Riverside: A South Carolina Slave Community* (Urbana: University of Illinois Press, 1984); John Scott Strickland, "Traditional Culture and Moral Economy: Social and Economic Change in the South Carolina Low Country, 1865–1910," in *The Countryside in the Age of Capitalist Transformation: Essays in the Social History of Rural America,* ed. Steven Hahn and Jonathon Prude (Chapel Hill: University of North Carolina Press, 1985), 141–78, and idem, "'No More Mud Work': The Struggle for the Control of Labor and Production in Low Country South Carolina, 1863–1880," in *The Southern Enigma: Essays on Race, Class, and Folk Culture,* ed. Walter J. Fraser Jr. and Winfred B. Moore Jr. (Westport, Conn.: Greenwood, 1983), 43–62; Philip Morgan, "Work and Culture: The Task System and the World of Lowcountry Blacks, 1700 to 1880," *William and Mary Quarterly,* 3d ser., 39 (Oct. 1982): 563–99; Julie Saville, *The Work of Reconstruction: From Slave to Wage Laborer in South Carolina, 1860–1870* (New York: Cambridge University Press, 1994).

5. Scholars interested in the origins of American social welfare policy would do well to consider the Reconstruction-era debates over welfare provisions, as well as the example of how freedwomen contested the gender- and race-biased imperatives of federal social policy in the postbellum South. In turn, the current litera-

ture on women and the welfare state raises important questions about women's relationship to the state that bear clear revelance to the history of Reconstruction. See Linda Gordon, ed., *Women, the State, and Welfare* (Madison: University of Wisconsin Press, 1990).

6. See Hilary McD. Beckles, *Natural Rebels: A Social History of Enslaved Black Women in Barbados* (New Brunswick: Rutgers University Press, 1989), and Marietta Morrissey, *Slave Women in the New World: Gender Stratification in the Caribbean* (Lawrence: University of Kansas Press, 1989).

7. The war's impact on plantation slavery is discussed in Richard H. Sewell, *A House Divided: Sectionalism and Civil War, 1848–1865* (Baltimore: Johns Hopkins University Press, 1988), 101–25; Paul W. Gates, *Agriculture and the Civil War* (New York: Knopf, 1965), 3–45; Emory M. Thomas, *The Confederate Nation, 1861–1865* (New York: Harper and Row, 1979), 236–42; and James L. Roark, *Masters without Slaves: Southern Planters in the Civil War and Reconstruction* (New York: Norton, 1977).

8. Charles Manigault, "The Close of the War—The Negro, etc.," R1, Ser. J. Pt. 4, *RABSP.*

9. Roger Ransom and Richard Sutch, *One Kind of Freedom: The Economic Consequences of Emancipation* (Cambridge: Cambridge University Press, 1977), 44–47 and 232–36; Leon F. Litwack, *Been in the Storm So Long: The Aftermath of Slavery* (New York: Random House, 1974), 244–47; Herbert G. Gutman, *The Black Family in Slavery and Freedom 1750–1925* (New York: Pantheon, 1976), 167–68; Lawrence N. Powell, *New Masters: Northern Planters During the Civil War and Reconstruction* (New Haven: Yale University Press, 1980), 108–9; Eric Foner, *Reconstruction: America's Unfinished Revolution, 1863–1877* (New York: Harper and Rowe, 1988), 84–87; J. Jones, *Labor of Love*, 58–63; and Jaynes, *Branches without Roots*, 229–31.

10. See, for example, William Cohen, *At Freedom's Edge: Black Mobility and the Southern White Quest for Racial Control, 1861–1875* (Baton Rouge: Louisiana State University Press, 1991), 14, and Gutman, *The Black Family*, 167–68. Leon F. Litwack suggests that by insisting that their wives withdraw from the workforce, freedmen attempted to "reinforce their position as the head of the family in accordance with the accepted norms of the dominant society" (*Been in the Storm So Long*, 245), but in a following paragraph he also portrays withdrawal as a strategy by which freedwomen gained control over the allocation and conditions of their paid labor.

11. Gerald Jaynes argues that freedwomen's withdrawal from the labor market was a rational response to the decline in their wages and also reflected the greater cost-effectiveness of women's independent agriculture in family gardens (Jaynes, *Branches without Roots*, 228–31); Jacqueline Jones asserts, "Only at home could [freedwomen] exercise considerable control over their own lives and those of their husbands and children and impose a semblance of order on the physical world" (*Labor of Love*, 58).

12. In 1977, Roger L. Ransom and Richard Sutch offered the first quantitative estimate of the extent of freedwomen's withdrawal from plantation labor (*One Kind of Freedom*). Their work has since been used to support many assertions about the prevalence of women's withdrawal, despite the implicit and explicit limitations of

the Ransom and Sutch estimates. These include a failure to confirm planters' statements about the sexual division of labor on plantations by consulting overseer records; an overreliance on secondary sources, including the much-criticized work of Fogel and Engerman in *Time on the Cross;* and the use of Freedmen's Bureau estimates of work apparently without consideration for the propagandistic intent of those sources (for example, South Carolina agents repeatedly insisted that freedpeople should work ten hours a day, a notion widely rejected by lowcountry freedpeople). Ransom and Sutch did not investigate how plantation size, the process and organization of plantation production, or any other variation in the farm and plantation economies of the cotton South affected the amount of work performed by women in slavery or freedom, yet the authors assert that their findings can be generalized to the entire cotton South.

Other historians have ignored or overlooked the limitations of Ransom and Sutch's findings. Jacqueline Jones uses *One Kind of Freedom* as the basis for her assertion about the prevalence of withdrawal (in *Labor of Love*), but also emphasizes that first-hand observations about withdrawal were common (58–63). As Leon Litwack did, Jones groups together domestic servants and field hands in her discussion of withdrawal, implying that freedwomen responded similarly to very different work conditions (Litwack, *Been in the Storm So Long,* 244–47). In an important contribution to the discussion of women's withdrawal from wage work, Jones challenges the suggestion that freedwomen sought to "play the lady" or were forced to withdraw by husbands; she respects freedwomen's choices to allocate their labor in what they saw as the best interests of themselves and their families. That approach has also been used by Lawrence Powell, who suggests that freedwomen were among the most militant of former slaves in the effort to control their labor (*New Masters,* 108–9). Powell offers no explanation of how women's labor militancy was reconciled with their decision to withdraw from labor conflict. Both Powell and Jones attempt to contextualize women's withdrawal in terms of the exploitation and oppression they encountered in the postbellum organization of free labor.

In *Branches without Roots,* Gerald Jaynes challenges the presumption of universality underlying the manner in which historians have described freedwomen's work choices, contrasting the rate of women's participation in different plantation systems—finding significantly less participation by women in postbellum sugar plantation agriculture, as opposed to cotton plantation agriculture (228–33). Jaynes, paying careful attention to the process and organization of production, attributes the difference to the distinct labor demands of the two crops. Jaynes also asserts that recognition of the rapid decrease in women's agricultural wages in the immediate postwar period should be fundamental to any consideration of the supply or withdrawal of women's labor. He argues that the purchasing power of women's wage work lagged behind the value of women's unpaid social and reproductive labor, making "withdrawal" a logical and rational choice. Jaynes thus draws our attention to significant factors that create variation in patterns of women's participation in wage labor after the war.

13. J. H. Easterby, ed., *The South Carolina Rice Plantation as Revealed in the Papers of Robert F. W. Allston* (Chicago: University of Chicago Press, 1945), 54.

14. James M. Clifton, ed., *Life and Labor on Argyle Island: Letters and Documents*

of a Savannah River Rice Plantation, 1833–1867 (Savannah: Beehive, 1978), x; Coclanis, *Shadow of a Dream,* 69–70; Philip D. Morgan, "Black Society in the Lowcountry, 1760–1810," in *Slavery and Freedom in the Age of the American Revolution,* Ira Berlin and Ronald Hoffman, eds. (Charlottesville: University Press of Virginia, 1983), 93; and John B. Boles, *Black Southerners, 1619–1869* (Lexington: University Press of Kentucky, 1984), 75.

15. Elizabeth W. Allston Pringle, *Chronicles of Chicora Wood* (Boston: Christopher Publishing House, 1940), 15; George P. Rawick, ed., *The American Slave: A Composite Autobiography* (Westport, Conn.: Greenwood, 1972), Vol. 3, South Carolina, Pt. 3, 92.

16. Indigo production became a very profitable secondary export crop on many eighteenth-century rice plantations, since its processing could be performed at slack times in rice production. While indigo culture undoubtedly contributed to the growth of the lowcountry plantation regime, the industry suffered during the Revolution and ultimately producers in America could not compete with those in India. See Gray, *History of Agriculture,* 1:293–96.

17. Edward Pearson offers a penetrating analysis of the lowcountry's agricultural revolution in "From Stono to Vesey: Slavery, Resistance, and Ideology in South Carolina, 1739–1822" (Ph.D. diss., University of Wisconsin, 1992), esp. chap. 2. A detailed account of South Carolina's transition from frontier to a plantation society can be found in Peter H. Wood, *Black Majority: Negroes in Colonial South Carolina from 1670 through the Stono Rebellion* (New York: Knopf, 1974), and Russell R. Menard, "The Africanization of the Lowcountry Labor Force," in *Race and Family in the Colonial South,* ed. Winthrop D. Jordan and Sheila L. Skemp (Jackson: University Press of Mississippi, 1987), 81–108; Daniel C. Littlefield, *Rice and Slaves: Ethnicity and the Slave Trade in Colonial South Carolina* (Baton Rouge: Louisiana State University Press, 1981), and Coclanis, *Shadow of a Dream.* On Africans' introduction of rice agriculture to Louisiana, see Gwendolyn Mindlo Hall, *Africans in Colonial Louisiana* (Baton Rouge: Louisiana State University Press, 1992).

18. Gray, *History of Agriculture,* 1:279–80, 2:722. The new rice plantations were limited to a narrow strip of the coast—lower North Carolina, South Carolina, and upper Georgia—where tidal action raised and lowered the level of water in freshwater rivers by six to seven feet, providing the necessary force to fill and drain the fields.

19. David Doar, in *Rice and Rice Planting in the South Carolina Low Country* (Charleston, S.C.: The Charleston Museum, 1936), 41, estimates the size and distribution (by river) of South Carolina rice plantations, noting that nearly 160 million pounds of rice was produced on 227 South Carolina plantations in 1850. I present here his findings in table form.

Location	Number of Rice Plantations	Acres Devoted to Rice Cultivation
Savannah River (South Carolina side)	18	5,635
Combahee River	34	12,591
Ashepoo River	14	3,295

Edisto River	9	4,970
Cooper River	41	6,050
Santee River	39	16,660
Sampit River	7	n.a.
Black River	16	4,335
Pee Dee River	22	n.a.
Waccamaw River	27	n.a.

20. Herbert Ravenel Sass and D. E. Huger Smith, *A Carolina Rice Plantation of the Fifties* (New York: Morrow, 1936), 22–25.

21. Captain Basil Hall, *Travels in North America, in the Years 1827 and 1828* (1830), quoted in *The Plantation South,* ed. Katherine M. Jones (Indianapolis: Bobbs-Merrill, 1957), 101.

22. In the most detailed exploration of African ethnicity and planter preference within the context of the South Carolina slave trade, Daniel C. Littlefield argues that one result of South Carolina's planter preferences was that the slave trade focused on regions where women were less available to the trade (*Rice and Slaves*). Littlefield's argument concurs with that made by Claire C. Robertson and Martin A. Klein in *Women and Slavery in Africa* (Madison: University of Wisconsin Press, 1983) about the impact of African control over the Atlantic slave trade. See also Robertson's review essay, "The Perils of Autonomy," in *Gender and History* 3, no. 1 (Spring 1991): 91–96.

23. John Davis, *Personal Adventures and Travels of Four Years and a Half in the United States of America* (1817), quoted in K. Jones, *The Plantation South,* 84.

24. Louis De Vorsey Jr., ed., *De Brahm's Report of the General Survey in the Southern District of North America* (Columbia: University of South Carolina Press, 1971), 94.

25. On the demography of African slave imports to South Carolina, see Littlefield, *Rice and Slaves,* 56–68; P. Morgan, "Black Society in the Lowcountry," 83–100; Wood, *Black Majority,* 150–66; and Menard, "Africanization." Scholars agree that increasing numbers of healthier Creoles in the slave population accelerated the rate of natural increase in the slave population to a far greater extent than balanced sex-ratios. Fragmentary evidence suggests that certain other demographic improvements—for example, in (Creole) women's age at first birth and in birth-spacing intervals—also increased the rate at which the slave population reproduced itself by the early national period.

26. P. Morgan, "Black Society in the Lowcountry," 83–141.

27. See Littlefield, *Rice and Slaves,* for a full exploration of African ethnicities and the South Carolina slave trade.

28. Boles, *Black Southerners,* 75. Georgetown District was established as a local administrative and judicial division in 1769, extending jurisdiction over several parishes established by South Carolina's Anglican church in 1721. In 1865, parishes were abolished as election units; by 1868, the state's districts were replaced by a county system of governance (George C. Rogers Jr., *The History of Georgetown County, South Carolina* [Columbia: University of South Carolina Press, 1970], 1–6).

29. Coclanis, *Shadow of a Dream,* 113.

30. On the lowcountry slave population, see Rogers, *History of Georgetown County,* 342–43, 359; Boles, *Black Southerners,* 75, 107; Gray, *History of Agriculture,* 1:481, 529, 531; Sherman L. Ricards and George M. Blackburn, "A Demographic History of Slavery: Georgetown County, South Carolina, 1850," *South Carolina Historical Magazine* 76 (Oct. 1975): 216–19; and P. Morgan, "Black Society in the Lowcountry," 85–86, 88, 93, 94, 129.

31. Sidney W. Mintz and Richard Price, *An Anthropological Approach to the Afro-American Past: A Caribbean Perspective* (Philadelphia: Institute for the Study of Human Issues, 1976), 35.

32. Wood, *Black Majority,* 324–25; Margaret Washington Creel, *"A Peculiar People": Slave Religion and Community-Culture among the Gullahs* (New York: New York University Press, 1988), 161–66.

33. "This is one of the Singular facts connected with our negro population," asserted one lowcountry planter; that people of African descent "thrive, and are healthy in the midst of our rice fields, and hot summer sun," while whites "sink under their influence" (Edward Thomas Heriot to [My Dear Cousin], Apr. 1854, Edward Thomas Heriot Family Papers, PL). See also Easterby, *South Carolina Rice Plantation,* 9.

34. Vorsey, *De Brahm's Report,* 94.

35. See Charles Manigault to Louis Manigault, 27 Mar. 1859, in Clifton, *Life and Labor,* 284; James M. Clifton, "The Rice Driver: His Role in Slave Management," *South Carolina Historical Magazine* 82 (Oct. 1981): 331–53; William L. Van Deburg, *The Slave Drivers: Black Agricultural Labor Supervisors in the Antebellum South* (New York: Oxford University Press, 1979); and Joyner, *Down by the Riverside,* 65–70.

36. See Robert Barnwell Rhett's Plantation Account Book, 1853–1874, in the Robert Barnwell Rhett Papers, PL.

37. See Rawick, *The American Slave,* Vol. 2, South Carolina, Pt. 1, 110–11, on cooperation among slaves. In 1858, the rice planter James R. Sparkman asserted that it was "customary (*and never objected to*) for the more active and industrious hands to assist those who are slower and more tardy in finishing their daily task" (Easterby, *South Carolina Rice Plantation,* 346).

38. P. Morgan, "Work and Culture," 569–74.

39. R. King Jr., "On the Management of the Butler Estate . . . . ," *Southern Agriculturist,* Dec. 1828. Many lowcountry planters and overseers held similar opinions about independent production by slaves. See B. McBride, "Directions for Cultivating the Various Crops Grown at Hickory Hill," *Southern Agriculturist,* May 1830: "All my slaves are to be supplied with sufficient land, on which encourage, and even compel them to plant and *cultivate* a crop. . . . This crop can be tended during their idle hours, after task work is done, which otherwise would be spent in the perpetration of some act that would subject them to severe punishment." In his essay "On the General Management of a Plantation" (*Southern Agriculturist,* July 1831), W. W. Hazard stated that "to encourage industry and increase the comfort and contentment of these people, I allow every one, a task of ground, and a half task for every child capable of working." The habits and customs set by the larger planters had an impact on how other slaveowners in the lowcountry treated their slaves: Mrs. Julia R. Speaks, a small farmer in Beaufort County, noted that she "allowed

my slaves a good many privileges. I gave them land to plant and allowed them to make something for themselves in their spare time. I also allowed them to raise Hogs and Poultry" (Affidavit by Mrs. Julia R. Speaks, 12 May 1875, claim of Harriet Smith, Beaufort County, SC, case files, Approved Claims, Ser. 732, Southern Claims Commission, 3d Auditor, RG 217). The topic of slaves' independent production and marketing activities has been the subject of considerable debate over the proper characterization of slaves' economic activities: as an integral part of plantation economies or, alternately, as a breach in those systems—and in some ways, an indirect challenge to them. Despite their differences, most scholars would probably agree with Dale Tomich that "slaves themselves created and controlled a secondary economic network which originated within the social and spatial boundaries of the plantation but which allowed for the construction of an alternative way of life that went beyond it" (Tomich, "Une Petite Guinee: Provision Ground and Plantation in Martinique, 1830–1848," in *Cultivation and Culture: Labor and the Shaping of Slave Life in the Americas,* ed. Ira Berlin and Philip D. Morgan [Charlottesville: University Press of Virginia, 1993], 222; see also the introductory essay by Berlin and Morgan, *Cultivation and Culture,* 1–45).

Chapter 1: "Women Always Did This Work"

The chapter title quotes from Duncan Clinch Heyward's observations about the sexual division of labor on rice plantations; see his memoir, *Seed from Madagascar* (Chapel Hill: University of North Carolina Press, 1937), 31.

1. P. Morgan, "Black Society in the Lowcountry," 97.

2. This finding is based on a small sampling of lowcountry plantation records from the quarter century preceding the war. Female slaves constituted the majority of all field hands on ten of the thirteen South Carolina plantations that were sampled. Furthermore, on only two of the sampled South Carolina plantations did male prime or full field hands outnumber female prime hands; in nine instances, female prime hands were either equal in number to (3) or outnumbered (6) male prime field hands (in two cases, the records did not include task ratings). An additional three Georgia plantations were also examined, and all included a majority of female prime field hands. See "List of Task Hands on Dirleton, 12 Feb. 1859," in Dirleton Plantation Memo Book, 1859–1864, James Ritchie Sparkman Papers (SCHS), R9, Ser. B, *RABSP;* "Task Hands Birdfield Jany. 1 1858," MS Vol. bd., 1857–1859, James Ritchie Sparkman Papers (SCL), R6, Ser. B, *RABSP;* William Elliott's Plantation Book for Pon Pon, 1841–1851, Subseries 5.1, Elliott-Gonzales Family Papers; Murry Hill Plantation Book, 1858, Habersham Elliott Papers; "1844, Negroes at work in the field," Springwood Plantation Lists, William Ervine Sparkman Papers, the latter three all at SHC; also, Exeter Plantation Book, 1846–1871, Jacob Rhett Motte Papers, and Hopeton Slave Inventory, 1861, Francis Porteus Corbin Papers, both at PL; "List of Negroes on Plantations, Property of Jos. Blake," including Bonny Hall, Pleasant Hill, New Ground, Parkes, Blakefield, and True Blue Plantations, Mitchell-Pringle Family Papers, SCHS; List of Negroes on Waverly Planta-

tion [1835 or 1836], Robert Francis Withers Allston Family Papers, SCL; and Clifton, *Life and Labor,* 248–49.

Hilary McD. Beckles found that once the Barbadian plantation regime progressed beyond its early frontier years, slave women also outnumbered slave men as field hands on plantations (*Natural Rebels,* 11). Beckles argues that "the more developed the colony as a plantation system, the greater the tendency for the normalization of sex ratios, moving from a male predominance under frontier conditions, to female predominance with maturity" (19). The similar development of slave women's role in the lowcountry rice regime offers support to Beckles's argument that slave women's role in the plantation economy makes their labor central, not peripheral, to the study of plantation slavery.

3. Ira Berlin and Philip D. Morgan, "Labor and the Shaping of Slave Life in the Americas," in their *Cultivation and Culture,* 1. Frances Fox Piven and Richard A. Cloward make a parallel point in *Poor People's Movements: Why They Succeed, How They Fail* (New York: Vintage, 1977): "people experience deprivation and oppression within a concrete setting, not as the end product of large and abstract processes, and it is the concrete experience that molds their discontent into specific grievances against specific targets" (20).

4. Easterby, *South Carolina Rice Plantation,* 126. According to the overseer at Charles Manigault's Hermitage plantation, January work left Manigault's slaves "coughing, blowing, sneezeing, and shivering" (K. Washington Skinner to Charles Manigault, 24 Jan. 1852, in Clifton, *Life and Labor,* 89). For a general discussion of rice cultivation, see James C. Darby, "On Planting and Managing a Rice Crop," in *Southern Agriculturist,* June 1829.

5. Although neither planters, nor overseers, nor slaves have left us a record of the conscious choices that led to this sexual division of labor at this time, it is interesting to note that a century earlier, in the 1750s, slave women and children were responsible for cutting down and burning bushes and shrubs when new fields were prepared (trees were removed by slave men). See Vorsey, *De Brahm's Report,* 94.

6. Frances Anne Kemble, *Journal of a Residence on a Georgian Plantation in 1838–1839* (1863; rpt., Athens: University of Georgia Press, 1984), 179.

7. Duncan Clinch Heyward, *Seed from Madagascar* (Chapel Hill: University of North Carolina Press, 1937), 28–29. On women burning stubble, see also Frederick Law Olmsted, *A Journey in the Seaboard Slave States, with Remarks on Their Economy* (New York: Dix and Edwards, 1856), 423; Louis Manigault to Charles Manigault, 1 Mar. 1853, in Clifton, *Life and Labor,* 142; and entries for 7 Jan. 1853, 17 Jan. 1855, and 19 Feb. 1857, Mulberry Plantation Journals, 1853–1889, Vol. 1, SCHS.

8. Olmsted, *Journey in the Seaboard States,* 481; see also 482.

9. Kemble, *Journal of a Residence,* 155; K. Washington Skinner to Charles Manigault, 21 Jan. 1852, in Clifton, *Life and Labor,* 87; and Lewis Cecil Gray, *History of Agriculture in the Southern United States to 1860,* 2 vols. (Washington, D.C.: Carnegie Institution, 1933), 2:727.

10. Kemble, *Journal of a Residence,* 178. See also Heyward, *Seed from Madagascar,* 30.

11. See Leslie Howard Owens, *This Species of Property: Slave Life and Culture in the Old South* (New York: Oxford University Press, 1976), 39, for a brief discussion of slave women's handling of plows. On the handling of plows exclusively by slave men in the lowcountry, see Easterby, *South Carolina Rice Plantation,* 315–16; Patience Pennington [pseud., Elizabeth W. Allston Pringle], *A Woman Rice Planter* (New York: Macmillan, 1913), 78; D. E. Huger Smith, *A Charlestonian's Recollections, 1846–1913* (Charleston, S.C., 1950), 20; Clifton, *Life and Labor,* 87; and Mulberry Plantation Journals, 1853–1889, Vol. 2, passim, SCHS. In these and other records, planters and overseers refer to "ploughmen" but very rarely discussed the sexual division of labor in rice cultivation. The gender of the slaves was frequently lost through such references as "all the hands hoeing today."

12. Wood, *Black Majority,* 28–34, and Smith, *A Charlestonian's Recollections,* 23–24.

13. For a precise description of this hierarchy, see Smith, *A Charlestonian's Recollections,* 19.

14. Barbara Bush, "Towards Emancipation: Slave Women and Resistance to Coercive Labour Regimes in the British West Indian Colonies, 1790–1838," *Slavery and Abolition* 5 (Dec. 1981): 222–23.

15. Kemble, *Journal of a Residence,* 156; Olmsted, *Journey in the Seaboard States,* 432.

16. See, for example, entries for 9 Jan. 1853 and 14 Feb. 1867, Mulberry Plantation Journals, 1853–1889, Vol. 1, SCHS.

17. Olmsted, *Journey in the Seaboard States,* 397. Henry William Ravenel often wrote in the *Southern Agriculturist* about the benefits of manuring. See also the John B. Milliken Plantation Journals, R8, Ser. B, *RABSP.*

18. For an overview of the work required in maintaining a rice plantation's irrigation system, see James C. Darby, "On the Embanking and Preparation of Marsh Land, for the Cultivation of Rice," *Southern Agriculturist,* Jan. 1829.

19. Hall, *Travels in North America,* in K. Jones, *The Plantation South,* 100.

20. Contrary to the argument made by Eugene Genovese (*Roll, Jordan, Roll: The World the Slaves Made* [New York: Pantheon, 1974], 489), that slave women were generally assigned lighter tasks, or the argument made by Joyner (*Down by the Riverside,* 45), that lowcountry slave women were not assigned tasks involving mudwork, there is considerable evidence that slave women were regularly assigned very difficult and strenuous tasks maintaining and repairing plantation irrigation systems. I attribute our different findings to variations between what planters said about their treatment of slave women and what the daily work records, which I have studied extensively, reveal about actual labor assignments. For examples, see Louis Manigault to Charles Manigault, 9 Apr. 1853 and 6 Jan. 1854, in Clifton, *Life and Labor,* 150, 165; Heyward, *Seed from Madagascar,* 30; entries for 26 and 27 Jan. and 25 Feb. 1859, "Richmond" Overseer Journal, 1859–1860, Charleston District, South Carolina, R7, and entries for 7 and 9 Mar. 1854, "Mulberry" Journal, and 12 Mar. 1858, R. Meynardie Overseer Account, both in John B. Milliken Plantation Journals, 1853–1859, Charleston District, South Carolina, R8, both in Ser. B, *RABSP.*

21. *Southern Agriculturist,* Nov. 1833.

22. Even this particular work in maintaining the irrigation systems was not performed exclusively by slave men; on some plantations, while slave men cut lumber for use in repairing the wooden floodgates, slave women were sent to haul the cut lumber back to the plantation. See E. B. Heyward, "Hopewell Plantation Journal," Jan.–Feb. 1857, R12, Ser. A, Pt. 2, *RABSP.*

23. Easterby, *South Carolina Rice Plantation,* 346. The planter William E. Sparkman was among those who distributed spades only to his slave men; see "1844: Springwood Plantation act. Tools," William Ervine Sparkman Papers, SHC.

24. Heyward, *Seed from Madagascar,* 31. The Georgetown planter James R. Sparkman distributed spades only to his prime male hands on Dirleton, whereas the Savannah River planter Louis Manigault had both male and female slaves at work, in 1837, cutting new ditches (presumably with spades) on his plantation. See James R. Sparkman Papers, MS vol. bd., 1853–1859 (Dirleton), R6, Ser. A, Pt. 2, and Charles Izard Manigault, "Plantation Work 1837," in Louis Manigault Papers, R4, Ser. F, Pt. 2, both in *RABSP.*

25. K. Washington Skinner to Charles Manigault, 8 Feb. 1852, in Clifton, *Life and Labor,* 91.

26. Louis Manigault to Charles Manigault, 7 Mar. 1852, in Clifton, *Life and Labor,* 94.

27. Richard James Arnold and his overseer assigned slave women the complete range of tasks associated with "mudwork," including cleaning, widening, and deepening ditches and canals; clearing and digging new drains, trunks, canals, dams, and banks. See the entries for 16, 18, and 19 Jan. 1847 and 26 Jan. 1849, Richard James Arnold Journal, 1847–49, Arnold and Screven Family Papers, SHC. For similar examples see the entry for 24 Feb. 1849, Comingtee Plantation Book, Vol. 5 (1849–71), John and Keating Simons Ball Papers, SHC; entries for Jan. and Apr. 1857 in the Plantation Account Book, 1853–74, Robert Barnwell Rhett Papers, PL; and Clifton, *Life and Labor,* passim.

28. Olmsted, *Journey in the Seaboard States,* 470.

29. Sass and Smith, *A Carolina Rice Plantation,* 26.

30. R. F. W. Allston, "Sea-Coast Crops," *Southern Agriculturist,* July 1854.

31. Ibid.; Heyward, *Seed from Madagascar,* 31.

32. Pennington, *A Woman Rice Planter,* 74.

33. Ibid.

34. Allston, "Sea-Coast Crops."

35. Pennington, *A Woman Rice Planter,* 12.

36. Clifton, *Life and Labor,* xxii.

37. Nathaniel Heyward's Water Culture, 1802, Heyward Family Papers, SHC.

38. Kemble, *Journal of a Residence,* 164.

39. Olmsted, *Journey in the Seaboard States,* 387. In *Chronicles of Chicora Wood,* Elizabeth W. Allston Pringle noted that twice yearly, planters in the Georgetown area sent out a number of hands, proportioned to their landholding, to repair the roads under the direction of one of the planters (20).

40. Allston, "Sea-Coast Crops." The assignment of shucking corn to both male and female slaves suggests there was a potentially significant contrast in the processes and traditions on cotton and rice plantations. Drawing exclusively on up-

country sources, Eugene Genovese has observed that slaves (as opposed to over-seers or planters) adhered to a rigid sexual division of labor during corn shucking and in the social activities that attended the corn harvest. This sexual division of labor emphasized elements of masculine authority and male prowess that, accord-ing to Genovese, were important manifestations of slaves' control over the process of production. A construction of gender that deemphasized women's competence, he concluded, was an important "weapon for joint resistance to dehumanization" (Genovese, *Roll, Jordan, Roll,* 315–19). In making this argument, Genovese was vague on two points: whether the sexual division of labor he described governed corn shucking done for both the planter and the slaves themselves; and in which regions of the South the practice occurred.

41. Heyward, *Seed from Madagascar,* 31.

42. Hall, *Travels in North America,* in K. Jones, *The Plantation South,* 101.

43. Allston, "Sea-Coast Crops"; Heyward, *Seed from Madagascar,* 40.

44. Doar, *Rice and Rice Planting,* 49.

45. Jesse T. Cooper to Charles Manigault, 24 Aug. 1849, in Clifton, *Life and Labor,* 72.

46. Olmsted, *Journey in the Seaboard States,* 474 (my emphasis).

47. One plantation mistress recalled slave women spreading sheaves of rice on a large tarpaulin; the women used flails—long sticks with a shorter stick attached by leather thongs—to beat the rice, and then used large, shallow baskets, called winnowing baskets, to throw the rice "up high—over & over—mean while singing 'blow wind blow'" as the chaff was blown aside and the heavy grain fell back into the baskets. See "Recollections by Harriot Lucas Huger Elliott, wife of John Barn-well Elliott," in Habersham Elliott Family Papers, SHC.

48. Charles Manigault to Robert Habersham and Son, 1 Feb. 1847, in Clifton, *Life and Labor,* 48.

49. See, for example, Charles Manigault's 1844 plantation journal, in Clifton, *Life and Labor,* 10.

50. Heyward, *Seed from Madagascar,* 176.

51. Ibid.

52. Olmsted, *Journey in the Seaboard States,* 2:61.

53. On children's labor, see Gray, *History of Agriculture,* 2:729; "Employment of Children Collecting Manure," *Southern Agriculturist,* Apr. 1831; Summerville, "On the Collecting of Manures, and Keeping of Cattle and Hogs," *Southern Agricultur-ist,* May 1831; "Account of the Management of Pushee [*sic*], the Residence of Dr. Henry Ravenel," *Southern Agriculturist,* July 1831; Allston, "Sea-Coast Crops"; Pen-nington, *A Woman Rice Planter,* 35–36; Heyward, *Seed from Madagascar,* 41–42; and Easterby, *South Carolina Rice Plantation,* 165.

54. Heyward, *Seed from Madagascar,* 105.

55. Ibid., 105–6.

56. James Ritchie Sparkman, "List of Negroes Feb. 12 1859" and "List of Task Hands on Dirleton, 12 Feb. 1859," in Dirleton Plantation Memo Book, 1859–1864, James Ritchie Sparkman Papers, SCHS, R9, Ser. B, *RABSP;* "Task Hands 1847 June," MS vol. bd., 1827–45; "List of Negroes Belonging to Ja. R. Sparkman 1 January 1845," MS vol. bd., 1845–64; "Negroes on Birdfield 1st March 1851," MS vol. bd.,

1850–57; "Dirleton 1858" and "Task Hands Birdfield Jany. 1 1858," MS vol. bd., 1857–59; and "Task Hands May 1861," MS vol. bd., 1859–61, James Ritchie Sparkman Papers (SCL), all on R6, Ser. A, Pt. 2, *RABSP.*

57. Heyward, *Seed from Madagascar,* 179.

58. See entries for Jan. 1849, Richard James Arnold Journal, 1847–49, Arnold and Screven Family Papers, SHC.

59. Rawick, *The American Slave,* Vol. 2, South Carolina, Pt. 1, 107–14.

60. Heyward, *Seed from Madagascar,* 179.

61. King, "On the Management of the Butler Estate."

62. On skilled work among slave women, see Pringle, *Chronicles of Chicora Wood,* 13, 91, 335; Heyward, *Seed from Madagascar,* 102–3, 177; and Easterby, *South Carolina Rice Plantation,* 27, 33, 58, 86, 153.

63. Easterby, *South Carolina Rice Plantation,* 58.

64. Pringle, *Chronicles of Chicora Wood,* 13, 91.

65. King, "On the Management of the Butler Estate."

66. Doar, *Rice and Rice Planting,* 31–32.

67. Ibid.

68. Skilled occupations among slave men included those carried out in the carpenter's shop, where sometimes a half dozen carpenters working under a head carpenter built flats, lighters, floodgates, rowboats, canoes, and maintain the plantation buildings. At the blacksmith's shop, horses were shod, and the wheels and axles of plantation carts and wagons were repaired. Boatmen sailed the planter's schooner, which transported the crop to Charleston, or navigated rice-laden flats to inland markets. Other slave men served as the trunkminders and watchmen, the coopers who built barrels in which the harvested rice was shipped, the engineers and millers who operated and maintained the threshing and pounding mills; in some places, there were also stockminders, hostlers, and hunters. See Heyward, *Seed from Madagascar,* 102, 103, 105, 124, 127, 164; Clifton, *Life and Labor,* 59; and Smith, *A Charlestonian's Recollections,* 19, 20, 22, 24, 26.

69. Clifton, *Life and Labor,* 46–47.

70. The fact that R. F. W. Allston's driver, Tommy, had erred in his judgment and consequently "been abandon'd by his hands" gave Allston "reason to think less of his qualification as a Driver" (Easterby, *South Carolina Rice Plantation,* 164). This suggests that some slaves could have wielded a degree of control over the appointment of drivers.

71. Easterby, *South Carolina Rice Plantation,* 176; Mary Elliott Johnstone refers to this incident on an unspecified plantation in her letter to Mrs. William Elliott, [1857], Elliott-Gonzales Family Papers, SHC; Clifton, *Life and Labor,* 46–47.

72. Easterby, *South Carolina Rice Plantation,* 33.

73. Rawick, *The American Slave,* Vol. 3, South Carolina, Pt. 4, 2–3.

74. One ex-slave, Abby Mishow, a young girl at the time of the Civil War, told her WPA interviewer that having been brought up in the "yard," and as the daughter of the plantation seamstress, she knew nothing about the lives of field hands; even her food and clothing differed from theirs. Rawick, *The American Slave,* Vol. 3, South Carolina, Pt. 3, 197–99.

75. Elizabeth Fox-Genovese, in *Within the Plantation Household,* offers the best

sustained study to date of slave women's domestic labor and the social relations shaping it. Deborah Gray White's pathbreaking monograph on slave women, *Ar'n't I A Woman*, also provides an insightful analysis of slave women and domestic service. The labor I describe draws from their research, but also from the descriptions of domestic life provided in the correspondence and autobiographical literature of lowcountry elites such as the Allstons, the Manigaults, Frances Kemble, the Ravenels, the Smiths, and the Hugers.

76. Pringle, *Chronicles of Chicora Wood*, 158–59.

77. Ibid., 61.

78. Charles Manigault to Louis Manigault, 17 Jan. 1860, in Clifton, *Life and Labor*, 291. One Sea Island houseservant was glad to return to the fields after being whipped by her owner until her arms and back were covered with scars (William F. Allen Diary, typescript, p. 136, William F. Allen Family Papers, State Historical Society of Wisconsin). See also William Elliott to Mrs. Anne Hutchinson Smith Elliott, 11 Feb. 1856, Elliott-Gonzales Family Papers, SHC.

79. Based on slave lists for plantations belonging to Charles Manigault in 1845, and plantations belonging to James R. Sparkman in 1847 and 1858. See Clifton, *Life and Labor*, 31–32, and James Ritchie Sparkman, "Task Hands 1847 June," MS vol. bd., 1827–45, and "Dirleton 1858" as well as "Task Hands Birdfield Jany. 1 1858," MS vol. bd., 1857–59, James Ritchie Sparkman Papers, R6, Ser. A, Pt. 2, *RABSP*. It should be noted that Gowrie was an "absentee" plantation; it lacked a permanent planter residence and thus employed far fewer servants than was typical on rice plantations.

80. Hall, *Travels in North America*, in K. Jones, *The Plantation South*, 102.

81. Clifton, *Life and Labor*, 152, 183.

82. Easterby, *South Carolina Rice Plantation*, 34; Rawick, *The American Slave*, Vol. 2, South Carolina, Pt. 1, 308–15; and Kemble, *Journal of a Residence*, 108.

83. Rawick, *The American Slave*, Vol. 2, South Carolina, Pt. 2, 305.

84. Clifton, *Life and Labor*, 192, and Easterby, *South Carolina Rice Plantation*, 347. See also the comment by Edmund Ravenel that "Juno's appearance would determine her value," especially if she were "a fine looking woman in good condition," in Edmund Ravenel to H. W. Ravenel, 26 Mar. 1857, in folder marked 4 Apr. 1844–4 Dec. 1866, Henry William Ravenel Papers, SCL.

85. Olmsted, *Journey in the Seaboard States*, 435–36.

86. William Elliott to Emily, 7 Aug. 1858, Elliott-Gonzales Family Papers, SHC.

87. Rawick, *The American Slave*, Vol. 2, South Carolina, Pt. 1, 112, 110.

88. Ibid., Pt. 2, 311.

89. Ibid., Pt. 1, 119.

90. Kemble, *Journal of a Residence*, 160; see also 74, 79, 175.

91. Ibid., 170, 187, 214–15, 229–30.

92. Easterby, *South Carolina Rice Plantation*, 53.

93. Ibid., 346; Sass and Smith, *A Carolina Rice Plantation*, 13, 70; Doar, *Rice and Rice Planting*, 33; and Kemble, *Journal of a Residence*, 99–100, 291. In contrast to the myth perpetuated by lowcountry whites, that their slaves easily withstood the region's blazing heat and humidity, Charles Manigault's overseer describes the unhealthy effect of summer heat on slaves, in Clifton, *Life and Labor*, 83.

94. Heyward, *Seed from Madagascar,* 165.

95. Plantation Journal [1844], in Clifton, *Life and Labor,* 8–9.

96. Charles Manigault to Louis Manigault, 18 Oct. 1856, in Clifton, *Life and Labor,* 230.

97. Heyward, *Seed from Madagascar,* 57; Olmsted, *Journey in the Seaboard States,* 480–83; A Black River Planter, "Observations on the Bearded Rice," in *Southern Agriculturist,* Nov. 1830.

98. Olmsted, *Journey in the Seaboard States,* 480.

99. Rawick, *The American Slave,* Vol. 2, South Carolina, Pt. 1, 113.

100. Charles Manigault to Anthony Barclay, 15 Apr. 1847, in Clifton, *Life and Labor,* 53–54.

101. Benjamin Allston to Robert F. W. Allston, 17 June 1860 (typescript), in Robert F. W. Allston Family Letters, Vol. 3, R. F. W. Allston Papers, SCL.

102. Easterby, *South Carolina Rice Plantation,* 263.

103. Stephen F. Clark to Charles Manigault, 25 Sept. 1855, in Clifton, *Life and Labor,* 198.

104. In his study of South Carolina slave runaways, Philip Morgan has found that "petit marronage was an accepted fact of life for South Carolina planters." Morgan found that four-fifths of reported female runaways (in contrast to two-thirds of the male runaways) were suspected of running away for the purpose of "visiting." Runaway slave women were clearly acting to maintain and strengthen family and community ties, a theme discussed in chapter 2, below. See Philip D. Morgan, "Colonial South Carolina Runaways: Their Significance for Slave Culture," *Slavery and Abolition* 6, no. 3 (1985): 58, 67, 72–73.

105. Rawick, *The American Slave,* Vol. 2, South Carolina, Pt. 1, 147 and Pt. 2, 167; Clifton (*Life and Labor,* 153, 175, 177, 178) details the 1854 exodus of five slaves who, recently purchased by Charles Manigault from Charles Ball, did not like the location of their new owner's plantation (Savannah River rice plantations apparently having a bad reputation among mainland lowcountry slaves). The five slaves, including two "young goddesses" and an "old woman" who was "very troublesome & has a bad influence on all the rest," returned to the Ball plantation to plead their case with Mrs. Ball; "they went off because they were afraid of going to the Savannah River." The five were returned to the new owner, who instructed his overseer to bring the old woman "to her bearings," with "a plantation talk," and a visit to the Savannah workhouse, if necessary. See also Clifton, *Life and Labor,* 305, 310.

106. For the opposing argument—that pregnancy and childbirth induced women in particular to accept their status of slaves—see, for example, Gerda Lerner, "Women and Slavery," in *Slavery and Abolition* 4 (Dec. 1983): 175.

107. Kemble, *Journal of a Residence,* 170, and see also 114, 179, 187.

108. Testimony of Henry McMillan before the American Freedmen's Inquiry Commission, [1863], filed with O-328 1863, Letters Received, Ser. 12, RG 94 [K-78].

109. Kemble, *Journal of a Residence,* 179; Easterby, *South Carolina Rice Plantation,* 346.

110. Easterby, *South Carolina Rice Plantation,* 346.

111. Ibid., 101.

112. Testimony of Henry McMillan before the American Freedmen's Inquiry Commission, [1863], filed with O-328 1863, Letters Received, Ser. 12, RG 94 [K-78].

113. Kemble, *Journal of a Residence*, 245.

114. John M. Hawks to Esther Hill Hawks, 17 May 1862, Esther Hill Hawks Papers, LC.

115. In 1844, Charles Manigault's overseer complained that there were five pregnant women on the plantation, "which weakens the force very much." See A. R. Bagshaw to Charles Manigault, 14 Aug. 1844, in Clifton, *Life and Labor*, 15.

116. Rawick, *The American Slave*, Vol. 2, South Carolina, Pt. 2, 298–307, 310–11. Horry's reference, that bloodstains from a whipped slave's wounds permanently marked—and memorialized—the inhumane treatment of slaves, occurs frequently in African-American oral traditions and family legends about the experience of slavery. See, for example, the stories repeated to Dorothy Spruill Redford in North Carolina, in Redford's *Somerset Homecoming: Recovering a Lost Heritage* (New York: Doubleday, 1988), 189.

117. Rawick, *The American Slave*, Vol. 2, South Carolina, Pt. 2, 304.

118. Affidavit by Lydia Alston, 13 Nov. 1907; affidavit by Amos Gadsden, 13 Nov. 1907; affidavit by Prince Brown, 25 Nov. 1907, all in pension file of Murphy Allston, WC 1887, Civil War Pension Files, RG 15.

119. Rawick, *The American Slave*, Vol. 2, South Carolina, Pt. 2, 167.

120. Testimony of Solomon Bradley [1863], filed with O-328 1863, Letters Received, Ser. 12, RG 94 [K-75].

121. Clifton, *Life and Labor*, 135, 155, 160, 224; and Easterby, *South Carolina Rice Plantation*, 156.

Chapter 2: *"Ties to Bind Them All Together"*

The chapter title is from advice given by a planter to his son, about purchasing slaves in groups that include family or community members, so that the slaves "then in a strange place have ties to bind them all together." Otherwise, he warned, "they dont assimilate . . . & all goes wrong with them" (Clifton, *Life and Labor*, 239).

1. See, for example, J. Jones, *Labor of Love*, 58. Using a different approach, Deborah Gray White has been one of the few historians to insist that a narrow focus on the nuclear slave family has deflected our attention away from exploring the slave family's relationship to the larger community of slaves; see White, *Ar'n't I a Woman?* White's approach seems particularly applicable to the study of lowcountry slave women and their communities.

2. I use "culture" here as it has been defined by the historian Margaret Washington Creel: the "creative, adaptive, dynamic patterns of behavioral meanings, which are inherited and historically transmitted through rituals, symbols, and systems of communications that represent societal understanding, awareness, and conceptions of life." Creel, *"A Peculiar People,"* 1.

3. Littlefield, *Rice and Slaves,* 65. Allan Kulikoff has noted that male African slaves in Virginia planned an uprising in light of their inability to find wives (Kulikoff, "The Beginnings of the Afro-American Family in Maryland," in *The American Family in Social-Historical Perspective,* ed. Michael Gordon, 2d ed. (New York: St. Martin's, 1978), 446.

4. Joyner, *Down by the Riverside,* 120–26; Easterby, *South Carolina Rice Plantation,* 348; K. Jones, *The Plantation South,* 99, 136; and Doar, *Rice and Rice Planting,* 31.

5. Pringle, *Chronicles of Chicora Wood,* 53, 63–64; Easterby, *South Carolina Rice Plantation,* 30.

6. The Sparkman and Allston plantations might be considered typical of the lowcountry in that both can be traced to pre-Revolution land grants, and that by 1850 both the land and a core group of slaves (including many third- and fourth-generation slave families) had been retained over the course of several decades, despite the disruptions associated with the transfer of ownership from one generation to the next. Both plantations also included large numbers of slaves purchased or inherited from other lowcountry planters. James R. Sparkman, Dirleton Plantation Memo Book, 1859–1864, James Ritchie Sparkman Papers, R9, Ser. B, *RABSP;* Rogers, *History of Georgetown County,* 208, 277; Robert F. W. Allston, Register of Births and Deaths on True Blue, 1855 MS vol. bd., R. F. W. Allston Papers, SCL; and Easterby, *South Carolina Rice Plantation,* 20, 28–30. On the evolution of eighteenth-century lowcountry slave society and family formations, see P. Morgan, "Black Society in the Lowcountry," esp. 124–29.

7. Testimony of Harry McMillan [1863], filed with O-328 1863, Letters Received, Ser. 12, RG 94 [K-78].

8. Testimony of Robert Smalls [1863], filed with O-328 1863, Letters Received, Ser. 12, RG 94 [K-76].

9. Testimony of Lydia Alston, 13 Nov. 1907, testimony by Rebecca Wright, 13 Nov. 1907, testimony by Amos Gadsden, 13 Nov. 1907, all in pension file of Murphy Allston, WC 18887, Civil War Pension Files, RG 15.

10. Testimony by Lucy Brown, 12 Aug. 1890, pension file of Sandy Brown, WC321403, Civil War Pension Files, RG 15. It was not uncommon for slave parents to use surnames in this manner as a way of strengthening family ties; for another instance, see testimony by Benjamin Baker, 15 May 1901, pension file of Benjamin Baker, WC935415, Civil War Pension Files, RG 15. Although Baker's biological father was his master, he was given the name of his slave mother's husband.

11. Testimony by John Swinton, 7 May 1907; testimony by Sawney Simmons, 7 May 1907; and testimony by Rebecca Mention, 7 May 1907, all in pension claim of Sandy White, WC 626577, Civil War Pension Files, RG 15.

12. Testimony by Mary Nesbit (nee Higgins), 1 July 1901, pension file of Brutus Nesbit, WO 542840, Civil War Pension Files, RG 15.

13. Testimony by Nelly Thompson, 25 May 1894, in pension claim of Hardy Mayrant, WC 398031, Civil War Pension Files, RG 15.

14. Testimony of Affy Lawton, 5 May 1875, and of Ellen Woodruff (nee Corsee), 3 May 1875, both in pension file of Moses Graham, WC 173264, Civil War Pension Files, RG 15.

15. Testimony of Rebecca Allston, 16 July 1912, in pension claim of Nathaniel Allston, WC 746108; and testimony of Eliza Coit, 21 Mar. 1901, in pension claim of Prince [Albert] Coit, WC 7915, all in Civil War Pension Files, RG 15.

16. Rawick, *The American Slave,* Vol. 3, South Carolina, Pt. 3, 167–68.

17. Testimony of Mary Green, 12 Apr. 1894, in pension file of Luck Green, WC 397867, Civil War Pension Files, RG 15.

18. William Sweet to Adele Allston, Oct. 1864, Allston Family Papers, SCHS.

19. Testimony by Rina Green, 24 July 1901, in pension claim of Hector Green, WC 432779, Civil War Pension Files, RG 15.

20. Testimony of Rebecca Allston, 16 July 1912, in pension claim of Nathaniel Allston, WC 746108; for similar examples, see affidavit by Tira Cohen, 26 Sept. 1907, in pension claim of Caesar Cohen, WO 878010, and testimony by Rina Green, 24 July 1901, in pension claim of Hector Green, WC 432779, all in Civil War Pension Files, RG 15.

21. Testimony of Nelly Thompson, 25 Apr. 1894, pension claim of Hardy Mayrant, WC 398031, Civil War Pension Files, RG 15; and Joyner, *Down by the Riverside,* 65, 75.

22. Testimony by Eliza Coit, 18 Apr. 1892, in pension claim of Prince [Albert] Coit, WC 7915, Civil War Pension Files, RG 15; and Rogers, *History of Georgetown County,* 354.

23. Testimony of Jane Myers, 14 Apr. 1894, and testimony of Mary Green, 12 Apr. 1894, in pension file of Luck Green, WC 397867, Civil War Pension Files, RG 15.

24. For a description of planter involvement in planning and celebrating slave weddings, see Joyner, *Down by the Riverside,* 138.

25. Rogers, *History of Georgetown County,* 353–54.

26. Testimony of Annie Frazier, 1 Sept. 1909, in pension file of Daniel Frazier, WC 695221, Civil War Pension Files, RG 15. See also the Reverend Alexander Glennie's Parish Diary, which records the slave marriages he performed in Georgetown's All Saints Parish between 1852 and 1859 (Reverend Alexander Glennie, Parish Diary, 1832–1859, R9, Ser. B, *RABSP*). The Allston family correspondence also describes slaveowners' participation in planning and celebrating slave weddings (Easterby, *South Carolina Rice Plantation,* 171, 453–54).

27. Planter memoirs, correspondence, and instructions to overseers—as well as overseers' plantation journals—are consistent in noting the distribution of material support exclusively through slave women. For an overview of what Charles Joyner describes as the "material environment of the slave," see chapter 3 of his monograph *Down by the Riverside,* 90–126.

28. Cheryll Ann Cody, "Naming, Kinship, and Estate Dispersal; Notes on Slave Family Life on a South Carolina Plantation, 1786–1833," *William and Mary Quarterly,* 3d Ser., 39 (Jan. 1982): 193, 208–9.

29. Margaret Washington Creel eloquently presents this interpretation of lowcountry family formation in her essay, "Gullah Attitudes toward Life and Death," in *Africanisms in American Culture,* ed. Joseph E. Holloway (Bloomington: Indiana University Press, 1990), 69–97, as well as more generally in her monograph, *"A Peculiar People."*

30. Clifton, *Life and Labor,* 185, 191–92.

31. See, for example, Kenneth Stampp's discussion of slave families in *The Peculiar Institution: Slavery in the Ante-Bellum South* (New York: Knopf, 1956), 340–47.

32. Rawick, *The American Slave,* Vol. 2, South Carolina, Pt. 1, 167–71.

33. Randol Beckett explained that "my father titled Beaty in slave time, but he took the name Beckett after freedom, and when I came out of the war, I titled after my father" (testimony of Randol Beckett, 8 Mar. 1911, in pension file of Randol Beckett AKA Ward, WC 742386, Civil War Pension Files, RG 15). The pension records of black Civil War veterans from the lowcountry contain many examples of sons claiming the names of their fathers, as well as name changes by sons to follow the example of their fathers after freedom. The same records reveal that slave girls also took their father's last names. See the testimony of Frank Pyotte, 27 Mar. 1901, in pension file of Frank Pyotte [AKA Pyatte], IC 918604; testimony of William Washington, 8 Apr. 1901, in pension file of William Washington, WC 585991; testimony of Daniel Robinson, 8 Apr. 1901, in pension file of Daniel Robinson, IC 2560487; affidavit by Benjamin Weston, 28 Mar. 1898, in pension file of Benjamin Huger, IC 974352; and testimony of Mary Nesbit, 1 July 1901, in pension claim of Brutus Nesbit, WO 542840, all in Civil War Pension Files, RG 15.

34. Entries for 24 and 25 Feb. 1850, Comingtee Plantation Book, John and Keating Simons Ball Papers, SHC.

35. Clifton, ed., *Life and Labor,* 239; Easterby, *South Carolina Rice Plantation,* 151.

36. Clifton, *Life and Labor,* 249–50.

37. Robert Manson Myers, *The Children of Pride: A True Story of Georgia and the Civil War* (New Haven: Yale University Press, 1972), 255.

38. William Elliott to Anne Hutchinson Smith Elliott, 11 Feb. 1856, Elliott-Gonzales Family Papers, SHC.

39. Testimony of Robert Smalls [1863], filed with O-328 1863, Letters Received, Ser. 12, RG 94 [K-76]; testimony of Laura M. Towne [1863], filed with O-328 1863, Letters Received, Ser. 12, RG 94 [K-73]; testimony of Henry G. Judd [1863], filed with O-328 1863, Letters Received, Ser. 12, RG 94 [K-74]. General Benjamin F. Butler, commanding Union forces in tidewater Virginia, first designated fugitive slaves as "contraband of war" in 1861, when he developed a new policy of treating runaway slaves as part of the enemy's property and thus vulnerable to confiscation.

40. J. Jones, *Labor of Love,* 38–43, and Genovese, *Roll, Jordan, Roll,* 489–90.

41. James R. Sparkman, in recording his various slave purchases for one of his plantations, noted that he bought six slave women, of which five were mothers, and whose children Sparkman also purchased. Of three slave men purchased, all were bought singly, without family or mates. See James R. Sparkman, MS vol. bd., 1845–64, R6, Ser. A, Pt. 2, *RABSP.*

42. The sexual division of labor in contemporary African societies is discussed by Jeanne K. Henn, "Women in the Rural Economy: Past, Present, and Future," in *African Women South of the Sahara,* ed. Margaret Jean Hay and Sharon Stichter (New York: Longman, 1984), 1–10.

43. King, "On the Management of the Butler Estate," 526.

44. Mamie Garvin Fields, with Karen Fields, *Lemon Swamp and Other Places: A Carolina Memoir* (New York: Free Press, 1983), 59–60.

45. Pennington, *A Woman Rice Planter,* 74.

46. Entries for Dec. 1856, Hopewell Plantation Journal, MS vol. bd., R12, Ser. A, Pt. 2, *RABSP.*

47. On independent production among lowcountry slaves, see chapter 1; P. Morgan, "Work and Culture"; and idem, "The Ownership of Property by Slaves in the Mid-Nineteenth-Century Low Country," *Journal of Southern History* 49 (Aug. 1983): 399–420.

48. On the sexual division of labor in household production, see Joyner, *Down by the Riverside,* 122–23; Henry W. Ravenel, "Recollections of Southern Plantation Life," *Yale Review* 25 (Summer 1936): 753; Pringle, *Chronicles of Chicora Wood,* 55; Heyward, *Seed from Madagascar,* 78.

49. Rawick, *The American Slave,* Vol. 3, South Carolina, Pt. 4, 67–68.

50. This argument is addressed at length by Ira Berlin and Philip D. Morgan in "Labor and the Shaping of Slave Life in the Americas," in *Cultivation and Culture: Labor and the Shaping of Slave Life in the Americas,* ed. Berlin and Morgan (Charlottesville: University of Virginia Press, 1993), 1–45.

51. McBride, "Directions for Cultivating the Various Crops."

52. J. H. Easterby, "South Carolina Through New England Eyes: Almira Coffin's Visit to the Low Country in 1851," *South Carolina Historical Magazine* 45 (1944): 131–32.

53. See, for example, John Campbell, "As 'A Kind of Freeman'? Slaves' Market-Related Activities in the South Carolina Upcountry, 1800–1860," 131–69; John T. Schlotterbeck, "The Internal Economy of Slavery in Rural Piedmont Virginia," 170–81; and Roderick A. McDonald, "Independent Economic Production by Slaves on Antebellum Louisiana Sugar Plantations," 182–208, all in *Slavery and Abolition,* 12, no. 1 (May 1991).

54. King, "On the Management of the Butler Estate"; McBride, "Directions for Cultivating the Various Crops"; Hazard, "On the General Management of a Plantation"; and affidavit by Mrs. Julia R. Speaks, 12 May 1875, claim of Harriet Smith, Beaufort County, SC, case files, Approved Claims, Ser. 732, Southern Claims Commission, 3d Auditor, RG 217.

55. Hazard, "On the General Management of a Plantation."

56. Testimony of Harriet Smith, 12 May 1875, claim of Harriet Smith, Beaufort County, SC, case files, Approved Claims, Ser. 732, Southern Claims Commission, 3d Auditor, RG 217.

57. Entry for 12 May 1849, Comingtee Plantation Book, Keating Simons Ball Papers, Ser. F, Pt. 2, *RABSP.*

58. See Clifton, *Life and Labor,* 271.

59. Testimony of Rose Goethe and Mrs. Eliza Peeples, 14 May 1875, claim of Rose Goethe, Beaufort County, SC, case files, Approved Claims, Ser. 732, Southern Claims Commission, 3d Auditor, RG 217.

60. Summary by S. O. Aldis et al., and testimony of Pompey Smith, 24 Nov. 1874, claim of Pompey Smith, Beaufort County, SC, case files, Approved Claims, Ser. 732, Southern Claims Commission, 3d Auditor, RG 217.

61. Testimony of Eliza Washington, 26 Mar. 1875, claim of Eliza Washington, Beaufort County, SC, case files, Approved Claims, Ser. 732, Southern Claims Commission, 3d Auditor, RG 217.

62. Testimony of Robert Bryant, claim of Robert Bryant, Beaufort County, SC, case files, Approved Claims, Ser. 732, Southern Claims Commission, 3d Auditor, RG 217.

63. Ravenel, "Recollections of Southern Plantation Life," 750–51.

64. Olmsted, *Journey in the Seaboard States,* 439.

65. Alexander Frasier et al., Agreement signed 17 Apr. 1836, Folder 22, Vander-Horst Family Collection, SCHS.

66. Heyward, *Seed from Madagascar,* 183.

67. Ravenel, "Recollections of Southern Plantation Life," 757.

68. P. Morgan, "Work and Culture," 592. Slave women also defended what they apparently perceived as slaves' inheritance rights; on the death of Stephen, a re-captured runaway slave, his mother, Nancy, requested through the overseer at Nightingale Hall that the planter send Stephen's things to her as soon as possible, so that she could give them to his surviving child (W. Sweet to Adele Allston, 2 Nov. 1864, Allston Family Papers, SCHS).

69. Capt. Thomas Pinckney to Col. John Say, 18 June 1863; Williams Middleton to General [Walker], 13 June 1863; Proceedings of a Board of Investigation Convened at McPhersonville, South Carolina. . . , 2 July 1863, all in claim of Williams Middleton, Confederate Papers Relating to Citizens or Business Firms, R443, M346, War Department Collection of Confederate Records, RG 109.

70. Testimony of William Drayton, 20 Feb. 1874, claim of William Drayton, Beaufort County, SC, case files, Approved Claims, Ser. 732, Southern Claims Commission, 3d Auditor, RG 217.

71. Testimony of Ann Goethe, 26 Nov. 1874, claim of Ann Goethe, Beaufort County, SC, case files, Approved Claims, Ser. 732, Southern Claims Commission, 3d Auditor, RG 217.

72. Testimony of Plenty Green, 27 Mar. 1875, claim of Plenty Green, Beaufort County, SC, case files, Approved Claims, Ser. 732, Southern Claims Commission, 3d Auditor, RG 217.

73. Testimony of Harriet Smith, 12 May 1875, claim of Harriet Smith, Beaufort County, SC, case files, Approved Claims, Ser. 732, Southern Claims Commission, 3d Auditor, RG 217.

74. Testimony of Julia R. Speaks, 5 July 1878, claim of Benjamin Tyson, Beaufort County, SC, case files, Approved Claims, Ser. 732, Southern Claims Commission, 3d Auditor, RG 217.

75. Statement by Special Commissioner E. M. Epping, 24 Nov. 1874, claim of Pompey Smith, Beaufort County, SC, case files, Approved Claims, Ser. 732, Southern Claims Commission, 3d Auditor, RG 217.

76. Former slave Benjamin Tyson insisted, "I worked Hard and made money." Testimony of Benjamin Tyson, 5 Oct. 1877, claim of Benjamin Tyson, Beaufort County, SC, case files, Approved Claims, Ser. 732, Southern Claims Commission, 3d Auditor, RG 217.

77. Rupert Sargent Holland, ed., *Letters and Diary of Laura M. Towne, Written*

from the Sea Islands of South Carolina, 1862–1884 (1912; rpt., New York: Negro Universities Press, 1969), 28.

78. Unfortunately, the sources documenting slave women's independent production offer little insight into women's control over the proceeds. If wartime and postbellum experiences are at all indicative of antebellum patterns, however, it would appear that women closely guarded their earnings.

79. Joyner, *Down by the Riverside,* 19. Over one thousand slaves lived on the six plantations belonging to the premier rice-planting family of John J. Ward.

80. Boles, *Black Southerners,* 107.

81. Joyner, *Down by the Riverside,* 33–40.

82. Rogers, *History of Georgetown County,* 328.

83. Jame R. Sparkman, MS vol. bd., 1845–64, R6, Ser. A, Pt. 2, *RABSP.*

84. Clifton, *Life and Labor,* 241; Easterby, *South Carolina Rice Plantation,* 151.

85. On the Allston plantations, see Easterby, *South Carolina Rice Plantation,* 18–23, 28–35; Rogers, *History of Georgetown County,* 263, 276, 328–29; and Joyner, *Down by the Riverside,* 23–24.

86. The significance of multigenerational ties and extended kin networks to the formation and transmission of the slave community was frequently lost on planters, who had their own reasons for emphasizing the nuclear family as the dominant social structure of the slave quarters. See Cody, "Naming, Kinship, and Estate Dispersal," and Joyner, *Down by the Riverside,* 31.

87. Robert Wilson, D.D., *An Address Delivered Before the St. John's Hunting Club at Indianfield Plantation, St. John's Berkeley, 4 July 1907* (Charleston, S.C., 1907), 11. For additional discussion of the significance of close and extended kin to slave communities, see also Mintz and Price, *An Anthropological Approach,* 34; and Gutman, *The Black Family,* chap. 5.

88. Boles, *Black Southerners,* 60–63.

89. Wilson, *An Address Delivered Before the St. John's Hunting Club.*

90. Margaret Creel Washington posits that "symbolic fellowship, respect, and veneration" of departed family members, along with belief in "life after death, and in the significance of that future life" led lowcountry slaves to integrate ancestors into the community's spiritual and secular life (Creel, *"A Peculiar People,"* 54–55). Sidney Mintz and Richard Price also identify the crucial significance of burial grounds to both history and genealogy as part of the larger "set of broadly shared ideas brought from Africa" (Mintz and Price, *An Anthropological Approach,* 35–36). In interviewing descendants of Georgia lowcountry slaves, researchers in the Depression-era Georgia Writer's Project found that local burial grounds in Georgia continued to have importance even to lowcountry people who had migrated north: "The custom of bringing the dead back to their original home for interment is also prevalent throughout coast Georgia. . . . 'Dey alluz brings um back tuh bury um ef dey kin git duh money, cuz yuh see duh spirit'll jis wanduh roun an nebuh be satisfied lessen it brung back home tuh be buried,'" explained Susie Branch. Georgia Writers' Project, *Drums and Shadows: Survival Studies among the Georgia Coastal Negroes* (1940; rpt., Athens: University of Georgia Press, 1986), 77.

91. Affidavit by Nellie Thompson, 25 Apr. 1894, pension file of Handy Mayrant, WC 398031, Civil War Pension Files, RG 15 (Mrs. Thompson, in her early six-

ties at the time of her statement, was one of the six hundred former slaves once owned by R. F. W. Allston, and still a resident of Chicora Wood plantation).

92. Affidavit of Mary Ann Johnson, 21 Oct. 1909, pension file of Mingo Cooper, WC 691815, Civil War Pension Files, RG 15.

93. Affidavit of Carolina Ellis, 9 Mar. 1903, pension file of Jack Hemmingway, IC 259698, Civil War Pension Files, RG 15.

94. Affidavit of Rose Simmons, 3 Jan. 1910, pension file of Daniel Frazier, WC 695221, Civil War Pension Files, RG 15.

95. Affidavit of Frank Pyotte, 22 Mar. 1902, pension file of Randol Beckett AKA Ward, WC 742386; and affidavit of John Swinton, 7 May 1907, pension file of Sandy White, WC 626577, both in Civil War Pension Files, RG 15.

96. Testimony of Bristo Habersham, 25 May 1901, pension file of Frank Duncan, WC 753197, Civil War Pension Files, RG 15.

97. Affidavit of Grace Brown, 21 Mar. 1901, pension file of Sandy Days, WC 510041, Civil War Pension Files, RG 15.

98. Testimony of Eliza Coit, 21 Mar. 1901, pension file of Prince Coit, WC 7915, Civil War Pension Files, RG 15. For a similar claim to community membership by way of "raisen," see the testimony of Hannah Johnson, 10 Oct. 1893, pension file of Michael Tucker, WC 386131, Civil War Pension Files, RG 15.

99. Testimony of Henry G. Judd [1863], filed with O-328 1863, Letters Received, Ser. 12, RG 94 [K-74].

100. See chapter 1, above.

101. Darlene Clark Hine, "Rape and the Inner Lives of Black Women in the Middle West: Preliminary Thoughts on the Culture of Dissemblance," *Signs* 14 (Summer 1989): 912–20.

102. See chapter 7 for a discussion of family conflict and domestic violence in postbellum South Carolina.

103. Thomas L. Webber makes this argument for slave women across the South in *Deep Like the Rivers: Education in the Slave Quarter Community, 1831–1865* (New York: Norton, 1978), 162–67.

104. My understanding of lowcountry "spiritual mothers" owes much to a paper presented by Margaret Washington Creel, titled "Cultural Transmission and Female Diviners in the Gullah Slave Society," at the November 1989 meeting of the Southern Historical Association.

105. Margaret Washington Creel's scholarship also supports Deborah Gray White's assertion that a narrow focus on the slave family obscures the family's relationship to the community and women's role in both settings. According to Creel, "kinship was important, but the Gullah concept of household did not necessarily mean filial attachment, but all those living within a family and community structure, with the rights, duties, and privileges therein" (Creel, *"A Peculiar People,"* 281).

106. See Creel, "Gullah Attitudes towards Life and Death," in Holloway, *Africanisms in American Culture,* 71; idem, *"A Peculiar People,"* 179; Joyner, *Down by the Riverside,* 154–59, and Rogers, *History of Georgetown County,* 349–51, 356, 357. Certainly many lowcountry planters would have agreed with James R. Sparkman's assessment, that the religious instruction of the slaves made them more manageable (Joyner, *Down by the Riverside,* 157).

107. A visitor to the lowcountry in 1857 revealed that the Reverend Alexander Glennie, an Episcopalian minister to Georgetown-area plantations, had at least one slave woman serving as "class leader." See Rogers, *History of Georgetown County,* 357–58.

108. Creel, in *"A Peculiar People"* (chap. 7, 211–51), provides an overview of Sea Island efforts to Christianize slaves. For a parallel study of planters, religion, and slaves on the mainland lowcountry, see Joyner, *Down by the Riverside,* chap. 5 (141–71).

109. Holland, *Letters and Diaries of Laura M. Towne,* 20–22, 56, 140, 144–45; Elizabeth Ware Pearson, ed., *Letters from Port Royal, 1862–1868* (1906; rpt., New York: Arno, 1969), 43–44, 186, 222, 250, 303–4; Allen diary, 56, 140.

110. Kemble, *Journal of a Residence,* 118–119.

111. Recounted by Robert W. Gordon, member of the Society for the Preservation of Spirituals, in Augustine T. Smythe et al., *The Carolina Low-Country* (New York: Macmillan, 1931), 201.

112. Women's organized community roles took a range of forms in different West African societies. The Poro (among men) and Sande (among women) secret societies dominated community life in several Upper Guinea groups, and informed the organization of community among Gullah slaves. Among the Ibo people of the Calabar region of West Africa, women's gatherings (*mikiri*) were the base of women's political power, the setting for self-rule and the articulation and protection of women's interests. Judith Van Allen, "'Sitting on a Man': Colonialism and the Lost Political Institutions of Igbo Women," *Canadian Journal of African Studies* 6 (1972): 165–81. See also Victor C. Uchendu, "Slaves and Slavery in Igboland, Nigeria," in *Slavery in Africa: Historical and Anthropological Perspectives,* Suzanne Miers and Igor Kopytoff, eds. (Madison: University of Wisconsin Press, 1977), 121–32. Margaret Washington Creel rightfully argues these West African antecedents place Gullah "seeking" in a larger cultural context of community creation. Although Creel is among those historians who assert that the Igbo (or Ibo) people were "shunned" by Carolinian slave traders, Daniel Littlefield (*Rice and Slaves*) argues that in fact slave *men* from this region were shunned, and that slave women were most available from this region. See the introduction, above, and Creel, *"A Peculiar People,"* 35.

113. K. Jones, *The Plantation South,* 101, 189.

Chapter 3: "A Hard Fight for We"

The chapter title quotes from Elizabeth Botume's rendering of a slave mother's account of the impact of war on slave families; see Elizabeth Hyde Botume, *First Days amongst the Contrabands* (1893; rpt., New York, 1968), 155.

1. On the wartime home front, see Berlin et al., *Destruction of Slavery,* chap. 9.

2. Entry for 22 Nov. 1861, John Berkeley Grimball Diary, SHC.

3. One of the best general overviews of the wartime crisis in slavery can be found in Roark's *Masters without Slaves,* especially chap. 3. Charles Edward Cauthen, in

South Carolina Goes to War, 1860–1865 (Chapel Hill: University of North Carolina Press, 1950), offers a very useful study of South Carolina's secession crisis, and Clarence L. Mohr carefully traces the wartime collapse of slavery in Georgia in *On the Threshold of Freedom: Masters and Slaves in Civil War Georgia* (Athens: University of Georgia Press, 1986). Also useful is Bell Irvin Wiley's classic study of wartime slavery, *Southern Negroes, 1861–1865* (New Haven: Yale University Press, 1938).

4. According to a census taken by South Carolina's comptroller general, James A. Black, between November 1862 and November 1864 the lowcountry districts lost 27,589 slaves, or 21 percent of the 1862 slave population. Some, but not all of the loss, may be accounted for by an increase (of 20,727 slaves) in the upcountry population (see [James A. Black], *Report of the Comptroller General to the Legislature of South Carolina, November 1864* [Columbia, S.C.: Charles P. Pelham, 1864]). The impact of the naval blockade and other aspects of the war on plantation slavery are discussed in Sewell, *A House Divided,* 101–25; Gates, *Agriculture and the Civil War,* 3–45; and Thomas, *The Confederate Nation,* 236–42.

5. Clifton, *Life and Labor,* 320; C. Vann Woodward, ed., *Mary Chesnut's Civil War* (New Haven: Yale University Press, 1981), 464, and see also 48, 78, 234; Mary Elliott Johnstone to Mamma [Mrs. William Elliott], [?] 15, 1861 or 1862, Elliott-Gonzales Family Papers [ser. 1.7, folder 67], SHC.

6. For discussion of wartime shortages, see Bell Irvin Wiley, *Southern Negroes,* chap. 2; Mary Elizabeth Massey, *Ersatz in the Confederacy: Shortages and Substitutes on the Southern Homefront* (1952; rpt. Columbia: University of South Carolina Press, 1993); George C. Rable, *Civil Wars: Women and the Crisis of Southern Nationalism* (Urbana: University of Illinois Press, 1989), chap. 5.

7. Thomas P. Ravenel to My Dear Wife [Mrs. Elizabeth Wilson Ravenel], 24 Nov. 1861, Thomas Porcher Ravenel Papers, R2, Ser. B, *RABSP.*

8. Henry William Ravenel notes that the interruption of trade with Northern ports was resulting in higher prices by May 1861. See Henry Arney Robinson Childs, ed., *The Private Journal of Henry William Ravenel, 1859–1887* (Columbia: University of South Carolina Press, 1947), 69, 116. By September 1864, slaves owned by the lowcountry planter Benjamin Huger had been without shoes for nearly three years (Benjamin Huger to James Pringle, 18 Sept. 1864, James R. Pringle Papers, PL). See also Wiley, *Southern Negroes,* 28–32, and Childs, *Private Journal,* 160.

9. Ann VanderHorst to Arnoldus VanderHorst, 11 Oct. 1861, VanderHorst Family Collection, SCHS.

10. Easterby, *South Carolina Rice Plantation,* 315: shoes were provided to boathands, plowhands, the driver, and the key house servant.

11. J. R. Walker to Mrs. Robert Smith, 18 Feb. 1864, James R. Pringle Papers, PL.

12. Easterby, *South Carolina Rice Plantation,* 313–14, 316, 295.

13. Berlin et al., *Destruction of Slavery,* 151. Although the woman lived as a slave in lowcountry Georgia, her account of wartime burdens is suggestive of slave women's experiences in South Carolina as well.

14. Yates Snowden, "The Planters of St. John's," *Transactions of the Huguenot Society of South Carolina,* no. 21 (1915): 23; see also Wiley, *Southern Negroes,* 54–58, and Childs, *Private Journal,* 130.

15. Marjorie Spaulding Kell to Blanche Kell, 12 July 1862, John McIntosh Kell Papers, PL.

16. Easterby, *South Carolina Rice Plantation,* 288.

17. Charles Petigru Allston to Adele Petigru Allston, 11 Feb. 1864, R. F. W. Allston Family Papers, SCL; Maj. W. H. Echols to Lt. Col. D. B. Harris, 7 Sept. 1863, Letters Received, E-72, Dept. of SC, GA, & FLA, Records of Military Commands, RG 109. Slave diets were also affected by the food shortages that occurred when Confederate authorities approved the impressment of food for military consumption from local producers and markets, and when Confederate soldiers made a habit of stealing provisions from nearby plantations to add variety to their sparse rations. By April 1863, all producers were required to contribute a tax-in-kind of one-tenth their produce for market to the Confederacy (Massey, *Ersatz in the Confederacy,* 37). Official impressment and improvised provisioning not only removed produce from the marketplace and thus from civilian consumption, but also frightened producers. Unable to purchase slave rations on the open market, some lowcountry planters devoted more acres to provision crops and expected slave laborers to produce what could no longer be purchased, adding to slaves' workload and to the incremental disruption of the work routine and social relations of lowcountry rice agriculture—the basis of slave labor for more than five generations (Entry for Apr. 1862, Thomas Porcher Ravenel Plantation Book [1855–74], in Thomas Porcher Ravenel Papers, 1731–1899, R2, Ser. B, *RABSP;* and Childs, *Private Journal,* 129).

18. William Capers to Sir [Louis Manigault], 19 June 1862, Louis Manigault Papers, R6, Ser. F, Pt. 2, *RABSP,* and Clifton, *Life and Labor,* 343.

19. Clifton, *Life and Labor,* xliii, 343; Thos. P. Ravenel to [My Dear Wife], 24 Nov. 1861, Thomas Porcher Ravenel Papers, R2, Ser. B: Selections from the South Carolina Historical Society, *RABSP;* Heyward, *Seed from Madagascar,* 74, 182.

20. Ella Lonn, *Salt as a Factor in the Confederacy* (New York: Walter Neale, 1933), 43, 108. Lonn's work provides the best general discussion of the significance of the salt shortage and the efforts to meet wartime demands. On lowcountry shortages and the responses by planters, see also Easterby, *South Carolina Rice Plantation,* 205, and Navy *OR,* Ser. I, Vol. 13, 202–3.

21. The state executive council first passed a resolution offering loans as well as insurance against enemy attacks on coastal saltworks on 21 May 1862; the loans were greatly enlarged by the state convention later in the war (Charles E. Cauthen, ed., *Journals of the South Carolina Executive Councils of 1861 and 1862* [Columbia: South Carolina Archives Department, 1956], 183, and idem, *South Carolina Goes to War,* 150–51). See also Wiley, *Southern Negroes,* 61, and Childs, *Private Journal,* 160. By the end of 1862, there were some 120 saltmaking establishments within Charleston's city limits alone, producing 4,000 bushels per day.

22. Navy *OR,* Ser. I, Vol. 13, 458. Twelve slaves belonging to the Allstons constructed and operated a saltmaking camp on the coast near Georgetown beginning in 1862, and they produced about twenty-two bushels of salt every week or ten days—and continued their operations through 1864. That year, despite occasional attacks by the federal blockading fleet, the Allstons earned nearly eight thousand dollars from the sale of slave-produced salt to South and North Carolinians. Neighboring planters operated similar works; one, Col. Daniel W. Jordan, had his

slaves producing fifty bushels of salt per day by December 1862. Although documentation of individual plantation saltmaking operations is scattered at best, overseer reports for Robert F. W. Allston's Chicora Wood plantation for July–November 1862 included reports on the amount of salt being produced (Easterby, *South Carolina Rice Plantation*, 270–75, 457). See also claim no. 4, R. F. W. Allston, R14, and J. Izard Middleton to Genl. Jordan, 8 Sept. 1863, R683, both in Confederate Papers Relating to Citizens or Business Firms, M346, War Department Collection of Confederate Records, RG 109; R. F. W. Allston to General Pemberton, 22 July 1862, Letters, Telegrams and Reports, 1861–62, E-75, Dept. of SC, GA, & FL, Records of Military Commands, RG 109; and H. H. W. [Wilson] to My Dearest Marie, Dec. 1862, H. H. Wilson Papers, SCL.

23. H. H. W. [Wilson] to My Dearest Marie, Dec. 1862, H. H. Wilson Papers, SCL. See also Lonn, *Salt as a Factor*, 247 n. 15. According to Lonn, South Carolina's high-salinity coastal waters produced one bushel of salt for every sixty to one hundred gallons of seawater boiled down.

24. Easterby, *South Carolina Rice Plantation*, 314–15.

25. Saltmaking was only one of many activities for which wartime conditions prompted the reallocation of slave resources away from rice agriculture. On the Allston plantations, the cultivation and processing of sugar cane during the war was similarly disruptive: not only was it an unfamiliar crop for the plantation labor force, but the labor was untasked and demanding, and the processing of the harvested cane especially difficult. It was agricultural labor over which slaves had no traditional source of power or control. See Easterby, *South Carolina Rice Plantation*, 188, 299–303.

26. See Easterby, *South Carolina Rice Plantation*, 313–17.

27. Childs, *Private Journal*, 129, 176; Gates, *Agriculture and the Civil War*, 30; Easterby, *South Carolina Rice Plantation*, 173. Confederate policies relating to staple crop production played an important role in the reallocation and disruption of slave labor on lowcountry long-staple cotton plantations. Confederate officials urged planters in 1861 to produce more corn and less cotton; by late 1862 and 1863, the Confederate states were passing numerous laws to insure that food, not cotton, dominated wartime agriculture. Lowcountry plantations devoted to long-staple cotton were, by 1863, required by state law to limit cotton production to one and a half acres per prime hand. In 1862 and 1863, the planter Henry W. Ravenel believed his neighboring planters were patriotically complying with the wartime effort to feed Confederate troops, but Charleston newspapers described the many imaginative ways in which planters subverted the restrictive legislation.

28. Easterby, *South Carolina Rice Plantation*, 203, 316–17. Dr. Francis S. Parker sold at least $11,726 worth of rice to the Confederate quartermaster in a two-year period; R. F. W. Allston, $10,078. Allston, along with several other lowcountry planters, also found a steady market for beef, corn, and fodder in the Confederate Quartermaster. See Dr. F. S. Parker, vouchers dated 16 Sept. 1862–16 July 1864, R772, and R. F. W. Allston, vouchers dated 13 June 1862–7 Mar. 1864, R14, Confederate Papers Relating to Citizens or Business Firms, M346, War Department Collection of Confederate Records, RG 109.

29. As one South Carolinian argued, "The same necessity which justifies the

conscription of the white man, justifies the impressment of the negro" (*Journal of the Convention of the People of South Carolina Held in 1860, 1861, and 1862, Together with the Ordinances, Reports, Resolutions, etc.* [Columbia, S.C.: 1862], 677).

30. While it is possible that slaveowers could have tried to answer their assessments for slave labor with slave women as well as men, the evidence overwhelmingly suggests that only men were impressed for defense work. The possible discrepancy between impressment policies and practice may be due in part to the basis of impressment mechanisms in the provision of slave labor for work on public roads. Public road duty assessments specified slave men but offered some leeway by which slave women could be provided instead (an 1825 Act of the General Assembly allowed the exemption of male servants if able-bodied slave women were substituted). The fact that Frederick Law Olmsted observed lowcountry slave women engaged in road repairs supports the likelihood that slave women were substituted for slave men in road duty (Olmsted, *Journey in the Seaboard States,* 387); it also raises the possibility that such substitution may have been attempted in response to impressment. In studying the impressment of enslaved Virginians, Ervin L. Jordan Jr. found one instance where two counties attempted to meet their quotas by forwarding slave women, only to have Confederate officials return the women to their owners (Jordan, *Black Confederates and Afro-Yankees in Civil War Virginia* [Charlottesville: University Press of Virginia, 1995], 63). In the variety of sources I examined (Confederate and state-generated materials, as well as private manuscripts), I found no record of a slave woman's impressment for labor on coastal fortifications.

31. Clarence L. Mohr's investigation and discussion of the exclusion of slave women from impressment points to such an interpretation; see his book *On the Threshold of Freedom,* esp. 172–75 and 182–83. Mohr believes that the exclusion of slave women from slave hiring and impressment reflected the drive toward maximizing profit and the opinion held by employers that slave women were incapable of working as hard as slave men (172). This interpretation would not be supported by my research in lowcountry South Carolina antebellum plantation practices.

32. In defending the Confederate impressment policy to state legislators, Gen. P. T. G. Beauregard pointed out that the policy excluded "the large number of negro women available for and actually employed in field labor," suggesting that the exclusion of slave women was seen, at least in part, in light of the need to continue plantation operations (quoted in Berlin at al., *Destruction of Slavery,* 714). A single proposal for the exclusive impressment of slave women—to harvest and thresh the rice on the exposed plantations of the Ashepoo and Combahee River plantations in 1862—seems to offer some support for this view of slave women as the core of the agricultural workforce. Thomas Jordan to Gen'l. W. S. Walker, 10 Nov. 1862, Chap. 2, Vol. 22, p. 230, Letters Sent, Dept. of SC, GA, & FLA, Records of Military Commands, RG 109 [F-161].

33. One lowcountry planter noted that for the greater part of 1863 and 1864, most of his "prime men" were absent from the rice fields, at work on local fortifications; see Clifton, *Life and Labor,* 348.

34. Easterby, *South Carolina Rice Plantation,* 170; entries for 12 and 30 Jan.

1861, Margaret Ann Morris [Meta] Grimball Diary, SHC; Clifton, *Life and Labor,* 316; Childs, *Private Journal,* 46. General Beauregard initiated a system of fortifications stretching "from Winyah Bay to Hilton Head, including Bull's Bay, Cole's and Battery Islands, North and South Edisto, and both sides of the entrance to Port Royal." These works were constructed immediately after the defenses of Charleston Harbor had been strengthened and multiplied. See R. S. Ripley, "Charleston and Its Defences in the Late 'War between the States,'" in *Year Book—1885, City of Charleston, So. Ca.* (Charleston, S.C.: News and Courier Book Presses, 1886), 347–48, as well as Rogers, *History of Georgetown County,* 388–89; and Col. Walter Gwynn to F. W. Pickens, 23 Dec. 1860, Governors' Papers, SCDAH.

35. Planters controlled the supply of slave laborers, provided their transportation to the coast, and either accompanied their slaves themselves or sent along an overseer; see entries for 12 and 30 Jan. 12 1861, Margaret Ann Morris [Meta] Grimball Diary, SHC; Clifton, *Life and Labor,* 316; and Childs, *Private Journal,* 46.

36. Confederate General J. C. Pemberton came to the conclusion after the first year of war that planters' volunteering of slave labor "is not to be relied on at all, each owner of slaves judging apparently the value of the work, by what amount of protection, his individual interest may seem to derive from it" (General J. C. Pemberton to Hon. I. W. Hayne, 22 Mar. 1862, Chap. 2, Vol. 21, pp. 10–11, Letters Sent and Received by Gen. J. C. Pemberton, Dept. of SC, GA, & FL, Records of Military Commands, RG 109).

37. In a secret session during 1861, the state executive council first empowered the military commander to impress slaves from the immediate vicinity of Charleston, a move which it withheld from public knowledge (Cauthen, *South Carolina Goes to War,* 147).

38. The fall of Forts Henry and Donelson and the repositioning of Confederate troops away from the coast into the interior of the Confederacy had left Pemberton with a much-reduced force (Rogers, *History of Georgetown County,* 396–98). See also Gen. J. C. Pemberton to Genl. S. Cooper, 27 Mar. 1862, pp. 16–17; Gen. J. C. Pemberton to Maj. L. A. Washington, 8 Apr. 1862, pp. 25–27; Gen. J. C. Pemberton to Genl. R. E. Lee, 10 Apr. 1862, pp. 29–30; Gen. J. C. Pemberton to Hon. James Chesnut, 18 Apr. 1862, pp. 33–34, and 26 July 1862, pp. 92–94, all in Chap. 2, Vol. 21, Letters Sent and Received by Gen. J. C. Pemberton, and S. J. Gaillard et al. to Maj. General J. C. Pemberton, 23 Aug. 1862, Letters, Telegrams, and Reports, 1861–62, all in Dept. of SC, GA, & FL, Records of Military Commands, RG 109. See also D. W. Jordan to Hon. G. Randolph, 3 Aug. 1862, Letters, Telegrams, and Reports, 1861–62, E-75, Dept. of SC, GA, & FL, Records of Military Commands, RG 109.

39. The first effort to spread the burden of impressment to the rest of the state occurred in May 1862; it was then quickly revoked until September, when the state's executive council finally yielded to military pressure and began impressing slaves from across the state (I. W. Hayne to General Pemberton, undated telegram, reprinted in Cauthen, *Journals,* 199, 216; see also *Journal of the Convention of the People of South Carolina,* 221, 233, 240, 246, 248, 250, 256–57, 677). By November 1862, impressment ceased once again because of the abolition of the executive council and the invalidation of its acts by the state legislature. See Cauthen,

Journals, xiii. In the wake of the November collapse of the impressment plan, Governor Pickens proposed the creation of a permanent force of slave laborers, a plan that General Beauregard endorsed but the legislature rejected (Cauthen, *South Carolina Goes to War,* 178). Not until February 1863 did the state legislature restore impressment. Governor Bonham, newly elected, forwarded a copy of South Carolina's new law to Confederate Secretary of War James A. Seddon, but Seddon warned Bonham that the Confederate government could not be held responsible or liable for the loss of South Carolinian slaves who escaped or were captured by the enemy. It would be nearly three months before the Confederate Congress would pass legislation assuming such liability. See *OR,* Ser. IV, Vol. 2, 266–70, and Cauthen, *South Carolina Goes to War,* 179. For Confederate legislation finally assuming liability, see *OR,* Ser. IV, Vol. 2, 469–72.

40. Confederate States of America, *Public Laws of the Confederate States of America* (Richmond: R. M. Smith, 1862), 103–4, and Wiley, *Southern Negroes,* 118–19.

41. Cauthen, *Journals,* 283, 285; idem, *South Carolina Goes to War,* 279–80.

42. James Tupper, *Report of the Auditor of South Carolina, on Claims Against the State for Slaves Lost in Public Service* (Columbia, S.C., 1864), 4; Cauthen, *South Carolina Goes to War,* 180; and William Shannon to Governor Bonham, 26 Aug. 1863, Box 33, Letters Received, E-72, Dept. of SC, GA and FL, Records of Military Commands, RG 109. Governor Bonham informed Secretary of War Seddon that impressment "has created more dissatisfaction and discontent than any other duties the Citizens have had to perform." M. L. Bonham to G. T. Beauregard, 15 Jan. 1863, in Governors' Papers, SCDAH.

43. By December 1863, less than 20 percent of the slaves called for were supplied (*OR,* Ser. I, Vol. 28, Pt. 2, 533, and Cauthen, *South Carolina Goes to War,* 181–83). During the last year and a half of the war, the Confederate Congress hastened to amend the impressment procedures to answer the complaints and dissatisfaction of planters and to increase the numbers of both enslaved and free African-American laborers available to the Confederate cause. Exemptions for house servants and an increase in the payments made to slaveowners who complied with impressment were coupled with amendments that extended the age of slaves eligible for impressment to fifty years. The term of impressment was also extended to sixty days. The Secretary of War was authorized by the Confederate Congress to impress up to twenty thousand slaves, but no more than one-fifth of a planter's eligible slaves were to be impressed at one time. Taking their lead from state action, Congress also stipulated that slaves were to be impressed only after free negroes had been taken (*OR,* Ser. IV, Vol. 3, 208). A related but futile effort—one extensively and vigorously debated—was the formulation of legislation approving the enlistment of slave men into the Confederate military, passed 13 March 1865, so late in the war that even President Davis recognized its limited utility (Confederate States of America, *Journal of the Senate of the Confederate States of America* [Second Congress, First and Second Session] [Washington, D.C., 1904–5], 704).

44. Cauthen, *Journals,* 111; W. W. Harlee to Genl. J. C. Pemberton, 27 Mar. 1862, and D. W. Jordan to Hon. G. W. Randolph, 3 Aug. 1862, both in Letters, Telegrams, and Reports, 1861–62, E-75, Dept. of SC, GA, & FL, Records of Military Commands, RG 109.

45. D. W. Jordan to Hon. G. Randolph, 3 Aug. 1862, Letters, Telegrams, and Reports, 1861–62, E-75, Dept. of SC, GA, & FL, Records of Military Commands, RG 109.

46. The conditions of slave encampments in and near Charleston Harbor are frequently described in the correspondence of the Department of South Carolina, Georgia, and Florida; see Major D. B. Harris to General Beauregard, 26 Nov. 1862, Edwin White to Capt. W. H. Echols, 2 Dec. 1862, Maj. Wm. H. Echols to Genl. R. S. Ripley, 14 Mar. 1863, Major Henry Bryan to Col. A. Roman, 27 and 31 July 1863, all in Letters Received, E-72, Dept. of SC, GA, & FL, Records of Military Commands, RG 109. See also Maj. W. H. Echols to Capt. J. Howard, 31 July 1863, Chap. 3, Vol. 14, 34; Lt. J. Guignard to Maj. W. H. Echols, 12 Aug. 1863, Chap. 3, Vol. 14, 87, both in Letters and Telegrams Sent, Engineer's Office at Charleston, Records of Commands in South Carolina, Records of Local Commands, RG 109; General Beauregard to R. L. Brodie, 24 Oct. 1863; Gen. Beauregard to Maj. Motte Pringle, 24 Oct. 1863; and Gen. Beauregard to Col. D. B. Harris, 9 Dec. 1863, all three in Chap. 2, Vol. 32, pp. 186 and 392, Letters Sent, Dept. SC, GA, & FL, Records of Military Commands, RG 109. See also the *OR,* Ser. I, Vol. 14, 974.

47. D. W. Jordan to Hon. G. Randolph, 3 Aug. 1862, Letters, Telegrams, and Reports, 1861–62, E-75, Dept. of SC, GA, & FL, Records of Military Commands, RG 109; Claims of Slaves Lost in Public Service, Ft. Sumter Hospital, Oct. 1863– Dec. 1864, SCDAH; entries for 30 Nov. and 3 Dec. 1861, and 20 July 1863, Thomas Porcher Ravenel Plantation Book, 1855–1874, Thomas Porcher Ravenel Papers, R1, Ser. B, *RABSP.* Some superintendents of impressed labor, apparently ignorant of the impact of wartime shortages on lowcountry slaves, attributed the poor condition of impressed slaves to planter negligence, or the "unloading" of undesirable slave men on impressment agents. *OR,* Ser. I, Vol. 28, Pt. 2, 534–35.

48. Myers, *Children of Pride,* 878. From November 1862 to March 1863, one-third of the impressed slave men working at Charleston either became sick or ran away (*OR,* Ser. I, Vol. 14, 827).

49. On wartime slave labor in South Carolina, see *OR,* Ser. IV, Vol. 3, 829–31; Major Henry Bryan to Col. A. Roman, 27 July 1863, Letters Received, E-72, Dept. of SC, GA, & FL, Records of Military Commands, RG 109; F. W. Pickens to General Beauregard, 5 Nov. 1862, Governors' Papers, SCDAH; entries for 1 Jan. 1861, 10 Feb. 1864, 16 July 1864, 27 Dec. 1864, Thomas Porcher Ravenel Diary, 1855–65; entry for 31 Dec. 1860, Thomas Porcher Ravenel Plantation Book, 1855–74, both in Thomas Porcher Ravenel Papers, R2, Ser. B, *RABSP;* Childs, *Private Journal,* 50, 103, 104, 132, 179–80. For a more general discussion of slave labor throughout the Confederacy, see Wiley, *Southern Negroes,* 113–14; James H. Brewer, *The Confederate Negro: Virginia's Craftsmen and Military Laborers, 1861–1865* (Durham, N.C.: Duke University Press, 1969), 11, 114; Bernard H. Nelson, "Confederate Slave Impressment Legislation, 1861–1865," *Journal of Negro History* 31, no. 4 (1946): 398. On the injuries sustained by slave laborers, see C. A. Grasser to Maj. Thomas Jordan, 20 Aug. 1863, and J. J. Ryan to R. L. Singletary, 9 Oct. 1863, both in Letters Received, E-72, Dept. SC, GA, & FL, Records of Military Commands, RG 109.

50. Entry for 30 Nov. 1861, Thomas Porcher Ravenel Plantation Book, 1855–1874, Thomas Porcher Ravenel Papers, R2, Ser. B, *RABSP,* and *OR,* Ser. I, Vol. 14, 959.

51. Jonathan J. Clarke to Major J. W. Alexander, 11 Oct. 1864, Governors' Papers, SCDAH.

52. Major Henry Bryan to Col. A. Roman, 27, 31 July 1862, Letters Received, E-72, and Gen. Beauregard to Col. D. B. Harris, 31 Oct. 1863, Chap. 2, Vol. 32, Letters Sent, both in Dept. of SC, GA, & FL, and G. Thos. Cox to General Jordan, 31 Aug. 1863, Gen. P. T. G. Beauregard Papers, E-116, Collections of Officers' Papers, all in Records of Military Commands, RG 109.

53. See F. W. Pickens to President Davis, 29 July 1862, and F. W. Pickens to General Beauregard, 5 and 25 Nov. 1862, both in Governors' Papers, SCDAH; Myers, *Children of Pride*, 861–62. Lowcountry planters—and other South Carolinians—were especially critical of the decisions made concerning defense works under the command of General Pemberton, in the spring and summer of 1862. See Ripley, "Charleston and Its Defences," 354–55; Easterby, *South Carolina Rice Plantation*, 170; and *OR*, Ser. I, Vol. 14, 914. The labor agent appointed by the state of South Carolina, William M. Shannon, conceded that planters felt that "the Confederate authorities had hitherto trifled with them by calling for slaves for thirty days, keeping them for ninety; by retaining their tools and implements, which they could not resupply; by sending their negroes home without or with insufficient rations" (*OR*, Ser. I, Vol. 14, 912–13).

54. *Correspondence Relating to Fortification of Morris Island and Operations of Engineers, Charleston, S.C., 1863* (New York: John C. Caulon, 1878), 7–8, 27.

55. "Sister" to Emmie, 2 Mar. 1863, Elliott-Gonzales Family Papers, SHC, and *OR*, Ser. I, Vol. 28, Pt. 2, 533.

56. Gen. Beauregard to Capt. R. H. Colcock, 17 Oct. 1863, Chap. 2, Vol. 32, p. 133, Letters Sent, Dept. of SC, GA, & FL, Records of Military Commands, RG 109; Maj. W. H. Echols to Lt. Col. D. B. Harris, 18 Aug. 1863, Chap. 3, Vol. 14, 110, and Maj. W. H. Echols to Lt. Col. D. B. Harris, 12 Sept. 1863, Chap. 3, Vol. 14, p. 236, both in Letters and Telegrams Sent, Engineer Office at Charleston, Records of Commands in South Carolina, Records of Local Commands, RG 109; Maj. Henry Bryan to Col. A. Roman, 28 Aug. 1863, Letters Received, E-72, Dept. of SC, GA, & FL, Records of Military Commands, RG 109. See also Childs, *Private Journal*, 139.

57. Gen. Beauregard to Brig. Genl. Henry A. Wise, 8 Nov. 1863, Chap. 2, Vol. 32, p. 260, Letters Sent, Dept. of SC, GA, & FL, Records of Military Commands, RG 109, and Maj. D. B. Harris to Brig. Genl. Thos. Jordan, 23 Feb. 1863, General P. G. T. Beauregard's Papers, E-116, Collections of Officers' Papers, Records of Military Commands, RG 109.

58. See, for example, Maj. W. H. Echols to Lt. Col. D. B. Harris, 5 Aug. 1863, Chap. 3, Vol. 14, p. 51, Letters and Telegrams Sent, Engineer Office at Charleston, Records of Commands in South Carolina, Records of Local Commands, RG 109. For reports of escaped impressed slaves, see entry for 30 Dec. 1861, Thomas Porcher Ravenel Plantation Book, 1855–74, Thomas Porcher Ravenel Papers, R2, Ser. B, *RABSP;* Childs, *Private Journal*, 138–39; Testimony of Mack Duff Williams, 24 Aug. 1872, claim of Mack Duff Williams, Charleston County, SC, case files, Approved Claims, Ser. 732, Southern Claims Commission, RG 217; *OR*, Ser. IV, Vol. 3, 1018–26.

59. Pringle, *Chronicles of Chicora Wood*, 356–57, and Easterby, *South Carolina Rice Plantation*, 196–97.

60. F. W. Pickens to General Beauregard, 5 Nov. 1862, Governors' Papers, SCDAH; Maj. Wm. H. Echols to Lt. Col. D. B. Harris, 7 Sept. 1863, Letters Received, E-72, Dept. of SC, GA, & FL, Records of Military Commands, RG 109; Maj. D. B. Harris to Maj. W. H. Echols, 9 July 1863, Papers of Gen. P. G. T. Beauregard, Collections of Officers' Papers, E-116, Records of Military Commands, RG 109.

61. Cauthen, *Journals,* 283; idem, *South Carolina Goes to War,* 179; Mary Elliott Johnstone to Mamma [Mrs. William Elliott], 29 Dec. 1862, Elliott-Gonzales Family Papers, SHC; Lt. Col. C. K. Huger to Col. E. VanderHorst, 17 Dec. 1862, Vander-Horst Family Papers, SCHS; F. W. Pickens to General Beauregard, 5 Nov. 1862, Governors' Papers, SCDAH; and John F. Marszalek, ed., *The Diary of Miss Emma Holmes, 1861–1866* (Baton Rouge: Louisiana State University Press, 1994), 284.

62. Maj. W. H. Echols to Lt. Col. D. B. Harris, 26 Aug. 1863, Chap. 3, Vol. 14, p. 155, Letters and Telegrams Sent, Engineer Office at Charleston, Records of Commands in South Carolina, Records of Local Commands, RG 109; Maj. Wm. H. Echols to Lt. Col. D. B. Harris, 7 Sept. 1863, and Maj. Henry Bryan to Col. A. Roman, 28 Aug. 1863, both in Letters Received, E-72, Dept. of SC, GA, & FL, Records of Military Commands, RG 109; G. Thos. Cox to General Jordan, 13 Aug. 1863, Papers of Gen. P. G. T. Beauregard, E-116, Officers' Papers, Records of Military Commands, RG 109. Still other planters responded to calls for labor by returning the same sick or disabled slaves who had already been worked half to death and sent home by military authorities (Maj. D. B. Harris to General Thomas Jordan, 9 Jan. 1863, Papers of Gen. P. G. T. Beauregard, E-116, Collections of Officers' Papers, Records of Military Commands, RG 109).

63. *OR,* Ser. IV, Vol. 3, 1023; see also Cauthen, *South Carolina Goes to War,* 183. Indeed, one Charleston County slave accustomed to hiring his own time— Mack Duff Williams—twice escaped from impressment and gained protection from his employer, whose farm had been hard hit by impressing officers. Although still a slave, Williams had managed to reject his new master in preference for the old. Testimony of Mack Duff Williams, 24 Aug. 1872, claim of Mack Duff Williams, Charleston County, SC, case files, Approved Claims, Ser. 732, Southern Claims Commission, RG 217.

64. F. W. Pickens to General Beauregard, 5 Nov. 1862, Governors' Papers, SCDAH.

65. Ann VanderHorst to Arnoldus VanderHorst, 19 Aug. 1863, VanderHorst Family Collection, SCHS; *OR,* Ser. IV, Vol. 2, 978–79. VanderHorst was not the only Charlestonian fearful of an apparent rise in the autonomy of the city's black population; fifty-five Charleston women, suspicious of the loyalty of slave men in the city, petitioned the governor to exempt more white men from the draft to protect the women from "the mercy of the treacherous negroes," who numbered over five thousand within a five-mile radius of the city (*The South Carolinian,* 6 Dec. 1864).

66. Testimony of Mary Orr, 12 Nov. 1877, claim of Mary Orr, and testimony of John Cochran, 18 Sept. 1877, claim of John Cochran, both in Beaufort County, SC, case files, Approved Claims, Ser. 732, Southern Claims Commission, 3d Auditor, RG 217. Also, see testimony of Rebecca Smith, 26 Mar. 1875, claim of Rebecca Smith, Barred and Disallowed Case Files, Records of the U. S. House of Representatives, RG 233; testimony of Alexander Jones and William Jenkins, 12 Nov.

1877, claim of Mary Orr; testimony of Charles J. Williamson, 20 Sept. 1877, claim of Charles J. Williamson; testimony of Thomas Jackson, 22 Mar. 1875, claim of Thomas Jackson; testimony of Thomas W. Jackson, 19 Sept. 1877, claim of Thomas Cochran, all in Beaufort County, SC, case files, Approved Claims, Ser. 732, Southern Claims Commission, 3d Auditor, RG 217.

67. Responding to an apparent escape attempt in 1864, Adele Allston instructed her overseer to have "Toney hired to the Government to work on the fortifications until the war is over" (Easterby, *South Carolina Rice Plantation,* 292). For other accounts of "dumping," see also Marszalek, *Diary of Miss Emma Holmes,* 252. Elias VanderHorst responded to the escape of about thirty of his slave men by hiring out eighteen of those who remained to work on the railroad coal fields in North Carolina; see "List of Seventeen Negro Men . . . ," 30 Oct. 1862, Folder 26, Vander-Horst Family Collection, SCHS.

68. See Childs, *Private Journal,* 65, 110, 121, 128, 132, 194, 201; Easterby, *South Carolina Rice Plantation,* 194, 204–5, 266–67, 269, 270, 272, 273, 277, 302; and Woodward, *Mary Chesnut's Civil War,* 304.

69. Wayne K. Durrill, in his study of wartime Washington County, North Carolina, describes how one family coped with the problems of wartime separation because of hiring; see *War of Another Kind: A Southern Community in the Great Rebellion* (New York: Oxford University Press, 1990), 160–61.

70. See Major Lee Hutson, Chief Quartermaster, Consolidated Report of Persons and Articles Hired and Roll of Enlisted Men Employed by the Quartermaster's Department in SC, GA & FL, Feb., Apr., May, and June 1863; Major Motte A. Pringle, Quartermaster, Report of Persons and Articles Employed and Hired at Charleston, SC, Feb. & Mar. 1863; Capt. J. S. Coles, Assistant Quartermaster, Report of Persons and Articles Hired and Roll of Enlisted Men Employed by the Quartermaster's Department in SC, GA, & FL, Apr. 1863, all in Records of Civilian Employment, E-78, Dept. of SC, GA, & FL, Records of Military Commands, RG 109.

71. Brewer, *The Confederate Negro,* 40–41, 61, 69, 86, 95, 97, 98, 106, 133. See also Jordan, *Black Confederates,* 54–55. Clarence L. Mohr found very similar patterns in his unsurpassed study of impressed and hired slave labor in wartime Georgia; see his *On the Threshold of Freedom,* 128–35.

72. The twenty-three South Carolina hospitals for which there are extant records include sixteen that employed slaves; see South Carolina's Hospital Muster Rolls in the Records of the Surgeon General's Office, Records of the Medical Department, RG 109.

73. J. M. Zohler to Williams Middleton, 9 Nov. 1862, Middleton Family Papers, SCHS.

74. Easterby, *South Carolina Rice Plantation,* 202, 204, 205.

75. Allan Maifarlam[?] to Elias VanderHorst, 18 Mar. 1863, VanderHorst Family Papers, SCHS.

76. An overseer would later report that Toney and "the Rest of the gange that ware to go with him . . . is all caught and in Jail," although Lizzie and her family apparently avoided recapture. The escape is described in Easterby, *South Carolina Rice Plantation,* 199, 289–92, and in Adele Petigru Allston to Charles Petigru Allston, 11, 20 July 1864, R. F. W. Allston Family Papers, SCL.

77. Saville, in *Work of Reconstruction,* 45n, cites a source indicating that in March 1864, the population of agricultural workers was 57 percent female, 27 percent male, and 16 percent children.

78. John Eaton, *Grant, Lincoln and the Freedmen: Reminiscences of the Civil War* (1907; rpt., New York: Negro Universities Press, 1969), 3; Berlin et al., *Destruction of Slavery,* 23, 39-40, and *Wartime Genesis,* 27.

79. Berlin et al., *Wartime Genesis,* document 8, p. 125.

80. Rose, *Rehearsal for Reconstruction;* Powell, *New Masters;* and Berlin et al., *Destruction of Slavery,* and *Wartime Genesis.*

81. Berlin et al., *Destruction of Slavery,* 103-56; the specific provisions concerning slave women and children are discussed in Berlin, Reidy, and Rowland, *Black Military Experience,* 15n.

82. Clifton, *Life and Labor,* 319-20.

83. Ibid., 319, 313.

84. James M. McKim, "The Freed Men of South Carolina" (Philadelphia: Willis P. Hazard, 1862), 2.

85. Easterby, *South Carolina Rice Plantation,* 185-86.

86. *OR,* Ser. I, Vol. 28, Pt. 2, 255.

87. Not only were his former slaves celebrating with music and dancing; "the House . . . with the exception of the Piano . . . was completely turned up side down & inside out," and the slaves were "not doing any work upon the Plantations" although the fields were "white with cotton." The slaves, of course, were "not inclined to come" off the islands with the planters (Thom. R. S. Elliott to Mother [Ann H. S. Elliott], [1861], Elliott-Gonzales Family Papers, SHC).

88. Entry for 10 Feb. 1862, Henry William Ravenel Journal, SCL.

89. Wm. E. LeRoy to Admiral S. F. Dupont, 25 Apr. 1862, Vol. 3 (Apr.–June 1862), pp. 81–84, Squadron Letters, South Atlantic Squadron, Ser. 30, RG 45 [T-543]; Flag Officer Commanding S. F. DuPont to Secretary of Navy Gideon Welles, 25 Apr. 1862, R139, M89; and *OR,* Ser. I, Vol. 6, 36, 76–78, 91–92; and Rogers, *History of Georgetown County,* 396–98.

90. William Elliott to General [?], 1861, Elliott-Gonzales Family Papers, SHC.

91. F. W. Pickens to President Davis, 12 June 1862, Governors' Papers, SCDAH; John L. Clifton to Father, 5 Apr. 1862, John L. Clifton Papers, PL.

92. Lowcountry slaveowners documented their losses in response to a published call from South Carolina's Senator James L. Orr, for testimony relating to violations of the usages of war by U.S. forces; their claims are located in Confederate Papers Relating to Citizens or Business Firms, M346, War Department Collection of Confederate Records, RG 109 (an index to South Carolinian claimants, titled "A Report of the Committee under a resolution of the Senate to ascertain losses etc. . . . . sustained by the people of South Carolina by depredations of the enemy," is filed under James L. Orr, R760). See also Confederate States of America, *Journal of the Congress of the Confederate States of America* (Second Session), 404.

93. Capt. Francis D. Lee to Capt. M. P. King, 19 July 1862, Letters, Telegrams, and Reports, E-75, Dept. of SC, GA, & FL, Records of Military Commands, RG 109.

94. Charles Nordhoff, *The Freedmen of South-Carolina; some account of their*

appearance, character, condition, and peculiar customs (New York: Charles T. Evans, 1863), 20.

95. Thomas Wentworth Higginson, *Army Life in a Black Regiment* (1869; rpt., New York: Norton, 1984), 235. Additional accounts of family escapes can be found in the testimony of Elizabeth Grant, 15 Oct. 1902, in the pension file of her husband, Lester Grant, WC 580312, Civil War Pension Files, RG 15, and in the slave narrative of Gabe Lance, formerly the slave of Frank Heriot (Rawick, *The American Slave,* Vol. 3, South Carolina Narratives, Pts. 3 and 4, pp. 91–93.

96. William H. Grimball to John Berkeley Grimball, 10 June 1863, John Berkeley Grimball Papers, PL.

97. Thomas Wentworth Higginson, "Up the Edisto," *Atlantic Monthly,* Aug. 1867, 159–60.

98. On the various modes of escape by groups of slaves, see, for example, the logbook of the USS *Gem of the Sea,* entries for 13, 14 July, 17 Aug., 19 Sept. 1862; and the logbook of the USS *Albatross,* entries for 9, 20, 28 June 1862, all in RG24. See also Adele Petigru Allston to Benjamin Allston, 30 Oct. 1862, and Adele Petigru Allston to Charles Petigru Allston, 29 Mar. 1863, R. F. W. Allston Family Papers, SCL, as well as Easterby, *South Carolina Rice Plantation,* 189–90, 192.

99. Heyward, *Seed from Madagascar,* 131. Grimball's slaves escaped in nearly equal numbers of men and women (entry for 3 Mar. 1862, John Berkeley Grimball Diary, SHC); see also Mary Elliott Johnstone to Mamma [Mrs. William Elliott], 2 Mar. [1862], Elliott-Gonzales Family Papers, SHC.

100. Comdr. Geo. A. Prentice to Flag Officer S. F. DuPont, 25 May 1862, R139, M89; logbook of the USS *Albatross,* entry for 22 May 1862, RG 24.

101. [Elias VanderHorst], "List of Negroes Who Ran Away to the Enemy . . . ," VanderHorst Family Papers, SCHS.

102. Rogers, *History of Georgetown County,* 402, 406–7. Mariah Heywood, an ex-slave, recalled the execution of one of the men, Nemo Ralston: each of his limbs was tied to a different horse and Ralston was stretched to his death. Rawick, *The American Slave,* Vol. 2, South Carolina, Pt. 2, 287–88.

103. Adele Petigru Allston to Charles Petigru Allston, 25 July 1862, R. F. W. Allston Family Papers, SCL.

104. Mary Elliott Johnstone to Mamma [Mrs. William Elliott], n.d. (folder 193), Elliott-Gonzales Family Papers, SHC.

105. William Ervine Sparkman Diary, 1862, William Ervine Sparkman Papers, SHC.

106. Nordhoff, *Freedmen of South-Carolina,* 2.

107. In a typical example, a Union gunboat approached Charles Ball's Cedar Hill plantation and left with several slaves—including two brothers of William Gaillard. Gaillard, a teenager at the time, hadn't even known that the gunboat had been to the plantation until some time later. See testimony of William Gaillard, 9 Mar. 1904, pension file of Andrew Gaillard, Civil War Pension Files, RG 15.

108. John Emory Bryant to Emma Spaulding, 3 June 1863, John Emory Bryant Papers, PL; Mrs. M. M. Grimball to John Berkeley Grimball, 15 July 1863 and H. H. Manigault to J. Berkeley Grimball, 14 July 1863, both in John Berkeley Grimball Papers, PL.

109. Nordhoff, *Freedmen of South-Carolina*, 13.

110. Adam and Diana's separation is discussed in M. M. Grimball to John B. Grimball, 18 July 1863, [?] Bowman to John B. Grimball, 24 July 1863, and Lewis M. Grimball to J. B. Grimball, 30 Aug. 1863, all in John Berkeley Grimball Papers, PL.

111. North Island apparently served as a temporary camp, holding contrabands until their passage could be arranged to the larger and more permanent camps at Beaufort, and Hilton Head, or one of the other Sea Island locations. See Logbook, U.S.S. *Gem of the Sea*, entries for 15, 16 July; 25 Aug.; 1, 5, 18, 27 Sept. 1862; Logbook, U.S.S. *Pochahontas*, 24 Aug. 1862; Logbook, U.S.S. *Sebago*, entry for 16 Mar. 1863; Logbook, U.S.S. *Nipsic*, entry for 8 Dec. 1864, all in RG24.

112. A full accounting of the sale of Sea Island land and the consequences for contrabands can be found in Berlin et al., *Wartime Genesis*, 87–122; Rose, *Rehearsal for Reconstruction*, chap. 7; and Julie Saville, "A Measure of Freedom: From Slave to Wage Worker in South Carolina, 1860–1868" (Ph.D. diss., Yale University, 1986), chap. 2.

113. Botume, *First Days amongst the Contrabands*, 67. Captain E. W. Hooper, a superintendent over contraband plantations, also noted in 1863 that while Sea Island "natives" lived in their old cabins, over three thousand refugees had been crowded into whatever shelter was available. See testimony by Capt. E. W. Hooper [1863], filed with O-328 1863, Letters Received, Ser. 12, RG 94 [K-82]. As bad as conditions were for mainland refugees, they were far worse in other parts of the South, particularly in the Mississippi Valley; see Berlin et al., *Wartime Genesis*, chap. 3.

114. Berlin et al., *Wartime Genesis*, 88–89; Saville, "A Measure of Freedom," 55.

115. Botume, *First Days amongst the Contrabands*, 16; Berlin et al., *Wartime Genesis*, 270–71.

116. Botume, *First Days amongst the Contrabands*, 50–51.

117. Nordhoff, *Freedmen of South-Carolina*, 11.

118. Berlin et al., *Wartime Genesis*, 78–79.

119. Nordhoff, *Freedmen of South-Carolina*, 3.

120. Berlin et al., *Wartime Genesis*, document 26, pp. 218–19. The disproportionate employment of men in the Hilton Head quartermaster's department is attributable to the number of single men employed. Children appear to have been employed as well.

121. Superintendent Sam B. Broad to Capt. Hazard Stevens, 15 and 17 Apr., 16 May 1862; Superintendent J. B. Strong to Capt. Lambert, 3 Oct. 1862, all in Letters Sent, Ser. 3117; see also the reports of John E. Webster in 1863, in Consolidated Morning Reports, Ser. 3118, all in Beaufort, SC, Contraband Dept., RG 105. See also McKim, *Freedmen of South-Carolina*, 26; Berlin et al., *Wartime Genesis*, 110, 147, 317; testimony of Captain E. W. Hooper [1863], filed with O-328 1863, Letters Received, Ser. 12, RG 94 [K-82]; Susie King Taylor, *Reminiscences of My Life in Camp with the 33rd U.S. Colored Troops, Late 1st South Carolina Volunteers: A Black Woman's Civil War Memoirs*, ed. Patricia W. Romero and Willie Lee Rose, (1902; rpt., New York: Marcus Wiener, 1988), 42, 91; Saville, "A Measure of Freedom," 54–57.

122. Testimony of Judge A. D. Smith, [1863], filed with O-328 1863, Letters Received, Ser. 12, RG 94 [K-71].

123. See, for example, Testimony of Captain E. W. Hooper before the American Freedmen's Inquiry Commission, [June 1863], filed with O-328 1863, Letters Received, Ser. 12, RG 94 [K-82].

124. Rose offers a full exploration of the wartime Sea Island experience in *Rehearsal for Reconstruction*. See also Saville, "A Measure of Freedom," esp. chap. 2.

125. Jonathan Lewis Whitaker to Mrs. Julia A. Whitaker, 2 May 1864, Jonathan Lewis Whitaker Papers, SHC.

126. Virginia Matzke Adams, ed., *On the Altar of Freedom: A Black Soldier's Civil War Letters from the Front, Corporal James Henry Gooding* (Amherst: University of Massachusetts Press, 1991), 110–11.

127. Berlin et al., *Wartime Genesis,* 316–19.

128. General Orders No. 130, Headquarters Dept. of the South, 6 Sept. 1864, Vol. 31/43, DS, pp. 164–65, General Orders, Ser. 4124, Dept. of the South, RG 393, Pt. 1 [C-1334]; Col. P. P. Brown to Maj. Gen. J. G. Foster, 28 May 1864, Letters Received, Ser. 4277, Provost Marshal of the Department of the South, RG 393, pt. 1 [C-1543].

129. Berlin et al., *Wartime Genesis,* 317.

130. Dr. Esther Hill Hawks, a trained physician who came to the Sea Islands as a teacher for the Freedmen's Aid Society, noted that the men targeted by recruiters "were suspicious and reluctant—and not til after they received their first wages did they feel confidence in the good intentions of the Government towards them" (Gerald Schwartz, ed., *A Woman Doctor's Civil War: Esther Hill Hawks' Diary* [Columbia: University of South Carolina Press, 1984], 40).

131. The resumption of conscription came just following the introduction of the wartime draft in March 1863; however, Northern states were not authorized to fill their draft quotas with black enlisted men from the Confederate states until July 1864 (Berlin, Reidy, and Rowland, *Black Military Experience,* 7–15).

132. Berlin et al., *Wartime Genesis,* 77, and document 37, p. 274.

133. The most complete history of wartime black enlistment in lowcountry South Carolina, with particular attention to the families of black soldiers, can be found in Berlin, Reidy, and Rowland, *Black Military Experience.* On the employment of contrabands as military laborers, see also *OR,* Ser. I, Vol. 28, Pt. 2, 255. The military experience of black soldiers and their families is explored in chapter 4.

134. The quotes are by General Rufus Saxton in a letter to Secretary of War Edwin Stanton. See Berlin et al., *Wartime Genesis,* 328.

135. Berlin et al., *Wartime Genesis,* 314–16; see also 166–68.

136. Schwartz, *A Woman Doctor's Civil War,* 34; testimony of Brigadier General Rufus Saxton before the AFIC, [1863], O-328 1863, Letters Received, Ser. 12, RG 94 [K-70]; on the rape of teen-aged contraband girls by Union officers and soldiers see also the *New York Times,* 11 Apr. 1867.

137. Nordhoff, *Freedmen of South-Carolina,* 4.

138. Holland, *Letters and Diaries of Laura M. Towne,* 144–45.

139. John Emory Bryant to Emma Spaulding, 15 Sept. 1862, John Emory Bryant Papers, PL.

140. Descriptions of these activities among the women in the contraband camps are found in Holland, *Letters and Diaries of Laura M. Towne,* 20–22, 56, 140, and in E. W. Pearson, *Letters from Port Royal,* 43–44, 186–87, 250, 303–4.

141. Rose, *Rehearsal for Reconstruction,* 229–36.

142. Berlin et al., *Wartime Genesis,* 326–27.

143. Sister [?] to Emmie [?], 26 [?], [1862], and Mary Elliott Johnstone to Mamma [Mrs. William Elliott], 21 [?] [1863], both in Elliott-Gonzales Family Papers, SHC; Easterby, *South Carolina Rice Plantation,* 291–92; Ann VanderHorst to Arnoldus VanderHorst, 1 Apr. 1862, VanderHorst Family Papers, SCHS; and Clifton, *Life and Labor,* 320–21.

144. Pringle, *Chronicles of Chicora Wood,* 33. In 1861, Henry William Ravenel described his slaves as "contented and loyal" (Childs, *Private Journal,* 66–67). A contrasting description of slaves came from a Georgetown-area overseer, who reported that the slaves "doant seem to care to obay orders & Jack the Drive[r] is not behaveing write[;] he dont talk write before the People" (Easterby, *South Carolina Rice Plantation,* 310).

145. Local authorities and the Confederate provost guard also extended their surveillance to the communities of free people of color, a close watch by a group that was violent enough to be portrayed by slave and free alike as nothing short of a lynch mob. See testimony by John Cochran, 18 Sept. 1877, claim of John Cochran, and testimony of Thomas Jackson, 22 Mar. 1875, claim of Thomas Jackson, both in Beaufort County, SC, case files, Approved Claims, Ser. 732, Southern Claims Commission, RG 217.

146. William Elliott to General [?], [1861], Elliott-Gonzales Family Papers, SHC; F. W. Pickens to President Davis, 12 June 1862, Governors' Papers, SCDAH; John L. Clifton to Father, 5 Apr. 1862, John L. Clifton Papers, PL.

147. Mary Elliott Johnstone to Mamma [Mrs. William Elliott], 28 June 1862, Elliott-Gonzales Family Papers, SHC; Rogers, *History of Georgetown County,* 396–97.

148. *Journal of the Convention of the People of South Carolina, Held in 1860, 1861 and 1862* (Columbia, S.C., 1862), 343.

149. *OR,* Ser. I, Vol. 14, 588–90, 609.

150. Ibid., Ser. IV, Vol. 2, 978–79; Ser. I, Vol. 14, 541, 588–89, 609.

151. Clifton, *Life and Labor,* 314.

152. Marszalek, *Diary of Miss Emma Holmes,* 237.

153. Entry for 8 Mar. 1862, John Berkeley Grimball Diary, SHC, and Clifton, *Life and Labor,* 337, 338, 339.

154. Sister to Emmie, 2 Mar. [1863], and Mary Elliott Johnstone to Mamma [Mrs. William Elliott], 21 [?] [1863], both in Elliott-Gonzales Family Papers, SHC.

155. William Elliott to William Elliott, 15 Aug. 1862, Elliott-Gonzales Family Papers, SHC, and Elias VanderHorst to Arnoldus VanderHorst, 26 Dec. 1862, VanderHorst Family Papers, SCHS.

156. Berlin et al., *Wartime Genesis,* 251; Clifton, *Life and Labor,* 331; and Charles Manigault to Mr. Capers, 26 Jan. 1862, Louis Manigault Papers, PL.

157. Capers later recognized the limits of his powers of surveillance and control when he admitted that Big George, if not sold, would run off again (Clifton, *Life and Labor,* 325).

158. William Capers to Louis Manigault, 14 Aug. 1863, Louis Manigault Papers, R6, Ser. F, Pt. 2, *RABSP*.

159. Testimony by Mack Duff Williams, 24 Aug. 1872, claim of Mack Duff Williams, ? County, SC, case files, Approved Claims, Ser. 732, Southern Claims Commission, RG 217.

160. Testimony by John Cochran, 18 Sept. 1877, claim of John Cochran, and testimony of Thomas Jackson, 22 Mar. 1875, claim of Thomas Jackson, both in Beaufort County, SC, case files, Approved Claims, Ser. 732, Southern Claims Commission, RG 217.

161. Quoted in Rogers, *History of Georgetown County,* 407.

162. Testimony by Job Mayz[e]ck, 11 Mar. 1873 and 19 Nov. 1878, claim of Job Mayzeck, Disallowed Claims, RG 233; testimony by Alonzo Jackson, 17 Mar. 1873, claim of Alonzo Jackson, Georgetown County, SC, case files, Approved Claims, Ser. 732, Southern Claims Commission, RG 217. When Jackson offered this testimony and described the execution, the special commissioner interviewing him commented that "the rebels tried colored people very often in this way, to frighten them."

163. Pringle, *Chronicles of Chicora Wood,* 22.

164. Easterby, *South Carolina Rice Plantation,* 306-7, 310.

165. Ibid., 314, 316, 309; Adele Petigru Allston to Charles Allston, 8 July 1863, R. F. W. Allston Family Papers, SCL.

166. Entry for 22 Nov. 1862, John Berkeley Grimball Diary, SHC.

167. Mary [Elliott Johnstone] to Mamma [Mrs. William Elliott], undated, Elliott-Gonzales Family Papers, SHC.

168. W. H. Elliott to [?], undated, Elliott-Gonzales Family Papers, SHC.

169. Easterby, *South Carolina Rice Plantation,* 204.

170. Thomas R. S. Elliott to Mother [Anna Hutchinson Smith Elliott], [1861], Elliott-Gonzales Family Papers, SHC.

171. Clifton, *Life and Labor,* 320-21; see also Daniel H. Huger Smith, Alice R. Huger Smith, and Arney R. Childs, eds., *Mason Smith Family Letters* (Columbia: University of South Carolina Press, 1950), 56-57.

172. Mary [Johnstone Elliott] to Mamma [Mrs. William Elliott], [n.d.], Elliott-Gonzales Family Papers, SHC. See also Ann VanderHorst to Arnoldus VanderHorst, 1 Apr. 1862, Vanderhorst Family Collection, SCHS.

173. Mary Elliott Johnstone to Mamma [Mrs. William Elliott], 15 [?] [1863], and Mary Elliott Johnstone to Mrs. William Elliott, 2 Feb. [1862], Elliott-Gonzales Family Papers, SHC; Marjorie Spaulding Kell to Blanche Kell, 19 Nov. 1861, John McIntosh Kell Papers, PL; Smith, Smith, and Childs, *Mason Smith Family Letters, 56-57.*

174. Easterby, *South Carolina Rice Plantation,* 292. See also B. J. Sellers to Williams Middleton, 26 Nov. 1863, Middleton Papers, SCHS; Mary Elliott Johnstone to Mamma [Mrs. William Elliott], 2 Feb. [1862?], Elliott-Gonzales Family Papers, SHC.

175. John Berkeley Grimball Diary, pp. 19-20, 29-30, SHC.

176. Smith, Smith, and Childs, *Mason Smith Family Letters,* 44-45; Mary Elliott Johnstone to Mrs. William Elliott, 8 June [1862], Elliott-Gonzales Family Papers, SHC.

177. "An Ordinance to provide for the Removal of Negroes and other Property from portions of the State which may be Invaded by the Enemy," *Journal of the Convention of the People of South Carolina, Held in 1860, 1861 and 1862, Together with the Ordinances, Reports and Resolutions, etc.* (Columbia, S.C., 1862), 779–82.

178. *Report of the Special Committee of Twenty-One, On the Communication of His Excellency Governor Pickens, Together with the Reports of Heads of Departments, and Other Papers* (Columbia, S.C.: R. W. Gibbes, 1862), 121–23. "The Military gives no protection to the planters[;] *they* say move your negroes, but if you attempt that they are off," complained one plantation mistress to her husband (Ann Vander-Horst to Arnoldus VanderHorst, 1 Apr. 1862, VanderHorst Family Collection, SCHS). But those planters who ignored Confederate orders to evacuate lost many of their slaves in the course of Union naval raids, including a particularly devastating raid in 1863 when more than seven hundred rice plantation slaves were carried off to Union lines (*OR*, Ser. I, Vol. 14, 293–308; Botume, *First Days amongst the Contrabands*, 50, 51, 53; and Smith, Smith, and Childs, *Mason Smith Family Letters*, 44–45).

179. Much to the consternation of area rice planters, Confederate troops were ordered to withdraw from Georgetown early in April 1862. Rogers, *History of Georgetown County*, 397–98.

180. Easterby, *South Carolina Rice Plantation*, 176–77, 188. By 31 May 1862, the federal navy basically had free rein in Winyah Bay and the river systems of the Georgetown area. The rice crops, saltmaking works, and slaves in the area became the targets of federal naval operations intended to deprive Confederate forces the use of the same. See *OR*, Ser. I, Vol. 14, 347–48.

181. Easterby, *South Carolina Rice Plantation*, 189–90. Slaves belonging to the Middletons, the Reads, the Westons, and the Lowndes had left during 1862.

182. This figure is based on an analysis of slave liens—loans secured by lowcountry planters from the state—for removal between April and December 1862, including only those liens that named the slaves and therefore allowed some estimation of the sex ratio. These records report the removal of 1,175 slaves, of whom 421 were adult men, 618 adult women, and an additional 136 composed largely of unnamed infants, but also a few illegible names (of unassignable sex). See the Papers of the Commission for the Removal of Negroes and Property, 1862–63, SCDAH.

183. B. T. Sellers to Mr. Williams Middleton, 5 Dec. 1863, Williams Middleton Papers, SCL.

184. Evidence of the particular vulnerability of slave women to removal is particularly strong in the testimony by freedwomen in the pension applications of lowcountry black veterans. See, for example, affidavit by Eliza Coit, 10 Mar. 1897, in pension claim of Prince Albert Coit, WC 7915; affidavits by Susan Haywood, 10 Oct. 1893, Julia Tucker, 9 Oct. 1893, Mary Atkinson, 10 Oct. 1893, and Hannah Johnson, 10 Oct. 1893, all in pension claim of Michael Tucker, WC 386131; and affidavits by Prince Brown, 25 Nov. 1907, Lydia Alston, 13 Nov. 1907, and Rebecca Wright, 13 Nov. 1907, all in pension claim of Murphy Allston, WC 18887, Civil War Pension Files, RG 15.

185. William Grimball to John Berkeley Grimball, 26 Mar. 1862, John Berke-

ley Grimball Papers, PL, and Mary Elliott Johnstone to Mrs. William Elliott, [1863], Elliott-Gonzales Family Papers, SHC.

186. Heyward, *Seed from Madagascar,* 131–33.

187. Smith, Smith, and Childs, *Mason Smith Family Letters,* 57.

188. William Capers to Louis Manigault, 20 Aug. and 24 Sept. 1863, Louis Manigault Papers, R6, Ser. F, Pt. 2, *RABSP.*

189. Easterby, *South Carolina Rice Plantation,* 283, 202, 300.

190. Clifton, *Life and Labor,* 322–23.

191. For testimony about the impact of removal on slave women and their families, see affidavits by Julia Tucker, 9 Oct. 1893, Susan Heyward, 10 Oct. 1893, Mary Atkinson, 10 Oct. 1893, Ann Davis, 10 Oct. 1893, and Hannah Johnson, 10 Oct. 1893, all in pension file of Michael Tucker, WC 386131, Civil War Pension Files, RG 15; affidavits by Eliza Coit, 10 Mar. 1897 and 21 Mar. 1901, both in pension file of Prince [Albert] Coit, WC 7915, Civil War Pension Files, RG 15; and affidavit by Rebecca Wright, 13 Nov. 1907, in pension file of Murphy Allston, Civil War Pension Files, RG 15. On assaults against slave women, see testimony by Lydia Alston, 13 Nov. 1907, claim of Murphy Allston, Civil War Pension Files, WC 1887, RG 15; William Capers to Louis Manigault, 14 Aug. 1863, Louis Manigault Papers, R6, Ser. F, Pt. 3, *RABSP.*

192. Easterby, *South Carolina Rice Plantation,* 177, 194; Smith, Smith, and Childs, *Mason Smith Family Letters,* 49–50.

193. Wilkes to Wm. Middleton, 2 and 8 Nov. 1862, Middleton Papers, SCHS. When William Mason Smith moved his slaves inland, the slaves were forced to leave behind about one hundred hogs and a large quantity of poultry. Although Smith intended to sell the stock and reimburse his slaves for their losses, the provisions would have been far more valuable to them than the cash. See Smith, Smith, and Childs, *Mason Smith Family Letters,* 59, 61.

194. Antagonism between lowcountry and upcountry whites had several manifestations, from the high rents charged by upcountry whites to the characterization of lowcountry elite women as selfish and lazy. See, for example, Lalla Pelot to Julia, 30 June [?], Lalla Pelot Papers, PL; entry for 12 Apr. 1862, Margaret Ann Morris [Meta] Grimball Diary, and Mary Elliott Johnstone to Mrs. William Elliott, 15 Mar. [1863], Elliott-Gonzales Family Papers, both in SHC. The theft of hogs and cattle from local farmers by refugeed slaves fueled that hostility; see Pringle, *Chronicles of Chicora Wood,* 361–62; Easterby, *South Carolina Rice Plantation,* 280, 289; and Jno. L. McDaniel to General [Beauregard], 10 Dept. 1863, Letters Received, E-72, Records of the Dept. of SC, GA, & FL, Records of Military Commands, RG 109.

195. Mary Elliott Johnstone to Mrs. William Elliott, undated [ss 1.12.15.1], folder 192, Elliott-Gonzales Family Papers, SHC, and Marszalek, *Diary of Miss Emma Holmes,* 220, 306. The arrival of one lowcountry planter and several slave women provoked a "written warning—from the citizens of crab creek, mud creek, willow little river, and other parts of the country to remove from the state within a week all of his negroes until the war is over or failing to do so—they will come and remove Mr. L. *with* his negroes—not choosing to leave their wives and children—among so many negroes" (Mary Elliott Johnstone to Mrs. William Elliott, 3 Aug. [1862], Elliott-Gonzales Family Papers, SHC). The threats were backed by occasions

of mob action, and lowcountry planters rallied toggether in self-defense against the bands of "lawless conscripts" (Mary Elliott Johnstone to Mrs. William Elliott, undated, folder 192, Elliott-Gonzales Family Papers, SHC). Not entirely unaware of the consequences of removal for upcountry residents, the state acted to allay the anxiety and quell the hostile reactions of upcountry residents to the influx of slaves by requiring the presence of an overseer at the location of all removed slaves, under penalty of a hefty fine. See Cauthen, *Journals,* 87.

196. Mary Elliott Johnstone to Mrs. William Elliott, undated, folder 192, Elliott-Gonzales Family Papers, SHC.

197. When William Mason Smith moved his slaves inland, he did so without giving them any advance warning, in order to prevent any organized resistance to the move. The slaves managed to bring some baggage with them, but a last-minute move could hardly have provided the opportunity to pack well. See Smith, Smith, and Childs, *Mason Smith Family Letters,* 56–57.

198. Jno. Bottom to Louis Manigault, 13 Apr. 1863, William Capers to Louis Manigault, 11 Apr. 1863 and 13 Apr. 1863, Louis Manigault Papers, PL.

199. Myers, *Children of Pride,* 1015.

200. A. H. Elliott to [?], undated letter fragment, Elliott-Gonzales Family Papers, SHC.

201. Heyward, *Seed from Madagascar,* 132.

202. Adele Petigru Allston to Benjamin Allston, 30 June 1864, R. F. W. Allston Family Papers, SCL.

203. Jno. Bottom to Louis Manigault, 13 Apr. 1863, William Capers to Louis Manigault, 11 Apr. 1863 and 13 Apr. 1863, Louis Manigault Papers, PL.

204. Brenda Stevenson, ed., *The Journals of Charlotte Forten Grimké* (New York: Oxford University Press, 1988), 444–45.

205. A. H. Elliott to ?, undated letter fragment, Elliott-Gonzales Family Papers, SHC.

206. Easterby, *South Carolina Rice Plantation,* 204.

207. Clifton, *Life and Labor,* 346, 347, 350; testimony by B. J. Sellers, 15 Mar. 1872, claim of Edward Middleton, Charleston County Claims, Southern Claims Commission, RG 217.

208. See Mary Elliott Johnstone to [?], [1861], same to Mrs. William Elliott, 7 Sept. [1863], and [?] ["Your Affectionate Brother"] to Emily, 11 Dec. 1863, all in Elliott-Gonzales Family Papers, SHC; and Marrietta Heyward to Louis Manigault, 10 Apr. 1863, Louis Manigault Papers, PL. See also the entries for 1862 and 1863, passim, William Ervine Sparkman's Diary, SHC, and Easterby, *South Carolina Rice Plantation,* 22, 205–6, 279. Other planters coped with the expense of removal by hiring out their slaves to various upcountry employers, assuming that they would be "fed and taken care of during the war." It was reported, however, that "a large number of them died from the want of care and change of locality, and those necessary comforts to which they had been accustomed." Even the employers of refugeed slaves lacked the resources to feed the slaves they hired (*New York Times,* 14 May 1865).

209. Easterby, *South Carolina Rice Plantation,* 205–6.

210. [?] to Lalla Pelot, 2 Apr. 1864, Lalla Pelot Papers, PL.

Chapter 4: "Without Mercy"

The chapter title quotes from the observation of one of the officers leading Union troops through the South Carolina countryside, that his soldiers robbed and mistreated slaves "without mercy" (*OR,* Ser. I, Vol. 47, Pt. 1, 487).

1. Quoted in Joseph T. Glatthaar, *The March to the Sea and Beyond: Sherman's Troops in the Savannah and Carolinas Campaigns* (New York: New York University Press, 1985), 140.

2. Glatthaar, *March to the Sea,* 54.

3. Williamson, *After Slavery,* 24; Navy *OR,* Ser. I, Vol. 14, 260–62, 274–75; and Rogers, *History of Georgetown County,* 416–18.

4. Entries for 16, 26, 27 Feb. and 1, 2 Mar. 1865, in the Private Journal of Henry William Ravenel, typescript, SCL; see also Ravenel's memoir of the closing moments of war in his essay "Recollections of Southern Plantation Life."

5. Jervey and Ravenel, *Two Diaries,* 3.

6. Ibid., 29.

7. Harriet R. Palmer, MS Memoir, 15–16. Early in March, a Santee River rice plantation slave reported that "eight of the ten fellows [planter] W. Porcher had carried with him had come back, they pretended they had got separated from & lost their master at Kingstree." Writing from the USS *Potomska,* on the Cooper River, Commander Montell observed that the slaves of the Cooper River rice planter Col. Singleton, a "rank secessionist," had been "herded together the night previous for the purpose of being transported" to a safer spot, "but several succeeded in escaping from their Master" (Commander F. M. Montell to Admiral Jno. A. Dahlgren, 20 Feb. 1865, Ser. 30, Squadron Letters—South Atlantic Blockading Squadron, T-579). See also Smith, Smith, and Childs, *Mason Smith Family Letters,* 161–62.

8. Easterby, *South Carolina Rice Plantation,* 206–8.

9. Jervey and Ravenel, *Two Diaries,* 5; see also the entry for 23 Feb. 1865, in the Private Journal of Henry William Ravenel, typescript, SCL. Major General William T. Sherman described how "Wheeler's cavalry . . . had, by details of negro laborers, felled trees, burned bridges, and made obstructions to impede our march" in the lowcountry. See *OR,* Ser. 1, Vol. 47, Pt. 1, 19.

10. Several months later, a Freedmen's Bureau agent noted that Confederate deserters "ravaged" the Combahee River area "to a fearful extent, . . . taking provisions clothing cooking utensils & everything movable from the defenceless colored people." Combahee Ferry Land Report by G. G. Batchelder, 9 Oct. 1865, Land Reports, Ser. 3177, Combahee Ferry, SC, RG 105.

11. Jervey and Ravenel, *Two Diaries,* 5.

12. Ibid., 7–9, 15–16.

13. Ibid., 4; Harriet R. Palmer MS Memoir, 16; Smith, Smith, and Childs, *Mason Smith Family Letters,* 175.

14. Jervey and Ravenel, *Two Diaries,* 9.

15. Rawick, *The American Slave,* Vol. 2, South Carolina, Pt. 2, 159–60; testimony of Dennis Hazel, 18 Mar. 1873, in claim of Alonzo Jackson, Georgetown County, SC, case files, Approved Claims, Ser. 732, Southern Claims Commission, 3d Audi-

tor, RG 217; testimony of John Frederick and testimony of Edward Brown, 15 Mar. 1872, both in claim of Edward Middleton, Charleston County, SC, case files, Approved Claims, Ser. 732, Southern Claims Commission, 3d Auditor, RG 217.

16. One popular Northern magazine described Confederate guerrillas in the border states, for example, as men "to whom an act of cruelty and outrage is a good joke. To cause the innocent to suffer, to perform deeds of unparalleled atrocity and wickedness, is their daily work" (*Harper's Weekly,* 17 Jan. 1863, 40–42).

17. One wartime diarist, Sarah Morgan, of Baton Rouge, felt that Butler's order gave Union soldiers license to insult and outrage Southern ladies at will. From the pages of her diary, Morgan threatened to use her knife against "the first man who attempts to Butlerize—or brutalize—(the terms are synonymous) me!" (Charles East, ed., *The Civil War Diary of Sarah Morgan* [Athens: University of Georgia Press, 1991], 77.) A Georgia diarist, Ella Gertrude Clanton Thomas, similarly reacted to news of Butler's order, noted the widespread attention it received in the Southern press, as well as the fact that General Beauregard read it to his troops. She described the order as an incentive for Southern white men "to protect the honour of their women. Numerous instances have occurred of men attempting to defend their wives subjected to brutal passion, having been shot down" (Virginia Ingraham Burr, ed., *The Secret Eye: The Journal of Ella Gertrude Clanton Thomas, 1848–1889* [Chapel Hill: University of North Carolina Press, 1990], 207). Mary Chesnut noted that his orders "are in everybody's mouth. We hardly expected from Massachusetts behavior to shame a Comanche" (Woodward, *Mary Chesnut's Civil War,* 378–79). Pauline DeCaradeuc Heyward, a South Carolinian, also commented on the outrageous conduct of "Beast" Butler (Mary D. Robertson, ed., *A Confederate Lady Comes of Age: The Journal of Pauline DeCaradeuc Heyward, 1863–1888* [Columbia: University of South Carolina Press, 1992], 34).

18. Missouri's guerrilla warfare, for example, included rape and what Michael Fellman describes as "symbolic" or "near rape"; see *Inside War: The Guerrilla Conflict in Missouri During the American Civil War* (New York, 1989), 205–23.

19. Kate M. Stoney to Rear Admiral Dahlgren, 24 Mar. 1865, Dahlgren Papers, PL.

20. Myers, *Children of Pride,* 1230.

21. Harriet R. Palmer, MS Memoir, "Ballsdam, March 1865," p. 35, Palmer Family Papers, SCL.

22. Easterby, *South Carolina Rice Plantation,* 211; Smith, Smith, and Childs, *Mason Smith Family Letters,* 184–85.

23. For reasons explored by Darlene Clark Hine in her essay "Rape and the Inner Lives of Black Women," former slave women may have chosen to shield "the truth of their inner lives and selves from their oppressors" and not disclose to Northern or Southern whites (who authored most of the sources we have about this period) the facts of the assaults they endured. Most of the extant testimony we have by former slave women about their experiences during the closing weeks of war focuses on their loss of property and is contained in the applications of lowcountry men and women to the Southern Claims Commission for reimbursement for goods confiscated by the Union forces. Observations by Northern and Southern whites of the assaults against slave women may tell us what happened,

but they provide little insight into the actual experience and response by the slave women themselves.

24. Former slaves such as William Young, once a slave driver on a Waccamaw River rice plantation, saw a direct relationship between Union occupation and freedom; he asserted that slaves "became free when the Yankees took Georgetown during the last year of the war" (Testimony of William Young, 6 Jan. 1874, claim of William Young, Disallowed Claims, RG 233).

25. Entry for 22 Feb. 1865, John Snider Cooper Diary, PL.

26. Alonzo Reed to Mother, 25 Feb. 1865, Alonzo Reed Papers, PL; and Childs, *Private Journal,* 219.

27. Henry William Ravenel, entries for 27 Feb. and 2 Mar. 1865, in the Private Journal of Henry William Ravenel, typescript, SCL.

28. Joseph Glatthaar's *March to the Sea* portrays the great range of sentiment among Sherman's soldiers about slavery and the fate of slaves (see esp. 40–41, 52–65). Glatthaar also asserts that the Carolinas campaign was far more grueling than the march to Savannah. Extremely difficult forays through the swamplands of the lowcountry made Sherman's troops into harsh messengers of Sherman's edict that Southern people be made to understand that "the Confederate armies were no longer capable of protecting its citizens and that life outside the Union was much worse than life inside the Union" (100).

29. From the first arrival of Union troops on the South Carolina Sea Islands, they were authorized to "avail" themselves of the "services" of slaves. By 1865, lowcountry contrabands were regularly carried into Beaufort and employed in the engineer, commissary, and quartermaster's departments. See Berlin et al., *Destruction of Slavery,* 114–15; and *OR,* Ser. I, Vol. 47, Pt. 2, 83. On relations between Union troops and lowcountry slaves, see Glatthaar, *March to the Sea,* chaps. 3, 7, and 8, passim.

30. According to John Richard Dennett, special correspondent to the *Nation,* there wasn't a slave's house in the path of Sherman's troops that hadn't been ransacked when they crossed into North Carolina, nor was there a modestly dressed or shod slave who wasn't forced by the Union soldiers to stop and "trade" clothing. See Dennett, *The South as It Is, 1865–1866,* ed. Henry M. Christian (1965; rpt., Athens: University of Georgia Press, 1986), 177.

31. Joseph T. Glatthaar provides an excellent study of the actions of Sherman's troops in the Carolinas in *March to the Sea,* esp. chaps. 7 and 8.

32. Testimony of Robert Bates, 13 Mar. 1873, in claim of Job Mayzeck, Disallowed Claims, RG 233.

33. Entry for 9 Feb., 1865, John Snider Cooper Diary, and Alonzo Read to Mother, 25 Feb. 1865, Alonzo Read Papers, both at PL.

34. Testimony by Ceasar Deas, 27 Mar. 1875, claim of Ceasar Deas, Beaufort County, SC, case files, Approved Claims, Ser. 732, Southern Claims Commission, 3d Auditor, RG 217.

35. Testimony of Cupid Hamilton, 26 Mar. 1875, claim of Cupid Hamilton, Disallowed Claims, RG 233; see also Jervey and Ravenel, *Two Diaries,* 35; testimony of Benjamin J. Sellers, 15 Mar. 1872, claim of Edward Middleton, Charleston County, SC, case files, Approved Claims, Ser. 732, Southern Claims Commission, 3d Auditor, RG 217.

36. Testimony of Luke Green, 26 Mar. 1875, claim of Cupid Hamilton, Disallowed Claims, RG 233.

37. Testimony by Eliza Washington, 26 Mar. 1875, claim of Eliza Washington, Beaufort County, SC, case files, Approved Claims, Ser. 732, Southern Claims Commission, 3d Auditor, RG 217.

38. One of the commanders of Union forces in South Carolina, for example, decried the pillaging of houses as "disgraceful and demoralizing to this army" and "disgraceful to our arms and shocking to humanity." He noted that the homes of free blacks had even "been stripped of the necessary bedclothes and of family apparel." His threat of arrest and punishment for soldiers caught in such acts would have been difficult to enforce. See *OR,* Ser. I, Vol. 47, Pt. 2, 184–85.

39. Rawick, *The American Slave,* Vol. 2, South Carolina Narratives, Pt. 2, 153–54. Brig. Gen. James D. Morgan, commanding the Second Division of the Fourteenth Army Corps in its march through South Carolina, noted with regret that some of the men under his command "have mistaken the name and meaning of the term foragers, and have become under that name highwaymen, with all their cruelty and ferocity and none of their courage; their victims are usually old men, women, and children, and negroes, whom they rob and maltreat without mercy"(*OR,* Ser. I, Vol. 47, Pt. 1, 487).

40. Testimony of Rebecca Smith, 16 Mar. 1874, claim of Rebecca Smith, Disallowed Claims, RG 233.

41. Sherman and other officers would later forget their instrumental role in creating this state of dependence, and instead perpetuated a stereotype of lowcountry freedpeople as tending "naturally" toward "laziness" and dependence on the federal government for support. This stereotype would help to shape federal policy in the postwar South. This is discussed more fully in following chapters. See also testimony by James Mole, 26 Feb. 1875, claim of Sarah Harvey, Disallowed Claims, RG 233.

42. Testimony by Eliza Washington, 26 Mar. 1875, claim of Eliza Washington, Beaufort County, SC, case files, Approved Claims, Ser. 732, Southern Claims Commission, 3d Auditor, RG 217.

43. Testimony of Luke Green, 26 Mar. 1875, claim of Cupid Hamilton, Disallowed Claims, RG 233.

44. Testimony of Rebecca Smith, 17 July 1871, claim of Rebecca Smith, Disallowed Claims, RG 233.

45. Testimony by Agnes Jackson, 24 Mar. 1875, Beaufort County, SC, case files, Approved Claims, Ser. 732, Southern Claims Commission, 3d Auditor, RG 217.

46. *OR,* Ser. I, Vol. 47, Pt. 1, 1027.

47. Ibid., *OR,* Ser. I, Vol. 47, Pt. 1, pp. 1027, 1032.

48. Easterby, *South Carolina Rice Plantation,* 210.

49. Entry for 16 Apr. 1865, John Snider Cooper Diary, PL.

50. Ibid.

51. See Berlin et al., *Wartime Genesis,* 339–40.

52. Rose, *Rehearsal for Reconstruction,* 272.

53. Maj. Genl. R. Saxton to Maj. Genl. M. C. Meigs, 6 Apr. 1865, Quartermaster General Consolidated Correspondence File, 1794–1915, Box 720, RG 92.

54. Edward Magdol, *A Right to the Land: Essays on the Freedmen's Community*

(Westport, Conn.: Greenwood, 1977), 102–3. See also Smith, Smith, and Childs, *Mason Smith Family Letters,* 189.

55. Smith, Smith, and Childs, *Mason Smith Family Letters,* 205, 224.

56. Civil War historians owe a great debt to W. E. B. Du Bois for making this point. See his classic work, *Black Reconstruction in America, 1860–1880* (1935; rpt., New York: Atheneum, 1985). More recently, Leon F. Litwack elaborated on this thesis in *Been in the Storm So Long.*

57. Elizabeth Catherine Palmer Porcher to My Dear Husband, 23 Mar. 1865, typescript, Palmer Family Papers Folder, SCL.

58. N. S. Harless to Adele Petigru Allston, 22 Apr. 1865, Robert F. Allston Family Letters, SCL.

59. Elizabeth Catherine Palmer Porcher to My Dear Husband, 23 Mar. 1865, typescript, Palmer Family Papers Folder, SCL.

60. Childs, *Private Journal,* 238–39.

61. See the entry for 12 Mar. 1865 in the Private Journal of Henry William Ravenel, typescript, SCL.

62. Clifton, *Life and Labor,* 350.

63. Jervey and Ravenel, *Two Diaries,* 10–11; Harriet R. Palmer MS Memoir, p. 16, Palmer Family Papers, SCL.

64. Entry for 6 Mar. 1865, John Snider Cooper Diary, PL.

65. Exceptions to these extemporaneous reactions were celebrations organized by white missionaries on the Sea Islands, as well as those among Charleston's black elite, where the congregants of the city's black churches celebrated a day of National Thanksgiving. Also, on 1 January, an "old-fashioned barbacue" was the centerpiece of a secular emancipation celebration. See the *South Carolina Leader,* 9 and 16 Dec. 1865, and Smith, Smith, and Childs, *Mason Smith Family Letters,* 181, 188. Williamson (*After Slavery,* 49) describes many upcountry village-wide celebrations of emancipation on New Years' and Independence Day in 1870. William H. Higgins Jr., in *O Freedom! Afro-American Emancipation Celebrations* (Knoxville: University of Tennessee Press, 1987), argues that Southern emancipation celebrations continued out of slave holidays and religious observances, while Northern emancipation celebrations included a range of landmark events, including the abolition of the foreign slave trade, emancipation in the British West Indies, and Lincoln's preliminary emancipation (xviii–xix, 34–36).

66. This and the following quotation are from Jesse Belflowers to Mrs. [Adele] Allston, 18 Mar. 1865, R. F. Allston Papers, SCHS.

67. John Drayton to Williams Middleton, 2 June 1865, Middleton Papers, SCHS.

68. Entry for 16 Apr. 1865, John Snider Cooper Diary, PL.

69. Elizabeth Catherine Palmer Porcher to [My Dear Husband], 23 Mar. 1865, Palmer Family Papers Folder, SCL; Charles Manigault, "The Close of the War—The Negro, etc.," Manigault Family Papers, R1, Ser. J, Pt. 4, *RABSP.*

70. Easterby, *South Carolina Rice Plantation,* 328–29; untitled eight-page typescript, Trapier Family Papers Folder, 1861–29 Sept. 1910, and Catherine Palmer Porcher to [?], 23 Mar. 1865, typescript, Palmer Family Papers Folder, both in SCL; Jervey and Ravenel, *Two Diaries,* 10, 12, 35–36; Lt. Jarvis O'Kane to Rear Admiral Dahlgren, 7 Mar. 1865, Letters Received by the Secretary of the Navy, M89.

71. One particular plantation mistress had no doubt that the kind of wreck-

age done to the planter residence was purely malicious in intent. See Alberta Morel Lachicotte, *Georgetown Rice Plantation* (Columbia: University of South Carolina Press, 1955), 123. Willie Lee Rose and Julie Saville also found the nature of this kind of destruction unmistakably motivated, at least in part, by revenge. See Rose, *Rehearsal for Reconstruction,* 106–7, and Saville, "A Measure of Freedom," 51–52.

72. Nordhoff, *Freedmen of South-Carolina,* 7–8.

73. Henry L. Swint, *Dear Ones at Home: Letters from Contraband Camps* (Nashville: Vanderbilt University Press, 1966), 186.

74. My interpretation of these events is indebted, in part, to James C. Scott, *Domination and the Arts of Resistance: Hidden Transcripts* (New Haven: Yale University Press, 1990), especially chap. 8.

75. Easterby, *South Carolina Rice Plantation,* 328.

76. Francis LeJau Frost to Father, 31 July 1865, Alston-Pringle-Frost Papers, SCHS.

77. "Charges and Specifications against Jack a freedman," "Charges and Specifications against Cato, a freedman," and "Charges and Specifications against Andrew, a freedman," encl. in Olney Harleston to Capt. F. W. Leidtke, 11 Apr. 1866, Ser. 3277, RG 105.

78. Easterby, *South Carolina Rice Plantation,* 209–11.

79. Ibid., 213.

80. Ibid.

81. Charles Manigault, "The Close of the War—The Negro, etc.," Manigault Family Papers, R1, Ser. J, Pt. 4, *RABSP.*

82. Jervey and Ravenel, *Two Diaries,* 36, and Smith, Smith, and Childs, *Mason Smith Family Letters,* 223.

83. Easterby, *South Carolina Rice Plantation,* 206–8.

84. Charles Manigault, "The Close of the War—The Negro, etc." Manigault Family Papers, R1, Ser. J, Pt. 4, *RABSP;* Easterby, *South Carolina Rice Plantation,* 210–11, 312. While still a slave, Lavinia had been sent to the Plantersville Allston residence by the overseer in October 1864 to "take care of the House & the furniture," and consequently made this claim on the house and furniture as her own.

85. In the highly publicized trial three months later, Arnell and one of the band members were sentenced and executed by hanging, while the remaining members were sentenced to hard labor in a New York penitentiary (*Charleston Daily Courier,* 9 Sept. 1865). Army officers later complained about the excessive cost of the well-attended trial and execution.

86. This group of freedmen, also tried by military commission, was sentenced to hard labor. Reuben Tomlinson to Bvt. Major Genl. R. Saxton, 15 Sept. 1865, Letters Received, Ser. 3126, 6th Subdistrict, Charleston, SC, RG 105, and *Charleston Daily Courier,* 11 Sept. 1865. Another incident in which a "band of negroes" attacked a planter is described in Smith, Smith, and Childs, *Mason Smith Family Letters,* 237.

87. Freedmen's military posturing during the closing weeks of war may have had deep roots in lowcountry slave culture, given the organization of both the Stono Rebellion and the conspiracy that Denmark Vesey attempted to lead. Both incidents offer evidence of lowcountry slave men's deployment of paramilitary styles

in organizing and, in the case of the Stono Rebellion, in carrying out armed slave resistance. See Edward A. Pearson, *Designs against Charleston: The Transcript of the Denmark Vesey Conspiracy of 1822* (University of North Carolina Press, forthcoming) and "From Stono to Vesey."

88. Jervey and Ravenel, *Two Diaries,* 10, 12, 35; Elizabeth Catherine Palmer Porcher to My Dear Husband, 23 Mar. 1865, typescript, Palmer Family Papers Folder, SCL.

89. *Charleston Daily Courier,* 11 Sept. 1865.

90. Statement by W. M. Robertson, 14 Aug. 1865, encl. in Lt. W. Wood to Lt. S. Baker, 16 Sept. 1865, Letters Received, Ser. 2384, Subdistrict of Coosawatchie, SC, RG 393, No. 141, DS, Pt. 2 [C-1593].

91. *OR,* Ser. I, Vol. 47, Pt. 1, 1042–43.

92. Harriet R. Palmer, MS Memoir, 22, Palmer Family Papers, SCL.

93. Thomas Porcher Ravenel, entry for 3 Mar. 1865, Thomas Porcher Ravenel Diary, 1855–65, Thomas Porcher Ravenel Papers, 1731–1899, R1, Ser. B, *RABSP.*

94. James Scott, in *Domination and the Arts of Resistance,* observes that "The first public unveiling of the hidden transcript frequently sets in motion a crystallization of public action that is astonishingly rapid" (223).

95. North of the Santee River toward Georgetown, numerous abandoned plantations, including Rosemont, Kensington, Wee-Haw, Keithfield, Weymouth, Ingleside, and Hagley, were looted and burned by former slaves. Undated anonymous typescript, in Trapier Family Folder, 1861–29 Sept. 1910, SCL.

96. Easterby, *South Carolina Rice Plantation,* 328.

97. Ibid., 209–11.

98. Ibid., 206–8.

99. Henry William Ravenel, entry for 6 Mar. 1865, Private Journal of Henry William Ravenel, typescript, SCL.

100. The Georgetown militia was particularly incited by the sweep of local plantations by black Union soldiers of the 54th Massachusetts and the 32d and 102d USCT as part of a Union raid through the area during the first three weeks of April. On the Union occupation of Georgetown, see Capt. H. S. Stellwagon to Rear Admiral Dahlgren, 27 Mar. 1865, Ser. 30, Squadron letters—South Atlantic Squadron, Mar.–May 1865, 157–61, T-581; Navy *OR,* Ser. 1, Vol. 16, 260–62, 268, 272–73, 274–75, 278; Rogers, *History of Georgetown County,* 416–17; Easterby, *South Carolina Rice Plantation,* 206–9.

101. Dennett, *The South as It Is,* 195.

102. Henry William Ravenel, entry for 6 Apr. 1865, Private Journal of Henry William Ravenel, typescript, SCL.

103. Ibid.

104. See Bettina Aptheker's essay, "Woman Suffrage and the Crusade against Lynching, 1890–1920," in her collection titled *Woman's Legacy: Essays on Race, Sex, and Class in American History* (Amherst: University of Massachusetts Press, 1982), 53–76.

105. Accounts of the activities of the scouts and the freedmen in the Charleston District neighborhood of Pineville can be found in Harriet R. Palmer's MS Memoir, 27–29, in the Palmer Family Papers, SCL; Private Journal of Henry Wil-

liam Ravenel, entries for Mar. and Apr., esp. 22 Mar. 1865, typescript, SCL; entries for 27 Feb.–3 Mar. 1865, in the Thomas Porcher Ravenel Diary, 1855–65, Thomas Porcher Ravenel Papers, 1731–1899, R1, Ser. B, *RABSP;* Jervey and Ravenel, *Two Diaries,* 13, 17–18, 38–42.

106. Harriet R. Palmer, MS Memoir, "Ballsdam, March 1865," pp. 27–29, 35, Palmer Family Papers, and Henry William Ravenel, entry for 9 Apr. 1865, Private Journal of Henry William Ravenel, typescript, both at the SCL; and Jervey and Ravenel, *Two Diaries,* 13, 17–18, 38–42.

107. Entry for 22 Mar. 1865, Private Journal of Henry William Ravenel, typescript, SCL.

108. Jervey and Ravenel, *Two Diaries,* 38–43.

109. LeeAnn Whites offers a lucid analysis of the relational position occupied by Southern white men in the introduction to her study, *The Civil War as a Crisis in Gender: Augusta, Georgia, 1860–1890* (Athens: University of Georgia Press, 1995).

110. *OR,* Ser. I, Vol. 47, Pt. 1, 1042–43.

111. Henry William Ravenel, entry for 21 June 1865, in the Private Journal of Henry William Ravenel, typescript, SCL.

112. Litwack, *Been in the Storm So Long,* 94.

113. *OR,* Ser. I, Vol. 47, Pt. 2, 641.

114. Joseph T. Glatthaar, *Forged in Battle: The Civil War Alliance of Black Soldiers and White Officers* (New York: Free Press, 1990), 209–10.

115. *OR,* Ser. I, Vol. 47, Pt. 3, 98. Within a week, Potter reported having collected together 2,500 contrabands, which he sent down to Charleston on military transports (*OR,* Ser. I, Vol. 47, Pt. 3, 176).

116. See Descriptive Books for 34th and 128th U.S. Colored Infantries, Regimental Books and Papers, USCT, RG 94, and *OR,* Ser. I, Vol. 47, Pt. 1, 1026–27. Approximately 450 former slave men enlisted into the 128th U.S. Colored Infantry. South Carolina slave men also appeared on the rosters for various other black regiments, including Northern regiments and the three South Carolina regiments created primarily among Sea Island contrabands, including the 21st, 33d, and 34th U.S. Colored Infantry. For Major General Foster's comments on the slow rate of enlistment among slave men, see *OR,* Ser. I, Vol. 47, Pt. 2, 210.

117. At least 5,462 adult slave men from South Carolina served in the Union army during the course of the war, representing about 8 percent of the state's adult slave male population (not including the large number of South Carolina slaves enlisted into Northern units such as the 54th Massachusetts or the 104th USCT). Another 25 percent of total wartime Navy enlistment involved black sailors, or a total of 29,511. According to one researcher, a minimum of 117 of these were from South Carolina. See Berlin, Reidy, and Rowland, *Black Military Experience,* 12, and David Lawrence Valuska, "The Negro in the Union Navy: 1861–1865" (Ph.D. diss., Lehigh University, 1973), 55. For soldiers as well as for their families, the experience of enlistment in the spring of 1865 was significantly different from the experience of slaves who had enlisted—or been drafted—in the earlier years of war. Like the majority of Sea Island, Florida, and Georgia slaves mustered into the early South Carolina black regiments, lowcountry slave men who escaped from the mainland earlier in the war and enlisted in the army and the navy faced continual assignment to

menial labor and periods of service without pay or with less pay than that received by white soldiers. Those members of the early South Carolina regiments struggled for the right to enlist, to end constant assignments to fatigue duty, to assume a soldier's role in the battlefield, and to receive a full soldier's pay for their service to their country. They also fought for some guarantee of the safety of their families. These initial battles over African Americans' right to equality in military service paved the way and improved conditions for the men who enlisted in the army at the close of the war. Slave men who enlisted in the navy, where equal pay and a far greater degree of integration was the wartime norm, avoided many of the conflicts that occurred in the army as a result of institutionalized discrimination against black soldiers. See Glatthaar, *Forged in Battle,* 169–206, and Herbert Aptheker, "The Negro in the Union Navy," *Journal of Negro History* 32 (Apr. 1947): 179–80.

118. Affidavit by Harriet Lemmon, 4 May 1908, and by Cain Nesbit, 1 May 1908, in pension file of Cain Nesbit (AKA Piatt), WC 938695, Civil War Pension Files, RG 15.

119. Testimony of Gabriel Brown, 24 Feb. 1907, in pension file of Pompey Gray, WC 570700, Civil War Pension Files, RG 15.

120. Affidavit by Rina Green, 24 July 1901, in pension file of Hector Green, WC 432779; deposition of Cain Nesbit, 1 May 1908, in pension file of Cain Nesbit (AKA Piatt), WC 938695; affidavit of Jacob Vandross, 21 July 1902, in pension file of Jacob Nadrus (AKA Vandross), IC 554729, Civil War Pension Files, RG 15.

121. Affidavit by Frederick Allston, 11 Aug. 1905, in pension claim of Cain Mayhams [AKA Mayhem], MC 596808, Civil War Pension Files, RG.

122. Affidavit by Frederick Allston, 11 Aug. 1905, in pension file of Cain Mayhams (AKA Mayhem), MC 596808; affidavit of Ann Frazier, 30 Dec. 1909, and affidavit of Benjamin Weston, 31 Dec. 1898, in pension file of Daniel Frazier, WC 695221, Civil War Pension Files, RG 15.

123. The literature on Civil War military service and masculinity is small but growing. See Reid Mitchell, "Soldiering, Manhood, and Coming of Age: A Northern Volunteer," David W. Blight, "No Desperate Hero: Manhood and Freedom in a Union Soldier's Experience," and Jim Cullen, "'I's a Man Now': Gender and African American Men," all in Clinton and Silber, *Divided Houses,* 43–91. Also important are several recent monographs on African-American men and their military experience: see R. J. M. Blackett, ed., *Thomas Morris Chester, Black Civil War Correspondent* (Baton Rouge: Louisiana State University Press, 1989); Virginia M. Adams, *On the Altar of Freedom;* Edwin S. Redkey, ed., *A Grand Army of Black Men: Letters from African-American Soldiers in the Union Army, 1861–1865* (New York: Cambridge University Press, 1992); David W. Blight, *Frederick Douglass' Civil War: Keeping Faith in Jubilee* (Baton Rouge: Louisiana State University Press, 1989), esp. chap. 7; Glatthaar, *Forged in Battle;* and Berlin, Reidy, and Rowland, *Black Military Experience,* 517–22.

124. Testimony of Col. [Thomas W.] Higginson [1863], O-328 1863, Letters Received, Ser. 12, RG 94 [K-81].

125. *OR,* Ser. I, Vol. 47, Pt. 2, 210. In 1863, a white commander of a black North Carolina regiment echoed a similar sentiment: "they have been slaves and are just learning to be men" (Berlin, Reidy, and Rowland, *Black Military Experience,* 493).

126. Higginson, *Army Life in a Black Regiment,* 221.

127. Wilson Gallant, a slave from Chicora Wood plantation when he enlisted, practiced drilling in Beaufort for six months before his company was finally given guns. They remained, drilling and performing guard duty, in Beaufort. According to one member, when they were joined by new recruits, some of whom were also from the Georgetown area, "we learned them to drill." When not drilling, Gallant was detailed to help dismount guns at Hilton Head and to transport provisions between Charleston and Morris Island (affidavit by Wilson Gallant, 30 Jan. 1902 and 16 May 1901, pension claim of Wilson Gallant, IC 717471, Civil War Pension Files, RG 15). Another former slave from Georgetown who enlisted, Nat Allston, also drilled constantly and performed heavy labor, "in the way of handling lumber and transporting same, from different places to Beaufort for repairing wharf's etc" (affidavit by Nat Allston, 13 Aug. 1895, pension claim of Nathaniel Allston, WC 746108, Civil War Pension Files, RG 15).

128. For an overview of medical theories that were not only racist but also supported the notion of the physical disposition of black people toward slavery, see Walter Fisher, "Physicians and Slavery in the Antebellum Southern Medical Journal," *Journal of the History of Medicine* 23 (1968): 36–49; J. D. Guillory, "The Pro-Slavery Arguments of Dr. Samuel A. Cartwright," *Louisiana History* 9 (1968): 209–27; and Nancy Kreiger, "Shades of Difference: Theoretical Underpinnings of the Medical Controversy on Black/White Differences in the United States, 1830–1870," *International Journal of Health Services* 17, no. 2 (1987): 259–78.

129. Affidavit by Archa Ward [AKA Robinson], n.d. [1892], pension claim of Archa Ward [AKA Robinson], WC 882864, and affidavit by Abram Trappier, 25 Apr. 1911, pension claim of Abram Trappier, IC 2510275, Civil War Pension Files, RG 15. On the navy's belief that black sailors were physiologically "better suited" to hard labor in the heat and humidity of the lowcountry, see Valuska, "Negro in the Union Navy," 37–49, and Rear Admiral Commanding S. F. DuPont to Hon. Gideon Welles, 26 Aug. 1862, South Atlantic Squadron, Letters from Officers Commanding Squadrons, RG 45 [T-552]. See also Henry W. Ravenel, entry for 24 June 1865, in the Private Journal of Henry William Ravenel, typescript, SCL. For a discussion of similar sentiments held by white officers toward black troops, see Glatthaar, *Forged in Battle,* 81–90. Medical theories of race differences and their impact on lowcountry slavery are discussed by Wood in *Black Majority,* 63–91. A general discussion of the health of black soldiers can be found in Berlin, Reidy, and Rowland, *Black Military Experience,* 633–37.

130. Rear Admiral Commanding S. F. DuPont to Hon. Gideon Welles, 26 Aug. 1862, RG 45 [T-552].

131. Thus, former slavewomen like Elizabeth Grant could assert that she was with her husband "almost all the time he was in the army," from his enlistment to his discharge. See the testimony by Elizabeth Grant, 13 June 1904, pension file of Lester Grant, WC580312, Civil War Pension Files, RG 15. The account by the adolescent brother of Private Cain Mayhams, of Company D, offers another example. Cain's brother went to Beaufort to visit Cain and stayed three weeks before he returned to their home on John Pyatt's Georgetown plantation. Affidavit by Fred

G. Mayhams, 9 Aug. 1905, in pension claim of Cain Mayhams [AKA Mayhem], MC 596808, Civil War Pension Files, RG 15.

132. Col. Wm. B. Barton to Brig. Genl. R. Saxton, 5 Dec. 1863, enclosing Lt. Col. Augie G. Bennet to Capt. Wm. L. M. Burger, 30 Nov. 1863, Letters Received, 21st U.S. Colored Infantry, Regimental Books and Papers USCT, RG 94 [G-302].

133. Testimony of General Rufus Saxton [1863], O-328 1863, Letters Received, Ser. 12, RG 94 [K-70].

134. See OR, Ser. I, Vol. 47, Pt. 2, 33–35.

135. Adams, On the Altar of Freedom, 110–11.

136. Ibid. Although Gooding seems to be referring here to the popular portrayal (especially in geography primers) of New Zealanders as ferocious cannibals, he had actually served prior to the war as a sailor on board a whaling ship with three Pacific Islanders (see p. xxiv). See also Redkey, Grand Army of Black Men, 75.

137. Adams, On the Altar of Freedom, 110–11; Berlin et al., Wartime Genesis, 183.

138. Berlin et al., Wartime Genesis, 318n.

139. General Orders No. 130, Headquarters Dept. of the South, 6 Sept. 1864, Vol. 31/43, DS, pp. 164–65, General Orders, Ser. 4124, Dept. of the South, RG 393, Pt. 1 [C-1806]; Col. P. P. Brown to Maj. Gen. J. G. Foster, 28 May 1864, Letters Received, Ser. 4277, Provost Marshal of the Department of the South, RG 393, Pt. 1 [C-1543]).

140. Affidavit by Washington Rutledge, 13 Nov. 1901, in pension claim of Washington Rutledge, WC 801129, Civil War Pension Files, RG 15.

141. Testimony by Cain Nesbit, 1 May 1908, pension claim of Cain Nesbit [AKA Piatt], WC 938695, Civil War Pension Files, RG 15.

142. Affidavit by Julia Tucker, 9 Oct. 1893, and testimony by Frank Coleman, 9 Oct. 1893, pension claim of Michael Tucker, WC 386131, Civil War Pension Files, RG 15.

143. Testimony by Richard Humbert, 26 June 1902, pension claim of Brutus Nesbit, WO 542840, Civil War Pension Files, RG 15.

144. Affidavit by Ann Frazier, 30 Dec. 1909, and affidavit by Ben Huger and January Mitchell, 17 Dec. 1894, in pension claim of Daniel Frazier, WC 695221, Civil War Pension Files, RG 15.

145. Berlin, Reidy, and Rowland, Black Military Experience, 30, 493.

Chapter 5: "The Simple Act of Emancipation"

The chapter title quotes from a speech made at the November 1865 Freedmen's Convention held in Charleston, where one delegate asserted that "the simple act of emancipation, if it stops there, is not worth much." See Proceedings of the Colored People's Convention of the State of South Carolina Held in Zion Church, Charleston, November 1865 (Charleston, S.C., 1865).

1. Charles Manigault, "The Close of the War—The Negro, etc.," Manigault Family Papers, R1, Ser. J, Pt. 4, RABSP.

2. Ibid.

3. John Drayton to Williams Middleton, 2 June 1865, Middleton Family Papers, SCHS.

4. J. J. Pringle Smith to Mrs. Robert Smith, 4 May 1865, Middleton Family Papers, SCHS.

5. Major James P. Roy to Lt. Col. W. L. M. Burger, 9 Dec. 1865, Letters Received, Ser. 4109, Dept. of the South, RG 393, Pt. 1. Roy notes that medical attention came from the freedpeople's "own female doctors; or nurses."

6. H. G. Judd to Maj. Genl. Saxton, Asst. Comr. Bureau Freedmen &c., 29 Aug. 1865, R34, M869.

7. Williams Middleton to F. Francis Fisher, 29 Aug. 1865, Middleton Family Papers, SCHS.

8. Col. Isaac Dyer to Lieut. C. B. Fillebrown, 2 Aug. 1865, Ser. 4112, Letters Received, Department of the South, RG 393, Pt. I; 9. J. A. Alden to General [R. Saxton], 30 Aug. 1865, R34, M869.

9. H. G. Judd to Brvt. Maj. Genl. R. Saxton, 29 Aug. 1865, R34, M869.

10. J. Bachman to Miss E. Elliott, 11 Sept. 1865, Elliott-Gonzales Family Papers, SHC.

11. H. G. Judd to Maj. Gen. R. Saxton, Asst. Com. Freedmen's Affairs, &c., 1 Aug. 1865, R34, M869.

12. Childs, *Private Journal,* 222.

13. Major James P. Roy to Lt. Col. W. L. M. Burger, 9 Dec. 1865, Letters Received, Ser. 4109, Dept. of the South, RG 393, Pt. 1.

14. The April expedition up the Santee drew over a thousand contrabands who followed the troops back to the coast. Also during April, General E. H. Potter commanded a drive inland from Georgetown to destroy the Summerville-Camden railroad. On his troops' return march to Georgetown, they were followed by thousands of former slaves who had been rationed off the countryside. The newly freed slaves and troops stripped the area of anything they could eat. Most of these former slaves were subsequently transported to the Sherman Reserve. See *OR,* Ser. I, Vol. 47, 1032, and Williamson, *After Slavery,* 24–25. Williamson surmises that the fugitives who followed Potter's troops from Camden back to the lowcountry were all "making their way to freedom," but I find it more likely that many of the fugitives may have, in effect, been making a forced march, the interior countryside having been ravaged of provisions.

15. Dennett, *The South as It Is,* 229.

16. H. G. Judd to Maj. Gen. Saxton, 29 Aug. 1865, R34, M869.

17. H. G. Judd to Bvt. Maj. Gen. R. Saxton, 1 Aug. 1865, R34, M869.

18. Many had to overcome the schemes and manipulations of former owners and mistresses who feared the loss of the servants on whom they had relied so heavily. Mary Pringle, for example, refused to provide transportation for her former domestic slaves to return to their lowcountry homes from the upcountry refuge to which she had carried them during the war; Pringle suspected that if her former servant Cretia were reunited with her fellow servants and especially her sons, who were "established in a home of their own," Cretia would herself prefer to live with friends or family rather than her employer (Mary M. Pringle to Rebecca Brewton

Pringle Frost, 5 Oct. 1865, Alston-Pringle Frost Papers, SCHS). E. P. Smith suspected that servant women, if returned to the coast, would abandon their jobs to seek out family and mates—"Mary in search of her husband and Ann in search of her lover." For this and other examples see E. P. Smith to Susan Middleton, 1, 7, 10 June 1865, Middleton Family Manuscripts [microfiche edition], SCHS, and also Mrs. J. B. Grimball to J. B. Grimball, 5 Jan. 1866, John Berkeley Grimball Papers, PL.

19. Eager to defend her place in the antebellum social heirarchy of public life, the woman added, "I never pretend to dispute place with them but look very pityingly at them and say 'poor ignorant thing you know no better'" (Cousin M. [?] to Celia [?], 11 June 1865, Porcher Family Papers, SCHS).

20. *New York Times,* 14 and 22 May 1865; Schwartz, *A Woman Doctor's Civil War,* 130–33.

21. Harriet R. Palmer, MS Memoir, Ballsdam, St. Stephen's Parish, Charleston District, Mar. 1865, in Palmer Family Papers, SCL.

22. Unfortunately, Julia, Ben, and their children were murdered by white guerrilla forces before they made it to Charleston. See E. P. Smith to Susan Middleton, 10 June 1865, Middleton Family Papers, SCHS. On James Redpath's work as superintendent of schools in Charleston, see Schwartz, *A Woman Doctor's Civil War,* 125–26.

23. On the motives drawing freedpeople to Charleston, see E. P. Smith to Susan Middleton, 1, 7, 10, 15 June 1865, Middleton Papers, SCHS; Mary M. Pringle to Rebecca [?], 5 Oct. 1865, Alston-Pringle-Frost Papers, SCHS.

24. Schwartz, *A Woman Doctor's Civil War,* 141–42.

25. Jas. Lynch to Arnoldus VanderHorst, 31 May 1865, VanderHorst Family Papers, SCHS.

26. *New York Times,* 14 May 1865.

27. Ibid., 14 June 1865.

28. The twelve hundred refugees, black and white, who had been sent to Summerville by the army found the provision of government rations there drastically reduced by order of General Hatch in July (Col. James C. Beecher to Major Gen. R. Saxton, 28 July 1865, R34, M869).

29. Jas. Lynch to Arnoldus VanderHorst, 3 May 1865, VanderHorst Family Papers, SCHS.

30. Childs, *Private Journal,* 219.

31. Elizabeth Catherine Palmer Porcher to My Dear Husband, 23 Mar. 1865, in Palmer Family Papers Folder, SCL. See also Easterby, *South Carolina Rice Plantation,* 209–11.

32. Elizabeth Catherine Porcher to Philip Edward Porcher, 27 Mar. 1865, Palmer Family Papers, SCL; Elizabeth Pringle Smith to Susan Middleton, 10 June 1865, Middleton Place Papers, SCHS.

33. Pringle, *Chronicles of Chicora Wood,* 239–42.

34. Rawick, *The American Slave,* Vol. 2, South Carolina Narratives, Pt. 1, 158.

35. Ibid., Pt. 2, 177–82.

36. Wm. G. Roberts to Capt. Upham, 13 Sept. 1865, Letters Received, Ser. 2384, Subdistrict of Coosawatchie, SC, RG 393, DS, Pt. 2, No. 141 [C-1581].

37. H. G. Judd to Maj. Genl. R. Saxton, Asst. Comr. Bureau Freedmen &c., 29 Aug. 1865, R34, M869.

38. E. W. Pearson, *Letters from Port Royal,* 304.

39. Testimony by Bashie Ladson, 20 May 1910, in pension file of Abraham Ladson, WC 704591, Civil War Pension Files, RG 15.

40. Nordhoff, *Freedmen of South-Carolina,* 7–8.

41. Whitelaw Reid, *After the War: A Tour of the Southern States, 1865–1866,* (1866; rpt., ed. C. Vann Woodward, New York: Harper and Row, 1965), 59.

42. Thos. McFeely to Mr. Tomlinson, 27 Aug. 1865, Letters Received, Ser. 3126, Charleston SAC, 6th Subdistrict, RG 105; George C. Fox, Monthly Land Report, Georgetown District, SC, 31 Oct. 1865, Misc. Records, Ser. 3212, Georgetown, SC, Subasst. Comr., RG 105; G. G. Batchelder, Monthly Land Report, Combahee Ferry, SC, 9 Oct. 1865, Abandoned Land Reports, Ser. 3177, Combahee Ferry, SC, Agt., RG 105; H. C. Judd, Monthly Land Report, St. Bartholomew's Parish, SC, n.d. [1865], R. Tomlinson, Monthly Land Report, Prince George's Parish, SC, and St. John's Berkeley, St. Thomas, and St. Stephen's Parishes, SC, n.d. [1865], all in Abandoned Land Reports, Ser. 2932, South Carolina Assistant Commissioner's Records, RG 105.

43. Gen. James C. Beecher to Lieut. M. N. Rice, 21 Jan. 1866, Letters and Reports Received, Ser. 4112, Depart. of SC, RG 393, pt. 1; and Gen. James C. Beecher to Lt. M. N. Rice, 12 and 15 Jan. 1866, Letters Received, Ser. 4109, Dept. of SC, RG 393, pt. 1. Freedwomen on Jehossee Island joined with freedmen who "say with one voice, they will not remain there to till the soil if [the U.S.] Gov. recognizes Mr. Aiken's right to the property—They will seek some other place where they can have the right to say, what shall be planted, & what shall not" (J. A. Alden to General [Saxton], 30 Aug. 1865, R34, M869).

44. Childs, *Private Journal,* 245–46.

45. Statements by Jane Pringle, 8 Dec. 1865, Vol. 190, Registered Letters Received, Ser. 3202, SC Asst. Comr., RG 105, and R. Tomlinson, Report of Abandoned Land, [?] 1865, R33, M869.

46. H. G. Judd to Maj. Genl. R. Saxton, Asst. Comr. Bureau Freedmen &c., 29 Aug. 1865, R34, M869.

47. Geo. C. Fox to Lieut. Col. A. J. Willard, 2 Nov. 1865, Registered Letters Received, Ser. 3202, Georgetown District, RG 105.

48. See Eric L. McKitrick, *Andrew Johnson and Reconstruction* (Chicago: University of Chicago Press, 1960), 48–49, and Magdol, *Right to the Land,* 156–57.

49. Lt. Col. A. J. Willard to Capt. Geo. W. Hooker, 20 Oct. 1865, Vol. 156, DS, 8–10, Letters Sent, Ser. 2389, 4th Subdist., Military Dist. of Charleston, RG 393, Pt. 2, No. 142 [C-1614].

50. Childs, *Private Journal,* 223; Easterby, *South Carolina Rice Plantation,* 208–9; Rogers, *History of Georgetown County,* 419–21.

51. Easterby, *South Carolina Rice Plantation,* 210.

52. One plantation mistress reported, "*Every one* is therefore taking the oath & are Making contracts with their negroes." E. P. Smith to My Dear Daughter [Susan Middleton], 1 June 1865, Middleton Family Papers, SCHS.

53. Childs, *Private Journal,* 222.

54. Easterby, *South Carolina Rice Plantation,* 209.

55. Ibid., 211.

56. Pringle, *Chronicles of Chicora Wood,* 272–73. The overseer had mentioned

in an earlier report that many of the young men and boys had already left the plantation to enlist in the army (Easterby, *South Carolina Rice Plantation,* 328).

57. Francis LeJau Frost to Father, 31 July 1865, Alston-Pringle-Frost Papers, SCHS.

58. See "Contract, S. L. Horry, Edward Frost, Trustee, with Freed people Santee, Georgetown Dist., August 1, 1865," Labor Contracts, Ser. 3210, Georgetown, SC, Subasst. Comr., RG 105; Lt. Col. B. B. Murry[?] to "The Freed men and women residing on the plantation . . . ," 8 Aug. 1865, Alston-Pringle-Frost Papers, SCHS.

59. F. L. Frost to My dear Mamma [Mrs. Edward Frost], 28 Dec. 1865, Alston-Pringle-Frost Papers, SCHS.

60. Jervey and Ravenel, *Two Diaries,* 35–36.

61. Ibid., 18; Lt. J. O'Kane to Rear Admiral John A. Dahlgren, 7 Mar. 1865, Letters Received by the Secretary of the Navy, M89.

62. Smith, Smith, and Childs, *Mason Smith Family Letters,* 236.

63. The former slaves apparently chastised the overseer for reporting their actions to Allston, and the overseer hastily wrote again to Allston, "dont say any thing a bout it to aney one of the People. . . thay are just Ready to eat me up for it" (Easterby, *South Carolina Rice Plantation,* 209–11, 328–29).

64. Childs, *Private Journal,* 219, 221; Gabriel Edward Manigault Autobiography, 484, Manigault Family Papers, R2, Ser. J, Pt. 4, *RABSP.*

65. Col. J. C. Beecher, Special Orders No. 15, Summerville, SC, 5 Aug. 1865, R34, M869.

66. On the evolution of the contract labor system and its relationship to free labor ideology, see Holt, "'An Empire Over the Mind,'" and Powell, *New Masters,* esp. 73–96.

67. *OR,* Ser. I, Vol. 47, 256.

68. For a brief overview of the Louisiana origins of the labor contract system, see Foner, *Reconstruction,* 54–56; a more detailed account is given in Berlin et al., *Wartime Genesis,* 347–77.

69. Hatch's final instructions to lowcountry planters do not appear in the *OR,* although the correspondence leading up to those instructions is included. Furthermore, in the version printed in the *Charleston Courier* of 26 April 1865, there is no indication that Hatch's communication to lowcountry planters was in the form of orders or even a circular, although the internal language of the communication refers to its directives as orders. See *OR,* Ser. I, Vol. 47, 256, 274–75; the *Charleston Courier,* 26 Apr. 1865; entry for 6 May 1865, Private Journal of Henry William Ravenel, typescript, SCL.

70. See reports from South Carolina in the *New York Herald* for 4, 21, 28 June, 13, 19 July, 21 Aug., 13 Sept. 1865.

71. *New York Herald,* 21 Aug. 1865.

72. Ibid., 6 July 1865.

73. Ibid., 13 July 1865.

74. *OR,* Ser. I, Vol. 47, Pt. 3, 619.

75. Williamson, *After Slavery,* 64–65.

76. *New York Herald,* 21 June, 13 July 1865.

77. Berlin, Reidy, and Rowland, *Black Military Experience,* 752–54.

78. James E. Sefton, *The United States Army and Reconstruction, 1865–1877* (Baton Rouge: Louisiana State University Press, 1967), 52; General Gillmore to General L. Thomas, 20 Aug. 1865, Ser. 15, DS, RG 98.

79. Gillmore and Stanton's concerns are expressed in documents reprinted in Berlin et al., *Black Military Experience,* 746–47.

80. Col. James C. Beecher recorded a wave of appeals from lowcountry freed-people seeking enforcement of contract terms that specified the provision of rations by planters; see James Chaplin Beecher Journal, 1865, and Memorandum Book, 1865–66, James Chaplin Beecher Papers, PL.

81. Capt. Charles C. Soule to Maj. Genl. O. O. Howard, 12 June 1865, Miscellaneous Records, Ser. 3169, District of Columbia, SC, RG 105 (this letter was apparently misfiled under the Columbia district records, and instead should have been filed under the Orangeburg District records). On the large numbers of lowcountry freedpeople still refugeed in Orangeburg during 1865, see Col. E. A. Kozlay to Maj. H. W. Smith, 28 Nov. 1865, R34, M869.

82. See, for example, Lieut. Col. A. J. Willard to F. D. Hodges, 26 Dec. 1865, Letters Received, Ser. 4112, RG 393, Pt. 1, DS.

83. Lieut. Col. A. J. Willard to Capt. Geo. S. Hooker, 7 Nov. 1865, Vol. 156, DS, p. 19, Letters Sent, Ser. 2389, Georgetown Dist., DS, RG 393, Pt. 2, No. 142 [C-1614].

84. Ibid.

85. Eric Foner offers a concise overview of the bureau's project in *Reconstruction,* 67–69; for the bureau's organization and activities in South Carolina, see Martin Abbott, *The Freedmen's Bureau in South Carolina, 1865–1872* (Chapel Hill: University of North Carolina Press, 1967).

86. On the establishment of the Freedmen's Bureau in South Carolina, see Laura Josephine Webster, *The Operation of the Freedmen's Bureau in South Carolina* (1916, rpt., New York: Russell and Russell, 1970), 19–26; Abbott, *The Freedmen's Bureau,* 9–15, 66–69; and Williamson, *After Slavery,* 61–63. On the absence of Georgetown agents, see Col. Gobin to Maj. Gen. Gillmore, 7 Sept. 1865, Ser. 4109 Letters Received, RG 393, Pt. 1, DS. On the role and responsibilities of the bureau's predecessors (the Quartermaster Departments' Superintendents of Freedmen), see U.S. Congress, *House Executive Documents,* 39th Congress, 1st Session, No. 11, "Report of the Commissioner of the Bureau of Refugees, Freedmen, and Abandoned Lands," 18 Dec. 1865, 2, 13.

87. See Major General O. O. Howard, "Report of the Commissioner of the Bureau of Refugees, Freed Men, and Abandoned Lands," Dec. 1865, House Executive Doc. No. 11, 39th Congress, 1st Session, p. 27, where Howard notes that in South Carolina, "A very large number of contracts were made for last year by the military authorities, and none by the bureau." See also E. P. Smith to My Dear Daughter [Susan Middleton], 1 June 1865, Middleton Family Papers, SCHS.

88. See Foner, *Reconstruction,* 68–70, 142–44; Abbott, *The Freedmen's Bureau,* 7–16, 37–40; Webster, *Operation of the Freedmen's Bureau,* 19–23.

89. See H. G. Judd to Maj. Genl. R. Saxton, 29 Aug. 1865, G. Pillsbury to Maj. Gen. Saxton, 27 Aug. 1865, and Capt. H. J. Hawkins to Lt. Clous, 13 Aug. 1865, all in R34, M869; and H. G. Judd to Maj. O. D. Kinsman, 12 Oct. 1865, and C. C. Bowen to Maj. O. D. Kinsman, 20 Oct. 1865, in R20, M869.

90. *New York Times,* 3 Aug. 1865.

91. *New York Herald,* 22 and 25 Oct. 1865.

92. See Schwartz, *A Woman Doctor's Civil War,* 151, and see also 157–58, 198; and Glatthaar, *Forged in Battle,* 240–41.

93. H. G. Judd to Maj. Genl. R. Saxton, Asst. Comr. Bureau Freedmen &c., 29 Aug. 1865, R34, M869.

94. Col. J. C. Beecher, Commanding 2d Subdistrict, Special Orders No. 15, 5 Aug. 1865, enclosed in Col. J. C. Beecher to Capt. Taylor, 7 Sept. 1865, R34, M869.

95. Wm. G. Roberts to Capt. Upham, 13 Sept. 1865, Letters Received, Ser. 2384, Subdistrict of Coosawatchie, SC, RG 393, DS, Pt. 2, No. 141 [C-1581].

96. Col. James C. Beecher to Maj. Genl. R. Saxton, 28 July 1865, R34, M869; Acting Assistant Commissioner G. Pillsbury to Maj. Gen. Saxton, 27 Aug. 1865, and Acting Assistant Commissioner G. Pillsbury to Col. James C. Beecher, 16 Aug. 1865, enclosed, R34, M869.

97. Quoted in Sefton, *The United States Army,* 47.

98. G. Pillsbury to Col. James C. Beecher, 16 Aug. 1865; and Col. James C. Beecher to Gilbert Pillsbury, Esq., Supt. &c., 11 Aug. 1865, both enclosed in G. Pillsbury to Maj. Gen. Saxton, 27 Aug. 1865, R34, M869; Col. J. C. Beecher, Commanding 2d Subdistrict, Special Orders No. 15, 5 Aug. 1865, enclosed in Col. J. C. Beecher to Capt. Taylor, 7 Sept. 1865, R34, M869.

99. Entry for 18 Nov. 1865, James Chaplin Beecher Journal, 1865, PL.

100. Col. James C. Beecher to Gilbert Pillsbury, Esq., Supt. &c., 11 Aug. 1865, enclosed in G. Pillsbury to Maj. Gen. Saxton, 27 Aug. 1865, R34, M869.

101. Ibid.

102. The remainder of the contracts were witnessed and approved either by Thomas McFeely, Georgetown's Superintendent of Freedmen (wartime predecessor of the Freedmen's Bureau, under the Quartermaster's Department), or by George Fox, the assistant commissioner of the bureau for Georgetown District. The number of extant labor contracts for the District of Georgetown—112—is probably very close to the total number of contracts in the district that year, according to a report in early September noting that only 105 contracts had been signed in the district. Of the estimated 18,000 freedpeople in Georgetown at that time, only about 2,700 were laboring under the contract system; McFeely, by then the general superintendent and acting subassistant commissioner of the Freedmen's Bureau, estimated that another 3,000 labored on abandoned plantations in the district. For Georgetown labor contracts, see Ser. 3210 and 3211, Labor Contracts, Georgetown, SC, Subasst. Comr., RG 105. On the administration of the contracts by the army and the Freedmen's Bureau, see Thomas McFeely to Mr. Tomlinson, 27 Aug. 1865, Letters Received, Ser. 3126, Charleston, SC, Subasst. Comr., RG 105; Col. Gobin to Maj. Gen. Gillmore, 7 Sept. 1865, Letters Received, Ser. 4109, RG 393, Pt. 1, DS; Charles F. Folsom to Brig. Gen. J. P. Hatch, 22 May 1865, Letters Received, Ser. 2420, Northern District DA, RG 393, Pt. 2, No. 145 [C-1665]; and Affidavit by George C. Fox, 6 Feb. 1866, Letters Sent Ser. 2389, Vol. 156, DS, RG 393, Pt. 2.

103. Of the 112 extant contracts from Georgetown District, slightly more than 20 percent were with small groups of laborers—under twenty, but often less than ten—in which freedwomen were less than a third of the contracted hands. Such

small operations, unusual in the local rice economy, might suggest the appearance of temporary turpentine operations, a source of cash for both local rice planters and renters in the unsettled state of the lowcountry plantation economy (Gabriel Edward Manigault, Autobiography, 508, Manigault Family Papers, R2, Ser. J, Pt. 4, *RABSP*). The war had stimulated demand for turpentine, while decreasing its production, so high prices drew the attention of those who were not able to resume rice production. The prevalence of male laborers' names on the contracts would support this speculation, since skilled turpentine workers would have been men, while women would have been more prevalent on farming operations. On the larger contracts (more than twenty workers), freedmen and freedwomen were nearly equally represented. The extant labor contracts for Georgetown District are located in Labor Contracts, Ser. 3210, Records of the Georgetown, SC, Subasst. Comr., RG 105. See also the records of labor contracts reported to the Assistant Commissioner (Reports of Contracts Approved in the Subdistricts, Ser. 2930, SC, Assistant Commissioner, RG 105, reproduced in R42, M869).

104. Although printed labor contracts were rarely used in 1865, many of the contracts bore identical terms and wording, suggesting that the troops dispatched throughout the lowcountry to see that contracts were signed may have carried with them a model contract. See Mrs. A. P. Allston, Chicora Wood Plantation, with Freed-people, Pee Dee, Georgetown Dist., 1865, Labor Contracts, Ser. 3210, Georgetown, SC, Subasst. Comr., RG 105.

105. John A. Hume with Freed people, Georgetown District, 7 June 1865; Daniel Bath with Freed people, Mill Creek, Waccamaw, Georgetown District, 6 July 1865; D. H. Smith with Freed people, Georgetown District, June 1865, all in Labor Contracts, Ser. 3210, Georgetown, SC, Subasst. Comr., RG 105.

106. Fitzsimmons with Freed people, Georgetown District, 2 June 1865, and Thos. W. Bath with Freed people, Mill Creek, Pee Dee, Georgetown District, 6 July 1865, both in Labor Contracts, Ser. 3210, Georgetown, SC, Subasst. Comr., RG 105.

107. The estimate of Georgetown's black population was made in early September 1865 by an officer stationed at Georgetown in his report to the commander of the Department of South Carolina. See Col. Gobin to Maj. Gen. Gillmore, 7 Sept. 1865, Letters Received, Ser. 4109, Department of SC, RG 393, Pt. 1, DS.

108. Wm. G. Roberts to Capt. Upham, 13 Sept. 1865, Letters Received, Ser. 2384, Subdistrict of Coosawatchie, SC, RG 393, DS, Pt. 2, No. 141 [C-1581].

109. Williams Middleton to J. Frances Fisher, 17 Nov. 1865, Middleton Family Papers, SCHS.

110. Readers familiar with the work of James C. Scott, in particular his monograph *Domination and the Arts of Resistance,* will recognize my reliance here on his dynamic and revealing analysis of confrontations between dominant and subordinate groups, one I find particularly useful to understanding the changing relations between former slaveowners and former slaves in the postbellum South.

111. Entry for 24 Aug. 1865, James Chaplin Beecher Memorandum Book, 1865–66, James Chaplin Beecher Papers, PL.

112. Wm. G. Robert to Captain [Upham], 20 Nov. 1865, Ser. 2384, Letters Received, Subdistrict of Coosawatchie, RG 393, Pt. 2, No. 141 [C-1581], and W. M. Robertson, Statement of the Conduct of the Colored People former Slaves of the

Est. W. McBride from Feb. 5th 1865 to the 15th Sept. 1865, 15 Sept. 1865, encl. in Lt. W. Wood to Lieut. S. Baker, 16 Sept. 1865, Letters Received, Ser. 2384, RG 393, DS, Pt. 2, No. 141 [C-1593].

113. W. M. Robertson, Statement of the Conduct of the Colored People.

114. See, for example, Benjamin R. Bostick to Capt. Upham, 17 Oct. 1865, Letters Received, Ser. 2384, Subdistrict of Coosawatchie, SC, RG 393, DS, Part 2, No. 141 [C-1585]; Capt. [J. J. Upham] to Lt. J. W. Clous, 10 Sept. 1865, Vol. 154/304, DS, 11–13, Letters Sent, Ser. 2383, Subdist. of Coosawatchie, RG 393, DS, Pt. 2, No. 141 [C-1595]; and Col. Gobin to Major General Gillmore, 7 Sept. 1865, Letters Received, Ser. 4109, Dept. of SC, RG 393, Pt. I.

115. C. C. Bowen to Major H. W. Smith, 30 Nov. 1865, RG 105 [A-7073].

116. Although the planters convinced the commander of the army post at Georgetown that the public health was endangered, the commander's superiors were apparently not persuaded. See Lt. Col. A. J. Willard to Capt. Geo. W. Hooker, 20 Oct. 1865, 8–10, Vol. 156, DS, Letters Sent Ser. 2389, RG 393, Pt. 2, No. 142 [C-1614], and Ben Allston et al. to Col. Willard, 30 Oct. 1865, Letters Received, Ser. 2392, 4th Subdist., Mil. Dist. of Charleston, SC, RG 393, Pt. 2, No. 142 [C-1602]. In the Georgia lowcountry, some planters were eventually forced to employ Irish migrant workers to repair and maintain the rice plantation irrigation systems. See Frances Butler Leigh, *Ten Years on a Georgia Plantation since the War* (1883; rpt. New York: Negro Universities Press, 1969), 104.

117. Statement by W. W. Robertson, 15 Sept. 1865, enclosed in Lt. W. Wood to Lieut. S. Baker, 16 Sept. 1865, Letters Received, Ser. 2384, Subdistrict of Coosawatchie, SC, RG 393, DS, Part 2, No. 141 [C-1593]; see also various entries for Aug. 1865, James Chaplin Beecher Memorandum Book, 1865–66, James Chaplin Beecher Papers, PL.

118. G. G. Batchelder, Monthly Report of Abandoned or Confiscated Lands, 9 Oct. 1865, Ser. 3177, Combahee Ferry, SC, Land Reports, RG 105; Ralph Ely to Captain J. A. Clark, 8 Dec. 1865, Western District, SC, Letters Received, Ser. 4112, RG 393, DS.

119. Wm. G. Roberts to Capt. Upham, 13 and 28 Sept. 1865, Letters Received, Ser. 2384, Subdistrict of Coosawatchie, SC, RG 393, DS, Pt. 2, No. 141 [C-1581]. Robert complained from Beech Branch about husbands' bringing wives back to the plantation, then going off and leaving the women behind. J. S. Bostick to Capt., n.d. [Sept. 1865?], Letters Received, Ser. 2384, Subdistrict of Coosawatchie, SC, RG 393, DS, Pt. 2, No. 141 [C-1588].

120. Benj. R. Bostick to Capt. Upham, 17 Oct. 1865, Letters Received, Ser. 2384, Subdistrict of Coosawatchie, SC, RG 393, DS, Pt. 2, No. 141 [C-1585].

121. William J. Robert to Captain [Upham], 20 Nov. 1865, Letters Received, Ser. 2384, Subdistrict of Coosawatchie, RG 393, Pt. 2, No. 141 [C-1581].

122. *New York Herald,* 5 and 13 Sept., 22 Oct. 1865; and J. S. Bostick to Capt., n.d. [Sept. 1865?], Letters Received, Ser. 2384, Subdistrict of Coosawatchie, SC, RG 393, DS, Pt. 2, No. 141 [C-1588].

123. Entry for 10 Aug. 1865, James Chaplin Beecher Memorandum Book, 1865–66, James Chaplin Beecher Papers, PL; see also Elizabeth Catherine Porcher to Philip Edward Porcher, 23 Mar. 1865, typescript, Folder 19, Palmer Family

Papers, SCL; Easterby, *South Carolina Rice Plantation*, 208; Col. James C. Beecher to Gilbert Pillsbury, 11 Aug. 1865, and G. Pillsbury to Col. James C. Beecher, 16 Aug. 1865, both in R34, M869.

124. G. G. Batchelder to Maj. Genl. R. Saxton, 10 Oct. 1865, R20, M869.

125. Reuben Tomlinson to Maj. O. D. Kinsman, 27 Sept. 1865, Unregistered Letters Received, R20, M869.

126. G. Pillsbury to Maj. H. W. Smith, 30 Dec. 1865, Unregistered Letters Received, R20, M869.

127. Several historians have grappled with Johnson's motives, Howard's response to the revocation of Sherman's "promise" of land, and Saxton's reluctance to follow Johnson's directives. For a full discussion of the players and their motives, see William S. McFeely, *Yankee Stepfather: General O. O. Howard and the Freedmen* (New Haven: Yale University Press, 1968), 45–148; Foner, *Reconstruction*, 50–60, 159–61; Claude F. Oubre, *Forty Acres and a Mule: The Freedmen's Bureau and Black Land Ownership* (Baton Rouge: Louisiana State University Press, 1978), 46–71; and Williamson, *After Slavery*, 79–86. Edward Magdol offers an excellent discussion of freedmen's perceptions of the "promise" of land and their response to Circular 15; see Magdol, *Right to the Land*, 161–65.

128. Despite Johnson's clear instructions to Howard in September, Howard, Saxton, and military officials sympathetic to the freedpeoples' land claims created a series of bureaucratic obstacles to delay the process of restoration. One of the key obstructionists in South Carolina was the commander of the 128th USCT, one of the black regiments drawn almost entirely from lowcountry South Carolina. See Williamson, *After Slavery*, 79–80, and Abbott, *The Freedmen's Bureau*, 55–65.

129. See Eric Foner's excellent synthesis of the literature on Presidential Reconstruction in *Reconstruction*, 176–227.

130. This interpretation is supported in part by the petition of fifty Georgetown residents to Governor Perry, early in November, requesting the removal of black troops—seen by whites as antagonists in the effort to force freedpeople into labor contracts—and by the insistence of white civilians that force, administered by white troops, would have to be used to get former slaves to prepare the plantations for the next year's crops. See Petition by 50 Citizens of Georgetown District to Governor Perry, 3 Nov. 1865, Governors' Papers, SCDAH.

131. Francis Butler Simkins and Robert Hilliard Woody, *South Carolina during Reconstruction* (Chapel Hill: University of North Carolina Press, 1932), 48–50; see Williamson, *After Slavery*, 74–77, for a complete description of the black code.

132. Col. Isaac Dyer to Lieut. C. B. Fillebrown, 2 Aug. 1865, Ser. 4112 Letters Received, Department of the South, RG 393, Pt. 1.

133. Undated newspaper clipping, Manigault Family Papers, Frame 187, R2, Ser. J, Pt. 4, *RABSP*.

134. J. Bachman to Miss E. Elliott, 11 Sept. 1865, Elliott-Gonzales Family Papers, SHC.

135. Jervey and Ravenel, *Two Diaries*, 36.

136. E. P. Miliken to Col. R. N. Gourdin, 14 Aug. 1865, Robert N. Gourdin Papers, PL; Jervey and Ravenel, *Two Diaries*, 42–43.

137. Col. Gobin to Maj. Gen. Gillmore, 7 Sept. 1865, Letters Received, Ser. 4109, 1st Subdistrict, Eastern District of SC, RG 393, Pt. 1, DS; Mary M. Pringle to [?], 10 Oct. 1865, Alston-Pringle-Frost Papers, SCHS.

138. Julie Saville offers a complete analysis of the organized movements among Sea Islanders to resist restoration; see Saville, *Work of Reconstruction,* 85–101.

139. Articles and announcements published before and after the convention in the *South Carolina Leader* indicate the role of Charleston's black congregations, including groups such as "the Ladies of the African M. E. Church," in preparing for the event (*South Carolina Leader,* 21 Oct., 9, 16 Dec. 1865, 31 Mar. 1866). The convention delegates elected at local meetings represented Charleston (22 delegates), Colleton and Richland (4 each), Prince George Winyaw, Sumter, and Orangeburg (3 each), Kershaw (2), and Beaufort, Chester, Greenville, John's Island, and Goose Creek (1 each). The determination that the delegates were elected representatives is based on the fact that the convention assigned a committee on credentials, and on evidence that a meeting to elect delegates was held in Georgetown. See Lt. Col. A. J. Willard to Capt. Geo. W. Hooker, 19 Nov. 1865, pp. 8–10, Vol. 156, DS, Letters Sent, Ser. 2389, RG 393, DS, Pt. 2, No. 142 [C-1614]; *Proceedings of the Colored People's Convention of the State of South Carolina, Held in Zion Church, Charleston, November 1865* (Charleston, S.C., 1865), and Holt, *Black Over White,* 15.

140. See Major James P. Roy to Lt. Col. W. L. M. Burger, 9 Dec. 1865, Letters Received, Ser. 4109, Department of SC, RG 393, Pt. 1.

141. Henry Bram and Ishmael Moultrie were among the Edisto Islanders who organized the islanders in their efforts to obtain land and to petition President Johnson for their right to purchase land; see Magdol, *Right to the Land,* 161–64. On the 1865 South Carolina freedmen's convention, see Holt, *Black Over White,* 9–26, and Foner, *Reconstruction,* 112–13.

142. Williamson, *After Slavery,* 71–77.

143. The convention delegates protested to the citizens of the state as well as to members of the U.S. Senate and House of Representatives concerning several points: their exclusion from the franchise; the exclusion of their testimony from courts of law; restrictions of their rights to engage in business; limitations on their access to education; the wholesale refusal to sell freedpeople land; and the racist misrepresentation of freedpeople in the state's newspapers and journals. South Carolina's freedmen's convention provides a conservative contrast to the Mississippi convention. Although the latter followed a similar course of events, it also responded to that state's black code—the handiwork of Mississippi's constitutional convention—which was very similar to the code being developed in South Carolina. But the Mississippi freedmen's convention clearly articulated and directly attacked the black code's implications for black agricultural workers. The Mississippi freedmen, describing themselves as representatives of the state's "laboring class," warned Mississippi legislators "to carefully consider the Fixed laws that govern labor and capital," arguing that "what is the Laborers interest in the capitalists interest. Without Labor you are bankrupt without Labor we are paupers." Addressing a letter to President Johnson, the same freedmen insisted that in the face of continued oppression by the rebels, freedmen "will not consent to die by

peace meals" but instead "will die as our brothers have on the field of battle." See *Official Proceedings of the Colored Convention for the State of Mississippi, 22–25 Nov. 1865,* and three resolutions (Nov. 1865), M-82 1866, Letters Received, Ser. 15, Washington Hdqrs., RG 105 [A-9223], and *Proceedings of the Colored People's Convention of the State of South Carolina, Held in Zion Church, Charleston, November, 1865* (Charleston, S.C., 1865).

144. Lieut. Col. A. J. Willard to Captain Geo. W. Hooker, 7 Nov. 1865, pp. 170–20, Vol. 156, DS, Letters Sent, Ser. 2389, Dept. of the South, RG 393, Pt. 2, No. 142 [C-1614].

145. Dennett, *The South as It Is,* 364.

146. Ibid., 227.

147. Smith, Smith, and Childs, *Mason Smith Family Letters,* 245.

148. F. L. Frost to Mrs. Edward Frost, 28 Dec. 1865, Alston-Pringle-Frost Papers, SCHS; T. S. R. Elliott to Emmie [?], 19 Dec. 1865, Elliott-Gonzales Papers (Ser. 1.7 F 79), SHC; William Middleton to J. Francis Fisher, 1 Nov. 1865, Middleton Family Papers, SCHS. See also Foner, *Reconstruction,* 158–64, and Williamson, *After Slavery,* 79–83.

149. Charges and Specifications against Sergeant Frances Mildenburger, enclosed in R. Tomlinson to Mr. Stephen Dorr, 18 Sept. 1865, Letters Received, Ser. 4112, RG 393, Pt. 1, DS, and C. C. Bowen to Thomas Doar, 19 Oct. 1865, Letters Received, Ser. 4112, RG 393, Pt. 1, DS.

150. Petition of 50 citizens from Georgetown District to Governor Perry, 3 Nov. 1865, Governors' Papers, SCDAH.

151. Ibid.

152. Governor James L. Orr to Maj. Gen. D. E. Sickles, n.d., Governors' Papers, SCDAH.

153. Jane Pringle to Major Genl. D. Sickles, 19 Dec. 1865, P 1865, Letters Received, Ser. 2392, 4th Subdist., Mil. Dist. of Charleston, RG 393, Pt. 2, No. 142 [C-1604].

154. The fear of insurrection was somewhat pervasive across the South in 1865; see Williamson, *After Slavery,* 249–52; Litwack, *Been in the Storm So Long,* 426–30; and Dan T. Carter, "The Anatomy of Fear: The Christmas Day Insurrection Scare of 1865," *Journal of Southern History* 42 (Aug. 1976): 345–64.

155. D. E. Sickles to James L. Orr, 17 Dec. 1865, Governors' Papers, SCDAH.

156. Smith, Smith, and Childs, *Mason Smith Family Letters,* 234, 236.

Chapter 6: "In Their Own Way"

The chapter title quotes from a rice planter's complaint that his former slaves now insisted "they will only work in their own way & at such times as they see fit"; see W. St. J. Mazyck to Col. Smith, 4 Feb. 1866, Ser. 2392 Letters Received, RG 393, Pt. 2, No. 142.

1. This point is eloquently made by Sharon Ann Holt in her essay "Making Freedom Pay: Freedpeople Working for Themselves, North Carolina, 1865–1900," *Journal of Southern History* 60 (May 1994): 228–62.

2. See Geo. E. Pingree to Maj. Edw. Deane, 31 Aug. 1867, R35, M869, and "Recent Election in South Carolina: Testimony Taken by the Select Committee on the Recent Election in South Carolina," House Miscellaneous Document No. 31, 44th Congress, 2d Session (Washington, D.C.: Government Printing Office, 1877), pp. 15, 19, 24, 27, 35, 38, 40, 55, 63.

3. This question has been explored by Catherine Clinton in "Reconstructing Freedwomen," in Clinton and Silber, *Divided Houses,* 306–19, and by Laura F. Edwards in "Sexual Violence." For an example of violence against lowcountry freedwomen, see Lt. Col. Garrett Nagle, Report of Outrages Committed, 31 July 1866, Colleton District, Ser. 3353, RG 105.

4. F. L. Frost to Mrs. Edward Frost, 28 Dec. 1865, Alston-Pringle-Frost Papers, SCHS.

5. Jane Pringle to Maj. Gen. D. Sickles, 19 Dec. [1865], Letters Received, Ser. 2392, 4th Subdist., Military Dist. of Charleston, SC, RG 393, DS, Pt. 2, No. 142 [C-1604]; Lt. Col. Garrett Nagle to Maj. A. M. L. Crawford, 30 Nov. 1867, Eastern District of Colleton, Ser. 3353, RG 105; and Geo. A. Williams to Maj. Edw. Deane, 13 Dec. 1867, Charleston, Reports of Conditions and Operations, R35, M869.

6. The agent "took precautions" in the event that an insurrection might occur, by placing guards on the district's principle roads and ferries and accepting the assistance of local armed white militia. Bvt. Lieut. Col. B. F. Smith to Bvt. Maj. H. W. Smith, 4 Jan. 1866, R21, M869.

7. Foner, *Reconstruction,* 244.

8. Abbott, *The Freedmen's Bureau,* 20.

9. On Gillmore's dismissal, see E. W. Pearson, *Letters from Port Royal,* 321. See also Abbott, *The Freedmen's Bureau,* 18–19.

10. Following Johnson's February veto of the Freedmen's Bureau Bill, including its three-year extension on the possessory titles freedpeople held to Sea Island lands, the bureau and the military department in the state yielded to the inevitability of restoration (with some officials acting to slow the process, and others seeing restoration as the answer to a speedy transition to free labor on the turbulent Islands). By March 1866, the possessory titles were subject to closer scrutiny, and those freedpeople who held no title or who had settled on land other than that specified in the title were subject to eviction. This accelerated the process of restoration, but it also increased the number and extremity of conflicts between returning planters and freedpeople. See Abbott, *The Freedmen's Bureau,* 60–62; Foner, *Reconstruction,* 161–63; and Williamson, *After Slavery,* 84–86.

11. *Charleston Daily Courier,* 31 May 1866. Another indication that lowcountry freedpeople experienced very strong—perhaps unique—ties to their home plantations was the lesser degree of emigration among them compared to that of freedpeople from upcountry districts. While upcountry freedpeople chose to emigrate to areas where land was available under the Homestead Act, lowcountry freedpeople were determined to gain control over the land where they had lived and labored for generations. Upcountry bureau agents describe emigration to Florida, Mississippi, and Texas in J. Greene to Maj. Ed. L. Deane, 31 Jan. 1867, Columbia, and in Lieut. Col. A. P. Caraher to Maj. Edw. Deane, 31 Jan. 1867, Unionville, both in Reports of Conditions and Operations, R35, M869.

12. The resistance to restoration on the islands is described in James C. Beecher to Lieut. M. N. Rice, 31 Jan. and 7 Feb. 1866; James C. Beecher to Maj. Smith, 31 Jan. 1866; James C. Beecher to Lt. Clark, 6 Feb. 1866; and James C. Beecher to Hon. Charles Sumner, 7 Feb. 1866, all in the James Chaplin Beecher Papers, PL. Resistance on the mainland is noted in Mary [Elliot Johnstone] to Mamma [Mrs. William Elliott], 24 Jan. [1866], Elliott-Gonzales Family Papers, SHC; Williams Middleton to Eliza M. Fisher, 11 Dec. 1865, and B. T. Sellers to Williams Middleton, 15 Feb. 1866, both in Middleton Family Papers, SCHS.

13. Quoted by a reporter in a lengthy reprint from the Savannah *Weekly Republican* appearing in the *Charleston Daily Courier,* 24 Jan. 1867; see also 23 Jan. 1867. On Jehossee plantation, see Major James P. Roy to Lt. Col. W. L. M. Burger, 9 Dec. 1865 and 1 Feb. 1866, both in Letters Received, Ser. 4109, Dept. of SC, RG 393, Pt. 1. On Delta plantation, see Joseph P. Reidy, "Aaron A. Bradley: Voice of Black Labor in the Georgia Lowcountry," in *Southern Black Leaders of the Reconstruction Era,* ed. Howard N. Rabinowitz [Urbana: University of Illinois Press, 1982], 288; *Charleston Daily Courier,* 23, 24, and 31 Jan. 1867; Henry Brandt to Lt. Col. H. W. Smith, 30 Nov. 1866, Rice Hope, Reports of Conditions and Operations, R34, M869; and Sgt. Henry Brandt to Lt. Wm. Stone, 13 Jan. 1868, Rice Hope, Reports of Conditions and Operations, R35, M869.

14. Henry Brandt to H. W. Smith, 28 May 1867 and Henry Brandt to Maj. Edw. L. Deane, 31 Mar. 1867, both in Rice Hope, Reports of Conditions and Operations, R35, M869; Lt. Col. B. F. Smith to Maj. Genl. Devens, 20 Jan. 1866, Letters Received, Ser. 2392, 4th Subdist., Mil. Dist. of Charleston, SC, RG 393, Pt. 2, No. 142; and George C. Fox to Lt. Col. A. J. Willard, 2 Nov. 1865, Registered Letters Received, Ser. 3202, Georgetown, SC, Subasst. Comr., RG 105.

15. W. C. Munnerlyn to Maj. Genl. Saxton, 29 Dec. 1865, Unregistered Letters Received, R21, M869; Geo. C. Fox, Monthly Land Report for the State of South Carolina, 31 Oct. 1865, Misc. Records, Ser. 3212, Georgetown, SC, Subasst. Comr., RG 105.

16. Rogers, *History of Georgetown County,* 407; Testimony of Job Mayzeck, 11 Mar. 1873, claim of Job Mayzeck, Disallowed Claims, RG 233; and *OR,* Ser. IV, Vol. 2, 978–79.

17. Describing his position as head cooper on Keithfield, Hazel proclaimed, "I was the boss over all" (testimony of Dennis Hazell, 18 Mar. 1873, claim of Alonzo Jackson, Southern Claims Commission, RG 217); see also testimony of Dennis Hazel, 12 Mar. 1873, claim of Job Mayzeck, Disallowed Claims, RG 233.

18. Testimony of Dennis Hazel, 4 Apr. 1866; statement of Francis S. Parker Jr., 4 Apr. 1866; Charges and Specifications against Jim, Job, and Stewart, 2 Apr. 1866; Charges against Sukey, 1 Apr. 1866; Charges against Becky, 1 Apr. 1866; Francis S. Parker Jr. to Col. Smith, 31 Mar. 1866, and undated, unsigned list of fourteen names, all in Letters Received, Ser. 2392, 4th Subdist., Mil. Dist. of Charleston, SC, RG 393, Pt. 2, No. 142 [C-1606]. See also Lt. Col. Smith to Capt. M. N. Rice, 7 Apr. 1866, Vol. 156, DS, pp. 62–63, Letters Sent, Ser. 2389, 4th Subdist., Mil. Dist. of Charleston, SC, RG 393, Pt. 2, No. 142; Capt. B. F. Smith to Major H. W. Smith, 6 Apr. 1866, Reports of Conditions and Operations, Georgetown, R34, M869; and Capt. B. F. Smith, "Semi-Monthly Report of Persons Ar-

rested," 15 May 1866, Reports of Arrests of Civilians, Ser. 4161, Department of the Carolinas, RG 393, Pt. 1.

19. Lt. Col. A. J. Willard to Capt. Geo. W. Hooker, 20 Oct. 1865, Vol. 156, DS, pp. 8–10, Letters Sent, Ser. 2389, 4th Subdist., Mil. Dist. of Charleston, SC, RG 393, Pt. 2, No. 142 [C-1614].

20. Planters' exaggerated hopes for what restoration could accomplish are well documented in Smith, Smith, and Childs, *Mason Smith Family Letters.*

21. Major James P. Roy to Lt. Col. W. L. M. Burger, 9 Dec. 1865 and 1 Feb. 1866, both in Letters Received, Ser. 4109, Dept. of SC, RG 393, Pt. 1.

22. *Charleston Daily Courier,* 24 Jan. 1866; William Bull Pringle to Gen. Sickles, 18 Jan. 1866, RG 98; Bvt. Lt. Col. B. F. Smith to 1st Lt. M. N. Rice, 21 Jan. 1866, Vol. 156, DS, pp. 40–41, Letters Sent, Ser. 2389, 4th Subdist., Military Dist. of Charleston, RG 393, Pt. 2, No. 142 [C-1616]; Bvt. Lt. Col. B. F. Smith to 1st Lt. M. N. Rice, 21 Jan. 1866, Vol. 156, DS, pp. 40–41, Letters Sent, Ser. 2389, 4th Subdistrict, Military Dist. of Charleston, RG 393, Pt. 2, No. 142 [C-1616]; Wm. R. Maxwell to Genl. Sickles and Genl. Bennet, 1 Mar. 1866, Letters Received, Ser. 2392, RG 393, Pt. 2, No. 142.

23. Capt. D. T. Corbin to Major H. W. Smith, 30 Apr. 1866, Mt. Pleasant, Reports of Conditions and Operations, R34, M869, and Capt. Hoge to Maj. Neide, 19 May 1868, Charleston, Reports of Conditions and Operations, R35, M869.

24. Mary Elliott Johnstone to Mamma [Mrs. William Elliott], 24 Jan. 1866, Elliott-Gonzales Papers, SHC.

25. F. L. Frost to Mrs. Edw. Frost, 28 Dec. 1865, Alston-Pringle-Frost Papers, SCHS.

26. Wms. Middleton to Father, 15 Feb. 1866, Middleton Family Papers, SCHS.

27. W. St. J. Mazyck to Col. Smith, 4 Feb. 1866, Letters Received, Ser. 2392, 4th Subdist., Mil. Dist. of Charleston, SC, RG 393, Pt. 2, No. 142.

28. Affid. by Geo. C. Fox, 6 Feb. 1866, No. 156, DS, Letters Sent, Ser. 2389, 4th Subdist., Mil. Dist. of Charleston, SC, RG 393, Pt. 2, No. 142; Lt. Col. B. F. Smith to Lt. M. N. Rice, 20 Feb. 1866, Vol. 156, DS, pp. 53–54, Letters Sent, Ser. 2389, 4th Subdist., Mil. Dist. of Charleston, SC, RG 393, Pt. 2, No. 142 [C-1616].

29. B. B. Gen. James C. Beecher to Lt. M. N. Rice, 21 Jan. 1866, Ser. 4112, Letters Received, RG 393.

30. See the restoration order issued by Genl. Saxton, 29 Nov. 1865; Wms. Middleton to Eliza M. Fisher, 11 Dec. 1865 and 1 Mar. 1866; B. T. Sellers to Wms. Middleton, 15 Feb. 1866; Wms. Middleton to J. Francis Fisher, 1 Apr. 1866; Edward Middleton to Wms. Middleton, 24 Apr. 1866, all in Middleton Family Papers, SCHS.

31. Elias VanderHorst to Mrs. VanderHorst, 9 and 16 Feb. 1866, VanderHorst Family Papers, SCHS.

32. Williams Middleton to J. F. Fisher, 14 Dec. 1865, Middleton Family Papers, SCHS.

33. On resistance to contract labor, see W. St. J. Mazyck to Col. Smith, 4 Feb. 1866, Letters Received, Ser. 2392, 4th Subdist., Mil. Dist. of Charleston, SC, RG 393, Pt. 2, No. 142; Gen. James C. Beecher to Lieut. M. N. Rice, 21 Jan. 1866, Letters and Reports Received, Ser. 4112, Dept. of SC, RG 393, Pt. 1; and Maj. Genl.

Charles Devens Jr. to Lieut. Col. W. M. L. Burger, 28 Feb. 1866, Vol. 70, DS, pp. 552–55, Letters Sent, Ser. 2413, Northern District, DS, RG 393, Pt. 2, No. 145 [C-1676]. By February 1866, one lowcountry post commander found that freedpeople's delay in contracting for the year helped them secure contracts for one-half, rather than one-third, the harvest; see Bvt. Lieut. Col. B. F. Smith to 1st Lieut. M. N. Rice, 20 Feb. 1866, Vol. 156, DS, pp. 53–54, LS, Ser. 2389, 4th Subdist., Mil. Dist. Of Charleston, RG 393, Pt. 2, No. 142 [C-1616]. On freedpeople's use of delay as a tactic, see also the *Charleston Daily Courier,* 22 Jan. 1867, and A. M. L. Crawford to Maj. E. L. Deane, 12 Aug. 1867, Charleston, Reports of Conditions and Operations, R35, M869.

34. John Izard Middleton to Williams Middleton, 14 Jan. 1866, Middleton Family Papers, SCHS.

35. R. I. Middleton to Brother, 16 Sept. 1867, Middleton Family Papers, SCHS.

36. Examples of freedpeople using delay as a tactic in contract negotiations can be found in Lieut. Col. B. F. Smith to Lt. M. N. Rice, 21 Jan. 1866, Vol. 156, DS, pp. 40–41, Letters Sent Ser. 2389, 4th Subdist., Mil. Dist. of Charleston, RG 393, Pt. 2, No. 142 [C-1616]; Maj. Genl. Chas. Devens Jr. to Lieut. Col. W. M. L. Burger, 28 Feb. 1866, Vol. 70, DS, pp. 552–55, Letters Sent, Ser. 2413, Northern Dist., DS, RG 393, Pt. 2, No. 145 [C-1676]; Lieut. John C. Chance to Maj. E. L. Deane, 6 Feb. 1867, Unregistered Letters Received, Ser. 3203, Georgetown, SC, Subasst. Comr., RG 105; and A. M. L. Crawford to Maj. E. L. Deane, 12 Aug. 1867, Charleston, Reports of Conditions and Operations, R35, M869.

37. *Charleston Daily Courier,* 22 Jan. 1867.

38. Lt. Col. B. F. Smith to 1st Lieut. M. N. Rice, 4 Jan. 1866, Letters and Reports Received Relating to Freedmen and Civil Affairs, Ser. 4112, Dept. of SC, RG 393, Pt. 1, DS.

39. Lieut. Col. B. F. Smith to 1st Lieut. M. N. Rice, 21 Jan. 1866, pp. 40–41, Vol. 156, DS, Letters Sent, Ser. 2389, 4th Subdist., Mil. Dist. of Charleston, RG 393, Pt. 2, No. 142 [C-1616].

40. In 1866 the subassistant commissioner over several Santee River–area parishes asserted that it was simply "ignorance" that made freedpeople distrustful of their former masters, and he believed it was his job to try and persuade the freedpeople otherwise (Capt. D. T. Corbin to Maj. H. W. Smith, 28 Feb. 1866, Mt. Pleasant, Reports of Conditions and Operations, R34, M869). Part of the bureau's responsibility became the education of the freedpeople in order to enlighten them to the "principle that the interests of capital and labor are identical" (Maj. H. W. Smith to Capt. D. T. Corbin, 28 Feb. 1866, Mt. Pleasant, Reports of Condition and Operations, R34, M869; Gen. R. K. Scott, Circular Letter to the Landlords and Laborers of the State of South Carolina, 26 Dec. 1866, *Charleston Daily Courier,* 5 Jan. 1867). Once the freedpeople were enlightened, they would perform as free laborers; they would, for example, be more willing to sign contracts, which many of the illiterate former slaves avoided out of fear that the papers would return them to slavery (Gen. R. K. Scott to Maj. Gen. O. O. Howard, 21 Feb. 1866, reprinted in U.S. Senate, *Senate Executive Documents,* 39th Cong., 1st Sess., No. 27, p. 25).

41. Maj. Gen. D. E. Sickles to James L. Orr, 17 Dec. 1865, Governors' Papers, SCDAH; Sefton, *The United States Army,* 70–73.

42. See, for example, Capt. F. W. Liedtke to Maj. H. W. Smith, 1 Feb. 1866, R34, M869.

43. R. H. Nesbit to Col. B. F. Smith, 20 Apr. 1866, Letters Received, Ser. 2392, RG 393, DS, Pt. 2, No. 142 [C-1609].

44. Major General Charles Devens Jr. to Lieut. Col. W. M. L. Burger, 28 Feb. 1866, pp. 552–55, Vol. 70, DS, Letters Sent, Ser. 2413, Northern District, DS, RG 393, Pt. 2, No. 145 [C-1676]; see also Hattie [Harriet Rutledge] to Mamma [Anne Hutchinson Smith Elliott], "Monday 11th" [1867–67], Elliott-Gonzales Papers, SHC.

45. Brig. Gen. James C. Beecher to Maj. Gen. R. Saxton, 10 Jan. 1866, Unregistered Letters Received, Ser. 2923, SC Assistant Commissioner, RG 105 [A-7050].

46. Smith, Smith, and Childs, *Mason Smith Family Letters,* 273.

47. Brig. Genl. James C. Beecher to Maj. Gen. R. Saxton, 10 Jan. 1866, Unregistered Letters Received, Ser. 2923, SC Assistant Commissioner, RG 105 [A-7050].

48. Ibid.; Major General Charles Devens Jr. to Lieut. Col. W. M. L. Burger, 28 Feb. 1866, pp. 552–55, Vol. 70, DS, Letters Sent, Ser. 2413, Northern District, DS, RG 393, Pt. 2, No. 145 [C-1676]; Brvt. Brig. Genl. Comdg. James C. Beecher to Hon. Charles Sumner, 7 Feb. 1866, James Chaplin Beecher Papers, PL.

49. Eric Foner describes the ideological work that contracts were intended to accomplish, and their shortcomings in operation, in *Reconstruction,* 164–67. Garret Nagle, bureau agent for Colleton District in 1866 and the man who adjudicated over two hundred instances of contract violations, believed that "nearly all the freedpeople who were discharged from plantations had very little idea of what they had contracted for. They were under the impression that when their usual tasks were finished they were at liberty to do as they pleased, regarding their contract as meaning so much work per day in the field and when the crop is harvested to have their share" (Garret Nagle to Col. H. W. Smith, 1 Nov. 1866, R34, M869). His suspicions were shared by former slaveowners; in 1865, Caroline Ravenel, describing her uncle's reading of the contract to his former slaves, stated, "I don't believe they understood a word [of it], & when they said they did not understand, he told them it meant they might stay just as they were, or go" (Smith, Smith, and Childs, *Mason Smith Family Letters,* 225–26).

50. F. L. Frost to Mrs. Edw. Frost, 28 Dec. 1865, Alston-Pringle-Frost Papers, SCHS.

51. For orders from the Department of the South to withhold rations (complaining of the bureau's continued "improvident" disbursal of the same), see U.S. War Department, "Annual Report of the Secretary of War [1866]," *House Executive Documents,* 39th Cong., 2d Sess., no. 3, p. 60; on the bureau's decision to limit the issuing of rations, see William Elliott to Mother (Anne Hutchinson Smith Elliott), 25 Mar. 1866, Elliott-Gonzales Papers, SHC. See also Wms. Middleton to J. Francis Fisher, 1 Apr. 1866, and Edward Middleton to Wms. Middleton, 24 Apr. 1866, both in Middleton Family Papers, SCHS.

52. Eric Foner properly points out that while the approval of the bureau was not required by law, it is true that the bureau in South Carolina refused to intervene in any labor conflict when the existing contract had not received bureau approval; lowcountry planters were, in fact, highly motivated to secure bureau approval for this reason, and also because freedpeople seemed more inclined to

concede to contracts in the presence of bureau agents or U.S. soldiers (Foner, *Reconstruction,* 164–67).

53. Garret Nagle to Col. H. W. Smith, 1 Nov. 1866, R34, M869.

54. Jane Pringle, a planter, pleaded with Georgetown military authorities, "We are powerless—with you lies the solution of the problem" (Jane Pringle to Major Genl. Sickles, 7 Feb. 1866, Ser. 2393, Letters Received, Georgetown District, RG 393, DS, Pt. 2, No. 142 [C-1604]).

55. Heyward, *Seed from Madagascar,* 154–55.

56. Barney [Edward Barnwell Heyward] to Tab [Catherine Heyward], 5 May 1867, Heyward Family Papers, SCL.

57. Extant labor contracts for Georgetown indicate over 4,000 laborers entered into labor contracts in this district alone, out of an estimated 130,000 laborers who signed contracts throughout the state. See Labor Contracts, Ser. 3210 and 3211, Georgetown, SC, RG 105; and Abbott, *The Freedmen's Bureau,* 73.

58. Some of this agreement, of course, stems from the circulation of printed contract forms. The following discussion of labor contracts draws from series 3106 (Beaufort labor contracts), 3120 (Berkeley), and 3211 (Georgetown), RG 105, and includes contracts from 1866 and 1867.

59. Contract made between A. G. Heriot and freedmen [*sic*], 1 Feb. 1866, Labor Contracts, Ser. 3211, Georgetown, SC, Subasst. Comr., RG 105.

60. See, for example, contracts between J. J. Anderson and freedpeople, 8 Feb. and 5 Mar. 1866; W. A. Bissent and freedpeople, 1 Jan. 1866; Dr. A. M. Forster and freedpeople, 1 Jan. 1866; Mrs. Jane Pringle and freedpeople, 22 Jan. 1866, all in Labor Contracts, Ser. 3211, Georgetown, SC, Subasst. Comr., RG 105.

61. Contract between W. J. Magill & D. W. Jordan and freedpeople, 12 Feb. 1867, Labor Contracts, Ser. 3211, Georgetown, SC, Subasst. Comr., RG 105.

62. See contracts between Charles Alston Sr. and freedpeople, 1 Jan. 1866; William M. Hazzard and freedpeople, 29 Jan. 1866; Mrs. R. S. Izard and freedpeople, 27 Feb. 1866; and Col. Ben Allston and freedpeople, 27 Feb. 1866, all in Labor Contracts, Ser. 3211, Georgetown, SC, Subasst. Comr., RG 105.

63. Contracts between Benjamin P. Fraser and freedpeople, 20 Jan. 1866, Labor Contracts, Ser. 3211, Georgetown, SC, Subasst. Comr.; Cornelius V. S. Wilson and freedpeople, 20 Feb. 1866, John G. Shoolbred and Jack Chisolm, 26 Apr. 1866, and William Sinkler and freedpeople, 8 Jan. 1866, all three in Labor Contracts, Ser. 3120, Berkeley, SC, Subasst. Comr.; W. C. Daniel and freedpeople, 4 Mar. 1867, Labor Contracts, Ser. 3106, Beaufort, SC, Subasst. Comr., all five in RG 105. For disputes that arose over the discriminatory enforcement of fencing laws and regulations, see Mr. G. Gibbs to Captain, 12 May 1866, Testimony, Reports, and Other Records Relating to Court Cases and Complaints, Ser. 3284, Moncks Corner, SC, Subasst. Comr., RG 105; and Capt. F. W. Liedtke to Thomas Ferguson, 5 Sept. 1866, and T. B. Ferguson to Capt. F. W. Liedtke, 5 Sept. 1866, both enclosed in Capt. F. W. Liedtke to Maj. A. M. L. Crawford, 7 Sept. 1866, Letters Received, Ser. 3277, Moncks Corner, SC, Subasst. Comr., RG 105. Fencing and land usage continued to bring freedpeople and planter families into conflict; freedpeople on Esther Palmer's plantation complained about the damage her ducks did to their independent rice crops until she finally fenced them

in (only to have the ducks stop laying eggs, to her annoyance); see E.C.P. to Hattie, 24 May 1868, Palmer Family Papers, SCL.

64. Mr. G. Gibbs to Capt., 12 May 1866, Testimony, Reports, and Other Records Relating to Court Cases and Complaints, Ser. 3284, Moncks Corner, SC, Subasst. Comr., RG 105.

65. See contracts between Dr. A. M. Forster and freedpeople, 1 Jan. 1866; W. Porter Sr. and freedpeople, 1 Jan. 1866; E. P. Coachman and freedpeople, 1 Jan. 1866; and H. S. Thomson and freedpeople, 12 Jan. 1866, all in Labor Contracts, Ser. 3211, Georgetown, SC, Subasst. Comr., RG 105.

66. See contracts between Williams Middleton and freedpeople, 26 Mar. 1866, Labor Contracts, Ser. 3106, Beaufort, SC, Subasst. Comr. and W. J. Magill & D. W. Jordan and freedpeople, 12 Feb. 1867, Labor Contracts, Ser. 3211, Georgetown, SC, Subasst. Comr., both in RG 105.

67. Printed contracts, Ser. 3210, Georgetown, SC, Subasst. Comr., RG 105.

68. Contract between Wm. R. Maxwell and Freedpeople, 27 Feb. 1866, Labor Contracts, Ser. 3210, and Contract between William R. Maxwell and Freedmen, 27 Feb. 1866, Labor Contracts, Ser. 3211, Georgetown, SC, Subasst. Comr., RG 105; and William R. Maxwell to General Sickles and General Bennet, 1 Mar. 1866, Letters Received, Ser. 2392, 4th Subdist., Mil. Dist. of Charleston, RG 393, Pt. 2, No. 142.

69. This scenario is described by Leigh in *Ten Years on a Georgia Plantation since the War,* 26.

70. Although I disagree with this part of Strickland's interpretation, my overall understanding of the work culture of lowcountry African Americans has been greatly influenced by his insightful essay "Traditional Culture"; for the point about which we disagree, see especially 146–47.

71. *Charleston Daily Courier,* 31 May 1866.

72. Lieut. Col. B. F. Smith to Brig. General O. H. Hart, 25 Apr. 1866, Vol. 156, DS, pp. 66–67; and Lt. Col. B. F. Smith to Lt. Col. H. W. Smith, 30 June 1866, Vol. 156, DS, p. 77, both in Letters Sent, Ser. 2389, 4th Subdist., Mil. Dist. of Charleston, RG 393, Pt. 2, No. 142.

73. Olney Harleston to General [Scott], 21 Jan. 1867, Testimony, Reports, and Other Records Relating to Court Cases and Complaints, Ser. 3284, Moncks Corner, SC, Subasst. Comr., RG 105.

74. [?] McKim to Capt. F. W. Liedtke, 25 June 1866, and J. Calhoun Cain to Capt. F. W. Liedtke, 11 Aug. 1866, both in Letters Received, Ser. 3277, Moncks Corner, SC, Subasst. Comr., RG 105.

75. Barney [Edward Barnwell Heyward] to Tab [Catherine Heyward], 5 May 1867, Heyward Family Papers, SCL.

76. John William DeForest, *A Union Officer in the Reconstruction,* ed. James H. Croushore and David Morris Potter (New Haven: Yale University Press, 1948), 94.

77. *Charleston Daily Courier,* 25 May 1866; Olney Harleston to General R. K. Scott, 21 Jan. 1867, Testimony, Reports, and Other Records Relating to Court Cases and Complaints, Ser. 3284, Moncks Corner, SC, Subasst. Comr., RG 105.

78. The labor contracts discussed here are located in Ser. 3210 and 3211, Labor Contracts, Georgetown, SC, Subasst. Comr., RG 105. Information from addi-

tional contracts that are not extant can be found in the Reports of Contracts Approved in the Subdistricts, Ser. 2930, SC Assistant Commissioner, RG 105, reproduced in R42, M869.

79. Readers are cautioned against drawing conclusions about the overall declining number of contracting hands, as indicated in table 1, since we have no reason to believe the extant contracts represent the universe of contracts made. Several factors affected the gender ratio of contract signatures, including the absence of men who were enlisted in the service and instances when men signed for their families (although the task system made this far less likely than did the sharecropping system).

80. I use these figures in an illustrative, rather than a conclusive, manner. For example, I report only raw numbers and percentages because I suspect it would be inappropriate to suggest, with more refined statistical methods, that the data represented here comprise a complete representation of postbellum labor arrangements. As noted above, freedpeople often ignored or challenged the terms of their contracts in the course of a year; planters, too, frequently altered the terms of the contracts or violated their specifications. Furthermore, judging from the total number of contracts that are extant for Georgetown District, there were more plantations operating without labor contracts than operating with them. For these and other reasons, the contracts can be considered only a closed universe, rather than representative of all plantation labor in this particular lowcountry district.

81. The rice planter E. B. Heyward noted in 1867 that the freedwomen he employed as field laborers worked slowly and seemed indifferent about the success of his crop. Heyward also noted that the freedmen and freedwomen on his plantation had planted independent rice crops as well. Despite Heyward's assertion that freedwomen were "doing nothing," it appears that they were tending the poultry, the provision crops, and their own rice crops, besides working (however indifferently) in Heyward's rice fields. See E. B. Heyward to Tab, 5 May 1867, Heyward Family Papers, SCL.

82. Based on slave lists from plantations belonging to Charles Manigault in 1845 (Clifton, *Life and Labor,* 31–32) and from plantations belonging to James R. Sparkman in 1847 and 1858 ("Task Hands 1847 June," MS vol. bd., 1827–45, and "Dirleton 1858" and "Task Hands Birdfield Jany. 1 1858," MS vol. bd., 1857–59, James Ritchie Sparkman Papers, R6, Ser. A, Pt. 2, *RABSP*).

83. Elizabeth Catherine Porcher to Philip Edward Porcher, 23 Mar. 1865, typescript, Folder 19, Palmer Family Papers, SCL.

84. Jervey and Ravenel, *Two Diaries,* 13.

85. Harriet R. Palmer, MS Memoir, Mar. 1865, p. 23, Palmer Family Papers, SCL.

86. Rawick, *The American Slave,* Vol. 2, South Carolina, Pt. 2, 179–80. In Burr, *The Secret Eye,* Ella Thomas, a slaveower, describes a very similar postwar scene where a young girl, a house servant who was previously her slave, conspired with her mother (who had been sold away for bad behavior) to "escape" from the Thomas household, much to Thomas's disappointment (267–68).

87. Jervey and Ravenel, *Two Diaries,* 42.

88. C. Vann Woodward and Elisabeth Muhlenfeld, eds., *The Private Mary Chesnut: The Unpublished Civil War Diaries* (New York: Oxford University Press, 1984), 246.

89. Alice A. Palmer to Hattie, 20 July and 2 Aug. 1865, Folder 19, Palmer Family Papers, SCL.

90. Alice A. Palmer to Hattie, 17 Oct. 1866, and Elizabeth Catherine Porcher to Hattie, 25 Oct. 1865, both in Palmer Family Papers, SCL. See also Major Jos. Totten to Inspector General, 9 May 1866, T-19 1866, Letters Received, Ser. 15, RG 159 [J-51], for a description of the changes freedwomen made in domestic service.

91. Elizabeth Catherine Porcher to [My Dear Hattie], 5 Aug. [1866], and E. L. Porcher to Harriet [?], [1870], Palmer Family Papers, SCL.

92. Meta M. Grimball to J. B. Grimball, 5 Jan. 1866, John Berkeley Grimball Papers, PL.

93. Hattie [Harriet Rutledge Elliott Gonzales] to Mama [Ann Hutchinson Smith Elliott], Monday 11th [1867–68], Ser. 1.8, Elliott-Gonzales Papers, SHC.

94. Mary Elliott Johnstone to Mrs. William Elliott, 10 Jan. 1866, Ser. 1.7, Elliott-Gonzales Papers, SHC.

95. E. C. P. to Hattie, [1866] and 24 May 1868, both in Palmer Family Papers, SCL.

96. Alice Palmer to [My Dear Hattie], 19 Sept. 1866, Palmer Family Papers, SCL.

97. Elizabeth Catherine Porcher to Hattie, 25 Oct. 1865, Palmer Family Papers, SCL.

98. E. C. P. to Hattie, 25 Sept. and 28 Nov. 1867, Palmer Family Papers, SCL.

99. E. C. P. to Hattie, [1866], Palmer Family Papers, SCL.

100. Mary Elliott Johnstone to Mrs. William Elliott, 10 Jan. 1866, and Mary Elliott Johnstone to Ralph E. Elliott, 9 July 1865, both in Ser. 1.7, Elliot-Gonzales Papers, SHC.

101. Elizabeth Fox-Genovese has explored white women's identities as mistresses of households in *Within the Plantation Household,* esp. chap. 2, "The View from the Big House."

102. Emily Elliott to Mary Elliott Johnstone, 21 Sept. 1866, Elliott-Gonzales Papers, SHC.

103. On the spread of disease through the lowcountry population, see Smith, Smith, and Childs, *Mason Smith Family Letters,* 205, 224, and Williams Middleton to F. Francis Fisher, 29 Aug. 1865, Middleton Family Papers, SCHS (microtext edition).

104. See Gaines M. Foster, "The Limitations of Federal Health Care for Freedmen, 1862–1868," *Journal of Southern History* 48 (Aug. 1982): 350–72.

105. Howard's report was among many by authors described as the "intelligent" and "public-spirited" "farming interest" of the country; see Rev. C. W. Howard, "Conditions and Resources of Georgia," in the *Report of the Commissioner of Agriculture for the Year 1866* (Washington, D.C., 1867), 567–80.

106. Howard, "Conditions and Resources," 573–74.

107. Fitzhugh quoted in George M. Frederickson, *The Black Image in the White Mind: The Debate on Afro-American Character and Destiny, 1817–1914* (New York: Harper and Row, 1971), 56.

108. Herbert Gutman offers an incisive discussion of how slaveowners both observed slave family ties and refused to recognize how slave culture sustained such relationships and behavior; see *The Black Family,* 291–93.

109. E. Francis Fischer to Williams Middleton, 10 Feb. 1866, Middleton Family Papers, SCHS.

110. On rape, violence, and women's experience of slavery, see Catherine Clinton, "'Southern Dishonor': Flesh, Blood, Race, and Bondage," in *In Joy and In Sorrow: Women, Family, and Marriage in the Victorian South,* ed. Carol Blesser (New York: Oxford University Press, 1991), 52–68.

111. Howard, "Conditions and Resources," 567–80.

112. C. P. [?illeg.] to Mary Elliott Johnstone, 2 Mar. 1868, Ser. 1.8, Elliott-Gonzales Papers, SHC.

113. Edwin M. Tilton to Col. Smith, 18 Jan. 1866, Vol. 156, DS, Letters Sent, Ser. 2392, Post of Georgetown, SC, RG 393, Pt. 2, No. 142; and Gen. James C. Beecher to Lieut. M. N. Rice, 21 Jan. 1866, Letters and Reports Received, Ser. 4112, Department of SC, RG 393, Pt. 1.

114. B. H. Pinners to Col. Smith, 1 May 1866, Letters Received, Ser. 2392, Post of Georgetown, SC, RG 393, Pt. 2, No. 142.

115. Edwin M. Tilton to Col. Smith, 16 Jan. 1866, Letters Received, Ser. 2392, Post of Georgetown, SC, RG 393, Pt. 2.

116. B. H. Pinners to Col. Smith, 1 May 1866, Letters Received, Ser. 2392, Post of Georgetown, SC, RG 393, Pt. 2, No. 142.

117. For example, on Nightingale Hall, one of the Allston plantations in Georgetown, a freedman by the name of Mack "had charge of the plantation, was chosen by the negroes," according to a neighbor. See affidavit by William Sweet, 16 Apr. 1866, Letters Received, Ser. 2392, Post of Georgetown, SC, RG 393, Pt. 2, No. 142.

118. Olney Harleston to Capt. F. W. Liedtke, 16 Mar. 1866, Letters Received, Ser. 3277, Moncks Corner, SC, Subasst. Comr., RG 105 [A-7182].

119. J. Rees Ford to Lieut. Col. B. H. Smith, 20 Mar. 1866, Letters Received, Ser. 2392, Post of Georgetown, SC, RG 393, Pt. 2, no. 142.

120. Capt. G. M. Montell, 17 Nov. 1865, Charleston, Unregistered Letters Received, R20, M869. Bryant was in jail for three weeks for this offense, until his wife, Dolly Bryant, appealed to the local bureau agent, revealing that Bryant Montell responded to Bryant's curse by beating Bryant over the head with his pistol, and telling the Bryants that "they were not free, but that he had charge of them and the place." Montell also beat Bryant's brother for begging Montell to stop beating Bryant. See O. D. Kinsman, 4 Dec. 1865, Charleston, Unregistered Letters Received, R20, M869.

121. Jane Pringle to Major General D. Sickles, 7 Feb. 1866, Letters Received, Ser. 2392, Post of Georgetown, SC, RG 393, DS, Pt. 2, No. 142 [C-1604].

122. U.S. Senate, *Senate Executive Documents,* 39th Cong., 2d Sess., No. 6, p. 116.

123. Williams Middleton to Francis Fisher, 15 Feb. 1866, Middleton Family Papers, SCHS.

124. E. C. P. to Hattie, 25 Oct. 1865, Palmer Family Papers, SCL.

125. For an example of the the violence which accompanied these searches, see Affidavit of Austin Elmore, 24 Sept. 1866, Colleton Dist., Ser. 3353, RG 105.

126. Lt. Col. B. F. Smith to Capt. M. N. Rice, 20 Feb. 1866, Vol. 156, DS, pp. 53–54, Letters Sent, Ser. 2389, 4th Subdist., Mil. Dist. of Charleston, RG 393, Pt. 2, No. 142 [C-1616].

127. C. Wilson to Major O'Brien, 18 July 1866, Testimony, Reports, and Other Records Relating to Court Cases and Complaints, Ser. 3284, Moncks Corner, SC, Subasst. Comr., RG 105.

128. Entry for 10 Oct. 1866, Vol. 239, Register of Complaints, Ser. 3283, Moncks Corner, SC, Subasst. Comr., RG 105; Smith, Smith, and Childs, *Mason Smith Family Letters,* 264–65; Contract between A. G. Heriot and Freedmen, 1 Feb. 1866, Labor Contracts, Ser. 3211, Georgetown, SC, Subasst. Comr., RG 105.

129. The account of the Singleton case, which appears in the next several paragraphs, comes from testimony of George Singleton, Annette Manigault, Rachel Taylor, and Richard White, 9 Mar. 1868; statement by Rene Ravenel, 11 Mar. 1868; Special Orders No. 158, Major General Ed. R. S. Canby, 11 July 1868, all in George Singleton vs. John Henry Porcher and Samuel Ravenel, Proceedings of Provost Courts, Military Tribunals, and Post Court-Martial Cases Tried in North and South Carolina, Ser. 4257A, Judge Advocate, RG 393. For a similar, although less detailed, record of how white men used the pretense of searching freedpeople's homes as a means of terrorizing freedpeople, see the freedman Austin Elmore's charges against Peter Bird, who entered the Elmore home, beat Austin, his wife, and his mother with a pistol and an iron, and smashed earthenware, provisions, and other property in the cabin; in affidavit by Austin Elmore, 24 Dec. 1866, Misc. Records, Ser. 3353, Summerville, SC, Subasst. Comr., RG 105.

130. Although other testimony was somewhat ambiguous, Rachel Tayor emphasized that Samuel Ravenel "exposed [Mrs. Singleton's] person." Mrs. Singleton appears to have been deeply affected by the intrusion; according to Taylor, she "took sick right off after the search" (Lt. F. W. Liedtke to Lt. H. R. Anderson, 22 Jan. 1868).

131. Capt. F. W. Liedtke to Major, 31 Aug. 1866, R34, M869.

132. Lt. Col. Garrett Nagle to Major A. M. L. Crawford, 31 Dec. 1866, R34, M869; Alice Palmer to [My Dear Hattie], 19 Sept. 1866, Palmer Family Papers, SCL.

133. Affidavit by Andrew, 11 Jan. 1866; affidavit by Wm. R. Maxwell, 18 Jan. 1866; affidavit by Harry Goudin, 13 Jan. 1866; affidavit by Washington Gary, 16 Jan. 1866, and affidavit by Corporal Charles Freck, 17 Jan. 1886, all in Letters Received, Ser. 2392, 4th Subdist., Mil. Dist. of Charleston, RG 393, Pt. 2, No. 142.

134. Benj. Huger to Dear Sir, 9 Sept. 1866, Letters Received, Ser. 3277, Moncks Corner, SC, Subasst. Comr., RG 105; William Elliott to Mother, 16 June 1866, Elliott-Gonzales Papers, SHC; J. M. Hucks to Arnoldus VanderHorst, 8 Apr. 1867, VanderHorst Family Papers, SCHS.

135. Capt. E. H. Read to Lieut. John C. Chance, 3 Jan. 1867, Georgetown Dist., Ser. 2273, Letters Received, RG 393, DS, Pt. 2, No. 132 [C-1619]; Major General R. K. Scott to James L. Orr, 17 Dec. 1866, Ser. 2916, Vol. 11, p. 303, RG 105 [A-7109].

136. See Scott's Circular #2, *Charleston Daily Courier,* 23 Jan. 1867.

137. John M. Hucks to Arnoldus VanderHorst, 4 Feb. 1867, VanderHorst Family Papers, SCHS.

138. E. Frost to F. L. Frost, 2 Dec. 1867, Alston-Pringle-Frost Papers, SCHS.

139. On the hiring of Chinese workers, see John B. Grimball to Arthur Grimball, 18 June 1866, John Berkeley Grimball Papers, PL; and a printed invitation, circulated among lowcountry planters, to a meeting to discuss the possibility of

recruiting Chinese labor (printed invitation, dated 8 May 1866, in Middleton Family Papers, SCHS); see also Williams Middleton to J. F. Fisher, 17 May 1866, in same collection. See also A. C. Jones to L. Manigault, 18 Aug. 1869, Louis Manigault Papers, PL. On the employment of Irish men, see F. L. Frost to his wife, 22 Nov. 1867, Alston-Pringle-Frost Papers, SCHS, and James B. Heyward to Louis Manigault, 17 Jan. 1876, Louis Manigault Papers, PL.

140. Gabriel Edward Manigault Autobiography, p. 92, Manigault Family Papers, Ser., J, Pt. 4, *RABSP.*

141. The patterns of planter responses to the war and emancipation are insightfully analyzed by Roark in *Masters without Slaves,* esp. 207–9.

142. Lt. James M. Johnston to Maj. A. M. L. Crawford, 31 Dec. 1866, Charleston, Reports of Conditions and Operations, R35, M869; for a nearly identical comment, see Capt. F. W. Liedtke to Major, 31 Aug. 1866, R34, M869.

143. E. B. Heyward to Catherine Heyward, [1867], Heyward Family Papers, SCL.

144. Olney Harleston to General [?], 21 Jan. 1867, Letters Received, Ser. 3277, Moncks Corner, SC, Subasst. Comr., RG 105; Gabriel Edward Manigault Autobiography, p. 510, Manigault Family Papers, Ser. J, Pt. 1, *RSABP.*

145. Capt. D. T. Corbin to Assist. Adj. Gen. O. D. Kinsman, 3 Feb. 1866, Testimony, Reports, and Other Records Relating to Court Cases and Complaints, Ser. 3284, Moncks Corner, SC, Subasst. Comr., RG 105; see also Capt. F. W. Liedtke to Major A. M. L. Crawford, 31 Aug. 1866; Garret Nagle to Lt. J. M. Johnson, 30 Nov. 1866; and Garret Nagle to Maj. A. M. L. Crawford, 31 Dec. 1866, all in R34, M869; Olney Harleston to General, 21 Jan. 1867, Ser. 3284, RG 105; M. Williams to J. Berkeley Grimball, 13 June 1869, John Berkeley Grimball Papers, PL; contract between Milton Leverett and Freedmen and women, 1 Feb. 1866, and between Williams Middleton and B. F. Sellars and freedmen and women, 26 Mar. 1866, both in Labor Contracts, Ser. 3106, Beaufort, SC, Subasst. Comr., RG 105.

146. See R. Y. Dwight to Capt. F. W. Liedtke, 24 July 1866, Letters Received, Ser. 3277, Moncks Corner, SC, Subasst. Comr., RG 105; Asst. Comr. Edw. L. Deane to Lieut. John C. Chance, n.d. [prob. Sept. 1867], Unregistered Letters Received, Ser. 3203, Georgetown, SC, Subasst. Comr., RG 105.

147. Williams Middleton to J. F. Fisher, 14 Dec. 1865, Middleton Family Papers, SCHS.

148. M. Williams to J. Berkeley Grimball, 13 June 1869, John Berkeley Grimball Papers, PL.

149. M. Martin to J. Berkeley Grimball, 15 Aug. 1869, John Berkeley Grimball Papers, PL.

150. Lt. Col. Garret Nagle to Major A. M. L. Crawford, 31 Dec. 1866, R34, M869.

151. For a standard contract form of this type, see contract between John E. Walls and freedpeople, 6 Mar. 1866, Labor Contracts, Ser. 3106, Beaufort, SC, Subasst. Comr., RG 105. On the inflated prices charged by planters ("the planters will add at least [50] fifty per cent to the price of everything they purchase for the plantation"), see Garret Nagle to Major A. M. L. Crawford, 31 Dec. 1866, R34, M869.

152. Capt. F. W. Liedtke to Major, 31 Aug. 1866, R34, M869; also see Bvt. Lt. Col. Geo. A. Williams to Bvt. Maj. Scott, 1 Feb. 1867, R35, M869.

153. See also Easterby, *South Carolina Rice Plantation,* 232.

154. *New York Herald,* 13 June 1866; see Strickland, "Traditional Culture," 156–57, and Foner, "The Emancipated Worker," in *Nothing But Freedom,* 74–110. See also J. B. Heyward to Louis Manigault, 4 Sept. 1877, Louis Manigault Papers, PL.

155. E. C. P. to Hattie, 4 Aug. 1866, Palmer Family Papers, SCL.

156. Alice Palmer to Hattie, 8 Jan. 1868, Palmer Family Papers, SCL.

157. Benjamin Huger et al. to General [?], 1 Sept. 1866, Ser. 2273, Letters Received, RG 393, DS, Pt. 2, No. 132 [C-1615].

158. John Dennett describes the extent of trade and barter among freedpeople at Beaufort: "more than in any other district of the South in which I have yet travelled, the Negroes seem to form a part of the commercial world. I was constantly overtaking them or meeting them going into the town with produce to sell, or returning with their purchases, the load being sometimes made into a bundle or laid in a flat basket and carried mile after mile on the head" (Dennett, *The South As It Is,* 201).

159. See, for example, contract between F. W. Ford and freedpeople, 1 Jan. 1867, Labor Contracts, Ser. 3211, Georgetown, SC, Subasst. Comr., RG 105.

160. The antebellum customary right of independent production and trade is discussed at length in chapter 1. On efforts to restrict both in postwar South Carolina, see Lieut. Col. A. J. Willard to Capt. Geo. W. Hooker, 20 Oct. 1865, and 7 Nov. 1865, pp. 8–10 and 17–20, Vol. 156, DS, Letters Sent, Ser. 2389, RG 393, DS, Pt. 2, No. 142 [C-1614]; Lieut. Col. A. J. Willard to Capt. F. D. Hodges, 26 Dec. 1865, Letters Received, Ser. 4112, RG 393, Pt. 1, DS; affidavit by S. B. Callicut, 29 Dec. 1865, in Letters Received, Ser. 2392, RG 393, Pt. 2, No. 142; *Charleston Daily Courier,* 22 Nov. 1865; Benjamin Huger et al. to General [?], 1 Sept. 1866, Letters Received, Ser. 2273, RG 393, DS, Pt. 2, No. 132 [C-1651]; and Lieut. Col. B. F. Smith, General Orders No. 2, 3 Sept. 1866, p. 33, Vol. 157/331, DS, General and Special Orders, Ser. 2394, RG 393, Pt. 2.

161. Williams Middleton to Eliza Fisher, 1 Mar. 1866, Middleton Family Papers, SCHS.

162. *Charleston Daily Courier,* 5 Jan. 1867; Bvt. Maj. Gen. R. K. Scott, "Circular Letter," 13 Sept. 1867, Unregistered Letters Received, Ser. 3203, Georgetown, SC, Subasst. Comr., RG 105; Bvt. Lt. Col. Garret Nagle to Bvt. Maj. A. M. L. Crawford, 31 Oct. 1867, Misc. Records, Ser. 3353, Summerville, SC, Subasst. Comr., RG 105. The conflict over whether freedpeople could choose to work as croppers (and reject winter mudwork on the plantation) threatened to bring Keithfield back to the brink of a violent eruption in 1867. When Francis Parker threatened to dismiss freedpeople if they did not continue to work on the plantation that November, the freedman Israel "in a violent manner called out that 'No more work was to be done on the plantation after today—that no charge or forfeit could be enforced against the laborers,' or words to that effect—all for the purpose & with the view of causing a turbulent spirit & to raise a disturbance on the plantation," according to Parker (statement of Francis Parker, 11 Nov. 1867; Bvt. Major E. W. Everson to Bvt. Maj. Edw. L. Deane, 23 Oct. 1867, enclosing copy of Bvt. Maj. E. W. Everson to Mr. Francis S. Parker, 22 Oct. 1867, all in Unregistered Letters Recieved, Ser. 3203, Georgetown, SC, Subasst. Comr., RG 105).

163. John Scott Strickland has described the two-day system as allowing far

more independence to black agricultural workers than workers enjoyed under market capitalism. See Strickland, "Traditional Culture," especially 154–55.

164. Lieut. Col. B. F. Smith to Lieut. Col. H. W. Smith, 30 June and 31 July 1866, Georgetown, Reports of Conditions and Operations; and Capt. F. W. Liedtke to Lt. A. M. L. Crawford, 30 June 1866, both in R34, M869.

165. Maj. Edw. F. O'Brien to Maj. A. M. L. Crawford, 5 Sept. 1866, Mt. Pleasant, Reports of Conditions and Operations, R34, M869.

166. L. W. Winningham to Major O'Brien, 18 Aug. 1866, Testimony, Reports, and Other Records Relating to Court Cases and Complaints, Ser. 3284, Moncks Corner, SC, Subasst. Comr., RG 105; William Elliott Jr. to Mother [Ann Hutchinson Smith Elliott], 25 Mar. 1866, Elliott-Gonzales Family Papers, SHC.

167. R. Y. Dwight to Maj. Gen. R. K. Scott, 22 Aug. 1866, Registered Letters Received, Ser. 3277, Moncks Corner, SC, Subasst. Comr., RG 105; L. W. Winningham to Major O'Brien, 18 Aug. 1866, Testimony, Reports, and Other Records Relating to Court Cases and Complaints, Ser. 3284, Moncks Corner, SC, Subasst. Comr., RG 105.

168. Olney Harleston to Capt. F. W. Liedtke, 16 Mar. and 23 Aug. 1866, Letters Received, Ser. 3277, Moncks Corner, SC, Subasst. Comr., RG 105 [A-7182].

169. Lt. John L. Chance to Lt. H. Neide, 20 June 1867, Unregistered Letters Received, Ser. 3203, Georgetown, SC, Subasst. Comr., RG 105.

170. Brev. Maj. R. K. Scott to Major General O. O. Howard, 7 Oct. 1867, Misc. Records, Ser. 2956, Asst. Comr., RG 105.

171. Henry Hammond, *South Carolina: Resources and Population, Institutions and Industries* (Charleston, S.C.: Walker, Evans and Cogswell, 1883), 30.

172. M. Williams to John Berkeley Grimball, 6 Nov. 1868, and John Berkeley Grimball to Wife, 19 Jan. 1866, John Berkeley Grimball Papers, PL; see also Williams Middleton to Eliza, 27 Jan. 1867, Middleton Family Papers, SCHS. On the economy of the two- or three-day system, see Gabriel Manigault to Brother, 19 Nov. 1876, Louis Manigault Family Papers, PL. Gabriel estimated that the initial investment in a 300–acre rice crop could be reduced from $5,000 to $3,000 by employing the two-day system. He based his estimates on the savings reported by South Carolina planters then using the system. See also B. T. Sellars to Williams Middleton, 9 Mar. 1866, Middleton Family Papers, SCHS. This issue is also raised in Jaynes, *Branches without Roots,* 156–57.

173. Thavolia Glymph outlines the important changes over time in the share-wage system in her essay, "Freedpeople and Ex-Masters: Shaping a New Order in the Postbellum South, 1865–1868," in Glymph and Kushma, *Essays,* 48–72.

174. Gabriel Manigault to Brother, 19 Nov. 1876, Louis Manigault Family Papers, PL.

175. Lt. John Chance to Lt. H. Neide, 20 June 1867, Unregistered Letters Received, Ser. 3203, Georgetown, SC, Subasst. Comr., RG 105.

176. For accounts of the division of labor according to gender under the two-day system, see Lt. John L. Chance to Lt. H. Neide, 20 June 1867, Unregistered Letters Received, Ser. 3203, Georgetown, SC, Subasst. Comr., RG 105; J. M. Johnston to Lt. Col. H. W. Smith, 31 May 1867, Edisto, R35, M869. On how households headed by mothers fared under the two-day system, see [?] McKim to Maj. D. T.

Corbin, 11 July 1866, Letters Received, Ser. 3277, Moncks Corner, SC, Subasst. Comr., RG 105.

177. Elizabeth Catherine Porcher to Hattie [?], 12 Feb. 1868, Palmer Family Papers, SCL. The same system continued in 1869 on this plantation; see Elizabeth Catherine Porcher to Hattie [?], 28 Jan. 1869, Palmer Family Papers, SCL.

178. Cathie Porcher to [her aunt], 22 Jan. 1870, Palmer Family Papers, SCL.

179. See, for example, contract between William C. Daniell and freedpeople, 4 Mar. 1867, Labor Contracts, Ser. 3106, Beaufort, SC, Subasst. Comr., RG 105.

180. The bureau agent in rural Charleston District noted in 1866 that "during the time between the laying by of the crops and the harvesting, no work connected with the present crop is necessary to be done, and this has caused some serious disagreements on several plantations where the freedpeople because of want of provisions desired to work out for wages" (Capt. F. W. Liedtke to Major, 31 Aug. 1866, R34, M869); see also Martin Williams to J. B. Grimball, 6 Nov. 1868, John Berkeley Grimball Papers, PL.

181. A potential lessee of one of Grimball's plantations noted that in local competition for contract laborers, Edward Barnwell had succeeded with his offer of the work-rent system (M. M. Clement to J. B. Grimball, 13 Jan. 1869, John Berkeley Grimball Papers, PL). The competition between planters for the lowcountry workforce strained relations between planters; see Williams Middleton to Eliza M. Fisher, 9 Feb. 1867, Middleton Family Papers, SCHS, and also J. M. Hucks to Arnoldus VanderHorst, 11 Mar. 1867, and John Lewis to A. VanderHorst, 23 Mar. 1867, in VanderHorst Family Papers, SCHS. James R. Sparkman charged his neighbor, the planter Ralph Izard, with violating the "courtesy of a high-toned gentleman and neighbor" by undercutting Sparkman's contract with freedpeople. Sparkman reprimanded Izard, pointing out that "without this comity & courtesy between neighbors, the system of contracts in which we are all interested must prove more embarassing & the freedmen themselves become so demoralized as to be entirely beyond control" (James R. Sparkman to Lt. Chance, 20 Mar. 1867, encl. James R. Sparkman to Ralph Izard, 18 Mar. 1867, both in Unregistered Letters Received, Ser. 3203, Georgetown, SC, Subasst. Comr., RG 105. See also Lt. John C. Chance to Bvt. Maj. Edw. L. Deane, 11 Apr. 1867, Unregistered Letters Received, Ser. 3203, Georgetown, SC, Subasst. Comr., RG 105).

182. Williams Middleton to Eliza M. Fisher, 9 Feb. 1867, Middleton Papers, SCHS.

183. Elizabeth Catherine Porcher to Hattie [?], 12 Feb. 1868, Palmer Family Papers, SCL. The same system continued in 1869 on this plantation; see Elizabeth Catherine Porcher to Hattie [?], 28 Jan. 1869, Palmer Family Papers, SCL.

184. A. M. L. Crawford to Maj. Edw. L. Deane, 17 Oct. 1867, Charleston, and J. M. Johnston to Lieut. Col. H. W. Smith, 31 May 1867, Edisto, both in Reports of Conditions and Operations, R35, M869; and L. P. Wagner to Maj. E. F. O'Brien, 1 Feb. 1867, Testimony, Reports, and other Records Relating to Court Cases and Complaints, Ser. 3284, Moncks Corner, SC, Subasst. Comr., RG 105.

185. J. M. Johnston to Lt. Col. H. W. Smith, 31 May 1867, Edisto Island, Reports of Conditions and Operations, R35, M869.

186. This description of bureau ideology is based on Thomas Holt's analysis of free labor ideology in his essay "'An Empire Over the Mind.'"

187. James L. Orr to General R. K. Scott, 6 Dec. 1866, Ser. 2916, Vol. 11, p. 303, RG 105 [A-7109]. In October 1867, Assistant Commissioner Scott instructed local agents that "in no case should [freedpeople] be asked to perform labor necessary for another season's Crop unless they are under Contract for that Crop" (Endorsement by Bvt. Maj. Gen. R. K. Scott, 25 Oct. 1867, in on Bvt. Maj. E. W. Everson to Bvt. Maj. Edw. L. Deane, 23 Oct. 1867, Unregistered Letters Received, Ser. 3203, Georgetown, SC, Subasst. Comr., RG 105).

188. Lacy Ford reviews South Carolina's lien law in his essay "Labor and Ideology in the South Carolina Up-Country: The Transition to Free-Labor Agriculture," in *The Southern Enigma: Essays on Race, Class, and Folk Culture,* ed. Walter J. Fraser Jr. and Winfred Moore Jr. (Westport, Conn.: Greenwood, 1983), 32.

189. L. P. Wagner to Major E. F. O'Brien, 1 Feb. 1867, and endorsement by Major Edw. L. Deane, 7 Feb. 1867, Testimony, Reports, and Other Records Relating to Court Cases and Complaints, Ser. 3284, Moncks Corner, SC, Subasst. Comr., RG 105.

190. Lt. Col. Geo. A. Williams to Maj. Edw. L. Deane, 7 Mar. 1867, Charleston, Reports of Conditions and Operations, R35, M869.

191. Circular, 18 June 1867, Maj. Geo. A. Williams, Orders and Circulars Received, Ser. 3279, Moncks Corner, SC, Subasst. Comr., RG 105; Lt. W. M. Wallace to Bvt. Maj. E. W. H. Read, 8 Jan. 1867, Georgetown Dist., Ser. 2273, Letters Received, RG 393, DS, Pt. 2, No. 132 [C-1619]; Geo. A. Williams to Maj. Edw. Deane, 16 Sept. 1867, M869, R35; J. E. Lewis to Maj. L. Walker, 31 Jan. 1868, Grahamville, Reports of Conditions and Operations, R35, M869. Lewis reported that freedpeople in several parishes in Beaufort District rejected wage and share labor; "they are still holding out with such unanimity as to lead to the belief that they have been instructed from some source not to contract except upon their own terms which are that they will work two days each week for the planter." He complained, "The freedpeople obstinately hold to it," despite the fact that the local bureau authorities disapproved of such arrangements and would not advance provisions to anyone working under such contracts.

192. Freedwomen's political activism and its integral role in Republican party politics is particularly well documented during the 1876 elections, coinciding with a period of intense labor conflict on lowcountry rice plantations. Federal investigators heard extensive testimony about freedwomen's organized and, in many instances, armed monitoring of male voters, to prevent them from voting for the Democratic ticket. The state Republican party was alleged to call directly on freedwomen not to let their husbands "put you back in slavery" (*House Miscellaneous Documents,* 44th Congress, 2d Sess., No. 31, Pt. 2, pp. 15, 19, 24, 35, 38, 40, 55, 63, 64).

Chapter 7: "And So to Establish Family Relations"

The chapter title quotes from the testimony of a wartime plantation superintendent about how best to encourage family relations among the contrabands; he suggested establishing a family meal hour by law and furnishing the contrabands with tablecloths and table settings. See Testimony of Frederick A. Eustis before the AFIC, [1863], filed with O-328 1863, Letters Received, Ser. 12, RG 94 [K-80].

1. C. V. J. Wilson to Major O'Brien, 19 July 1866, Testimony, Reports and Other Records Relating to Court Cases and Complaints, ser. 3284, Moncks Corner, SC, Sub-asst. Comr., RG 105. The quotation in the following paragraph is from this same source.

2. See, for example, Harold D. Woodman, "The Reconstruction of the Cotton Plantation in the New South," in Glymph and Kushma, *Essays,* 106–11.

3. Eric Foner, *Politics and Ideology in the Age of the Civil War* (New York: Oxford University Press, 1980), 73–75, 100–103; see also David Montgomery, *Beyond Equality: Labor and the Radical Republicans* (New York: Knopf, 1967). Free labor, as Eric Foner puts it, had been "sanctified by the North's triumph" and "would emerge from the war further strengthened as a definition of the good society, and underpinning of Republican party policy, and a starting point for discussions of the postwar South" (Foner, *Reconstruction,* 29).

4. Holt, "'An Empire Over the Mind,'" 287–88. Harold D. Woodman notes that emancipation, although necessary for the rise of a free labor system, "was not sufficient in itself to create that system" ("Reconstruction of the Cotton Plantation," 101). See also Foner, *Reconstruction,* 28.

5. Mary McIntosh, "The State and the Oppression of Women," in *Feminism and Materialism: Women and Modes of Production,* ed. Annette Kuhn and AnnMarie Wolpe (Boston: Routledge and Kegan Paul, 1978), 259; Varda Burstyn, "Masculine Dominance and the State," *Socialist Register* (1983): 59–62; Joan Wallach Scott, "Gender: A Useful Category of Historical Analysis," in *Gender and the Politics of History* (New York: Columbia University Press, 1988), esp. 42–49. Jeanne Boydston brilliantly traces the importance of gender relations and ideas about gender to the emergence and nature of nineteenth-century wage systems in *Home and Work: Housework, Wages, and the Ideology of Labor in the Early Republic* (New York: Oxford University Press, 1990), esp. xviii and 160. Historians of Reconstruction have been slow to incorporate scholarship on the significance of gender into their study of the era. Eric Foner has recently argued that the benefits of emancipation as envisioned by Northern congressmen did not encompass any explicit, separate effort to alter gender conventions (Foner, "The Meaning of Freedom in the Age of Emancipation," *Journal of American History* 81, no. 2 [Sept. 1994]: 455–56). This is an argument that is limited by the premise that gender was not an integral part of the "concrete historical realities" shaping Northern policy (which would exclude, for example, the pastoralization of women's housework and the undervaluation of women's paid labor); see Boydston, *Home and Work,* chap. 7.

6. Foner, *Reconstruction,* 142–70. On masculinity and free labor ideology, see Nina Silber, *The Romance of Reunion: Northerners and the South, 1865–1900* (Chapel Hill: University of North Carolina Press, 1993), 21, 24–26.

7. The quote is from an elaboration on free labor by a northern Sea Island cotton planter, Edward Atkinson, quoted in Woodman, "Reconstruction of the Cotton Plantation," 104.

8. On the significance of intrafamily gender relations in the North, see Boydston, *Home and Work.*

9. Holt, "'An Empire Over the Mind,'" esp. 303.

10. On the racial attitudes shaping white Northerners' views of the South, see Rose, *Rehearsal for Reconstruction,* 159–66; Foner, "Reconstruction and Free Labor," in *Politics and Ideology,* 97–127; Frederickson, *Black Image,* chaps. 4 and 6; and David R. Roediger, *The Wages of Whiteness: Race and the Making of the American Working Class* (New York: Verso, 1991), esp. 170–81. I cannot refrain here from pointing out my own difference of opinion with Frederickson's evaluation of "romantic racialism" as benign. However paternalistic Port Royal's humanitarians may have been, their policies—as noted in earlier chapters—had sometimes devastating consequences for contrabands. Neither were the Port Royal missionaries unchanged *during* the war in their racial attitudes, as noted by Elizabeth Botume in her memoir, *First Days amongst the Contrabands,* 113.

11. Gen. James C. Beecher to Lieut. M. N. Rice, 21 Jan. 1866, Letters and Reports Received Relating to Freedmen and Civil Affairs, Ser. 4112, Dept. of SC, RG 393, Pt. 1.

12. Herbert Gutman offers a probing discussion of the overlap in *The Black Family,* 294–304. See also Silber, *Romance of Reunion,* 140–41.

13. Holt, "'An Empire Over the Mind,'" 303. This change in racial beliefs and attitudes becomes particularly apparent when contrasted to the wartime racial attitudes of the Gideonites and military officials who came to the federally occupied Sea Islands during the war. The testimony they gave to the American Freedmen's Inquiry Commission (AFIC) in 1863 conveys a strong belief in the role of slavery in shaping black life and character in the South. What George Frederickson had labeled as "romantic racialism," he points out, found its "most authoritative and complete presentation" in the AFIC report (Frederickson, *Black Image,* 124). The commission's report on the conditions and behavior of Sea Island contrabands also had a clear political intent, its antislavery members hoping to offer a "blueprint" for Reconstruction consistent with the goals of Radical Republicans. Informants in the Port Royal community of missionaries and military officials also hoped the report would reflect well on their endeavors with the contrabands. To the extent that the contrabands bore a propensity for lying and immorality, most informants agreed, these were the results of slavery; under federal protection and encouragement, they were abandoning "their cringing, bowing, and scraping before white men" in favor of "more spirit and manliness and independence." That is, what Northern whites viewed as the characterological habits of slavery that had set enslaved African Americans apart from Northern whites (and from Northern African-Americans, as Charlotte Forten Grimké pointed out) could be unlearned under Northern tutelage and military service. (Brenda Stevenson, editor of the Grimké journal, has noted that "like the other teachers and missionaries who came to instruct the contraband, Charlotte was sometimes both amused and repulsed by the social and religious practices of the Sea Island blacks," but Grimké was also "quick to explain that their cultural expression and lifestyles, which seemed peculiar and sometimes crude to Northerners, were largely a result of their past as slaves" [Stevenson, *Journals of Charlotte Forten Grimké*]). Many military and civilian agents hoped to uplift and civilize the oppressed race—not to a level of equality with whites, but above its state of servility—by abolition but also by imparting

to former slaves the legal protections, cultural apparatus, and value system of a free labor society. See testimony of Henry Judd before the AFIC, [1863], O-328 1863, LR, Ser. 12, RG 94 [K-74]; testimony of Brigadier General Rufus Saxton before the AFIC, [1863], O-328 1863, LR, Ser. 12, RG 94 [K-70]; testimony of Elbridge Gerry Dudley before the AFIC, [1863], O-328 1863, LR, Ser. 12, RG 94 [K-77]; testimony of Alexander Ketchum before the AFIC, [1863], O-328 1863, LR, Ser. 12, RG 94 [K-79]; testimony of Laura M. Towne before the AFIC, [1863], O-328 1863, LR, Ser. 12, RG 94 [K-73]; testimony of B. K. Lee before the AFIC, [1863], O-328 1863, LR, Ser. 12, RG 94 [K-72]; see also Nordhoff, *Freedmen of South-Carolina;* Stevenson, *Journals of Charlotte Forten Grimké;* and Botume, *First Days amongst the Contrabands.*

14. See Amy Dru Stanley, "Beggars Can't Be Choosers: Compulsion and Contract in Postbellum America," *Journal of American History* 78, no. 4 (Mar. 1992): 1265–93, 1289 quoted; Holt, "'An Empire Over the Mind,'" 286; and Jonathan A. Glickstein, "'Poverty Is Not Slavery': American Abolitionists and the Competitive Labor Market," in *Antislavery Reconsidered: New Perspectives on the Abolitionists,* ed. Lewis Perry and Michael Fellman (Baton Rouge: Louisiana State University Press, 1979), 195–218.

15. Howard, of course, was not alone in predicting the eventual extinction of African Americans as a race; James Roark points out the contributions of several white South Carolinians to the development of this idea, in *Masters without Slaves,* 166–67.

16. Botume, *First Days amongst the Contrabands,* 160, 154–56.

17. Berlin et al., *Wartime Genesis,* 317; and testimony of Capt. E. W. Hooper before the American Freedmen's Inquiry Commission, [1863], filed with O-328 1863, Letters Received, Ser. 12, RG 94 [K-82]. Men and women alike contributed to this discussion of slaves and slave family life; Laura Towne seems to have been alone among her colleagues in raising what she felt was the problem of the mistreatment of slave women by their husbands. Testimony of Laura M. Towne before the AFIC, [1863], O-328 1863, Letters Received, Ser. 12, RG 94 [K-73].

18. Testimony of Frederick A. Eustis before the AFIC, [1863], filed with O-328 1863, Letters Received, Ser. 12, RG 94 [K-80]; testimony of Laura M. Towne before the AFIC, [1863], filed with O-328 1863, Letters Received, Ser. 12, RG 94 [K-73].

19. See the testimony of Henry Judd before the AFIC, [1863], O-328 1863, LR, Ser. 12, RG 94 [K-74]; testimony of Brigadier General Rufus Saxton before the AFIC, [1863], O-328 1863, LR, Ser. 12, RG 94 [K-70]; testimony of Elbridge Gerry Dudley before the AFIC, [1863], O-328 1863, LR, Ser. 12, RG 94 [K-77]; testimony of Alexander Ketchum before the AFIC, [1863], O-328 1863, LR, Ser. 12, RG 94 [K-79]; testimony of Laura M. Towne before the AFIC, [1863], O-328 1863, LR, Ser. 12, RG 94 [K-73]; testimony of B. K. Lee before the AFIC, [1863], O-328 1863, LR, Ser. 12, RG 94 [K-72]; Nordhoff, *Freedmen of South-Carolina* and Botume, *First Days amongst the Contrabands.* Jacqueline Jones has made a similiar point about missionary teachers among Georgia contrabands and freedpeople in *Soldiers of Light and Love: Northern Teachers and Georgia Blacks, 1865–1873* (1980; rpt. Athens: University of Georgia Press, 1992), chap. 6.

20. Rose, *Rehearsal for Reconstruction,* 236.

21. Abbott, *The Freedmen's Bureau,* 105–6.

22. Ibid., 105–7.

23. Williamson, *After Slavery,* 307–8.

24. Gen. R. K. Scott, General Orders Number 6, 7 Feb. 1866; Gen. R. K. Scott, General Orders No. 19, 14 June 1866, and General Orders No. 2, 18 Jan. 1868, Orders and Circulars, R36 M869. In March 1866, Gen. O. O. Howard, Commissioner of the Freedmen's Bureau, instructed each assistant commissioner to draw up specific rules regarding marriage between freedpeople; see the circular issued by Maj. Gen. O. O. Howard, 2 Mar. 1866, appended to Maj. Gen. O. O. Howard to Secretary of War Hon. E. M. Stanton, 1 Nov. 1866, in U.S. Congress, *House Executive Documents,* 39th Cong., 2d Sess., No. 1, 756–57.

25. Charges against Billy and Martin Aesop, Vol. 239, Register of Complaints, Ser. 3283, Moncks Corner, SC, Subasst. Comr., 1866, RG 105. Although the state's 1868 constitution included a divorce clause, which was further expanded by an 1870 statute, divorce reform was repealed by 1878. Apparently, no divorce had been granted during the ten years when the possibility existed; see Glenda Riley, *Divorce: An American Tradition* (New York: Oxford University Press, 1991), 69–71.

26. *New York Times,* 11 Apr. 1867.

27. Gutman, *The Black Family,* 414.

28. Botume, *First Days amongst the Contrabands,* 158–59; Reid, *After the War,* 126; E. W. Pearson, *Letters from Port Royal,* 103–4.

29. See, for example, Charlotte Forten Grimké's comments, quoted in Sterling, *We Are Your Sisters,* 282.

30. Testimony of Randol Ward, 22 Mar. 1902, pension claim of Randol Beckett [AKA Ward], WC 742386, Civil War Pension Files, RG 15; testimony of Sina Grant, 8 June 1912, pension claim of Frank Duncan [AKA Grant], WC 753197, Civil War Pension Files, RG 15; testimony of Bashie Ladson, 20 May 1910, pension claim of Abraham Ladson, WC 704591, Civil War Pension Files, RG 15. Several lowcountry freedpeople had marriage certificates signed by the assistant commissioner of the Freedmen's Bureau in South Carolina; see, for example, the marriage certificates included in the pension claim of Sandy Days, WC 510041, and in the pension claim of Cain Mayhams [AKA Mayhem], WC 596769, both in Civil War Pension Files, RG 15.

31. Testimony by Lucy Brown, 5 Nov. 1890, pension claim of Sandy Brown, WC 321403, Civil War Pension Files, RG 15; testimony of Mary Nesbit, 1 July 1901, pension claim of Brutus Nesbit, WO 542840, Civil War Pension Files, RG 15; testimony by Toney Alston, 4 Oct. 1905; testimony by Susan Grant, 29 Sept. 1905, and testimony by Judith Swinton, 19 May and 4 Oct. 1905, all in pension claim of Aaron Grant, WC 607660, Civil War Pension Files, RG 15.

32. R. H. Nesbit to Col. B. H. Smith, 20 Apr. 1866, Letters Received, Ser. 2392, Post of Georgetown, SC, RG 393, Pt. 2, No. 142.

33. Testimony of Rebecca Allston, 16 July 1912, pension claim of Nathaniel Allston, WC 746108, Civil War Pension Files, RG 15.

34. Testimony of Washington Rutledge, 13 Nov. 1901, pension claim of Washington Rutledge, WC 801129, Civil War Pension Files, RG 15; testimony of Bethel

Deas, 9 Jan. 1920, pension claim of Israel Carr, WC 882726, Civil War Pension Files, RG 15; testimony of Charlotte Washington, 13 July 1901, pension claim of Frank Duncan [AKA Grant], WC 753197, Civil War Pension Files, RG 15; A. P. Caraher to [Maj. Edw. L. Deane], 30 Sept. 1867, Unionville, Reports of Conditions and Operations, R35, M869; and *New York Times,* 20 Apr. 1867.

35. Botume, *First Days amongst the Contrabands,* 154–55.

36. S. L. Bennet to Maj. J. P. Roy, 1 Feb 1868, Charleston, Reports of Conditions and Operations, R35, M869; statement by Mr. Herland, quoted in Capt. L. Walker to Maj. Neide, 12 Mar. 1868, Aiken, Reports of Conditions and Operations, R35, M689.

37. For example, see the testimony by Eliza Coit, 10 Mar. and 21 Mar. 1901, pension claim of Prince Coit, WC 7915; testimony of Emma Drayton, 4 Dec. 1899, testimony of Grace Brown, 4 Dec. 1899, and Marriage Certificate, 5 May 1867, all in pension claim of Sandy Days, WC 510041; and testimony of Annie Frazier, 1 and 13 Sept., 15 Oct., 30 Dec. 1909, all in pension claim of Daniel Frazier, WC 695221, all in Civil War Pension Files, RG 15.

38. Testimony of Ellen Cooper, 20 Oct. 1909, and testimony of Mary Ann Richardson, 21 Oct. 1909, in pension claim of Mingo Cooper, WC 691815, Civil War Pension Files, RG 15.

39. James Bracey vs. Regina Toney, Oct. 1867, Provost Court Marshal Records, Ser. 4257, RG 393.

40. Berkeley to Mother, 18 Mar. 1866; John Berkeley Grimball to Wife, 19 Jan. 1866; and Lease with Robert Deas, 8 July 1868, all in John Berkeley Grimball Papers, PL. For a wartime example, see Botume, *First Days amongst the Contrabands,* 160–61.

41. *New York Times,* 11 Apr. 1867.

42. Testimony of Lydia Alston, 13 Nov. 1907; testimony by Adam Brewer, 13 Nov. 1907; testimony by Rebecca Wright, 13 Nov. 1907; testimony by Amos Gadsden, 13 Nov. 1907, all in pension claim of Murphy Allston, WC 18887, Civil War Pension Files, RG 15.

43. Testimony of Lucy Brown, 12 Aug. and 2 Nov. 1890, pension claim of Sandy Brown, WC 321403, Civil War Pension Files, RG 15.

44. Botume, *First Days amongst the Contrabands,* 124–27.

45. Testimony by William Grice, 25 Apr. 1894, and testimony by Jane Mayrant, 25 Apr. 1894, in pension claim of Hardy Mayrant, WC 398031, Civil War Pension Files, RG 15.

46. *New York Herald,* 19 July 1865; see also the entry for 20 May 1865, in Childs, *Private Journal,* 237–38.

47. James Chapin Beecher Journal and Memorandum Book, 1865–66, entries for 12, 15, 19, 21 Aug. 1865, PL.

48. *New York Times,* 20 Apr. 1867.

49. This was certainly the case when the provost marshal at Georgetown apprenticed three children to a local white man when their mother died and their stepfather believed he could no longer support the entire family. The children's biological father, having separated from his wife and children during the war when he escaped to a Union gunboat, returned to claim the children, who had found a

way to inform him of their mother's death and their apprenticeship. See 1st Lieut. John C. Chance to Bt. Maj. Edw. L. Deane, 30 Jan. 1867, and endorsement by A. A. Comr. Genl. Scott, 31 Jan. 1867, Labor Contracts, Ser. 3210, Georgetown, SC, Sub-asst. Comr., RG 105.

50. In antebellum North Carolina, apprenticeships and fostering also had a history of being used to regulate sexuality and race relations, and encouraged the exploitation of child labor (Bynum, *Unruly Women,* 99–103).

51. Assistant Commissioner Rufus Saxton issued Circular No. 4, addressing the issue of apprenticeship, on 19 Oct. 1865, according to a newspaper clipping in the assistant commissioner's files; see Receipts, contained in Misc. Records, 1865–68, Assistant Commissioner's Office, Ser. 2956, RG 105.

52. See Howard, "Conditions and Resources," 567–80.

53. Charles Manigault, "The Close of the War—The Negro, etc.," frame 542, Manigault Family Papers, R1, Ser. J, Pt. 4, *RABSP.*

54. *New York Times,* 11 Feb. 1866.

55. Superintendent G. Pillsbury to Maj. O'Brien, 22 Aug. 1866, Testimony, Reports, and Other Records Relating to Court Cases and Complaints, Ser. 3284, Moncks Corner, SC, Subasst. Comr., RG 105.

56. F. W. Liedtke to Lt. Col. H. W. Smith, 31 July 1866, Moncks Corner, Reports of Conditions and Operations, R34, M869.

57. Rebecca Scott, "The Battle Over the Child: Child Apprenticeship and the Freedmen's Bureau in North Carolina," *Prologue* 10 (Summer 1978): 101–13. On Assistant Commissioner Scott's willingness to overrule apprenticeships in prefer-ence for parental custody, see Lieut. John C. Chance to Lt. Col. H. W. Smith, 16 May 1867, Unregistered Letters Received, Ser. 3203, Georgetown, SC, Subasst. Comr., and 1st Lt. John C. Chance to Bt. Maj. Edw. L. Deane, 30 Jan. 1867 and endorsement by Gen. Scott, 31 Jan. 1867, Labor Contracts, Ser. 3210, Georgetown, SC, Subasst. Comr., all in RG 105. For an example of a local agent's unwillingness to override an existing apprenticeship to allow a mother custody of her son, see John C. Chance to Bvt. Lieut. Col. H. W. Smith, 23 Oct. 1866, endorsement by D. W. Bennet, 6 Nov. 1866, and endorsement by Bt. Maj. Edw. L. Deane, 13 Nov. 1866, in Registered Letters Received, Ser. 3202, Georgetown, SC, Subasst. Comr., RG 105.

58. Foner, *Reconstruction,* 201–2. On the indenturing of freedchildren to former owners, see Gen. B. F. Foust, Attny. Genl., to Lt. Col. H. W. Smith, 14 Nov. 1866, and enclosures, Ser. 4109, RG 393, DS, Pt. 1, and Lieut. John C. Chance to Lt. Col. H. W. Smith, 16 May 1867, enclosing Robt. C. Grier to "the Comsr Freedmens Bureau, Charleston S.C. General," 12 May 1867, and John Gould to "The Asst. Commissioner Freedmen's Bureau," 11 May 1867, in Unregistered Letters Received, Ser. 3203, Georgetown, SC, Subasst. Comr., RG 105.

59. Gen. B. F. Foust to Lt. Col. H. W. Smith, 14 Nov. 1866, enclosing testimony and proceedings in The State vs. Wm. Cade, 1866, Letters Received, Ser. 4109, Department of the South, RG 393, Pt. 1.

60. On Susannah Durr's appeal, see Lt. F. W. Liedtke to Major A. M. L. Craw-ford, 5 Apr. 1867, Letters Received, Ser. 4280, 2d Mil. Dist., RG 393, Pt. 1 [SS-186]. Examples of contested child apprenticeships can be found in Lt. John C. Chance to Lt. Col. H. W. Smith, 16 May 1867, Unregistered Letters Received, Ser. 3203,

Georgetown, SC, Subasst. Comr., RG 105, where an eight-year-old orphan's uncle "objects to the Boy being bound to anyone." See also Lt. John C. Chance to Lt. H. W. Smith, 23 Oct. 1866, Unregistered Letters Received, Ser. 3203, Georgetown, SC, Subasst. Comr., RG 105, where a mother's efforts to contest an apprenticeship were denied on the grounds that "the mother was and is in no condition to provide for her son." See also Ira Berlin, Francine C. Cary, Steven F. Miller and Leslie S. Rowland, "Family and Freedom: Black Families in the American Civil War," in *History Today* 37 (Jan. 1987): 8–15, and R. Scott, "Battle Over the Child," 101–13.

61. Lieut. F. W. Leitke to Brvt. Maj. A. M. L. Crawford, 5 Apr. and 5 June 1867, Letter Received, Ser. 4280 Provost Marshal General, 2d MD L-31 (1867) RG 393, DS, Pt. 1 [SS-186].

62. First Lieut. John C. Chance to Bvt. Maj. Edw. L. Deane, 27 Feb. 1867, and endorsement, 2 Mar. 1867, by Maj. Edw. L. Deane, in Registered Letters Received, Ser. 3202, Georgetown, SC, Subasst. Comr., RG 105.

63. Abbott, *The Freedmen's Bureau,* 38–39.

64. Superintendent G. Pillsbury to Maj. O'Brien, 22 Aug. 1866, Testimony, Reports, and Other Records Relating to Court Cases and Complaints, Ser. 3284, Moncks Corner, SC, Subasst. Comr., RG 105. See also Litwack, *Been in the Storm So Long,* 379–82.

65. *New York Times,* 11 Feb. 1866.

66. Major General O. O. Howard, "Report of the Commissioner of the Bureau of Refugees, Freedmen, and Abandoned Lands," in U.S. Congress, *House Executive Documents,* 39th Cong., 1st Sess., No. 11, pp. 15, 23, 34. My reading of the bureau's efforts to define some former slaves as dependents has benefited from an essay by Nancy Fraser and Linda Gordon, "A Genealogy of Dependency: Tracing a Keyword of the U.S. Welfare State," *Signs* 19 (Winter 1994): 309–36.

67. U.S. War Department, "Annual Report of the Secretary of War [1866]," 60.

68. Gen. James C. Beecher to Lt. M. N. Rice, 21 Jan. 1866, Letters and Reports Received Relating to Freedmen and Civil Affairs, Ser. 4112, Dept. of SC, RG 393, Pt. 1.

69. U.S. War Department, "Annual Report of the Secretary of War [1866]," 61.

70. Williams Middleton to Father, 15 Feb. 1866, Middleton Family Papers, SCHS.

71. See Gen. J. Greene to Maj. Gen. H. W. Smith, 31 May 1867, Columbia, Reports of Conditions and Operations, R35, M869, and Circular Letter, 12 Dec. 1866, Maj. Gen. R. K. Scott, *Charleston Daily Courier,* 5 Jan. 1867.

72. General Orders No. 1, 1 Jan. 1866, in the *Charleston Daily Courier,* 23 Jan. 1866; and Col. E. A. Kozlay to Maj. H. W. Smith, 29 Jan. 1866, Orangeburg, Reports of Conditions and Operations, R34, M869. See also U.S. War Department, "Annual Report of the Secretary of War [1866]," 710.

73. S. Goings to Maj. E. F. O'Brien, 7 Jan. 1867, and endorsement by Gen. R. K. Scott, 7 Feb. 1867, Testimony, Reports, and Other Records Relating to Court Cases and Complaints, Ser. 3284, Moncks Corner, SC, Subasst. Comr., RG 105.

74. See Monthly Transportation Reports, 1866–68, Ser. 2955, SC Assist. Comr., RG 105.

75. T. P. Mikell, an Edisto Island planter, helped thirty-seven of his former slaves apply for free transportation from Sumter back to Edisto late in 1866; see Aaron

Simons et al., to Gen. Scott, 21 Dec. 1866, Monthly Transportation Reports, Ser. 2955, SC Assist. Comr., RG 105.

76. For example, Rose Butler, a pregnant freedwoman who was discharged from her plantation for leaving without the permission of the planter, was dismissed without penalty to her husband, who worked on the same plantation; see Agent C. V. Wilson to Major O'Brien, 19 July 1866, Testimony, Reports, and Other Records Relating to Court Cases and Complaints, Ser. 3284, Moncks Corner, SC, Subasst. Comr., RG 105. See also Wm. Postell Ingraham to Capt. F. M. Liedtke, 11 June 1866, Letters Received, Ser. 3277, Moncks Corner, SC, Subasst. Comr., RG 105.

77. *Charleston Daily Courier,* 23 Jan. 1866.

78. Barney [E. B. Heyward] to Tab [Catherine Heyward], 5 May 1867, Heyward Family Papers, SCL.

79. Scott's General Orders No. 9, issued on 29 June 1866, were printed in the *Charleston Daily Courier,* 3 July 1866. See also J. C. McKim to Dear Sir, 11 July 1866, Letters Received, Ser. 3277, Moncks Corner, SC, Subasst. Comr., RG 105.

80. See, for example, R. Y. Dwight to Capt. F. W. Leidtke, 24 July 1866, Letters Received, Ser. 3277, Moncks Corner, SC, Subasst. Comr., RG 105, and the printed labor contract form (issued by the South Carolina Assistant Commissioner of the Bureau in 1866) in the Middleton Family Papers, SCHS; quote is from William Postell Ingraham to Capt. F. W. Leidtke, 11 June 1866, Letters Received, Ser. 3277, Moncks Corner, SC, Subasst. Comr., RG 105.

81. *Charleston Daily Courier,* 5 Jan. 1867.

82. Endorsement, Office of Assistant Commissioner, 4 Apr. 1866, in Lieut. O. F. Lemon to Major H. W. Smith, 29 Mar. 1866, Letters Received, Ser. 3318, Rice Hope Plantation, SC, RG 105 [A-7166].

83. Lt. John L. Chance to 1st Lieut. H. Neide, 20 June 1867, endorsement by Bvt. Maj. Gen. R. K. Scott, 28 June 1867, Unregistered Letters Received, Ser. 3203, Georgetown, SC, Subasst. Comr., RG 105.

84. See contracts between F. W. Ford and Freedpeople, 1 Jan. 1867, and between Col. Ben Allston and Freedmen and Freedwomen, 2 Feb. 1867, both in Labor Contracts, Ser. 3210, Georgetown, SC, Subasst. Comr., RG 105.

85. The quoted comments are from Linda Gordon, *Heroes of Their Own Lives: The Politics and History of Family Violence* (New York: Viking, 1988), 3.

86. Charleston Dist. Agent A. M. L. Crawford estimated that 11 of 145 cases he adjudicated for June 1866 related to marriages or family disputes. See A. M. L. Crawford to H. W. Smith, 1 July 1866, Charleston, Reports of Conditions and Operations, R34, M869.

87. Maj. J. W. DeForest to Maj. Edw. Deane, 25 Sept. 1867, Greenville; Capt. George E. Pingree to Maj. Edw. L. Deane, 1 May 1867, Darlington; and A. P. Caraher to "Sir," 30 June 1867, Unionville, all in Reports of Conditions and Operations, R35, M869.

88. Entry 59, p. 31, Vol. 254, Register of Complaints, Ser. 3309, Orangeburg, SC, Subasst. Comr., RG 105.

89. Register of Complaints, 1867, Ser. 3085, Barnwell Dist., SC, Subasst. Comr., RG 105.

90. See Thomas D. Morris, "Equality, 'Extraordinary Law,' and Criminal Justice: The South Carolina Experience, 1865–66," *South Carolina Historical Magazine* 83, no. 1 (1982): 15–33; Maj. Geo. A. Williams to E. L. Deane, 31 Dec. 1866, Charleston, Reports of Conditions and Operations, R34, M869; Lt. F. W. Liedtke to Major [A. M. L. Crawford], 5 Apr. 1867, Letters Received, Ser. 4280, 2d Military District RG 393, Pt. 1 [SS-186]; Abbott, *The Freedmen's Bureau,* 99; Sefton, *The United States Army,* 30–34; U.S. Senate, *Senate Executive Documents,* 39th Cong., 2d Sess., No. 6, 116; and Webster, *Operation of the Freedmen's Bureau,* 24–26, 40–46.

91. Register of Complaints, 1866–1867, Ser. 3309, Orangeburg, SC, Subasst. Comr., RG 105; Provost Judge A. S. Hitchcock to Lieut. Louis V. Caziare, 20 May 1868, U.S. vs. Scipio Perry, 20 May 1868, Proceedings of Provost Courts, Military Tribunals, and Post Courtmartial Cases Tried in North and South Carolina, Ser. 4257, Judge Advocate, RG 393, Pt. 1. Sometimes, it was not the battered wife but instead a parent who sought bureau or miliary intervention; one father brought his son-in-law before the provost court, charging that the husband had whipped his wife only two or three weeks after her recent confinement. In this case, the wife was not willing to testify against her husband, who excused the incident by explaining that he whipped her "for jawing me." The provost court found him not guilty.

92. Towne, *Letters and Diary,* 184, and the testimony of Elbridge Gerry Dudley before the AFIC, [1863], O-328 1863, Letters Received, Ser. 12, RG 94 [K-77]. Not all wartime observers blamed family violence on freedmen; one of Saxton's aides, Capt. E. W. Hooper, simply noted that the marriage relation "brings them to blows oftener than anything else" [testimony of Capt. E. W. Hooper before the AFIC, [1863], O-328 1863, LR, Ser. 12, RG 94 [K-82].

93. Capt. Geo. E. Pingree to Major Deane, 16 Mar. 1867, Darlington, Reports of Conditions and Operations, R35, M869.

94. *New York Times,* 11 Feb. 1866.

95. Testimony of Capt. E. W. Hooper before the AFIC, [1863], O-328 1863, LR, Ser. 12, RG 94 [K-82].

96. Seaboro vs. Seaboro, 6 Mar. 1867, and Chisolm vs. Chisolm, 13 Mar. 1867, both in Register of Complaints, Ser. 3103, Beaufort, SC, Subasst. Comr., RG 105.

97. Register of Complaints, Vol. 94, Ser. 3085, Barnwell, SC, Subasst. Comr., RG 105.

98. The United States vs. James Anderson, 7 Apr. 1868, South Carolina Provost Court Proceedings, Ser. 4257, RG 393, Pt. 1.

99. James Bracey vs. Regina Toney, Oct. 1867, South Carolina Provost Court Proceedings, Ser. 4257, RG 393, Pt. 1.

100. Proceedings, Nancy Bacon vs. Titus Bacon, 31 Mar. 1868, Ser. 4257, South Carolina Provost Court Proceedings, RG 393, Pt. 1.

101. Register of Complaints, Vol. 182, Ser. 3192, Darlington, SC, RG 105.

102. M. A. Holland to Col. Reede, 10 Nov. 1867, Letters Received, Ser. 2392, RG 393, Pt. 2, No. 142.

103. Flora Murphy to Maj. D. Corbin, 23 May 1866, Testimony, Reports, and Other Records Relating to Court Cases and Complaints, Ser. 3284, Moncks Corner, SC, Subasst. Comr., RG 105.

104. Testimony by Sarah Waite and Paul Waite, 29 Jan. 1867, in U.S. vs. Hester Scott, Provost Court for Sea Islands, Wadmalaw Island, SC, 30 Jan. 1867, Ser. 4257, RG 393.

105. Register of Complaints, Vol. 254, Ser. 3309, Orangeburg, SC, Subasst. Comr., RG 105.

106. Capt. Geo. E. Pingree to Major Deane, 16 Mar. 1867, Darlington, Reports of Conditions and Operations, R35, M869.

107. Holt, "'An Empire Over the Mind,'" 288.

108. Testimony of Frederick A. Eustis before the AFIC, [1863], filed with O-328 1863, Letters Received, Ser. 12, RG 94 [K-80]. See also Litwack, *Been in the Storm So Long,* 240, 245–46.

109. O. F. Lemen to H. W. Smith, 29 Mar. 1866, Letters Received, Ser. 3318, Rice Hope Plantation, SC, RG 105.

110. On race and gender and their impact on the construction of women's dependency in the nineteenth-century United States, see Gwendolyn Mink, "The Lady and the Tramp: Gender, Race, and the Origins of the American Welfare State," in Gordon, *Women, the State, and Welfare,* 92–122.

111. Gen. R. K. Scott, Circular Letter to the Landlords and Laborers of the State of South Carolina, 25 Dec. 1866, Headquarters, Assistant Commissioner, BRFAL, Charleston, SC, printed in *Charleston Daily Courier,* 5 Jan. 1867.

112. Julie Saville has touched briefly but insightfully on the political and economic significance of domestic production among lowcountry freedpeople in her article "Grassroots Reconstruction: Agricultural Labour and Collective Action in South Carolina, 1860–1868," *Slavery and Abolition* 12, no. 3 (Dec. 1991): 173–82.

113. Military and civilian agents of Reconstruction developed an elaborate set of policies intervening in lowcountry African-American family life. For example, on 1 Jan. 1866, Maj. D. E. Sickles issued General Orders No. 1 from the headquarters of the Department of South Carolina in Charleston, which encouraged the eviction from plantations of the wives and children of any freedmen found to be in violation of labor contract terms, regardless of the preferences or conduct of women and children (printed copy, Middleton Family Papers, SCHS). The sweeping marriage rules instituted by the bureau, intended to encourage legal ceremonies among those married while slaves, contradicted the actual conditions and disregarded the preferences of lowcountry African Americans, so that a new and elabrate set of marriage rules had to be issued to address the confusion and damage imposed by the initial effort. See Gen. R. K. Scott, General Orders No. 6, 7 Feb. 1866, and General Orders No. 2, 18 Jan. 1868, Orders and Circulars, R36, M869; M. French, Marriage Rules, 1866, Miscellaneous Records, Ser. 2956, SC Asst. Comr., RG 105; and the circular issued by Maj. Gen. O. O. Howard to Secretary of War Hon. E. M. Stanton, 1 Nov. 1866, in U.S. Congress, *House Executive Documents,* 39th Cong., 2d Sess., No. 1, pp. 756–57.

114. Myers, *Children of Pride,* 1310.

115. W. St. J. Mazyck to Col. Smith, 4 Feb. 1866, Letters Received, Ser. 2392, 4th Subdist., Mil. Dist. of Charleston, RG 393, Pt. 2, No. 142.

116. These consequences included, by the end of the century, the failure of the region's staple-crop plantation economy. The reasons for this failure are many; one

was the continued insistence by African-American men and women that they enter the labor market when and how they judged best. John Scott Strickland describes the impact of the transition to free labor on the lowcountry's rice economy in his essay "Traditional Culture," 141–78.

BIBLIOGRAPHY

Primary Sources

Manuscript Collections

William R. Perkins Library, Duke University, Durham, North Carolina
    James Chaplin Beecher Papers
    John Emory Bryant Papers
    John Snider Cooper Diary
    Francis Porteus Corbin Papers
    Dahlgren Papers
    Thomas Rhett Smith Elliott Papers
    Robert Newman Gourdin Papers
    John Berkeley Grimball Papers
    Edward Thomas Heriot Papers
    John McIntosh Kell Papers
    Louis Manigault Papers
    Jacob Rhett Motte Papers
    Lalla Pelot Papers
    James R. Pringle Papers
    Alonzo Reed Papers
    Robert Barnwell Rhett Papers
    Sanders Family Papers
South Carolina Department of Archives and History, Columbia, South Carolina
    Governors' Papers
      James L. Orr
      Francis Pickens
    State Auditor Records
      Claims of Slaves Lost in Public Service, 1862–64
      Papers of the Commission for the Removal of Negroes and Property, 1862–63
      Miscellaneous Papers, 1861–65
South Caroliniana Collection, University of South Carolina, Columbia, South Carolina
    Allston Family Papers
    Robert F. W. Allston Papers
    Heyward Family Papers
    Williams Middleton Papers
    Palmer Family Papers
    Porcher-Ford Families Papers

Prince Frederick's Protestant Episcopal Church Records (Plantersville, South Carolina)

Prince George Winyah Protestant Episcopal Church Records (Georgetown, South Carolina)

Henry William Ravenel Papers

Read-Lance Families Papers

James Ritchie Sparkman Collection

Trapier Family Papers

Paul D. Weston Papers

H. H. Wilson Papers

South Carolina Historical Society, Charleston, South Carolina

Allston Family Papers

Alston-Pringle-Frost Papers

Sandford William Barker Plantation Records

Confederate States, Army Records

P. Gourdin Plantation Records

Elizabeth Heyward Jervey Time Books

Manigault Family Papers

Middleton Place Papers

Mitchell-Pringle Papers

Porcher Family Papers

Henry Ravenel Papers

Richmond Plantation Overseer Journal

VanderHorst Family Papers

John Joshua Ward Account Book

Paul Weston Papers

Southern Historical Collection, University of North Carolina, Chapel Hill, North Carolina

Richard James Arnold Papers

Arnold and Screven Family Papers

John and Keating Simons Ball Papers

Confederate Engineer Department Papers

Louis DeSaussure Plantation Record

Elliott-Gonzales Family Papers

Habersham Elliott Papers

Federal Soldiers' Letters

John Edwin Fripp Papers

Jeremy Francis Gilmer Papers

Gregorie and Elliott Family Papers

John Berkeley Grimball Diary

Meta (Morris) Grimball Diary

Grimball Family Papers

Heyward Family Papers

Heyward and Ferguson Family Papers

James Barnwell Heyward and Robert Barnwell Heyward Papers

H. A. Johnson Papers

Manigault Family Papers
Ravenel Family Papers
William Ervine Sparkman Papers
Trapier Family Papers
Jonathan Lewis Whitaker Papers
Wisconsin State Historical Society Manuscript Collection, Madison, Wisconsin
William F. Allen Family Papers

Manuscripts on Microfilm

Stampp, Kenneth M., ed. *Records of Ante-Bellum Southern Plantations from the Revolution through the Civil War.* Frederick, Md.: University Publications of America, c. 1985–c. 1996.
Series A: Selections from the South Caroliniana Library, University of South Carolina, Columbia, South Carolina
Heyward Family Papers
Series B: Selections from the South Carolina Historical Society, Charleston, South Carolina
Reverend Alexander Glennie Parish Diary
Glover Family Papers
Dr. Andrew Hasell Medical Account Book
John B. Milliken Plantation Journals, 1853–89
Henry Ravenel Papers
Thomas Porcher Ravenel Papers
"Richmond." Overseer Journal, 1859–60
John Sparkman Plantation Book
Joshua John Ward Plantation Journals
Paul D. Weston Papers
Series F: Selections from the Manuscript Department, Duke University Library, Part 2: South Carolina and Georgia
Keating Simons Ball Papers, Comington Plantation Book
Alfred Huger Letterbooks
Louis Manigault Papers
"Rockingham" Plantation Journal

National Archives

National Archives Microfilm Publication M346: Confederate Papers Relating to Citizens or Business Firms, RG 109
National Archives Microfilm Publication M869: Records of the Assistant Commissioner for the State of South Carolina, Bureau of Refugees, Freedmen, and Abandoned Lands, 1865–70
National Archives Microfilm Publication M89: Letters Received by the Secretary of Navy from Commanding Officers of Squadrons ("Squadron Letters"), 1841–86
Record Group 15: Records of the Veterans Administration
Record Group 24: Records of the Bureau of Naval Personnel

Record Group 45: Naval Records Collection of the Office of Naval Records and Library
Record Group 56: General Records of the Department of the Treasury
Record Group 58: Records of the Internal Revenue Service
Record Group 94: Records of the Adjutant General's Office, 1780s–1917
Record Group 105: Records of the Bureau of Refugees, Freedmen, and Abandoned Lands
Record Group 109: The War Department Collection of Confederate Records
Record Group 217: Records of the United States General Accounting Office
Record Group 233: Records of the United States House of Representatives
Record Group 393: Records of the United States Army Continental Commands, 1821–1920

Published Letters, Diaries, and Reminiscences

Adams, Virginia M., ed. *On the Altar of Freedom: A Black Soldier's Civil War Letters from the Front: Corporal James Henry Gooding.* Amherst: University of Massachusetts Press, 1996.
Blackett, R. J. M., ed. *Thomas Morris Chester, Black Civil War Correspondent.* Baton Rouge: Louisiana State University Press, 1989.
Botume, Elizabeth Hyde. *First Days amongst the Contrabands.* 1893; rpt., New York: Arno, 1968.
Burr, Virginia Ingraham, ed. *The Secret Eye: The Journal of Ella Gertrude Clanton Thomas, 1848–1889.* Chapel Hill: University of North Carolina Press, 1990.
Childs, Arney Robinson, ed. *The Private Journal of Henry William Ravenel, 1859–1887.* Columbia: University of South Carolina Press, 1947.
Clifton, James M., ed. *Life and Labor on Argyle Island: Letters and Documents of a Savannah River Rice Plantation, 1833–1867.* Savannah: Beehive, 1978.
Cooley, Rossa B. *Homes of the Freed.* New York: New Republic, 1926.
Cooper, Anna Julia. *A Voice from the South By A Black Woman of the South.* 1892; rpt., New York: Negro Universities Press, 1969.
Correspondence Relating to Fortification of Morris Island and Operations of Engineers, Charleston, S.C., 1863. New York: John C. Caulon, 1878.
DeForest, John William. *A Union Officer in the Reconstruction.* Edited by James H. Croushore and David Morris Potter. New Haven: Yale University Press, 1948.
Dennett, John Richard. *The South as It Is, 1865–1866.* Edited by Henry M. Christian. 1965; rpt., Athens: University of Georgia Press, 1986.
De Vorsey, Louis, Jr., ed. *De Brahm's Report of the General Survey in the Southern District of North America.* Columbia: University of South Carolina Press, 1971.
East, Charles, ed. *The Civil War Diary of Sarah Morgan.* Athens: University of Georgia Press, 1991.
Easterby, J. H., ed. *The South Carolina Rice Plantation As Revealed in the Papers of Robert F. W. Allston.* Chicago: University of Chicago Press, 1945.
———. "South Carolina through New England Eyes: Almira Coffin's Visit to the Low Country in 1851." *South Carolina Historical Magazine* 45 (1944): 127–36.

Eaton, John. *Grant, Lincoln and the Freedmen: Reminiscences of the Civil War.* 1907; rpt., New York: Negro Universities Press, 1969.

Harper, Frances. "Colored Women of America." *English Women's Review* (15 Jan. 1878): 10–15.

Higginson, Thomas Wentworth. *Army Life in a Black Regiment.* 1869; rpt., New York: Norton, 1984.

————. "Up the Edisto." *Atlantic Monthly,* Aug. 1867, 157–65.

Holland, Rupert Sargent, ed. *Letters and Diary of Laura M. Towne, Written from the Sea Islands of South Carolina, 1862–1884.* 1912; rpt., New York: Negro Universities Press, 1969.

Jervey, Susan R., and Charlotte St. J. Ravenel. *Two Diaries from Middle St. John's, Berkeley, South Carolina, February–May 1865.* South Carolina: St. John's Hunting Club, 1921.

Jones, Katherine M., ed. *The Plantation South.* Indianapolis: Bobbs-Merrill, 1957.

Kemble, Frances Anne. *Journal of a Residence on a Georgian Plantation in 1838–1839.* 1863; rpt., Athens: University of Georgia Press, 1984.

Leigh, Frances Butler. *Ten Years on a Georgia Plantation since the War.* 1883; rpt., New York: Negro Universities Press, 1969.

Marszalek, John F., ed. *The Diary of Miss Emma Holmes, 1861–1866.* Baton Rouge: Louisiana State University Press, 1994.

McKim, James M. *The Freed Men of South Carolina.* Philadelphia: Willis P. Hazard, 1862.

Myers, Robert Manson, ed. *The Children of Pride: A True Story of Georgia and the Civil War.* New Haven: Yale University Press, 1972.

New England Freedmen's Aid Society. *Second Annual Report.* Boston: New England Freedmen's Aid Society, 1864.

Nordhoff, Charles. *The Freedmen of South-Carolina; some account of their appearance, character, condition, and peculiar customs.* New York: Charles T. Evans, 1863.

Olmsted, Frederick Law. *A Journey in the Seaboard Slave States, with Remarks on Their Economy.* New York: Dix and Edwards, 1856.

Pearson, Elizabeth Ware, ed. *Letters from Port Royal, 1862–1868.* 1906; rpt., New York: Arno, 1969.

Pennington, Patience [pseud. Elizabeth W. Allston Pringle]. *A Woman Rice Planter.* New York: Macmillan, 1913.

Pringle, Elizabeth W. Allston. *Chronicles of Chicora Wood.* Boston: Christopher Publishing House, 1940.

Proceedings of the Colored People's Convention of the State of South Carolina, Held in Zion Church, Charleston, November, 1865. Charleston, S.C., 1865.

Ravenel, Henry W. "Recollections of Southern Plantation Life." *Yale Review* 25 (Summer 1936): 748–77.

Rawick, George P., ed. *The American Slave: A Composite Biography.* 19 vols. Westport, Conn.: Greenwood, 1972.

Reid, Whitelaw. *After the War: A Tour of the Southern States, 1865–1866.* Edited by C. Vann Woodward. 1866; rpt., New York: Harper and Row, 1965.

Rosengarten, Theodore. *Tombee: Portrait of a Cotton Planter, with The Journal of Thomas B. Chaplin (1822–1890).* Edited by Susan W. Walker. New York: McGraw-Hill, 1987.

Sass, Herbert Ravenel, and D. E. Huger Smith. *A Carolina Rice Plantation of the Fifties.* New York: Morrow, 1936.

Schwartz, Gerald, ed. *A Woman Doctor's Civil War: Esther Hill Hawks' Diary.* Columbia: University of South Carolina Press, 1984.

Smith, D. E. Huger. *A Charlestonian's Recollections, 1846–1913.* Charleston: Carolina Art Association, 1950.

Smith, Daniel E. Huger, Alice R. Huger Smith, and Arney R. Childs, eds. *Mason Smith Family Letters, 1860–1868.* Columbia: University of South Carolina Press, 1950.

Smythe, Augustine T., et al. *The Carolina Low-Country.* New York: Macmillan, 1931.

Snowden, Yates. "The Planters of St. John's." *Transactions of the Hugenot Society of South Carolina* 21 (1915): 16–30.

Stevenson, Brenda, ed. *The Journals of Charlotte Forten Grimké.* New York: Oxford University Press, 1988.

Swint, Henry L. *Dear Ones at Home: Letters from Contraband Camps.* Nashville: Vanderbilt University Press, 1966.

Taylor, Susie King. *Reminiscences of My Life in Camp with the 33rd U.S. Colored Troops, Late 1st South Carolina Volunteers: A Black Woman's Civil War Memoirs.* Edited by Patricia W. Romero and Willie Lee Rose. 1902; rpt., New York: Marcus Wiener, 1988.

Wilson, Robert, D.D. *An Address Delivered Before the St. John's Hunting club at Indianfield Plantation, St. John's Berkeley, 4 July 1907.* Charleston, 1907.

Woodward, C. Vann, ed. *Mary Chesnut's Civil War.* New Haven: Yale University Press, 1981.

Woodward, C. Vann, and Elizabeth Muhlenfeld, eds. *The Private Mary Chesnut: The Unpublished Civil War Diaries.* New York: Oxford University Press, 1984.

Year Book—1885, City of Charleston, So. Ca. Charleston, S.C.: News and Courier Book Presses, 1886.

Published Public Documents

Annual Report of the Acting Commissioner and Architect of the New State House, for the Fiscal Year 1863. Columbia, S.C., 1863.

[Black, James A.]. *Report of the Comptroller General to the Legislature of South Carolina, November 1864.* Columbia, S.C.: Charles P. Pelham, 1864.

Cauthen, Charles E., ed. *Journals of the South Carolina Executive Councils of 1861 and 1862.* Columbia: South Carolina Archives Department, 1956.

Confederate States of America. *Journal of the Congress of the Confederate States of America, 1861–1865.* Vol. 1. *Journal of the Provisional Congress of the Confederate States of America.* S. Doc. 234, 58th Congress, 2d Session, Ser. 4610. Washington, D.C., 1904.

———. *Journal of the Congress of the Confederate States of America, 1861–1865.* Vols. 2–4. *Journal of the Senate of the Confederate States of America.* S. Doc. 234, 58th Congress, 2d Session, Ser. 4611–13. Washington, D.C., 1904.

———. *Journal of the Congress of the Confederate States of America, 1861–1865.* Vols. 5–7. *Journal of the House of Representatives of the Confederate States of America.* S. Doc. 234, 58th Congress, 2d Session, Ser. 4614–18. Washington, D.C., 1905.

———. *Public Laws of the Confederate States of America.* Richmond: R. Smith, 1862.

Gibbes, R. W. *Regulations for the Medical Department of the Military Forces of South Carolina.* Columbia, S.C., 1861.

Journal of the Convention of the People of South Carolina Held in 1860, 1861, and 1862, Together with the Ordinances, Reports, Resolutions, etc. Columbia, S.C., 1862.

Report of the Chief of the Department of Justice and Police, to the Governor and Executive Council. Part 3: *On the Special Action of the Department of Justice and Police.* Columbia, S.C., 1862.

Report of the Commissioner of Agriculture for the Year 1866. Washington, D.C., 1867.

Report of the Comptroller General to the Legislature of South Carolina, November 1862. Columbia, S.C., 1862.

Report of the Special Committee of Twenty-One, On the Communication of His Excellency Governor Pickens, Together with the Reports of Heads of Departments, and Other Papers. Columbia, S.C.: R. W. Gibbes, 1862.

Tupper, James. *Report of the Auditor of South Carolina, on Claims Against the State for Slaves Lost in Public Service.* Columbia, S.C., 1864.

U.S. Congress. *Report of the Joint Committee on Reconstruction.* Washington, D.C., 1866.
———. *Report of the Commissioner of the Bureau of Refugees, Freedmen, and Abandoned Lands.* House Reports, 39th Congress, 1st Session, No. 11.

U.S. Navy Department. *Official Records of the Union and Confederate Navies in the War of the Rebellion,* 30 vols. Washington, D.C., 1894–1922.

U.S. Senate. *Report of Carl Schurz on the States of South Carolina, Georgia, Alabama, Mississippi, and Louisiana.* Senate Executive Documents, 39th Congress, 1st Session, Ex. Doc. No. 2.
———. *Reports of the Assistant Commissioners of the Freedmen's Bureau Made Since December 1, 1865.* Senate Executive Documents, 39th Congress, 1st Session, Ex. Doc. No. 27.
———. *Report of 21 December, 1866, by the Commissioner of Freedmen.* Senate Executive Documents, 39th Congress, 2d Session, Ex. Doc. No. 6.

U.S. War Department. *The War of the Rebellion: A Compilation of the Official Records of the Union and Confederate Armies.* 128 vols. Washington, D.C., 1880–1901.

Newspapers and Journals

Charleston Daily Courier (Charleston, South Carolina)
Daily South Carolinian (Charleston, South Carolina)
New York Herald
New York Times
Pee Dee Times (Georgetown, South Carolina)
South Carolina Leader (Charleston, South Carolina)
Southern Agriculturist

Secondary Sources

Abbott, Martin. *The Freedmen's Bureau in South Carolina, 1865–1872.* Chapel Hill: University of North Carolina Press, 1967.

Adams, Virginia M., ed. *On the Altar of Freedom: A Black Soldier's Civil War Letters from the Front: Corporal James Henry Gooding.* Amherst: University of Massachusetts Press, 1991.

Aptheker, Bettina. *Woman's Legacy: Essays on Race, Sex, and Class in American History.* Amherst: University of Massachusetts Press, 1982.

Aptheker, Herbert. "The Negro in the Union Navy." *Journal of Negro History* 32 (1947): 169–200.

Armstrong, Thomas F. "From Task Labor to Free Labor: The Transition along Georgia's Rice Coast, 1820–1880." *Georgia Historical Quarterly* 64 (Winter 1980): 432–47.

Beale, Francis. "Double Jeopardy: To Be Black and Female." In *The Black Woman: An Anthology,* edited by Toni Cade. New York: New American Library, 1970.

Beckles, Hilary McD. *Natural Rebels: A Social History of Enslaved Black Women in Barbados.* New Brunswick: Rutgers University Press, 1989.

Bell, Malcolm, Jr. *Major Butler's Legacy: Five Generations of a Slaveholding Family.* Athens: University of Georgia Press, 1987.

Bentley, George R. *A History of the Freedmen's Bureau.* Philadelphia: University of Pennsylvania Press, 1955.

Berkeley, Kathleen C. "'Colored Ladies Also Contributed': Black Women's Activities from Benevolence to Social Welfare, 1866–1896." In *The Web of Southern Social Relations: Work, Family, and Education,* edited by Walter J. Fraser, Jr., R. Frank Saunders, Jr., and Jon L. Wakelyn. Athens: University of Georgia Press, 1985.

Berlin, Ira. "Time, Space, and the Evolution of Afro-American Society on British Mainland North America." *American Historical Review* 85 (Feb. 1980): 44–78.

Berlin, Ira, Francine C. Cary, Steven F. Miller, and Leslie S. Rowland. "Family and Freedom: Black Families in the American Civil War." *History Today* 37 (Jan. 1987): 8–15.

Berlin, Ira, Barbara J. Fields, Thavolia Glymph, Joseph P. Reidy, and Leslie S. Rowland, eds. *Freedom: A Documentary History of Emancipation, 1861–1867.* Series I, Vol. 1, *The Destruction of Slavery.* Cambridge: Cambridge University Press, 1985.

Berlin, Ira, Thavolia Glymph, Steven F. Miller, Joseph P. Reidy, Leslie S. Rowland, and Julie Saville, eds. *Freedom: A Documentary History of Emancipation.* Series I, Vol. 3, *The Wartime Genesis of Free Labor: The Lower South.* Cambridge: Cambridge University Press, 1990.

Berlin, Ira, Steven Hahn, Steven F. Miller, Joseph P. Reidy, and Leslie S. Rowland. "The Terrain of Freedom: The Struggle Over the Meaning of Free Labor in the U.S. South." *History Workshop Journal* 22 (Autumn 1986): 108–30.

Berlin, Ira, and Ronald Hoffman, eds. *Slavery and Freedom in the Age of the American Revolution.* Charlottesville: University Press of Virginia, 1983.

Berlin, Ira, and Philip D. Morgan, eds. *Cultivation and Culture: Labor and the Shaping of Slave Life in the Americas.* Charlottesville: University Press of Virginia, 1993.

Berlin, Ira, Joseph P. Reidy and Leslie S. Rowland, eds. *Freedom: A Documentary History of Emancipation, 1861–1867.* Series II, *The Black Military Experience.* Cambridge: Cambridge University Press, 1982.

Blackett, R. J. M., ed. *Thomas Morris Chester, Black Civil War Correspondent.* Baton Rouge: Louisiana State University Press, 1989.

Blassingame, John W. *The Slave Community: Plantation Life in the Antebellum South.* New York: Oxford University Press, 1972.

Blight, David W. *Frederick Douglass' Civil War: Keeping Faith in Jubilee.* Baton Rouge: Louisiana State University Press, 1989.

Boles, John B. *Black Southerners, 1619–1869.* Lexington: University Press of Kentucky, 1984.

Boydston, Jeanne. *Home and Work: Housework, Wages, and the Ideology of Labor in the Early Republic.* New York: Oxford University Press, 1990.

Bozzoli, Belinda. "Marxism, Feminism and South African Studies." *Journal of South African Studies* 9 (Apr. 1983): 138–71.

Brewer, James H. *The Confederate Negro: Virginia's Craftsmen and Military Laborers, 1861–1865.* Durham, N.C.: Duke University Press, 1969.

Brown, Elsa Barkley. "Negotiating and Transforming the Public Sphere: African American Political Life in the Transition from Slavery to Freedom." *Public Culture* 7 (1994): 107–46.

———. "Womanist Consciousness: Maggie Lena Walker and the Independent Order of Saint Luke." *Signs: A Journal of Women in Culture and Society* 14 (Spring 1989): 610–33.

Brown, Kathleen M. *Good Wives, Nasty Wenches, and Anxious Patriarchs: Gender, Race, and Power in Colonial Virginia.* Chapel Hill: University of North Carolina Press, 1996.

Burstyn, Varda. "Masculine Dominance and the State." *Socialist Register* (1983): 59–62.

Burton, Orville Vernon. *In My Father's House Are Many Mansions: Family and Community in Edgefield, South Carolina.* Chapel Hill: University of North Carolina Press, 1985.

Bush, Barbara. *Slave Women in Caribbean Society, 1650–1838.* Bloomington: Indiana University Press, 1990.

———. "Towards Emancipation: Slave Women and Resistance to Coercive Labour Regimes in the British West Indian Colonies, 1790–1838." *Slavery and Abolition* 5 (Dec. 1981): 222–43.

Bynum, Victoria E. *Unruly Women: The Politics of Social and Sexual Control in the Old South, 1840–1865.* Chapel Hill: University of North Carolina Press, 1992.

Calhoun, Craig. *The Question of Class Struggle: Social Foundations of Popular Radicalism during the Industrial Revolution.* Chicago: University of Chicago Press, 1982.

Carter, Dan T. "The Anatomy of Fear: The Christmas Day Insurrection Scare of 1865." *Journal of Southern History* 42 (Aug. 1976): 345–69.

———. *When the War Was Over: The Failure of Self-Reconstruction in the South.* Baton Rouge: Louisiana State University Press, 1985.

Cauthen, Charles Edward. *South Carolina Goes to War, 1860–1865.* Chapel Hill: University of North Carolina Press, 1950.

Cell, John. *The Highest Stage of White Supremacy: The Origins of Segregation in South Africa and the American South.* Cambridge: Cambridge University Press, 1982.

Channing, Steven A. *Crisis of Fear: Secession in South Carolina*. New York: Norton, 1974.

Clifton, James M. "The Rice Driver: His Role in Slave Management." *South Carolina Historical Magazine* 82 (Oct. 1981): 331–53.

———. "Twilight Comes to the Rice Kingdom: Postbellum Rice Culture on the South Atlantic Coast." *Georgia Historical Quarterly* 62 (Summer 1978): 146–52.

Clinton, Catherine. "'Southern Dishonor'" Flesh, Blood, Race, and Bondage." In *In Joy and in Sorrow: Women, Family, and Marriage in the Victorian South,* edited by Carol Blesser. New York: Oxford University Press, 1991.

Clinton, Catherine, and Nina Silber, eds. *Divided Houses: Gender and the Civil War.* New York: Oxford University Press, 1992.

Coclanis, Peter A. *The Shadow of a Dream: Economic Life and Death in the South Carolina Low Country, 1670–1920*. New York: Oxford University Press, 1989.

Cody, Cheryll Ann. "Naming, Kinship, and Estate Dispersal: Notes on Slave Family Life on a South Carolina Plantation, 1786–1833." *William and Mary Quarterly,* 3d Ser., 39 (Jan. 1982): 192–211.

———. "There Was No Absalom on the Ball Plantations: Slave-Naming Practices in the South Carolina Low Country, 1720–1865." *American Historical Review* 92 (June 1987): 563–96.

Cohen, William. *At Freedom's Edge: Black Mobility and the Southern White Quest for Racial Control, 1861–1875*. Baton Rouge: Louisiana State University Press, 1991.

Cox, LaWanda. *Lincoln and Black Freedom: A Study in Presidential Leadership*. Columbia: University of South Carolina Press, 1981.

Creel, Margaret Washington. "Gullah Attitudes toward Life and Death:" In *Africanisms in American Culture,* edited by Joseph E. Holloway. Bloomington: Indiana University Press, 1990.

———. *"A Peculiar People": Slave Religion and Community-Culture among the Gullahs*. New York: New York University Press, 1988.

Davis, Angela. "Reflections on the Black Woman's Role in the Community of Slaves." *Black Scholar* 3 (December 1971): 3–15.

Dethloff, Henry C. *A History of the American Rice Industry, 1685–1985*. College Station: Texas A & M University Press, 1988.

Doar, David. *Rice and Rice Planting in the South Carolina Low Country.* Contributions from the Charleston Museum, No. 8. Charleston: The Charleston Museum, 1936.

Du Bois, W. E. B. *Black Reconstruction in America, 1860–1880*. 1935; New York: Atheneum, 1935.

Duncan, Russell. *Freedom's Shore: Tunis Campbell and the Georgia Freedmen*. Athens: University of Georgia Press, 1986.

Durrill, Wayne K. *War of Another Kind: A Southern Community in the Great Rebellion*. New York: Oxford University Press, 1990.

Dusinberre, William. *Them Dark Days: Slavery in the American Rice Swamps*. New York: Oxford University Press, 1996.

Edwards, Laura F. "Sexual Violence, Gender, Reconstruction, and the Extension of Patriarchy in Granville, North Carolina." *North Carolina Historical Review* 68, no. 3 (1991): 237–60.

Engerman, Stanley L. "Economic Adjustments to Emancipation in the United States and British West Indies." *Journal of Interdisciplinary History* 13 (Autumn 1982): 191–220.

Escott, Paul D. *After Secession: Jefferson Davis and the Failure of Confederate Nationalism.* Baton Rouge: Louisiana State University Press, 1978.

Farnham, Christie. "Sapphire? The Issue of Dominance in the Slave Family, 1830–1865." In *"To Toil the Livelong Day": America's Women at Work, 1780–1980,* edited by Carol Groneman and Mary Beth Norton. Ithaca: Cornell University Press, 1987.

Faust, Drew Gilpin. "Altars of Sacrifice: Confederate Women and the Narratives of War." *Journal of American History* 76 (1990): 1200–1228.

———. *The Creation of Confederate Nationalism: Ideology and Identity in the Civil War South.* Baton Rouge: Louisiana State University Press, 1988.

———. "'Trying to Do a Man's Business': Slavery, Violence, and Gender in the American Civil War." *Gender and History* 4, no. 2 (1992): 197–214.

Fields, Barbara J. "The Advent of Capitalist Agriculture: The New South in a Bourgeois World." In *Essays on the Postbellum Southern Economy,* edited by Thavolia Glymph and John J. Kushma. College Station: Texas A & M University Press, 1985.

———. "Ideology and Race in American History." In *Region, Race, and Reconstruction: Essays in Honor of C. Vann Woodward,* edited by J. Morgan Kousser and James M. McPherson. New York: Oxford University Press, 1982.

———. *Slavery and Freedom on the Middle Ground: Maryland during the Nineteenth Century.* New Haven: Yale University Press, 1985.

Fields, Mamie Garvin, with Karen Fields. *Lemon Swamp and Other Places: A Carolina Memoir.* New York: Free Press, 1983.

Fisher, Walter. "Physicians and Slavery in the Antebellum Southern Medical Journal." *Journal of the History of Medicine* 23 (1968): 36–49.

Fitzgerald, Michael William. "The Union League Movement in Alabama and Mississippi: Politics and Agricultural Change in the Deep South during Reconstruction." Ph.D. diss., University of California, Los Angeles, 1986.

Fogel, Robert William, and Stanley L. Engerman. *Time on the Cross: The Economics of American Negro Slavery.* Boston: Little, Brown, 1974.

Foner, Eric. *Free Soil, Free Labor, Free Men: The Ideology of the Republican Party before the Civil War.* New York: Oxford University Press, 1970.

———. "The Meaning of Freedom in the Age of Emancipation." *Journal of American History* 81, no. 2 (Sept. 1994): 435–60.

———. *Nothing But Freedom: Emancipation and Its Legacy.* Baton Rouge: Louisiana State University Press, 1983.

———. *Politics and Ideology in the Age of the Civil War.* New York: Oxford University Press, 1980.

———. *Reconstruction: America's Unfinished Revolution, 1863–1877.* New York: Harper and Row, 1988.

Ford, Lacy. "Labor and Ideology in the South Carolina Up-Country: The Transition to Free-Labor Agriculture." In *The Southern Enigma: Essays on Race, Class, and Folk Culture,* edited by Walter J. Fraser Jr. and Winfred Moore Jr. Westport, Conn.: Greenwood, 1983.

Foster, Gaines M. "The Limitations of Federal Health Care for Freedmen, 1862–1868." *Journal of Southern History* 48 (Aug. 1982): 350–72.

Fox-Genovese, Elizabeth. "Strategies and Forms of Resistance: Focus on Slave Women in the United States." In *Resistance: Studies in African, Caribbean, and Afro-American History,* edited by Gary Y. Okihiro. Amherst: University of Massachusetts Press, 1986.

———. *Within the Plantation Household: Black and White Women of the Old South.* Chapel Hill: University of North Carolina Press, 1988.

Frankel, Noralee. "The Southern Side of 'Glory': Mississippi African-American Women during the Civil War." In *"We Specialize in the Wholly Impossible": A Reader in Black Women's History,* ed. Darlene Clark Hine, Wilma King, and Linda Reed. Brooklyn: Carlson, 1995.

Fraser, Nancy, and Linda Gordon. "A Genealogy of Dependency: Tracing a Keyword of the U.S. Welfare State." *Signs: A Journal of Women in Culture and Society,* 19, no. 2 (1994): 309–36.

Frederickson, George M. *The Arrogance of Race: Historical Perspectives on Slavery, Racism, and Social Inequality.* Middletown, Conn.: Wesleyan University Press, 1988.

———. *The Black Image in the White Mind: The Debate on Afro-American Character and Destiny, 1817–1914.* New York: Harper and Row, 1971.

———. *The Inner Civil War: Northern Intellectuals and the Crisis of the Union.* New York: Harper and Row, 1965.

Gates, Paul W. *Agriculture and the Civil War.* New York: Knopf, 1965.

Genovese, Eugene D. *Roll, Jordan, Roll: The World the Slaves Made.* New York: Pantheon, 1974.

———. *The World the Slaveholders Made: Two Essays in Interpretation.* New York: Random House, 1971.

Gerteis, Louis S. *From Contraband to Freedman: Federal Policy Toward Southern Blacks, 1861–1865.* Westport, Conn.: Greenwood, 1973.

Giddings, Paula. *Where and When I Enter: The Impact of Black Women on Race and Sex in America.* New York: William Morrow, 1984.

Gillette, William. *Retreat from Reconstruction, 1869–1879.* Baton Rouge: Louisiana State University Press, 1979.

Glatthaar, Joseph T. *Forged in Battle: The Civil War Alliance of Black Soldiers and White Officers.* New York: New York University Press, 1985.

———. *The March to the Sea and Beyond Sherman's Troops in the Savannah and Carolinas Campaigns.* New York: Free Press, 1985.

Glickstein, Jonathan A. "'Poverty Is Not Slavery': American Abolitionists and the Competitive Labor Market." In *Antislavery Reconsidered: New Perspectives on the Abolitionists,* edited by Lewis Perry and Michael Fellman. Baton Rouge: Louisiana State University Press, 1979.

Glymph, Thavolia. "Freedpeople and Ex-Masters: Shaping a New Order in the Postbellum South, 1865–1868." In *Essays on the Postbellum Southern Economy,* edited by Thavolia Glymph and John J. Kushma. College Station: Texas A & M University Press, 1985.

Glymph, Thavolia, and John J. Kushma, eds. *Essays on the Postbellum Southern Economy.* College Station: Texas A & M University Press, 1985.

Goldin, Claudia. "Female Labor Force Participation: The Origin of Black and White Differences, 1870 and 1880." *Journal of Economic History* 37 (1977): 87–108.

————. "'N' Kinds of Freedom: An Introduction to the Issues." *Explorations in Economic History* 16 (1979): 8–30.

Gordon, Linda. *Heroes of Their Own Lives: The Politics and History of Family Violence.* New York: Viking, 1988.

————, ed. *Women, the State, and Welfare.* Madison: University of Wisconsin Press, 1990.

Gray, Lewis Cecil. *History of Agriculture in the Southern United States to 1860.* 2 vols. Washington, D.C.: Carnegie Institution, 1933.

Groneman, Carol, and Mary Beth Norton, eds. *"To Toil the Livelong Day": America's Women at Work, 1780–1980.* Ithaca: Cornell University Press, 1987.

Guillory, J. D. "The Pro-Slavery Arguments of Dr. Samuel A. Cartwright." *Louisiana History* 9 (1968): 209–27.

Gutman, Herbert G. *The Black Family in Slavery and Freedom, 1750–1925.* New York: Pantheon, 1976.

————. "Work, Culture, and Society in Industrializing America, 1815–1919." *American Historical Review* 78 (1973): 531–88.

Hahn, Steven. *The Roots of Southern Populism: Yeoman Farmers and the Transformation of the Georgia Upcountry, 1850–1890.* New York: Oxford University Press, 1983.

Hahn, Steven, and Jonathan Prude, eds. *The Countryside in the Age of Capitalist Transformation: Essays in the Social History of Rural America.* Chapel Hill: University of North Carolina Press, 1985.

Hall, Douglass. "The Flight from the Estates Reconsidered: The British West Indies, 1838–42." *Journal of Caribbean History* 10–11 (1978): 7–24.

Hammond, Harry. *South Carolina: Resources and Population, Institutions and Industries.* Charleston, S.C.: Walker, Evans and Cogswell, 1883.

Hay, Margaret Jean, and Sharon Stichter, eds. *African Women South of the Sahara.* New York: Longman, 1984.

Hewitt, Nancy A. "Beyond the Search for Sisterhood: American Women's History in the 1980s." *Social History* 10 (Oct. 1985): 299–321.

Heyward, Duncan Clinch. *Seed from Madagascar.* Chapel Hill: University of North Carolina Press, 1937.

Higginbotham, Elizabeth Brooks. "The Metalanguage of Race." *Signs: A Journal of Women in Culture and Society* 17 (Winter 1992): 251–74.

Higgins, William H., Jr. *O Freedom! Afro-American Emancipation Celebrations.* Knoxville: University of Tennessee Press, 1987.

Hine, Darlene Clark. "Lifting the Veil, Shattering the Silence: Black Women's History in Slavery and Freedom." In *The State of Afro-American History: Past, Present and Future,* edited by Darlene Clark Hine. Baton Rouge: Louisiana State University Press, 1986.

————. "Rape and the Inner Lives of Black Women in the Middle West: Preliminary Thoughts on the Culture of Dissemblance." *Signs: A Journal of Women in Culture and Society* 14 (1989): 912–20.

————, ed. *The State of Afro-American History: Past, Present, and Future.* Baton Rouge: Louisiana State University Press, 1986.

Hine, Darlene Clark, Wilma King, and Linda Reed, eds. *"We Specialize in the Wholly Impossible": A Reader in Black Women's History.* Brooklyn: Carlson, 1995.

Hine, Darlene Clark, and Kate Wittenstein. "Female Slave Resistance: The Economics of Sex." *Western Journal of Black Studies* 3 (Summer 1979): 123–27

Holt, Sharon Ann. "Making Freedom Pay: Freedpeople Working for Themselves, North Carolina, 1865–1900." *Journal of Southern History* 60 (May 1994): 228–62.

Holt, Thomas. *Black Over White: Negro Political Leadership in South Carolina during Reconstruction.* Urbana: University of Illinois Press, 1977.

———. "'An Empire Over the Mind': Emancipation, Race, and Ideology in the British West Indies and the American South." In *Region, Race and Reconstruction: Essays in Honor of C. Vann Woodward,* edited by J. Morgan Kousser and James M. McPherson. New York: Oxford University Press, 1982.

———. *The Problem of Freedom: Race, Labor, and Politics in Jamaica and Britain, 1832–1938.* Baltimore: Johns Hopkins University Press, 1992.

hooks, bell. *Ain't I a Woman: Black Women and Feminism.* Boston: South End Press, 1981.

Jaynes, Gerald David. *Branches without Roots: Genesis of the Black Working Class in the American South, 1862–1882.* New York: Oxford University Press, 1986.

Jones, Jacqueline. *Labor of Love, Labor of Sorrow: Black Women, Work, and the Family from Slavery to the Present.* New York: Basic Books, 1985.

———. "'My Mother Was Much of a Woman': Black Women, Work, and the Family Under Slavery." *Feminist Studies* 8 (Summer 1982): 235–69.

———. *Soldiers of Light and Love: Northern Teachers and Georgia Blacks, 1865–1873.* 1980; rpt., Athens: University of Georgia Press, 1992.

Jordan, Ervin L., Jr. *Black Confederates and Afro-Yankees in Civil War Virginia.* Charlottesville: University Press of Virginia, 1995.

Jordan, Winthrop. *White Over Black: American Attitudes Toward the Negro, 1550–1812.* Chapel Hill: University of North Carolina Press, 1968.

Joyner, Charles. *Down by the Riverside: A South Carolina Slave Community.* Urbana: University of Illinois Press, 1984.

Kolchin, Peter. *First Freedom: The Responses of Alabama's Blacks to Emancipation and Freedom.* Westport, Conn.: Greenwood, 1972.

———. "Reevaluating the Antebellum Slave Community: A Comparative Perspective." *Journal of American History* 70 (December 1983): 579–601.

Kousser, J. Morgan, and James M. McPherson, eds. *Region, Race, and Reconstruction: Essays in Honor of C. Vann Woodward.* New York: Oxford University Press, 1982.

Kreiger, Nancy. "Shades of Difference: Theoretical Underpinnings of the Medical Controversy on Black/White Differences in the United States, 1830–1870." *International Journal of Health Services* 17, no. 2 (1987): 259–78.

Lachicotte, Alberta Morel. *Georgetown Rice Plantations.* Columbia: University of South Carolina Press, 1955.

Lebsock, Suzanne. *The Free Women of Petersburg: Status and Culture in a Southern Town, 1784–1860.* New York: Norton, 1984.

Lerner, Gerda. *Black Women in White America: A Documentary History.* New York: Pantheon, 1972.

———. *The Majority Finds Its Past: Placing Women in History.* New York: Oxford University Press, 1979.

———. "Women and Slavery." *Slavery and Abolition* 4 (Dec. 1983): 173–98.

Levine, Lawrence W. *Black Culture and Black Consciousness: Afro-American Folk Thought from Slavery to Freedom.* New York: Oxford University Press, 1977.

Littlefield, Daniel C. *Rice and Slaves: Ethnicity and the Slave Trade in Colonial South Carolina.* Baton Rouge: Louisiana State University Press, 1981.

Litwack, Leon F. *Been in the Storm So Long: The Aftermath of Slavery.* New York: Random House, 1974.

Lonn, Ella. *Salt as a Factor in the Confederacy.* New York: Walter Neale, 1933.

Magdol, Edward. *A Right to the Land: Essays on the Freedmen's Community.* Westport, Conn.: Greenwood, 1977.

Mann, Susan A. "Slavery, Sharecropping, and Sexual Inequality." *Signs: A Journal of Women in Culture in Society* 14, no. 4 (1989): 774–98.

Massey, Mary Elizabeth. *Ersatz in the Confederacy: Shortages and Substitutes on the Southern Homefront.* 1952; rpt., Columbia: University of South Carolina Press, 1993.

McCurry, Stephanie. *Masters of Small Worlds: Yeoman Households, Gender Relations, and the Political Culture of the Antebellum South Carolina Low Country.* New York: Oxford University Press, 1995.

McFeely, William S. *Yankee Stepfather: General O. O. Howard and the Freedmen.* New Haven: Yale University Press, 1968.

McIntosh, Mary. "The State and the Oppression of Women." In *Feminism and Materialism: Women and Modes of Production,* edited by Annette Kuhn and Ann-Marie Wolpe. Boston: Routledge and Kegan Paul, 1978.

McKitrick, Eric L. *Andrew Johnson and Reconstruction.* Chicago: University of Chicago Press, 1960.

McPherson, James M. *The Negro's Civil War.* New York: Pantheon Books, 1965.

———. *The Struggle for Equality: Abolitionists and the Negro in the Civil War and Reconstruction.* Princeton: Princeton University Press, 1964.

Menard, Russell A. "The Africanization of the Lowcountry Labor Force." In *Race and Family in the Colonial South,* edited by Winthrop D. Jordan and Sheila L. Skemp. Jackson: University Press of Mississippi, 1987.

Miers, Suzanne, and Igor Kopytoff, eds. *Slavery in Africa: Historical and Anthropological Perspectives.* Madison: University of Wisconsin Press, 1977.

Mintz, Sidney W. *Caribbean Transformations.* Baltimore: Johns Hopkins University Press, 1974.

———. "Slavery and the Rise of Peasantries." *Historical Reflections* 6 (Summer 1979): 213–42.

———. "Was the Plantation Slave a Proletarian?" *Review* 2 (Summer 1978): 81–98.

Mintz, Sidney W., and Richard Price. *An Anthropological Approach to the Afro-American Past: A Caribbean Perspective.* Philadelphia: Institute for the Study of Human Issues, 1976.

Mohr, Clarence L. *On the Threshold of Freedom: Masters and Slaves in Civil War Georgia.* Athens: University of Georgia Press, 1986.

Montgomery, David. *Beyond Equality: Labor and the Radical Republicans, 1862–1872.* New York: Knopf, 1967.

Moore, John Hammond. "Getting Uncle Sam's Dollars: South Carolinians and the Southern Claims Commission, 1871–1880." *South Carolina Historical Magazine* 82 (July 1981): 248–62.

Morgan, Lynda. *Emancipation in Virginia's Tobacco Belt, 1850–1870.* Athens: University of Georgia Press, 1992.

Morgan, Philip D. "Black Society in the Lowcountry, 1760–1810." In *Slavery and Freedom in the Age of the American Revolution,* edited by Ira Berlin and Ronald Hoffman. Charlottesville: University Press of Virginia, 1983.

———. "Colonial South Carolina Runaways: Their Significance for Slave Culture." *Slavery and Abolition* 6, no. 3 (1985): 57–78.

———. "The Ownership of Property by Slaves in the Mid-Nineteenth-Century Low Country." *Journal of Southern History* 49 (Aug. 1983): 399–420.

———. "Task and Gang Systems: The Organization of Labor on New World Plantations." In *Work and Labor in Early America,* edited by Stephen Innes. Chapel Hill: University of North Carolina Press, 1988.

———. "Work and Culture: The Task System and the World of Lowcountry Blacks, 1700 to 1880." *William and Mary Quarterly,* 3d ser., 39 (Oct. 1982): 563–99.

Morris, Thomas D. "Equality, 'Extraordinary Law,' and Criminal Justice: The South Carolina Experience, 1865–66." *South Carolina Historical Magazine* 83, no. 1 (1982): 15–33

Morrissey, Marietta. *Slave Women in the New World: Gender Stratification in the Caribbean.* Lawrence: University of Kansas Press, 1989.

Mullin, Michael. "Women, and the Comparative Study of American Negro Slavery." *Slavery and Abolition* 6 (May 1985): 25–40.

Nelson, Bernard H. "Confederate Slave Impressment Legislation, 1861–1865." *Journal of Negro History* 31, no. 4 (1946): 392–410.

Oakes, James. *The Ruling Race: A History of American Slaveholders.* New York: Knopf, 1982.

———. *Slavery and Freedom: An Interpretation of the Old South.* New York: Knopf, 1990.

Oubre, Claude F. *Forty Acres and a Mule: The Freedmen's Bureau and Black Land Ownership.* Baton Rouge: Louisiana State University Press, 1978.

Owens, Leslie Howard. *This Species of Property: Slave Life and Culture in the Old South.* New York: Oxford University Press, 1976.

Pearson, Edward A. *Designs against Charleston: The Denmark Vesey Trial of 1822.* Chapel Hill: University of North Carolina Press, forthcoming.

———. "From Stono to Vesey: Slavery, Resistance, and Ideology in South Carolina, 1739–1822." Ph.D. diss., University of Wisconsin, 1992.

Peirce, Paul Skeels. *The Freedmen's Bureau: A Chapter in the History of Reconstruction.* Iowa City: University of Iowa Press, 1904.

Powell, Lawrence N. *New Masters: Northern Planters during the Civil War and Reconstruction.* New Haven: Yale University Press, 1980.

Rabinowitz, Howard N., ed. *Southern Black Leaders of the Reconstruction Era.* Urbana: University of Illinois Press, 1982.

Rable, George C. *Civil Wars: Women and the Crisis of Southern Nationalism.* Urbana: University of Illinois Press, 1989.

Raboteau, Albert J. *Slave Religion: The "Invisible Institution" in the Antebellum South.* New York: Oxford University Press, 1978.

Radley, Kenneth. *Rebel Watchdog: The Confederate States Army Provost Guard.* Baton Rouge: Louisiana State University Press, 1989.

Ransom, Roger L., and Richard Sutch. *One Kind of Freedom: The Economic Consequences of Emancipation.* Cambridge: Cambridge University Press, 1977.

Redkey, Edwin S., ed. *A Grand Army of Black Men: Letters from African-American Soldiers in the Union Army, 1861–1865.* New York: Cambridge University Press, 1992.

Reidy, Joseph P. "Aaron A. Bradley: Voice of Black Labor in the Georgia Lowcountry." In *Southern Black Leaders of the Reconstruction Era,* edited by Howard N. Rabinowitz. Urbana: University of Illinois Press, 1982.

Ricards, Sherman L., and George M. Blackburn. "A Demographic History of Slavery: Georgetown County, South Carolina, 1850." *South Carolina Historical Magazine* 76 (Oct. 1975): 215–24.

Riley, Glenda. *Divorce: An American Tradition.* New York: Oxford University Press, 1991.

Ripley, C. Peter. *Slaves and Freedmen in Civil War Louisiana.* Baton Rouge: Louisiana State University Press, 1976.

Roark, James L. *Masters without Slaves: Southern Planters in the Civil War and Reconstruction.* New York: Norton, 1977.

Robertson, Claire C., and Martin A. Klein, eds. *Women and Slavery in Africa.* Madison: University of Wisconsin Press, 1983.

Robinson, Armstead L. "Beyond the Realm of Social Consensus: New Meanings of Reconstruction for American History." *Journal of American History* 68 (Sept. 1981): 276–97.

———. "The Difference Freedom Made: The Emancipation of Afro-Americans." In *The State of Afro-American History,* edited by Darlene Clark Hine. Baton Rouge: Louisiana State University Press, 1986.

———. "'Plans dat Comed from God': Institution Building and the Emergence of Black Leadership in Reconstruction Memphis." In *Towards a New South? Studies in Post-Civil War Southern Communities,* edited by Orville Vernon Burton and Robert C. McMath. Westport, Conn.: Greenwood, 1980.

Roediger, David R. *The Wages of Whiteness: Race and the Making of the American Working Class.* London: Verso, 1991.

Rogers, George C., Jr. *The History of Georgetown County, South Carolina.* Columbia: University of South Carolina Press, 1970.

Rose, Willie Lee. *Rehearsal for Reconstruction: The Port Royal Experiment.* 1964: rpt., New York: Vintage, 1967.

———. *Slavery and Freedom.* Edited by William W. Freehling. New York: Oxford University Press, 1982.

Saville, Julie. "Grassroots Reconstruction: Agricultural Labor and Collective Action in South Carolina, 1860–1868." *Slavery and Abolition* 12, no. 3 (1991): 173–82.

———. "A Measure of Freedom: From Slave to Wage Worker in South Carolina, 1860–1868." Ph.D. diss., Yale University, 1986.

———. *The Work of Reconstruction: From Slave to Wage Laborer in South Carolina, 1860–1870.* New York: Cambridge University Press, 1994.

Savitt, Todd L. *Medicine and Slavery: The Diseases and Health Care of Blacks in Antebellum Virginia.* Urbana: University of Illinois Press, 1978.

Scott, James C. *Domination and the Arts of Resistance: Hidden Transcripts.* New Haven: Yale University Press, 1990.

Scott, Joan Wallach. *Gender and the Politics of History.* New York: Columbia University Press, 1988.

Scott, Rebecca. "The Battle Over the Child: Child Apprenticeship and the Freedmen's Bureau in North Carolina." *Prologue* 10 (Summer 1978): 101–13.

Sefton, James E. *The United States Army and Reconstruction, 1865–1877.* Baton Rouge: Louisiana State University Press, 1967.

Sewell, Richard H. *A House Divided: Sectionalism and the Civil War, 1848–1865.* Baltimore: Johns Hopkins University Press, 1988.

Shick, Tom W., and Don H. Doyle. "The South Carolina Phosphate Boom and the Stillbirth of the New South, 1867–1920." *South Carolina Historical Magazine* 86 (Jan. 1985): 1–31.

Silber, Nina. *The Romance of Reunion: Northerners and the South, 1865–1900.* Chapel Hill: University of North Carolina Press, 1993.

Simkins, Francis Butler. *South Carolina during Reconstruction.* Chapel Hill: University of North Carolina Press, 1932.

Smith, Alfred Glaze, Jr. *The Economic Adjustment of an Old Cotton State: South Carolina, 1820–1860.* Columbia: University of South Carolina Press, 1958.

Stacey, Judith. *Patriarchy and Socialist Revolution in China.* Berkeley: University of California Press, 1983.

Stack, Carol B. *All Our Kin: Strategies for Survival in a Black Community.* New York: Harper and Row, 1974.

Stampp, Kenneth M. *The Era of Reconstruction, 1865–1877.* New York: Knopf, 1965.

———. *The Peculiar Institution: Slavery in the Ante-Bellum South.* New York: Knopf, 1956.

Stanley, Amy Dru. "Beggars Can't Be Choosers: Compulsion and Contract in Postbellum America." *Journal of American History* 78, no. 4 (Mar. 1992): 1265–93.

Sterling, Dorothy, ed. *We Are Your Sisters: Black Women in the Nineteenth Century.* New York: Norton, 1984.

Stevenson, Brenda. "Distress and Discord in Virginia Slave Families, 1830–1860." In *In Joy and in Sorrow: Women, Family and Marriage in the Victorian South,* edited by Carol Blesser. New York: Oxford University Press, 1991.

Strickland, John Scott. "'No More Mud Work': The Struggle For Control of Labor and Production in Low Country South Carolina, 1863–1880." In *The Southern Enigma: Essays on Race, Class, and Folk Culture,* edited by Walter J. Fraser Jr. and Winfred B. Moore Jr. Westport, Conn.: Greenwood, 1983.

———. "Traditional Culture and Moral Economy: Social and Economic Change in the South Carolina Low Country, 1865–1910." In *The Countryside in the Age of Capitalist Transformation: Essays in the Social History of Rural America,* edited by Steven Hahn and Jonathan Prude. Chapel Hill: University of North Carolina Press, 1985.

Stuckey, Sterling. *Slave Culture: Nationalist Theory and the Foundations of Black America.* New York: Oxford University Press, 1987.

Terborg-Penn, Rosalyn. "Black Women in Resistance: A Cross-Cultural Perspective." In *Resistance: Studies in African, Caribbean, and Afro-American History,* edited by Gary Y. Okihiro. Amherst: University of Massachusetts Press, 1986.

Terborg-Penn, Rosalyn, Andrea Rushing, and Sharon Harley, eds. *Women in Africa and the African Diaspora.* Washington, D.C.: Howard University Press, 1987.

Thomas, Emory M. *The Confederate Nation: 1861–1865.* New York: Harper and Row, 1979.

Trexler, Harrison A. "The Opposition of Planters to the Employment of Slaves as Laborers by the Confederacy." *Mississippi Valley Historical Review* 27 (1940): 211–24.

Valuska, David Lawrence. "The Negro in the Union Navy: 1861–1865." Ph.D. diss., Lehigh University, 1973.

Van Allen, Judith. "'Sitting on a Man': Colonialism and the Lost Political Institutions of Igbo Women." *Canadian Journal of African Studies* 6 (1972): 165–81.

Van Deburg, William L. *The Slave Drivers: Black Agricultural Labor Supervisors in the Antebellum South.* New York: Oxford University Press, 1979.

Walker, Clarence E. *A Rock in a Weary Land: The African Methodist Episcopal Church during the Civil War and Reconstruction.* Baton Rouge: Louisiana State University Press, 1982.

Webber, Thomas L. *Deep Like the Rivers: Education in the Slave Quarter Community, 1831–1865.* New York: Norton, 1978.

Webster, Laura Josephine. *The Operation of the Freedmen's Bureau in South Carolina.* 1916; rpt., New York: Russell and Russell, 1970.

White, Deborah Gray. *Ar'n't I A Woman? Female Slaves in the Plantation South.* New York: Norton, 1985.

————. "Female Slaves: Sex Roles and Status in the Antebellum Plantation South." *Journal of Family History* 8 (Fall 1983): 248–61.

White, E. Frances. "Africa on My Mind: Gender, Counter Discourse and Africa-American Nationalism." *Journal of Women's History* 2 (Spring 1990): 73–97.

Whites, LeeAnn. *The Civil War as a Crisis in Gender: Augusta, Georgia, 1860–1890.* Athens: University of Georgia Press, 1995.

Wikramanayake, Marina. *A World in Shadow: The Free Black in Antebellum South Carolina.* Columbia: University of South Carolina Press, 1973.

Wiley, Bell Irvin. *Southern Negroes, 1861–1865.* New Haven: Yale University Press, 1938.

Williamson, Joel. *After Slavery: The Negro in South Carolina during Reconstruction, 1861–1877.* Chapel Hill: University of North Carolina Press, 1965.

Wood, Betty. "Prisons, Workhouses, and the Control of Slaves Labor in Low Country Georgia, 1763–1815." *Slavery and Abolition* 8 (December 1987): 247–71.

Wood, Peter H. *Black Majority: Negroes in Colonial South Carolina from 1670 through the Stono Rebellion.* New York: Knopf, 1974.

Woodman, Harold D. "The Reconstruction of the Cotton Plantation in the New South." In *Essays on the Postbellum Southern Economy,* edited by Thavolia Glymph and John J. Kushma. College Station: Texas A & M University Press, 1985.

Woody, R. H. "The Labor and Immigration Problem of South Carolina During Reconstruction." *Mississippi Valley Historical Review* 18 (1931): 195–212.

Woofter, T. J., Jr. *Black Yeomanry: Life on St. Helena Island.* New York: Henry Holt, 1930.

Wright, Gavin. "Freedom and the Southern Economy." *Explorations in Economic History* 16 (1979): 90–108.

INDEX

242, 247, 248, 260, 263, 265; legislation regarding, 241, 249; new and renewed, 241–45, 245–46; regulation of, 241–43, 267–68, 248, 249; reunion, complications of, 241–42, 245–46, 250; significance of, 242–47, 267–68; slave, 51–54, 57–58, 243–45; wedding ceremonies (slave), 53. *See also* Families, freed; Families, slave; weddings

Maxwell, James, 63

Maxwell, William R., 203–4, 221

Mayhams, Cain, 138

Mayrant, Hardy, 52

Mayrant, Jane, 248

Mayrant, William, 96

Mayzeck, Job, 106

Mayzck, Sallie, 192–93

McMillan, Harry, 51

Meade, George G., Maj. Gen., 165–66

Middleton, Eliza, 143

Middleton, Oliver, 194

Middleton, Williams, 63, 128, 195, 224, 226

Midwives, 219–20

Migration, 162, 172, 173, 176, 198–200, 208–9, 223, 257–60, 324n.14, 324–25n.18

Miliken, E. P., 181

Militia Act (July 1862), 92

Ministers, 102, 242, 244; slave preachers, 53, 106

Missionaries (Northern), 91, 97–98, 103–4, 142, 157, 237–38, 239–40

Mitchell, Rina, 53

Mobs, 159–60, 185, 191–93

Moncks Corner (South Carolina), 228, 229, 230

Mortality: among freedpeople, 149–51; wartime, 79, 83

Moultrie, Ishmael, 182,

Moultrie, Magdalen, 192–93

Mudwork, 22–23, 25; and Chinese hired laborers, 345–46n.139; historians' misreading of, 22–23, 279n.20; and Irish hired laborers, 222–23, 331n.116; and labor contracts, 172, 202; rejected by freedpeople, 175, 196, 204, 222–23, 226, 227; and sexual division of labor, 22–23, 81–82, 278nn.24, 27. *See also* Plantation labor, postbellum; Plantation laborers, postbellum

Murphy, Flora, 265

Myers, Jane, 53

Nagle, Garret, 200

Nesbit, Brutus, 52, 143, 244

Nesbit, Cain, 138, 143

Nesbit, Mary, 244

Nesbit, Rebecca, 53, 245

Nordhoff, Charles, 103

North Santee River, 129, 160, 161

Olmsted, Frederick Law, 21, 37–38, 40

Orangeburg (South Carolina), 166

Orr, James, 185–86, 231

Orr, Mary, 86

Overseers, 14–15, 20, 30, 33, 37–39, 41, 42, 43–44, 58, 78, 85, 89, 105–6, 107, 111–12, 113, 118, 123, 129, 160–61, 214–17, 217–20, 224–25, 227; attacked by freedpeople, 127–30, 131, 192–93; rejected by freedpeople, 160–61, 162, 185, 194–95, 214–17. *See also* Task system

Parker, Francis S., 85, 105, 107, 192–93

Paternalism, 174; rejected by former slaves, 132, 174. *See also* Planters

Paternity, 51, 51–52, 55

Pee Dee River, 9, 110, 143, 163

Pension files, Civil War, 66–67

Perry, Benjamin, 179, 185

Perry, Leah, 262

Petigru, James, 92–93

Pickens, Francis W., 85, 93

Pierce, Edward, 70–71

Pineville (South Carolina), 13, 133–34, 135

Plantation agriculture: African expertise, 9; provision crops, 14, 25; rice, compared to cotton and sugar, 14, 15, 20, 25, 39; rice cultivation, 9, 12, 14–15, 19–27, 37–45, 108–10; wartime, 80–81. *See also* Gender; Overseers; Plantation labor, antebellum; Plantation laborers, postbellum; Plantations; Planters; Slave drivers; Slave men; Slave women; Task system; West Africans

Plantation households, 34–37

Plantation labor, antebellum: artisanal, 30–33; cooperation among slaves in performing, 29–30; domestic service, 34–37; slave, 8–12, 14–15, 19–46; war's

LESLIE A. SCHWALM is an assistant professor of history at the University of Iowa

Books in the Series Women in American History

Women Doctors in Gilded-Age Washington: Race, Gender, and
Professionalization   *Gloria Moldow*

Friends and Sisters: Letters between Lucy Stone and Antoinette Brown
Blackwell, 1846–93   *Edited by Carol Lasser and Marlene Deahl Merrill*

Reform, Labor, and Feminism: Margaret Dreier Robins and the Women's Trade
Union League   *Elizabeth Anne Payne*

Private Matters: American Attitudes toward Childbearing and Infant Nurture in
the Urban North, 1800–1860   *Sylvia D. Hoffert*

Civil Wars: Women and the Crisis of Southern Nationalism   *George C. Rable*

I Came a Stranger: The Story of a Hull-House Girl   *Hilda Satt Polacheck;
edited by Dena J. Polacheck Epstein*

Labor's Flaming Youth: Telephone Operators and Worker Militancy, 1878–1923
Stephen H. Norwood

Winter Friends: Women Growing Old in the New Republic, 1785–1835
Terri L. Premo

Better Than Second Best: Love and Work in the Life of Helen Magill
Glenn C. Altschuler

Dishing It Out: Waitresses and Their Unions in the Twentieth Century
Dorothy Sue Cobble

Natural Allies: Women's Associations in American History   *Anne Firor Scott*

Beyond the Typewriter: Gender, Class, and the Origins of Modern American
Office Work, 1900–1930   *Sharon Hartman Strom*

The Challenge of Feminist Biography: Writing the Lives of Modern American
Women   *Edited by Sara Alpern, Joyce Antler, Elisabeth Israels Perry, and
Ingrid Winther Scobie*

Working Women of Collar City: Gender, Class, and Community in Troy, New
York, 1864–86   *Carole Turbin*

Radicals of the Worst Sort: Laboring Women in Lawrence, Massachusetts, 1860–
1912   *Ardis Cameron*

Visible Women: New Essays on American Activism   *Edited by Nancy A. Hewitt and Suzanne Lebsock*

Mother-Work: Women, Child Welfare, and the State, 1890–1930
Molly Ladd-Taylor

Babe: The Life and Legend of Babe Didrikson Zaharias   *Susan E. Cayleff*

Writing Out My Heart: Selections from the Journal of Frances E. Willard, 1855–96   *Carolyn De Swarte Gifford*

U.S. Women in Struggle: A *Feminist Studies* Anthology
Edited by Claire Goldberg Moses and Heidi Hartmann

In a Generous Spirit: A First-Person Biography of Myra Page
Christina Looper Baker

Mining Cultures: Men, Women, and Leisure in Butte, 1914–41   *Mary Murphy*

Gendered Strife and Confusion: The Political Culture of Reconstruction
Laura F. Edwards

The Female Economy: The Millinery and Dressmaking Trades, 1860–1930
Wendy Gamber

Mistresses and Slaves: Plantation Women in South Carolina, 1830–80
Marli F. Weiner

A Hard Fight for We: Women's Transition from Slavery to Freedom in South Carolina   *Leslie A. Schwalm*

University of Illinois Press
1325 South Oak Street
Champaign, Illinois 61820-6903
www.press.uillinois.edu